NeXTSTEP™ PROGRAMMING
STEP ONE: Object-Oriented Applications

TELOS, The Electronic Library of Science, is an imprint of Springer-Verlag New York, with publishing facilities in Santa Clara, California. Its publishing domain encompasses the natural and physical sciences, computer science, mathematics, and engineering. All *TELOS* publications have a computational orientation to them, as *TELOS'* primary publishing strategy is to wed the traditional print medium with the emerging new electronic media in order to provide the reader with a truly interactive multimedia information environment. To achieve this, it is important that every *TELOS* publication delivered on paper also have an associated electronic component. This can take the form of book/diskette combinations, book/CD-ROM packages, books delivered via networks, electronic journals, newsletters, plus a multitude of other exciting possibilities. Since *TELOS* is not committed to any one technology, any delivery medium can be considered.

The range of *TELOS* publications extends from high end research level reference works through textbook materials for the higher education audience, practical handbooks for working professionals, as well as more broadly accessible science, computer science, and high technology trade publications on the lower end of the publishing spectrum. Many *TELOS* publications are interdisciplinary in nature, and most are targeted for the individual buyer, which dictates that *TELOS* publications be priced accordingly.

Of the numerous definitions of the Greek word "telos," the one most representative of our publishing philosophy is "to turn," or "turning point." We perceive the establishment of the *TELOS* publishing program to be a significant step towards attaining a new plateau of high quality information packaging and dissemination in the interactive learning environment of the future. *TELOS* welcomes you to join us in the exploration and development of this frontier as a reader and user, an author, editor, consultant, strategic partner, or in whatever other capacity might be appropriate, by contacting us directly.

THE ELECTRONIC LIBRARY OF SCIENCE

3600 PRUNERIDGE AVENUE, SUITE 200
SANTA CLARA, CALIFORNIA 95051

Simson L. Garfinkel • Michael K. Mahoney

NeXTSTEP™
PROGRAMMING

STEP ONE: Object-Oriented Applications

 Diskette included

 THE ELECTRONIC LIBRARY OF SCIENCE

 Springer-Verlag

Simson L. Garfinkel
52½ Pleasant Street
Cambridge, MA 02139 USA

Michael K. Mahoney
Department of Computer Engineering
and Computer Science
California State University
Long Beach, CA 90840-8302 USA

TELOS, The Electronic Library of Science, Santa Clara, CA is an imprint of Springer-Verlag New York, Inc.

Publisher: Allan M. Wylde
Publishing Coordinator: Cindy Peterson
Production Editor: Henry Krell
Electronic Production Advisor: Howard Ratner
Cover Designer: Rudy Zenthner
Promotions Manager: Jacqueline Jeng
Manufacturing Supervisor: Vincent Scelta

Library of Congress Cataloging-in-Publication Data
Garfinkel, Simson.
    NeXTSTEP programming : step one, object-oriented applications /
Simson L. Garfinkel, Michael K. Mahoney.
        p.   cm.
    Includes bibliographical references and index.
    ISBN 0-387-97884-4. — ISBN 3-540-97884-4
    1. NeXT (Computer)—Programming. 2. NeXTSTEP. 3. Object-oriented
programming (Computer science)
I. Mahoney, Michael K. II. Title.
QA76.8.N49G37 1993
005.4′3—dc20   92-39585

The center computer graphic on the cover of this book is used with the permission of NeXTWORLD.

Negatives prepared from authors' FrameMaker files.
Printed and bound by Hamilton Printing Co., Rennselaer, NY.
Printed in the United States of America.

9 8 7 6 5 4 3 2 1   Printed on acid-free paper.

ISBN 0-387-97884-4 Springer-Verlag New York Berlin Heidelberg
ISBN 3-540-97884-4 Springer-Verlag Berlin Heidelberg New York

To my parents, Marvin and Marian, who have put up with my addiction to computers since before I could type.

Simson

To Louise, Nina, and Timmy.

Michael

Preface

Welcome!

This book is about programming computers running NeXTSTEP. It's a no-nonsense, hands-on book that teaches programmers how to write application programs that take full advantage of NeXTSTEP, the operating environment from NeXT Computer Inc.

Writing programs for NeXTSTEP is fundamentally different than writing programs for other computers, because NeXTSTEP represents a radical departure from conventional programming environments. One writes NeXTSTEP programs by building systems of related but distinct parts, or *objects*, and connecting them together to form an integrated whole. Confining different aspects of a program to different pieces makes those pieces easier to design, implement, debug, and reuse. This is what is known as *object-oriented programming*.

NeXTSTEP embodies the principles of object oriented programming from its user interface down to its very core. This greatly simplifies the task of interfacing application programs with the NeXTSTEP operating environment. The downside is that it makes the NeXTSTEP environment very different from the environments to which most programmers are accustomed: there's a steep curve to climb when learning to program in this easy-to-program environment (sounds strange, but it's true).

We wrote this book out of frustration: at the time, there was no single book that explained step-by-step how to write programs for NeXTSTEP. Instead, a programmer trying to approach the platform was confronted by the NeXT technical documentation and the source-code for several dozen example programs. There was no mention of style, program structure or design considerations. It seemed that there was a black art to writing programs for the black computer, along with a priesthood which promised that newcomers *might* one day become members – once we paid our dues.

With this book, we've paid a lot of your dues for you.

This book is for anybody who knows how to program in C and wants to do something substantial with NeXTSTEP. Our goal is to get you up-and-running as quickly as possible. This isn't a textbook or a reference manual – Brad Cox (the inventor of Objective-C) and the technical writing department at NeXT have already written those. This book is instead a jumping-off point. Consequently, we will occasionally sacrifice depth for breadth and brevity. You won't learn all of the options of Interface Builder or all the obscure methods that the Text object implements by reading this book. But you'll acquire the conceptual framework necessary to understand NeXT's excellent documentation, enabling you to discover what you need to know about the Text object and everything else.

All of the examples in this book were developed and tested under both version 2.1 and 3.0 of the NeXTSTEP operating environment. (When we write NeXTSTEP 2.1 this includes NeXTSTEP 2.0, 2.1, and 2.2.) Although NeXTSTEP 3.0 offers many features not found in the 2.1 operating system, from the programmer's point of view the two releases are actually quite similar. Furthermore, we've tried to limit the subject matter of this book to those underlying concepts and features of the operating system – the parts that haven't changed much since the initial release of NeXTSTEP 1.0 in 1989.

One significant difference between NeXTSTEP 2.1 and NeXTSTEP 3.0, however, lies with Interface Builder, the powerful development tool for building application interfaces and application projects. With NeXTSTEP 3.0, NeXT split the 2.1 version of Interface Builder into two distinct programs: Interface Builder 3.0 and Project Builder. Nevertheless, the two 3.0 tools contain essentially the same functionality as the single 2.1 Interface Builder tool.

To help deal with this difference, we've explained how to use Interface Builder under both 2.1 and 3.0. We've also covered explanatory information about Project Builder, where appropriate.

What is NeXTSTEP?

NeXTSTEP is the object-oriented environment that runs on NeXT, 80486-based, and possibly other computers. It is the main reason that the NeXT computer is different, both for users and programmers.

From the user's point of view, NeXTSTEP is the unified graphical operating environment that makes a computer running it easy to use:

- Display PostScript, a version of Adobe's PostScript imaging system that displays information on a computer's screen.
- Workspace, NeXTSTEP's graphical interface to the UNIX file system.
- Mail, Digital Librarian, the Edit editor, and other NeXT-supplied application programs.

- The Preferences and Defaults system, which lets users store their preferences for individual programs without having to directly modify special files stored in their home directories.

From the programmer's point of view, NeXTSTEP includes:

- The NeXT Application Kit, a collection of Objective-C objects which gives NeXTSTEP its distinctive look-and-feel.
- The NeXTSTEP Sound and Music Kits, for writing programs that make noise.
- The NeXTSTEP Database Kit, DBKit, for writing programs that access databases.
- The streams package, which allows interprocess communication, archiving of information, and direct mapping of files.
- The C threads package, for writing multi-threaded applications.
- The Mach operating system.

Using NeXTSTEP gives your program the characteristic NeXTSTEP look-and-feel. Although every application program is different, NeXTSTEP makes it easier for all applications to work in similar ways, which in turn makes it easier for people to learn new application programs.

NeXTSTEP also makes it easier for application programs to work with each other. Because of its object-oriented nature, NeXTSTEP applications can easily provide services and special functions to other application programs running on the same computer or across the network.

Using NeXTSTEP also speeds your development time. Programmers who have gone through NeXT's Developer's Training Camp report that they can develop an application three to ten times faster under NeXTSTEP than under Microsoft Windows or X Windows. Indeed, it is so easy to develop an application under NeXTSTEP that many large companies are purchasing NeXT computers specifically to develop their own custom, in-house applications: the increased programmer productivity justifies the purchase decision!

What You Need

In order to try out the examples in this book, you will need a computer running the Extended Edition of the NeXTSTEP Software Release 2.0, or later. The Extended Edition contains everything you need to develop a

NeXTSTEP application, including the NeXT's GNU C compiler (developed by the Free Software Foundation), the assembler, linker, all of the libraries, and all of the "include" files (files that are included into your C program with the #include and #import directives). The Extended edition also contains on-line documentation, a variety of demonstration programs, source-code for many of these programs, and a variety of other tools, such as the TeX document processing system and the complete works of William Shakespeare.

If you have a NeXTcube or a NeXTstation with a 400MB hard disk or larger, you've already got the Extended Edition: it comes installed as standard software on your system.

If you have a NeXTstation with a 105MB hard disk, you're out of luck: there's just no way to make the files and programs that you need for the development environment fit onto this hard disk and still have room left to do anything useful. Your best bet is to buy a 400MB (or larger) external hard disk, put the Extended Edition on it, and boot it as your main disk: use the internal hard disk for backup and for virtual memory swapping space.

If you have a NeXTstation with a 200MB or 250MB hard disk, you can copy the individual files that you need to develop programs and still have some breathing space left over to do some serious work. Don't worry about copyright restrictions: the Standard Edition includes a license for the Extended Edition. Just copy the files from a friend or a friendly computer store. The files are also on the NeXTSTEP 3.0 CD-ROM.

If you are using an Intel 486-based computer with NeXTSTEP 486, then you must specially purchase the Developer's Edition if you wish to write programs.

Programming with NeXTSTEP 2.1

Below we list the directories and files that you need for changing the NeXTSTEP 2.1 Standard Edition into something you can program with.

Directories:

```
/lib, /usr/lib/nib, /usr/include
```

Files (programs) in `/bin`:

```
ar                    file
ld                    segedit
as                    g++filt
```

```
nm                  size
cc                  gdb
nm++                strip
cc++                kgdb
otool               ebadexec
ranlib              pswrap
kl_ld 1
```

Library Files:

```
/usr/lib/*.a
```

Note: UNIX libraries are files that end with the extension **.a**. If you copy a library with the **cp** command, you will need to run **ranlib** on the library to "refresh" the date stored in it.

Programming with NeXTSTEP 3.0

With NeXTSTEP 3.0, many of the special files and directories that you need to write programs have been moved to the **/NextDeveloper** directory. Symbolic links have been left in their place for backwards compatibility. For example, the directory **/usr/include** is now a symbolic link to **/NextDeveloper/Headers**. This change makes it substantially easier to do development on a NeXTSTEP 3.0 system with a small hard disk: Simply make the **/NextDeveloper** directory on your hard disk be a symbolic link to the same directory on the CD-ROM drive containing the NeXTSTEP 3.0 release. Alternatively, if you have a workstation on a network, you can mount the developer's directory from another computer with a larger hard disk.

Additional Programs

Besides the bare minimum, NeXTSTEP comes with a lot of documentation and additional programs that make programming a pleasure. Below we list the directories and programs that will make programming with NeXTSTEP a lot easier.

```
/NextLibrary/Documentation/NextDev
/NextLibrary/Documentation/UNIX
/usr/lib/emacs
/usr/bin/etags
```

1. **/usr/bin/kl_ld** and **kgdb** are only needed if you wish to do *kernel* programming.

The Organization of this Book

This book is designed to teach you how to write sophisticated NeXTSTEP applications. Although we do not assume prior knowledge with NeXT or any other window-based operating environment, we do assume familiarity with programming in general and the ANSI C language in particular.

This book is divided into five main sections, two appendices, and a floppy disk.

Part 1

The first part of this book introduces NeXTSTEP, NeXTSTEP programming, and the Objective-C language in which NeXTSTEP is written.

Chapter 1, "Introduction to the NeXTSTEP Graphical User Interface," is a brief tutorial on how to *use* NeXTSTEP and the NeXTSTEP GUI. Although people familiar with NeXTSTEP can skip it, it contains many hints and short-cuts that even experienced NeXT users may not be familiar with.

Chapter 2, "NeXTSTEP Development Tools," contains an overview of NeXT's Edit text-editor, brief descriptions of how to build icons and use the HeaderViewer and Librarian documentation access tools, and a discussion of compiling and debugging programs in NeXTSTEP's UNIX environment.

Chapter 3, "Creating a Simple Application With Interface Builder," introduces Interface Builder, NeXT's revolutionary program for drawing and wiring together objects in application interfaces. We'll use it to create a tiny application that plays a sound and updates a text field when the user moves a slider.

Chapter 4, "Creating an Application Without Interface Builder," builds an application program from the ground up using just Objective-C and the NeXTSTEP Application Kit. This gives you a hands-on feel for what Interface Builder is actually doing. We also use this chapter to introduce the syntax and framework of the Objective-C language.

Part 2

The second part of this book is focused upon building a simple application program – a calculator – which we slowly extend through four chapters.

Chapter 5, "Building a Project: A Four Function Calculator," introduces the calculator project. In this chapter we create the calculator's window and build a simple Objective-C object that handles the math. At the end of the chapter you'll have a working four-function calculator.

In Chapter 6, "Nibs and Icons," we add an Info Panel to the calculator application. This gives us an opportunity to provide further background on Interface Builder. This chapter finally explains what "nib" (NeXT Interface Builder) files really are. We also clarify NeXTSTEP's system of outlets, connections and actions. At the end of this chapter, we show you how to add an icon to your application so that it will display nicely from NeXTSTEP's Workspace File Viewer.

Chapter 7, "Delegation and Resizing," introduces the concept of *delegation* – designating objects to perform functions for other objects. In this chapter we make the four-function calculator work with other bases (octal, hexadecimal, and binary) and use delegation to set the initial base. In the second half of the chapter, we use an example of programmatically resizing a window to introduce NeXTSTEP's **Window** and **View** classes.

Chapter 8, "Events and Responders," introduces the responder chain, the chain of objects that NeXTSTEP uses to process events (such as key presses and mouse clicks). At the end of the chapter we use our new found knowledge to modify the calculator so that you can enter numbers by typing on the keyboard, instead of just clicking with the mouse.

Chapter 9, "Mach and the Window Server," provides background on the Mach operating system, upon which NeXTSTEP is based, and the Display PostScript window server that NeXTSTEP uses to draw on the screen.

Part 3

The third part of this book focuses on building a new application program called MathPaper. MathPaper is like a word processor, except when you hit return, the application program solves the equation that you typed in the window. The application uses a back-end mathematical processor called Evaluator to do its work.

Chapter 10, "MathPaper and Multiple Windows," introduces the MathPaper application and shows you how to write application programs that control multiple windows. We also build MathPaper's back end in this chapter.

In Chapter 11, "Spawning Multiple Processes and the Text Object," we tie MathPaper's front end and back end together with a **Process** object that can spawn subprocesses. MathPaper is fully functional by the end of this chapter.

Chapter 12, "Text and Rich Text," discusses Microsoft's Rich Text format, which NeXTSTEP uses to encode information such as font, point size, and alignment into a text stream. We use Rich Text to make MathPaper's output look more professional.

Chapter 13, "Saving, Loading, and Printing," introduces NeXTSTEP's facilities for dealing with document files. We show how to register a file name extension with the Workspace Manager, how to archive information into streams, and how to save and load files with the Save and Load panels. We also show how to receive messages from the Workspace to open a file. These messages are sent when a user double-clicks on a file icon.

Part 4

The fourth section of this book is about drawing in NeXTSTEP **View**s with Display PostScript. These chapters assume some familiarity with the PostScript language, but you can probably pick it up along the way if you need to.

In Chapter 14, "Drawing with Display PostScript," we show the basics of how to put lines and letters into a NeXTSTEP window. We do this by making an animated Info Panel for the MathPaper application.

Chapter 15, "Draw Yourself: All About NeXTSTEP Views," leaves Math-Paper. We spend the whole chapter exploring the View class in general and the **drawSelf::** method in particular.

Chapter 16, "GraphPaper: A Multi-Threaded Application with a Display List," introduces GraphPaper, a complex application that graphs a formula in two-dimensions. This application is multi-threaded, meaning that it has several execution threads and does several different things at the same time. It uses the same Evaluator back end that MathPaper used.

Chapter 17, "Color," shows how to draw color with Display PostScript and NeXTSTEP.

Chapter 18, "View Resizing and Mouse Tracking," shows how to catch two kinds of events with **View**s: resizes and mouse clicks. We do this by modifying the GraphPaper application so that it can display the value of the (x,y) pairs of the graph for wherever the user places the mouse.

Part 5

The last part of this book fills out topics that haven't been covered anywhere else – things that you don't need to get your application going, but that you do need to make it polished.

Chapter 19, "Zooming and Saving Graphics Files," shows how to put a zoom-button on a view to zoom in or zoom out. We also show how to save a graphics image as an Encapsulated PostScript file or as a TIFF bitmap image.

Chapter 20, "The Pasteboard and Services," shows how to put data on the Pasteboard and take it off. We also show how to make GraphPaper a NeXTSTEP Service, so you can graph equations that are in other application programs.

Chapter 21, "Preferences and Defaults," shows how to build a multi-view Preference panel and how to save its contents into the defaults database.

Appendices

In "Appendix A: Source Code Listings," we've included complete source code listings for the three major applications in this book: Calculator, MathPaper, and GraphPaper.

"Appendix B: References," lists other books that you might find helpful in programming NeXTSTEP.

Floppy Disk

The 1.44MB floppy disk included with this book contains the complete source code for the programs that we develop during the course of each chapter. The data is provided in the form of a single file that has been processed with the UNIX **compress** and **tar** commands. The disk is in MS-DOS file format so that you can read it on either a NeXTstation, an industry-standard personal computer running NeXTSTEP 486, or any PC running MS-DOS.

To unload the program files from the floppy, it is necessary to copy the file into one of your directories and process the file. The simple instructions on how to do this are located on the floppy disk in a file called **README**.

We recommend that you use this floppy disk as a *last resort*. You'll learn more about programming NeXTSTEP if you take the time to type in the demonstration programs, rather than simply loading them off the floppy disk and running them. We've provided the disk so you have something to fall back upon in the event that the programs you type in don't work.

Conventions Used in this Book

The following conventions are used in this book:

Italics	are used to identify *arguments* in function and method prototypes. Italics are also used to emphasize new terms and concepts when they are introduced.
Bold	is used for file and directory names, and Objective-C class and method names. (Note that NeXT's documentation does *not* use bold for class names.)
`Constant Width Text`	is used for programming examples and UNIX shell output. **`Bold`** constant width text means the text (code, commands) was *inserted*.
`localhost>`	is the UNIX C shell prompt, which you can access from the NeXTSTEP Terminal application.

This book was designed by Michael K. Mahoney and is set in Times and `Courier`. It was produced entirely on NeXT Computers. The book was built and formatted using FrameMaker 3.0. The screen shots were "grabbed" using the Grab application. The icons were built in IconBuilder. The code was written using Emacs and Edit.

Acknowledgments

Bringing this book from an idea to final publication took a lot of time on the part of a lot of people. The initial idea for the book came from Marc Davis, Simson's office mate at the MIT Media Laboratory. Simson started writing this book in October 1990.

Michael came on board in November 1991, having wanted to write a NeXTSTEP book for a couple of years. He had written and presented Interface Builder tutorials at ACM Computer-Human Interface (CHI) Conferences in Seattle, New Orleans, and Monterey that were subsequently placed at the Purdue and Oregon archives, but they concentrated more on building graphical user interfaces than on programming. He and Simson actually "met" through a posting on Usenet about NeXTSTEP books!

Matt Wagner at Waterside productions believed in the book. Mark Hall, Simson's first editor, gave him the courage to keep going on the book when he felt like quitting. David Shapiro, our second editor, gave much needed support. Our third editor at Springer, Allan Wylde, saw the project through to completion and opened the door to an exciting CD-ROM distribution associated with the book.

Allan Wylde has also opened to the door for us to write "STEP TWO" and "STEP THREE" books on NeXTSTEP programming. These books would cover advanced topics such as the PhoneKit, database and the DBKit, and 3D graphics and the 3DKit. These kits were introduced in NeXTSTEP 3.0.

We are proud that this book is the very first book to be published by TELOS, Springer-Verlag's "The Electronic Library of Science." By publishing with TELOS, we are able not only to bring a paper book into print, but we have also opened the door to electronic publishing of this book's contents. Look for a CD-ROM related to this book – possibly with an indexed version of the book with more information and interactive examples – at some point in the future. Fill out the perforated card in the book and mail it so TELOS can keep you apprised of the latest details on this exciting possibility. We'd like to thank Howard Ratner and Henry Krell at Springer, and Cindy Peterson and especially Allan Wylde at TELOS for their help with the production and editing of this book.

Lots of people at NeXT and elsewhere provided a lot of help: Mike Hawley (originally at NeXT, now at the MIT Media Lab) gave Simson his first introduction to the computer in 1988. Adam Hertz was responsible for getting Simson a NeXT cube in 1990 and writing Simson's first series of programs on it. Bob Clover (originally at CSU Long Beach, now at Cal Poly San Luis Obispo) was responsible for getting Michael his first NeXTcube in January 1989. It was part of the initial California State University system-wide purchase of 44 NeXTcubes. Bruce Blumberg and Randy Nelson put up with Michael and Simson (respectively) at (separate) NeXT developer camps. Simson's stay was arranged by Jeanne Etcheverry. Jayson Adams provided technical support and gave us programs that we could tear apart to see how they worked. David Spitzler provided moral support. Alan Belanger, Matt Black, Alison Bomar, Dave Bradley, Henry Chiu, Janet Leimer, Yvette Perry, John Powell, Lorraine Rapp, Chuck Schneebeck, Stein Tumert, and Dennis Volper were of great help to Michael at CSULB.

NeXT's Developer Support Team was exceptional – especially Julie Zelenski and Sharon Zakhour – in debugging the examples in this book. A big thank-you to all of DST!

Claude Anderson "beta tested" the book with his SE 103 class at Rose Hulman University during the spring of 1992. Claude found many, many typos and problems with our example programs, and we are indebted to him for his time and effort. Other early copies of this book were reviewed by Ali Ozer at NeXT, Eric Bergeson at Objective Technologies, Inc., Charles L. Perkins at The Cube Route, Inc., Suzanne Woolf at SRI International, William Ballew of Aerospace Corp., and John Glover at the University of Houston.

The **tiny** programs in Chapter 4 were based on a program posted to the Usenet newsgroup comp.sys.next by Larry Shupe of the University of Washington on 26 September 1990.

Authors' Biographies

Simson L. Garfinkel is Senior Editor at *NeXTWORLD* Magazine, an IDG publication dedicated to following the world of NeXTSTEP computers. He is also president of Simson Garfinkel and Associates, a Cambridge-based company that develops NeXTSTEP applications.

Simson started programming NeXT computers in 1990, when he wrote NeXT's CD-ROM file system under contract for NeXT Computers, Inc. He learned to program in Objective-C and use Interface Builder several months later when he entered the doctoral program at the Massachusetts Institute of Technology's Media Laboratory.

Simson earned a Master's degree in Journalism at Columbia University in 1988. He has published over 150 articles in newspapers and magazines, and is the co-author (with Gene Spafford) of *Practical UNIX Security*, a comprehensive book about the UNIX operating system and security issues. He holds three undergraduate degrees from MIT.

Simson L. Garfinkel
Fifty two and one half Pleasant St.
Cambridge, MA 02139

Michael K. Mahoney is Professor and Chair of the Computer Engineering and Computer Science Dept. at California State University, Long Beach. He started programming a NeXT Computer in January 1989 and attended NeXT Developer's Camp in May 1989. He has conducted several semesters of NeXTSTEP software development seminars at CSULB and led training in industry for Mahoney Consulting and the Anderson Software Group.

Michael has given presentations on Object-Oriented Programming and NeXTSTEP's Interface Builder at ACM meetings in Seattle, Los Angeles, Monterey, and New Orleans. He regularly teaches courses on Computer Graphics, User Interface Design, and Discrete Mathematics. He is currently directing several students who are developing 3D computer graphics applications in the NeXTSTEP environment.

Michael is founder and President of SCaN, the Southern California NeXT Users' group, which meets monthly at various sites in Los Angeles County. He is also co-editor of *SCaNeWS*, SCaN's newsletter, which can be obtained from the `nova.cc.purdue.edu` archive site.

Michael earned his Ph.D. in mathematics at the University of California, Santa Barbara in 1979. He has published papers in computer graphics, computer science education and mathematics. He won campus-wide teaching awards at both UCSB and CSULB.

Michael K. Mahoney
Dept. of Computer Engineering and Computer Science
California State University, Long Beach
Long Beach, CA   90840-8302

This book may be ordered by calling (800) 777-4643, which can be easily remembered as (800) SPRINGER.

Corrections and comments concerning this book may be sent to the following e-mail address:

`nextbook@csulb.edu`

Brief Contents

Contents

Preface vii

1

Introduction to the NeXTSTEP Graphical User Interface 1

2   *NeXTSTEP Development Tools 47*

3   *Creating a Simple Application With Interface Builder 69*

6

Nibs and Icons 167

9   *Mach and the Window Server   247*

10   *MathPaper and Multiple Windows   259*

11 *Spawning Multiple Processes and the Text Object 287*

12 *Text and Rich Text 307*

13 *Saving, Loading, and Printing 323*

14 *Drawing with Display PostScript 353*

15 *Draw Yourself:*
All About NeXTSTEP Views 381

16   *GraphPaper: A Multi-Threaded Application with a Display List   407*

17   *Color 449*

18   *View Resizing and Mouse Tracking 471*

21 *Preferences and Defaults 533*

Appendix A: Source Code Listings 555

1

Introduction to the NeXTSTEP Graphical User Interface

NeXTSTEP is both a graphical user interface (or GUI – pronounced "gooey") and an application program development environment. In order to write applications which function well in this environment, a developer should first become proficient at using it. This means knowing NeXT's GUI guidelines and how applications are structured well enough to accomplish tasks quickly and efficiently. You can then use this knowledge to write applications which provide better interfaces for others.

This chapter contains an introduction to the NeXTSTEP GUI and its guidelines. No previous experience with NeXTSTEP is assumed. All screen shots will be taken from NeXTSTEP 3.0, but most of the discussion applies to NeXTSTEP 2.1 as well. When there are significant differences between the two NeXTSTEP releases, we'll point them out. You can use this chapter (and this book) regardless of which release you are using.

What Makes NeXTSTEP So Special?

The NeXTSTEP GUI is special because it provides an easy-to-use interface to a powerful version of the industry standard UNIX operating system called *Mach*. It's the interface to all NeXTSTEP applications including the

Workspace Manager, a program which lets you manage what goes on in the *workspace*, or screen environment. The Workspace Manager is like the Macintosh Finder or Microsoft Windows' Program and File Managers in that you use it to start up programs and manage the file system. Unlike these programs, however, the Workspace Manager enables you to harness the power of a much more powerful underlying engine, and it manages to do this without being difficult to use. For example, using the Workspace Manager, a user could copy 10 MB of files from one disk to another, launch (run) several programs, open and print an 80 page document, recursively change the permissions on files, and view a graphics file in a panel, all at the same time!

NeXTSTEP is also special because of its embedded imaging model, *Display PostScript*. (An *imaging model* does the actual drawing on the screen or on a printer.) Display PostScript, a superset of the industry standard *PostScript* page description language, provides true WYSIWYG ("wizzy-wig" or what-you-see-is-what-you-get) capability because the imaging model for printing is the same as that for the screen. This is a marvelous asset for any application that uses text or graphics (what application doesn't?).

Where NeXTSTEP shines brightest, however, is in its development environment. As you'll discover by reading this book, the object-oriented environment of NeXTSTEP makes it surprisingly easy to design new applications and then turn them into working programs. Our main tool will be *Interface Builder*, a powerful system for building applications. With Interface Builder, you can create menus, windows, controls, etc., and make connections between them graphically. Interface Builder allows easy access to the *Application Kit*, a set of over 50 powerful self-contained classes which define and create objects for use by your applications. We'll discuss these powerful tools in great depth later.

An Overview of the Graphical User Interface

Figure 1 contains a screen shot of a typical NeXTSTEP 3.0 user's screen. (NeXTSTEP 2.1 looks very similar – we'll discuss the differences in the section "New Features in the NeXTSTEP 3.0 Interface" on page 43.) The screen background, called the *workspace*, is dark gray. The Workspace Manager is the active application with its main menu at the upper left, its **File** submenu attached to the main menu, and its **Tools** submenu, "torn off" from the main menu, below the other menus. The Workspace Manager's File Viewer is the main window in the top middle and its Inspector panel is

FIGURE 1. NeXTSTEP 3.0 Screen

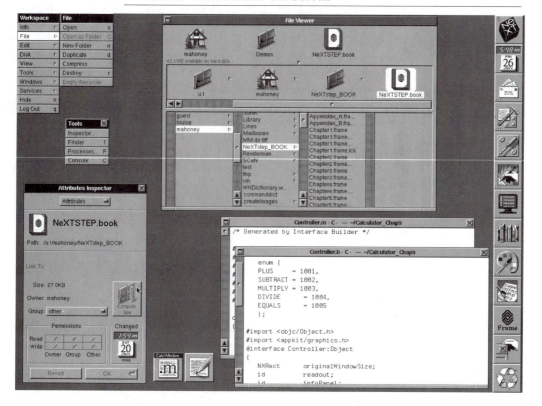

at the bottom left of the screen. (A *panel* is a special type of window which gives information about or instructions to an application.) The Inspector panel contains a matrix of switches to set file permissions, and buttons labeled **Revert** and **OK** to cancel or activate permission choices. We'll discuss these screen objects in more detail later in this chapter.

The *Application Dock* at the right of Figure 1 contains 13 icons, the first 12 representing applications (programs) and the last representing the Recycler. The NeXT icon, which represents the Workspace Manager application, is always at the top of the dock and doubles as a handle. You can grab the NeXT icon to drag the dock downward to create more screen real estate or back upward to see more of the dock.

The *Recycler* icon at the bottom of the dock represents a *folder* (directory) where files can be stored for deletion or restoration later. It works like the Macintosh Trash Can – files are deleted *only* when you choose the **Empty**

Recycler command from the Workspace **File** submenu. The little ball inside the recycler symbol means that the recycler has files inside it, waiting to be emptied.

The text windows with white backgrounds and the two icons at the bottom middle of the screen in Figure 1 belong to the *Edit* application. The titled icon on the left is an Edit *miniwindow,* which represents an Edit text window that was miniaturized. The icon next to it is Edit's freestanding application icon. Larger copies of these two icons are at the left of this paragraph. Although the Edit application is running, it is not *active* in the sense that it's not the application in the foreground (the Workspace Manager application is) and Edit's main menu is not displayed. You can activate the Edit application by clicking in one of Edit's text windows or double-clicking one of the Edit icons. If the Edit application icon was in the dock then it would not appear as a freestanding icon.

Basic Principles of the NeXTSTEP User Interface

NeXTSTEP was designed with the idea that the user interface should be consistent across all applications. Consistency helps users because they don't have to learn a new set of rules to perform basic operations as they move from application to application. (Think of how easy it is to drive different brands of automobiles – no additional training is required because they all have steering wheels, brakes, and accelerators which work the same way.) NeXTSTEP's consistency means that windows in different applications have the same look and functionality, mouse clicks and drags perform the same kinds of actions, common menu commands are in the same place and have the same names, keyboard alternatives, and so on. The overall look and feel of NeXTSTEP applications is the same. Contrast this with the haphazard way interfaces to DOS applications have been developed over the years, and you'll begin to see why we like NeXTSTEP so much.

NeXTSTEP puts you in charge of your workspace and its windows. Through preferences, inspectors, resize bars, icon dragging and other means you can change the size, visibility, and location of most windows, decide how much of your dock is visible and which application icons are in it, change the size of most text, and even determine which icons represent your folders.

With NeXTSTEP, the primary instrument that you use to interact with the computer is the mouse. Compared with the computer's keyboard, the mouse seems more natural for most users because using the mouse is a better analogy for how we interact with objects in the real world. For example, if a window in the workspace represents a piece of paper on a desk, then it is more natural for a user to move that window by dragging the window to a new place on the screen than by typing a sequence of keyboard commands. On the other hand, you may wish to learn some of the common keyboard alternatives (such as Command-x for **Cut** and Command-v for **Paste**) and use them to increase your efficiency.

The Mouse

There are two basic things that you can do with a mouse: move it and click its buttons. From these basic actions, several different mouse events (actions) can be derived:

- **clicking** – pressing and releasing a mouse button *(mouse down* and *mouse up)* without changing the position of the mouse
- **multiple-clicking** – pressing and releasing a mouse button two or three times quickly without changing the position of the mouse
- **dragging** – pressing and holding down a mouse button and then moving the mouse (and thus the cursor); release the mouse button to end dragging
- **pressing** – pressing and holding down a mouse button in place; release the mouse button to end pressing

Clicking (or single-clicking) is used to select an object or location on the screen. For example, you can click a button or menu command to select some action, click an icon or file name in a list to select it for further action, click in a window to bring it in front of other windows, or click on a piece of text to select an insertion point.

Multiple-clicking extends the action of clicking. For example, you can click on a piece of text to select an insertion point, double-click to extend the action to selecting the nearest word, and triple-click to select the entire line or paragraph. You can click a file icon in the File Viewer to select a file and double-click the icon to open the file in its associated application.

Dragging is used primarily to move an object or define a range. For example, you can drag a window's title bar to move the window, drag a miniwindow to reposition it in the workspace, or drag the knob on a slider or scroller to select a value or scroll through a window, respectively. You can also use dragging to define a range of characters in a text area, graphics in a drawing area, or icons in a file area. The last two operations use a technique known as *rubberbanding*, where a lightly drawn rectangle indicates the range of selection.

Pressing is used mainly as a substitute for repeated single-clicks. For example, you can repeatedly click a scroll button to move through the contents of a document window, or you can simply press the scroll button.

One *chooses* menu commands, *clicks* buttons or icons, *selects* items in a list, *drags* icons across the workspace, *drags* across items in a list (e.g. files in a browser), and *presses* on a button.

Although the NeXTSTEP mouse has two buttons, they initially work the same way. Through NeXTSTEP's Preferences application it is possible to make one of the mouse buttons bring up the main menu for the active application.

Mouse Action Paradigms

It's not crucial for users to know NeXTSTEP's mouse action paradigm terminology because most NeXTSTEP actions seem natural and people don't have to think about them. However, mouse action paradigms (patterns, archetypes) and their terms should be clearly defined to you as a NeXTSTEP developer. You need to be aware of the paradigms so you won't disrupt their naturalness for users of your applications. You also need to understand the terminology in order to properly use the procedures which come with NeXTSTEP, as well as understand NeXT's documentation. Below we list the four NeXTSTEP mouse action paradigms together with some examples:

- **Direct manipulation** – A user drags a window's title or resize bar and the window moves or is resized, or clicks in a partially obscured window and the window is reordered to the front, or drags the icon of a file to the recycler icon. The user *directly manipulates* these objects.

- **Target selection** – A user drags across a sequence of characters to select them for a change in font, or drags a rectangle around several graphics objects to select them for copying.

- **Targeted action through control**s – A user clicks a button and a text font changes, drags a slider knob and the size of an object changes, or clicks a menu command and a panel appears. We'll discuss *control* objects in depth later in this chapter.

- **Modal tool selection** – A user clicks a pencil or rectangle icon in a palette of tools in a graphics editor to select a drawing tool and the cursor changes to indicate the mode of drawing. The word "modal" implies that the program has distinct modes. When an application is in a modal state, some (or most) of its commands may be unavailable, or subsequent mouse actions may be specific to that mode.

Fortunately for developers most responses to direct manipulation and target selection by the mouse are handled automatically by NeXTSTEP objects and the *Window Server*. For example, you don't have to do anything to make a button highlight or a window move; NeXTSTEP button objects automatically highlight when clicked and the NeXTSTEP Window Server handles all window movements. On the other hand, an action in response to a change in a control object (e.g., button, scroller, menu cell) or a cursor change in response to a modal tool selection is usually handled explicitly by the developer.

Cursors

The NeXTSTEP cursor is a graphics image 16 pixels square which moves with the mouse. Moving the mouse quickly will move the cursor farther than moving it slowly – even if the distance moved is the same. Picking up the mouse and placing it elsewhere does not change the position of the cursor.

There are many different shapes the cursor can take depending on the context. The cursor can change in response to entering or exiting a window or graphics area and in response to tool or target selection. The most common cursors are shown below. The *hot spot*, or the location of the screen referred to by the cursor, depends on the type of cursor currently displayed.

Arrow – the most common cursor; for selecting, clicking, etc.; the hot spot is at the tip of the arrow. For certain operations (e.g., moving a file in the NeXTSTEP 3.0 Workspace) the interior of the arrow will turn white ( ).

I-bar – for text input positioning, editing, etc.; the hot spot is at the middle.

Spinning disk – a "wait" cursor; indicates that the computer is performing an operation that must be completed before you can continue your work in *that* application; however, you may activate *another* application (e.g., by clicking in one of its open windows) and not have to wait. The hot spot is in the middle.

Pencil – for drawing lines in a graphics editor or other such program; the hot spot is at the tip.

Crosshair – for drawing shapes such as rectangles or circles in a graphics editor; the hot spot is at the middle.

Two-pages – indicates a copying operation is about to take place in the Workspace Manager or other application. The hot spot doesn't matter, since this cursor only appears when the user is dragging another object.

Link cursor – indicates that a link (reference) operation is about to take place in the Workspace Manager or other application. Like the two-pages cursor, the hot spot doesn't matter.

Window Types

Other than the cursor, everything you see on the screen, including icons, menus and panels are windows. On-screen objects fall into ~~five~~ seven principle [a] categories:

- Standard Windows
- Panels
- Menus
- Pop-up Lists
- Pull-down Lists
- Miniwindows
- Freestanding and Docked Icons

Standard Windows

A *standard window* is the main working area of an application. The window containing the file being edited in a word processor or the image being manipulated in a drawing program is a standard window. Most standard windows, like the Edit text windows in Figure 1 and the window in Figure 2 below, will have a resize bar and both *miniaturize* and *close* buttons. They will usually contain vertical or horizontal scrollers when the window contents are too large to fit in the window. An application can have many standard windows open at the same time.

FIGURE 2. Standard Window

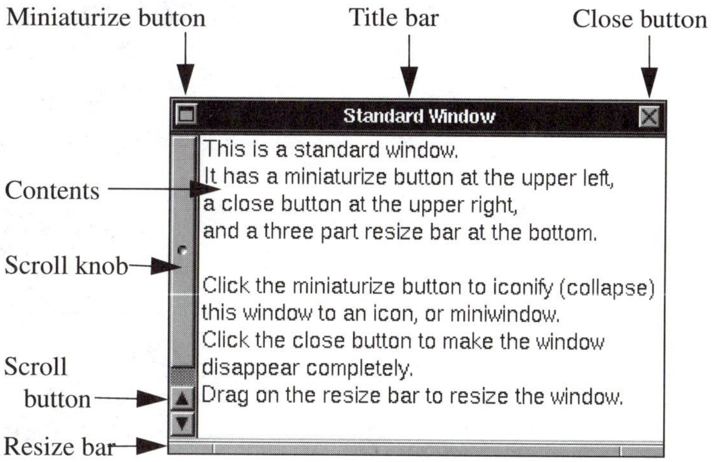

Miniaturize button   Title bar   Close button

Contents

Scroll knob

Scroll button

Resize bar

Standard Window

This is a standard window.
It has a miniaturize button at the upper left,
a close button at the upper right,
and a three part resize bar at the bottom.

Click the miniaturize button to iconify (collapse)
this window to an icon, or miniwindow.
Click the close button to make the window
disappear completely.
Drag on the resize bar to resize the window.

Panels

A *panel* supports the work done in the main window of an application by providing information to the user or a vehicle for the user to give instructions to the application. Panels fall into two groups, *attention* panels and *control* panels.

An attention panel requires a user response before work can be done in any other window of the application and will disappear after serving its purpose. Attention panels may be brought up as a result of a menu command (e.g., **Print**), or as a warning to give the user a chance to take corrective steps (e.g., a panel that interrupts a close window command to allow the user to save an altered file). A NeXTSTEP attention panel should appear in the middle of the screen, in front of any other window that might be present, and remain on-screen until it has served its purpose, even if another application becomes active.

A control panel is used to give instructions to an application and is brought up by a menu command. It can arise anywhere and, under normal circumstances, should remain on-screen only while its application is active. You close a control panel by clicking on its close button. See Figure 3 for examples of panels.

FIGURE 3. Attention and Control Panels

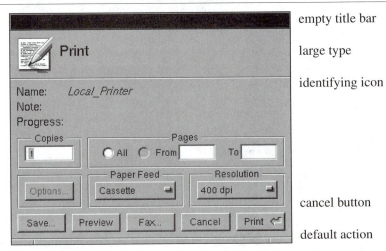

empty title bar

large type

identifying icon

cancel button

default action

an attention panel in the Edit application

title

close button

a control panel in the Workspace application

Menus

A *menu* contains a vertical list of commands and submenus, or menu cells, which can be chosen with the click of a mouse button. An arrowhead at the right of a menu cell indicates a submenu whereas a character indicates a *keyboard alternative*, or key equivalent, to the mouse. Key alternatives are used in combination with one of the *Command* keys at the bottom of the keyboard. Menu commands which bring up panels are followed by three dots. Grayed-out (or dimmed) menu commands are disabled in the application's current context. Submenus may be "torn off" and placed anywhere on the screen. Menus and submenus should float on top of all other windows (except attention panels) and be visible only when the associated application is active. In NeXTSTEP 3.0, the locations of the main menu and torn-off submenus are automatically remembered between application launches. See Figure 4 below for examples of menus.

FIGURE 4. **Menus and Submenus**

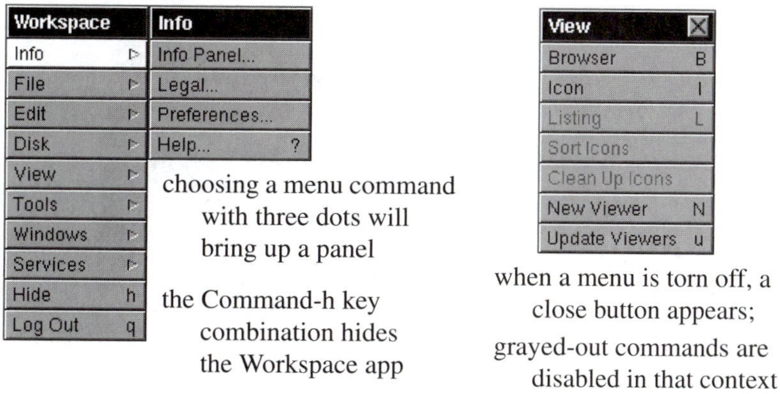

choosing a menu command
with three dots will
bring up a panel

the Command-h key
combination hides
the Workspace app

when a menu is torn off, a
close button appears;

grayed-out commands are
disabled in that context

Pop-Up Lists

A *pop-up list* is a menu-like list that appears *on top of* a button when the button is pressed. It is used in a window or panel instead of a series of mutually exclusive switches to save space. Unlike menu commands, pop-up-list commands should set a state rather than initiate an action. To select a command from a pop-up-list, a user would press the pop-up list button, drag to the desired command and finally release the mouse button. The chosen command remains atop the pop-up-list button representing the chosen state. Pop-up lists are sometimes given *numeric* keyboard alternatives (e.g. Command-1). See Figure 5 below for an example of a pop-up list.

FIGURE 5. Pop-Up List

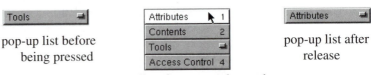

pop-up list before
being pressed

pop-up list after mouse dragged
from Tools to Attributes

pop-up list after
release

Pull-Down Lists

A *pull-down list* is a menu-like list that appears *below* a button when the button is pressed. Commands in a pull-down list should initiate actions much like menu commands. A command is selected from a pull-down list in the same way as from a pop-up list. Unlike a pop-up list, the title on a pull-down list doesn't change. Pull-down lists aren't very common because submenus are usually more appropriate. See Figure 6 below for an example of a pull-down list.

FIGURE 6. Pull-Down List

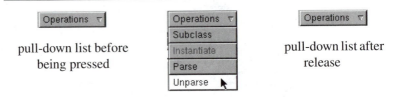

pull-down list before
being pressed

pull-down list after mouse dragged
from Operations to Unparse

pull-down list after
release

Pop-up and pull-down lists are little windows which float on top of other windows. However, they act more like controls because they prompt an action when one of their commands is chosen. We'll discuss controls in the section titled "Controls" on page 16.

Miniwindows

A *miniwindow* is a small (icon size) *titled* window representing a window that's been miniaturized. To expand the window to its original size and position, double-click the miniwindow. See Figure 7 below for an example of a window and its associated miniwindow, and Figure 1, "NeXTSTEP 3.0 Screen," on page 3 for an example of a miniwindow in the workspace.

FIGURE 7. Window and Associated Miniwindow

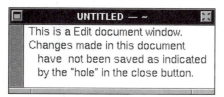

a standard window before being miniaturized; miniaturize it by clicking
the button at the upper left

miniwindow representing
the standard window
at the left;

double-click it to make it
normal size

Freestanding and Docked Icons

Application icons are icons that represent application programs. An application icon may be either *docked*, meaning that it is in the user's dock, or
freestanding, meaning that it isn't. See Figure 1, "NeXTSTEP 3.0 Screen,"
on page 3 for examples of each.

A docked application may either be running or not. If the application is *not*
running, three dots appear in the application icon's lower left corner. If the
application is launched by double-clicking its docked icon (or an associated file name or icon in the File Viewer), the three dots will disappear.

On the other hand, if an application without a docked icon is launched from
the File Viewer or by other means, then the Workspace Manager places its
application icon at the bottom of the workspace. This icon is freestanding
in the sense that it can be moved by direct manipulation, unlike the docked
icon for a running application. See Figure 8 below.

FIGURE 8. Freestanding and Docked Icons

the Edit icon as it would appear
freestanding or in the dock
when Edit is running

the Edit icon as it would appear
in the dock when Edit is not
running; note the three dots

Main and Key Windows

The *key* window is the standard window or panel which will respond to keyboard actions. It always has a *black* title bar. The *main* window is the standard window where a user does most of his or her work (e.g., a document window in a word processor or image window in a graphics editor). Most of the time the main window is also the key window because a user works in the main window most of the time. A main window relinquishes its key window status temporarily while a user gives instructions to an application in a panel. During this time the main window is not the key window, and has a *dark gray* title bar.

For example, if you are editing a file and choose the **Print** menu command, a Print panel will appear. The Print panel will temporarily become the key window and let you choose how many copies to print from the keyboard. The document window would still be the main window but would not accept key strokes.

Standard windows which are neither key nor main windows have *light gray* title bars. An application can only have one key and one main window at any given instant. The following table lists the three possibilities for a *standard window*:

If the standard window's title bar is:	Then the standard window is:
black	both the key window and the main window
dark gray	the main window but not the key window
light gray	neither the key window nor the main window

The following table lists the two possibilities for a *panel*, which can never be the main window and thus cannot have a dark gray title bar:

If the panel's title bar is:	Then the panel is:
black	the key window but not the main window
light gray	neither the key window nor the main window

Figure 9 contains a partial screen shot of two standard windows and the Print panel from the NeXTSTEP 3.0 Edit application. The Print panel is the key window (black title bar) and will respond to any keyboard actions (e.g., if a user types the "4" key then the selected number of copies, "1" in Figure 9, will change to "4"). The standard window titled "Window_1" is the main window (dark gray title bar) and was also the key window before the Print menu command was chosen. The standard window titled "Window_2" is neither the key nor the main window (light gray title bar).

FIGURE 9. **Main, Key, and Standard Windows**

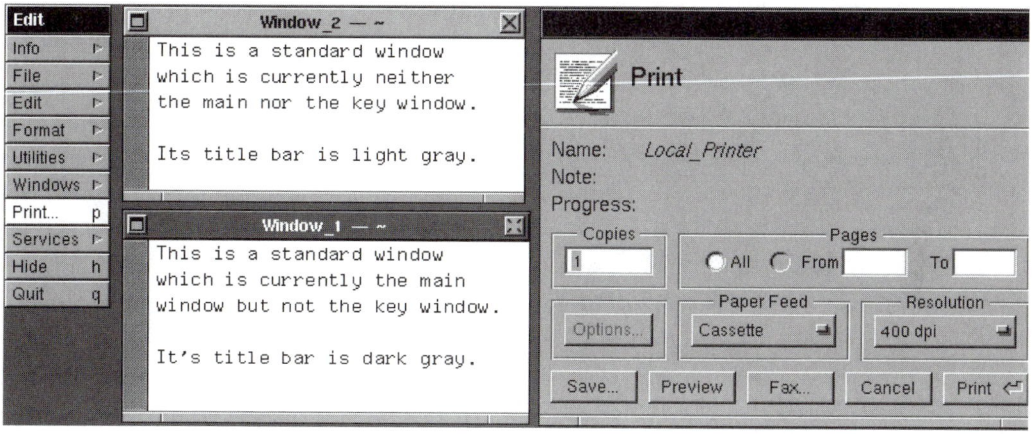

Window Order

When using NeXTSTEP on a large display there are often 30 or more windows on-screen (recall that icons, menus, and panels are all special types of windows). Without a clear window ordering scheme a user's screen would often be in chaos and the GUI would lose much of its ease of use. For example, suppose a new user had spent hours writing a document within an application without saving his work and an attention panel for that application demanded his action before he could save the document. If the attention panel was completely hidden by other windows then the user might think he had a hung application, resign himself to losing hours of work and kill the application (or worse, reboot). If the attention panel was front and center then this probably wouldn't happen. As another example, suppose a user couldn't find a menu for an application you wrote because it was hidden under several windows. The user wouldn't be very productive if she had to find the menu whenever she needed it and wouldn't have a great desire to use your application again.

To prevent this from happening, NeXTSTEP organizes the on-screen windows into seven levels (or tiers). If two windows belong to the same level then either one may be in front. However, if two windows belong to different levels and occupy the same screen space, then the one in the higher level is always in front. The seven levels are listed below from front to back:

1. spring-loaded windows (e.g., pop-up lists, pull-down lists, and menus which pop up at the cursor location in response to a mouse click – see "Configuring Your Workspace, Step by Step" on page 23 for examples)

2. attention panels

3. main menu

4. submenus

5. docked application icons

6. control panels

7. all other windows

Controls

NeXTSTEP *controls* are on-screen objects which perform like physical control devices we use every day. Consider the example of a car stereo system that has an on-off switch with indicator light, a row of buttons to select a radio station, a sliding knob to set volume, and a push button for ejecting a tape. Each of these devices is a control device with a different functionality. The on-off switch is a toggle, the radio buttons allow a choice of one out of many, the slider sets a level or value, and the push button forces an action. All of these physical control devices have analogous on-screen controls in NeXTSTEP.

There are seven standard control types in the NeXTSTEP user interface:

- Buttons
- Menu Commands
- Text fields
- Sliders
- Scrollers
- Browsers and Selection Lists
- Color Wells

Buttons

On-screen buttons fall into two main groups: *action* buttons and *two-state* buttons. An action button performs a single task such as opening a panel, saving a file, or closing a window. A two-state button sets a single feature or attribute on or off, such as whether or not text symbols should be shown in a document or borders should be shown around graphics objects in an image. In the stereo system analogy the eject button is an action button while the on-off switch is a two-state button. The set of car radio buttons is analogous to a matrix (group) of two-state buttons, each indicating whether the associated radio station is selected or not. There is more structure to this matrix of radio buttons, however, because only one of the two-state buttons may be selected at any one time.

Menu Commands

Menus are hierarchically arranged sets of buttons. Pop-up and pull-down lists are special kinds of menus. Menus are discussed extensively in "Menu Guidelines and Keyboard Alternatives" on page 29.

Text Fields

A *text field* is a rectangular area which can display a single line of text. The text is usually *editable*, so the user can change it, and *selectable*, so the user can drag across it or multiple-click it for subsequent cut, copy, and paste operations. Text fields are often arranged in groups where the Tab key can move the selection from one text field to the next. When the user types some text and then hits the Return key, the text field usually makes something happen; typically the text is read and some action is performed with it (e.g., a file is saved under a name typed into a text field in a Save panel).

Sliders and Scrollers

Scrollers let you scroll through a text or graphics area which is larger than the displayed view. *Sliders* let you set a value (e.g., floating point, integer) and are often accompanied by a text field displaying the value. You can grab a scroll or slider knob anywhere to drag it. You can also click anywhere in a scroller or slider well for larger movements. The middle of the knob will move to the position clicked.

The *size* of a scroll knob within the scroller well indicates the relative size of what you see compared with the total area. Thus in Figure 10 we see slightly more than half of the icons at the top of the Preferences window. Scrollers often contain scroll *buttons* for slow, consistent scrolling through an area. See the standard window in Figure 2 for a vertical scroller with scroll buttons.

FIGURE 10. Sliders and Scroller

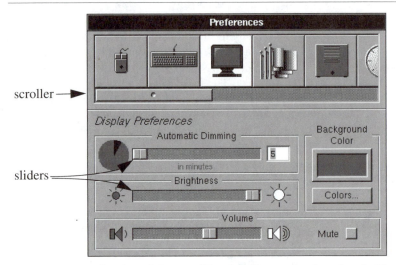

the size of the *scroll* knob indicates that less than half the icons above it are visible

the size of a *slider* knob doesn't change

Browsers and Selection Lists

Figure 11 below contains examples of a *browser* and a *selection list*. They are similar in that they both allow the user to select one or more items in a list. The difference is that a browser uses multiple lists to show data, such as files and folders, that's organized hierarchically, whereas a selection list contains a single list. The user can select an item in one of these controls by clicking it and then hitting Return to force an action, or by simply double-clicking the item for the same action.

Color Wells

A *color well* is used to select and manipulate colors. If you press the mouse down inside the color area of a color well (the white area in the color well at the left) and drag outward, you will drag out a chip of "color" which can be dropped on another on-screen object. Alternatively, you can click the mouse on the edge of a color well and bring up a Color panel, which can be

FIGURE 11. **Browser and Selection List**

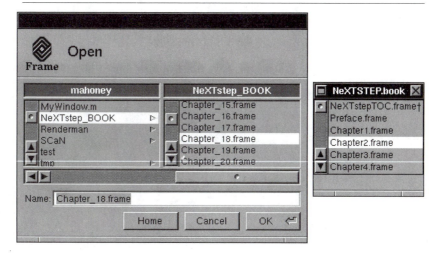

used to change the color well's color. Figure 10 above contains an example of a color well to change the background color. Color wells are explained in more detail in Chapter 17.

The Workspace Manager Application

The Workspace Manager application (or simply *Workspace* with a capital "W") is a special application in NeXTSTEP because it oversees the GUI environment and allows easy access to all other applications. The NeXT icon at the left represents the Workspace application just as the Edit icon represents the Edit application. At any time you can activate the Workspace Manager by double-clicking the NeXT icon at the top of the dock – it's always visible. Although the Workspace Manager is special it acts like other applications in most ways. It has a main menu, submenus, panels, windows, etc. which can be manipulated just as those for other applications. We begin our in-depth discussion of the Workspace Manager with the File Viewer.

The File Viewer

The *File Viewer* is the best creation we've seen for manipulating files in a hierarchical file system. Figure 1, "NeXTSTEP 3.0 Screen," on page 3 displays the files in a home folder with the *Browser* view. Figure 12 below shows a NeXTSTEP 3.0 File Viewer displaying the files in the **/NextApps** folder with the *Icon* view (some of the files in the **/NextApps** folder are different in NeXTSTEP 2.1). A UNIX-like listing of files called a *Listing* view is also available. The commands for choosing these views are available in the Workspace Manager's **View** submenu or via key alternatives.

FIGURE 12. File Viewer with Icon View of the /NextApps Folder

A File Viewer is made up of three major parts, the *shelf*, the *icon path*, and the *browser* (so named even though it might display an Icon or Listing view). The shelf is the area below a File Viewer's title bar which stores icons representing any type of folder or file. The icon in the upper left corner of the shelf you see on login always represents your home folder, normally a house icon. To place a file or folder icon on the shelf, simply drag it from the icon path or browser and release it in the shelf area. To take a file or folder icon off your shelf, drag it off and drop it in the workspace.

You should use the shelf mainly to store icons representing folders and document files you access frequently. (The shelf can also store file icons representing applications, but the dock is usually a better place because it cannot store any other type of icon.) A single click on any folder icon on the shelf opens that folder in the browser. Thus folders you access regularly are only a click away.

Double-clicking any document file icon on the shelf will launch (or activate) the associated application and open that file within the application.
Thus document files you need to edit or view regularly are only a double-
click away.

The shelf is also a handy place to temporarily put files or folders when
moving them from one folder to another. We'll show you how to do this
and also how to make your shelf resizable in the step-by-step exercises
later in this chapter.

The icon path in the middle of a File Viewer shows an ordered sequence of
icons which represents the path from the root folder to the current working
folder, whose files and folders are shown in the browser. If there are too
many folders to fit in the icon path, then a scroller allowing access to all the
icons appears just below the icon path.

Any folder can be represented with a custom icon simply by including an
icon file named "**.dir.tiff**" in the folder. The iconic image contained in the
"**.dir.tiff**" file shows up as the folder icon for the folder which contains the
file. We normally use the icon images at the left to represent our home folders. The size of the images doesn't matter – the Workspace Manager automatically scales the image to icon size. The icon displayed when the folder
opens can also be customized by including a file named "**.opendir.tiff**" in
the folder.

The Workspace Menu Structure

Workspace	
Info	▷
File	▷
Edit	▷
Disk	▷
View	▷
Tools	▷
Windows	▷
Services	▷
Hide	h
Log Out	q

As with all NeXTSTEP applications, the Workspace Manager menu structure is hierarchical. All but the last two items in the Workspace main menu
contain little triangles (arrowheads) at the right which indicate submenus.
To see a submenu, simply click the appropriate item in the main menu. The
submenu displayed will be attached to the main menu and will remain visible until another item in the main menu is chosen. If you want to hide an
attached submenu without choosing another command, then click the highlighted main menu item again. If you want to keep a submenu displayed at
all times when the Workspace is active, simply "tear off" the submenu from
the main menu by dragging its title bar. A close button will appear for a
torn off submenu so that the submenu may be closed when it's no longer
needed. Figure 13 shows the hierarchical nature of the submenus for the
NeXTSTEP 3.0 Workspace Manager application (NeXTSTEP 2.1 is very
similar). This hierarchy is typical of NeXTSTEP applications.

FIGURE 13. Workspace Manager Hierarchical Menu Structure

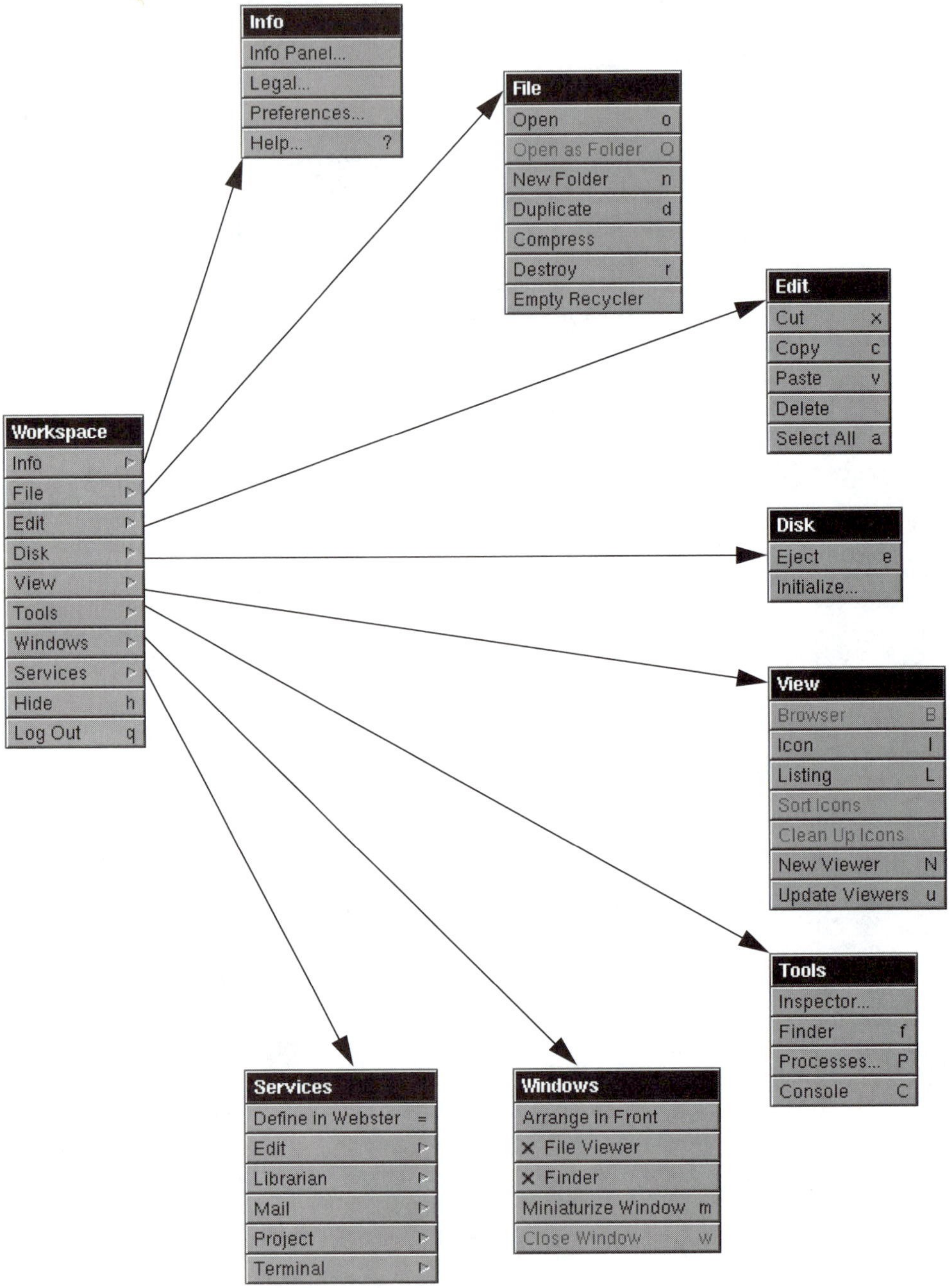

Info	
Info Panel...	
Legal...	
Preferences...	
Help...	?

File	
Open	o
Open as Folder	O
New Folder	n
Duplicate	d
Compress	
Destroy	r
Empty Recycler	

Edit	
Cut	x
Copy	c
Paste	v
Delete	
Select All	a

Workspace	
Info	▷
File	▷
Edit	▷
Disk	▷
View	▷
Tools	▷
Windows	▷
Services	▷
Hide	h
Log Out	q

Disk	
Eject	e
Initialize...	

View	
Browser	B
Icon	I
Listing	L
Sort Icons	
Clean Up Icons	
New Viewer	N
Update Viewers	u

Tools	
Inspector...	
Finder	f
Processes...	P
Console	C

Services	
Define in Webster	=
Edit	▷
Librarian	▷
Mail	▷
Project	▷
Terminal	▷

Windows	
Arrange in Front	
✕ File Viewer	
✕ Finder	
Miniaturize Window	m
Close Window	w

Workspace Manager Panels

There are several Workspace Manager panels which you should use regularly. These include the Preferences and Help panels, accessible via the **Info** submenu, and the Inspector, Finder and Processes panels, all accessible via the **Tools** submenu. All of these panels will be discussed in this chapter.

Configuring Your Workspace, Step by Step

This section takes you on a guided-tour of the NeXTSTEP Workspace Manager and Preferences applications. All the steps work under both NeXTSTEP 3.0 and NeXTSTEP 2.1. The screen shots are all from NeXT-STEP 3.0. We'll discuss the additional NeXTSTEP 3.0 configuration features in "New Features in the NeXTSTEP 3.0 Interface" on page 43.

To get the most out of these steps, we recommend that you follow them precisely. For example, start by logging in and do not close any windows or panels unless requested to do so. If you do not follow a step precisely or if you skip a step, then subsequent steps may not make sense.

1. **Log in** to a NeXTSTEP environment. To do this, you must have a username and a password. (If you just bought your NeXTSTEP computer, you will automatically be logged into the **me** account. For further information about user names and passwords, see NeXT's documentation.)

2. **Move your File Viewer around the workspace** by dragging its title bar. Any window, panel, or menu can be moved in this way.

3. **Make sure you are viewing files in your File Viewer in Browser mode** by choosing **View→Browser** from the Workspace menu (i.e. the **View** submenu item followed by the **Browser** menu command). If you are already in Browser mode, the menu item will be grayed out.

4. **Remove all the icons from your dock** (except for the NeXT and Recycler icons which are permanent) by dragging them from the dock and dropping them into the workspace (background).

    you can Command-drag the recycler from the dock

    If any applications are running, you must quit them before they can be dragged out of your dock. Running applications are those whose application icons do *not* contain 3 dots at the lower left corner. To quit a running application, double-click its icon and choose Quit from its main menu. Don't quit the Workspace application – that logs you out!

5. **Select the /NextApps folder (directory) in your File Viewer** by clicking the leftmost folder icon (probably a NeXT display monitor) in its icon path and selecting **NextApps** in the browser.

6. **Add the Preferences application to your dock** by selecting it in the browser, dragging its icon from your icon path and dropping it just below the NeXT icon in your dock.

7. **Add the Mail, Terminal, Edit, Librarian, and Webster applications to your dock** in a similar fashion. Only one application at a time can be dropped into the dock. If your machine isn't connected to a network you'll probably want to remove **Mail** later.

8. **Select the /NextDeveloper/Demos folder in your File Viewer** by selecting **NextDeveloper** and then **Demos** in your browser.

9. **Add Billiards** or any other interesting applications you like to your dock as was done above. There are so many demos that you'll have to drag the vertical scroll knob downward to see them all. You may also want to add applications from **/NextDeveloper/Apps** and **/LocalApps** to your dock. **/NextDeveloper/Apps** is the folder where some (*most* in NeXTSTEP 3.0) development tools are located. **/LocalApps** is the folder where third party applications are usually installed.

10. **Drag the NeXT icon at the top of your dock down as far as it will go and then drag it back up to the top of the screen.** The NeXT icon remains visible so you can always retrieve your dock and activate the Workspace application. Note that you can add "real estate" to your screen working area when necessary.

    Some application icons change to indicate something. For example, the running Preferences icon is a clock and the running Mail icon shows a sheaf of letters to indicate that you have new mail. You may wish to have these icons near the top of your dock so you can drag part of the dock below the screen and still see those "indicator" icons.

11. **Experiment with the different ways of displaying files in your File Viewer** by choosing **View→Icon** and **View→Listing** from the Workspace menu. **Sort Icons** only works in **Icon View** mode, which is why it may be grayed out.

12. **Put your File Viewer back in Browser mode**.

    You can keep the **View** submenu exposed by clicking Workspace's **View** main menu command without sliding it off onto the **View** submenu. NeXTSTEP is unlike many other GUIs in that submenus can always be made to "stay up."

13. **Bring up another File Viewer** by choosing **View→New Viewer**.

The new File Viewer has a *close button* in its title bar whereas the original File Viewer doesn't. You can't close your original File Viewer but you can miniaturize or hide it if you like. Note also that the new File Viewer opens the same folder as the original File Viewer.

14. **Reorder the File Viewer windows** by alternately clicking in one and then the other. This is known as "click-to-focus."[1]

15. **Close the new File Viewer** by clicking its close button.

16. **Close the View submenu** by choosing **View** from the Workspace main menu.

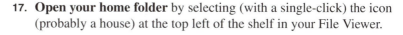 17. **Open your home folder** by selecting (with a single-click) the icon (probably a house) at the top left of the shelf in your File Viewer.

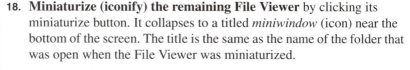 18. **Miniaturize (iconify) the remaining File Viewer** by clicking its miniaturize button. It collapses to a titled *miniwindow* (icon) near the bottom of the screen. The title is the same as the name of the folder that was open when the File Viewer was miniaturized.

19. **Move the miniwindow around the screen** by dragging any part of it.

Note that the miniwindow will not cover the dock or menus, because it is in a lower tier (see "Window Order" on page 15).

20. **Expand this File Viewer** to its former size (and position) by double-clicking its miniwindow.

21. **Open the Workspace Manager Preferences panel** by choosing **Info→Preferences** from the Workspace menu. See Figure 14.

Note that the color of the File Viewer's title bar turned dark gray, indicating that it is the main window but not the key window.

 22. **Force the Preferences, Mail, and Terminal applications to auto-launch following login** by clicking the switches next to their names and then the **Set** button in the Workspace Manager Preferences panel.

 23. **Change the contents of the Preferences panel** by pressing the pop-up list button titled "**Dock**," dragging to "**Shelf**" and releasing the mouse button. Note that "**Shelf**" is the new title on the pop-up list.

---

1. Many workstations that use the X Windows window system use *point-to-focus* (or *mouse-to-focus*) rather than click-to-focus. With point-to-focus, windows become active when you move the cursor on top of them. Point-to-focus can result in commands being accidentally sent to the wrong application if your mouse is bumped. This is one of the reasons that NeXTSTEP doesn't use this interaction system. On the other hand, some people prefer point-to-focus because it requires less clicking.

FIGURE 14. Workspace Manager Preferences Panel

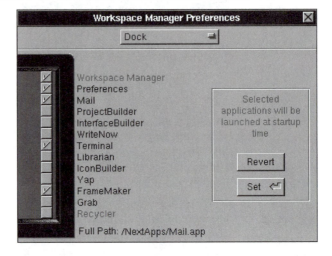

24. **Make your File Viewer shelves resizable** by clicking the **Resizable Shelf**" *switch* button. Note the *new knob* (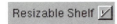) at the bottom middle of your shelf.

25. **Close the Workspace Manager Preferences panel** by clicking its close button (or by typing Command-w). (Note that there are other useful preferences, such as **Disk Options**, which can be set here.)

26. **Make your File Viewer taller** by pressing on the middle part of its resize bar (at the bottom of the File Viewer) and dragging downward.

27. **Enlarge the shelf** in your File Viewer by pressing its **knob** ( ) and dragging it downward about an inch.

28. **Hide the Workspace Manager** by choosing **Hide** from the Workspace main menu. **Activate the Workspace Manager** by double-clicking the NeXT icon in your dock.

29. **Launch the Preferences application** by double-clicking its icon in your dock. Note the new main menu at the upper left corner of the screen. **Preferences** has become the *active* application.

    not running

    The Preferences *application* lets you set *global* preferences which work across applications whereas a Preferences *panel* within an application lets you set preferences only for that particular application.

30. **Change the speed at which the cursor moves relative to your mouse movement** by clicking the **mouse icon button** atop the Preferences window (if necessary) and then clicking one of the four choices in the **Mouse Speed** box. See Figure 15.

FIGURE 15. Mouse, Date & Time Preferences

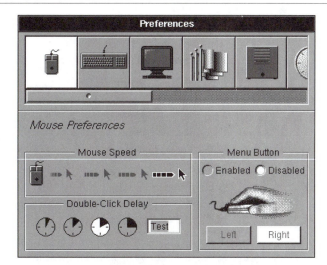

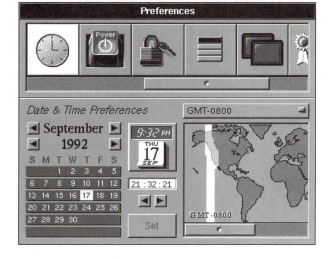

Preferences
application icon
(while running)

31. **Choose an application font** (one which shows up in your File Viewer and other windows on subsequent login) by clicking the **NeXTcube icon button** in the Preferences window, clicking the **Set Font (or Font Panel) button** and then selecting a font from the Font Panel (finish by clicking the **Set** button in the Font panel). Choose a size in the range 10-14. Close the Font Panel by clicking its close box.

32. **Choose a system beep** by selecting a sound from the list of choices in the box titled "**System Beep**".

33. **Choose a clock style** by clicking the **clock icon button** atop the Preferences window and then the **clock button** in the middle repeatedly until your favorite clock style appears. See Figure 15.

    You can change the time by clicking the arrow buttons and the time zone by dragging on the vertical white time line.[1]

34. **Choose a default menu position** for *all* applications by clicking the **menu icon button** atop the Preferences window (you may have to first drag the **scroll knob** below the icons to the right) and then dragging the little menu in the **Menu Location** box. The best menu position for most people is at the top left of the screen.

35. **Force your File Viewer and other file windows to display UNIX system files** by clicking the "UNIX" button atop the Preferences window (drag the scroll knob, if necessary) and then clicking the "**UNIX Expert**" switch.

    Dot files (those whose names begin with a "."") and files in the **/bin**, **/etc**, and other *system* folders will immediately show up in your File Viewers, Open and Save Panels, etc. (Being a "UNIX Expert" in NeXTSTEP 2.1 also enables you to create **UNIX Shell windows** from the Workspace **Tools** submenu on subsequent login.)

36. **Make your new clock style choice show up in the dock** by choosing **Hide** from Preferences' main menu. Note that the Workspace Manager automatically becomes the *active* application (since it was the active application just before Preferences was activated).

37. **See all of your new system preferences take effect** by logging out and logging back in. Note the applications which auto-launch in your dock and the new text style in your File Viewer.

38. "**Tear off**" **the Workspace Tools submenu** by choosing **Tools** from the Workspace main menu and then dragging the **Tools** submenu title bar downward about an inch. Note the *new close button* in the title bar.

39. **Again choose the Tools submenu item** from the Workspace main menu and note that the *attached* submenu won't stay up (because the **Tools** submenu has been torn off).

40. **Log out** (or type Command-q).

---

1. Often networked workstations are configured so that only the superuser can change the time.

Menu Guidelines and Keyboard Alternatives

Developers should follow NeXTSTEP's menu guidelines carefully so users of their applications can learn and work faster. Common menu structure and commands are crucial to better productivity within a GUI. In this section we discuss most of the NeXTSTEP menu and associated keyboard alternative guidelines. For further details see the *NeXTSTEP User Interface Guide* (available using **anonymous ftp** at NeXT archive sites).

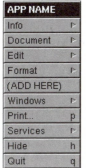

A keyboard alternative (equivalent) is a way of manipulating a graphical object (usually a menu) using the keyboard rather than the mouse. It works by typing a single key (perhaps modified by the shift key) while pressing one of the Command keys near the bottom of the NeXT keyboard. Experienced users use keyboard alternatives because they are faster than manipulating the mouse. Using the mouse is a more natural way to manipulate graphical objects, but it's often slower and less convenient because either the user's hands are already on the keyboard, or mouse (cursor) movements across a screen are time-consuming and clumsy.

A keyboard alternative usually substitutes for a click of a menu command, but may also substitute for a pop-up list command. In the latter case the alternative key should be a digit (e.g., Command-2 activates the second item down from the top of a pop-up list). Since most keyboard alternatives are common across applications, a user will only need to use 10-20 of them to speed up his work considerably. The most common and useful keyboard alternatives are listed in the tables below. Others can be seen in the screen shots of the menus themselves.

Main Menu

The main menu for an application should *always* display the application's (possibly abbreviated) name in the title bar and contain **Info**, **Services**, **Hide** and **Quit** commands. The other commands in the menu on the left are application dependent, but if included should be placed in the order shown. If additional main menu commands such as **Tools**, **Page**, **View**, etc. are included, then they should be inserted where "**(ADD HERE)**" is located.

A submenu command is sometimes *promoted* up a level to the main menu if it's essential to the application. For example, the **Font** or **Find** commands might be promoted from the **Format** or **Edit** submenu to the main menu in a word processor. If this decision is made, then the promoted commands should immediately follow the submenus where they would normally be found. Thus a promoted **Font** command would follow **Format** in the main menu.

Keyboard Alternative	Main Menu Command
Command-p	Print
Command-h	Hide
Command-q	Quit

Info Submenu

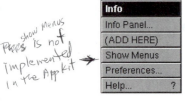

Info submenu commands should allow users to get information about the application as a whole, and set preferences for the application as a whole. Additional commands, such as those to bring up a **License** or **Copyright** panel, should be added immediately after the **Info Panel** command. The **Show Menus** command will show all the menus of the application, but is not implemented in NeXTSTEP release 2.1 or earlier. **Help** is the only command with a key alternative because it's the only command used often enough to warrant one. The **Info Panel** command should never have a keyboard alternative.

Show Menus is not implemented in the AppKit [handwritten note]

Document (or File) Submenu

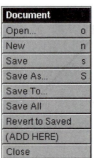

Document submenu commands affect a document or file as a whole. They can be used to open, create, or save almost any kind of document or file that is appropriate to the particular application. The title "**Document**" should be used when the application can open, create, or save files containing *text*, such as a word processor. Other possible titles for this type of menu are "**Model**" (for spreadsheets), "**Image**" (for graphics file), "**Game**" (for games), but not "**Window**" as it's not very specific and would confuse users with the "**Windows**" submenu (discussed below). As with the main menu, not all of the commands in the **Document** submenu at the left are required, but if included should be ordered as shown. **Save As** and **Save To** will both save the contents of the main window to a file with a new name, but only **Save As** will change the name of the file in the main window itself.

Keyboard Alternative	Document Menu Command
Command-o	Open
Command-n	New
Command-s	Save
Command-S	Save As

Edit Submenu

Edit submenu commands can be used to manipulate text, graphics and other objects in the *key* window. Their keyboard alternatives are perhaps the most worthwhile to learn because they are used often in a variety of places. They can be used in most text and graphics areas in any main window or panel which is the key window. **Edit** submenu key alternatives are very convenient, especially for right-handed people, because they can be performed easily with your left hand while your right hand is on the mouse. Occasionally the **Find** command is promoted from the **Edit** submenu to the main menu.

Keyboard Alternative	Edit Menu Command
Command-x	Cut
Command-c	Copy
Command-v	Paste
Command-z	Undo
Command-a	Select All

Find Submenu

Find submenu commands allow easy access to Find *panel* choices such as finding a character string and finding the next or previous appearance of the same string. The **Enter Selection** command enters the current selected text into the Find panel's Find field for subsequent searches.

Keyboard Alternative	File Menu Command
Command-f	Find, Find Panel
Command-g	Find Next
Command-d	Find Previous

Format Submenu

Format submenu commands affect the *layout* of text and graphics documents. Usually the **Font** command is a choice in the **Format** submenu, but it can be promoted to the main menu. The only common keyboard alternative is for **Page Layout**, which brings up a standard panel with portrait, landscape, page size, and other choices.

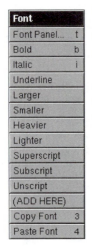

Font Submenu

Font submenu commands such as **Bold** and **Italic** affect one aspect of text font. There are several other common **Font** submenu commands which affect font size and style but are not shown here. You can find out what these common commands are by exploring Edit and Interface Builder. The **Font Panel** command brings up a standard panel with font family, type-face, and size choices.

Keyboard Alternative	Menu Command
Command-t	Font Panel
Command-b	Bold
Command-i	Italic

Windows Submenu

Windows submenu commands apply to windows within the active application. The **Miniaturize** and **Close Window** commands apply only to the *key* window (which might be a panel). The **Arrange in Front** command will arrange all *main* windows for the active application *front and center* in a cascaded fashion. The **Window_1** and **Window_2** commands in the submenu at the left were added dynamically as *main* windows for the application were opened. Choosing one of them will make that window the key window and bring it to the front.

The particular **Windows** menu shown above belongs to the Edit application we saw in Figure 9, "Main, Key, and Standard Windows," on page 15. The contents of **Window_2** had been saved, but the contents of **Window_1** had not, as indicated by the symbols on the left of the menu cells and the close buttons in Figure 9. The number of items in the **Windows** submenu grows and shrinks dynamically as *main* windows are opened and closed in an application.

Keyboard Alternative	Menu Command
Command-m	Miniaturize Window
Command-w	Close Window

Services Submenu

Services submenu commands allow for communication between different programs. Most services take the selected text or object in the key window and perform some sort of function. For example, if you select a word and then use the Librarian service **Search**, the word will be searched in NeXT-STEP's Digital Librarian application.

Working with the File System, Step by Step

The Workspace Manager's main use is for managing files stored on your computer's hard and floppy disks, and over the network. This section shows you many of Workspace's operations and menu commands for managing files. All the steps work under both NeXTSTEP 3.0 and NeXTSTEP 2.1. The screen shots are all from NeXTSTEP 3.0. If you're using 3.0, see the section "New Features in the NeXTSTEP 3.0 Interface" on page 43.

To get the most out of these steps, we recommend that you follow them precisely.

1. **Log in**.

2. **Open your home folder (directory)** by selecting (with a single-click) the icon (probably a house) at the top left of the shelf in your File Viewer.

3. **Create a new folder under your home folder** by choosing **File→New Folder** from the Workspace menu (i.e. **File**, then **New Folder**).

4. **Make sure the text "NewFolder" in the icon path of the File Viewer is selected** (in dark gray) as in the screen shot at the left. If it isn't, then double-click the text "**NewFolder**" to select it.

5. **Rename the New Folder "stuff"** by entering "stuff" on the keyboard. As before, *enter* means hit the Return key after typing the text.

6. **Make your stuff folder easily accessible** by dragging its icon from your icon path and dropping it on your shelf. Whenever you need to access the stuff folder, all you need to do is click its icon on the shelf. It works much like a radio button in your car.

7. **Open the /NextLibrary/Sounds folder** in your File Viewer by simply entering "**/NextLibrary/Sounds**" (the Workspace Finder panel automatically opens) on the keyboard. While you are typing the Finder is the *key window* (black title bar) and the File Viewer is the *main window* (dark gray title bar). See Figure 16 below.

    In NeXTSTEP 3.0 it's possible that a separate *folder window* opened in this step; it depends on how the Finder option in the Preferences panel is set. If this occurred, then close the folder window after Step 15 below is completed.

    UNIX file names are *case sensitive* – an uppercase "A" is a different character than a lowercase "a" – so be sure to use the correct capitalization. Also, use *forward* slashes as separators, and do not type the quotes.

    FIGURE 16. Workspace Finder Panel

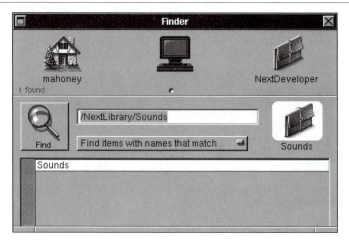

8. **Select the Funk.snd file** by clicking the file name "**Funk.snd**" in the browser. Note the **Funk.snd** icon in the icon path.

9. Without releasing the mouse button, drag the **Funk.snd** icon from the icon path so it's on top of the **stuff** folder icon on your shelf.

    Note that the folder icon "opens" and the cursor changes to a little *two-page* (⬚) *icon*. This indicates that a *copy* operation is about to take place.

10. **Now drop (i.e., release the mouse button)** the **Funk.snd icon** atop the **stuff** folder icon and note that "**Copying...**" appears at the lower right corner of your shelf.

While they are being executed in the background, copy, move, and other file operations are indicated by small text in the lower *right* corner of your shelf. These operations are in the *background* in the sense that you may request that other Workspace operations be performed simultaneously.

The small text in the lower *left* corner of your shelf indicates the amount of free space remaining on the disk containing the folder.

11. Again **drag the Funk.snd icon from the icon path and drop it atop the stuff folder icon on your shelf**. Your chosen *system beep* sounds and the Workspace Processes panel opens to alert you that the file **Funk.snd** already exists in your **stuff** folder. See Figure 17 below and note the *two-page* (⌔) icon in the Processes panel to the left of the file being copied.

12. **Stop the copy operation** by clicking the **Stop** button in the Processes panel.

13. **Move the Processes panel to a relatively unused area of the screen,** say just below the Workspace main menu. Do not close the Processes panel as we'll use it later.

14. **Hear the contents of the Funk.snd file** by double-clicking its icon in your icon path. The **Sound** (**SoundPlayer** in NeXTSTEP 2.1) application in **/NextDeveloper/Demos** automatically launches. Play the sound by clicking the **Play** button.

15. **Quit the active Sound** (or **SoundPlayer**) **application** by choosing **Quit** at the bottom of its menu. Note that the previous active application, namely the Workspace Manager, automatically becomes active.

16. **Discover which applications are running** in the Workspace by pressing on the **Background** pop-up list button and dragging to **Applications** in the Processes panel. (If it's not displayed, you can display the Processes panel by choosing the **Tools→Processes** command.) The applications listed as running in your Processes panel probably differ from those in Figure 17.

The **Kill button** in Figure 17 provides a simple way to quit applications which are *hung* (unable to continue processing). If an application is hung then double-click the NeXT icon to activate the Workspace application, open the Processes panel, select the hung application from the list of running applications and click the **Kill** button. Do *not* use this method to quit an application unless it is hung.

17. **Open your home folder** as in Step 2 above.

FIGURE 17. **Workspace Processes Panel**

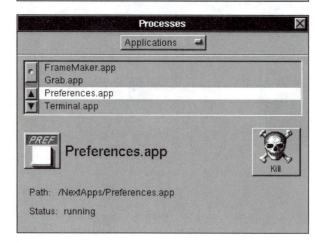

18. **Create another new folder called "junk" under your home folder**
    by typing Command-n (the *key alternative* for **File→New Folder**), and
    renaming "**NewFolder**" as in Steps 4-5 above. To type Command-n
    hold down one of the Command keys while typing the "n" key.

19. **Make your junk folder easily accessible** by dragging its icon from
    your icon path and dropping it on your shelf.

20. **Open the stuff folder** by clicking its icon on your shelf.

21. **Select the file Funk.snd** in your browser (use a *single*-click).

22. **Make a copy of the Funk.snd file in the stuff folder** by choosing **File→Duplicate** from the Workspace menu (or type Command-d). Note that "**Duplicating...**" appears at the lower right corner of your shelf and you soon have a new file named "**CopyOfFunk.snd**" in your browser.

23. **Without releasing the mouse button, drag the Funk.snd icon from the icon path so it's atop the junk folder icon on your shelf.**

move
cursor
in 3.0

The two-page cursor does *not* appear this time, instead the cursor remains an arrow (and turns *white* in NeXTSTEP 3.0). The arrow indicates that the file **Funk.snd** will be *moved* to the **junk** folder, *not copied*.

24. **Release the mouse button** and check the contents of the **stuff** and **junk** folders. Note that the **Funk.snd** file appears only in the **junk** folder. "**Moving...**" would have appeared at the bottom right of your shelf if the move operation took longer.

Move
vs.
Copy

If you are the owner of both folders and they reside on the same physical disk, then the file in the *drag-and-drop* operations above is moved, not copied. Otherwise, the file is copied. This behavior also applies when you drag and drop *multiple files* or *folders*.

25. **Open the junk folder** by selecting its icon in your shelf.

26. **Select the Funk.snd** file in your browser.

mahoney

27. **Without releasing the mouse button, drag the Funk.snd icon from your icon path atop each of the icons in your shelf and your icon path.** Some of the folder icons (e.g., your **home icon**) change to "open" icons indicating that you have permission to move or copy files into those folders.

28. **Keeping the mouse button pressed, drag the Funk.snd icon atop the stuff folder icon on your shelf and press an Alternate key.** Note that the *two-page* cursor appears. Release the mouse button while pressing the *Alternate* key and note that the **Funk.snd** file is *copied* into the **stuff** folder.

You have *forced a copy* by using the *Alt* key.

29. **Open the junk folder "as a folder"** by first clicking the **junk** icon in your icon path and then choosing **File→Open as Folder** from the Workspace menu (or type Command-O).

The new *folder window* that opens functions the same as a File Viewer except that it can only access files located under the **junk** folder.

30. **Close the junk folder window** by clicking its close button.

Note that a file called "**.dir3_0.wmd**" ("**.dir.wmd**" in NeXTSTEP 2.1) is automatically saved in the **junk** folder. This file contains information about the folder window such as its location, size, and shelf icons. This information will be used the next time you open **junk** *as a folder*. (If the "**.dir3_0.wmd**" doesn't show up, then type Command-u (or choose to *update* the File Viewer. If it still doesn't show up, then you didn't turn on the *UNIX Expert* switch in the Preferences application.)

31. Use the Workspace **Finder** together with **file name completion** to open the **/NextDeveloper/Examples/PostScript** folder as follows:

    (a) type "**/NextD**" and then the *Escape* (**Esc**) key

    (b) type "**/E**" and then the Escape key again,

    (c) type "**/Po**" and then the Escape key one more time.

    (d) hit the **Return** key

    Note how the folder names are completed when the Escape key is typed. Partially typed folder (or file) names must be unique to be completed. The system beep will alert you if the name isn't completed.

5 items

32. **Select multiple files in your browser** by pressing the mouse button down on "**Arrows.eps**" and dragging downward across five file names. When you release the mouse button a *hand-of-cards* icon representing the files appears in your icon path. (In NeXTSTEP 2.1, the number of selected files is *not* displayed beneath the hands-of-cards icon.)

33. **Deselect the CircularText.eps file** in the browser by holding down a *Shift* key while clicking the name "**CircularText.eps**".

    This action is known as *Shift-clicking*. It *toggles* whether the object you click is selected or not.

34. **Drag the hand-of-cards icon** (which now represents only four files) **and drop it on your shelf**.

35. **Launch the Preview application and see the contents of all selected** "**.eps**" (Encapsulated PostScript) **files** simultaneously by simply double-clicking the hand-of-cards icon in your icon path.

    If an application other than Preview was launched then the account you're using has been configured so that "**.eps**" files launch that other application. This was done in the Workspace Inspector panel which we'll discuss later.

36. **Hide the application that was launched in the previous step** by typing Command-h. Note how all the windows displaying "**.eps**" files "hide" behind the freestanding (or docked) application icon.

37. **If you see a freestanding icon** near the bottom left of the screen, **then move it around the screen** by dragging any part of it. If you can't see one, then either there isn't one (because the application icon is in the dock) or it may be hidden behind windows which cover the bottom left of your screen. In the latter case, move the windows.

    As with miniwindows, an application icon will not cover the dock or menus (or attention panels if any were on the screen) once it's released; however, it "floats" above other windows.

38. **Activate the application** by double-clicking its freestanding (or docked) icon.

39. **Move your File Viewer without activating the Workspace Manager** by *Alt-dragging* its title bar.

    Alt-dragging (i.e., holding down an Alternate key while dragging) lets you rearrange an application's windows without having to activate the application.

40. **Send the File Viewer to the back** (i.e., behind other windows) by *Command-clicking* on its title bar (i.e., pressing a Command key while clicking the mouse on the title bar).

41. **Cycle through all the windows and panels on the screen** by holding down a Command key while repeatedly pressing the up (or down) arrow key. Note how you can find hidden windows in non-active applications without changing the active application.

42. **Quit the application** (probably Preview) displaying the "**.eps**" files.

43. **Copy the files represented by the hand-of-cards icon to your junk folder** by dragging the icon from your shelf and dropping it atop the **junk** folder icon which is also on your shelf. Watch the Processes panel and note that all the files are copied.

    You can *drag-and-drop* icons from the File Viewer's shelf, icon path, or browser (in Icon view) to any other area of the File Viewer – or any other application that accepts *drag-and-drop*.

44. **Open your junk folder** by clicking its icon on your shelf.

45. **Select your new Compositing.eps and Funk.snd file**s by clicking **Compositing.eps** and then *Shift-clicking* **Funk.snd** in your browser.

    Shift-clicking lets you to *select* or *deselect* files (or folders) when they aren't consecutive in a browser listing.

46. **Drag the hand-of-cards icon representing the two files and drop it on the recycler icon** at the bottom of your dock. Note that this hand-of-cards icon looks like the previous one (except the number of items). Moving, copying or deleting hands-of-cards can be dangerous.

    The *ball* in the middle of the recycler icon indicates that the recycler contains files.

47. **See which files are stored in the recycler** by double-clicking the recycler icon. The Recycler *window* opens.

48. **Recover the "recycled" Funk.snd file** by dragging it from the recycler and dropping it on the **junk** folder icon on your shelf (or icon path).

49. **Delete the file(s) in the recycler** by choosing **File→Empty Recycler** from the Workspace menu. Close the Recycler window.

50. **Select the Arrows.eps file** in your **junk** folder in your File Viewer.

51. **Make a link to the Arrows.eps file** in the **stuff** folder by *Control*-dragging the **Arrows.eps** file icon from your icon path and dropping it on your **stuff** folder. Note that the cursor changes to the link cursor (🔗) to indicate that a UNIX file link is being made. The **Arrows.eps** *entry* in the **stuff** folder is a *reference* to the **Arrows.eps** file in **junk**.

52. **Inspect the attributes of your junk folder** by selecting it in your File Viewer and choosing **Tools→Inspector** from the Workspace menu. See Figure 18 below. If necessary move the Inspector panel so it doesn't cover any part of your File Viewer.

53. **Determine the size (in bytes) of your junk folder** by clicking the **Compute Size** button in the Attributes Inspector panel. Note that "Sizing..." appears at the lower right corner of your shelf.

54. **Change the permissions of your Arrows.eps file** by first selecting it in your browser. Then click the **Read-Group** and **Read-Other** switches in the permissions matrix in the Attributes Inspector panel, and click **OK**. Now other users can't read your **Arrows.eps** file.

55. **Inspect the contents of your Arrows.eps file** by pressing the **Attributes** pop-up list button, dragging to **Contents**, and then clicking the **Display** button (if necessary). See Figure 18 above.

56. **Determine which tool (application) will be activated to inspect** *any* **file with an ".eps" extension** in the File Viewer by dragging to **Tools** in the Inspector panel pop-up list. The highlighted application icon indicates the application (probably Preview) which was activated when the "**.eps**" files were double-clicked in a previous step. You can change the tool by selecting a different application icon in the panel.

FIGURE 18. Workspace Inspector Panels

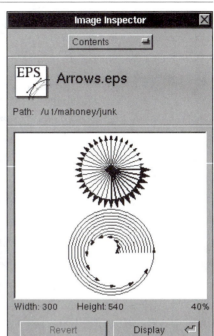

57. **Determine which tool will be activated to inspect any file with a
    ".snd" extension** in the File Viewer by selecting **Funk.snd** in your
    browser. The **SoundPlayer** (or **Sound**) application is (probably) the
    current tool.

58. **Inspect the contents of your Funk.snd file** by typing Command-2
    (the key alternative for the Contents Inspector) and clicking the **Play**
    button to play the sound from the Workspace application.

    Whenever the Workspace application is active you can use the key
    alternatives Command-1, Command-2, Command-3, and Command-4
    to access the Attributes, Contents, Tools, and Access Control Inspec-
    tors, respectively. These are worth remembering because they work
    even when the Inspector panel is closed.

59. **Inspect the contents of your junk folder** by selecting it in your File
    Viewer and looking in the Inspector panel. Note that you can sort files
    in the **junk** folder in various ways and can also *recursively* change
    permissions of the files (and folders, if any existed) under a folder. (In
    NeXTSTEP 3.0 you need to drag to **Access Control** in the Inspector's
    pop-up list, or type Command-4, to recursively change permissions.)

60. **Open Librarian.app "as a folder"** by navigating to **/NextApps** in your File Viewer, selecting **Librarian.app**, and choosing **File→Open as Folder** from the Workspace menu.

61. **View files in the Librarian.app folder window in Listing mode** by choosing **View→Listing** from the Workspace menu. See Figure 19.

    Librarian.app looks like a simple file but is actually a folder which contains "**.tiff**" images and other files and folders which support the Librarian application. The folder **Librarian.app** is called an *app wrapper.*

FIGURE 19. Librarian.app Opened as a Folder

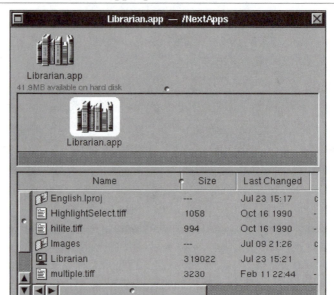

62. **Clean up your workspace** by closing the Librarian application folder and the Workspace Inspector panel.

63. **Log out**.

New Features in the NeXTSTEP 3.0 Interface

Our discussion so far has been applicable to both NeXTSTEP 3.0 and NeXTSTEP 2.1, even though the screen shots are all from NeXTSTEP 3.0. In this section we'll list most of the *new* features of the NeXTSTEP 3.0 GUI which are *not* available in NeXTSTEP 2.1.

Workspace Manager 3.0 Menus: New Commands

? • **Info→Help**   brings up the Workspace Help panel for hypertext-like help (see Figure 20 below). Read the first few sections on getting help in the panel for a quick introduction. Holding down the Control and Alternate keys simultaneously (or Help key on a new keyboard) brings up the "question mark" help cursor seen at the left.

FIGURE 20. Workspace Manager Help Panel

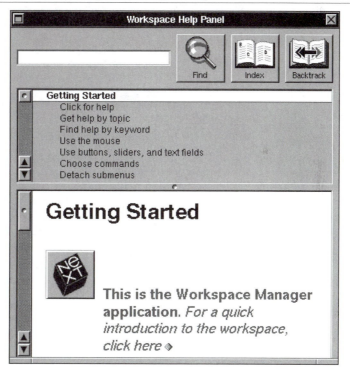

• **File→Compress**   will ~~using~~ use the standard UNIX **compress** command to compress any file selected in the File Viewer (to save space) and give it the ".**compressed**" file extension. When the **.compressed** file is subsequently selected this menu command will change to **File→Decompress**. Choosing **File→Decompress** will decompress the file and restore the original file. Note the new "compressed" icon at the left of the page. The **File→Compress** command will also compress a *folder* to a single file. When compressing a folder, **File→Compress** uses the standard UNIX **tar** command in addition to the UNIX **compress**.

- **View→Clean Up Icons**   organizes the icons in the File Viewer's browser area in Icon view mode only.

- **Tools→New Shell**   has been *deleted* in NeXTSTEP 3.0.

- **Windows→Arrange in Front**   was described in generic terms earlier in this chapter. It was omitted from the NeXTSTEP 2.1 Workspace Manager for some reason (probably a bug or an oversight).

- **Services→Project**   will add a file to a programming project or build a project directly from the Workspace (see Chapter 5 for details).

- **Services→Terminal**   will perform UNIX commands in a Terminal window. The commands available can be determined by the user in the Terminal application (**Info→Terminal Services** menu command).

Workspace Manager 3.0 Panels: New Features

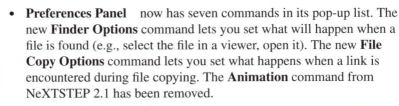

- **Preferences Panel**   now has seven commands in its pop-up list. The new **Finder Options** command lets you set what will happen when a file is found (e.g., select the file in a viewer, open it). The new **File Copy Options** command lets you set what happens when a link is encountered during file copying. The **Animation** command from NeXTSTEP 2.1 has been removed.

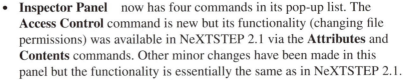

- **Inspector Panel**   now has four commands in its pop-up list. The **Access Control** command is new but its functionality (changing file permissions) was available in NeXTSTEP 2.1 via the **Attributes** and **Contents** commands. Other minor changes have been made in this panel but the functionality is essentially the same as in NeXTSTEP 2.1.

- **Finder Panel**   is more functional because a user may store folders to search in a bookshelf-like area at the top of the panel. See Figure 16, "Workspace Finder Panel," on page 34 for an example.

- **Initialize Disk Panel**   will now format floppy disks in NeXT, DOS, or Macintosh format. See Figure 21 below.

NextApps, NextDeveloper/Apps Folders in NeXTSTEP 3.0

Most NeXTSTEP 3.0 development tools (applications) reside in the **/NextDeveloper/Apps** folder (see Figure 22 below). **InterfaceBuilder**, which was in the **/NextApps** folder in NeXTSTEP 2.1, and **Yap** (PostScript code

FIGURE 21. **Initialize Disk Panel in NeXTSTEP 3.0**

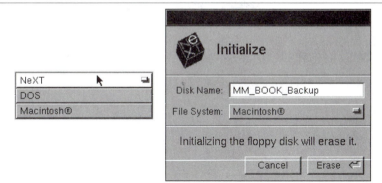

FIGURE 22. **NextDeveloper/Apps Folder in NeXTSTEP 3.0**

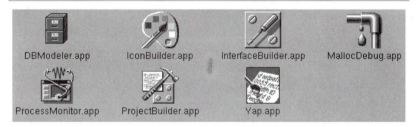

builder and previewer), which was in the **NextDeveloper/Demos** folder in NeXTSTEP 2.1, have both been moved to **NextDeveloper/Apps** in NeXT-STEP 3.0. **HeaderViewer**, a valuable new developer's tool for accessing on-line information, can be found in the 3.0 **NextDeveloper/Demos** folder.

InterfaceBuilder has been split into two applications: **InterfaceBuilder** (3.0) which only builds interfaces (**.nib** files) and a new development tool, called **ProjectBuilder**, which takes over the project building capability of the NeXTSTEP 2.1 **InterfaceBuilder**. Another new development tool, called **IconBuilder**, makes it easy to build icons for applications, files, and folders, and replaces the buggy (but innovative) **Icon** application from NeXTSTEP 2.1. We believe all of these changes make life better for NeXTSTEP developers.

The NeXTSTEP 3.0 **NextApps** folder (see Figure 23 below) contains one new application, called **Grab**, which will grab screen shots. It's similar to the **Grab** application in **NextDeveloper/Demos** from NeXTSTEP 2.1, but is more stable and can now take "timed" screen shots. **Grab** was used to capture all of the graphics images in this text.

The **Installer** application has been moved from **/NextApps** to **/NextAdmin** in NeXTSTEP 3.0. The **Preview** application now previews **.tiff** (as well as PostScript) images. **Mathematica** (except for educational customers) and **WriteNow** are no longer bundled. If you own them, re-install them to the **/LocalApps** folder, where third party applications are normally installed.

FIGURE 23. NextApps Folder in NeXTSTEP 3.0

Preferences Application: New Features

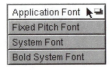

There are several *great* new features in the NeXTSTEP 3.0 **Preferences** application. In the **General Preferences** (cube icon) section you can change the menu font (**System Font**) and title bar font (**Bold Font**) for all menus, windows, and panels. This will be greatly appreciated by people who don't see well and people who give on-line demonstrations to groups. In the **Display Preferences** (monitor icon) section you can now change the background color (see Figure 10, "Sliders and Scroller," on page 18) and in the new **Services Preferences** you can choose services you want to appear in applications.

Summary

Although there is far more to learn about using NeXTSTEP, this brief introduction is probably enough to get you started. In the next chapter, we will look at some of the NeXTSTEP developer's tools. Then in Chapter 3, we'll start creating our first program.

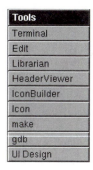

2

NeXTSTEP Development Tools

There are several bundled NeXTSTEP applications which are very useful when you are writing NeXTSTEP programs. The *Terminal* application enables you to work in a UNIX terminal emulator setting and perform numerous programming related operations. The *Edit* application provides an easy way to enter, edit, and debug code files. The *(Digital) Librarian* and *HeaderViewer* are tools which will search through on-line documentation. *IconBuilder (Icon* in NeXTSTEP 2.1) provides an easy way to build application and document icons for your applications. The standard UNIX *make* program is used to determine which parts of your program need to be compiled and calls the compiler. The GNU debugger, *gdb*, is useful for debugging your programs and will work together with Edit.

Interface Builder will actually build your application's user interface from your (mostly graphical) specifications. It will save your on-screen user interface design by saving the user interface object specifications in a file. *Project Builder* (Interface Builder in NeXTSTEP 2.1) will create skeletal source code files and specify how they can be compiled together to make a stand-alone executable file (program). In other words, Interface Builder together with Project Builder will build an application for you without any programming whatsoever! Of course, the application won't have much of a computational engine (back end) unless you add application-specific code, but it will have a pretty face and will run. We'll see how to use Interface Builder in the next chapter and Project Builder in Chapter 5.

We discussed the locations of all of these development tools, except **make** and **gdb**, near the end of Chapter 1. Both **make** and **gdb** are located in the standard UNIX directory **/bin**. From now on we'll call directories "directories" rather than "folders," unless the context demands otherwise.

As with Chapter 1 we will write this chapter for users of both NeXTSTEP 3.0 and NeXTSTEP 2.1, and take most screen shots from NeXTSTEP 3.0.

The Terminal Application

The NeXTSTEP Terminal application provides you with windows that function like conventional terminals connected to your computer. This gives you a conventional interface for running standard UNIX editors, debuggers, and other programs which do not have NeXTSTEP interfaces.

Figure 1 shows a screen shot of a Terminal window running *vi*, the visual editor available with every version of UNIX. The UNIX shell in effect (csh) and the number of text columns and rows is shown in the window's title bar (you must set a Terminal preference for the size to appear in NeXTSTEP 3.0). Terminal windows work like most VT100 terminals and thus we'll only discuss the NeXTSTEP improvements here.

FIGURE 1. Terminal Application's Main Menu and Window

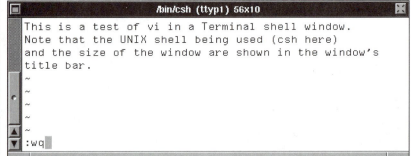

Terminal's main menu in Figure 1 contains most of the standard NeXT-STEP main menu commands. As required there are **Info**, **Services**, **Hide** and **Quit** commands (in the correct positions) and the Preferences panel can be accessed from the **Info** submenu.

Figure 2 shows the Terminal 3.0 *window* preferences available, including those that set the window size, font, and shell exit behavior. The pop-up list on the left of Figure 2 shows that you have a great deal of control over your Terminal's behavior. (The Terminal Preferences panel in NeXTSTEP 2.1 looks quite different, but lets you set many of the same the preferences.)

When you print, take note of the buttons in the Print panel's **Range** box (**Extent** box in 2.1), which lets you print all the text output to the window (which is stored in a buffer), the selected text, or simply what's visible in the window.

FIGURE 2. Terminal Preferences Panel in NeXTSTEP 3.0

Perhaps the most useful Terminal submenu is **Shell**, in the main menu's second slot where **Document** or **File** usually sits. The name "**Shell**" makes sense in the second slot because its **New** command creates a new shell window in the Terminal application, just as **New** creates a new file or document in an editor application.

The **Shell→Steal Keys** command in the **Shell** submenu turns a Terminal shell window into a "point-to-focus" style window, like those that other UNIX GUIs support. Use this mode when you're debugging a running application using **gdb**, the GNU debugger, in a Terminal window. You can type debugger commands without deactivating your running application and therefore not affecting the application's state in any way – important while debugging. For example, suppose you click the **Steal Keys** command, run **gdb** in a shell window, start an application called MyApp from **gdb**, and test MyApp's menu commands. While MyApp remains active you could move the cursor into the Terminal shell window (which would temporarily become the key window) and type **gdb** debugging commands, thereby "stealing" keystrokes from MyApp.

Next we'll run you through a few steps so you can become familiar with the Terminal application. These steps work in the Terminal applications for both NeXTSTEP 3.0 and NeXTSTEP 2.1.

1. **Launch the Terminal application** (from your dock or **/NextApps**). A UNIX shell window will likely open (if it doesn't, then choose **Shell→New** and check your Terminal preferences). See Figure 3.

FIGURE 3. Terminal UNIX Shell Window in NeXTSTEP 3.0

```
/bin/csh (ttyp1) 80x24
localhost> cd /NextApps
localhost> ls -l
total 11
drwxr-xr-x  3 root      1024 Apr  6 12:57 Edit.app/
drwxr-xr-x  3 root      1024 Apr  6 12:57 FaxReader.app/
drwxr-xr-x  3 root      1024 Apr  2 21:30 Grab.app/
drwxr-xr-x  3 root      1024 Apr  2 21:36 Librarian.app/
drwxr-xr-x  3 root      1024 Apr  6 12:57 Mail.app/
dr-xr-xr-x 17 root      1024 Apr  6 12:57 Preferences.app/
drwxr-xr-x  3 root      1024 Mar 26 03:54 Preview.app/
dr-xr-xr-x  3 root      1024 Mar 23 13:14 PrintManager.app/
dr-xr-xr-x  3 root      1024 Mar 22 11:42 Quotations.app/
dr-xr-xr-x  3 root      1024 Mar 22 12:00 Terminal.app/
dr-xr-xr-x  3 root      1024 Mar 22 12:17 Webster.app/
localhost> ps aux
USER      PID  %CPU %MEM VSIZE RSIZE TT STAT  TIME COMMAND
root      215   7.4  2.2 1.80M  536K p1 R     0:00 ps aux
mahoney   129   7.1 24.5 24.2M 5.88M ?  S     7:11 - console (WindowServer)
root      139   2.2  7.8 4.55M 1.88M ?  S     0:21 /NextApps/Terminal.app/Term
root        0   0.3  7.2 16.0M 1.72M ?  R N  34:39 (kernel idle)
root       -1   0.0  0.0    0K    0K ?  SW    0:00 <mach-task>
root        2   0.0  1.0 1.52M  256K co S     0:00 /etc/mach_init -xx
root        3   0.0  3.7 5.02M  920K ?  SW    0:02 /usr/etc/kern_loader -n
root       55   0.0  1.2 1.42M  288K ?  S     0:00 /usr/etc/syslogd
```

2. **Change the directory by typing the UNIX command** "**cd /NextApps**" in this UNIX Shell window followed by **Return** (which may be a "bent arrow" on your keyboard). Include the space but not the quotes and remember that UNIX is case-sensitive.

3. **List all the files in the /NextApps directory** by entering "**ls -l**" in the window. We'll use the term *enter* to indicate that the command should be followed by hitting the **Return** key. (The screen shot is from NeXTSTEP 3.0 – some of the files in the **/NextApps** directory in NeXTSTEP 2.1 are different.)

Note that **Librarian.app** is actually a *directory*, not a simple file as it appears in the File Viewer. (The first character in the directory listing output for **Librarian.app** is the letter "**d**" for directory.) We showed how to open *app wrapper* directories from the Workspace in Chapter 1.

4. **List all running processes** by entering "**ps aux**" in the window ("**ps**" is the UNIX command that lists all of the processes currently running on the computer). A scroller appears when the total text output is larger than the window. (To see the list of processes better, enlarge the window by dragging the right part of the window's resize bar to the right and enter "**ps auxww**".)

5. **See the text which scrolled outside the window** by dragging the scroll knob upward. The standard **Edit** submenu commands **Copy**, **Paste**, and **Select All** can be used in this window.

6. **Investigate the default database** by entering "**dread -l**" in the UNIX Shell window. This command lists defaults for your applications. For example, the listing *may* contain the following line:

    DataPhile AutoSaveFrequency 5

    This line contains a default value for the third party product, *DataPhile*, by Stone Design. To learn more about these defaults, enter "**man dread**" and "**man dwrite**" in the Terminal Shell window. ("**man**" is the UNIX on-line documentation facility for accessing UNIX manual pages. You can also access the manual pages through NeXTSTEP's (Digital) Librarian.)

    The default information is stored in a file under your ".NeXT" directory under your home directory. Look in this directory and you'll see other "hidden" information pertaining to your account such as your recycler (trash). We'll discuss the defaults database in more detail in Chapter 21.

7. **Hide the Terminal application** by choosing **Hide** from its main menu or by typing Command-h. Clicking the close button in the Terminal window only closes that window, not the application as a whole.

Edit – NeXTSTEP's Mouse-Based Editor

The Edit application will create and edit both ASCII and RTF (Rich Text Format) files. Since our primary focus is on writing applications, we'll step you through several useful Edit features which aid programmers working with ASCII code files.

Using Edit and Librarian, Step by Step

This section is a step-by-step guide to getting started with the Edit and Librarian applications. To get the most out of these steps, we recommend that you follow them precisely. If you do not follow a step precisely or skip a step, then subsequent steps may not make sense. These steps work with both NeXTSTEP 3.0 and NeXTSTEP 2.1. All screen shots were taken from NeXTSTEP 3.0.

1. Copy the **/NextDeveloper/Examples/AppKit/Lines** directory (**/NextDeveloper/Examples/Lines** in 2.1) to your home directory by navigating to the **Lines** directory in your File Viewer, dragging its icon and dropping it atop your home directory icon.

2. **Open *your* new Lines directory** in the File Viewer and select its **LinesView.h** file.

3. **Open the LinesView.h file and simultaneously launch Edit** by double-clicking the **LinesView.h** icon in your File Viewer's icon path.

4. **If you are running NeXTSTEP 3.0** and do *not* see the **Utilities** submenu item in Edit's main menu (a screen shot of the menu is at the lower left), then you need to change Edit to launch in *developer's mode*. To do this, choose **Info→Preferences** from Edit's menu, select **Developer Mode** (see Figure 4 below), click the **Set** button, and **Quit** Edit. Then open **LinesView.h** in Edit again.

5. Choose Edit's **Info→Preferences and look at the available Preferences** by pressing the pop-up list button near the top of the Preferences panel and dragging to the various options (see Figure 4). Note that *tabs* are set in the **Text Options** view. Close the Preferences panel.

6. **Open a "folder window" for the Lines directory** by choosing **File→Open Folder** from Edit's menu and entering "**~/Lines**" in the attention panel as in Figure 5 below. (In NeXTSTEP 2.1, the files in the folder window will differ slightly from the ones in Figure 5.)

7. **Open a "folder window" for the ancestor directory** by double-clicking the line "**../**" in the **Lines** folder window. See Figure 5. You can open any ancestor or descendent directory this way.

8. **Open the LinesView.m (*not* .h) file in a standard Edit window** by double-clicking its name in the **Lines** folder window.

9. **Select any complete line in the LinesView.m file** by *triple*-clicking it.

FIGURE 4. Edit Preferences in User and Developer Modes

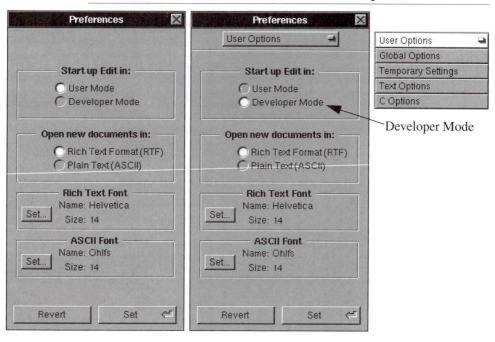

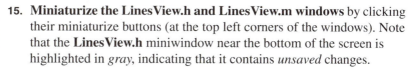

Developer Mode

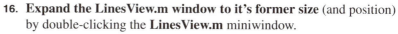

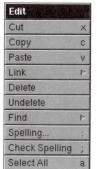

10. **Copy the selected line to the pasteboard** by choosing **Edit→Copy** from Edit's **Edit** submenu (or by typing the key alternative Command-c). See Edit's **Edit** *submenu* at the left of the page.

11. **Paste the contents of the pasteboard into the LinesView.h file** by first clicking in the **LinesView.h** window and then choosing **Edit→Paste** from Edit's menu (or typing Command-v).

12. **Select any complete word in LinesView.h** by double-clicking it.

13. **Delete the selected word** by hitting the Delete (Backspace) key.

14. **Insert the deleted word in a different position in LinesView.h** by clicking in a different position and choosing **Edit→Undelete**. (Note that **Undelete** is *not* the same operation as **Undo**.)

15. **Miniaturize the LinesView.h and LinesView.m windows** by clicking their miniaturize buttons (at the top left corners of the windows). Note that the **LinesView.h** miniwindow near the bottom of the screen is highlighted in *gray*, indicating that it contains *unsaved* changes.

16. **Expand the LinesView.m window to it's former size** (and position) by double-clicking the **LinesView.m** miniwindow.

FIGURE 5. Opening a Folder Window in Edit

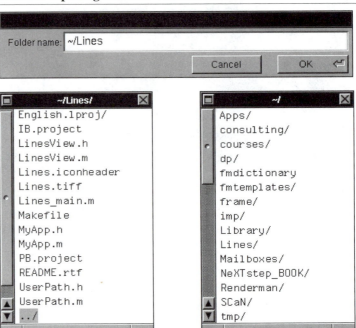

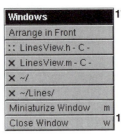

17. **Arrange all the directory and file windows front and center** by choosing **Windows→Arrange in Front** from Edit's menu. Note that the **LinesView.h** miniwindow expands and that the **X** in the **LinesView.h** menu command has a hole, indicating it contains *unsaved* changes. The **X** has the same meaning as it does inside a close button in a window's title bar.

18. **Undo all editing changes performed in the LinesView.h file since the last save** by choosing **File→Revert to Saved** in Edit's menu and then clicking **Revert** in the attention panel that is displayed.

19. **Bring the LinesView.m file to the front** by choosing **Windows→LinesView.m** from Edit's menu.

20. **Find the first instance of the "initFrame"** string by typing Command-f (or choosing **Edit→Find→Find Panel**) and entering "initFrame" in the Find Panel.

21. **Select the *entire* initFrame: method** (procedure) in **LinesView.m** by clicking just before the minus ("**-**") character in front of **initFrame** and then *Shift-clicking* just after the ending curly brace. See Figure 6 below.

Shift-clicking selects all of the text from the insertion point to the position where the shift-click occurs. Shift-clicking can also be used to extend or shorten a selection.

FIGURE 6. LinesView.m File With Selected Method

```
┌─────────────────────────────────────────────────────────────┐
│ □            LinesView.m - C -  — ~/Lines                 ☒ │
├─────────────────────────────────────────────────────────────┤
│                                                             │
│   @implementation LinesView                                 │
│ ○                                                           │
│   - initFrame:(NXRect *)rect                                │
│   {                                                         │
│                                                             │
│       [super initFrame:rect];                               │
│                                                             │
│     /* create a user path */                                │
│       userPath = newUserPath();                             │
│                                                             │
│       running = NO;                                         │
│                                                             │
│       return self;                                          │
│ ▲ }                                                         │
│ ▼                                                           │
└─────────────────────────────────────────────────────────────┘
```

22. **Select the** *body* **of the initFrame: method in the LinesView.m file** by double-clicking the opening curly brace on the line after the **initFrame:** header. The block contained between this curly brace and the matching closing curly brace should be selected.

23. **Contract the selected block** by choosing **Format→Structure→Contract Sel** from Edit's menu. The *white arrow* (⇨) indicates contracted code. See Figure 7 below.

24. **Expand the contracted blocks** by clicking the white arrows representing the blocks.

25. **Search for the initFrame: method in the on-line documentation** by double-clicking **initFrame** to select it and then choosing **Services→Librarian→Search**.

The Librarian application automatically launches (or activates) and a search for **initFrame** is made. If none are found, then click the **NeXT Developer** icon at the top of the Librarian window and then click the **Search** button in the window. See Figure 8 below.

FIGURE 7. LinesView.m File With Contracted Selection

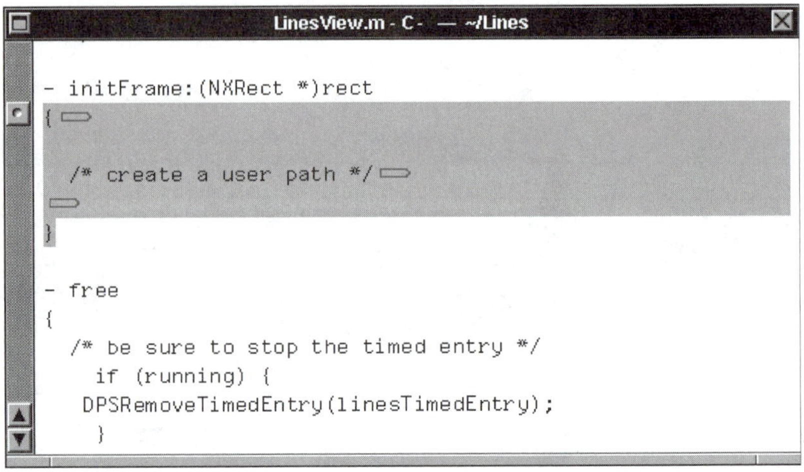

```
LinesView.m - C - — ~/Lines

- initFrame:(NXRect *)rect
{

  /* create a user path */


}

- free
{
  /* be sure to stop the timed entry */
    if (running) {
    DPSRemoveTimedEntry(linesTimedEntry);
    }
```

FIGURE 8. Librarian Bookshelf Window

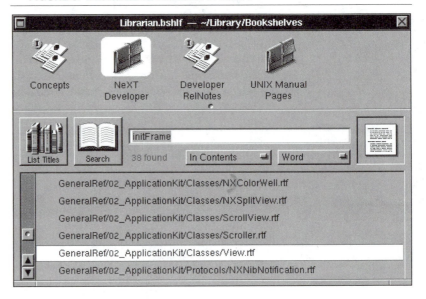

26. **Open the View.rtf file** containing the **initFrame:** documentation by double-clicking the line which ends with **View.rtf** in the Librarian window (you'll have to first drag the scroll knob downward). This line contains the path under the **/NextLibrary/Documentation/NextDev** directory where **View.rtf** is located.

27. **Find the next occurrence of initFrame** in the **View.rtf** file by clicking the **Find** button at the top right of the **View.rtf** window (or by typing Command-g).

28. **Copy any method header (e.g., initFrame) to the pasteboard** by *triple*-clicking it in the **View.rtf** file and choosing **Edit→Copy** from Librarian's menu (or by typing Command-c).

29. **Paste this method header into the LinesView.m file** by clicking in the **LinesView.m** window and choosing **Edit→Copy** from Edit's menu (or by typing Command-v). *Paste*

    Note how you can copy complicated headers or anything else from the on-line documentation to reduce spelling and capitalization errors.

30. **Click in the Librarian window and then hide the Librarian application** by choosing **Hide** from Librarian's menu (or by typing Command-h). Edit should become the active application (since it was the previous active application).

31. **Find out the line number where the insertion point resides in the LinesView.m file** by typing Command-l (or by choosing **Edit→Find→Line Range** in Edit's menu).

32. **Select line 2 in the LinesView.m file** by entering "**2**" in the **Line and Character Range** panel. This feature is very useful for finding where compiler errors are located because the compiler will tell you the line numbers where it found compiler errors.

33. **Select lines 3-14 in the LinesView.m file** by first typing Command-l to bring up the **Line and Character Range** panel and then typing **3:14** in the panel followed by **Return**.

34. **Quit** Edit.

HeaderViewer

HeaderViewer is a *great* new tool in NeXTSTEP 3.0 for finding and viewing information in NeXTSTEP toolkits and documentation. It's better than Librarian for finding information important for NeXTSTEP development. HeaderViewer can be found in the **/NextDeveloper/Demos** directory.

Figure 9 below contains the HeaderViewer's main window displaying documentation for the root **Object** class. If you dragged to **View Documentation** in the pop-up list, then the actual header file **Object.h** would appear. Note the variety of **Language Elements** in the left column of the browser.

FIGURE 9. Main Window in HeaderViewer

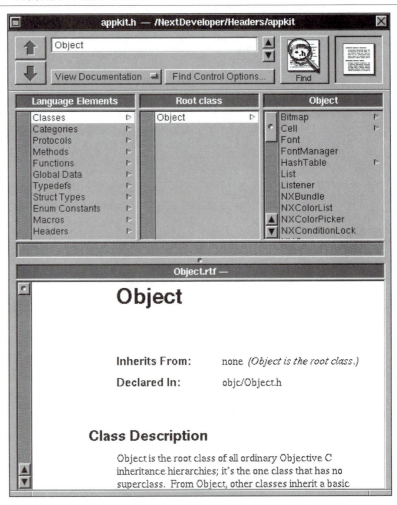

Creating Icons

Icons can be used to identify applications and documents belonging to applications in the Workspace. These icons are normally 48 x 48 pixels in size and have an alpha channel (for transparency information). In this section we'll show you how to create an icon. Then in Chapter 6 we'll show you how to use Project Builder (or Interface Builder in NeXTSTEP 2.1) to set up application and document icons for your own applications.

In NeXTSTEP 3.0, a bundled application called *IconBuilder* in the **/Next-Developer/Apps** directory can be used to create icons. In NeXTSTEP 2.1, a bundled application called *Icon* in the **/NextDeveloper/Demos** directory can be used to create icons. We'll step you through some of the basic features of both of these applications and create icons which can be used to represent applications, documents, or other things. Of course, you only need to go through the steps for the tool you'll be using.

Creating an Icon with IconBuilder in NeXTSTEP 3.0

1. Drag the **IconBuilder** application file icon into your dock (it's in the **/NextDeveloper/Apps** directory).

2. **Launch the IconBuilder application** by double-clicking its icon in your dock.

3. **Create a new icon** by choosing **Document→New** from **IconBuilder's** menu. An "UNTITLED" window with a 48 x 48 pixel icon pops up.

4. **Choose the rectangle drawing tool** (below the pencil) in the **Tools Palette** (see Figure 10 below). *The order of the tools may vary from that shown.*

5. **Open the Inspector panel** by choosing **Tools→Inspector** from **IconBuilder's** menu (see Figure 10). The type of rectangle we'd like to draw is already in effect.

6. Open the standard NeXTSTEP **Colors panel** by choosing **Tools→Colors** from **IconBuilder's** menu. See Figure 11 below. Take a couple of minutes to investigate how colors are selected in the four "color-picking" modes in the Colors panel.

7. **Change the rectangle color to dark gray** (or whatever color you want) in the **Colors panel.**

8. **Drag across the icon so it's completely gray.** Because the *rectangle* drawing tool is in effect, the cursor changes to the crosshair (+) while in the drawing area.

FIGURE 10. **IconBuilder's Tools Palette and Tools Inspector**

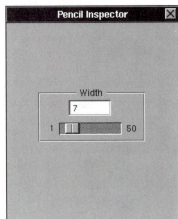

FIGURE 11. **Two Views of the Colors Panel in NeXTSTEP 3.0**

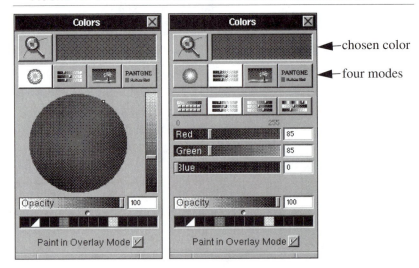

9.   **Choose the pencil tool** in the **Tools palette**.

10. **Change the color** (that the pencil tool will draw) **to black** in the **Colors panel**.

11. **Make the pencil width larger** by dragging the slider knob in the Pencil Inspector to about **7** (see Figure 10 above).

12. **Draw a "χ" symbol** or whatever else you want on top of the square gray icon. Note that the cursor changes to the pencil ( ) while in the drawing area.

13. **Save the image in your home directory** with the name "**MyIcon.tiff**" by choosing **Document→Save As** and entering "**~/MyIcon.tiff**".

14. **Quit** the **IconBuilder** application.

Creating an Icon with the Icon Application in NeXTSTEP 2.1

1. Drag the **Icon application** file icon into your dock (it's in the **/NextDeveloper/Demos** directory).

2. **Launch the Icon application** by double-clicking its icon in your dock.

3. **Open an existing icon file** (e.g., **BusyBoxApp.tiff** in the **/NextDeveloper/Examples/BusyBox** directory) by choosing **Image→Open** from **Icon**'s menu and finding the "**.tiff**" file. (This will insure that the size and properties of your icon will be correct.)

4. **Choose the rectangle drawing tool** (next to the white circle) in the **Tools Palette** (displayed at the left of the page).

5. **Change the rectangle color to gray** (or whatever you want) by choosing **Tools→Colors** to open the **Colors panel** and then clicking the color in the panel.

6. **Drag across the BusyBox icon so it's completely gray.** Because the *rectangle* drawing tool is in effect, the cursor changes to the crosshair (+) while in the drawing area.

7. **Choose the pencil tool** in the **Tools palette** (at the upper left).

8. **Change the color** (that the pencil tool will draw) **to black** in the **Colors panel**.

9. **Make the pencil width larger** by clicking in the "**Line Width**" box in the **Inspector panel**.

10. **Draw a "χ" symbol** or whatever else you want on top of the square gray icon. Note that the cursor changes to the pencil ( ) while in the drawing area.

11. **Save the image in your home directory** with the name "**MyIcon.tiff**" by choosing **Image→Save As** and entering "**~/MyIcon.tiff**".

12. **Quit** the **Icon** application.

Using an Icon to Represent a Directory in the File Viewer

As we mentioned in Chapter 1, any directory can be represented with a custom icon in your File Viewer simply by storing an icon file named "**.dir.tiff**" in the directory. Try this by renaming the **~/MyIcon.tiff** file you created above as **.dir.tiff**. Notice what happens to the house icon that represents your home directory – it turns into the icon you created above. The icon displayed when a directory "opens" to accept a file being copied or moved can also be customized by storing a file named "**.opendir.tiff**" in the directory.

make – The UNIX Program Building Utility

The UNIX **make** utility makes life much easier for developers because it creates your application (executable) from source files using instructions from a *Makefile*. A NeXTSTEP Makefile is a file containing instructions on how to compile and link all of an application's source files, including Objective-C, PostScript, TIFF, nib (the NeXT Interface Builder file containing interface specifications), and others. Life is especially easy for NeXTSTEP developers because a Makefile is automatically generated for a project by Project Builder (Interface Builder in NeXTSTEP 2.1). The NeXTSTEP **make** and Makefile work essentially the same as those in standard UNIX except that they support inclusion of the special sources mentioned above by a complex set of rules located in **/NextDeveloper/ Makefiles/app/app.make**.

A *target* of the **make** utility is usually an executable file, but there are other possible targets such as intermediate object code files, and manipulation of directories. To run **make** in a UNIX shell window, change to the directory containing the source files and Makefile and type **make target** at the command line. In the following table we list the possible **make** commands (with **target**s) and the corresponding tasks performed:

Command	Task
make (or make all)	(optimized) compile and link into an executable file named
make debug	compile and link into an executable file named **appname.debug** for use with **gdb**
make clean	removes all object and executable files
make install	installs the application into a chosen directory, such as **/LocalApps** or **~/Apps**

Command	Task
make installsrc	installs the source files into a chosen directory for archiving a completed project
make depend	generates a **Makefile.dependencies** file containing a dependency graph for the project
make diff	compares the source of two projects
make profile	compile and link into an executable named **appname.profile** for use with UNIX **gprof**
make help	lists the targets that can be made

gdb – Debugging Programs

gdb is the GNU Debugger, written by the Free Software Foundation. It is a powerful tool for looking inside a running program and trying to figure out why your program is not behaving as you expect it to. NeXT has specially modified **gdb** to be aware of Objective-C syntax and objects, and to work together with the Edit and Terminal applications.

You can use **gdb** either from the command line or from the Emacs editor in a Terminal shell window, and from Project Builder and Edit in NeXTSTEP 3.0. To debug the program **MyProgram.debug** with **gdb** at the Terminal shell command line, type:

```
localhost> gdb MyProgram.debug
```

(We'll use the convention that the commands you type are in **boldface**. localhost is the name of the host computer.)

To run **gdb** from Emacs, use the Emacs command:

```
M-X gdb <return>
```

After which Emacs will prompt you for:

```
Run gdb on file: /me/
```

(/me is the user's home directory.)

To which you should type the name of the file that you want to debug:

```
Run gdb on file: /me/MyProgram.debug <return>
```

The advantage to using **gdb** from Emacs is that Emacs will automatically split the screen into two windows, giving you a **gdb** buffer in one and following the program that you are debugging in the other. Many programmers find this an effective way to work.

gdb Commands

gdb is a complicated program with dozens of commands. Fortunately, you only need to know a very few basic commands.

Typically, when you are using **gdb**, you will set a *breakpoint* and then run your program until you reach that breakpoint. Your program will then automatically stop running and you will be free to inspect the contents of variables.

To set a breakpoint at:	Use this command:
line 53 in the file **myFile.m**	b myFile.m:53
the function **printer()**	b printer
the Objective-C method **drawPSInView:** in the class **Segment**	b [Segment drawPSInView:]

To run your program, type "**run**."

Once your program reaches a breakpoint (or if your program crashes), you will return to the **gdb** command-line. You can also interrupt your program's execution by typing Control-c. From the command-line, you may find the following commands useful in viewing your program's state.

gdb's "view" Command

The **view** command lets you view the source code associated with the executable code being debugged in the Edit application.

gdb's "where" Command

The **where** command shows a stack-trace of where your program is:

```
(gdb) where
#0 0x2324c in + [SList=0x0005e69c readFromFile: fn=(char *)
0x328f36 "/me/Database.sbook"] (SList.m line 25)
#1 0x20b48 in - [SLC=0x00329858 newDocFromFile: fn=(char *)
0x328f36 "/me/Database.sbook"] (SLC.m line 49)
```

```
#2 0x645a in - [AbstractDocController=0x00329858 openFile:
fn=(char *) 0x328f36 "/me/Database.sbook"]
(AbstractDocController.m line 110)
#3 0x1f112 in - [SBookController=0x0031a5f0 newDocForFile:
filename=(char *) 0x328f36 "/me/Database.sbook"]
(SBookController.m line 340)
#4 0x5c92 in - [AbstractAppController=0x0031a5f0 openNamedFile:
filename=(char *) 0x328f36 "/me/Database.sbook"]
(AbstractAppController.m line 181)
#5 0x5e00 in - [AbstractAppController=0x0031a5f0 autoLaunch]
(AbstractAppController.m line 219)
#6 0x5e5a in - [AbstractAppController=0x0031a5f0 appDidInit:
sender=(id) 0x32a074] (AbstractAppController.m line 228)
#7 0x1f8f0 in - [SBookController=0x0031a5f0 appDidInit:
sender=(id) 0x32a074] (SBookController.m line 535)
#8 0x6036dc8 in - [Application run]
#9 0x2643c in main (argc=1, argv=(char **) 0x3fffe1c)
(SBook_main.m line 11)
(gdb)
```

In this example, execution is currently at line 25 in the **SList.m** Objective-C file, at a method called **[SList readFromFile:]**. The argument to the method was "**/me/Database.sbook**."

gdb's "print" Command

You can use the **print** (**p** is a shortcut) command to display the value of a local variable:

```
(gdb) p fn
$2 = (char *) 0x328f36 "/me/Database.sbook"
(gdb)
```

You can also use the print command to run a function:

```
(gdb) p printf("this is a test %x\n",4211)
this is a test 1073
$3 = 0
(gdb)
```

In this example, **gdb** called the function **printf** which printed the line beginning "this is a test." The **printf** function itself then returned the value 0, which **gdb** printed.

You can also use the **print** command to send a message to an object:

```
(gdb) p [NXApp mainWindow]
$7 = 7176016
(gdb)
```

In this case, we sent the **mainWindow** message to the **NXApp** object. The returned value was 7176016. In order to understand what this returned value means, we must know that the **mainWindow** message returns the **id** of a **Window** object. We could use that **id** as the source of another message. For example, to ask that window what its title is, we could send it the **title** message. To see the printable string that is the window's title, we further need to cast the returned value into a **char ***:

```
(gdb) p [[NXApp mainWindow] title]
$8 = 3286712
(gdb) p (char *)[[NXApp mainWindow] title]
$9 = (char *) 0x3226b8 "Address Book"
(gdb)
```

We can also look at the instance variables of the window object:

```
(gdb) p (id)[NXApp mainWindow]
$10 = (id) 0x6d7f50
(gdb) p *(id)[NXApp mainWindow]
$11 = {
  isa = 0x4034bd0;
  nextResponder = 0x0;
  _reserved = 0x0;
  frame = {
    origin = {
      x = 255;
      y = 310;
    };
    size = {
      width = 610;
      height = 488;
    };
  };
  contentView = 0x31bf40;
  delegate = 0x6d8810;
  firstResponder = 0x6d7f50;
...
(gdb)
```

Using gdb in NeXTSTEP 3.0

Debug

In NeXTSTEP 3.0, the easiest way to use **gdb** is to click the **Debug** button in Project Builder. It will compile your program (if necessary), launch the Terminal application and run **gdb** in a shell window (if necessary), load the symbol information into **gdb**, launch the Edit application, and finally add a new menu item called **Gdb** to Edit's menu. All of this occurs by clicking a single button! Choosing the **Gdb** menu command in Edit brings up a panel which provides a graphical interface to most basic **gdb** commands. This panel for an application called **Calculator** can be seen in Figure 12 below.

FIGURE 12. Edit's gdb panel in NeXTSTEP 3.0

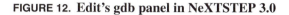

User Interface Design

Though not strictly a development *tool*, user interface design is certainly something that developers should concern themselves with. Most developers spend far too little time designing the user interface of an application when that is the part that makes a big first impression on most users. An application's user interface may very well determine its success or failure.

To properly address user interface design would take another book.[1] However, it's so important that we'll list a few tips below for novice designers.[2]

- *Create the user interface first.* Then the user interface will more likely be written for the user, and not the programmer. There's nothing worse than making an interface conform to code. Remember, you are writing your application for users, not yourself.

---

1. For example, see *Designing the User Interface* by Ben Shneiderman (Addison-Wesley) or *Software User Interface Design* by Deborah Mayhew (Prentice-Hall).

2. Thanks to Dave Grady of NeXT Computer, Inc. for most of these tips .

- *Don't put too many windows on the screen* immediately after your application is launched. If you do, the user will be confused and may not even know where the focus of your application lies.

- *Don't violate user's expectations.* In part, this means that you should follow the NeXTSTEP user interface guidelines for menus, windows, panels, and so on. As an example of such a violation, look at the location of the **Print** command in the main menu of the NeXTSTEP 2.1 Edit application. It violates the main menu guideline that **Print** should be immediately above **Services**. Another violation is the **Send** button in the mailbox windows of the NeXTSTEP 2.1 Mail application. To better reflect its function, the name of this button has been changed to **Compose** in NeXTSTEP 3.0.

- *Don't confuse the grouping of functionality.* Some applications are riddled with menus and panels which confuse functionality.

- *Provide sufficient WYSIWYG before a choice is set.* For example, in the standard NeXTSTEP 2.1 Font panel, the resulting font isn't displayed until *after* the **Set** button is clicked. The **Preview** button helps, but why not make the preview immediate? An example where the preview is excellent can be found in Lotus *Improv's* Format panel. The format of a spreadsheet cell is clearly displayed *before* the choice is set (thank goodness for that, since *Improv's* lack of **Undo** is a serious user interface problem).

Summary

In this chapter, we took a brief look at the NeXTSTEP development tools Terminal, Edit, Librarian, HeaderViewer, Icon Builder, Icon, **make**, and **gdb**. When using these applications, keep in mind that one can often be accessed from another through the **Services** menu.

In the next chapter we'll take a close look at Interface Builder, NeXTSTEP's powerful tool for building application interfaces, and create our first program.

3

Creating a Simple Application With Interface Builder

Figure 1 contains a screen shot of a typical NeXTSTEP 3.0 developer's screen (NeXTSTEP 2.1 looks similar). In the center of the screen are two Edit windows containing the source code for the Calculator program we'll create in later chapters. The two windows next to the dock on the right-hand side and the window with the title "**calculator.nib**" near the lower-left corner of the screen belong to the Interface Builder application. The window with the black title bar and the short menu are parts of the Calculator application's interface, which was being built in Interface Builder when the screen shot was taken. A very important icon in the dock is the icon for Interface Builder – a copy of it is at the left of this paragraph.

Interface Builder is NeXTSTEP's main development tool for writing applications. It lets you graphically design the windows that your application will use, together with all of their associated menus, buttons, sliders, and other objects. After you've put together the basic interface for your application, Interface Builder lets you "wire" together the parts (objects) and save all these specifications so that your application can use them when it runs.

People who aren't NeXTSTEP programmers often incorrectly call Interface Builder a prototyping tool. While Interface Builder *can* be used for building application prototypes, more often it's used to build the actual graphical user interface for a NeXTSTEP application. In NeXTSTEP 3.0

FIGURE 1. **Typical NeXTSTEP 3.0 Developer's Screen**

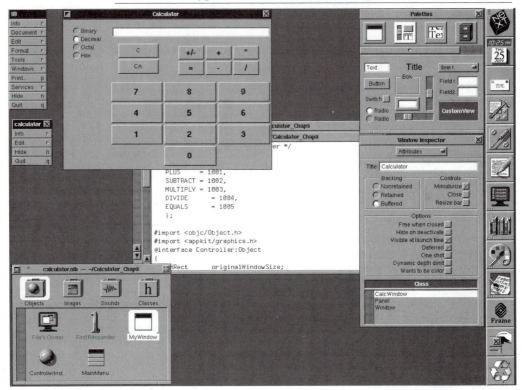

Interface Builder also works together with Project Builder – its icon is at the left of the paragraph – to provide a framework of source code to which a developer can add application-specific code. Interface Builder is much more than a prototyper; it is an integral part of the NeXTSTEP programming environment. (In NeXTSTEP 2.1 Interface Builder itself provides the framework mentioned above – there is no Project Builder.)

This chapter introduces you to Interface Builder. We'll build a *very* simple interface for an application and test it with Interface Builder's **Test Interface** command. We won't use this interface beyond this chapter; we won't even save it in a file. To keep things simple, we also won't build a complete project, and thus won't use Project Builder at all.

Getting Started with Interface Builder

1. Log in and hide the Workspace Manager.

2. If necessary, drag the Interface Builder icon into your dock. It's in the **/NextDeveloper/Apps** directory in NeXTSTEP 3.0 (**/NextApps** in NeXTSTEP 2.1).

3. Double-click the Interface Builder icon in your dock to launch the application.

Your screen should look similar to the screen shot in Figure 2 below. Interface Builder's main menu is in the upper-left corner, its Palettes window is near the upper-right corner of the screen, and its Inspector is below the Palettes window (you can specify which windows show up at launch time in Interface Builder's Preferences panel). Now that we've launched Interface Builder, we can start building our own application.

FIGURE 2. Interface Builder 3.0 Immediately After Launch

4. Choose **Document→New Application** from Interface Builder's menu (or type the keyboard alternative Command-n). See Figure 3 below. (In NeXTSTEP 2.1, this submenu is titled **File**, not **Document**.)

The screen has now become more interesting with the addition of three new objects. In the center of the screen in Figure 3 is a big empty window titled "**My Window**." Below Interface Builder's menu is another menu titled "**UNTITLED**." Don't try choosing commands from this menu right now – it's the main menu for the application that you are building. In subsequent chapters we show how you can tailor this menu with commands and sub-menus to suit a particular application. A larger picture of the **UNTITLED** menu appears in Figure 4 below.

FIGURE 3. New Application in Interface Builder

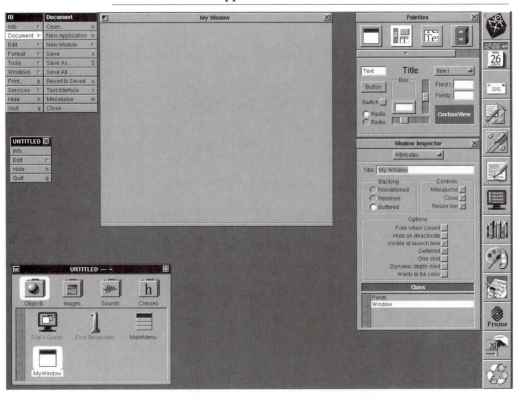

In the lower-left hand corner of the screen in Figure 3 is the *File window* for the new application. (A larger picture of it appears in Figure 4 below.) The File window and menu are titled "**UNTITLED**" because you have yet to give the application a name. (In NeXTSTEP 2.1, the File window's con-tents are arranged differently, but are essentially the same.)

FIGURE 4. Menu and File Window for a New Application

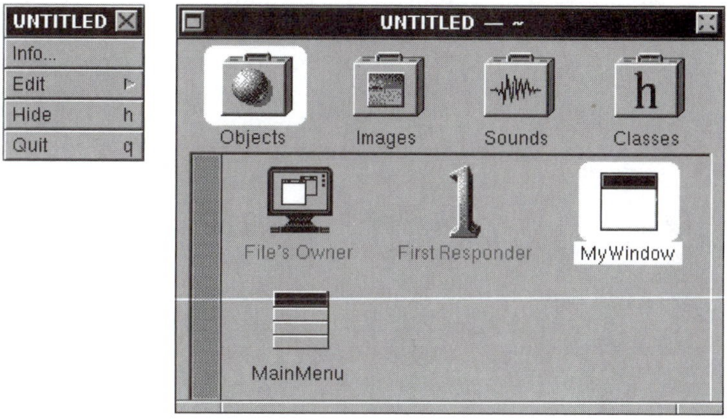

The "suitcase" icons in the File window in Figure 4 represent *resources* available to your application. The highlighted **Objects** suitcase icon in Figure 4 represents the objects in your application. If you add more windows or panels to your application, then icons representing these objects will also appear in this *Objects view* in the File window. If there are too many objects to be displayed in a File window of a given size, then you can drag the window's vertical scroll knob to see them all. You can also resize this window if you want. Generally, *every* window that has a scroller should be resizable – this is important to remember when you start designing your own applications.

The File window's close button ([X]) in its upper right-hand corner has a hole in its middle because the application being built hasn't been saved. The hole means that the contents of the window have been modified, or are *dirty*. After you save it, the button will change to this: [X].

Let's look at the individual objects in the Objects view for a *new* application, like the one in Figure 4.

The **File's Owner** icon represents the main object in charge of running your application. Normally this object is called "**NXApp**" and is of the **Application** class type. We'll go into the details of what this object is and what it does later; for now, just think of it as the thing that's controlling your program and providing an interface to the computer's hardware.

The **MainMenu** icon represents the new application's menu structure. Right now, this consists of the **UNTITLED** menu with its commands and the **Edit** submenu. The **Hide** and **Quit** commands are currently the only ones that have any effect.

The **MyWindow** icon represents the application's main window, the bland window titled "**My Window**" that Interface Builder created automatically when you chose **Document→New Application**. The File window will contain an icon for every standard window and panel in your application. If a window or panel in the application you're building isn't visible (perhaps it was closed to simplify the screen), then you can make it visible by double-clicking its icon in the File window.

A *Responder* is an object that receives and responds to *events*. Most events in NeXTSTEP come from the keyboard or the mouse. The First Responder icon represents your application's *key window*, the window (or panel) with the black title bar that receives keyboard events. If your program has more than one window which can become the key window, then the one that the First Responder icon represents will change as your program executes. You won't have to worry about this for a while.

Next we'll take a closer look at the three other views – Images, Sounds, and Classes – in the File window.

The **Images** suitcase (*Icons* suitcase in NeXTSTEP 2.1) icon in the File window represents the icons and other images that are available to the application. When you click the **Images** suitcase, Interface Builder will display the available images in the File window as in Figure 5 below. (In NeXTSTEP 2.1, a separate Icons window with similar contents opens.)

FIGURE 5. Images View in the File Window

Every NeXTSTEP application is provided with five system images for free: **NXradio**, **NXradioH**, **NXreturnSign**, **NXswitch**, and **NXswitchH**. You can add your own image by dragging its file icon from your Workspace File

Viewer and dropping it in the File window. Alternatively, you can add an image by pasting it into this window.

The **Sounds** suitcase is similar to the **Images** suitcase, except that it represents sounds rather than images. When you click the **Sounds** suitcase, Interface Builder will display icons for the available sounds in the File window as in Figure 6 below. (In NeXTSTEP 2.1, a separate Sounds window with similar contents opens.)

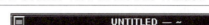
FIGURE 6. Sounds View in the File Window

Sounds are an integral part of many NeXTSTEP applications. Used appropriately, sounds can make an application easier and more fun to use. One very appropriate use of a sound is to alert the user to an unexpected event. For example, when you try to copy a file to a directory which contains a file with the same name, the Workspace Manager alerts you by playing your system beep. As another example, when the NeXT printer runs out of paper, the computer plays a recording of a woman with a British accent saying "your printer is out of paper" – a "sound" that will certainly grab your attention.

Every NeXTSTEP application is provided with six system sounds: **Basso**, **Bonk**, **Frog**, **Funk**, **Pop**, and **Tink**. These six sounds are located in the **NextLibrary/Sounds** directory. As with the Images view, you can add your own sounds to the application by dropping their file icons in the File windows or pasting them in place.

The **Classes** suitcase icon in the File window represents all of the Objective-C *classes* that your application "knows" about. (Classes define and create objects such as windows and buttons, as we'll see in subsequent chapters.) When you click the **Classes** suitcase, Interface Builder will display the hierarchy of available classes in the File window (In NeXTSTEP 2.1, a separate Classes window opens.) Commands available in this window let you add, modify and perform other operations on classes.

All of the icons in the Objects, Images, and Sounds views in the File window have their names displayed below them. Some of the names are in black, while others are in dark gray. You can change a name in black by double-clicking it and typing a new name. Changing an icon's name in the File window has no effect on the rest of the program. For instance, if you change the name of the icon **My Window** to **Steve's Window**, the window itself will still be titled **My Window**. These icon names are generally only for the convenience of the developer.

Adding Objects to Your Application

In this section we'll customize our new application's main window titled **My Window**. It's wonderful that Interface Builder automatically provides every new application with this window, but it's rarely the right size. Sometimes it's too small, usually it's too big. Fortunately, we can easily change its size by dragging its resize bar at the bottom.

5. Resize **My Window** to a height of about an inch and a width of about three inches by dragging its resize bar.

Notice that you don't need to know the exact height and width of this window to set its size; you simply resize it visually and you're done. This is a good example of the basic philosophy of Interface Builder – graphical things are best done graphically. It is this philosophy that is at the heart of NeXTSTEP's ease of programming. (On the other hand, you can resize the window to precise dimensions using the "Window inspector," if necessary.)

Adding a Button Object to Your Window

The Interface Builder Palettes window near the upper-right hand corner of the screen contains four (or more) palettes of objects which may be dragged into your application. By clicking one of the selector buttons near the top of the Palettes window, you can choose which one of the palettes is visible. This is called a *multi-view window*. (The File window is also a multi-view window.)

When Interface Builder launches, the Palettes window normally displays the *Views* palette. The 12 objects in this palette consist mainly of **Control** objects (see Chapter 1), and are labeled in Figure 7 below. You can drag an object from the Basic Views palette and drop it into any window or panel of the application you're building. Let's see how it works.

FIGURE 7. Views Palette

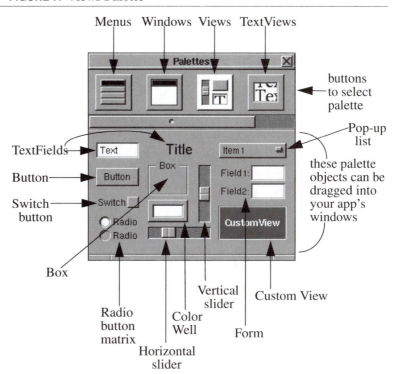

6. Add a button to your application by dragging the **Button** icon from the Palettes window and dropping it into the window titled **My Window**. The window should look something like this:

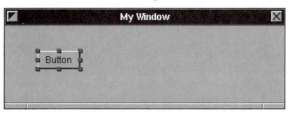

You can *resize* this new button by dragging any of the little dark gray squares, or *handles*, around the button's perimeter. You can *move* the button by pressing in the button's middle and dragging the button to the desired location within the window.

7. Resize the button so it's about twice as wide.

8. Move the button so it's in the same location as in the screen shot above.

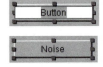

9. Change the name of the button. To do this, double-click the button's title ("Button") and the button's text will highlight in light gray to indicate it's been selected. You can then type anything you want. For example, if you type "Noise" (and then hit Return), you'll change the button's title to "Noise."

Now you've got a simple window with a button. Let's try it out!

10. Choose the **Document→Test Interface** menu command (or type the keyboard equivalent Command-r). (In NeXTSTEP 2.1, choose **File→Test Interface**.)

All of the Interface Builder windows including the Interface Builder menu will hide and you'll be left with your new application's main window and menu. It looks as though the application is running, but in fact we're only testing its interface – there is no executable file.

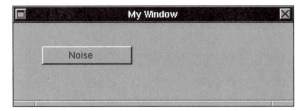

Notice that Interface Builder icon in your dock has changed from its original *build* mode to the "big Frankenstein switch" icon shown at the left. This new icon indicates that your program is now in *Test Interface* mode. You can move, resize, miniaturize, and even close **My Window**. Everything that's there works except the **Info** and **Edit** submenu commands (of course, the application doesn't do much.) Press the **Noise** button and note that it looks like a physical button that's been pushed – the white highlights and dark "shadows" around the edges of the button made it seem as though there's a light coming from the upper left.

11. Quit the Test Interface mode either by choosing **Quit** from the **UNTITLED** menu or by double-clicking the mutated Interface Builder icon in your dock.

Giving Your Button a Funky Sound

Next, we'll show how easy it is to add sound to a button.

Sounds

1. Click the **Sounds** suitcase icon in the File window to see the Sounds view. (In NeXTSTEP 2.1, you must *double*-click the icon.)

2. Drag one of the sound icons (e.g., **Funk**) and drop it on top of the **Noise** button in **My Window**. You'll see something like this:

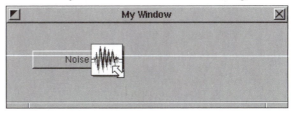

The link cursor means that the button is linked to the **Funk** system sound (In NeXTSTEP 2.1, the link cursor does *not* appear.)

Giving Your Button an Image

Next, we'll show how easy it is to make an image appear on a button.

Images

3. Click the **Images** suitcase icon in the File window to see the Images view.

4. Drag the **NXreturnSign** icon ( ) and drop it on top of the **Noise** button in **My Window**. You'll see something like this:

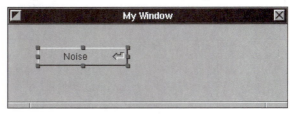

Normally you would only drop the **NXreturnSign** icon on a button to indicate that hitting the Return key has the same effect as clicking the button. But we're just starting out in this chapter and didn't want to have to create a special icon just to demonstrate this feature. The icon can be placed in a different location on the button using the Button Inspector window, which we'll discuss in a later chapter.

5. Choose **Document→Test Interface**. When you click the **Noise** button, you'll hear the sound that you dropped on top of the button.

6. Choose **Quit** from **UNTITLED**'s main menu to return to Interface Builder's build mode.

Objects, Messages, and Targets

The NeXTSTEP Application Kit is written in Objective-C, a hybrid language based on ANSI C and SmallTalk that was developed by Brad Cox. The principle building-block of object-oriented programs is the "object." Objects can be thought of as a combination of ANSI C variables and functions, but they are much more powerful than either alone.

Objective-C *objects* are self-contained code entities that communicate by sending messages to one another. A *message* is like a function call in a traditional programming language – it causes a procedure to be executed. But a message is unlike a function call in that it is sent to a specific object; it is not simply "called." These procedures, called *methods* in Objective-C, are "encapsulated" inside objects, and thus different objects can respond to the same message in different ways.

Unlike some object-oriented languages, Objective-C doesn't require that you know the type (*class*) of an object before you send it a message. This is known as *dynamic* or *run-time binding* – the message is bound to the object at run-time instead of compile-time. This allows for much greater flexibility, because certain decisions can be made following a user's action. For example, when a user chooses **Cut** from an application's **Edit** submenu, a **cut:** message is sent to a target object. If an application lets a user **cut** text, graphics, and other types of data, the **cut:** message would have varying targets which wouldn't be known until run-time. With run-time binding, the application doesn't need to know the class of the target object before the **cut:** message is sent.

Objects and Classes

Under NeXTSTEP, every on-screen object is represented by an Objective-C object inside the computer's memory. In our little demo application, there's a **Window** object that displays and controls the application's on-screen window, **My Window**, and there's a **Button** object that displays and controls the **Noise** button. There's yet another object for the application's **UNTITLED** main menu, and one additional object for each of the individual items (cells) inside the menu.

Every NeXTSTEP object belongs to a *class*, which both defines and creates the object. Many of the NeXTSTEP class names are fairly self-explanatory.

For example, the classes of the on-screen objects in the application described above are listed in the following table.

Object in the Application	Class
the window ("**My Window**")	Window
the button ("**Noise**")	Button
the main menu ("**UNTITLED**")	Menu
the menu items (**Info, Edit, Hide, Quit**)	MenuCell

There are three other objects present in this application that aren't immediately apparent because they have no obvious corresponding object on the screen. They are listed in the table below. (It's not imperative that you understand everything in the remainder of this section right now, but we're going to give it to you anyway.)

Object Name	Class	Purpose
NXApp	Application	The application's main controlling object.
[myWindow contentView]	View	Defines the content area of the window where the application can draw.
n/a	ButtonCell	The Button's supporting Cell object, which actually displays the button.

One of the objects in this table has a funny "name" with square brackets. The square brackets illustrate the Objective-C *messaging operator*. The statement **[myWindow contentView]** means "send the **contentView** message to the object called **myWindow** and return the result." The result is the name of the content **View** object inside **myWindow**. When the application starts up, we don't know the name for **myWindow**'s content **View** object. We can get it only by sending a message to the **myWindow** object (**myWindow** is the Objective-C variable name for the **Window** object with title "**My Window**").

Messaging is one of two major features that you need to learn about the Objective-C language in order to write NeXTSTEP programs. The other is constructing your own classes. The three bundled classes **Window**, **View** and **Application**, are the very heart and soul of NeXTSTEP. If you understand them, you understand a lot of what you need to know about the Application Kit to write NeXTSTEP programs.

Targets, Actions, and Connections

Many of the objects in the Application Kit, called **Control** objects, are set up so that when you manipulate an on-screen object, a *message* is automatically sent to a second object. The object that receives the message is the *target* of the sending object. The procedure (method) that the target is instructed to perform is called the *action*.

For example, when you choose the **Quit** menu command from an application's menu, the associated **MenuCell** object sends a **terminate:** message to the controlling object **NXApp** (also known as the **File's Owner**). You can think of this as calling a function called **terminate:** inside the **NXApp** object.

The **terminate:** message has the form **[NXApp terminate:self]**. The action is "**terminate:**" and **self** is an argument (which specifies the object that sent the message). This causes the **NXApp** object to execute its **terminate:** method, which terminates the program. Likewise, the **MenuCell** object associated with the **Hide** menu command sends the **hide:** message to **NXApp**, which causes **NXApp** to remove all the application's windows from the screen. The colons (**:**) shown above are actually part of the Objective-C method names!

To see how this all works in practice, we're going to add two more **Control** objects to **MyWindow**, a text field and a slider. First we'll put them in the window, and then we'll wire (connect) them together so that a message can be sent from the slider to the text field.

1. Drag the icons for the **TextField** and **Slider** objects (seen at the left of the page) from the Palettes window into **My Window**. When you're done, you should have something that looks like this:

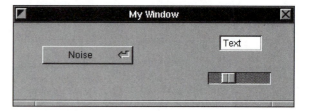

Next, we'll make a connection so that the **Slider** object can send a message to the **TextField** object whenever the **Slider** object's knob is moved.

2.   Hold down the Control key on the keyboard and drag from the **Slider** object to the **TextField** object (note the direction). You will see a "connection wire" appear between the two objects:

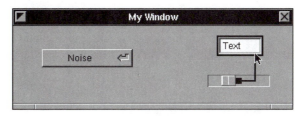

3.   Release the mouse button, and Interface Builder's *Connections* Inspector window will appear near the lower-right corner of the screen. See Figure 8 below. The Connections Inspector lets you make or break connections between objects.

Connections from a control object to another object have two parts: a *target* and an *action*. You already specified the **TextField** object as the *target* (or *receiver* or destination) of a message when you connected the **Slider** object to the **TextField**. You specify which *action* (method) the target should perform (in response to an event) in the Connections Inspector. Your choices are listed in the right hand column of the Connections Inspector window in Figure 8 below. (If you had connected the **Slider** object to a different target, say the **Button** object, then you would see a different list of actions in the Connections Inspector, because a **Button** object can perform a different set of actions than a **TextField** object.)

The action we'll use here is **takeDoubleValueFrom:**, which causes the **TextField** object to ask the *sender* (the **Slider** object) of the original message for its double (real number) value. This double value corresponds to the position of the **Slider** object's knob.

4.   Select the **takeDoubleValueFrom:** action in the Connections Inspector and then click the **Connect** button. (Alternatively, you can double-click the **takeDoubleValueFrom:** action.) After you make the connection, the **Connect** button becomes a **Disconnect** button, as in Figure 8, and the connection dot (●) appears next to the action name in the Inspector.

FIGURE 8. **Slider Inspector: Connections and Attributes**

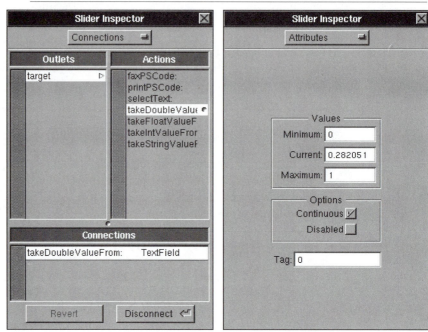

5. Test the interface again by choosing **Document→Test Interface**.

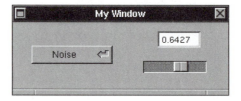

6. Drag the **Slider** object's knob. As you move it, the **TextField** object will update the number it displays according to the knob's position.

7. Choose **Quit** from **UNTITLED**'s main menu.

Figure 9 below shows the communication between the **Slider** and **Text-Field** objects. The mouse drag event causes the **Slider** to send the **take-DoubleValueFrom:** message to the target **TextField** object, which executes its **takeDoubleValueFrom:** method. The **takeDoubleValue-From:** method sends the **doubleValue** message back to the **Slider**, which returns the value **.6427** to the **TextField**, and then the **TextField** displays the result. (We didn't have to tell the **TextField** object's **takeDoubleValue-From:** action procedure to send the **doubleValue** message back to the

Slider; the **TextField** is smart enough to know how to get a double value from the *sending* object.) It may seem like a lot of overhead, but messaging is actually quite fast – only slightly slower than a standard function call.

FIGURE 9. Communication between Slider and TextField

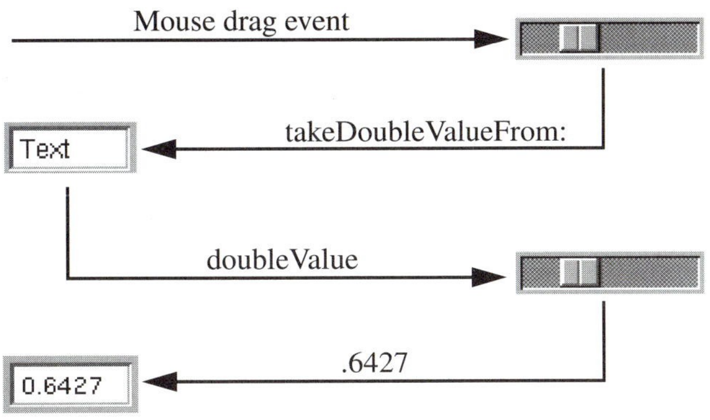

8. Select the **Slider** object (with a single-click) and drag to **Attributes** in the Inspector's pop-up list (or type Command-1) to bring up the **Slider**'s Attributes Inspector. A screen shot of it can be seen on the right of Figure 8 above.

Within the Slider Attributes Inspector you can specify the values that a slider will return at its minimum and maximum positions, its initial position, and whether it sends an action message to the target continuously as the slider is dragged, or only when it is released (**Continuous** or not). You can also disable the slider so that nothing happens when the user manipulates it and set a **Tag** so a slider can be distinguished from others in a matrix (group) of sliders. Every Application Kit object has its own Attributes Inspector.

9. Quit Interface Builder. There's no need to save the interface specifications.

Congratulations!

In this chapter, you've learned a little bit about the workings of Interface Builder and Objective-C. You've seen that on-screen objects have corresponding Objective-C objects inside the computer's memory. You've also seen a special class of object called a **Control**. A **Control** can have a *target*, which is another object that is automatically sent an *action* message to perform an *action* when the **Control** object is manipulated by the user.

In the next chapter, we'll cover the basics of Objective-C, NeXTSTEP's native programming language. We'll also take a look at the basic Objective-C classes that NeXTSTEP provides to make writing complicated programs much easier.

4

Creating an Application Without Interface Builder

What??? If Interface Builder is so wonderful, why would you want to write an application without it? Normally you wouldn't – using Interface Builder makes it dramatically easier to develop application programs with graphical user interfaces. But Interface Builder also hides a lot of the nuts-and-bolts of how NeXTSTEP application programs work. By showing the details of an application written without Interface Builder, we'll see Interface Builder's behind-the-scenes magic and learn a good deal about Objective-C and the NeXTSTEP Application Kit as well.

The *Tiny.m* Program

In this chapter, we'll discuss a small application called **Tiny.m** (the **.m** extension means that the file contains Objective-C code.) This program will bring up a menu which allows the user to quit. It will also bring up a window and draw a fancy pattern in it. See Figure 1 on the next page.

Before discussing the application in detail, we'll show you the complete source code for **Tiny.m**, which starts on the next page. Much of the code in **Tiny.m** which relates to on-screen objects will not be necessary when we combine Interface Builder with Objective-C, starting with the next chapter.

FIGURE 1. Tiny.m: Menu and Window

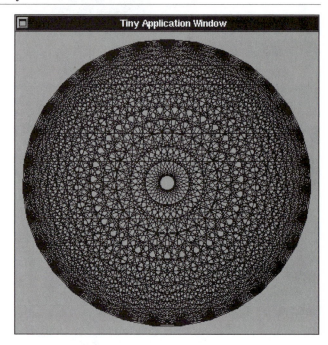

```
/* Tiny.m
 *
 *   A tiny NeXTSTEP application which creates a
 *   menu and a window and displays graphics
 *    in the window.
 */

#import <math.h>
#import <dpsclient/wraps.h>

#import <appkit/Application.h>
#import <appkit/Window.h>
#import <appkit/Menu.h>
#import <appkit/View.h>

void demo(void)
{
    id myWindow, myView, myMenu;
    NXRect graphicsRect;
    float f, g;        /* to draw the pattern */
    float pi = 2 * acos(0.0);
    const n = 31;
```

```
/* set up and display the window */
  NXSetRect(&graphicsRect, 100.0, 350.0,
            400.0, 400.0);     /* handy function */

  myWindow = [ [Window alloc]
             initContent: &graphicsRect
             style:       NX_TITLEDSTYLE
             backing:     NX_BUFFERED
             buttonMask:  NX_MINIATURIZEBUTTONMASK
             defer:       NO];
  [myWindow setTitle:"Tiny Application Window"];
  [myWindow display];

 /* set up the menu */
  myMenu = [ [Menu alloc] initTitle: "Tiny"];
  [myMenu addItem: "Quit"
          action: @selector(terminate:)
          keyEquivalent: 'q'];
  [myMenu sizeToFit];
  [NXApp   setMainMenu: myMenu];

 /* set up the View where the image will be drawn */
  myView = [ [View alloc] initFrame: &graphicsRect];
  [myView setOpaque: YES];

  [myWindow setContentView: myView];
  [myWindow makeKeyAndOrderFront: nil];

/* now do the drawing */
  [myView lockFocus];
  PSnewpath();
  PStranslate(200.0, 200.0);     /* place center */

  /* These lines trace two polygons with n sides and
   * interconnect all of the points...
   */

  for (f=0; f<2*pi; f+=2*pi/n) {
    for (g=0; g<2*pi; g+=2*pi/n) {
      PSmoveto( sin(f)*190.0, cos(f)*190.0 );
      PSlineto( sin(g)*190.0, cos(g)*190.0 );
    }
  }
  PSsetgray(NX_BLACK);
  PSstroke();

  /* Now send the drawing commands to the Window
   * Server.
```

```
    */

    [myWindow flushWindow];

    /* Unlock the PostScript focus */
    [myView unlockFocus];
}

void main()
{
    /* Create the application object.*/
    NXApp = [Application new];

    /* Display the menu, window, and graphic */
    demo();

    /* run the main event loop */
    [NXApp run];

    /* We get here when the user clicks Quit.
     * Free the application and go home.
     */
    [NXApp free];
}
```

Before we analyze the program, we suggest you type it in and save it in a file called **Tiny.m**. You can use any of the three programmer's editors which come with NeXTSTEP: Edit, GNU Emacs, or *vi*. If you're just starting out with UNIX, you'll probably want to use Edit, because it works like most other NeXTSTEP programs, has several nice features for writing code, and you learned how to use it in Chapter 2. Edit also has some powerful features for browsing a program's source code and interfacing directly with the **gdb**, the GNU debugger, and therefore we highly recommend it.

Many sophisticated programmers and system administrators use Emacs, from the Free Software Foundation. It's a powerful editor that's customizable. It also includes a graphical interface to **gdb** to make it easier to find out what's wrong with your programs when you make mistakes. One advantage of using Emacs is that it is available with most versions of UNIX.

The *vi* editor is the antique UNIX "visual" editor Bill Joy (of Sun Microsystems, Inc.) wrote. It's mostly there for historic reasons, but some people prefer it. Both Emacs and *vi* must be run from the NeXTSTEP Terminal application which was described in Chapter 2.

After you've typed the source code in the file **Tiny.m**, open up a Terminal window and compile it with the following command in **bold** type ("localhost>" is our UNIX command line prompt where "localhost" is the *host name* of the computer – yours may differ):

```
localhost> cc -Wall -o Tiny Tiny.m -lNeXT_s -lsys_s
localhost>
```

What you typed	What it means
`cc`	Invoke the C compiler. In NeXTSTEP, the C, Objective-C, and C++ compilers are all invoked with this same command. (If you wish to use C++ be sure that the appropriate libraries are properly installed.)
`-Wall`	Make the compiler list all warnings.
`-o Tiny`	Place the result of the compilation in the **Tiny** file.
`Tiny.m`	Compile the program in the **Tiny.m** file.
`-lNeXT_s`	Link the program with the **NeXT_s** library.
`-lsys_s`	Link the program with the **sys_s** library.

If the program compiles without errors, you can run it by typing its name:

```
localhost> Tiny
```

You should see the window displayed in Figure 1 above. To see the menu you must make **Tiny** the *active* application by clicking in its window or double-clicking its generic application icon (seen at the left) near the bottom of the screen (the icon does *not* have a title in NeXTSTEP 3.0).

Tiny.m: *line-by-line*

Neat? Now let's take a look at this program line-by-line.

```
/* Tiny.m
 *
 *   A tiny NeXTSTEP application which creates a
 *   menu and a window and displays graphics
 *    in the window.
 */
```

Like any well-written program, **Tiny.m** begins with a set of comments describing what the program does. Objective-C supports the standard

ANSI-C style of comments. That means that anything enclosed between a
/* and a */ is a comment. Anything on a line following a double-slash is a
comment as well. Thus:

```
/* this is a comment */
// This is a comment as well
```

Unfortunately, a lot of programs that process C source-code don't understand the double-slash syntax. This includes Emacs, *cb* (the C program
beautifier), and *indent* (a better C program beautifier).

The next block of statements are definitely Objective-C:

```
#import <math.h>
#import <dpsclient/wraps.h>

#import <appkit/Application.h>
#import <appkit/Window.h>
#import <appkit/Menu.h>
#import <appkit/View.h>
```

The Objective-C **#import** statement is a lot like C's **#include** statement,
with a twist: if the file specified in the **#import** statement has already been
#import-ed, it doesn't get **#import**-ed a second time. This is a real win,
because it avoids all sorts of "kludges" that C **#include** files are notorious
for, like this:

```
/* kludge.h:
* a kludgy C #include file
*/
#ifndef __KLUDGE__
#define __KLUDGE__
... /* code that we wanted to include, but just once
*/
#endif
```

With Objective-C, all you would have to use is:

```
#import <kludge.h>
```

This example checks to see if the symbol **__KLUDGE__** is defined and, if
it is not, defines the symbol and processes the rest of the **#include** file.
Objective-C's **#import** does all of this for you automatically.

Now then, what's being **#import**-ed? The first line should be familiar:
math.h contains the standard C language prototypes for the floating-point
math library. You need to include this file since **Tiny.m** uses the functions

sin() and **cos()** to create a graphical pattern. The next line includes the file **/usr/include/dpsclient/wraps.h**, which contains the prototypes for the PostScript (**PS**) functions that **Tiny.m** uses to display graphics.

The remaining **#import** statements bring in the definitions for **Application**, **Window**, **View** and **Menu**, which are all classes defined in the NeXT-STEP Application Kit. In the following section, we'll briefly divert our attention from **Tiny.m** to ramble a bit more about classes, objects, and methods. Then we'll resume our discussion of **Tiny.m**.

Classes and Objects, Methods and Messages

An Objective-C *object* is a self-contained programming unit containing both data and procedures which operate on that data. The data is stored in *instance variables* and the procedures are called *instance methods*. For example, a **Window** object, which controls an on-screen window, contains a **frame** instance variable which stores the window's size and an instance method **sizeWindow::** which sets the frame's **width** and **height**. The **Window** object is self-contained, or *encapsulated*, in the sense that instance variables such as **frame** are not directly accessible from outside the object – they may only be modified through methods. This ensures controlled access to, and the integrity of, the instance data and is called *data encapsulation*.

An Objective-C *class* defines and creates Objective-C (instance) objects. For example, the **Window** class defines the instance variables and methods which comprise **Window** objects, and creates **Window** objects (instances) according to the class definition. A class creates objects using a procedure called a *factory* or *class* method, so named because it builds new objects and is performed by the class rather than an instance object created by the class. In this sense a class is also an object, called a *factory* or *class* object.[1]

When a class creates an object using a factory method, it sets up memory for a new data structure containing the instance variables defined by the class. It does *not* make a copy of the instance methods that the object can perform. There is only one copy of the instance methods, and they are

---

1. This may be somewhat confusing to you if you already know C++, another "object-oriented" language based upon C. Objective-C and C++ are very different languages, largely because Objective-C has a run time system that handles messaging, while C++ doesn't.

stored as part of the class in memory. These instance methods are shared by all objects created by the class, which of course makes memory usage more efficient.

For example, suppose an application requires two on-screen windows. The application program will send two separate requests (messages) to the **Window** class to create two **Window** objects. Each **Window** object will contain its own class-defined data structure with its own copies of the instance variables such as **width** and **height**. If one of the **Window** objects is asked to perform the **sizeWindow::** method (which changes the window's **width** and **height**), then the window object will go to the **Window** class definition in memory for the actual **sizeWindow::** code, but will change only the **width** and **height** instance variables in its own data structure. An object is actually a data structure with a pointer to its class so it can access the shared methods. The Objective-C run time system is what brings it alive.

An Objective-C method is invoked by sending the object a *message*. Objective-C messages are enclosed in square brackets as follows:

```
[receiver message]
```

The *receiver* can be a factory or an instance object while *message* is a method name together with arguments. We will refer to the entire bracketed expression [*receiver message*] as a *message* as well; some people prefer to call it a *message expression*. There shouldn't be any confusion.

The terms *method* and *message* appear to be used interchangeably and may appear to mean the same thing, but they don't. A *method* is a procedure inside a class that's executed when you send that class or instance of that class a *message*.

For example, we could send the message **[Application new]** to the **Application** *class* to invoke the **new** *class* method, or the message **[NXApp run]** to an **Application** *object* to invoke the **run** *instance* method. As an example with arguments, we could send the message

```
[myWindow sizeWindow: 200 : 300]
```

to the **myWindow** object to invoke the **sizeWindow::** instance method. This message would change the size of **myWindow** to a width of 200 and a height of 300.

Objective-C adds only one new data type, **id**, to the C programming language. An **id** variable is a pointer to an object in the computer's memory.

(The variable **myWindow** in the previous paragraph could have been defined as an **id** variable.) An **id** variable is somewhat like the ANSI-C "**void ***" pointer: a "**void ***" can point to any kind of structure, while an **id** variable can point to an object of any class. This feature goes hand in hand with dynamic binding, Objective-C's ability to determine the class of the object receiving a message at run-time.

The Circle Class Example

Suppose you had an object called **aCircle**, which is an instance of a class called **Circle**. The **aCircle** object might respond to a **display** message which makes **aCircle** draw itself in a window. You would send this message with Objective-C as follows:

```
[aCircle display];
```

If you wanted to set the center of **aCircle** at position (x,y), you might send it another message:

```
[aCircle setX: 32.0 andY: 64.0];
```

Arguments always follow colons in messages, and thus a method has the same number of arguments as there are colons in its name. The colons are actually part of the Objective-C message, and thus the method above is named **setX:andY:**, not simply **setX** or even **setX andY.**

The **aCircle** object might also provide methods that let you find out the x and y locations of its center. We'll call these *accessor* methods because they give you access to a variable encapsulated inside the **aCircle** object. For example:

```
printf("The circle is centered at %f,%f\n",
       [aCircle x], [aCircle y] );
```

In this case, the methods **x** and **y** return floating point numbers and the output would be:

```
The circle is centered at 32.0,64.0
```

It's a good idea to add accessor methods to the classes you write: they hide the implementation details of how an object actually works. For example, the programmer who wrote the **Circle** class which built **aCircle** would likely arrange for **aCircle** to store the circle's center in instance variables. In this case, the methods **x** and **y** would simply return these stored variables. Alternatively, the programmer might be storing the locations of the corners of a square that is inscribed in the circle; in this case, the methods **x** and **y** would perform a calculation. By using the accessor methods, we remove the need to know how the value is computed from the calling program. This separates the classes in pieces of your program from each other. The classes communicate through well-defined interfaces. Their data is *encapsulated* and protected from the outside world.

Creating and Destroying Objects

We still need two more methods to make the **Circle** class usable: a way for creating new **Circle** objects (instances of the **Circle** class), and a way to destroy the circles when we are done with them. The "standard" Objective-C methods for doing this are called **alloc** and **free**. So the Objective-C code for drawing a circle on the screen might look like this:

```
id aCircle;

aCircle = [Circle alloc];
[aCircle init];

[aCircle setX: 32.0 andY: 64.0];
[aCircle setRadius: 10.0];
[aCircle display];
[aCircle free];
```

The **aCircle = [Circle alloc]** statement sends the **alloc** message to the **Circle** *class*, asking it to allocate memory (create) a new Circle object. Thus, **alloc** is a *factory* method. The other methods are *instance* methods, because they are invoked by messages that we send directly to a **Circle** *object*, in this example the circle object pointed to by the **id** variable **aCircle**. (By convention, class names begin with upper-case letters, while methods and instances begin with lower-case letters.)

Normally, if there's nothing obvious for a method to return, the object's method returns the **id** of the receiver object itself. (Remember that an **id** is a pointer to an object.) This enables us to "nest" messages like this:

```
[ [aCircle setX: 32.0 andY: 64.0] setRadius: 10.0];
```

Since all of the methods in the above example return the **id** of the **aCircle** instance itself (including the **alloc** message sent to the **Circle** *class*), we could be really cute and cryptic and write the above code like this:

```
id aCircle;

[[[[[Circle alloc]
        init]
```

```
        setX: 32.0 andY: 64.0]
        setRadius: 10.0]
        display]
        free];
```

This example might be a bit extreme, but the nesting technique is usually used with **alloc** and **init** methods as follows:

```
aCircle = [ [Circle alloc] init];
```

The advantage of separating creation (**alloc**) and initialization (**init**) into two methods has to do with the way that the NeXTSTEP virtual memory system works. For more information, look up the word *zone* and the method **allocFromZone** in Digital Librarian if you are curious.

Class Interface Definitions

In order to use a new class in your program, you need some way to tell the Objective-C compiler the name of your class, its instance variables, and its methods. This is done with a class interface definition – a fancy name for an include file that is brought to the compiler's attention with the **#import** directive.

Because **Circle** is a relatively simple class, it has a relatively simple class interface. Here it is:

```
#import <objc/Object.h>

@interface Circle:Object
{
  float x;
  float y;
  float radius;
}
+ alloc;
- init;
- setX: (float)x andY:(float)y;
- setRadius: (float)radius;
- (float) x;
- (float) y;
- display;
- free
@end
```

The following line begins the class interface:

```
@interface Circle : Object
```

This line tells the compiler that we're about to define the **Circle** class and that the **Circle** class inherits from the **Object** class. We'll discuss inheritance a bit later.

The next five lines define the *instance* variables that every **Circle** object contains. These variables are *private* to each object of type **Circle**; the only way you should access them is by sending messages to the object.

The eight lines which follow define methods. The **alloc** method is the one which creates new objects (or instances) of the **Circle** type (class). The plus sign ("+") means that it's a *factory* method; one that is invoked by a message you send to the **Circle** class itself, rather than to an instance of the **Circle** class. The other methods are preceded with minus signs ("-") which means that they are invoked by messages sent to class instances. (By the way, you can have class and instance methods with the same name; the Objective-C run-time system automatically figures out if you are sending the message to a class or an instance of that class.)

The methods **x** and **y** both return floating point numbers, while the other methods, including the factory method **alloc**, return the default return type **id**, a pointer to an object.

At this point, you know everything about the **Circle** class to use it effectively in one of your programs. Of course, you have no idea how the class is actually implemented but it doesn't really matter. That's the key to object-oriented programming: independent modules that work "as advertised" through well-documented interfaces, without forcing the programmer to understand the internals of *how* they work. This is known as *procedural (or functional) abstraction.*

One last point: although the words "sending a message" might suggest concurrency, message invocations are really little more than traditional C-language function calls.[1] If your program sends a message to an object, that object's corresponding method has to finish executing before your program can continue.

---

1. The Mach operating system, upon which NeXTSTEP is based, offers another kind of messaging called "Mach messages." Mach messages should not be confused with Objective-C messages.

The NeXTSTEP Classes Used by *Tiny.m*

Now that we know a little more about object-oriented programming and Objective-C, we can explain the following statements in the program **Tiny.m**:

```
#import <appkit/Application.h>
#import <appkit/Window.h>
#import <appkit/View.h>
#import <appkit/Menu.h>
```

These statements bring in the Objective-C class definitions for four important NeXTSTEP classes: **Application**, **Window**, **View**, and **Menu**. These classes implement the basic behavior of NeXTSTEP programs.

Every NeXTSTEP program has one, and only one, instance of the **Application** class. It's usually created inside the program's **main()** function by sending the **new** message to the **Application** class. (NeXTSTEP uses the **new** message to create a new object when you are only going to create *exactly one instance* of the object.)

The **Application** object is the most crucial object in the program because it provides the framework for program execution. The **Application** class connects the program to the Window Server, initializes the PostScript environment, and maintains a list of all the windows in the application. This enables it to receive events from the Window Server and distribute them to the proper **Window** objects, which in turn distribute the events to the proper objects inside the on-screen windows.

For example, if a user presses a button inside a window, then the Window Server gets a *mouse down* event from the hardware and passes it to the **Application** object of the program which owns the window. The **Application** object then passes the *mouse down* event to the proper **Window** object, which in turn passes it to the **Button object** that controls the on-screen button that was pressed.

The **Window** class is where the master control of your program's on-screen windows is defined. For every window that your program displays, there is an associated instance object of the **Window** class inside the computer's memory. You can send messages to **Window** objects that make the associated on-screen windows move, resize, reorder to the top of the window display list (placing themselves on top of the other windows) and perform many other operations.

The **View** class is the class which plays the most central role in NeXTSTEP applications. Many of the classes in the Application Kit, including all **Control** and **Text** classes, inherit from the **View** class (see the next section for the definition of *inherit*). **View** objects are responsible for drawing in windows and receiving events. Each **View** object can have any number of views that it contains, called *subviews*. When a window receives a mouse event, it automatically finds the correct **View** object to receive that event.

The **Menu** class implements the NeXTSTEP menu system. Methods in the **Menu** class allow you to create new menus, add items to them, display them, and perform other functions. Each item within the menu is actually handled by another class called **MenuCell**. You can look at the include file **/usr/include/appkit/MenuCell.h** if you are interested in seeing the methods that the **MenuCell** implements. In fact, all of the NeXTSTEP classes have interface (**.h**) files in the directory **/NextDeveloper/Headers/appkit** (or **/usr/include/appkit** in NeXTSTEP 2.1).

Inheritance

If you look at the file **/NextDeveloper/Headers/appkit/Menu.h**, you'll notice something curious in the **Menu** class interface:

```
@interface Menu : Panel
{
  ...
```

Also, if you look at the file **/NextDeveloper/Headers/appkit/Panel.h**, you'll see the following in the **Panel** class interface:

```
@interface Panel : Window
{
  ...
```

Unlike the **Circle** class we discussed above, the **Menu** class doesn't inherit directly from the **Object** class; instead, it inherits from the **Panel** class. In turn, the **Panel** class inherits from the **Window** class. This means that NeXTSTEP menus are really a special kind of panel with additional features. Panels, in turn, are special kinds of windows. As we go *down* the class inheritance chain from **Window** to **Panel** to **Menu**, each class has additional instance variables and custom behavior, where desired, but otherwise they basically work like objects from which they inherit. We say that the **Menu** class is a *subclass* of the **Panel** class and the **Panel** class is a subclass of the **Window** class. (If you've forgotten the distinction between a panel and a window you can look back in Chapter 1.)

"But wait! Aren't menus, panels, and windows different things?"

Yes and no. Although menus, panels, and windows look different on the NeXTSTEP screen, they are all types of windows that are displayed on the naked NeXTSTEP monitor's background. The only way to draw on NeXT-STEP's Display PostScript monitor is by creating a window. Therefore, menus and panels all need to be kinds of windows in order to be displayed. The easiest way to make it all work is to specify menus as a special kind of panel which itself is a special kind of window. This is called *inheritance*, and is another powerful feature of Objective-C.

The complete inheritance hierarchy of NeXTSTEP 2.1 Application Kit classes is shown in Figure 2 on the next page (these classes still exist in NeXTSTEP 3.0). Note the path

Menu : Panel : Window : Responder : Object

which contains the classes discussed above. **Responder** is the abstract superclass which contains the event responding mechanism of NeXTSTEP. The **Menu**, **Panel**, and **Window** classes inherit this mechanism, and therefore instances of these classes can respond to events. An *abstract super-class* is a class which contains the functionality needed and inherited by other classes, but instances of the class itself are rarely used. The **Object** class is another example of an abstract superclass. We'll return to our discussion of the **Responder** class later in this chapter.

Back to Tiny.m

The program **Tiny.m** consists of two functions: **demo()** and **main()**. As with C, every Objective-C program contains a function called **main()** which is called by the operating system to start the program. The **main()** function in **Tiny.m** isn't very complicated:

```
void main()
{
  /* Create the application object.*/
  NXApp = [Application new];

  /* Display the menu, window, and graphic */
  demo();

  /* run the main event loop */
  [NXApp run];
```

FIGURE 2. The Application Kit Hierarchy of Classes

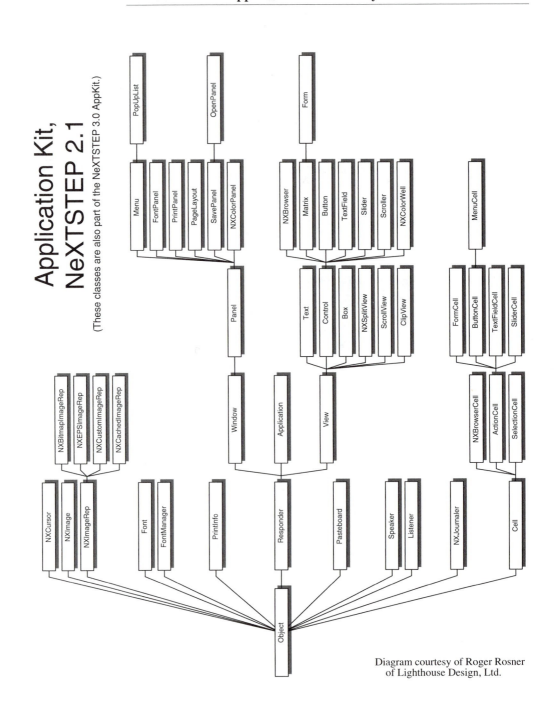

Application Kit,
NeXTSTEP 2.1
(These classes are also part of the NeXTSTEP 3.0 AppKit.)

Diagram courtesy of Roger Rosner
of Lighthouse Design, Ltd.

```
    /* We get here when the user clicks Quit.
     * Free the application and go home.
     */
    [NXApp free];
}
```

The first statement in the **main()** function above creates an **Application** *object* by sending the **new** message to the **Application** *class* (recall that every NeXTSTEP program must have exactly one **Application** object). The **id** of the new object is assigned to the *global* **id** variable **NXApp**. Global variables are a rarity in NeXTSTEP for style and software engineering reasons, but it makes sense to be able to send messages to the **Application** object from any part of the program because of its crucial role. (By the way, the name **NXApp** violates the convention that object names (pointers) start with a lower case letter; it's a very special object!)

The second statement in **main()** calls the function **demo()**, which contains the code which makes the **Tiny** program unique. We'll discuss this in detail in the next section.

The third statement, **[NXApp run]**, is a message to the **Application** *object* to run the program's main event loop. An *event loop* is a function that usually sits idle, waiting for the user to press a key on the keyboard, move or click the mouse, or for a timed event. The event loop is part of the **Application** class – you never see it (unlike event loops in some other window systems). The **run** method exits when the **NXApp** object gets sent a **terminate:** or **stop:** message; this usually happens when the user chooses the **Quit** menu command.

The last statement, **[NXApp free]**, is a message to the **Application** object to free any resources used by the application. Although you don't strictly need to do this – the underlying Mach operating system will automatically free those resources when the application exits – it's good programming style to free memory that you no longer need.

Windows, Menus, and the demo() Function

Now it's time to look at the workhorse of **Tiny.m**, the **demo()** function. We'll try to digest it in pieces. Below we list the first part of the function:

```
id myWindow, myView, myMenu;
NXRect graphicsRect;
id myWindow, myView, myMenu;
...
/* set up and display the window */
```

```
NXSetRect(&graphicsRect, 100.0, 350.0,
          400.0, 400.0);    /* handy function */
```

The NeXTSTEP Application Kit (known less formally as the "AppKit") provides a rich set of C **typedef**s for doing graphics. Perhaps the most common of these are **NXCoord, NXPoint, NXSize**, and **NXRect**, which are defined below. If you're interested, you can find them in the files **/NextDeveloper/Headers/dpsclient/event.h** and **/NextDeveloper/Headers/appkit/graphics.h**.

```
typedef float NXCoord;

typedef struct _NXPoint { /* point */
    NXCoord x, y;
} NXPoint;

typedef struct _NXSize { /* size */
    NXCoord width, height;
} NXSize;

typedef struct _NXRect { /* rectangle */
  NXPoint origin;
  NXSize size;
} NXRect;
```

The function **NXSetRect()** is simply a convenient shorthand for setting the **origin** and **size** of a rectangle. Instead of using

```
NXSetRect(&graphicsRect, 100.0, 350.0,
          400.0, 400.0);
```

we could have used (for the exact same effect):

```
graphicsRect.origin.x =    100.0;
graphicsRect.origin.y =    350.0;
graphicsRect.size.width =  400.0;
graphicsRect.size.height = 400.0;
```

The reason for setting up **graphicsRect** is to specify where the new window will be located and how big it will be. The window itself gets created in the next **Tiny.m** program line when the **alloc** message is sent to the **Window** class (**alloc** is a factory method).

The new instance object is then initialized within the nested message. The **id** of the new **Window** object that is created is assigned to the variable **myWindow**:

```
myWindow = [ [Window alloc]
```

```
initContent:  &graphicsRect
style:        NX_TITLEDSTYLE
backing:      NX_BUFFERED
buttonMask:   NX_MINIATURIZEBUTTONMASK
defer:        NO];
```

One of the many nice features of Objective-C is that, for the most part, arguments are labeled. It makes Objective-C programs easy to read, as we'll see in the discussion of arguments below.

initContent: &graphicsRect   Specifies where the window will be created and how large it will be. In this case, the location of the lower-left-hand corner is (100.0,350.0) and the size is 400 pixels square. (The screen origin, namely the point (0.0,0.0), is at the lower-left corner of the NeXT-STEP display.)

style: NX_TITLEDSTYLE   This tells the window server to display the window with a title bar. Most windows have title bars which contain a title. Windows that contain title bars without titles are usually attention panels such as the Open and Close panels. Freestanding and docked application icons are examples of a window without a title bar (yes, those icons are also windows). To obtain a window without a title bar, use the argument **NX_PLAINSTYLE** for its style. These and other choices are **#define**-ed in the file **/NextDeveloper/Headers/appkit/Window.h**.

backing: NX_BUFFERED   Windows can have three kinds of backing: retained, buffered, or none. *Retained* backing means that visible portions of the window that a program draws are written directly to screen memory, but that an off-screen buffer is set up to retain non-visible portions that are obscured by other windows. Thus if the window is covered by another window and then exposed, the Window Server can redraw it without any work on the part of your program. *Buffered* windows use the off-screen buffer as an input buffer, and the buffer's contents are transferred to the screen when the window is flushed. Windows with *no backing* have no off-screen memory; if they are covered and then exposed, they must be redrawn, and will momentarily flash white while that redrawing takes place. Usually, you will want to use a buffered window when working with NeXTSTEP.

buttonMask: NX_MINIATURIZEBUTTONMASK   This tells the Window Server which buttons to put in the window's title bar. The miniaturize button is the button which lets you iconify a window. That's the only button that we've chosen to provide for the user. We won't provide a close button.

defer:NO];   This tells the Window Server that we want our window created now, rather than later.

It's important to remember that all of these arguments make up a single Objective-C method, whose proper name is

```
initContent: style: backing: buttonMask: defer:
```

After this statement executes, the **myWindow** variable contains the **id** of the window that's been created. We can send messages to the window by sending messages to that **id**. The messages below set the window's title and force it to be displayed on the screen. (If the **display** message was omitted, then the window would be automatically displayed by the **Application** object when the main event loop starts up, but the window's title wouldn't show up.)

```
[myWindow setTitle: "Tiny Application Window"];
[myWindow display];
```

The next four statements create our application's main menu:

```
myMenu = [ [Menu alloc] initTitle: "Tiny"];
[myMenu addItem: "Quit"
        action: @selector(terminate:)
        keyEquivalent: 'q'];
[myMenu sizeToFit];
[NXApp  setMainMenu: myMenu];
```

The first statement creates and initializes a new **Menu** object with title "**Tiny**" and assigns the **id** of the object to the **id** variable **myMenu**. The second line adds a **Quit** menu item to **myMenu**. The argument **action:@-selector(terminate:)** specifies that the **terminate:** action method should be invoked when **Quit** is chosen (**@selector()** is a directive that returns the unique **unsigned int** identifier of a compiled method.) The **terminate:** action causes the **Application** object to stop the main event loop. The argument **keyEquivalent:'q'** specifies Command-q as the key alternative to the **Quit** menu command.

The second statement is for cosmetic reasons: it sends the **sizeToFit** message to instruct **myMenu** to recalculate its width and height to just fit the text of the menu cells that it contains and resize its window as necessary.

The last statement of the group above sends a message to **NXApp**, the **id** of the **Application** object that was created in **main()**, informing it that **myMenu** is the **id** of the application's main menu.

The next four statements create an object of the **View** class and set up the **Window** for drawing. We need to describe the **View** class before we discuss these statements thoroughly.

Views

The **View** class and its subclasses are the primary mechanism by which NeXTSTEP users and applications interact. Applications draw on the screen by first invoking **View** instance methods to establish communication with the Window Server (in particular, Display PostScript), and then by sending PostScript commands. Going the other way, the AppKit will send a message to an object of the **View** class when the user does something which creates an event, like clicking the mouse or pressing a key on the keyboard.

View objects represent rectangular chunks of screen real estate inside a window. Many of the interesting NeXTSTEP objects – sliders, buttons, matrices, the **Text** object, and so on – are instances of **View** subclasses. Likewise you, the programmer, usually use the **View** class by subclassing it. **View** is an *abstract superclass*; it contains the functionality that a lot of other classes need and therefore inherit, but instances of the **View** class itself are rarely used.

One of the most important methods in the **View** class is the **drawSelf::** method. The **drawSelf::** method in your **View** object is invoked when its containing view (or window) wants your view to draw itself. (NeXTSTEP invokes the **drawSelf::** method automatically for you.) In this example, however, we're just trying to make something that works, so we'll draw in the **View** object directly.

```
myView = [ [View alloc] initFrame: &graphicsRect];
[myView setOpaque: YES];
```

The first of the two statements above contains nested messages which create the **View** object, initialize it to the location and size of **graphicsRect**, and finally returns an **id** which is assigned to **myView**. The second statement sets the new **myView** object so it *covers* the area specified by **graphicsRect** (i.e., **myView** isn't transparent). You may have noticed a potential problem here: we've created **myView** with a size of 400×400, the same size as the content area of the **myWindow**, but it has an offset of 150×350 relative to the window's (0.0,0.0) origin. Don't worry, we'll take care of that before we do any drawing.

```
[myWindow setContentView: myView];
```

This statement sets up the **View** object that we've just created as the *content view* of the window that we created in the last section. Every window contains precisely one content view, which represents the area of the window that is accessible to the application program. That is, it contains the entire window except the title bar, border, and resize bar (if present). The **setContentView:** method also changes the offset and the size of the **View** object that we created so that it is precisely aligned with the window.

```
[myWindow makeKeyAndOrderFront: nil];
```

This statement sends the **makeKeyAndOrderFront:** message to **myWindow**, which places the window on top of all the other on-screen windows and makes it the *key* window, the window which accepts keyboard events. The argument **nil** doesn't do anything here. The **makeKeyAndOrderFront:** method contains the argument so a message invoking it can be set up within Interface Builder. We'll discuss this further in a later chapter.

Drawing with PostScript Inside a View Object

The remaining lines in the function **demo**() draw the fancy pattern shown in Figure 1. Before we continue, however, we should mention that the drawing code in this example is generally not the way drawing should be done in a window! (In fact very little in this example is the way NeXT-STEP programming should be done - it's here purely for pedagogical reasons.) The drawing code is just a quick *hack* to get something pretty displayed in a window, to help you get your feet wet. This hack isn't optimized so that it communicates in the most efficient manner possible with the PostScript interpreter; that's done with a program called **pswrap**. This hack also doesn't generate PostScript code in response to a request from the Window Server, which causes a problem if you want to print the window's contents. (If you draw on-screen correctly, then you can print with no additional code other than an invocation of a **View**'s **printPScode:** method.) But for now, this will do.

A pair of messages to the **myView** object bracket the drawing statements:

```
[myView lockFocus];
...
[myView unlockFocus];
```

The **lockFocus** and **unlockFocus** methods tell the Display PostScript interpreter that all of the drawing you're about to do (i.e., all the PostScript commands you're about to execute) will take place in the **myView** object. It is very important to **lockFocus** before you issue any PostScript commands. It is equally important to **unlockFocus** when you're done.

The next group of statements contain the declarations and PostScript commands (actually C functions that send PostScript commands to the window server) that cause the design to be drawn.

```
float f, g;
float pi = 2 * acos(0.0);
const n = 31;
...
  PSnewpath();
  PStranslate(200.0, 200.0); /* place center */

  for (f=0; f<2*pi; f+=2*pi/n) {
    for (g=0; g<2*pi; g+=2*pi/n) {
      PSmoveto( sin(f)*190.0, cos(f)*190.0 );
      PSlineto( sin(g)*190.0, cos(g)*190.0 );
    }
  }
  PSsetgray(NX_BLACK);
  PSstroke();                 /* paint through the path */
  [window flushWindow];
```

If you have programmed in PostScript before, these statements will look a little weird. NeXTSTEP's Display PostScript implementation is a strange blend of PostScript ideology with C-language syntax. Every Display Post-Script *operator* (e.g., **newpath**, **lineto**) has an equivalent C function (**PSnewpath()**, **PSlineto()**) known as a *single-operator* function. Most C programmers find them easier to understand than pure PostScript. The C-language PostScript bindings also free you from having to use PostScript's unusual looping constructs. Furthermore, it is generally faster to do looping and other sorts of calculations in a compiled language, like Objective-C, than in an interpreted language like PostScript.

When drawing a picture with PostScript, you first define the path, then use the **stroke** (or **fill**) operator to make the path appear. It's much like the way "STOP" is painted on our roads by government workers. First the stencil is cut out and then the paint is sprayed through. Display PostScript works the same way: first the path is cut out with the **newpath**, **moveto**, and **lineto** operators. Then the color is set with the **setgray** operator and drawn with the **stroke** operator. Sending the **flushWindow** message to **myWindow** causes the graphics buffer to make sure that everything is displayed on the screen. It is necessary to flush the window because it is **NX_BUFFERED**. (Normally, NeXTSTEP flushes the window for you automatically.)

This completes our discussion of the **Tiny** application. Next we'll discuss NeXTSTEP events and then modify **Tiny** to demonstrate event-handling.

Responding to Events

The previous section showed how you might use a NeXTSTEP **View** object to draw something on the screen. This section shows the other half of **View**'s functionality: intercepting (and processing) events.

An *event* is a specific action in space and time. NeXTSTEP supports many kinds of events. For example, mouse presses, mouse drags, window exposes, and pressing keys on the keyboard are all events. You can arrange for events to be passed to your program. Each event is represented by an **NXEvent** structure which contains fields in it that represent the time that the event took place, its location on the screen, and other information.

Here is the **NXEvent** structure which can be found in the same **event.h** file mentioned previously.

```
typedef struct _NXEvent {
    int type;              /* event type */
    NXPoint location;      /* mouse location */
    long time;             /* time since launch */
    int flags;             /* (Shift, Control, Alt) */
    unsigned int window;   /* window number of event */
    NXEventData data;      /* event type-dependent data */
    DPSContext ctxt;       /* PostScript context*/
} NXEvent, *NXEventPtr;
```

The **NXEventData** structure contains the raw data about each event, as provided by the Window Server. The **DPSContext** variable **ctxt** contains the PostScript drawing context identification (similar to a window) where the event originated. The other variables are self-explanatory.

NeXTSTEP supports 31 kinds of events types but only about half of them, such as *mouse-down* and *key-up*, are of interest to developers. They are **#define**-ed in the include file **events.h** and discussed in more detail later in this book. Each event has a unique integer. The **Application** object receives events and translates them from event numbers into Objective-C messages which are sent to the appropriate objects. The following list of methods are invoked as a result of these messages (**bold** indicates the method name).

```
- mouseDown: (NXEvent *)theEvent;
- rightMouseDown: (NXEvent *)theEvent;
- mouseUp: (NXEvent *)theEvent;
- rightMouseUp: (NXEvent *)theEvent;
- mouseMoved: (NXEvent *)theEvent;
- mouseDragged: (NXEvent *)theEvent;
- rightMouseDragged: (NXEvent *)theEvent;
```

```
- mouseEntered: (NXEvent *) theEvent;
- mouseExited: (NXEvent *) theEvent;
- keyDown: (NXEvent *) theEvent;
- keyUp: (NXEvent *) theEvent;
```

The names of these methods are also self-explanatory. They are defined for objects of the **Responder** class and all of its subclasses. In order for our programs to respond to most of these events in custom ways we simply have to implement (actually *override*) these methods in our own class implementations. With overriding, you can augment or replace the behavior of a method in the superclass of the class that has the same name.

Of the objects we've learned about so far, **Application**, **Window**, and **View** are all subclasses of the **Responder** class. They all receive events and either process them or pass them along. We'll learn more about events and responders as we learn more about NeXTSTEP.

An Introduction to Event Handling

One of the main functions of the Window Server is to send events to the application for which they are destined. For example, when you press the left mouse button in a window, the Window Server determines which application owns that window, and sends an **NX_LMOUSEDOWN** event to the **Application** object for that application. When you release the mouse button, the same **Application** object receives an **NX_LMOUSEUP** event.

After the **Application** object receives the event, it determines the **Window** object where the event occurred. The **Application** object then translates the event number into a **Responder** message. For example, the **NX_LMOUSEDOWN** event becomes a **mouseDown:** message, which is sent to the appropriate window where the event occurred. When the **Window** object receives the event, it determines in which one of its **View**s the event took place. It then sends the message to that **View** object. Thus, in order to handle events, we need to create a subclass of the **View** class and place an instance of it on the screen.

Tiny2: A Demonstration of Event Handling

Let's make this discussion concrete with a little example. We'll design a subclass of **View** which receives **mouseDown:** events and draws a small circle wherever the event occurs. After a few mouse clicks, the result might look like the picture in Figure 3 below.

FIGURE 3. Tiny2: Menu and Window

We first list the interface file for this subclass.

```
/*
 * CView.h
 *
 * Declare a subclass of the View class which
 * draws circles in response to mouse-clicks.
 */

#import <appkit/View.h>

@interface CView:View
{
}
- clear:sender;
- mouseDown:(NXEvent *)theEvent;
@end
```

According to the interface for the **CView** class, we're going to be defining two methods: **clear:** and **mouseDown:**. The **clear:** method is new; an object of the **View** class doesn't respond to it. On the other hand, the **mouseDown:** method is already in the ~~clear:~~ class (actually inherited from View the **Responder** class). By defining our own version of this method, objects of our subclass respond to the message first. This technique of re-defining a method inherited from a superclass is called *overriding* a method.

The class itself is defined in a separate implementation (**.m**) file called **CView.m.**

```
/* CView.m:
 *
 * Draw a circle when we get a mouse-click by
 * overriding mouseDown:
 * Set up a way to clear the screen with a clear:
 * method.
 */

#import "CView.h"
#import <dpsclient/wraps.h>

@implementation CView

/* Clear myself - the CView drawing area */
- clear:sender
{
   [self lockFocus];    /* Lock PostScript context */
   NXEraseRect(&bounds); /* Erase the drawing. */
   [window flushWindow]; /* update NOW */
   [self unlockFocus];
   return self;
}

/* respond to left mouse-down events */
- mouseDown:(NXEvent *)theEvent
{
/* declare a point variable;
 * get the location of the mouse-down event
 */
   NXPoint center = theEvent->location;

   /* convert the point from window coordinates
    * to View coordinates
    */
   [self convertPoint:&center fromView:nil];

   /* draw a circle of radius 10 */
   [self lockFocus];
   PSnewpath();
   PSarc(center.x, center.y, 10, 0, 360);
   PSsetgray(NX_BLACK);
```

```
      PSstroke();          /* paint through the path */
      [window flushWindow];
      [self unlockFocus];
      return self;
   }
@end
```

The **NXEraseRect(&bounds)** function call in the **clear:** method above needs some explaining. The purpose of the function is obvious from its name, but the **bounds** variable seems to come "out of nowhere." It is actually an instance variable of the **CView** class, although it doesn't appear to be because it wasn't declared in **CView.h**. It was declared to be an **NXRect** instance variable in the **View** class, and since **CView** inherits from the **View** class, all **View** instance variables are automatically instance variables in **CView**. The content of the **bounds** rectangle in the **CView** object will be initialized to the position and size of the **CView** object on the screen when the line

```
   myView = [ [CView alloc] initFrame: &graphicsRect]
```

is executed in the **demo()** function below. Thus, in short, the **NXEraseRect(&bounds)** function call clears the **CView** content area of the **Tiny2** window. (By the way, child classes inherit *all* of the instance variables in their parent class. They can also add their own instance variables.)

To use this new subclass of **View**, we'll have to make several changes to the function **demo()** in **Tiny.m**. If you plan on typing in this code, begin by making a copy of **Tiny.m** and renaming it **Tiny2.m**. Much of the code in the two programs is identical. A complete listing of **Tiny2.m** follows. We'll discuss its differences from **Tiny.m** after the listing.

```
   /* Tiny2.m
    *
    * A Tiny NeXTSTEP application which creates Menu,
    * Window, and CView objects and displays circles in
    * the window in response to mouseDown events.
    * Links to the CView class.
    */

   #import <dpsclient/wraps.h>
   #import <appkit/Application.h>
   #import <appkit/Window.h>
   #import <appkit/Menu.h>
   #import <appkit/MenuCell.h>
   #import "CView.h"   /* needed to create a CView */
```

```
void demo(void)
{
  id myWindow, myView, myMenu;
  NXRect graphicsRect;

/* set up and display the window */
  NXSetRect(&graphicsRect, 100.0, 350.0,
                           400.0, 400.0);
  myWindow = [ [Window alloc]
              initContent: &graphicsRect
              style:       NX_TITLEDSTYLE
              backing:     NX_BUFFERED
              buttonMask:  NX_MINIATURIZEBUTTONMASK
              defer:       NO];
  [myWindow setTitle: "Tiny2 Application Window"];
  [myWindow display];

/* set up the View where the image will be drawn */
  myView = [ [CView alloc] initFrame:&graphicsRect];
  [myView setOpaque: YES];

  [myWindow setContentView: myView];
  [myWindow makeKeyAndOrderFront: nil];

/* set up menu after myView; then set Clear target */
  myMenu = [ [Menu alloc] initTitle: "Tiny2"];

  [ [myMenu addItem: "Clear"
            action: @selector(clear:)
            keyEquivalent: 'k']
            setTarget: myView];

  [ [myMenu addItem: "Quit"
            action: @selector(terminate:)
            keyEquivalent: 'q']
    setTarget: NXApp];

  [myMenu sizeToFit];
  [NXApp setMainMenu:myMenu];
}

void main() /* identical to Tiny.m main() function */
{
  NXApp = [Application new]; /* create app */
  demo();                    /* setup window */
  [NXApp run];   /* run the event loop */
  [NXApp free];  /* free the application */
}
```

The first major change we made in **Tiny2.m** (from **Tiny.m**) is with the include files. The **Tiny2.m** program needs the interface defined in the **MenuCell.h** and **CView.h** files because we need to send a message to a new **MenuCell** object (titled "**Clear**") and we also need to create a new **CView** object. To create an instance of the **CView** class instead of the **View** class, we only had to change from this line:

```
myView = [ [View alloc] initFrame: &graphicsRect];
```

to this line:

```
myView = [ [CView alloc] initFrame: &graphicsRect];
```

By simply changing **View** to **CView**, we create a **CView** object with all of its associated behaviors. What are its behaviors? A **CView** object works exactly the same way as a **View** object, except that it responds to a **clear:** message and it handles **mouseDown:** events differently. The rest of its functionality is inherited from the **View** class.

The next major change we made was to add a new menu item titled **Clear**. This was done by the following statement:

```
[ [myMenu addItem: "Clear"
        action: @selector(clear:)
        keyEquivalent: 'k']
        setTarget: myView];
```

This is a little complicated. The **addItem** method you've seen before: it adds another menu item to the main menu; this menu item is called "**Clear**" and has a key-equivalent of "**k**". But what about the **setTarget: myView** part? It turns out that the **addItem:action:keyEquivalent:** message sent to **myView** returns the **id** of the **MenuCell** object that gets created for the new menu item. By setting the target of this menu item to **myView**, we arrange for the **clear:** message to be sent directly to the **CView** object (i.e., the target **myView**) that was created; the message doesn't have to be passed through any intermediate objects.

By the way, the reason we set up **myMenu** after **myView** in **Tiny2.m** is that we couldn't set the target object of the **Clear** menu command until **myView** existed.

Several less significant changes were made to **Tiny.m** to get **Tiny2.m**. We eliminated the code to draw the fancy pattern and we changed the titles of **myWindow** and **myMenu** to read "**Tiny2**" instead of "**Tiny**." Other than that, the rest of the code is the same.

To compile this program, type the command in **bold** below:

```
localhost> cc -Wall -o Tiny2 Tiny2.m CView.m \
                -lNeXT_s -lsys_s
```

The only differences from the previous compiler call is that we've changed names from **Tiny** to **Tiny2** and we command that **CView.m** be compiled as well. Run the program by typing:

```
localhost> Tiny2
```

Click the mouse in a few places on the window, and you'll end up with something like the picture in Figure 3 above. Have fun!

NeXTSTEP Capitalization Conventions

Programmers new to NeXTSTEP and Objective-C are often confused by NeXT's conventions for capitalization. Some words are capitalized, while others seem gratuitously lowercased. But the rules for capitalization are actually quite simple.

General Rules

NeXT uses capital letters to delimit embedded words, such as **mouseDown** and **lockFocus**. The underscore character (_) is used only in constants such as **NX_TITLEDSTYLE** and macros such as **NX_RAISE**(), so variable names like **invalid_variable** are generally not used.

Some NeXT classes and functions begin with the letters NX. Others don't. Generally, those classes that were part of the NeXTSTEP 1.0 release don't begin with the letters NX. With release 2.0, NeXT adopted the NX convention so that they would not use names for classes that might have already been used by third-party developers.

NeXT also uses the letters PS for PostScript bindings and DPS for Display PostScript bindings.

Objective-C Class Names

All Objective-C class names (like **Window** and **View**) begin with capital letters. Variables used to hold the **id**'s of class instances, like **myWindow**, begin with lower-case letters. (**NXApp** is an exception.)

Objective-C Methods

Method names begin with lower-case letters. Method names that are defined with a plus sign (**+**) are *class* or *factory* methods, while method names defined with a minus sign (**-**) are *instance* methods.

Methods have a colon for every argument. Thus the **setTitle:** method takes a single argument, **moveTo::** takes two arguments, and

```
initContent:contentRect:style:backing:buttonMask:
    defer:screen:
```

(a method that a **Window** object responds to) takes seven arguments.

NeXT uses method names beginning with an underscore (like **_display::**) for internal methods inside the Application Kit. These methods are not mentioned in the **#include** files and you should *never* use them, even if you think you know what they do. This is because method names with an underscore are not guaranteed to have the same function or even to exist between successive releases of the NeXTSTEP operating system. Furthermore, do not create your own method names with leading underscores: you may end up unwittingly overriding a method in the NeXTSTEP shared library, creating bizarre problems.

UNIX Variables and Functions

Unfortunately, the UNIX operating system follows no rules about capitalization or underscores. Most UNIX functions and variables are lower case without underscores, but there are exceptions. If a program that you write won't link for some unexplained reason, it is possible that a function that you have written has the same name as one that is built into the UNIX operating system.

Summary

In this chapter, we've written a program that used Objective-C but not Interface Builder. In the previous chapter, Chapter 3, we were limited by the tools that Interface Builder provided us with: there was no way to let the programmer create loops, do math, or perform most other tasks that we associate with "programming" a computational engine. We did lots of programming in this chapter, but we had to do all of the work and thinking about the mechanics of the program that Interface Builder did for us in Chapter 3.

The real power of the NeXT programming environment is that it lets you *combine* Interface Builder (and Project Builder) with Objective-C, taking advantage of each one for what it does best: Interface Builder for creating the interface and making connections which lead to message passing, and Objective-C for creating new classes and the actual writing of the computational engine. Throughout the rest of this book, we'll learn how to write powerful application programs while writing a relatively small amount of code.

5

Building a Project: A Four Function Calculator

In this chapter we'll build a simple calculator application with four functions: add, subtract, multiply, and divide. When we're done, our calculator will contain the menu and window shown below. In the process of building the calculator, we'll learn a lot more about Interface Builder, connections, and some of the commonly-used NeXTSTEP Application Kit (AppKit) classes.

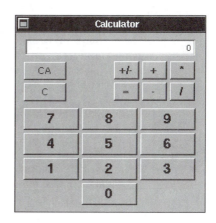

We've chosen to build a calculator as the first "real" application in this text for several reasons. First of all, calculators are familiar. We've all used one, and we sort of know how they work. (When creating an application, the first thing to understand is the problem to solve.) Second, calculators are useful. As programmers, we're constantly having to do silly little things like add two numbers together or convert a number from decimal to hexa-decimal (the hex part will be built in the next chapter). It's a tool that you can put to work after you build it.

More importantly, a calculator is a good starting-off point for budding NeXTSTEP developers. In subsequent chapters, we'll use the calculator as a building block for learning about NeXTSTEP graphics, printing, multiple windows, file handling, and many other features.

Creating your own calculator puts you in charge of its design. After all, there are so many different kinds of calculators: some are scientific, some financial, and some are just simple four function calculators. Our calculator will let you key in the sequence "3+4=" by clicking four buttons in a win-dow and will display (in order) 3, 3, 4, and 7 in a text output area. If you don't like the decisions we've made and want to change or add functions and features, go right ahead! Our aim is to give you the know-how to create your own applications.

Getting Started Building the Calculator Project

The six steps immediately below apply only to NeXTSTEP 3.0. If you are using NeXTSTEP 2.1, then you create a project in a much different way than in NeXTSTEP 3.0, and you should skip to "Building a Project in NeXTSTEP 2.1" on page 124.

1. Make sure the Project Builder (PB) and Interface Builder (IB) icons are in your dock and then launch PB from your dock. All you see is the main menu. See Figure 1 below.

2. Choose PB's **Project→New** menu command (or type Command-n) to create a new application. The **New Project** panel opens up. See Figure 2 below.

3. Type "**Calculator**" in the **Name** field of the **New Project** panel as in Figure 2 and then hit the Return (or Enter) key. A main window for the Calculator project opens. See Figure 3 below.

FIGURE 1. **Main and Project Menus in Project Builder**

ProjectBuilder		Project	
Info	▷	New...	n
Project	▷	Open...	o
Edit	▷	Open Makefile...	O
Files	▷	Save	s
Windows	▷	New Subproject...	
Services	▷	Add Help Directory	
Hide	h	Run Application	R
Quit	q	Debug Application	D

FIGURE 2. **New Project Panel in Project Builder**

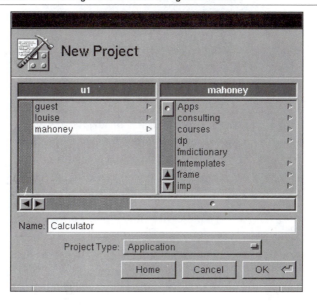

The main window in Project Builder contains five buttons just below its title bar. The two buttons on the left, **Run** and **Debug**, are "action" buttons that run and debug your project. The three buttons on the right, **Attributes**, **Files**, and **Builder**, select the content (or view) of what you see in the window, much like the buttons at the top of Interface Builder's Palettes window. We'll discuss these buttons in more detail later.

When you first see PB's main window the Files view is displayed. While in the Files view, the middle part of the main window contains an icon path similar that in a Workspace File Viewer. Below the icon path is a browser

FIGURE 3. Main Window in Project Builder

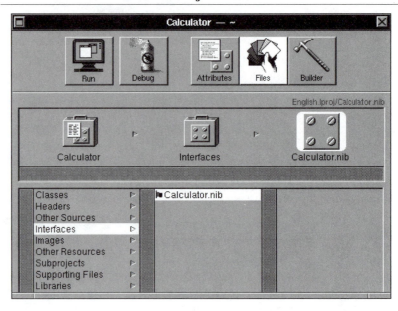

which contains a list of all the file types associated with a project. We'll discuss these different file types in "The Files in a Project" on page 159.

4. Click **Interfaces** in the main window's browser and then click **Calculator.nib** under **Interfaces**. The **Calculator.nib** file icon appears in the icon path as in Figure 3.

5. Double-click the **Calculator.nib** file icon in the main window's icon path. Interface Builder (IB) will automatically launch and display the **Calculator.nib** interface provided by PB, which includes a main menu titled "Calculator" and a main window titled "My Window." An associated File window is also displayed in the lower left corner of the screen.

6. In order to simplify the screen, click in Project Builder's main window and then type Command-h to hide Project Builder.

Skip the next section, which only applies to NeXTSTEP 2.1, and go directly to "Building the Calculator's User Interface" on page 126.

Building a Project in NeXTSTEP 2.1

1. Make sure the Interface Builder (IB) icon is in your dock and launch IB from your dock.

2. Choose IB's **File→New Application** menu command (or type Command-n) to create a new application. IB automatically provides an interface which includes a main menu titled "UNTITLED" and a main window titled "My Window." An associated File window containing objects and resources is also displayed in the lower left corner of the screen.

3. Choose IB's **File→Save** menu command (or type Command-s) to save this interface. When the **Save** panel pops up, enter (without the quotes or any spaces) "**Calculator/Calculator**" as the directory and file in which to save the application.

4. Since the directory that you specified (**Calculator/**) doesn't exist, IB will ask you if you want to create a new "path." (Actually, this is a standard feature of the NeXTSTEP Save panel object.) Click **Create**.

When you click **Create**, Interface Builder creates two things: a directory named **Calculator,** and a file named **Calculator.nib** in that directory. IB also changes the menu's title to "Calculator."

5. Choose IB's **File→Project** menu command to create a project.

In the lower-right hand corner of the screen, you'll see Interface Builder's Project Inspector, which is one of the views in IB's Inspector. There are four kinds of projects that IB can create. The **Application** choice is what you usually use; it tells IB that you're creating a project that's going to be compiled into an application program. The **Custom IB** and **IB Palette** choices are used for creating your own version of IB and your own IB palette, respectively. Your own palette can be added to IB and used just like the palettes delivered by NeXT. There are also a growing number of third-party commercial and public-domain palettes available for NeXTSTEP.

Subproject is used for managing projects that are too complicated to put everything in a single directory. This option lets you put nibs and source code into their own directories, which get separately compiled and linked into the main program.

6. Leave the selection on **Application** and click **OK** in IB's Project Inspector. This will create a NeXTSTEP 2.1 project consisting of a Makefile and three other supporting files in the **Calculator** directory. A fifth project file, **Calculator.nib** was already saved in the directory.

Now you'll see the "real" Project Inspector which lets you monitor all of the files that are part of your project. The **Add** button allows you to add files to your project, while the **Remove** button allows you to remove them.

If you want to edit a file, simply click the file's name in the right-hand column and click the **Open** button (alternatively, you can double-click the file's name). If the file is a nib file, Interface Builder will open up that nib's File window and display the nib's objects. Otherwise, Interface Builder will send a message to Workspace Manager asking it to open the file. This is very handy when you are creating class files, because you can go directly from IB to editing the class files in the Edit application.

Building the Calculator's User Interface

The **Calculator.nib** file created above is called, aptly enough, a *nib* file (*nib* stands for NeXT Interface Builder.) A nib file stores information about all of the user interface objects in your program – the windows, controls, menus, etc. and the connections between them – and the other objects that IB "knows about." When you compile and link your program, the program's nib file (or nib files, if the program uses more than one) gets bundled together with the program's executable code and stored in a *package* or *app wrapper* directory. This directory has an **.app** extension and looks like an executable application in the Workspace File Viewer.[1]

The nib files are stored in a NeXTSTEP proprietary binary format that is undocumented. Fortunately, it doesn't need to be documented – all of the management of the nib files is done by IB. IB is a nib editor: when it opens a nib file, it reads the specifications and displays the associated objects. After you make your modifications to the program, IB writes out a new nib file, replacing the old one.

Now that we've created the project we'll add and customize the windows, panels and menus needed for the Calculator's user interface.

Customizing the Main Window

The main window in the Calculator's interface, currently called "My Window," doesn't look anything like a calculator: it's the wrong shape, it shouldn't have a resize bar, and it doesn't even have the right name! Fortunately, these are all properties that we can easily change by using IB's Window Inspector.

---

1. In NeXTSTEP 2.1, nibs can also be stored directly in a *section* in the executable file. See Chapter 9 for more on sections.

To see the Window Inspector for a particular window, the window must be selected. You can select a window by simply clicking in its background, or by clicking its icon in the File window's Objects view. If you click an object (e.g., button) inside a window object in IB, then the button, not the window, will be selected.

In general, the title and contents of IB's Inspector panel change in response to which object in the interface is selected. When the Inspector changes in response to a selection, then you may still have to choose which aspect of the object you want to inspect: its attributes, connections, or something else. You can make this choice by dragging to it in the Inspector's pop-up list or by typing Command-1 for **Attributes**, Command-2 for **Connections**, and so forth.

Now we'll go through the steps to customize our Calculator's window.[1]

7. Select "My Window" in IB by clicking in the window's background.

8. If necessary, press the pop-up list button in the Window Inspector panel and drag to **Attributes** (or type Command-1). The Window Inspector should now look like the one on the left of Figure 4 below.

9. Change the **Title** from "My Window" to "Calculator" and hit Return.

10. Turn off the **Close** and **Resize Bar** attributes in the Window Inspector by clicking their switches so the check marks disappear; see the Inspector on the right of Figure 4. (In NeXTSTEP 2.1, you'll have to click the **OK** button to make the changes take effect.)

The resize bar in the now-renamed Calculator window will disappear. The close button will *not* disappear until the interface is tested or the application is running. This is so you can close the window to simplify the screen while building the interface.

Now resize the window to make it into the shape of a calculator.

Wait a minute! How do you resize the window if you just made the resize bar go away? Well, that's the purpose of the funny icon (▧) in the upper-left hand corner of the Calculator window. We'll refer to this as the *resize button*.

---

1. These steps work in both NeXTSTEP 3.0 and 2.1; however, the screen shots are all taken from NeXTSTEP 3.0 and may differ slightly in 2.1. Where there are significant differences between 2.1 and 3.0, we'll mention them in footnotes or parenthetic remarks.

FIGURE 4. **Window Inspector, Before and After**

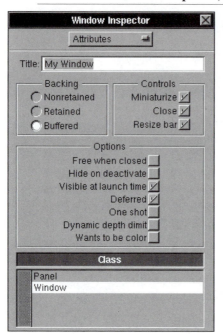

11. Click the resize *button* and the resize *bar* will temporarily reappear at the bottom of the Calculator window.

12. Resize the Calculator window so that it is about 3 inches square. After you resize the window, the resize bar will disappear again, so you might have to click the resize button several times if you wish to try several sizes.

Adding Controls in a Window

Next we'll drag the buttons and text display area that the Calculator application will need from Interface Builder's Palettes window into the **Calculator** window.

 13. Make sure the Views palette is visible by clicking the Views button at the top of IB's Palettes window.

14. Drag a **TextField** (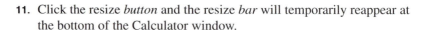) object from the Palettes window and drop it near the top left of the Calculator window. The window should look like the one on the left of Figure 5 below.

FIGURE 5. **Adding a TextField and a Button to a Window**

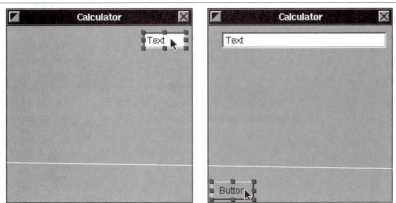

15. Drag the left-middle handle to the left to widen the **TextField** so that it is almost the width of the Calculator window, as in the window on the right of Figure 5.

16. Drag a **Button** (Button) object from the Palettes window and drop it in the lower left corner of the Calculator window as in Figure 5.

17. While holding the Alternate key on your keyboard, drag the upper-right-hand handle of the button up and to the right. Release the mouse button when there are four rows by three columns of buttons, as in the window on the left of Figure 6 below. Congratulations! You've just created a *matrix* of buttons.

FIGURE 6. **Adding a Matrix of Buttons to a Window**

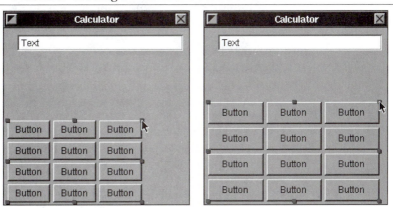

Matrix is one of the classes provided by the NeXTSTEP Application Kit. A **Matrix** object is a 2-dimensional array of other objects that are sub-classes of the NeXTSTEP **Cell** class.

Any **Cell** object can be displayed in a **Matrix**. Interface Builder automatically converts a **Control** and its associated **Cell** object into a **Matrix** and a group of **Cell** objects when you drag one of the **Control**'s resizing handles with the Alternate key pressed.

Every NeXTSTEP **Control** class, including **Button**, **Slider**, and **TextField**, has an associated **Cell** subclass (for example, **ButtonCell**, **SliderCell**, and **TextFieldCell**). These cell objects do the actual drawing of the controls that we put into the window.

NeXTSTEP uses combinations of objects because it is faster to draw in a **Cell** than in a **View**; there is less overhead. The corresponding **View** subclasses, **Button**, **Slider**, and **TextField**, are still used for handling events. Interface Builder hides this split personality between the **Control** and **Cell** from us and makes the control and its associated cell look like a single object. This is often a source of confusion for programmers new to NeXTSTEP.

18. *Without* pressing any modifier key, drag the upper-right handle of the **Button** matrix up and to the right. This time, the buttons will get bigger as in the Calculator window on the right of Figure 6.

Matrix Dragging Options

When you drag a handle on a matrix object, one of three things can happen depending on which modifier key is pressed. We saw the first two of these in the example above.

Modifier Key	Effect on the Cells in the Matrix
none	Changes the size of all cells in the matrix.
Alternate	Changes the number of cells in the matrix.
Command	Changes the spacing between cells.

The buttons in the **Matrix** we created above will be used to represent digit keys on our Calculator, and thus we'll change their names from "Button" to the 10 decimal digits (and disable the remaining two). We also need to set some less obvious attributes of the buttons, called *tags*, to make the buttons work properly. In order to explain how tags work and better understand why we make certain choices while creating an interface, we'll postpone finishing the interface to discuss the Objective-C class that we'll create to handle the button clicks.

Building the Calculator's Controller Class

It's time to start thinking about the Objective-C object that will control our Calculator – that is, respond to button clicks, calculate the values that the user wants, and display the results. By convention, this kind of object, which performs behind-the-scenes work and communicates with the user interface, is called a *controller*.

Controllers generally don't have main event loops; instead, they perform actions in response to events that are received and interpreted by other objects. A good rule of thumb is to place as little code in your controller as necessary. If it is possible to create a second controller that is only used for a particular function, do so – the less complicated you make your application's objects, the easier they are to debug. Our Calculator's controller will contain the code to perform the arithmetic and thus can be thought of as the *computational engine* or *back end* of the application.

Designing the Controller Class

NeXTSTEP doesn't provide you with a **Controller** class – it's up to you to write one for your particular application. (IB and the AppKit are fabulous but they can't do *everything* for you – at least not yet!)

Before you start coding, it's a good idea to sit down and think about your problem. What does the controller have to do? What sort of messages will it need to respond to? What sort of internal state does it have to keep in order to perform those functions? Recall that our Calculator will let a user key in the sequence "2*5=" by clicking four buttons in a window and will display (in order) 2, 2, 5, and 10 in a text output area. Thus for our Calculator, the answers are fairly straightforward.

What our Calculator must do:

- Clear the display and all internal registers (value holders) when a *clear* button is clicked.
- Allow the user to click a digit button on the numeric keypad and display the corresponding digit immediately after it is typed.
- Allow the user to click a function button (e.g., add, subtract).
- Clear the display when the user starts entering a second number.
- Perform the appropriate arithmetic operation when the user presses the "equals" button or another function button.

Our Calculator must also maintain the following state to perform these functions:

- The first number entered.
- The function button clicked.
- The second number entered.

It turns out that, in order to work properly, our controller object needs two more pieces of information:

- A flag that indicates when a function button has been clicked. If the flag is set, then the text display area (which we'll call **readout**) should be cleared the next time that a digit button is clicked, because the user is entering a second number.
- The location in the **readout** text display area where the numbers should be displayed.

If you think about it, what we are actually doing is using Objective-C to create a simulation of a real, physical calculator. That's what object-oriented programming is often about: constructing progressively better simulations of physical objects inside the computer's memory, and then running them to get real work done. When the simulation is functionally indistinguishable from the real-life object being simulated, the job is finished.

Creating the Controller Class

Every Objective-C class, except **Object**, is based on another class. The **Object** class itself is the most fundamental Objective-C class, because it defines the basic behavior of all objects and is at the root of all inheritance hierarchies. Since we don't need any other special behavior in our Calculator that is already defined in the AppKit, our **Controller** class will be a subclass of **Object**.

We'll start building our **Controller** class by subclassing it from **Object** in Interface Builder.

1.   Open the Classes view in IB's File window by clicking the Classes (**h**) suitcase icon.[1]

---

1. In NeXTSTEP 2.1, *double*-click the **Classes** suitcase icon in the File window. This will open up a *separate* Classes window.

2. Scroll to the far left in the Classes browser by clicking the left arrow
    ( ) several times, and then select the **Object** class by clicking it.
    See Figure 7 below.

The **Object** class name is displayed in gray, which means that you can't
change any of its properties or built-in behaviors without subclassing it. So
that's what we'll have to do.

3. Drag to **Subclass** in the **Operations** pull-down list. A new class called
    MyObject will appear under **Object** in the class hierarchy as in
    Figure 7 below.

FIGURE 7.   Classes View in Resource Window

4. Double-click the **MyObject** class name in the white text field area in
    the Class Inspector (at the lower right of the screen), change the name
    from **MyObject** to **Controller**, and hit Return.

You've just created a new class called **Controller**. Right now it doesn't do
anything different than the **Object** class. Next we'll give the **Controller**
class some custom behavior by adding some "outlets" and "actions."

Outlets and Connections

NeXTSTEP uses a powerful system called *outlets* and *connections* to give
you an easy way to send messages between user interface objects such as
windows, buttons, other controls, and your own custom objects. An *outlet*
is simply an instance variable in an Objective-C class that has the type **id**,
and thus can store a pointer to an object. The value of this instance variable
is usually the **id** of another object in the nib, i.e., a user interface object.

When an outlet is set to store the **id** of another object in the nib file, Interface Builder calls this a *connection.* NeXTSTEP automatically maintains connections for you. When object specifications are saved in a nib file, the connections we set up between them in IB are saved as well. These connections are automatically restored when the nib file is loaded back into IB.

For example, suppose that you have two object specifications in a nib file: object A and object B. Suppose also that object A contains an outlet that points to object B. When NeXTSTEP loads this nib file, it will first create new instances of object A and object B. NeXTSTEP will then automatically set the outlet in object A to point at object B. That is, it sets the outlet A to be the **id** of object B.

Outlets therefore give you an easy way to track down the **id** of objects that are dynamically loaded with nib files! They are the mechanism that NeXTSTEP gives you to "wire up" an interface without writing any code.

Adding Outlets to an Object

There are two ways to *add* outlets to a class. You can either add outlets by entering them in Interface Builder's Class Inspector, or you can add outlets "by hand" using an editor to type them into the class interface (**.h**) file for your class. In the latter case you have to tell IB to **Parse** the interface file so IB knows that the outlets exist for that class. We'll see how to add outlets in IB in this chapter and "by hand" in the next chapter.

Making the Connection

After adding an outlet, you use IB to *initialize* where it points. You do this by setting up a connection from the object containing the outlet to the object you want it to point to, and then choosing the outlet from the list of outlets in IB's Connections Inspector. When you make a connection between an outlet in an object and another object in IB, all IB does is set the instance variable in the first object to the **id** of the object to which it is connected. That's all!

In the steps below we'll add and initialize an outlet in IB.

5.   If necessary, select **Controller** in IB's File window and type Command-1 to display IB's Class Attributes Inspector.

6. If necessary, click the **Outlets** radio button in IB's Class Inspector. This tells IB that you want to edit the outlets in the **Controller** class. See Figure 8 below.[1]

7. Add an outlet called **readout**. Do this by clicking in the white text area near the bottom of the Class Inspector, typing "**readout**," and then clicking the **Add** button.

If you make a mistake, you can use the **Rename** button to change the name of an outlet. You can also use the **Edit→Cut** menu command to remove an outlet. When you're done, the Class Inspector should look like the one on the left in Figure 8 below.

FIGURE 8. Adding Outlets and Actions in the Class Inspector

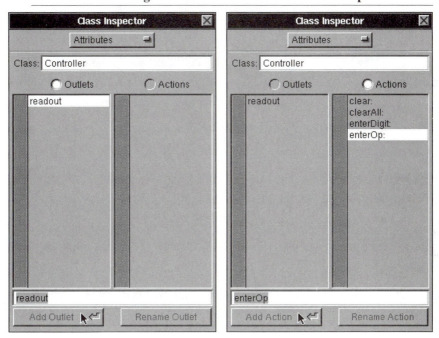

We'll use this **Controller** outlet to point to the text display area (**TextField**) object, so the **Controller** can send it messages. Next, we'll add action methods to the **Controller** class.

1. In NeXTSTEP 2.1, make sure the word **Outlet** is highlighted in black on the Outlet Action button in the Class Inspector (as it is here).

Adding Actions to the Controller

An "action" is a special type of Objective-C method. Action methods are special because they take a single argument called **sender**, the **id** of the object that sent the message which invoked the action method. Using Interface Builder, we can arrange for an object's action method to be automatically invoked in response to a user event, such as a button click, menu choice, or slider drag. Thus an action method is an "event handler."

In Chapter 3, the **takeDoubleValueFrom:** action method was used to make a **TextField** automatically take its value from the **Slider** object when the slider knob was moved (see Figure 9, "Communication between Slider and TextField," on page 85). Here we're going to create our own action methods in the **Controller** class and arrange to have them invoked when the user clicks our Calculator's buttons.

8. Click the **Actions** radio button in IB's Class Inspector. This tells IB that you want to edit the actions in the **Controller** class. See Figure 8 above.[1]

9. Add the following four actions to your **Controller** class (you don't have to type the colons (":") as IB will automatically append them):

```
clear:
clearAll:
enterDigit:
enterOp:
```

In light of our discussion of the design of the **Controller** class, the function of these four actions should seem fairly self-evident. The **Controller** Class Inspector should look like the one on the right in Figure 8 above.

Notice that there's only one action to handle all digit button clicks (**enterDigit:**) and only one action to handle all the function buttons (**enterOp:**). The way we determine which digit or function button is clicked is to use the single argument of these actions, the **id** of the *sender* of the message. By querying the sender of the message, the methods **enterDigit:** and **enterOp:** find out which digit or which function button was clicked and can then perform the appropriate action. This is a much more economic means of method dispatch than creating a separate method for each button on our Calculator – it takes less code but it runs virtually just as fast.

---

1. In NeXTSTEP 2.1, make sure the word **Action** is highlighted in black on the Actions-Outlets button in the Class Inspector.

Generating the Controller Class Files

We need to tell Interface Builder to create the **Calculator.h** *interface* and the **Calculator.m** *implementation* class files, so we can add the appropriate functionality and eventually compile them with the Objective-C compiler. Interface Builder's **Unparse** command generates these files from the class specifications we made in the File window and Class Inspector.

10. Make sure the **Controller** class is selected in the File window (Classes view) and then choose the **Unparse** operation from the **Operations** pull-down list.

11. Since creating these new files would obliterate any files with the same name that already exist, IB asks us to confirm the operation. (See the attention panel at the top of Figure 9 below.) Click **Yes**.

FIGURE 9. Unparse Attention Panels in Interface Builder

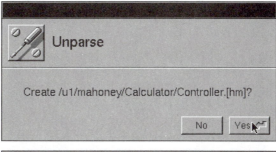

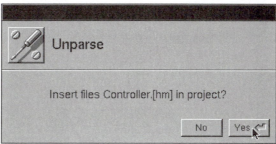

12. IB next asks if these files should be inserted into the project. (See the attention panel at the bottom of Figure 9.) Click **Yes**.

After you complete the last step above, the Project Builder tool reappears and displays the new **Controller** class implementation file, **Controller.m**, in the Files view as in Figure 10 below. The **Controller.h** class *interface* file appears under **Headers** in PB's Files view. These new **Controller** class files reside in the **~/Calculator** directory and contain only a skeleton of the

Controller class. In order to make our **Controller** work, we've got to write some Objective-C code.[1]

FIGURE 10. Controller Class in Project Builder

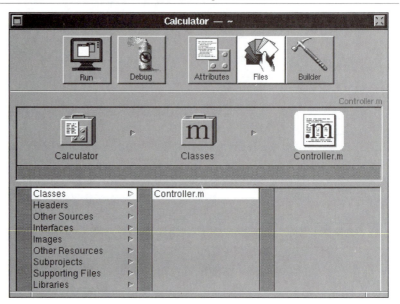

Adding Code to Make the Controller Class Work

In order to make the **Controller** work, we need to understand a little bit about four-function calculators. The basic four-function calculator has three registers: a X and a Y register, both of which hold numbers, and an operations register, which holds the current operation. The screen always displays the contents of the X register. Clicking a function button stores that function in the operation register and sets a flag. If the flag is set, then the next time a digit button is clicked, the number in the X register is moved to the Y register and the X register is set to 0.

We're going to get the **Controller** class working in stages, testing them one at a time. Generally, this is a good approach to writing any program, large or small. Object-oriented programming makes it easy to test the individual parts, because they are all fairly self-contained.

1. In NeXTSTEP 2.1, the Project Inspector reappears and displays the class files. Most of the information and functions available in IB's Project Inspector in NeXTSTEP 2.1 have been moved to Project Builder in NeXTSTEP 3.0.

First, we'll get numeric entry and the clear keys working. Later we'll handle the arithmetic functions.

13. Open the **Controller.h** class interface file in your favorite editor.

You can open the **Controller.h** file in the Edit application by double-clicking **Controller** in IB's File Window or by double-clicking **Controller.h** under **Interfaces** in PB's Files view.

Below we list the **Controller.h** file containing all the lines generated by Interface Builder in medium Courier type and all the lines you need to insert in **bold Courier type** (we'll use this type convention throughout the book when we mix "old" code with "new" code to be inserted).

```
/* Controller.h */

#import <appkit/appkit.h>

@interface Controller:Object
{
   id      readout;
   BOOL    enterFlag;
   BOOL    yFlag;
   int     operation;
   float   X;
   float   Y;
}

- clear:sender;
- clearAll:sender;
- enterDigit:sender;
- enterOp:sender;
- displayX;

@end
```

Interface Builder generated the first two (non-bold) lines because we subclassed **Object** to create the **Controller** class (**appkit.h** will import the **Object.h** class interface file)[1]. Since we added **readout** as an outlet in the Class Inspector, IB also generated the **id** declaration for **readout**. Finally, IB generated the four action method declarations because we added the four actions in IB's Class Inspector. Note the single argument **sender** for all of these action methods.

---

1. In NeXTSTEP 2.1, the **Object.h** class file is imported explicitly and **appkit.h** is not imported. We'll discuss **appkit.h** further on page 141.

14. Add the five new instance variables and one new method indicated by the lines that are shown in **bold** type in the **Controller.h** file above. We'll discuss the new **displayX** "non-action" method a bit later.

15. If necessary, open the **Controller.m** file in an editor. You can do this by double-clicking **Controller.m** under **Classes** in the PB's Files view.

Below we list the **Controller.m** file. As with the **Controller.h** file above, we list the lines generated by IB in medium type and the lines you need to insert in **bold type**.

```
#import "Controller.h"

@implementation Controller

- clear:sender
{
  X = 0.0;
  [self displayX];
  return self;
}

- clearAll:sender
{
  X = 0.0;
  Y = 0.0;
  yFlag = 0;
  enterFlag = 0;
  [self displayX];
  return self;
}

- enterDigit:sender
{
  if (enterFlag) {
    Y = X;
    X = 0.0;
    enterFlag = NO;
  }

  X = (X*10.0) + [ [sender selectedCell] tag];
  [self displayX];
  return self;
}

- enterOp:sender
{
    return self;
```

```
}

- displayX
{
  char buf[256];

  sprintf( buf, "%15.10g", X );
  [readout setStringValue: buf];
  return self;
}

@end
```

Interface Builder generated the line which imports **Controller.h** because every class implementation file must import its own interface file. Most of the other lines generated by IB are simply stubs for the action methods that we set up in the IB's Class Inspector. The lines IB generates in class files are more for convenience than anything else.

16. Insert the code shown in **bold** type above into the **Controller.m** file.

17. Save the **Controller.h** and **Controller.m** class files.

Note that the **Controller** sends messages to instances of the **TextFieldCell** and **Matrix** classes. For example, the newly added **displayX** method displays the contents of the X register by sending the **setStringValue:** message to **readout**, the outlet which we'll initialize in IB to point to the **TextFieldCell** object (near the top of the Calculator window).

When a message is sent to an object of a class, then the class interface file definition for that class should be **#import**-ed in the class definition. But **#import** statements for the **TextFieldCell** and **Matrix** class interface file definitions are not listed in the code above, so what's going on? Fortunately, the **#import "Controller.h"** line in **Controller.m** together with the **#import <appkit/appkit.h>** line in **Controller.h** take care of importing the **TextFieldCell** and **Matrix** class interface file definitions for us.[1] In fact, they import *all* Application Kit class definitions. This is very inefficient in NeXTSTEP 2.1 because compilation time is greatly increased.

---

1. If you're using NeXTSTEP 2.1, you'll have to insert the
    #import <appkit/appkit.h>
line yourself. Alternatively, you can include the **TextFieldCell** and **Matrix** class interface files explicitly for improved compilation efficiency. To do this, you would insert the following two lines at the top of either **Controller.h** or **Controller.m**:
    #import <appkit/TextFieldCell.h>
    #import <appkit/Matrix.h>

However, in NeXTSTEP 3.0 the AppKit class headers are all precompiled so it's okay to import them all. (A *precompiled header* file has been preprocessed and parsed, thereby improving compile time and reducing symbol table size.) This is why IB in NeXTSTEP 3.0 inserts the **#import <appkit/appkit.h>** line in all class interface files it generates.

The **clearAll:** method in the **Controller.m** file sets the X and Y registers to **0.0** and the two flags to false, and then sends the **displayX** message to **self** (the **Controller** object itself) to display **0.0** in the text display area. The **clear:** method is similar but only needs to set the X register to **0.0** and redisplay. We'll discuss the **enterDigit:** and **enterOp:** methods after we finish setting up the user interface and making all the connections.

Customizing Buttons and Making Connections

In this section we'll use Interface Builder to add more interface specifications to the **Calculator.nib** file, including customizing buttons and making several different types of connections between objects. In order to make connections which involve an object of the **Controller** class, we need a representation of it in IB.

Instantiating (Creating an Instance of) the Controller Class

Creating the *class* isn't enough: we also need to create an *object* that is a member of this class, called an *instance*. Then we have to arrange for the numeric keypad of buttons in the Calculator window to send action messages to the instance whenever these buttons are clicked.

1. Make sure the Classes view is displayed in IB's File window and then select the **Controller** class.

Classes

2. Choose the **Instantiate** command from the **Operations** pull-down list.

This will create an icon called **Controller** in the Objects view in the Calculator's File window as in Figure 11 below (IB automatically displays the Objects view). This icon represents an instance object of the **Controller** class; it can be used as the *target* object of action messages and also to initialize outlets. You can change the name **Controller** if you want; it isn't used for anything except your convenience.

FIGURE 11. **Controller Instance Object in File Window**

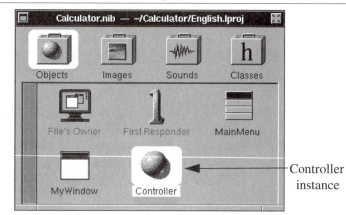

Controller
instance

Setting Up Titles and Tags for the Keypad Buttons

Next, we'll set up the buttons on the numeric keypad for the digits 0 through 9 and arrange for them to send messages to the **Controller** object. The **Controller** object needs to differentiate between the buttons somehow, so we'll assign them different integer *tags*.

3. Double-click the button at the upper-left of the matrix in the Calculator window. The button highlights in dark gray to indicate that it is selected, and the Attributes Inspector will display the button's attributes. See Figure 12 below.

4. Change the **Title** of the button from "Button" to "7" and hit Return.

5. Change the **Tag** of the button from **0** to **7**.[1]

A *tag* is a reference integer for a **Control** object and can be set and read in IB's Inspector panel. Tags are not used by the AppKit; rather, their purpose is to allow your program to distinguish cells (objects) in a matrix (or other controls) from one another when different cells of the matrix send the same message to an object.

For example, when one of the buttons in the matrix of digit buttons is clicked, we'll arrange for the **Matrix** object to send the **enterDigit:** message to our **Controller** object. The **Controller** object needs to know which button (i.e., which digit) was clicked, and thus sends a message back to the

---

1. In NeXTSTEP 2.1, you must click the **OK** or hit Return to make changes in the Inspector take effect.

FIGURE 12. Inspecting a Button's Attributes

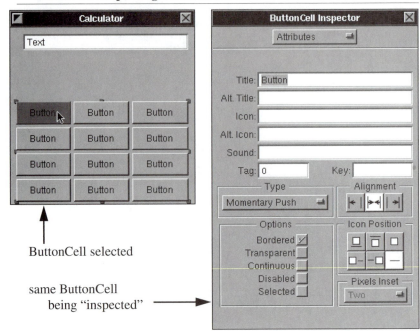

sender (**Matrix** object) to determine which of the button cells in the **Matrix** object was selected. The **Controller** can then get the tag for that cell and use it in the **enterDigit:** method as if it were a digit (since the tags will correspond to the digits on the buttons).

6. Change the titles and tags of the other keypad buttons to reflect the digits that they represent, as in Figure 13 below. The button with title 1 should have tag 1, the button with title 2 should have tag 2, etc. You can use the tab key to easily move between cells in the **Matrix**.

7. Double-click the lower-left hand button in the **Matrix** (which is invisible in Figure 13) to select it.

8. In the ButtonCell Inspector, *deselect* the **Bordered** switch, select the **Disabled** switch, delete the "Button" title, and hit Return. This will make the button disappear and become "unclickable."

9. Repeat Step 8 above for the lower-right hand button.

10. Click in the Calculator window background (where there are no buttons or text) to select the window, then click the button matrix *once* to select the matrix as a whole. Type Command-t to bring up the Font panel as in Figure 14 below.

FIGURE 13. **Customizing the Calculator's Buttons**

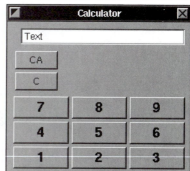

As with most NeXTSTEP applications, Interface Builder lets you change the font family, typeface, and size of most text it displays. (In NeXTSTEP 3.0, a user's Preferences application settings determine the font and size of the text in the window's title bar and menus.)

11. Choose the **Helvetica Bold 18 point** font as in Figure 14 below and then click the **Set** button. (If you pick a font that's too big, the buttons and the matrix will get bigger!) Your Calculator window should look like the one on the left in Figure 13 above.

FIGURE 14. **Font Panel in Interface Builder**

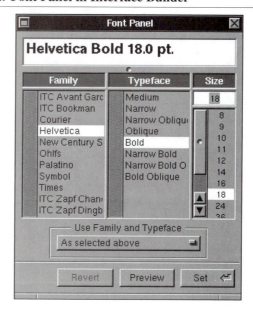

Making the Connections

12. Connect the button **Matrix** object to the **Controller** instance object by pressing the Control key on the keyboard and dragging the mouse cursor from the middle of the **Matrix** to the **Controller** instance object icon as in Figure 15 below.

FIGURE 15. The enterDigit: Action Connection

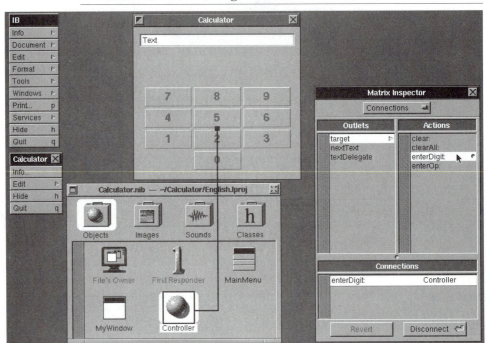

A small black square will appear in the middle of the **Matrix** and a "connection line" will connect the **Matrix** object to the **Controller** icon. Be careful to connect the *Matrix* and *not* one of the individual **Matrix** *buttons*!

When you release the mouse button, Interface Builder will display the Matrix Connections Inspector. You can determine the *source* object of the connection by the name in the title bar of the Inspector – in this case it should be *Matrix* Inspector. The column labeled **Actions** in the Matrix Inspector should include the four action methods we set up earlier in the *destination* object, namely the **Controller** instance.

13. Click the **enterDigit:** action and then click the **Connect** button in the Matrix Inspector. The dimple (✿) indicates the connection was made. See the Matrix Inspector at the right of Figure 15.

The connection we just made means the following: whenever a user clicks any one of the digit buttons in the matrix, the **Matrix** object will send the **enterDigit:** action message to an instance of our **Controller** class.

WARNING: It is easy to accidentally disconnect a connection by double-clicking in the wrong place in the Connections Inspector. Be careful!

Next, we'll add *clear* and *clear all* buttons in the **Matrix** object as we did with the digit buttons. This time, however, we'll connect the buttons *individually* to the **Controller** object, not as a matrix.

14. Add a second matrix of buttons above the digits matrix in the Calculator window. This new matrix should have two buttons with titles **CA** and **C** in a font such as Helvetica Bold 16 point.

Your window should look like the one on the right in Figure 13, "Customizing the Calculator's Buttons," on page 145. If you don't remember how to add a matrix to your window refer back to "Adding Controls in a Window" on page 128. If you can't find the Palettes window then choose in IB's **Tools→Palettes** menu command.

15. Double-click the **CA** button to select it. The ButtonCell Inspector, not the Matrix Inspector, should appear.

16. Connect the **CA** button to the **Controller** instance object icon by Control-dragging from the button to the icon and then double-clicking the **clearAll:** action in the ButtonCell Inspector (the double-click has the same effect as clicking the action name and then clicking the **Connect** button).

17. Similarly, double-click the **C** button to select it and then connect it to the **Controller** instance icon. This time, double-click on the **clear:** action.

You can make Interface Builder show you an existing connection from a source object by first selecting the source object and then clicking **target** or the action method with a dimple (✿) in the Connections Inspector.

18. Double-click the word "Text" in the **TextField** object and hit the Delete (Backspace) key to erase the word "Text."

19. If necessary, drag to Attributes in the TextField Inspector (or type Command-1).

20. *Deselect* the **Editable** option in the TextField Inspector so that the text in the **TextField** object is not editable.

21. Set the alignment to be right-justified by clicking the icon that looks like this:

The source of every Calculator connection we've made so far was a user interface object, while the destination was always the **Controller** object. In the next connection we make, the direction will be reversed; the source will be the **Controller** while the destination will be an interface object. This second type of connection requires an *outlet*.

22. Control-drag from the **Controller** instance object icon to the **TextField** object. The black "connection line" should look like the one in Figure 16 below.

FIGURE 16. **Making a Connection to Initialize an Outlet**

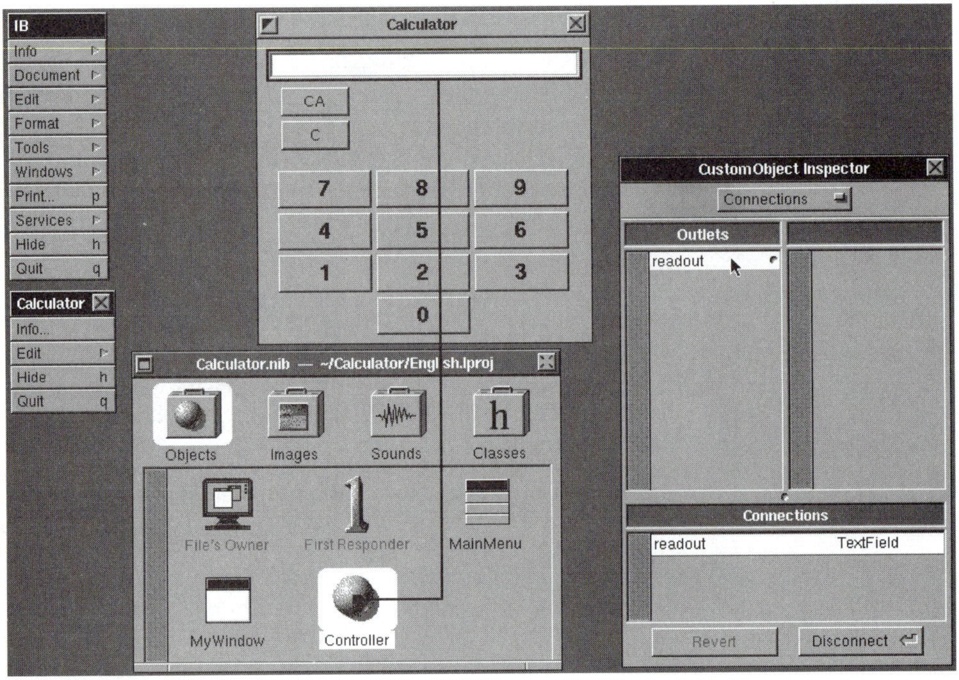

23. In the Connections Inspector, double-click the **readout** outlet to complete the connection.

Connecting the **readout** outlet to the **TextField** object causes the **readout** instance variable in the **Controller** object to get initialized to the **id** of the **TextField** when the nib section gets loaded at run time. Initializing an outlet in an instance object is the only way to determine the **id** of an object created with Interface Builder, and thus outlets must be used when sending messages to user interface objects.

24. Type Command-s in IB to save the **Calculator.nib** file.

Compiling and Running a Program

At this point, we're ready to test the keypad of digit buttons. In order to do this, we must compile the **Controller.m** and **Calculator_main.m** source code and link them together with the **Calculator.nib** file. (We'll discuss the **Calculator_main.m** source file in "The Files in a Project" on page 159.)

There are three ways to compile a NeXTSTEP program: from Project Builder, from a command line prompt, or from Emacs. We describe how to do each of these below using the target **make debug**.

Compiling and Running a Program from Project Builder

The steps below will compile (**make**, build) and run your Calculator program directly from Project Builder.

1. Activate PB and click the **Builder** button at the top of PB's main window to see the Builder view. (If you press the Command key and double-click the PB icon simultaneously, then PB will be activated and all other running applications will be hidden!)

2. In order to have PB use the **make debug** target, type "debug" in the **Args:** white text area as in Figure 17 below.

3. Start the compilation process by clicking the **Build** button in the Builder view. If there are no compile-time errors, then you should see the "Build succeeded" expression and compile log as in Figure 17. If an error occurred, see "Compiler Error Messages" on page 151 below.

4. To run your program directly from Project Builder, simply click the **Run** button at the top left of PB's main window.

This will run the **Calculator.debug** executable file which was created in your **~/Calculator** directory when the Calculator program successfully compiled. (**Calculator.debug** is actually a *directory* containing an executable file and the **Calculator.nib** file, among others.)

FIGURE 17. Compiling the Calculator Program in Project Builder

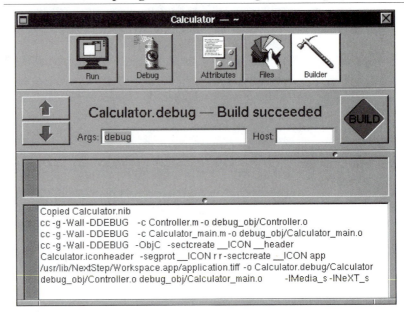

The main Calculator window and menu appear on the screen as in Figure 18 below.

5. Try the keypad to make sure every digit works. Clicking the buttons **1**, then **2**, then **3** should make the number "**123**" appear in the white text area. The **C** and **CA** keys should zero-out the values on the display. You should see the contents of Figure 18 on the screen. Note that the default application icon is the same one as on the **Run** button in PB.

6. Choose the Calculator's **Quit** menu command to exit the program.

Compiling and Running a Program in a Terminal Shell Window

To compile your Calculator program in a Terminal shell window, you can type the **bold** text below:

```
localhost> cd ~/Calculator
localhost> make debug
```

To compile your Calculator program within Emacs in a Terminal shell window, type:

```
M-x compile <Return>
```

Emacs will print:

FIGURE 18. Calculator Running in Workspace

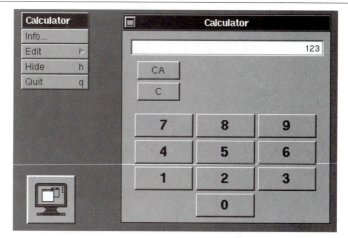

```
make
```

Type:

```
make debug <Return>
```

The compile log should look similar to that in Figure 17 above.

If everything compiled correctly, you now have an executable file called **Calculator.debug** in your **~/Calculator** directory. You can now run your program either by double-clicking the **Calculator.debug** icon in the Workspace File Viewer or by typing the following in a shell window:

```
localhost> open Calculator.debug
```

The **open** command sends a message to Workspace that it should open a file. This has the same effect as double-clicking an application icon in the Workspace Manager. See Figure 18 above.

Compiler Error Messages

Sometimes (many times!) code does not compile properly as can be seen in the Project Builder window in Figure 19 below.

If instead of a clean compile, you get compiler warning or error messages, you have probably made a typo at some point in the code. For example, the error message in Figure 19 was generated by removing a semicolon from the **displayX** method in the **Controller.m** file.

FIGURE 19. Build Failed in Project Builder

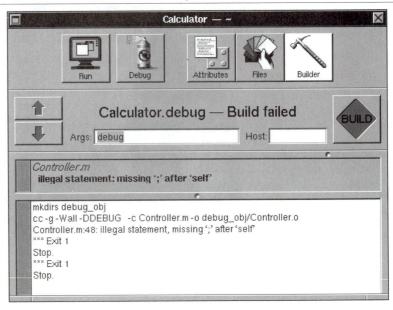

If you get any compiler errors, we suggest that you re-examine your code line-by-line, rather than resorting to the floppy disk included with this book. Examining your code is an important skill to develop, and when you are working on your own projects, you won't have a floppy disk with the completed program to fall back on.

 For the error reported here, you could open the **Controller.m** file in the Edit application, type Command-l to bring up the **Line and Character Range** panel, enter "48," the line where the error was reported, and inspect the code on line 48 and previous lines. You might also take some time to go back to Chapter 2 and review "gdb – Debugging Programs" on page 63.

 If you compiled your program in a Terminal shell window, then you would get essentially the same feedback as in Figure 19 above.

Tags and the enterDigit: Action Method

The **enterDigit:** method we added to the **Controller** class is invoked whenever a digit button is clicked. Let's look at it closely.

```
- enterDigit:sender
{
  if (enterFlag) {
    Y = X;
    X = 0.0;
    enterFlag = NO;
  }

  X = (X*10.0) + [ [sender selectedCell] tag];
  [self displayX];
  return self;
}
```

The first part of the function is self explanatory: if the **enterFlag** instance variable is set, then the value of the X register is copied into the Y register and both the X register and **enterFlag** are cleared. Note that the *scope* of instance variables (e.g., **enterFlag**) is the entire class definition. All methods within a class have access to all instance variables defined in that class.

The next line contains the magic: the value in the X register is multiplied by 10 and added to the returned value **[[sender selectedCell] tag]**. This performs a base 10 left-shift operation on X and then adds the last number pressed. Let's look at this nested method expression in pieces.

[sender selectedCell] sends the **selectedCell** message to the variable **sender**. When the **enterDigit:** method is invoked (called), **sender** is set to be the **id** of the object that sent the message, in this case the **Matrix** object. Clicking a button in a matrix selects that button. Thus the expression **[sender selectedCell]** returns the **id** of the **ButtonCell** object for the button that was clicked. **[[sender selectedCell] tag]** then sends the **tag** message to the **ButtonCell** object to get its tag. Since we set up the tag of each button on the keypad to be the value of that button, the expression **[[sender selectedCell] tag]** returns the numeric value of the digit that's on the button.

Adding the Four Calculator Functions

We still need to add the functions that perform the calculations to our Calculator. To do this, we'll first make some additions to the **Controller** class definition and then add the necessary on-screen function buttons.

1. Using an editor, insert the following enumerated data type after the **#import** directive in the **Controller.h** file.

```
enum {
    PLUS        = 1001,
    SUBTRACT    = 1002,
    MULTIPLY    = 1003,
    DIVIDE      = 1004,
    EQUALS      = 1005
};
```

These codes correspond to the tags that we will give the buttons in the arithmetic operations **Matrix**. The **Controller** object will determine the tag of the button that sends it the action message to decide which function button the user has clicked.

2. Using an editor, insert the lines in **bold** below into the method **enterOp:** in the **Controller.m** file.

```
- enterOp:sender
{
  if (yFlag) {           /* something is stored in Y */
    switch (operation) {
      case PLUS:
        X = Y + X;
        break;

      case SUBTRACT:
        X = Y - X;
        break;

      case MULTIPLY:
        X = Y * X;
        break;

      case DIVIDE:
        X = Y / X;
        break;
    }
  }

  Y     = X;
```

```
yFlag = YES;

operation = [ [sender selectedCell] tag];
enterFlag = 1;

[self displayX];
return self;
}
```

The **enterOp:** method is the real heart of our Calculator. It performs the arithmetic operation that was stored in the **operation** instance variable, sets up the registers and flags for another operation or another button click, and then displays the contents of the X register on the screen.

3. Activate Interface Builder and create a **Matrix** with two rows and three columns in the upper-right hand corner of your Calculator window. See Figure 20 below.

4. Set the title of each button to correspond with one of the six basic functions, as in Figure 20 below. Use a larger font (e.g., Helvetica Bold 16 pt.) so the titles are easily readable. Don't worry about the unary minus "**+/-**" button for now.

5. Set the tag of each button to correspond with the **enum** defined in the **Controller.h** file above.

6. Connect the function **Matrix** to the **Controller** by Control-dragging from the **Matrix** to the **Controller** instance icon and double-clicking the **enterOp:** action in the Matrix Inspector. This connection is similar to the one we made for the numeric keypad.

FIGURE 20. The Calculator Window with Six Function Buttons

7. Save the **Calculator.nib** and **Controller** class files.

8. Compile your program and run it. If you use PB, all you have to do is click the **Run** button and PB will **make** the program when necessary. All buttons except the unary minus should work as you expect.

For easy access, we recommend that you keep the Project Builder, Interface Builder, Edit, Terminal, and Librarian, and HeaderViewer application icons in your dock while developing applications.

When you want to switch applications, use NeXTSTEP's **Hide** command rather than **Quit** to suspend the current application. This keeps your screen clear, and avoids the wait of having applications start up again when you need them. A better technique is to use NeXTSTEP 3.0's new "activate and hide all others" command. If you press a Command key and double-click a docked application icon, then the application activates (or launches) as usual and *all other active applications will hide themselves!*

Adding Unary Minus to the Controller Class

We want the unary minus function (the button with the "**+/-**" on it) to change the sign of the number currently displayed in our Calculator's **readout**. One way to implement this function is to handle it with another **case** in the **switch** statement in the **enterOp:** method. You could give the "**+/-**" key its own tag and have the **enterOp:** method intercept it and perform the appropriate function. The problem with this approach is that the unary minus function has virtually nothing in common with the other arithmetic functions: it takes one argument instead of two and operates immediately on the displayed value. A far better way for implementing this function is to implement a new action method in the **Controller** class.

Using IB's Parse Command with a New Action Method

Adding new action methods to existing classes is slightly more difficult than creating the initial class definition. You wouldn't want to use Interface Builder to create the new methods as we did before, because IB's **Unparse** command will *replace* the existing class files (**Controller.h** and **Controller.m** here) and wipe out the source code you've added. Instead, you should edit the class files to add the new methods that you want, and then command Interface Builder to **Parse** the files to learn about the changes.

1. Using an editor, insert the **doUnaryMinus:** action method definition in `bold` below into **Controller.h**. (You can tell it's an *action* method because **sender** is the only argument.)

```
...
- clear:sender;
- clearAll:sender;
- enterDigit:sender;
- enterOp:sender;
- displayX;
- doUnaryMinus:sender;
@end
```

2. Using an editor, insert the entire **doUnaryMinus:** method below into **Controller.m**.

```
- doUnaryMinus:sender
{
  X = -X;
  [self displayX];
  return self;
}
```

It doesn't matter where you put this method in **Controller.m**, as long as it's between the directives **@implementation** and **@end**. However, we suggest you order the method implementations in the same way as the method declarations are ordered in the **Controller.h** class interface file.

Lastly, we have to tell Interface Builder about the new **doUnaryMinus:** method and set up a connection between the on-screen unary minus button and the **Controller**.

3. Activate IB and click the **Classes** suitcase icon in IB's File window to open the Classes view.

4. Select **Controller** in the class hierarchy in the Classes browser; recall it's a subclass of **Object** so you may have to scroll to the left.

5. Drag to **Parse** in the **Operations** pull-down list and you'll get the Parse panel in Figure 21 below. This panel tells us that the definition for **Controller.h** will be parsed from the edited file on disk.

6. Click **OK** in IB's Parse panel to parse the **Controller.h** file on disk. You should see the new **doUnaryMinus:** action method in the ButtonCell Inspector. See Figure 22 below.

7. Click the **Objects** suitcase icon in IB's File window to open the Objects view.

8. Double-click the unary minus button in the Calculator window. Make sure that the button, not the **Matrix** as a whole, has been selected.

FIGURE 21. **Interface Builder's Parse Panel**

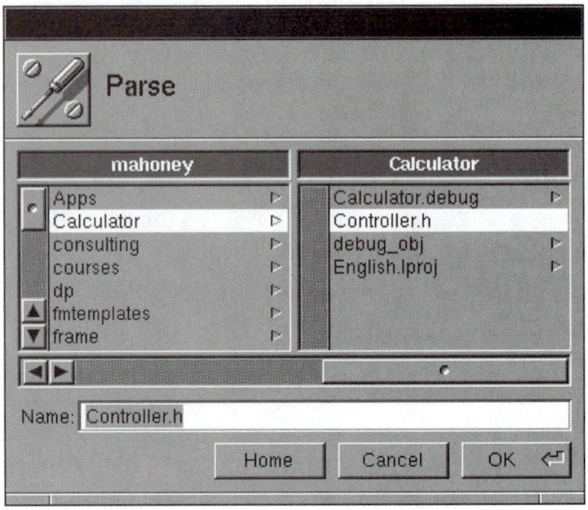

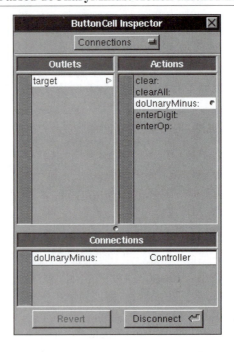

FIGURE 22. **Parsed doUnaryMinus: Action Method in Inspector**

9. Connect the unary minus button to the **Controller** by Control-dragging from the button to the **Controller** instance icon and double-clicking the **doUnaryMinus:** action in the ButtonCell Inspector. See Figure 22.

When a button in a **Matrix** object has its own target, the button's target overrides the target of the **Matrix**. So, when the user clicks on the unary minus button, the button will send the **doUnaryMinus:** message to its own target, rather than sending the **enterOp:** message to the target of the **Matrix**.

10. Save all pertinent files, **make** and run the program. The unary minus function should behave as expected.

You might be wondering why IB's **Parse** operation didn't bring in the definition of the **displayX** method in addition to the **doUnaryMinus:** method. The reason is that IB only looks for *action* methods when parsing a class interface (**.h**) file. An action method is a method declared in the form

```
- methodname:sender;
```

with a single argument called **sender**. As we'll see later, IB will also bring in *outlet* declarations when parsing a class interface file. These outlet declarations must be instance variables of the form

```
id outletname;
```

Action methods and outlets are the *only* types of information that Interface Builder learns about a class when it parses a class interface file.

The Files in a Project

If you've been checking your **~/Calculator** directory while stepping through this chapter you've noticed that several files were automatically created in it. In this section we'll discuss what these files contain and how they fit into a project.

Project Builder's Files view uses a browser to list each project file by type, as in Figure 23 below. You can change which type of files are displayed by clicking a file type (e.g., **Images**) in the left-hand column of the browser. In the table below we briefly discuss what each file type means.[1]

---

1. In NeXTSTEP 2.1, Interface Builder's built-in Project Inspector uses a similar browser to list each project file type by its file extension.

FIGURE 23. **Supporting Files in Project Builder**

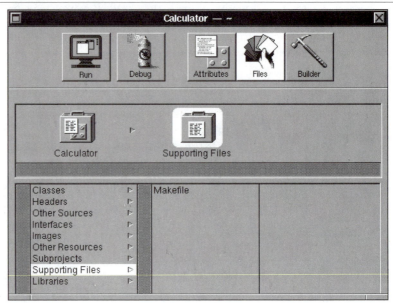

Several files are automatically placed in your project and project directory when you create a new project. Some of these, for example, **Makefile**, the **main()** function file (e.g., **Calculator_main.m**), and the Application Kit libraries, show up in PB's Files View.

File Type	Typical Extensions	Meaning
Classes	**.m**	Objective-C class implementation (e.g., **Controller.m**) source code files that you've created.
Headers	**.h**	Objective-C class interface (e.g., **Controller.h**) and C header files that you've created.
Other Sources	**.c, .m**	ANSI C (**.c**) and Objective-C (**.m**) source code files (e.g., **Calculator_main.m**).
Interfaces	**.nib**	NeXTSTEP Interface Builder files, which contain information on objects created in IB.

File Type	Typical Extensions	Meaning
Images	**.tiff**, **.eps**	TIFF (tag image file format, or bitmap) images and Encapsulated PostScript files.
Other Resources	**.psw**, **.snd**	Other "resource" files which don't fit any of the other types.
Subprojects	**.subproj**	Interface Builder subprojects.
Supporting Files		**Makefile** and any others.
Libraries	**.a**	Library files that are linked into your program (e.g., **/usr/lib/lib-NeXT_s.a**)

The Project Builder-generated Makefile

Every NeXTSTEP *project* directory needs a special file called *Makefile* (we discussed Makefiles and **make** targets (e.g., **make debug**) briefly in Chapter 2). The Makefile contains the specifications needed to tell the standard UNIX utility called **make** how to create directories, call the **cc** compiler, and do other tasks associated with building an application. If you've used Makefiles and **make** before, you'll be glad to know they work essentially the same way in NeXTSTEP; the big difference is that the Makefile is generated automatically for you by Project Builder. That's good news, because writing a Makefile in the traditional UNIX environment can be tedious and time-consuming.

The Makefile contains the names of all of the **nib**, Objective-C, **tiff** (bitmap), **snd** (sound), **psw** (PostScript), library, and other files that get linked together to produce your final application program. It can also contain installation information, include file dependencies, and other information.

Let's take a close look at the Makefile that Project Builder generated for us when we chose **Project→New** to create the Calculator project.

```
# Generated by the NeXT Project Builder.
#
# NOTE: Do NOT change this file --
#    Project Builder maintains it.
#
# Put all of your customizations in files called
# Makefile.preamble and Makefile.postamble
# (both optional), and Makefile will include them.
```

```
NAME = Calculator

PROJECTVERSION = 1.1
LANGUAGE = English

LOCAL_RESOURCES = Calculator.nib

CLASSES = Controller.m
HFILES = Controller.h
MFILES = Calculator_main.m

OTHERSRCS = Makefile

MAKEFILEDIR = /NextDeveloper/Makefiles/app
INSTALLDIR = $(HOME)/Apps
INSTALLFLAGS = -c -s -m 755
SOURCEMODE = 444

ICONSECTIONS = -sectcreate __ICON app \
    /usr/lib/NextStep/Workspace.app/application.tiff

LIBS = -lMedia_s -lNeXT_s
DEBUG_LIBS = $(LIBS)
PROF_LIBS = $(LIBS)

-include Makefile.preamble
include $(MAKEFILEDIR)/app.make
-include Makefile.postamble
-include Makefile.dependencies
```

Here's what most of the lines in this Makefile mean:

NAME=	Tells **make** the name of your application.
LOCAL_RESOURCES=	Lists the names of all nib files in your project.
CLASSES=	The Objective-C classes you've added.
HFILES=	The Objective-C and C header files added.
MFILES=	The Objective-C files that are not class implementation files.
MAKEFILEDIR=	Specifies the directory, **/NextDeveloper/Makefiles/app**, that should be searched for any Makefiles that are included. The standard included NeXT-STEP Makefile is **app.make**.

INSTALLDIR=	Specifies the directory where your program should be copied when you type "**make install**."
INSTALLFLAGS=	Specifies the flags passed to the **install** program when you type "**make install**."
SOURCEMODE=	When source code is archived in a directory in response to "**make installsrc**," SOURCEMODE specifies the UNIX file protection mode that these files should have. Mode 444 is read-only for all users.
LIBS=	Specifies which libraries should be linked into your program. The standard libraries are **libNeXT_s.a** and **libMedia_s.a**; they specify the NeXTSTEP Application Kit and a UNIX library.
DEBUG_LIBS=	Specifies which libraries should be used when the application is built in "debug mode."
ICONSECTIONS=	This line specifies the names of icons that should be linked into your application. They'll end up as sections of the executable file. **application.tiff** refers to the generic application icon we saw in Figure 18 above.
-include Makefile. preamble	Causes **make** to include the file called **Makefile.preamble**, if it exists in your project directory.
include $(MAKEFILEDIR)/ app.make	Includes the **/NextDeveloper/Makefiles/ app/app.make** file, which is the standard NeXTSTEP Makefile for compiling NeXT-STEP applications.
-include Makefile. postamble	Causes **make** to include the file called **Makefile.postamble**, if it exists in your project directory.
-include Makefile. dependencies	Causes **make** to include the file called **Makefile.dependencies**, if it exists in your project directory. This file is created by typing "**make depend**."

Since Project Builder (IB in NeXTSTEP 2.1) updates your project's Makefile, and since the Makefile is used to compile your program, it's important to keep PB up-to-date. When you add a file to your project, do it by using the PB, rather than modifying the Makefile directly. Indeed, you should *never* edit the Makefile directly; if you need to add commands not available via the Project Inspector, then put them in one of the files **Makefile.preamble** or **Makefile.postamble**, which are included in the Makefile if they exist in the project directory.

You can use the file **Makefile.dependencies** to tell **make** about dependencies created by **#include** and **#import** statements in your source code. This will force **make** to recompile a file if any of its included files are modified. From a UNIX shell command line, type "**make depend**" to create the file **Makefile.dependencies**: this will cause the C preprocessor to search for **#include** and **#import** statements and create a dependency file that **make** will include automatically.

To learn more about Project Builder's use of Makefiles, look at the master NeXTSTEP Makefile in **/NextDeveloper/Makefiles/app/app.make**.

The PB-generated main() Program File

We've seen that Project Builder (IB in NeXTSTEP 2.1) will generate a Makefile according to our specifications. PB will also generate an Objective-C file, **Calculator_main.m** in our example, containing an program's **main()** function. The **main()** function is where every Objective-C (and C) program begins. Below we list the generated **Calculator_main.m** file.

```
/* Generated by the NeXT Project Builder
   NOTE: Do NOT change this file --
   Project Builder maintains it.
*/

#import <appkit/Application.h>

void main(int argc, char *argv[]) {

  NXApp = [Application new];
  if ([NXApp loadNibSection:"Calculator.nib"
      owner:NXApp withNames:NO])
    [NXApp run];

  [NXApp free];
  exit(0);
}
```

Below we briefly discuss the executable statements in this **main()** function.

NXApp = [Application new];
This line contains a message to the **Application** class which creates a new **Application** object instance, and therefore sets up a connection to the Window Server. (Recall that every NeXTSTEP application needs precisely one **Application** object.) The **id** of this new object is assigned to the variable **NXApp**. **NXApp** is a global variable declared in **Application.h**, to make it easier to send messages to it from any part of your program.

[NXApp loadNibSection:"Calculator.nib"
  owner:NXApp withNames:NO]
This line sends the **loadNibSection:owner:withNames:** message to **NXApp**, which causes the **Calculator.nib** file to get "loaded" from the **Calculator.app** (or **Calculator.debug**) directory into your application's memory map. The objects that were specified in Interface Builder will be created in memory and any initialization that you've defined for these objects (e.g., the size of a button, an outlet to another object) automatically gets executed at this time.

[NXApp run];
This line sends the **run** message to **NXApp**, which causes the application's (**Application** object's) main event loop to run. The main event loop handles menu clicks, keystrokes and all of the other events to which an application can respond. Control doesn't return to **main()** until the object **NXApp** gets a **stop:** or **terminate:** message, usually in response to a user choosing the application's **Quit** menu item.

[NXApp free];
This line sends the **free** message to **NXApp**, which closes all the application's windows, breaks the connection to the Window Server, and frees the **Application** object that was created when the **new** message was sent to the **Application** class.

exit(0);
The standard C **exit()** library function which gracefully ends the application.

Every **main()** program file generated by NeXTSTEP has these same lines, although the name of the nib loaded is usually different. (Sometimes the class name **Application** is replaced by a subclass of the **Application** class.)

Other PB-generated Files

In addition to creating the Makefile, nib, and **main()** program files for a project, Project Builder created the following files for us:

- **PB.project** – a project file to keep track of all the parts of the project. If you look at this ASCII file in an editor, you'll see a lot of the same information as a Makefile.[1]
- **Calculator.iconheader** – contains information about application and document icons in your project; we didn't specify any of these icons in this chapter, so it contains the default icon names.
- **PB.gdbinit** – a **gdb** initialization file for this project.
- **English.lproj** – a *directory* which contains the information for an English language version of our project, including the **Calculator.nib** file in our example.

Summary

We did quite a bit in this Chapter! We started by building a "real" project with Project Builder. Then we used Interface Builder and Objective-C to build user interface objects, create and customize our own class, and connect these user interface objects with an object of our new class. We also learned a little more about Objective-C and some AppKit classes, and a lot about the files that PB generates. In the process we used all four of the operations that IB can perform on classes: **Subclass, Instantiate**, **Unparse**, and **Parse**.

In the next chapter, we'll add an Info Panel and some icons to our Calculator application and find out how to increase the efficiency of a NeXTSTEP application by using separate nib files.

---

1. In NeXTSTEP 2.1, the project file is called **IB.proj**, and there is no **PB.gdbinit** file or **English.lproj** directory.

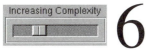

6

Nibs and Icons

In the previous chapter we created our simple four-function Calculator. Although our Calculator worked, it lacked a lot of the basic features of NeXTSTEP applications. In this and the following two chapters, we'll use our simple Calculator as a starting point and slowly expand it, adding new features one-by-one.

In the first half of this chapter, we'll create an Info Panel for our Calculator. The Info Panel performs the function of telling people about the author of the program. We will use the Info Panel to demonstrate how to manage multiple nib files within a single application. In the second half of this chapter, we'll see how NeXTSTEP allows you to specify an icon for an application and a directory. We'll assume you've read the section on creating icons with Icon Builder (Icon in NeXTSTEP 2.1) in Chapter 2.

Managing Multiple Nibs

When a NeXTSTEP application starts up, all of the objects stored in its main nib file are loaded into memory and initialized. This takes time: the more objects, the more time. And until the nib file is loaded, your program can't do anything else.

This can be real drag – especially if your program doesn't need most of the objects in the main nib file for normal operation. For this reason, NeXT-STEP lets you take objects that you don't use often and place them in separate nib files. These auxiliary nib files are loaded only when needed.

NeXT recommends that programs use auxiliary nib files for their Info Panel. As an experiment, start up Edit (or any other NeXTSTEP application) and choose the **Info Panel** menu command from the **Info** menu. You may see the NeXTSTEP spinning disk cursor (🌀) for a moment or two, and then the Info Panel will display. The delay is caused because Edit is loading the Info Panel's nib file into memory. If you click the Info Panel's close button and then choose **Info→Info Panel** again, you won't get any delay at all; this is because the panel, once loaded, stays in the computer's memory. Because Edit's Info Panel is stored in a separate nib, the user has to wait for the Info Panel to load only when he or she wants to see it – not every time the program is run.

Now we'll create a similar Info Panel nib for our Calculator. This will consist of three steps:

(i) Modifying the **Controller** class to load the nib and display the Info Panel.

(ii) Modifying the Calculator's main nib.

(iii) Creating the new nib for the Info Panel.

Modifying the Controller Class

To start, we'll modify the **Controller** object to add two things:

    infoPanel   An outlet that holds the **id** of the Info Panel.
    showInfo: A new action method that displays the Info Panel.

You might think that the easiest way to create the new outlet and action method is to add them in Interface Builder's Class Inspector, as we did in the previous chapter. This is precisely the wrong thing to do. The reason is that we've already added code to the **Controller.m** and **Controller.h** class files; if we use IB's **Unparse** command to generate new files, then we will lose all of the coding that we've added so far!

Instead, the thing to do is to add the new outlet and action method in the **Controller.m** and **Controller.h** files directly, and then use the IB's **Parse** command to read them into IB's internal description of the class. The new outlet and action will then appear in IB's Class Inspector and we'll be able to use them to make connections with user interface objects. (Recall that we **Parse**-d an *outlet* in the previous chapter; here we'll **Parse** a *method* as well.)

1. Using an editor, insert the two lines in `bold` type below into **Controller.h** and save the file. (In NeXTSTEP 2.1, you'll also have to import the **Application** class if you didn't previously import the entire AppKit. From now on we'll assume you imported the entire AppKit with the directive **#import <appkit/appkit.h>**.)

```
...
@interface Controller:Object
{
    id      readout;
    BOOL    enterFlag;
    BOOL    yFlag;
    int     operation;
    float   X;
    float   Y;
    id infoPanel;
}

- clear:sender;
- clearAll:sender;
- enterDigit:sender;
- enterOp:sender;
- displayX;
- doUnaryMinus:sender;
- showInfo:sender;
@end
```

The **infoPanel** outlet will hold the **id** of the Info Panel. The **showInfo:** action method will display the Info Panel in response to a menu choice.

2. Launch Project Builder (PB) by double-clicking the **PB.project** file icon in the **Calculator** project directory in the Workspace File Viewer. This will bring the entire project into PB. (In NeXTSTEP 2.1, double-click the **IB.proj** file in the project directory to launch IB.)

   We suggest you keep the **PB.project** file icon for your current project on your File Viewer's shelf for easy access.

3. Now double-click **Calculator.nib** in the Files view (under **Interfaces**) of PB's main window. This will open the **Calculator.nib** file in IB.

4. Open the Classes view in IB's File window by clicking the **Classes** (**h**) suitcase icon. (In NeXTSTEP 2.1, *double*-click the **Classes** suitcase icon in the File window to open up a *separate* Classes window.)

5. Select the **Controller** class (under **Object**) in the Classes browser.

6. Drag to **Parse** in the **Operations** pull-down list and you'll see IB's Parse panel. Click **OK** in the panel to parse new definition of the **Controller** class from the **Controller.h** file on disk.

Note the new **infoPanel** outlet and **showInfo:** action method in the Class Inspector as in Figure 1 below. (In NeXTSTEP 2.1 you'll get a different panel; click its **Replace** button. Type Command-1 to see the new declarations.)

FIGURE 1. New Outlet and Method in Class Inspector

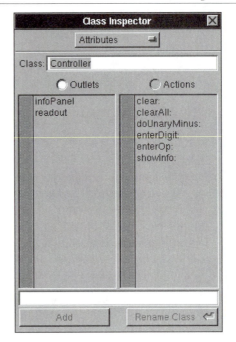

7. Using an editor, insert the entire new **showInfo:** method below into **Controller.m**. We suggest you place it just before the **@end** directive.

```
- showInfo:sender
{
    if (infoPanel == nil) {
        if (![NXApp
            loadNibSection: "info.nib"
            owner: self
            withNames: NO]) {
          return nil;              /* Load failed */
        }
    }
}
```

```
    [infoPanel makeKeyAndOrderFront: nil];
    return self;
}
```

All Objective-C instance variables are initialized to **nil** (0) when an object is created.[1] When the Calculator application starts up, the **infoPanel** outlet in the **Controller** instance will not be explicitly set, so its value will be **nil**. Thus, when the **showInfo:** method is invoked the first time, the "**if**" statement will cause the **loadNibSection:owner:withNames:** message to be sent to **NXApp**. (Recall that **NXApp** is the global variable which contains the **id** of the application's **Application** object.)

The **loadNibSection:owner:withNames:** method will load the nib for the Info Panel (which we'll call **info.nib**). Specifying **withNames:NO** avoids creating the object "names" associated with each object. (An object's name is the name that IB displays beneath the object's icon in the File window.) Names were used historically (in pre-NeXTSTEP 1.0 days!) to provide the same functionality achieved more cleanly with outlets today.

When the **info.nib** file is loaded, it will automatically initialize the **infoPanel** outlet to the **id** of the Info Panel. (We'll show you how to create the Info Panel and set up the initialization a bit later.) Finally, the **showInfo:** method will send the Info Panel the **makeKeyAndOrderFront:** message, which makes the Info Panel the key window and brings it to the front of the window display list (making it visible).

The second time the **showInfo:** method is called, the **infoPanel** outlet will already be initialized. Thus, the statement sending the **loadNibSection:-owner:withNames:** message will be skipped, preventing a second copy of the nib from being loaded. But since the nib that we loaded the first time through is still in memory, the Info Panel will be displayed without the loading delay.

Modifying the Main Calculator Nib

Next we'll create the **Info** command in the Calculator's main menu.

With NeXTSTEP Release 1.0, the **Info** command was one of the commands in the application's main menu. That is, you chose **Info** and the program's Info Panel popped up. Since NeXTSTEP 2.0, the **Info** command is

---

1. Note that Objective-C initializes *only* instance variables. Variables that are static or local to a method are still uninitialized, just like in standard ANSI-C.

properly located in the **Info** *submenu* with several other commands. Normally there are at least two commands in the **Info** submenu: **Info Panel** and **Preferences**. Other common commands you might want to add are **Help** and **Show Menus**. The first three of these commands bring up a panel and should thus be followed by three dots (e.g., "**Info...**"). The *NeXTSTEP User Interface Guide* says that bringing up a panel should be a safe and reversible option: a user should be able to make the panel go away by clicking a cancel or close button without any ill-effects for the application.

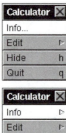

For reasons unknown to us, Interface Builder still provides NeXTSTEP version 1.0-style menus. Thus the Calculator's menu in IB looks like the top one at the left while we really want it to look like the bottom one and have the appropriate **Info** *submenu*.

To do this, follow these steps:

8.   Back in IB, click the "**Info...**" cell in the Calculator menu to select it.

9.   Type Command-x to cut the "**Info...**" menu cell out of the main menu.

10.   Click the menu icon button at the top of IB's Palettes window to see the Menus palette, which contains a selection of menu cells, as in Figure 2 below.

If the Palettes window isn't visible you can make it visible by choosing IB's **Tools→Palettes** menu command. The order of the buttons at the top of your Palettes window may differ; Palette order and loading can be set using IB's Preferences in NeXTSTEP 3.0.

FIGURE 2. Menus Palette in Interface Builder

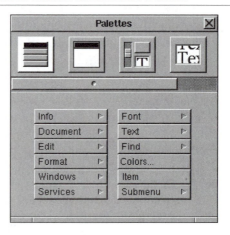

11. Drag the submenu from IB's Palettes window and drop it atop the **Calculator** menu just below the title bar, as in Figure 3 below. You'll see three **Info** submenu commands as at the right of Figure 3. Two commands are colored dark gray, which means that they are *disabled*.

FIGURE 3. Calculator Menus in Interface Builder

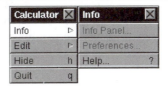

12. Select the **Info Panel** menu cell by clicking it.

13. *Enable* the **Info Panel** menu cell by deselecting (*no* check mark) the **Disabled** option in the MenuCell Inspector. See Figure 4 below. (In NeXTSTEP 2.1, you must click **OK** to make it happen.)

FIGURE 4. MenuCell Inspector

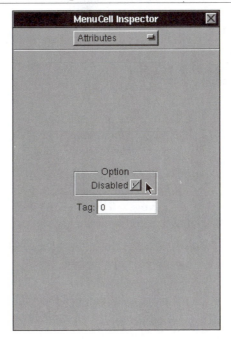

14. *Disable* the **Help** menu cell by first clicking it and then selecting the **Disabled** option in the MenuCell Inspector.

Objects

15. Open the Objects view in IB's File window by clicking the Objects suitcase icon. Note the **Controller** instance icon.

16. Connect the **Info Panel** menu cell to the **Controller** by Control-dragging from the menu cell to the **Controller** instance icon and double-clicking the **showInfo:** action method in the MenuCell Inspector.

   Connecting the **Info Panel** menu cell to the Controller instance actually sets the **MenuCell** object's **target** instance variable to be the **id** of the **Controller** instance.

Creating the Info Panel's Nib in NeXTSTEP 3.0

To complete the Info Panel addition we will create a *separate* nib for the Info Panel – the nib that gets loaded by the **loadNibSection:owner:withNames:** message that the **Controller**'s **showInfo:** method sends to the **NXApp** object.

This section only applies to NeXTSTEP 3.0. NeXTSTEP 2.1 auxiliary nibs are created much differently than in 3.0 and you should skip to "Creating the Info Panel's Nib in NeXTSTEP 2.1" on page 179.

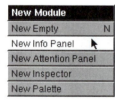

17. Choose IB's **Document→New Module→New Info Panel** command. You'll see a new Info Panel and File window as in Figure 5 below.

Note that there are now *two* File windows at the lower left of the screen, one for **Calculator.nib** and the other for the new nib that was created with IB's **Document→New Module→New Info Panel** command. The icon titled **Info** in the new File window represents the new Info Panel. (All commands in the **Document→New Module** submenu create new nibs and all nibs have their own File window.)

18. Type Command-s to save this new nib and you'll see a Save panel. See Figure 6 below. Note that IB automatically displays the directory (**Calculator/English.lproj** for *English* language nibs) where the new nib should be saved.

19. Type **info.nib** and click the **OK** button (we'll capitalize the names of main nibs and *not* capitalize the names of auxiliary nibs). IB will automatically display the attention panel in Figure 7 below. Click **Yes**.

   (Note that the name in the title bar of the new File window changes to **info.nib** and Project Builder automatically shows that the new nib has been added to the project.)

FIGURE 5. New Info Panel and Associated File Window

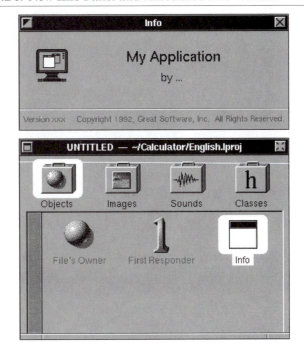

FIGURE 6. Save Panel for New Nib in Interface Builder

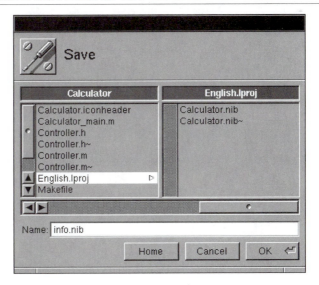

FIGURE 7. **Inserting a New Nib in a Project**

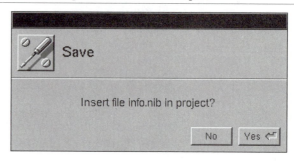

Project Builder displays **info.nib** as part of the Calculator project, as in Figure 8 below. When the program is compiled, the **info.nib** file will automatically be linked to the executable file because it is part of the Calculator project.

FIGURE 8. **info.nib in Project Builder's Main Window**

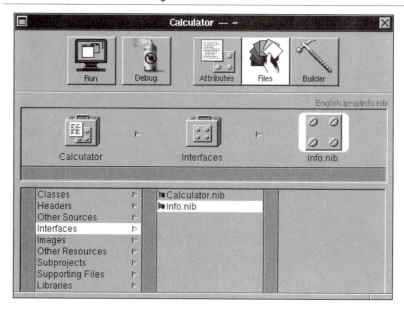

20. Double-click **info.nib** in PB's main window to reactivate **info.nib** in IB. (Any file you double-click in PB's Files view will open that file in the appropriate application.) This step may not be necessary.

21. Customize the text in the Info Panel with clicks, double-clicks and the keyboard. We customized our Info Panel as in Figure 9 below.

FIGURE 9. **Customized Info Panel**

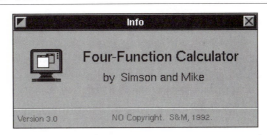

Don't worry about changing the Info Panel's icon – the default terminal icon on the left side of the panel – for now. We'll be replacing it with our own custom icon later in this chapter.

22. Click the **Classes (h)** suitcase icon in the **info.nib** (*not* **Calculator.nib**) File window to see the Classes view (browser) for this nib.

Each nib has its own list of classes that are available to that nib so be careful to make changes in the correct File window.

We want the **Controller** instance to load **info.nib** when the user chooses our Calculator's **Info→Info Panel** menu command. We've already set up the connection from the menu command to the **Controller**. We still have to set up communication between the **Controller** and the Info Panel, which is part of the separate **info.nib** file. As of now, **info.nib** doesn't even "know" that a **Controller** class exists (you can see this by looking at the subclasses of **Object** in the **info.nib** Classes view). We'll take care of this in the next few steps.

23. Select the **Object** class in the **info.nib** Classes view and then drag to **Subclass** in the **Operations** pull-down list. As we saw for **Calculator.nib** in Chapter 5, a new class called **MyObject** appears under **Object** in the class hierarchy.

24. Double-click the **MyObject** class name in the white text field area in the Class Inspector (at the lower right of the screen) and change the name from **MyObject** to **Controller**.

Now **info.nib** knows about *a* **Controller** class which is a subclass of **Object**; however, we'd like **info.nib** to know about the specific **Controller** class which contains the **infoPanel** outlet.

25. Drag to **Parse** in the **Operations** pull-down list and you'll get IB's Parse panel with our project's **Controller.h** file selected. (From now on, we'll abbreviate this by simply saying "**Parse** the **Controller** class definition.")

26. Click **OK** in IB's Parse panel to parse the **Controller.h** file on disk. You should see the **Controller**'s outlets and actions in the Class Inspector as in Figure 1, "New Outlet and Method in Class Inspector," on page 170.

Step 22 through Step 26 (inclusive) above can actually be performed in one simple step: simply drag the **Controller.h** icon from your File Viewer and drop it in the **info.nib** File window! IB will automatically insert the **Controller** class into the **info.nib** hierarchy and **Parse** the class definition on disk. We'll use this technique in subsequent chapters.

We need to make a connection from the **Controller** instance (created by **Calculator.nib**) to the Info Panel to initialize the **infoPanel** outlet. We can't do this using a different **Controller** instance instantiated by **info.nib**. It must be the same one that is instantiated by **Calculator.nib** because that's the one that will be controlling the program. The easiest way to do this is to use the **File's Owner**. The **File's Owner** is an object that "owns" a nib file; every loaded nib must have one. We'll arrange for the **Controller** instance created by **Calculator.nib** to be the **File's Owner** of **info.nib**. We'll discuss this further after the next few steps.

27. Click the Objects suitcase icon in the **info.nib** (*not* **Calculator.nib**) File window to see the Objects view for this nib.

28. Make **info.nib**'s **File's Owner** be of the **Controller** class by clicking the **File's Owner** icon in **info.nib**'s File window and then clicking **Controller** in the Class Inspector as in Figure 10 below (scroll upward, if necessary).

29. Make the **infoPanel** outlet in the **File's Owner** point to the Info Panel. Do this by Control-dragging from the **File's Owner** icon in the **info.nib** (*not* **Calculator.nib**) File window to the title bar of the Info Panel, and then double-clicking the **infoPanel** outlet in the **File's Owner** Connections Inspector.

When **info.nib** is loaded, it will create the Info Panel. It will then set the **infoPanel** outlet in the **File's Owner** object (the **Controller** object which loads **info.nib**) to the **id** of the newly-created panel.

*What is the **File's Owner**?* Recall the Objective-C statement in the **showInfo:** method in **Controller.m** which, when the program runs, loads **info.nib**:

```
[NXApp loadNibSection: "info.nib"
        owner: self
        withNames: NO])
```

FIGURE 10. File's Owner Inspector

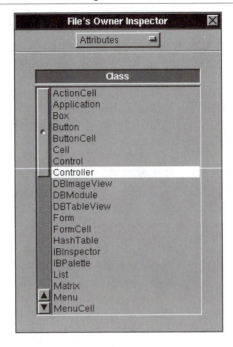

The *File's Owner* is the object that is specified by the **self** in the clause **owner:self**. In this case, the owner is the **Controller** instance (**self**) that sends the above message to **NXApp**. Thus the **infoPanel** outlet in the **Controller** instance is set to the **id** of the Info Panel that is loaded.

Setting **File's Owner** outlets and sending messages to a **File's Owner** object are the easiest ways to communicate between nibs.

30. To see that this all works, choose IB's **Document→Save All** command (to save both nibs), make sure the Controller class files are saved, and then compile and run the program.

The first time you choose the Calculator's **Info→Info Panel** menu command, there will be a slight delay before the Info Panel shows up. However, if you click the Info Panel's close button and then choose **Info→Info Panel** again, it should appear immediately.

Creating the Info Panel's Nib in NeXTSTEP 2.1

This section only applies to NeXTSTEP 2.1. If you're using NeXTSTEP 3.0, then skip to "Adding Icons to Your Application" on page 182.

To complete the Info Panel addition we will create a *separate* nib for the Info Panel – the nib that gets loaded by the **loadNibSection:owner:withNames:** message that the **Controller**'s **showInfo:** method sends to the **NXApp** object.

17. Choose IB's **File→New Module** command. You will see the New Module panel.

18. Change the name **MySubclass** to **Controller** and click **OK**. IB will create a *new* File window called **UNTITLED**.

Each Interface Builder File window corresponds to a nib file. The first thing to do is to give this new nib a name.

19. Choose **File→Save As** and save the new nib in the file **info.nib** in the project directory. The File window's title bar will change to reflect its new name.

20. Add the **info.nib** to your project. Type Command-6 and click the **Attributes/Files** button in IB's Project Inspector so that the word **Files** is highlighted. Click **.nib** in the **Type** column, then click the **Add** button. You'll get an Open panel.

21. Double-click the **info.nib** file name in the Open panel to add **info.nib** to your project. When the program is compiled, **info.nib** will automatically be linked to the executable file.

22. Create the **Info** panel. To do this, click the "Windows" button (seen at the left) at the top of Interface Builder's Palettes window.

23. Drag the icon labeled **Info** from the Palettes window and drop it somewhere (anywhere) in the middle of the screen. You'll see Interface Builder's default **Info** panel.

24. Customize the text in the Info Panel with clicks, double-clicks and the keyboard. We customized our Info Panel as in Figure 9 above.

Don't worry about changing the Info Panel's icon – the terminal icon on the left side of the panel – for now. We'll be replacing it with our own custom icon later in this chapter.

25. Double-click the **Classes** (.h) icon of the to **info.nib** File window to bring up the Classes window for this nib.

Each nib has its own list of classes that are available to that nib so be careful to make changes in the correct File window.

26. Select the **Controller** class in the Classes browser and then choose **Parse** from the **Operations** pull-down list. (From now on, we'll abbreviate this simply by saying "**Parse** the **Controller** class definition.")

We need to make a connection from the **Controller** instance (created by **Calculator.nib**) to the Info Panel to initialize the **infoPanel** outlet. We can't do this using a *different* **Controller** instance instantiated by **info.nib**. It must be the same instance that is instantiated by **Calculator.nib** because that's the one that will be controlling the program. The easiest way to make this connection is to use **info.nib**'s **File's Owner**. (A **File's Owner** is an object that "owns" a nib file; every loaded nib must have one.)

When we created a New Module we arranged for an object of the **Controller** class to be the **File's Owner** of **info.nib**. We'll discuss this further after the next few steps.

27. Make the **infoPanel** outlet in the **File's Owner** point to the Info Panel. Do this by Control-dragging from the **File's Owner** icon in the **info.nib** (*not* **Calculator.nib**) File window to the title bar of the Info Panel, and then double-clicking the **infoPanel** outlet in the **File's Owner** Connections Inspector.

    When **info.nib** is loaded, it will create the Info Panel. It will then set the **infoPanel** outlet in the **File's Owner** object (the **Controller** object which loads **info.nib**) to the **id** of the newly-created panel.

What is the File's Owner? Recall the statement in the **showInfo:** method in **Controller.m** which, when the program runs, loads **info.nib**:

```
[NXApp loadNibSection: "info.nib"
       owner: self
       withNames: NO])
```

The *File's Owner* is the object that is specified by the **self** in the clause **owner:self**. In this case, the owner is the **Controller** instance (**self**) that sends the above message to **NXApp**. Thus the **infoPanel** outlet in the **Controller** instance is set to the **id** of the Info Panel that is loaded.

Setting **File's Owner** outlets and sending messages to a **File's Owner** object are the easiest ways to communicate between nibs.

28. To show that this all works, choose IB's **File→Save All** command (to save both nibs), then compile and run the program.

The first time you choose the Calculator's **Info→Info Panel** menu command, it may take a moment for the Info Panel to display. However, if you click the Info Panel's close button and then choose **Info→Info Panel** again, it should appear immediately.

Adding Icons to Your Application

NeXTSTEP uses icons – little descriptive pictures – in many places to represent programs and their documents. NeXTSTEP also allows programs to change their icon while the program is running. For example, the NeXTSTEP Mail program uses the icon containing an envelope to represent the application. When you have new mail, the Mail program changes its icon to a sheaf of letters.

regular icon   sheaf of letters

Directories can also have icons. For example, the icon at the left, which looks like a book of NeXT documentation, is the icon for the directory **/NextLibrary/Documentation/NextDev/Summaries**.

NeXTSTEP icons are represented by standard TIFF (Tag Image File Format) files. All icons are displayed on a **48x48** pixel grid, although NeXTSTEP will automatically scale the icon that you provide if it is a different size. Icons are often stored 2-bits deep with alpha transparency information, although with the growing number of color computers running NeXTSTEP, color icons are becoming increasingly common.

If you want to use a color icon, you should store both a color icon and a black-and-white icon in the same file so that the icon will look good when it is displayed on a black-and-white system. Use the NeXTSTEP **tiffutil** utility if you need to put more than one TIFF image into a single file. Find out how to use it by searching the UNIX manual pages in Librarian.

Creating Icons

There are many ways to create icons in NeXTSTEP; any application which can save a graphic in a TIFF file can create an icon. The bundled icon building tool in NeXTSTEP 3.0 is Icon Builder, which resides in the **/Next-Developer/Apps** directory. The bundled icon building tool in NeXTSTEP 2.1 is Icon, which resides in the **/NextDeveloper/Demos** directory. We presented brief introductions to these icon building tools in Chapter 2 and we will therefore assume that you know how to create icons.[1]

---

1. For icon design guidelines we suggest you consult a book on user interface design, such as *Designing the User Interface* by Ben Shneiderman or *Software User Interface Design* by Deborah Mayhew.

We're not very good artists (certainly not as good as Keith Ohlfs!), but we did manage to create the icons in Figure 11 below. The one on the left will be used to represent our Calculator application while the one on the right will be used to represent our Calculator's project directory. They are displayed here in the *Obese Bits* format in the Icon Builder application. For a little variety, we've used Symbol font for the mathematical symbols in the application icon and Helvetica bold for them in the directory icon.

FIGURE 11. **Calculator Application and Directory Icons**

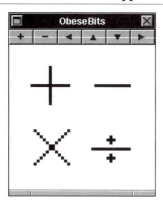 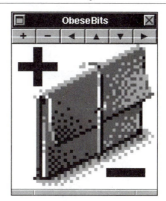

Strictly speaking, you don't have to create an icon for the Calculator directory. But it's nice to have one – it helps make the directory stand out when you look at it in the File Viewer. You don't have to make the Calculator directory's icon different from the Calculator itself; but you probably want to make them different, so you can tell them apart.

Once you've created a directory icon, save it in the Calculator directory with the name **.dir.tiff**[1]. The icon for the Calculator directory should change as in Figure 12 below. As you can see, we've created custom icons for our home directories as well.

---

1. You may also specify a TIFF to be shown while files are dragged into the directory by placing it in the directory with the name **.opendir.tiff.**

FIGURE 12. Calculator Directory Icon in File Viewer

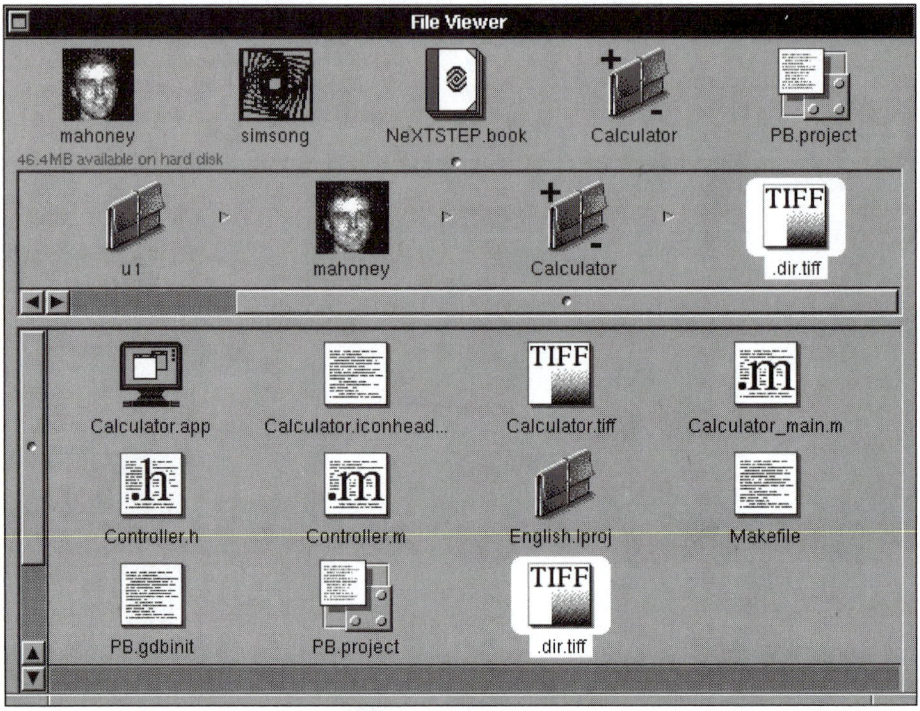

Changing the Calculator's Application Icon

To change the application icon for our Calculator, we'll assume you've saved an icon in the file **~Calculator/Calculator.tiff**. Then we'll tell Interface Builder to use this TIFF image for our Calculator's application icon. When the Calculator program is compiled, the TIFF image will automatically be included in the Calculator's Mach-O executable file. It will be stored in a section called **app** in the __ICON segment of the file (Mach-O files, *segments* and *sections* will be described in Chapter 9).

The following three steps only work in NeXTSTEP 3.0. If you're using NeXTSTEP 2.1, then skip to the section "Changing an Application Icon in NeXTSTEP 2.1" on page 187.

1. Back in Project Builder, click the **Attributes** button to display the attributes of your Calculator project.

Attributes

TIFF
Calculator.tiff

2. Drag the **Calculator.tiff** icon from your File Viewer and drop it in the
    Application Icon area at the lower left of the Attributes view in
    Project Builder. If necessary, the **Calculator.tiff** icon will be copied
    into the project directory. The icon should show up in the **Application
    Icon** well and (eventually) on the **Run** button as in Figure 13 below.

FIGURE 13. Application Icon in Project Builder

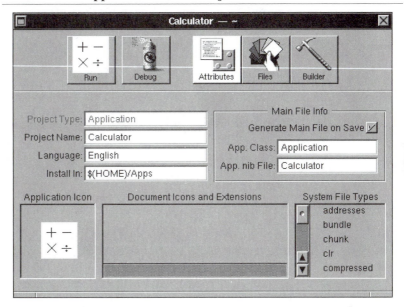

3. Compile and run your Calculator application by clicking the **Run**
    button in PB. PB's main window will change to the Builder view and
    your application will be compiled and run. See Figure 14 below.

Note that the **Calculator.debug** executable is linked again. However, the
code in the **Controller** class and **Calculator_main.m** files is *not* compiled
again because **make** is smart enough to know that their object code files in
the **~Calculator/debug_obj** directory are up-to-date.

If you look again at your **Calculator** directory in the File Viewer, you'll
see that the Calculator application icon has changed from the default to the
Calculator.tiff icon. You may need to choose Workspace's **View→Update
Viewers** menu command (or type Command-u) to force the Workspace
Manager to recognize the new icon.

FIGURE 14. **Builder View in Project Builder**

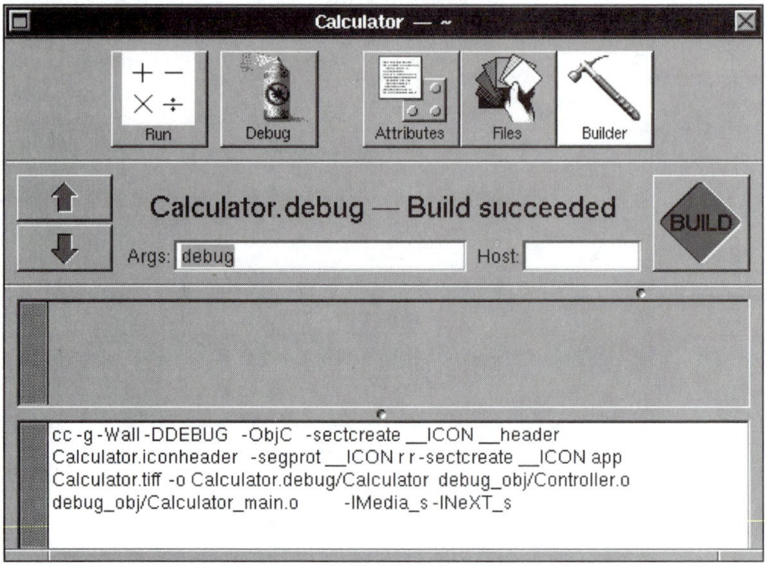

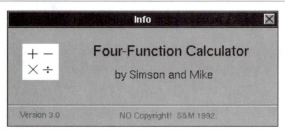

By adding the **Calculator.tiff** application icon we get one other benefit for free; the icon also shows up in the Info Panel! Run your Calculator application and choose **Info→Info Panel** to see it, as in Figure 15 below.

FIGURE 15. **Info Panel with Application Icon**

The reason the application icon shows up can be seen in Interface Builder. Get back into IB and click the icon in the Info Panel. The Button Inspector appears as in Figure 16 below because the icon is actually displayed on top of a disabled button. (Putting an image on a disabled button in a window is an easy way to display an image in a window.) In the Button Inspector, the **Icon** field contains **app**, the Mach-O section name for the application icon we added earlier.

FIGURE 16. **Button Inspector with Application (app) Icon**

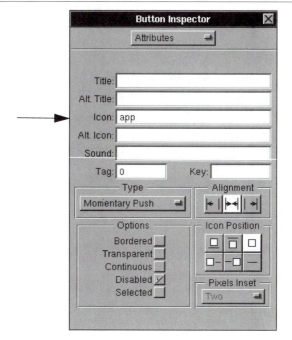

Changing an Application Icon in NeXTSTEP 2.1

The following six steps only work in NeXTSTEP 2.1. If you're using NeXTSTEP 3.0, then skip to "NeXTSTEP Images" on page 189.

1. Back in IB, click the **Attributes/Files** button in the Project Inspector so that the word **Attributes** is selected (in black).

2. Make sure the **App** icon well is highlighted (in white). Type "**Calculator.tiff**" in the **TIFF File** white text area, and then click **OK**. The **Calculator.tiff** icon should appear in the **App** icon well.

3. Build your Calculator application again either by choosing IB's **File→Make** menu command or by entering **make debug** in a shell window.

Note that the **Calculator.debug** executable is linked again. However, the code in the **Controller** class and **Calculator_main.m** files is *not* compiled again because **make** is smart enough to know that their object code files in the **~Calculator/debug_obj** directory are up-to-date.

If you look again at your **Calculator** directory in the File Viewer, you'll see that the **Calculator** application icon has changed from the default to the **Calculator.tiff** icon. You may need to choose Workspace's **View→Update Viewers** command (or type Command-u) to force the Workspace Manager to recognize the new icon.

There's still one little piece of unfinished business: the icon on our Calculator's Info Panel. Recall that when last saw the Info Panel it contained the default application icon (see Figure 9 above). Clearly, what we want is the Calculator's application icon, rather than the funny little default icon that Interface Builder gave us.

4. Back in IB, bring up the Info Panel (double-click its icon in the File window, if necessary) and click the funny little terminal icon so it's selected.

    The icon is actually a disabled button. Putting an image on a disabled button in a window is perhaps the easiest way to display an image in a window or panel.

5. Type Command-1 to bring up the Button Inspector.

NeXTSTEP lets you give a name to every icon associated with your application. The icons can be included in your application's executable file in the **__ICON** segment or stored in your application's *app wrapper* (*segments* will be described in Chapter 9; *app wrappers* were described on page 42). Interface Builder lets you specify the image that your button first displays when the program starts up. You can change the image displayed while your program is running by sending the button the **setIcon:** or **setImage:** message with the name of the icon or image you want to display.

6. Using the Button Inspector, change the icon name from **defaultappicon** to **app**. Click the **OK** button.

    You'll see the icon in your Info Panel change from the default application icon to Interface Builder's icon.

The Interface Builder icon is displayed because IB is the application program that is currently running (that is, when the **NXImage** object looks inside **__ICON segment** of the Mach-O file of the currently running program for an icon named **app**, it finds the IB icon.) However, when your **Info** panel is displayed inside your application program running by itself (rather than when it is displayed inside IB), the **app** icon displayed is the icon that you set as the Calculator's application icon, **Calculator.tiff**.

7. Build your Calculator application again either by choosing IB's **File→Make** menu command or by entering **make debug** in a shell window.

8. Run Calculator.debug and choose **Info→Info Panel.** The application icon should appear as in Figure 15, "Info Panel with Application Icon," on page 186.

NeXTSTEP Images

NeXTSTEP uses objects of the **NXImage** class to display both TIFF and EPS images on the Display PostScript screen. One of the nice features of **NXImage** is its facility for dealing with images by *name.* As we have seen, each image in a nib file or in the application wrapper is given a name; **NXImage** lets you retrieve these images by name and display them on the screen.

NeXT supplies 31 bitmap images which are available to every application via the **NXImage** class. Most of these images are used to construct the basic NeXTSTEP **Control** objects. For that reason, they are shown in Figure 17 on the next page on a light gray background. Notice that most of the icons have two images associated with them: a normal image and a highlighted version (whose name is the same as the normal image name but followed by a capital "H"). **Control** objects display the highlighted image when they are *selected*, and the unhighlighted image otherwise.

Many NeXT developers *enable* the application icon button, so that clicking it does something interesting. For example, clicking the icon might play a sound, display a "secret" message, or perform some sort of animation. There's really no limit to what you can do, as you can see by clicking the application icon in the Info Panels of the Preferences and Workspace Manager applications. To add your own magic, treat the application icon button like any other button: enable it and have it send a message to your **Controller** object (the **File's Owner** of the auxiliary nib file).

Adding Other Images to Your Application

There's no limit to the number of images that you can add to your application. To add an image to your project, simply drag the TIFF or EPS icon for that image file from your Workspace File Viewer into your application's File window in Interface Builder or main window in Project Builder. Note how the cute little suitcase icon "opens" when an image is dropped in the window – another great little feedback feature from NeXT! You can also paste images into the Icon view directly from the Pasteboard.

FIGURE 17. NeXT-supplied Images

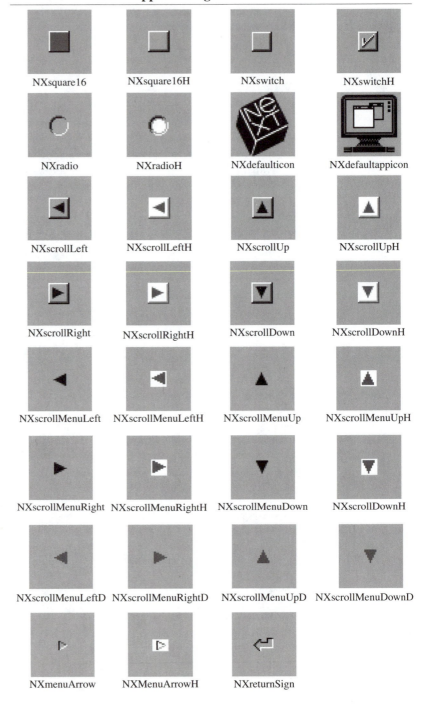

You can refer to your new icon by name, just like any of the other icons, and display it on a button or in any of your custom views. We'll show you how to display an image without using a button in a later chapter.

When you drag the image (e.g., **MyImage.tiff**) into your application's File window in IB, you'll be asked whether you want to add the image file to your project or create a local image, as in the attention panel in Figure 18 below. If you click **Create Local Image** then the image itself will be copied into the active nib in IB. If you click **Yes** then the image will be copied into the project directory and will show up under **Images** in Project Builder's Files view (this is also the case when you drop the image into Project Builder itself). Images that are stored in the nib file cannot easily be used by objects in other nibs. For this reason, it is usually better to store images in the project directory rather than in a nib.

FIGURE 18. Adding an Image to a Project

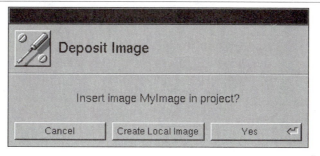

Summary

In the first part of this chapter, we added a second nib file to our Calculator application which provided it with an Info Panel. Using multiple nib files is a good way to speed the performance of your program: with multiple nibs, objects are only created when they need to be used.

In the second part of this chapter, we learned how to add two icons to our Calculator project: one for the project directory, the other for the application program itself. A side benefit of adding the application icon was that it automatically showed up in the Calculator's Info Panel (in NeXTSTEP 3.0).

In the next chapter, we'll learn about *delegation*, a powerful tool for controlling the functionality and extending the behavior of the NeXTSTEP Application Kit objects.

7

Delegation and Resizing

In this chapter, we are going to modify our Calculator so a user can choose to work with any of the following bases: base 2, 8, 10, and 16. To do this, we'll modify the **Controller** class to keep track of the current base and update the display accordingly. We'll also have to modify the keyboard-input routines to work with the proper base, called the *radix*, and ignore key presses (digit button clicks) that are invalid for a particular base. But most importantly, we will introduce the concept of *delegation*, a technique for specifying objects that perform functions for other objects. As for the user interface, we'll set up a matrix of radio buttons (for the user to change the base) and change the size of a window under program control.

Handling Different Bases

The first step toward making our Calculator work with more than one base is to put a control for changing the base in the Calculator window. We'll use a radio button matrix control, because it's both an input and an output at the same time (it shows a state and lets you change it). In addition to letting the user change the base, the radio button matrix indicates which base is currently selected, and shows at a glance all of the choices.

1. Open your Calculator project in Project Builder (PB) by double-clicking the **PB.project** file in the **Calculator** project directory.[1]

2. Open your project's main nib in Interface Builder (IB) by double-clicking **Calculator.nib** in PB's Files view (under the **Interfaces** file type).

3. Click the resize button (◨) in the Calculator window's title bar and extend the window about an inch to the left. See Figure 1 below.

FIGURE 1. Calculator with Radio Button Matrix

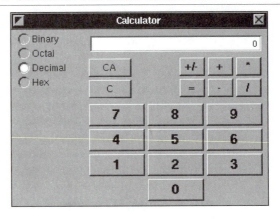

4. Drag a radio button matrix (◯ Radio / ◯ Radio) from IB's Palettes window and drop it on the left side of the Calculator window.

Radio button matrices work like the other button matrices we've used except that *exactly one* cell is always selected: the last button the user clicked. (They work the same as the buttons on a car radio.) Other than that, all the button matrices are essentially the same, with **tag** instance variables and **selectedCell** methods and all the other stuff that you get for free whenever you use the **Matrix** class.

5. While holding down an Alternate key, drag the bottom middle handle of the selected radio button matrix downward so that the matrix consists of four buttons.

1. In NeXTSTEP 2.1, double-click the **IB.proj** file in the **Calculator** project directory to bring the entire project into Interface Builder.

6. Label the buttons **Binary**, **Octal**, **Decimal**, and **Hex** and set the *tags* of the buttons to 2, 8, 10, and 16, respectively. (Double-click each radio button, type Command-1 to display the Button Attributes Inspector, and set the tags.)[1]

7. Make the **Decimal** radio button the selected one in the matrix by double-clicking it and then clicking the **Selected** switch in the Button Attributes Inspector. (Later we'll initialize the **Controller** object so that base 10 will be in effect when the application launches.)

Your Calculator window should now look like the one in Figure 1 above.

Modifying the Controller Class

To make the **Controller** work with this new matrix, we'll add a new action method called **setRadix:** which will be invoked whenever a radio button is clicked. This **setRadix:** method will find out which *base* was selected in the same way that the **enterDigit:** method in Chapter 5 found out which *digit* button was clicked: it will look at the selected cell within the matrix which sent it the message and set the radix depending on the selected cell's tag. To keep track of the radix that the user selected, we'll also add a new instance variable called **radix** to the **Controller** class.

Controller.h

8. Using an editor, insert the **radix** instance variable and the **setRadix:** action method declarations in **bold** below into **Controller.h**.

```
...
@interface Controller:Object
{
    id      readout;
    int     enterFlag;
    int     operation;
    int     yFlag;
    float   X;
    float   Y;
    id      infoPanel;
    int     radix;
}

- showInfo:sender;
- enterOp:sender;
- clearAll:sender;
- clear:sender;
- enterDigit:sender;
```

---

1. In NeXTSTEP 2.1, remember to click **OK** after setting the tags.

```
- doUnaryMinus:sender;
- showInfo:sender;
- setRadix:sender;
```

```
@end
```

9. Insert the **ltob()** *function* below into **Controller.m** before the
    @implementation directive.

```
char *ltob(unsigned long val, char *buf)
{
    int i;

    for (i=0; i<32; i++) {
        buf[i] = (val & (1<<(31-i)) ? '1' : '0');
    }
    buf[32] = '\0';

    for (i=0; i<32; i++) {
        if (buf[i] != '0') return (&buf[i]);
    }
    return (&buf[31]);
}
```

A function in your class implementation file can be used by any other part
of your program – it's a regular C language function. (The function does
not have access to the class instance variables because it is outside the class
implementation.) The **ltob()** function listed above changes a *long* integer
into an ASCII binary representation. It places that ASCII representation in
a buffer that is passed into the function, rather than an internal **static** buffer,
so that it will work properly in a multi-threaded environment. We need this
function because NeXTSTEP lacks a general purpose function for convert-
ing integers to ASCII-encoded strings of arbitrary bases.

10. Insert the **setRadix:** method below into **Controller.m** immediately
    before the **@end** directive.

```
- setRadix:sender
{
    radix = [ [sender selectedCell] tag];
    [self displayX];
    return self;
}
```

This method sets the **radix** instance variable to be the tag (2, 8, 10, or 16)
of the radio button cell that was clicked and updates the X register.

11. *Replace* the original **displayX** method in **Controller.m** with the new
    one below. The new lines, which handle the new bases, are in **bold**.

```
- displayX
{
  char buf[256];
  char bbuf[256];

  switch(radix) {
    case 10:
      sprintf( buf, "%15.10g", X );
      break;
    case 16:
      sprintf( buf, "%x", (unsigned int)X);
      break;
    case 8:
      sprintf( buf, "%o", (unsigned int)X);
      break;
    case 2:
      strcpy( buf, ltob( (int)X, bbuf ) );
      break;
  }

  [readout setStringValue:buf];
  return self;
}
```

This **displayX** method converts the contents of the X register to the base
(**radix**) that the user previously selected and displays the result in the Calculator window's text display area (recall that the **readout** outlet points to
the **TextField** object near the top of the Calculator window). Note that the
base is "known" to **displayX** through the **radix** instance variable. Since
radix is an instance variable, it is "global" within the class implementation
and thus accessible to any **Controller** method.[1]

In order for the **radix** instance variable to be set to the user-selected base,
we need to arrange for the radio button matrix to send the **setRadix:** message to the **Controller**. As always, when we need an on-screen object to
pass information to a custom object, we must set up a target-action connection in Interface Builder. But IB doesn't know about the **setRadix:** action
method yet, so we must first **Parse** the new **Controller** class definition.

12. Back in IB, open up the Classes view and **Parse** the new definition for
the **Controller** class to bring in the **setRadix:** action method
declaration (make sure you have first saved the **Controller** class files).

---

1. The **#import <string.h>** statement is required to use the **strcpy()** function.
The **#import <appkit/appkit.h>** statement imports **string.h** (and almost every
other header file you'll ever need, except your own class header files).

13. Connect the **Matrix** of radio buttons to the **Controller** instance icon (in the Objects view in IB's File window). Arrange for the **Matrix** to send the **setRadix:** action message to the **Controller** by double-clicking **setRadix:** in the Matrix Inspector.

14. Type Command-s to save **Calculator.nib**.

15. Finally, **make** and run your application. When it starts up, click the digit button labeled 9.

Wait! Nothing happens! What's wrong? Before you panic, try clicking the radio button labeled **Decimal**. The number 9 should appear. Then click the radio button labeled **Octal**. The display should change to 11. Click the **Binary** button and you'll see 1001.

The problem is a lack of initialization. Objective C initializes all of an object's instance variables to 0. That means that when our Calculator starts running, the **radix** instance variable has the value of 0. As a result, the **switch** statement in the **displayX** method doesn't execute any of the options – and no value gets displayed.

The solution is to create a new method in the **Controller** class which is invoked automatically when the program starts up. You can specify initialization methods with NeXTSTEP 3.0's **awakeFromNib** method. NeXTSTEP 3.0 will automatically call a method called **awakeFromNib**, if such a method exists, for every object it unarchives from a nib file once all of the objects have been unarchived and connected.

Another approach for setting an initial radix would be to create an **init** method for the **Controller** class.

The technique that we will use here to initialize the **Controller** object involves introducing a new technique called *delegation*, which we will use so that a method inside the **Controller** class is automatically called by the **NXApp Application** object when the program starts executing.

Delegation

NeXTSTEP uses a technique called *delegation* to allow objects to specify other objects, called *delegates*, to handle certain messages for them. Thus one object can delegate the responsibility for handling certain messages to another object. Delegation gives the programmer a system for modifying or controlling the behavior of NeXTSTEP's more complicated objects, such as **Application** and **Window**, without having to subclass them. Typically, delegation is used to control the behavior of an object or to invoke a method automatically in response to an action performed by the user.

An object sends its delegate specific messages under specific circumstances. Before the object sends the message, it checks to see if the delegate can respond to the message by interrogating the delegate with the **respondsTo:** message. If the delegate doesn't implement a method for a specific message, the message simply isn't sent! The object must do this, because if a delegate (or any object, for that matter) receives a message for which it doesn't have a corresponding method, the program will exit with an error.

For more information about **respondsTo:** and similar messages, see Digital Librarian's documentation on the **Object** class. The **respondsTo:** method is defined in the root **Object** class and thus is inherited by all other objects.

Did and *Will* Delegate Methods

NeXTSTEP has two principal kinds of messages which are sent to delegate objects: *Did* messages and *Will* messages. A *Did* message gets sent *after* a particular event takes place: it notifies the delegate object that something has occurred. For example, if you designate a delegate object for a **File's Owner** which is an instance of the **Application** class (or any subclass), that delegate will automatically get sent the following *Did* messages under the following conditions:

Did message	When the message is sent
appDidBecomeActive: *sender*	Sent to the **Application** object's delegate after the application is activated.
appDidHide: *sender*	Sent after the application is hidden.
appDidInit: *sender*	Sent after the application has been launched and initialized, but before it receives its first event.
appDidResignActive: *sender*	Sent after the application is deactivated.
appDidUnhide: *sender*	Sent after the application is unhidden.
appDidUpdate: *sender*	Sent after the **Application** object updates the application's windows.

A *Will* message gets sent *before* an event takes place. Some *Will* methods let you control the behavior of an **Application** object by the value your message returns. Here are the *Will* messages for an **Application** object:

Will message	When the message is sent
appWillInit: *sender*	Sent before the application is initialized. This method allows you to change the application's **Speaker** and **Listener** objects, which are used for inter-application communication.
appWillTerminate: *sender*	Sent when the **Application** object receives a **terminate:** message. This method lets you to clean up the application, such as shutting down databases and saving or closing any open files before it terminates. If this method returns **nil**, the application does not terminate.
appWillUpdate: *sender*	Sent before the **Application** object updates the application's windows.

Will methods let you do fairly complicated things with ease. For example, suppose you set up a delegate object for your application's **Application** object, and the delegate implements the **appWillTerminate:** method. When the user chooses the **Quit** menu command from your application, the **Application** object receives the **terminate:** message and in turn sends the **appWillTerminate:** message to its delegate. The delegate's **appWillTerminate:** method could then display a panel asking the user "Do you really want to quit?" If the user answers **No**, then the delegate returns **nil** to the **Application** object, and the application doesn't terminate. If the user answers **Yes**, the delegate returns **self**, and the application terminates.

Not every class in the Application Kit (AppKit) makes use of delegation; generally, anything that you want to do with delegation can be done just as well with subclassing. If you have a choice, use delegation: it is easier to debug and it affords you a greater opportunity to reuse your code from one project to another. It also frees you from having to subclass a lot of the AppKit classes. For most applications, you'll only need to subclass the **Object** or **View** classes.

The **Application** delegate method used most is **appDidInit:**, which automatically gets sent after an application is initialized but before it receives any events. We'll set up a delegate for our Calculator's **Application** object and use **appDidInit:** to set the initial radix and perform other initialization.

Specifying an Object's Delegate

An object's delegate is specified by an *outlet* instance variable called **delegate**. The following are the main AppKit classes that support delegates:

Class	Reason for Delegate
Application	To receive notification about the application's state.
Listener	To receive messages sent to your application from another application.
Matrix	For editing information stored inside a matrix.
NXBrowser	For filling the information stored in the browser.
NXImage	To notify the user program if an image isn't drawn.
NXJournaler	To control journaling.
NXSplitView	To control resizing.
SavePanel	To validate filenames.
Text	To control editing and interception of keystrokes.
Window	To receive window events and control resizing.

There are two ways to provide an object with a delegate:

(i) Connect the object to its delegate in Interface Builder.

(ii) Use the object's **setDelegate:** method.

But what should the delegate be? The answer to this question depends on your application. Sometimes you will create a special object whose sole mission in life is to be the delegate of one or more other objects. By using *one* object as the delegate for several other objects, you can centralize control for handling events for common objects. Other times, an object may serve double duty, being both the delegate for another object and having a life of its own.

In our example, we'll make our Calculator's **Controller** object be the delegate of the **Application** object. We'll do this for two reasons: first, the **Controller** is fairly simple. By making it the **Application**'s delegate, we eliminate the complexity of creating a second class.[1]

---

1. Creating too many classes to solve a particular problem is a common mistake of people new to object-oriented languages. It leads to *lasagna code* – code with too many layers stacked together. This is the object-oriented equivalent of spaghetti-code. Creating too *few* classes is also a common mistake of newcomers.

The second reason to make the **Controller** the **Application**'s delegate is that the initialization we want to perform – namely, setting the Calculator's radix – needs to be done inside the **Controller** object itself. Thus, the **Controller** is the logical object to be the **Application**'s delegate object.

Setting Up a Delegate Outlet in the Nib

We'll use Interface Builder to make our application's **Controller** instance the delegate of the **Application** object. Recall that the **File's Owner** object in the Objects view in the **Calculator.nib** File window represents the Calculator's **Application** object; it's the owner of **Calculator.nib** (see "The PB-generated main() Program File" on page 164 in Chapter 5 for further details).

1. Back in IB, Control-drag from the **File's Owner** icon to the **Controller** instance icon inside the **Calculator.nib** File window (Objects view). See Figure 2 on the next page.

2. Double-click the **delegate** outlet in the File's Owner Inspector to make the **Controller** instance the **Application**'s delegate. See Figure 2.

We'll need to add a new outlet to the **Controller** class so that the delegate method can determine the initial radio button (radix) that is selected in the on-screen matrix. This outlet, which we'll call **radixMatrix**, will be set to the **id** of the matrix of radio buttons.

3. Using an editor, insert the **radixMatrix** outlet into **Controller.h**.

```
...
@interface Controller:Object
...
    int radix;
    id   radixMatrix;
}
...
```

4. **Parse** the **Controller** class definition again so IB knows about the new **radixMatrix** outlet (make sure the **Controller.h** file has been saved).

5. Connect (Control-drag from) the **Controller** instance icon to the **Matrix** object containing the radio buttons and double-click the **radixMatrix** outlet in the CustomObject Connections Inspector. Be careful to connect the outlet to the **Matrix** object and not to one of the **Cell**s inside the **Matrix** (the text near the bottom of the CustomObject Inspector tells you the class of the destination object).

Next we'll create the delegate method in the **Controller** class.

FIGURE 2. **Setting up a Delegate in Interface Builder**

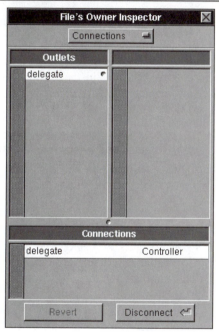

Adding the Delegate Method

To receive the application delegate's **appDidInit:** message in the **Controller**, all we need to do is create a method with the name **appDidInit:**. You can place this method between the **@implementation Controller** and **@end** statements. Alternatively, you can create a second set of **@implementation** and **@end** statements containing the delegate methods (that's what we've done below). This separate definition helps isolate those methods specifically for delegation from the methods used for other purposes.

6. Add the **ApplicationDelegate** code below *after* the original **@end** directive in **Controller.m**.

```
@implementation Controller(ApplicationDelegate)

- appDidInit:sender
{
    [self setRadix:radixMatrix];
    [self clearAll:self];

    return self;
}
@end
```

You can add as many **Controller** delegate methods as you like between the **@implementation Controller(ApplicationDelegate)** and **@end** directives. You can also use this syntax construct for adding methods to AppKit classes, but need you will to set up separate interface and implementation files. **ApplicationDelegate** is called a *category*. You cannot use a category to add new instance variables to a class, but methods in a category have full access to all of the instance variables defined in the object class itself. Next we show the matching class interface for the **Controller(ApplicationDelegate)** category.

7. Insert the **ApplicationDelegate** declaration code below *after* the original **@end** directive in **Controller.h**.

```
@interface Controller(ApplicationDelegate)
- appDidInit:sender;
@end
```

When the application starts up, the **Controller**'s **appDidInit:** method automatically gets executed. The **appDidInit:** method will then invoke the **Controller**'s **setRadix:** method, supplying **radixMatrix** as the **sender**. This simulates the user clicking one of the radio buttons. The **setRadix:** method looks at the **sender**, which points to the **Matrix** of radio buttons (recall we made a connection which made the **radixMatrix** outlet point to this **Matrix**), finds the selected cell and sets the **radix** variable appropriately. This is a little tricky because we're supplying a "phony" **sender**.

The **appDidInit:** method also calls the Calculator's **clearAll:** method, which clears all the Calculator's registers. (This **clearAll:** method is not strictly necessary, since all instance variables are initialized to 0, but it is the correct thing to do.)

8. **Make** your program and run it. This time, your Calculator should display the numbers as soon as you start clicking the keypad buttons.

Disabling Buttons for Better Multi-Radix Input

There is still a big problem with our Calculator: the keypad doesn't work correctly in any base except for decimal. The reason for this failure lies with the following statement in the **enterDigit:** method:

```
X = (X*10.0) + [ [sender selectedCell] tag];
```

This statement multiplies whatever is in the X register by 10 and adds the tag of a digit button each time one is clicked. Unfortunately, we don't want to multiply the X register by 10 if a radix other than base 10 is in effect – instead, we want to multiply by the current radix. So for a first pass, the **10.0** in this statement should be replaced with **radix**.

1. Using an editor, replace the **10.0** in the **enterDigit:** method in **Controller.m** with **radix** to get:

```
X = (X*radix) + [ [sender selectedCell] tag];
```

But that's not the *only* necessary change: we've also got to change the keypad so that particular buttons are deactivated when certain bases are selected. For example, a user shouldn't be able to press the 8 key when the **octal** base is chosen. Also, it would be nice to make buttons for the numbers **A, B, C, D, E**, and **F** appear when the user asks for **Hex** input.

Using a List Object to Directly Access Matrix Cells

Every NeXTSTEP button can be either *enabled* or *disabled*. If a button is disabled, the black labeling on the each button becomes gray, and the button won't depress when it's clicked. In the following steps, we'll modify the **setRadix:** method so that each time the radix is changed, the method will scan all of the buttons in the digit button matrix and disable the ones whose tag is equal to or greater than the new radix.

To scan all of the digit buttons in the **Matrix**, we'll need its **id**. We'll also need the **id** of each individual button that the matrix contains. As we will see, the **id** of each cell inside a **Matrix** object is stored in *yet another* Objective-C bundled object called a **List**. As it's name implies, a **List** object is used for making collections, or lists, of other objects.

2. Insert the **keyPad** outlet declaration in **bold** below into **Controller.h**.

```
...
@interface Controller:Object
{
...
  id   radixMatrix;
```

```
        id   keyPad;
}
...
```

The **keyPad** outlet will provide our program with the **id** of the digit button **Matrix** object when the application starts up. As usual, we'll arrange for this initialization in IB.

3.   Back in IB, **Parse** the new **Controller** class definition so IB knows about the new **keyPad** outlet (make sure **Controller.h** has been saved).

4.   Connect the newly-created **keyPad** outlet in the **Controller** instance to your Calculator's digit button **Matrix** object. As before, make sure you connect to the matrix and not a digit button within the matrix.

List is an important class for NeXTSTEP programmers: it's a generic class (actually called a *common* class) for maintaining a collection, or list, of other objects.[1] A **List** object has methods for:

- Adding an object to the list.
- Adding an object to the list if it isn't already there.
- Sending a message to every object in the list.
- Removing an object from the list.
- Counting the number of elements in the list.
- Accessing a specific element in the list by number.

Refer to the NeXTSTEP documentation for a detailed explanation of the **List** class (search for **List** in the Librarian application). **List** isn't strictly part of the AppKit; instead, it is one of the common classes that NeXT provides with Objective-C.

5.   *Replace* the old version of the **setRadix:** action method in **Controller.m** with the new one below (the new lines are in **bold**).

```
- setRadix:sender
{
    int i;
    id  cellList;

    radix = [ [sender selectedCell] tag];

    /* Disable the buttons that are
     * higher than selected radix
```

---

1. The **#import <objc/List.h>** statement is required to use the **List** class. The **#import <appkit/appkit.h>** statement imports **List.h** for us.

```
 */
cellList = [keyPad cellList];
for (i=0; i<[cellList count]; i++) {
  id cell = [cellList objectAt: i];
  [cell setEnabled: ([cell tag] < radix) ];
}

[self displayX];
return self;
}
```

We'll explain the new code in **setRadix:** line-by-line:

cellList = [keyPad cellList];
This line sends the **cellList** message to the **keyPad Matrix** object, which causes the object to return the **id** of the **List** object that holds all of the **Matrix**'s cells. Once we have the **id** of this **List** object, we can easily access the objects stored inside it.

for (i=0; i<[cellList count]; i++)
This line sets up a loop which will execute for each of the objects stored in the **List** object.

id cell = [cellList objectAt: i];
This line sets the **cell** local variable to be the **id** of the i'th element in the **List** object.

[cell setEnabled: ([cell tag] < radix)];
The expression "**[cell tag] < radix**" returns **YES** if **cell** should be enabled and **NO** if it shouldn't. (**YES** and **NO** are specified by **#define** operators in the file **/NextDeveloper/Headers/objc/objc.h**.) The outermost message then sets the cell to be enabled or disabled as appropriate for the current radix. For example, if the **radix** is 8 (octal), then all cells with tags less than 8 should be enabled (**YES**) while cells with tags at least 8 should be disabled (**NO**).

6. Save all pertinent files and **make** and run the Calculator program.

7. Enter the number 258. The main Calculator window should look like the one at the top of Figure 3 on the next page.

8. Now, click the **Binary** radio button. The number 258 should change to its binary representation, and the *numbers 2 through 9 on the digit buttons should turn gray*, as in the Calculator window at the bottom of Figure 3.

FIGURE 3. Calculator Window with Base 10 and Base 2

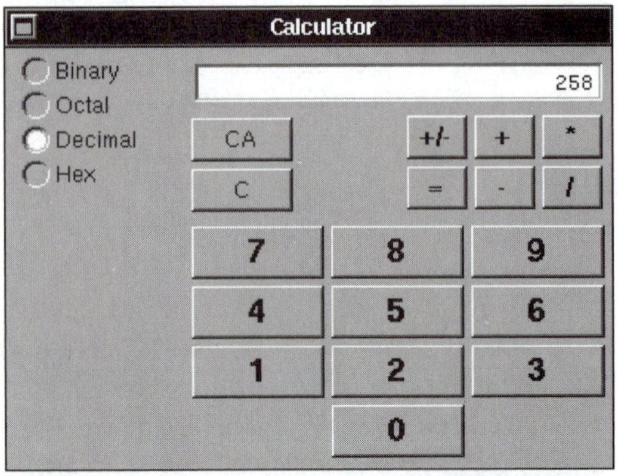

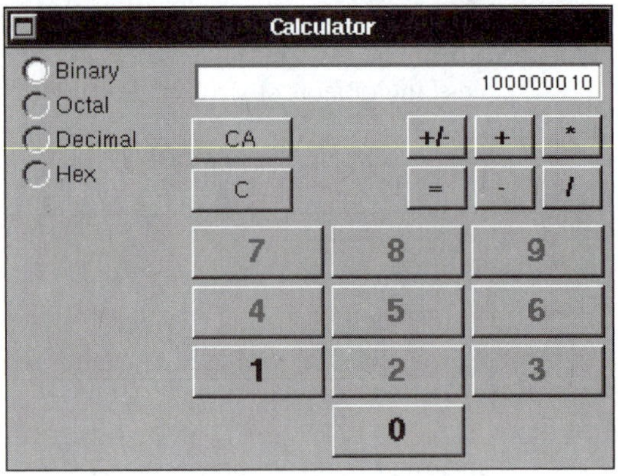

The numbers turn gray because NeXTSTEP buttons automatically display their titles in gray when they are disabled.

Coherence in Object-Oriented Programming

The changes to the **setRadix:** method bear mentioning, because they contain the essence of another important object-oriented concept: *coherence*. Being *coherent* means being logically or aesthetically ordered or integrated. In object-oriented programming, coherence means writing as little code as necessary by writing code that figures out what it needs to know when it runs, rather than having things pre-programmed. This way, if something changes, the code automatically reconfigures itself at run time.

In this example, the **setRadix:** method disables the buttons in the matrix that have a tag that is equal to or greater than the current radix – so, for example, the keys 2-9 don't work when you're in binary mode. But rather than *hard-coding* the keys the **setRadix:** method needs to disable for each radix, we have **setRadix:** find these keys by scanning through the associated **List** object which contains the matrix cells. Likewise, rather than *hard-coding* into **setRadix:** the *number* of buttons in the matrix, we have **setRadix:** determine the number by asking the **List** how many objects it contains. This way, we can change the number of cells in the matrix while in Interface Builder and not have to make any changes to the **setRadix:** method.

Resizing Windows Programmatically

We're not done with our Calculator because we still haven't built a system for entering the hexadecimal numbers **A**, **B**, **C**, **D**, **E**, and **F**. Probably the easiest way to enter these "numbers" is to add another 6 buttons to the keypad and put the letters on them. (Naturally, these buttons will have the tags 10 through 15.) Because we don't need to have these buttons displayed all the time, our NeXTSTEP Calculator will do something that no physical calculator can do: it will make itself bigger when it is in **Hex** mode (to have room for the extra buttons), and then make itself smaller when they are no longer needed.

To accomplish this magic, we'll widen the Calculator window and enlarge the keypad, adding the new digit buttons on the right-hand side. We'll also set the window back to its original size, covering the newly-added buttons.

To make all of this happen, we need to do the following:

(i)   Create the extra buttons for the keypad matrix on the right of the current digit button matrix. This new matrix will be bigger than the window, but the extra buttons will be off to the right-hand-side so you won't see them unless our Calculator is in hex mode.

(ii) Arrange for our Calculator to determine how much bigger it needs to grow in order to show the extra buttons.

(iii) Arrange for our Calculator to remember how big it is when it starts out, and to restore the window to that size when the user wants to make the extra buttons "disappear."

Modifying the Calculator's Interface

Follow these steps to modify our Calculator's interface to accommodate the additional buttons:

1. Back in IB, click the resize button (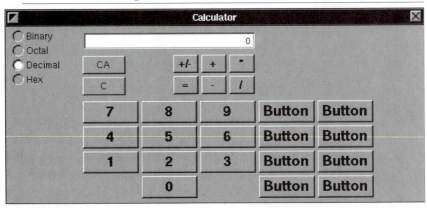) in the **Calculator** window's title bar and extend the window to the right, enough so that two more columns of digit buttons will fit.

2. (Single-) click the keypad matrix to select it.

3. While pressing the Alternate key, drag the center-right handle to the right, creating two new columns of buttons, as in the window at the top of Figure 4 below.

FIGURE 4. Adding the Hex Buttons A-F

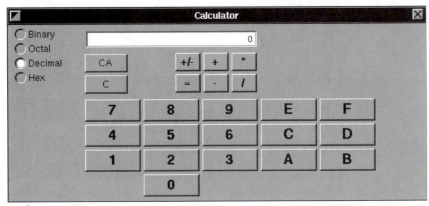

4. Select the **Disabled** attribute, deselect the **Bordered** attribute for the two new buttons in the bottom row, and remove their titles. See the window at the bottom of Figure 4.

5. Set up the tags and the titles for the buttons **A-F**. Set the tag for button **A** to the number 10, the tag for button **B** to 11, and so forth.

6. Resize the window so that you can't see the **A-F** buttons off to the right. Don't worry: they're still there. You just can't see them! Your Calculator should look like it did before we added the six additional buttons.

Notice that we haven't entered any sizes such as how big the matrix is, how big the Calculator window is, or how big the window has to grow. We simply don't need to find out this information ahead of time and *hardcode* it into our program. Instead, we'll have the **Controller** object send messages to the **Matrix** and **Window** objects to find out this information. The **Controller** will then calculate how much larger the window needs to grow in order to make the additional hex buttons visible, and send a message to the **Window** object to change its size accordingly.

Modifying the Controller Class

We need to modify the **Controller.h** and **Controller.m** files to make the window bigger when we switch to base 16 and smaller when we switch from base 16 to a different base.

7. Using an editor, insert a line in **bold** below into **Controller.h**.[1]

    ```
    ...
    @interface Controller:Object
    ...
        id      keyPad;
        NXRect originalViewSize;
    }
    ...
    ```

The new **originalViewSize** instance variable will hold the size of the Calculator window's *content view* before it is expanded. The *content view* of a window holds the contents of the window – all of the visible window except for the title bar, the black border, and the resize bar (if present).

8. Insert the line in **bold** below into the **appDidInit:** method in **Controller.m**.

    ```
    - appDidInit:sender
    {
        [self setRadix:radixMatrix];
        [self clearAll:self];
    ```

---

1. The **#import <appkit/graphics.h>** statement is required to use the **typedef** and **struct** definitions, such as **NXRect**, for NeXTSTEP graphical objects. The **#import <appkit/appkit.h>** statement imports **graphics.h** for us.

```
[ [ [keyPad window] contentView]
                    getFrame:&originalViewSize];

return self;
}
```

The innermost message, **[keyPad window]**, returns the **id** of the window containing our Calculator's keypad matrix. Sending this window the **contentView** message returns the **id** of the window's content **View**. Lastly, we ask that **View** for its frame (origin and size), and store the results in the **NXRect** variable **originalViewSize**. In this way, the application "remembers" the original size of our Calculator's window when it starts up. That's important, because after we make the Calculator window larger, there won't be any other record of the window's original (smaller) size.

9. *Replace* the old version of the **setRadix:** action method in **Controller.m** with the new one below (the *new* lines are in **bold**).

```
- setRadix:sender
{
  int  i;
  id   cellList;
  int  oldRadix   = radix;
  id   keyWindow  = [keyPad window];

  radix = [ [sender selectedCell] tag];

  /* Disable the buttons that are
   * higher than selected radix
   */
  cellList = [keyPad cellList];
  for (i=0; i<[cellList count]; i++) {
    id cell = [cellList objectAt: i];
    [cell setEnabled: ([cell tag] < radix) ];
  }

  if (radix==16 && oldRadix != 16) {
                            /* make window bigger */
    NXRect keyFrame;
    NXRect newWindowFrame;
    [keyPad getFrame:&keyFrame];

    [keyWindow getFrame:&newWindowFrame];
    NX_WIDTH(&newWindowFrame) +=
            NX_X(&keyFrame) + NX_WIDTH(&keyFrame)
            - NX_WIDTH(&originalViewSize)
            + 4.0;
    [keyWindow
```

```
                placeWindowAndDisplay:&newWindowFrame];
    }
    /* placeWindowAndDisplay: gives a cleaner redraw
     * when making the window bigger.
     */

    if (radix != 16 && oldRadix == 16) {
                        /* make window smaller */
       [keyWindow
         sizeWindow:NX_WIDTH(&originalViewSize)
                   :NX_HEIGHT(&originalViewSize)];
    }

    [self displayX];
    return self;
}
```

Don't worry if this code seems very complicated now. It uses a few methods in the **Window** and **View** classes that will be described shortly.

The two new declarations set up the **oldRadix** variable to contain the old radix and the **keyWindow** variable to contain the **id** of the window that contains the Calculator's keypad matrix. The actual changing of the Calculator window's size is done within the two "**if**" blocks that follow. The first "**if**" block makes the window bigger when switching to base 16 from another base. The second "**if**" block makes the window smaller when switching from base 16 to one of the others.

In the first case – making the window bigger – the program gets the size and position of the **keypad** matrix by sending it the **getFrame** message. All NeXTSTEP screen controls like **Matrix** and **Slider** are actually subclasses of the **View** class. All **View**s respond to the **getFrame:** message by returning the size of their "frame," or rectangular region in the window. The size returned is the size of the entire matrix, not just the part that is visible.

To calculate the width of the bigger window, the method first gets the current window's X coordinate using the **NX_WIDTH**() *macro*. It then adds to this X coordinate the width plus offset of the **keypad** matrix frame, subtracts the original width of the window, and adds a 4 pixel boundary.

The second "**if**" block – executed if the user is switching from base 16 to another base – simply restores the window to its original width stored in **originalViewSize**. Thus, it is not necessary to calculate how wide to make the window so that it correctly obscures the part of the **keypad** matrix that should be obscured.

10. Save all pertinent files and **make** and run your Calculator.

11. Click the **5**, **8**, and **7** digit buttons and then click the radio button labeled **Hex**. The **Calculator** window should change from the window at the top of Figure 5 to the window at the bottom. The number in the readout text area should change from **587** to **24b**.

12. Now click the **Binary** radio button and the window should return to its original size.

FIGURE 5. Calculator Window Changing Size Dynamically

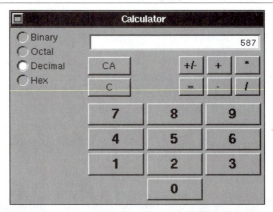

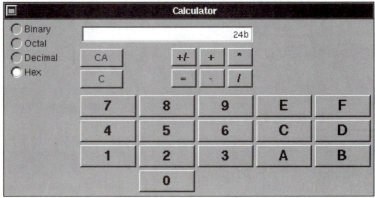

The Window and View Classes

In this section we'll describe the very important **Window** and **View** classes in more detail and list many of their most useful instance methods.

The Window Class

Window is one of the five most important classes in the Application Kit. If you want to be an effective NeXTSTEP programmer, it is important to be familiar with the variety and scope of **Window**'s many methods.

Every on-screen window displayed by a program is controlled by an instance object of the **Window** class. Each **Window** object receives events from a program's **Application** object. Most mouse events are sent to the object within the window where the mouse event took place (e.g., if an on-screen button is clicked, a **mouseDown:** message is sent to the corresponding **Button** object). Keyboard events get sent to the object that is the window's **firstResponder**, which will be described in detail in the next chapter.

Each window contains at least one instance of the **View** class (described below) called the window's *content view*. Although you can work directly with a window's content view, normally you will create subviews of the content view in which you do your actual drawing and event processing. We'll discuss these ideas in great depth in the following chapters.

Some of the most common instance methods for **Window** objects are listed alphabetically in the table below. We'll use the same type convention as is used in NeXTSTEP documentation. Methods are in **bold** type, arguments are in *italic* type, and data types are in normal type. Recall that if an argument's data type isn't specified (e.g., *sender*), then it's an **id** by default.

Window Instance Method	Purpose
center	Moves the window to the center of the screen.
contentView	Returns the **id** of the window's content view.
display	Displays the entire window, including borders, title bar, resize bar, and all contained views.

Window Instance Method	Purpose
getFrame: (NXRect *)*theRect*	Puts the window's frame into *theRect*. Tells you where the window is on the screen and how big it is.
makeKeyAndOrderFront: *sender*	Makes the window the key window and places it in front of all other windows on the screen.
moveTo: (NXCoord)*x* :(NXCoord)*y*	Places the lower-left hand corner of a window at a particular position on the screen.
orderOut: *sender*	Takes the window out of the screen list, which makes it invisible. The window is still in the Window Server's memory; you just can't see it! (The **Hide** menu command is implemented with this method.)
placeWindowAndDisplay: (const NXRect *)*frameRect*	Changes the size and location of a window and displays its contents.
performClose:*sender*	Simulates a user clicking the window's close button.
performMiniaturize: *sender*	Simulates a user clicking the window's miniaturize button.
setTitle: (const char *)*aString*	Sets the window's title in its title bar to *aString*.
setTitleAsFilename: (const char *)*aString*	Sets the window's title in its title bar to a file name.
sizeWindow: (NXCoord)*width* :(NXCoord)*height*	Sets the size of a window's content view to *width* by *height*.

All of the methods available to the **Window** class are described in the document **/NextLibrary/Documentation/NextDev/GeneralRef/02_ApplicationKit/Window.rtf**. Two easy ways to find and read this file are to use the Librarian and **/NextDeveloper/Demos/HeaderViewer** applications.

The View Class

View is the basic NeXTSTEP class for creating objects which draw in windows and respond to user events. Just as everything drawn on a NeXTSTEP screen is drawn in a window, practically everything drawn inside a window is drawn with the help of **View** objects. For example, the **Slider**, **TextField**, and **Button** classes are all subclasses of the **View** class.

Every window contains at least one view – the *content view*. This view covers the window except for the title bar, resize handles and black border. The window's content view automatically stretches and shrinks with the window when the window is resized.

Every view can have zero, one or more subviews. After a view draws itself, it redraws any of the objects in its subview hierarchy (more on view hierarchies later) whose appearance has been changed or altered. In this way, what is on the NeXTSTEP screen properly corresponds with what is stored in the computer's memory.

The **View** class is one of the most powerful abstractions in the NeXTSTEP Application Kit. Some of its most useful methods are listed below.

View Instance Method	Purpose
addSubview: *aView*	Adds *aView* as a subview to the **View**.
display	Causes the **View** to redisplay itself and all of its subviews by invoking the **drawSelf::** for all of these **View**s.
drawSelf :(const NXRect *)*rects* :(int)*rectCount*	Implemented by subclasses of the **View** class to draw themselves. This single method handles displaying on the NeXTSTEP screen, printing, faxing, and scrolling. It should invoked only by the **display** method, never directly.
findViewWithTag: (int)*aTag*	Searches a **View** and all of its subviews for a given tag.
lockFocus / unlockFocus	Locks/unlocks the PostScript focus on a **View**, so that all future PostScript drawing commands get executed in this **View**. If you are drawing inside a **drawSelf::** method, focus is automatically locked and unlocked for your program (by the **display** method).

View Instance Method	Purpose
printPSCode: *sender*	Tells a **View** to display at Print panel and redirect the PostScript code generated by a redisplay of this **View** – and all of its subviews – to the printer.
subviews	Returns the **List** object that contains all of a **View**'s subviews.
superview	Returns the **id** of a **View**'s superview.
tag	Return's the **View**'s tag. By default, **View**s have a tag of -1, but some **View**s (like **Control**s), allow you to change their tag to distinguish them.
window	Returns the **id** of the **View**'s window.

You can find the rest of the **View** methods using the Librarian or Header-Viewer applications.

Strong Typing with Objective-C

Although the **List** class provides a method called **objectAt:** for accessing elements in a list by number, some NeXTSTEP programmers access the objects inside a **List** object directly for improved performance. To do this, you need to use Objective-C's strong typing facility.

There are two ways that you can specify a variable that holds a pointer to an object in Objective-C. You can use the **id** type to declare a pointer to any kind of object. Alternatively, if you know in advance what kind of object you are going to have, you can construct a pointer to the specific object type specifically by using the object's class name as a type. Thus, a pointer to a **List** object can be declared like this:

```
id aList;
```

or it can be declared like this:

```
List *aList;
```

The second way of declaring **aList** is called *strong* (or *static*) *typing*. Strong typing provides better compiler type-checking and the ability to directly access public variables stored inside the **List** object. An object's public variables are those variables specified after the **@public** declaration. You access those variables with C's *arrow* (**->**) notation, just as if the variable **aList** was a pointer to a structure (which in fact, it is!).

You should generally refrain from using public variables in the classes that you design, because public variables make your objects less modular and more difficult to update without causing future problems. Using public variables also violates the notion of object encapsulation. Public variables are part of the language specification for those few cases when you need the utmost efficiency and speed. We will use them later in the GraphPaper application to access instance variables of an object without having to issue an Objective-C message.

Below are the variable declarations for the **List** class copied from the file **/NextDeveloper/Headers/objc/List.h**:

```
@interface List: Object
{
@public
  id *dataPtr;           /* data of the List object */
  unsigned numElements; /* Actual # of elements */
  unsigned maxElements; /* Total allocated elts. */
}
```

A **List** object has two public variables of interest:

* **dataPtr** – the array that holds the objects' **id**s, and
* **numElements** – the number of elements in the list.

The third variable, **maxElements**, simply holds the maximum number of elements that any particular **List** object can currently hold at location **dataPtr**. You don't normally need to concern yourself with this variable, because the **List** class automatically allocates more memory and relocates the array stored at **dataPtr** as necessary to accommodate the new data.

Just how much faster is accessing **@public** variables directly? On a 25 MHZ 68040 NeXTstation with 20 megabytes of RAM, we found accessing the **List** instance variables approximately 6 times faster than using the **objectAt:** method. Accessing an object with **objectAt:** took approximately 5.6 microseconds, while accessing an object directly took approximately 1 microsecond. So while using those **@public** variables *is* faster, in the big scheme of things it isn't a very significant speedup. Avoid using **@public** variables unless you have an extremely good reason to use them.

Summary

In this chapter we learned about delegation, a system which lets a programmer specify objects that should automatically be sent messages when certain events happen. We used delegation to catch the **Application** object's **appDidInit:** message, which is the standard technique for specifying code that should be run when an application is initialized.

Having done this, we modified our Calculator so that it could change its size using the **placeWindowAndDisplay:** and **sizeWindow::** methods. We then learned a little bit more about **Window** and **View** objects.

In the next chapter, we'll revisit our ongoing discussion of events – the basic data type used by NeXTSTEP to keep track of actions initiated by the user. We'll then see how events are handled by the **Responder** class, the abstract superclass of **Application**, **View**, and **Window** which contains much of the NeXTSTEP event handling mechanism.

8

Events and Responders

We had our first taste of events in Chapter 4, with the **tiny2** program that displayed little circles near the cursor whenever the mouse was clicked in the program's main window. In this chapter we'll learn more about events and the chain of objects that NeXTSTEP uses to respond to events. At the end of the chapter, we'll see how to catch events from the keyboard in our Calculator application.

Events and the Responder Chain

There are seven basic kinds of events with which NeXTSTEP programmers need concern themselves:

- Mouse events – generated by clicking or moving the mouse
- Keyboard events – generated in response to a keypress or release
- Timed events – for actions that happen periodically
- Cursor-Update events – generated when the cursor crosses the boundary of a predefined rectangular area (*tracking rectangle*) in a window
- Kit-Defined events – generated by the Application Kit when a window is moved, resized, exposed, or the application is activated or deactivated

- System-Defined events – generated by the system, for example, when the power is turned off
- Application-Defined events – defined and generated by your application

Of these, the mouse and keyboard events are the most important when writing most applications.

What Is An Event?

Simply put, an event is a message that the Window Server (described below) sends to an application in response to some action taken by the user. Pressing a key on the keyboard generates an event, as does releasing that same key. Pressing the mouse button in a window generates an event, as does releasing the mouse button (and moving the mouse).

The NeXTSTEP *Window Server* is a low-level process running in the background that is responsible for sending events to applications and displaying images on the screen. It isolates you from the particulars of the NeXT computer's hardware. We'll discuss the Window Server in detail in the next chapter.

Events drive applications. Every action that a user takes gets turned into an event by the Window Server and sent to the appropriate application. Each window has an *event mask* that it uses to tell the Window Server which events it wants to receive. Event masks will be described in more detail later.

What actually gets sent to the application is an event record, in the form of an **NXEvent** data structure. The **Application** object stores events in an event queue, a circular data structure which can hold up to 50 events.

The NXEvent Data Structure

When your program receives an event, it is packaged in an **NXEvent** data structure, as follows:

```
typedef struct _NXEvent {
    int type;              /* event type */
    NXPoint location;      /* mouse location */
    long time;             /* time since launch */
    int flags;             /* Shift, Control, Alt */
    unsigned int window;   /* event window number */
    NXEventData data; /* event type-dependent data */
    DPSContext ctxt;  /* event PostScript context */
} NXEvent, *NXEventPtr;
```

You can find this structure in the file **/NextDeveloper/Headers/dpsclient/event.h**. The first field in the structure is a 32-bit number that describes the kind of event that took place. NeXTSTEP supports 31 different kinds of events. The most important (which are also contained in the file **event.h**) are:

```
/* mouse events */
#define NX_LMOUSEDOWN      1    /* left mouse-down */
#define NX_LMOUSEUP        2    /* left mouse-up */
#define NX_RMOUSEDOWN      3    /* right mouse-down */
#define NX_RMOUSEUP        4    /* right mouse-up */
#define NX_MOUSEMOVED      5    /* mouse-moved event */
#define NX_LMOUSEDRAGGED   6    /* left mouse-dragged*/
#define NX_RMOUSEDRAGGED   7    /* right mouse-drag */
#define NX_MOUSEENTERED    8    /* mouse-entered */
#define NX_MOUSEEXITED     9    /* mouse-exited */

/* keyboard events */
#define NX_KEYDOWN         10   /* key-down event */
#define NX_KEYUP           11   /* key-up event */
#define NX_FLAGSCHANGED    12   /* flags-changed */

/* composite events */
#define NX_KITDEFINED      13   /* appkit-defined */
#define NX_SYSDEFINED      14   /* system-defined */
#define NX_APPDEFINED      15   /* app. defined */
#define NX_TIMER           16   /* timer */
#define NX_CURSORUPDATE    17   /* cursor tracking */
#define NX_JOURNALEVENT    18   /* journaling */
```

The **NXEvent** field called **location** is the point in the window's coordinate system where the event took place. You can convert this point from **Window** to **View** coordinates with the **View** method **convertPoint:fromView:** by specifying **nil** as the second argument.

Another important field is **data**, a C language *union* structure that contains the data of the event itself. Here is the definition of the union, also taken from **event.h**:

```
/* EventData type: defines data field of an event */
typedef union {

   struct { /* For mouse-down and mouse-up events */
      short  reserved;
      short  eventNum;/* unique button identifier */
      int    click;  /* click state of this event */
      int    unused;
```

```
      } mouse;

  struct { /* For key-down and key-up events */
    short   reserved;
    short   repeat;  /* nonzero if really a repeat */
    unsigned short charSet;/* character set code */
    unsigned short charCode;/* char code in set */
    unsigned short keyCode;/* device key number */
    short   keyData;   /* device-dependent info */
  } key;

  struct { /* For mouse-entered and mouse-exited */
    short   reserved;
    short   eventNum;    /* unique identifier */
    int     trackingNum; /* unique identifier */
    int     userData;    /* uninterpreted integer */
  } tracking;

  struct {
  /* For appkit-defined, sys-defined, app-defined
   * events
   */
    short     reserved;
    short     subtype; /* event subtype */
    union {
      float   F[2];  /* for compound events */
      long    L[2];  /* for compound events */
      short   S[4];  /* for compound events */
      char    C[8];  /* for compound events */
    } misc;
  } compound;

} NXEventData;
```

Normally you'll use this **data** field in methods that respond to keypress events to find out which key was pressed. That information is contained in the union element **data.key.charCode**. You can tell if the key press was an actual keypress or a repeat (caused by holding down the key) by looking at the element **data.key.repeat**.

Events and the Application Object

The NeXTSTEP **Application** object receives events from the Window Server and automatically translates them from event numbers into **Responder** methods. (**Responder** is the abstract superclass which contains the event responding mechanism of NeXTSTEP.) The following **Responder** methods are defined in the file **/NextDeveloper/Headers/app-kit/Responder.h**:

```
- mouseDown: (NXEvent *)theEvent;
- rightMouseDown: (NXEvent *)theEvent;
- mouseUp: (NXEvent *)theEvent;
- rightMouseUp: (NXEvent *)theEvent;
- mouseMoved: (NXEvent *)theEvent;
- mouseDragged: (NXEvent *)theEvent;
- rightMouseDragged: (NXEvent *)theEvent;
- mouseEntered: (NXEvent *)theEvent;
- mouseExited: (NXEvent *)theEvent;
- keyDown: (NXEvent *)theEvent;
- keyUp: (NXEvent *)theEvent;
- (BOOL)performKeyEquivalent: (NXEvent *)theEvent;
```

After the event is translated into a **Responder** method, it is sent to the appropriate window:

Responder method	Sent Where?
mouseDown: and **rightMouseDown:**	Sent to the window where the mouse down event occurred.
mouseUp: and **rightMouseUp:**	Sent to the window where the original mouse down event occurred.
mouseDragged: and **rightMouseDragged:**	Sent to the window where the mouse down event occurred.
mouseEntered:	Sent to the object specified when the tracking rectangle is created (see Chapter 18).
mouseExited:	Sent to the object specified when the tracking rectangle is created (see Chapter 18).
keyDown:	Sent to the *key* window.

Responder method	Sent Where?
keyUp:	Sent to the window that received the **keyDown:** event.
performKeyEquivalent:	Sent to every window that is of the **Panel** subclass.

Notice that the **Responder** methods all have the **NXEvent** structure as their only argument; this is the same **NXEvent** structure that the Window Server passes to the **Application** object, unmodified. No **Responder** (your own **View**s included) should ever change the contents of this structure.

Responders and the Responder Chain

The **View**, **Window**, and **Application** classes are all subclasses of the NeXTSTEP class called **Responder**. **Responder** is the main class for handling events. It's an *abstract superclass* because its functionality is used via instances of subclasses of **Responder**, rather than instances of **Responder** itself.

The **Responder** class declares a single instance variable called **nextResponder**, an **id** which points to another object. When a **Responder** object receives an event, such as a **mouseDown:** or a **keyDown:**, it tries to process the event. If it cannot do anything with the event, the **Responder** sends the event to its **nextResponder**. This forwarding happens automatically if a **Responder** subclass doesn't implement a particular **Responder** method, or if the method returns the value **nil**.

Application and **Window** objects contain their own instance variables (in addition to the **nextResponder** instance variable inherited from **Responder**) for the processing of keyboard events. An **Application** object contains an **id** pointer called **keyWindow**, which points to the window that is currently receiving keyboard events. A **Window** object contains an **id** pointer called **firstResponder**, which points to the **View** object inside the window that should be sent keyboard events when they are received from the **Application** object.

These linked **Responder**s are often called the *event* or *responder chain*. Graphically it looks like the diagram in Figure 1 below.

FIGURE 1. **Responder Chain of Events**

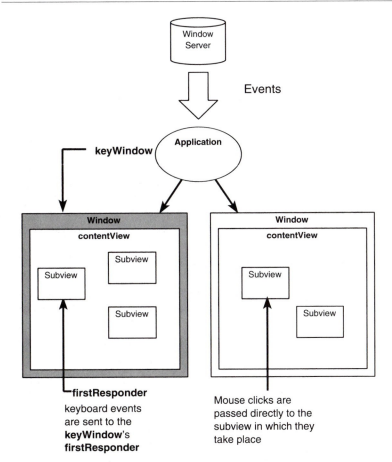

Mouse Event Handling

Here's what happens when you press a mouse button when the cursor is in a window:

(i)   The Window Server sends the **NXEvent** data structure for the event to your program's **Application** object.

(ii)   The **Application** object sends a **mouseDown:** message (with the same **NXEvent** structure as the argument) to the **Window** object which controls the window in which the cursor was located when the mouse press occurred.

(iii) The **Window** object uses the **hitTest:** message to determine the *subview* (i.e., the **View** object inside the window) in which the cursor was located when the mouse press occurred.

At this point, what follows depends on if the window is the key window or not.

(iv) If the window is already the key window, then the event gets sent to the subview where the mouse press occurred; or

If the window is not the key window, it makes itself the key window. It then sends the **acceptsFirstMouse** message to the subview. If the subview returns **YES**, the event is sent to it. If the view returns **NO**, no further processing takes place on the event.

Some **View**s, such as **Button** objects, accept the first mouse click. Thus you can click a button in a window (and have it do something) even when the window is not the key window. Other **View**s, such as the **Text** object, do not accept the first mouse click. This means that you must first click in the window to make it the key window before you can successfully click on an object inside the window. This prevents the cursor from moving inside a **Text** object in a window when you click in the window. As an example, try the following in the Edit application: open a file in Edit, activate another application, and then click in the Edit window. The cursor does not move to where you clicked because the **Text** object inside the Edit window returns **NO** when sent the **acceptsFirstMouse** message from the window.

If the **Window** object sends the event to the subview, the following additional processing takes place:

(v) If the subview cannot process the event, it sends the event to its **nextResponder**. The **nextResponder** of a **View** object is by default its superview – the **View** that contains the **View** receiving the event.

(vi) Inevitably, if none of the subviews can process the mouse click, it gets sent to the **Window**'s contentView. If the contentView cannot process the event, the event gets sent to *the contentView's* **nextResponder** – the Window itself.

For the most part, all of this handling of responders and first responders is automatic – you don't have to worry about it unless you are trying to do something non-standard.

Mouse events other than **mouseDown:** are handled a little differently. The **mouseUp:** event is sent to the **View** object that was sent the corresponding **mouseDown:** event, regardless of the position of the mouse when the button is released. This lets buttons that have been pressed know when they are released.

The **mouseEntered:** and **mouseExited:** events are sent to the "owner" object specified by the **setTrackingRect:inside:owner:tag:left:right:** message (more on these methods in Chapter 18). The **mouseMoved:** and **mouseDragged:** events are different from other events because they are sent continuously, and therefore tend to "drag" down the system performance. Use them only when necessary. (You can usually get around the need to catch **mouseMoved:** or **mouseDragged:** events by overriding other methods in the **Cell** or **Control** classes, or by creating your own modal loops.)

Keyboard Event Handling

Keyboard events are handled differently from mouse events because a keypress doesn't correspond to a particular point on the screen. Here's what happens when you press a key:

(i)   The Window Server sends the **NXEvent** data structure for the keyboard event to the active application's **Application** object.

At this point, what happens depends on whether or not a Command key is pressed (down). We'll continue our discussion assuming that a Command key is not down, and discuss the case when a Command key is down a bit later.

(ii)   Assuming that both Command keys are up, the **Application** object sends the **keyDown:** message to the **Window** object controlling the *key* window (via the **Application** object's **keyWindow** instance variable).

(iii)   The **Window** object that receives the **keyDown:** message sends the message to the window's **firstResponder**, which is usually a **View** that can handle keyboard events.

(iv)   If the **firstResponder** cannot handle the keyboard event, it sends the event to its **nextResponder**.

(v)   The **nextResponder** of the **Window**'s content **View** is the **Window** itself. If the keyboard event is returned to the **Window**, the computer's system beep is played.

On the other hand, if the Command key is down, the **Application** object sends the **commandKey:** message to every **Panel** object (including menus) in its window list, until one of the **Panel** returns YES. If one of the **Panel** returns YES, then the **Panel** translates the **commandKey:** message into a **performKeyEquivalent:** message for its **View**s. The **performKeyEquivalent:** message is then passed down the view hierarchy until it is sent to a **View** which will respond to the message. This is how NeXTSTEP makes tear-off menus work.

An Event Handling Example

Suppose you select two ASCII files (e.g., **Controller.h** and **Controller.m**) in your Workspace File Viewer and double-click the hand-of-cards icon to open the files in the Edit application. Two windows will be displayed and one will be the key window, say the one containing **Controller.h** (see Figure 2 below). If you then press a key, say "k," a keyboard event will be sent to the **Controller.h** window because it is the key window. Initially the key window is its own first responder, but it can't respond to this keyboard event message so the system beep will sound.

FIGURE 2. **Event Handling in Edit**

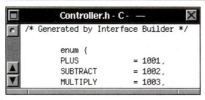

Now click anywhere inside the white **Text** object area in the **Controller.h** window and a cursor will appear at the location where you clicked. With this click you have made the **Text** object the first responder, and the **Window**'s **firstResponder** instance variable will be set accordingly. If you press the "k" key again, then a "k" will appear at the cursor location.

After you clicked in the **Text** object area, the **Window** sends the **acceptsFirstResponder** message to ask the **Text** object whether it wants to become the first responder. If the text displayed by a **Text** object is *editable* or *selectable*, as it is in Edit windows, then the **Text** object answers **YES**. The **Text** object's **acceptsFirstResponder** method would look something like this:

```
- (BOOL) acceptsFirstResponder
{
    return YES;
}
```

After the **Text** object answers **YES**, the **Window** tries to make it the first responder by sending the **makeFirstResponder:** message to itself (**self**) with a pointer to the **Text** object as the argument. The **makeFirstResponder:** method sends the **resignFirstResponder** message to the current first responder. If the current first responder refuses to relinquish its role, then it returns **nil** and the first responder doesn't change. In this example the **Window** is the current first responder and it returns **self**, which means that it will relinquish its role as first responder.

The **makeFirstResponder:** method then sends the **becomeFirstResponder** message to the potentially new first responder (the **Text** object). If an object refuses to become the first responder, then it returns **nil** and the **Window** again becomes the first responder. In this example the **Text** object returns **self**, which means that it will take on the first responder role. The **Window**'s **makeFirstResponder:** method finally sets the **firstResponder** instance variable to point to the **Text** object.

Now suppose you click in the **Text** object in the (other) **Window** object, the one displaying the **Controller.m** file contents. It receives a mouse-down event from Edit's **Application** object and becomes the key window. If you then press the "k" key, you will hear the system beep again because this **Window** is the first responder. A second click in the **Text** object area will make it the first responder and a cursor will appear.

The **Text** object uses the methods **becomeFirstResponder** and **resignFirstResponder** to control the display of the text cursor that is displayed at the point of entry. When it receives a **becomeFirstResponder** it displays the cursor; when it receives the **resignFirstResponder** message it erases it.

Action Messages and the Responder Chain

When we described how target and actions work in Interface Builder, we weren't entirely truthful. We said that if you specify a target and action for a button, the button sends that action message to that target. For example, when we connected the slider to the text field in Chapter 3 as in Figure 3 below, we said that the slider sent the **takeFloatValueFrom:** message to the **TextFieldCell**.

This isn't exactly true. Instead of having the **Slider** object send the message directly to the **TextField** object, NeXTSTEP uses **Control**'s **sendAction:to:** method to send the message (**Slider** is a subclass of **Control** and therefore inherits the **sendAction:to:** method). The reason for this is to allow some actions to be *context sensitive* – to change their behavior depending on which **View** and **Window** are currently selected.

FIGURE 3. Slider to Text Connection

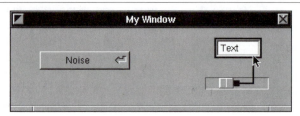

For example, suppose you had a simple window with three text fields, as in Figure 4 below. Suppose also that you chose the **Edit→Cut** menu command. NeXTSTEP needs some way of sending the **cut:** action message to the object containing the piece of text that you've selected. If the **Cut** menu cell had a specific target, say the first field, then the **cut:** message would often get sent to the wrong place.

FIGURE 4. Three Text Fields in a Window

If you look at the target of the **Cut** menu cell within Interface Builder, you'll see that it has been set to the **First Responder** icon (see Figure 5 below). Furthermore, if you look at the Connections Inspector in Figure 6

FIGURE 5. First Responder as a Target of an Action

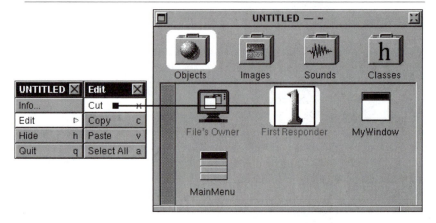

below, you'll see a wide choice of actions to which a **First Responder** object can respond. This is all especially confusing because *there is no First Responder class*. We describe what is happening below.

FIGURE 6. **Actions of the First Responder**

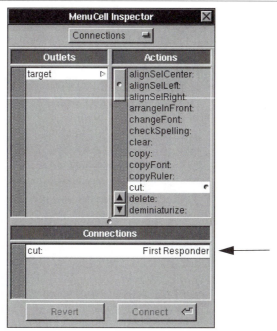

Interface Builder's target-action connections are implemented by the NeXTSTEP **ActionCell** class. The **ActionCell** class has an instance variable called **target** that holds the **id** of the object being sent the message, and an instance variable called **action** that holds an Objective-C encoding of the action method. Part of the Objective-C interface of the **ActionCell** class is shown below:

```
@interface ActionCell : Cell
{
    int     tag;
    id      target;
    SEL     action;
    id      _view;
}
```

If the **target** of an action message is **nil**, the **Control** object's **sendAction:to:** method determines an appropriate receiver for the action by checking a variety of objects. In order, the **Control** object:

(i) Begins with the **firstResponder** of the key window and follows the responder chain (via **nextResponder**s) to the **Window** object, searching for a **View** that can respond to the specific action.

(ii) If none of those **View**s can respond, the **Window**'s delegate object is checked to see if it can respond.

(iii) If the main window is different from the key window, the **Application** object checks the main window's responder chain and the main window's delegate.

(iv) If none of those views and delegates can respond to the action, the **Application** object tries to send the message to the **Application** object itself (**NXApp**) and, finally, to the **Application**'s delegate.

The search continues until an object is found that implements the action method, and the action method returns a value other than **nil**. If no object handles the message, the message is ignored.

Interface Builder's list of first responder methods in the Connections Inspector aren't defined anywhere: Interface Builder simply starts you off with the methods that NeXT thinks you'll need. You're free to add your own whenever you want (we'll do it in a later chapter).

Other Kinds of Events

Other kinds of events are processed in slightly different ways. *Window-moved*, *window-resized*, and *window-exposed* events are sent directly to the **Window** object associated with the event. The remaining NeXTSTEP events (application-defined events, system-defined events, timer events, cursor-update events, application-activate, and application-deactivate events) are handled directly by the **Application** object.

The Event Loop

Other than the **tiny.m** program in Chapter 4, we have not written a **main()** function for any of our NeXTSTEP applications. That's because, as we saw in "The Files in a Project" on page 159, Interface Builder automatically generates the **main()** function for its application.

Let's again look at the **Calculator_main.m** file, which contains the **main()** function used by our Calculator application.

```
#import <appkit/Application.h>

void main(int argc, char *argv[]) {

  NXApp = [Application new];
  if ([NXApp loadNibSection:"Calculator.nib"
      owner:NXApp withNames:NO])
    [NXApp run];

  [NXApp free];
  exit(0);
}
```

The first line in the **main()** function creates an instance of the **Application** object. The second line loads the nib section **Calculator.nib** from the executable, specifying the newly-created **Application** object as the nib's owner. (This is why Interface Builder uses the phrase **File's Owner** instead of **Application** in its File window: it's possible that something other than an **Application** object is specified in the **loadNibSection:ownerwith-Names:** method.)

The third line is the most important of all for events. It sends the **run** message to the **Application** object, **NXApp**. That's where a lot of the magic of NeXTSTEP begins.

The Application Event Loop

When the **Application** object receives the **run** message it starts the object's main event loop. The event loop is a section of code that reads events and performs appropriate functions for those events. This is the primary place where the **Application** object receives events from the Window Server. The event loop runs until the **Application** object gets sent a **stop:** or a **terminate:** message. A **stop:** message causes the **run** method to stop and control is returned to the caller. A **terminate:** message causes the application to quit gracefully and control is never returned to the caller.

The **Application** main event loop program does the following:

• If there is an event waiting, get it and process it.

• If there is a timed entry pending, execute it.

• If there is data received at a watched Mach port, read it and call the appropriate function.

- If there is data pending at a watched file descriptor, read it and call the appropriate function.

- Repeat until the **stop:** message is received.

The most common way of breaking out of the **Application**'s main event loop is by sending a **terminate:** message to **NXApp**. Here's what happens when the **terminate:** message is received:

(i)   If the **NXApp** object has a delegate that implements the **appWillTerminate:** message, this message is sent to the delegate.

(ii)   If the delegate's **appWillTerminate:** message returns **nil**, the **terminate:** method is aborted, and the main event loop continues to run.

(iii)   Otherwise, the application is terminated.

The fact that NeXTSTEP handles the main event loop for the programmer is one of the primary differences between programming in NeXTSTEP and programming in other window-based environments. By handling most events automatically, the programmer is freed from this tedious task, which in turn makes programs behave in a more reliable and unified fashion.

Nevertheless, NeXTSTEP does allow you to write your own event loop or take over the event loop while something out-of-the-ordinary is happening. Typically you would do this for a special purpose that isn't handled well by the Application Kit. For example, Interface Builder uses its own event loop when you Control-drag a connection from one object to another; the event loop exits when the mouse button is released.

You can use the NeXTSTEP function **NXGetOrPeekEvent()** or the **Application** method **getNextEvent:** to construct your own event loop. Both of these read the next event from the event queue. If you construct your own loop, you should be sure to set the event mask so that your event loop only receives the events that it wants. The other events will be saved until the main application event loop is running again.

Catching Keyboard Events for the Calculator

In the remainder of this chapter we'll make our Calculator easier to use by taking advantage of our new knowledge of events and the responder chain. The goal will be to let the user type digit keys on the keyboard instead of clicking buttons in the Calculator's window.

Subclassing the Window Class

We're going to accomplish our goal by subclassing the **Window** class to form a new class called **CalcWindow** and changing the class of our Calculator window to **CalcWindow**. Subclassing the **Window** class is a clever way to catch keyboard events that are not otherwise used by the application. (The key window is the ultimate recipient of any unused keyboard events since the **nextResponder** of a window's content **View** is the window itself.)

In addition to catching the keyboard events, a **CalcWindow** object needs to know what to do with them. To accomplish this, a **CalcWindow** object will scan the window for all buttons and make a table of each button that has a title consisting of a single character. Each time the **CalcWindow** object receives a keyboard event, it will consult this table to determine if there is a corresponding button that should act as if it has been "clicked."

The first step is to subclass the **Window** class in Interface Builder.

1. Open your Calculator project in Project Builder (PB) by double-clicking the **PB.project** file in the **Calculator** project directory.

2. Open your project's main nib in Interface Builder (IB) by double-clicking **Calculator.nib** in PB's Files view (under the **Interfaces** file type).

3. Select the **Window** class (under **Responder**) in the **Calculator.nib** File window (Classes view) and then drag to **Subclass** in the **Operations** pull-down list. Give this new subclass the name **CalcWindow**.

Next we'll change the class of the Calculator window to **CalcWindow**.

4. Select the main window titled "Calculator" in IB. To do this, click in its background or click its icon ("MyWindow") in the File window (Objects view) to avoid selecting an object in the window.

5. If necessary, type Command-1 to view the Window Attributes Inspector.

6. Click **CalcWindow** in the Window Attributes Inspector to change the Calculator window's class to **CalcWindow**, as in Figure 7 below.

7. Make sure the **CalcWindow** class is selected in IB's File window (Classes view) and then choose the **Unparse** operation from the **Operations** pull-down list.

FIGURE 7. Changing the Class of a Window

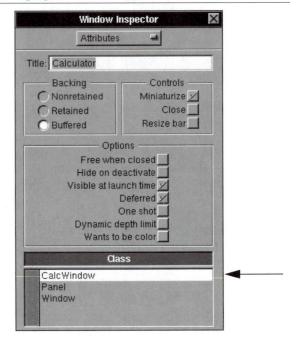

This step saves us a bit of typing by creating the skeleton **CalcWindow.h** and **CalcWindow.m** files in the project directory. There are no instance variables or methods in the files because we didn't specify any in IB. This step also adds the **CalcWindow** class to the project in Project Builder, something we'd have to do anyway.

Hash Tables

We will use a **HashTable** object to determine if incoming keyboard events match a button in the window. The **HashTable** class is provided by NeXT as an Objective-C common class. A **HashTable** object stores *key and value pairs*. When you store a *value* in a **HashTable** object, you provide a *key*. Later, when you present the **HashTable** object with the same *key*, you get the *value* back. Both the *key* and *value* can be any 32-bit value, including **id**, **int**, **void** * and **char** *. (To hash strings, you must use the **NXUniqueString()** function to turn the string into a unique 32-bit number.)

To implement the **CalcWindow** class, we'll use keyboard characters as the hash *keys* and the **id**s of the associated buttons as the *values*. To build the hash table, the **CalcWindow** object will search for all of the buttons contained in the window that have a single character title. The value stored in the hash table will be the **id** of the button.

Searching for Button Titles in the Calculator Window

In this section we'll implement the methods in the **CalcWindow** class that search for **Button** object titles and build a **HashTable** object as described above.

8.   Open the **CalcWindow.h** class interface file in your favorite editor and insert the five lines in **bold** below.[1]

```
#import <appkit/appkit.h>

@interface CalcWindow:Window
{
    id keyTable;
}

- findButtons;
- checkView:aView;
- checkButton:aButton;
- checkMatrix:aMatrix;
@end
```

The **keyTable** instance variable will point to the **HashTable** object. We'll use the four new methods to search the Calculator window for all of the buttons, as follows:

Method	Purpose
findButtons	Start searching the window's content **View**.
checkView: *aView*	Search *aView* object. If a **Button** object is found, check it with **checkButton:**. If a **Matrix** is found, check all of its buttons with **checkMatrix:**. If a subview is found, check it *recursively* with **checkView:**.

---

1. The only *required* imports are shown below. See **CalcWindow.m** for details.
#import <appkit/Matrix.h>
#import <appkit/Button.h>
#import <objc/HashTable.h>
#import <objc/List.h>
#import <NXCType.h>

Method	Purpose
checkButton: *aButton*	Check *abutton* to see if it has a single-character title. If so, add the button to the **HashTable** object with the title as its *key*.
checkMatrix: *aMatrix*	Check each of the buttons inside *aMatrix* by repeatedly invoking the **checkButton:** method.

Now we'll describe the implementations of each of these **CalcWindow** methods in detail. The **findButtons** method simply empties the **HashTable** object (**keyTable**) and then invokes the **checkView:** method for the window's **contentView** to set up the **HashTable**.

```
- findButtons
{
  /* check all the views recursively */
  [keyTable empty];
  [self checkView:contentView];
  return self;
}
```

The **checkView:** method is more interesting. It can be invoked with any **View** in the window as its argument and checks to see if the **View** is of the **Matrix** class, **Button** class, or neither. If the **View** is of the **Matrix** or **Button** class, **checkView:** invokes the **checkMatrix:** or the **checkButton:** method (respectively). Otherwise, **checkView:** gets the list of subviews for the **View** passed and invokes itself recursively for each one (yes, methods may invoke themselves recursively). In this manner, all of the **View**s in the window are processed. We need separate methods to check the **Matrix** and **Button** classes because the cells stored inside these objects are not subviews (because cells are not views). Here is the **checkView:** method:

```
- checkView:aView
{
  id  subViews    = [aView subviews];
  int numSubViews = [subViews count];
  int i;

/* Process the view if it's a Matrix or a Button. */
  if ([aView isKindOf: [Matrix class] ]) {
    return [self checkMatrix: aView];
  }

  if ([aView isKindOf: [Button class] ]) {
```

```
      return [self checkButton: aView];
    }

/* Recursively check all the subviews. */
    for (i=0; i<numSubViews; i++) {
      [self checkView:[subViews objectAt:i] ];
    }
    return self;
}
```

The **checkView:** method sends the **isKindof:** message to the **aView** object (**Matrix**, **Button**, or other) that is passed as an argument to determine its class. (The **class** factory method forces a *class object* to return its **id**.) If the **aView** object is of the **Matrix** or **Button** class then the **checkMatrix:** or **checkButton:** method is invoked. If not, then the **checkView:** method recursively invokes itself for all of the subviews contained within the **View**. Actually, the objects that are passed to **checkView:** are instances of *sub-classes* of the **View** class, not instances of **View** itself. But since they inherit from the **View** class we still refer to them as **View**s.

The **checkButton:** method checks a button to see if its title is a single character. If it is, the button is stored in the **keyTable** object (which is a **HashTable** object that we'll create when the **CalcWindow** object is initialized, as we'll see a bit later).

```
- checkButton:aButton
{
  const char *title = [aButton title];

/* Check for a cell that has a title that's exactly
 * one character long. Insert both uppercase and
 * lowercase versions for the user's convenience.
 */
  if (title && strlen(title)==1 &&
      [aButton tag] != 0x0c) { /* "c" for Clear */
    [keyTable insertKey: (void *)NXToLower(title[0])
            value: aButton];
    [keyTable insertKey: (void *)NXToUpper(title[0])
            value: aButton];
  }
  return self;
}
```

This method uses the **HashTable** instance method **insertKey:value:** to insert the button's **id**, namely **aButton**, into the **HashTable** object. The *key* is the single-character title of the button.

The **checkMatrix:** method checks all of the **Button** objects in a **Matrix**. **Matrix** objects must be checked separately because the **Button**s that they contain are not subviews of the **Matrix**. No doubt, this is done for performance reasons. It complicates our task, but not by much.

```
- checkMatrix:aMatrix
{
  id  cellList = [aMatrix cellList];
  int numCells = [cellList count];
  int i;

  for (i=0; i<numCells; i++) {
    [self checkButton: [cellList objectAt:i] ];
  }
  return self;
}
```

First this method gets the list of cells (**Button**s, in our example) that are contained in the **Matrix**. Then it invokes the **checkButton:** method for each one. Now we have the four methods we need to set up the **HashTable** object with *key-value* pairs.

Finishing Off the CalcWindow Class Implementation

The **CalcWindow** class requires two additional methods in order to work properly. The first is the method that actually handles the key-down events. The other is the method that initializes the **HashTable** object.

```
- keyDown:(NXEvent *)theEvent
{
  id button;

  button = [keyTable valueForKey:
          (void *)(int)theEvent->data.key.charCode];

  if (button) {
    return [button performClick:self];
  }
  return [super keyDown:theEvent];
}
```

This method is invoked only when a keyboard event is not otherwise handled by the **Responder** chain. It sends the **valueForKey:** message to the **HashTable** object (**keyTable**) to obtain the **id** for the **Button** whose title the same as the keyboard character (**data.key.charCode**) that was typed.

If no such **HashTable** *key* exists, **valueForKey:** returns **nil** and **keyDown:** passes the original message to its **super**(class), **Window**, so **Window** can handle the event. If the *key* does exist, then the **keyDown:** method sends the **performClick:** message to the **Button** whose **id** is stored for the *key*. The **performClick:** message causes the **Button** target object to perform as if it had been clicked. The message is not sent if the on-screen button is disabled.

Lastly, we need to set up an initialization method – the method that gets invoked automatically when the **CalcWindow** object is created and sets up the **HashTable** object.

Normally, we create initialization methods by simply overriding the **init** method. The difficulty in creating the initialization method for **CalcWindow** is that there are several different **Window** initialization methods from which to choose. If you use look in the **Window** class documentation or the file **/NextDeveloper/Headers/appkit/Window.h** (use the HeaderViewer application), you'll find the following three initialization methods:

```
- init

- initContent:(const NXRect *)contentRect
  style:(int)aStyle
  backing:(int)bufferingType
  buttonMask:(int)mask
  defer:(BOOL)flag;

- initContent:(const NXRect *)contentRect
  style:(int)aStyle
  backing:(int)bufferingType
  buttonMask:(int)mask
  defer:(BOOL)flag
  screen:(const NXScreen *)aScreen;
```

One of these methods is the designated initializer of the **Window** class. The *designated initializer* is the one initialization method that is guaranteed to be called by all of the other initialization methods. Thus, if you subclass a class, you need only write a method for the designated initializer method to catch all initialization events.

But which method is the designated initializer? Normally, it's the method that has the most arguments. But the **Window** class is different. The designated initializer is the second method listed. That's because the **initContent:style:backing:buttonMask:defer:** method was designated as the designated initializer before NeXTSTEP supported multiple screens (see the **screen:** argument in the last initialization method).

We discussed the **initContent:style:backing:buttonMask:defer:** method in detail in the section "Windows, Menus, and the demo() Function" on page 103. Below we override this method to create and initialize the **CalcWindow**.

```
- initContent:(const NXRect *)contentRect
    style:(int)aStyle
    backing:(int)bufferingType
    buttonMask:(int)mask
    defer:(BOOL)flag
{
  keyTable = [ [HashTable alloc] initKeyDesc:"i"];
  return [super initContent: contentRect
              style:       aStyle
              backing:     bufferingType
              buttonMask:  mask
              defer:       flag];
}
```

All this method does is to create a **HashTable** object (**keyTable**) with integer ("**i**") *keys* and then sends the identical message to its superclass (**Window**) to actually do the work of initializing the **CalcWindow** object. This method is invoked automatically whenever an instance of the **CalcWindow** class is created.[1]

Now it's time to put all this code into the **Calculator.m** file.

9.   Insert the code we've discussed above into **CalcWindow.m**. In particular, insert the *implementations* of the following *six* methods:

```
findButtons
checkView:
checkButton:
checkMatrix:
```

---

1. The keyTable could have been created on-demand in the **findButtons** method with a piece of code like this:
```
if(!keyTable){
    keyTable = [[HashTable alloc] initKeyDesc:"i"];
}
```
This style of on-demand allocation of resources is called *lazy allocation*. Using lazy allocation generally improves performance, because it defers creating objects until they are needed (recall our discussion of separate nib files). If they never are needed, they never get created. "It is always a good thing and something that developers should be encouraged to do," says NeXT's Ali Ozer.

We didn't use *lazy allocation* in our example because the **findButtons** method was already complicated enough, and because we wanted to show how to create a designed initializer for the **CalcWindow** subclass.

```
keyDown:
initContent:style:backing:buttonMask:defer:
```

Changes in the Controller Class

Lastly, we need to make a change to our Calculator's **Controller** class so that it invokes the **findButtons** method in the **CalcWindow** object to set up the **HashTable** object.

10. Insert the changes in **bold** below in **Controller.m**. Make sure you also delete the *triple*-nested message in the current **appDidInit:** method.

```
#import "Controller.h"
#import "CalcWindow.h"

@implementation Controller(ApplicationDelegate)

-appDidInit:sender
{
    id kwin = [keyPad window];

    [self setRadix:radixMatrix];
    [self clearAll:self];

    [ [kwin contentView] getFrame: &originalViewSize];
    [kwin findButtons];

    return self;
}
@end
```

The triple-nested message to get the **originalViewSize** has been simplified to a double-nested message because **kwin** already stores the **id** of the **Window** containing the **keyPad**.

11. Save all pertinent files and **make** and run your Calculator application.

12. If you press a number key on the keyboard, the corresponding button on the screen will highlight (due to **performClick:**) and the number will appear in the Calculator's readout text display area. Note also that you can use the symbols on the keyboard such as the plus ("**+**") and equals ("**=**") keys instead of clicking those buttons.

If your Calculator doesn't work properly, make sure that you've properly subclassed the Calculator's **Window** and properly set up the **CalcWindow** class definition.

Summary

In this chapter, we took a close look at events and the responder chain, and saw how they interact with the **Window** object. We'll periodically revisit these topics throughout the rest of the book, looking more closely at how events interact with the **View** class.

This chapter also marks the end of the evolution of our Calculator application. In the following chapter, we'll learn more about the system software that underlies NeXTSTEP. Then in Chapter 10 we'll start on a new application – *MathPaper* – which we'll use to learn about interprocess communication and controlling multiple main windows.

OSSoftware

9

Mach and the Window Server

If you've never worked with a multitasking operating system before, things may be getting a little confusing. How can you test your program by running it, when there's already at least two other programs, the editor and Interface Builder, running on your computer? How come we never need to worry about how much memory is left on the computer? And how is it that the computer can do more than one thing at a time? The answer to all of these question can be found in a single word: Mach.

The Mach Operating System

The NeXTSTEP environment is built "on top of" the Mach operating system, which was developed in the mid 1980s at Carnegie Mellon University. An *operating system* is the master control program that loads and runs other programs and controls a computer's input and output systems such as the keyboard, display, and disk drives. *Multitasking operating systems*, like Mach, allow more than one program to run at the same time on the same computer: the operating system automatically arbitrates between the various programs that are waiting to run, letting one program run for a few milliseconds, then another, then another. Each program gets its own *time slice* of system resources.

In addition to dividing the CPU between different programs that want to run, the operating system divides up the computer's memory and controls access to the computer's input and output devices. For example, the operating system makes sure that mouse events get sent to the correct program, even if more than one program is prepared to receive mouse events at a given instant.

Another important function of the operating system is to prevent running programs from interfering with each other. This is called *memory protection*. Without such protection, a wayward program could affect other programs or other users, could delete important files, or could even "crash" the entire computer system (users of the Apple Macintosh and PCs running DOS or MS-Windows are used to frequent crashes).

Conceptually, the NeXTSTEP Mach operating system consists of several parts which we'll describe in the following sections.

The Microprocessor

As of this writing, most computers running NeXTSTEP use the Motorola 68040 microprocessor, or central processing unit (CPU), to read and execute instructions and read and process data from the computer's memory. But since very little of Mach and NeXTSTEP are written in the 68040's native *assembly language*, NeXTSTEP can easily be ported to other microprocessors simply by recompiling the system and rewriting a small number of device drivers. Soon you should be able to get NeXTSTEP for computers based on the Intel 486 microprocessor (as well as others, we believe). This book, like the NeXTSTEP application development environment, is hardware independent; the information in it applies to NeXTSTEP running on any platform.

The Mach Microkernel

The Mach operating system consists of a small *microkernel* and a system support environment. One layer up from the hardware, the Mach microkernel manages the computer's memory and schedules computing time for the various programs that are ready to run.

The microkernel implements *virtual memory*, a system that uses the computer's hard disk to simulate a much larger block of random-access memory (RAM). Virtual memory is transparent to running programs (although it can slow them down considerably). A program that needs a 10 megabyte block of memory simply allocates a 10 megabyte block of memory; the microkernel automatically shuffles data from the computer's internal memory to the hard disk and back, as necessary. This is called *swapping* or *paging*.

The Mach microkernel oversees the creation of processes, or running programs. Mach further allows each process to create additional "lightweight" processes, called *threads,* which run independently of each other but run within the same program. Threads simplify writing programs which do more than one thing at the same time.

Mach also provides a highly-efficient system of interprocess communication using *Mach messages.* Messages can be sent from one thread to another, between processes, or even from one computer to another across the network.

The Mach microkernel is much smaller than traditional operating system kernels. Traditional operating system functions, like managing the file system, are performed by special-purpose programs called *servers* (not to be confused with special-purpose computers on a network). This allows for greater modularity, a more consistent programming interface, and the ability to configure a system without having to build a new kernel. For further information concerning Mach, see the NeXTSTEP *Operating System Software* manual.

The Mach System Support Environment

Sitting on top of the Mach microkernel is the operating system support environment, which provides UNIX 4.3BSD (Berkeley Software Distribution) compatibility. The Berkeley UNIX emulation provides NeXTSTEP with the UNIX file system (UFS) to manage files stored on the computer's hard disk and floppy disks, transparent networking (TCP/IP), support for the network file system (NFS), and a variety of other important features.

NeXTSTEP's UNIX environment also contains all of the device drivers for managing the computer's hardware devices, including the keyboard, the screen, the serial ports and the SCSI bus. UNIX is an intimate part of NeXTSTEP, and it is therefore important to understand how it manages users and processes.

Usernames and UIDs

Everyone who uses a computer running NeXTSTEP has a *username*. When you log in, your *username* gets translated into a unique number called your *user identifier*, or *UID*. (If you don't have to log into your NeXTSTEP computer in order to use it, then you are using the **me** account with no password.)

UNIX also uses some special system "users" for a variety of special purposes. There is **root**, also called the *super user*, which performs accounting and low-level system functions. The **uucp** user manages the UUCP (UNIX to UNIX copy) system. These users are not actually people who log in, but merely different UIDs used to run *daemons* (background processes - nothing evil about them) with different kinds of privileges.

If you use several different computers running NeXTSTEP on the same network, you should have the same UID on each of those computers, or else the Network File System (NFS) will not work properly. (Note, however, that it is *not* necessary that you have the same *username* on each of these systems.) Normally, this administrative task is taken care of by the NeXTSTEP *NetInfo* (network administrative information) system.

Processes, PIDs, and UIDs

Mach is a multitasking operating system. Every task that the computer performs at any given moment (such as the Window Server, the Preferences application, the Edit application) has an associated *process*. The process is the operating system's fundamental tool for controlling the computer. Normally, you can think of the terms *process* and *running program* as synonymous. But be careful: you can run more than one copy of a program at a time, in which case you would have only one program but *two* (or more) processes.

The Mach kernel assigns every running process a unique number called the *process identifier*, or *PID*. The first process that runs when the computer starts up is called **init**; this process is given the number 1. Any process can *fork*, and by doing, create a new process. All off the processes on your computer are descendents of process number 1.

Mach process numbers can range from 1 to 65535; the microkernel guarantees that no two active processes will ever have the same number.

Mach-O: The Mach Object File Format

NeXTSTEP stores object code and executable files in the Mach-O object file format. A complete description of the object file format resides in the **loader.h**, **nlist.h**, **stab.h**, and **reloc.h** include files in the **/NextDeveloper/Headers/mach-o/** directory. What follows is only a very brief description.

A typical NeXTSTEP program consists of a single Mach-O file which is made up of many *segments*. Each segment has a unique name. Segments are further subdivided into *sections*, which are again individually named. You can think of segments as directories and sections as files, all stored within a single Mach-O file.

Each Mach-O segment is used to store a different kind of data. The table below lists some of the segment names used by NeXTSTEP; you can also create your own.

Segment Name	Content
__PAGEZERO	Page 0 setup information for the Mach executable
__TEXT	680x0 executable code
__DATA	Program data and constants
__OBJC	Objective-C class information
__ICON	Program icons
__TIFF	TIFF images
__EPS	EPS images
__SND	Sound files
__LINKEDIT	Information for loading and dynamic linking.
__NIB	NeXT Interface Builder (nib) specifications. This segment is no longer created in NeXTSTEP 3.0.

The Mach **size** command displays the size of segments and sections in a Mach-O executable file. For example, take a look at the segments and sections in the Librarian application executable file by entering the following commands (in **bold**) in a shell window:

```
localhost> cd /NextApps/Librarian.app
localhost> size -m Librarian
Segment __PAGEZERO: 8192
Segment __TEXT: 122880
        Section __text: 104472
```

. . .   . . .

Mach provides a number of other tools, **otool** and **segedit** in particular, for manipulating the contents of a Mach-O executable file. You can use **otool** to print the contents of Mach-O files, and **segedit** for assembling new Mach-O files or taking apart old ones.

A variety of Application Kit objects will look in the Mach-O segment of a running program for their data. For example, an **NXImage** object may search the __ICON, __TIFF, or __EPS segments of a Mach-O executable in response to a **findImageNamed:** message. The **Application** object will search the __NIB segment for a nib (NeXT Interface Builder information) section inside the Mach-O executable in response to a **loadNibSection:-owner:** message. However, nib files created with Interface Builder in NeXTSTEP 3.0 cannot be included in Mach-O executables anymore. Instead, they remain separate files that are stored in the app wrapper.

For further information on all of these commands, search the on-line documentation and header files in the Librarian and HeaderViewer applications. Make sure both the **NeXT Developer** and **UNIX Manual Pages** "books" are selected in Librarian's main window (use *Shift-click* to select the second book).

The Window Server and Display PostScript

The NeXTSTEP Window Server is a low-level process running in the background that is responsible for two very important functions: drawing images on the screen and sending events to applications. The Window Server contains Adobe's Display PostScript (*DPS*) interpreter, which performs the actual drawing of lines, text, and pictures. The NeXTSTEP 3.0 DPS interpreter responds to a superset of Adobe's well-known PostScript Level 2 command set and therefore can display text in any font size and at any angle. The same interpreter is used for both the screen and the printer, so what you see on the screen is *exactly* what gets printed (except that the printer output looks better because of its higher resolution).

The Window Server manages the screen (or screens), the keyboard, the mouse and any printers. It assures that programs draw in their own rectangular piece of real estate on the screen, and sees to it that events destined for one program don't accidentally get sent to another. The Window Server frees you from having to worry about interactions between your program and other programs that might be running simultaneously. For all intents and purposes, you can design your program as if it is the only one running.

The Window Server also isolates you from the particulars of the computer's hardware. If your program is running on a NeXTSTEP computer that has a different sized screen, or a slightly different keyboard or mouse, these differences are automatically hidden from you by the Window Server.

PostScript

PostScript is a device-independent graphics description language which handles all aspects of line drawing, typesetting and image presentation on the computer's screen and printer. *Device-independent* means that Post-Script hides all differences in resolution from your program: to draw a line, you simply tell the PostScript interpreter to draw a line. PostScript automatically figures out which pixels on the screen (or dots on the printed page) should be turned on or turned off.

PostScript also handles output attributes such as line width and fill color. If you want to draw a dark gray line, you simply set the color to dark gray and draw the line. If the output device is black-and-white only, PostScript will automatically dither or halftone the line as necessary (*dithering* and *halftoning* are techniques for showing continuous-tone images on devices which can only display a few shades of color or black-and-white). If your output device can handle gray tones, PostScript automatically chooses values of gray according to what you selected.

When programming with color, PostScript allows you to specify color using a variety of color models – RGB, CMYK, HSB, or Pantone^{tm} color (NeXTSTEP 3.0 only) – and then, as with black and white, converts the color that you requested to what is appropriate to your display. This means that color PostScript programs can run on black-and-white displays, and *vice versa*. It also means that color output from a NeXTSTEP program looks as good as it possibly can on whatever display you use.

The Application Kit and the Window Server

Recall that the Application Kit is a collection of Objective-C classes that define and create objects for use by applications. In this section we'll describe how these objects communicate with the Window Server.

An application's **Application** object (recall that every NeXTSTEP application must have precisely one) is responsible for communication between the Application Kit objects in the application and the Window Server.

Because these communications are made through Mach ports, they can be made over the network, from different computers running NeXTSTEP. In other words, a NeXTSTEP application running on one computer can display its windows on a different computer running NeXTSTEP, over the network. (To do this, you need to launch the application program from the command line and specify the option **-NXHost**. Make sure that the account on the second computer has set the "Public Window Server" switch in the Preferences application.)

Window objects manage the application program's representation of windows on the screen. **Window** objects work together with the Window Server to handle window moved, window exposed, and other window events so that on-screen windows are always up-to-date.

The Application Kit classes' implementations are stored in a special file called a *shared library*. The shared library is automatically linked with your program when your program is run. This means that NeXT can make improvements in the Application Kit from release to release and those improvements are automatically reflected in your program when it runs on the newer release of the operating system. No recompiling is necessary! For example, NeXT added spell checking to the Application Kit's **Text** class between version 1.0 and 2.0; any 1.0 application that used a **Text** object can automatically use spell checking in 2.0 as a result. NeXT also added Fax capability to the **PrintPanel** class between releases 1.0 and 2.0, which means that any NeXTSTEP 1.0 program with a Print panel can automatically handle faxing. Shared libraries also make program images smaller, since the library isn't loaded into the program until it is loaded for execution.

You can find out which shared libraries an application depends on by using the **otool** command. Enter the following commands in **bold** to find out which shared libraries the Librarian application uses:

```
localhost> cd /NextApps/Librarian.app
localhost> otool -L Librarian
   /usr/shlib/libIndexing_s.A.shlib (minor version 1)
   /usr/shlib/libMedia_s.A.shlib (minor version 12)
   /usr/shlib/libNeXT_s.C.shlib (minor version 57)
   /usr/shlib/libsys_s.B.shlib (minor version 55)
localhost>
```

Seeing All the Processes

The Workspace Manager's Processes panel shows only those processes that were launched from the Workspace Manager (see Chapter 1). To see all of the processes, we can use the **ps** command in a UNIX shell window. The **ps** command has many different options, but by using the options **a**, **u**, and **x** we get a user-readable listing of all processes currently running.

Enter **ps -aux** in a shell window. Your listing should contain many of the same programs as in the listing in Figure 1 below, which was generated while running NeXTSTEP 2.1. Some of the processes running on your computer are bound to differ; it depends on which programs you are running and how your system is configured. Some of the commands in the COMMAND field in Figure 1 were truncated due to the 80 column width in our shell window; make your window wider and enter **ps -auxww** if you want to see the entire command.

The table below contains descriptions of the meaning of the different fields in the listing in Figure 1.

Field	Meaning
USER	**username** of the user who owns the process, usually **root** for processes run by the system or your **username** for processes run by you
PID	process identifier of each process
%CPU	percentage of the CPU time that the process is using
%MEM	percentage of physical memory the process is using
VSIZE	amount of virtual memory that the process is using
RSIZE	amount of process that is resident in physical memory
TT	terminal being used by the process; a "?" means that the process is not associated with any terminal
STAT	status of the process: **R** is running, **S** is stopped, **W** is waiting, **N** is "niced" (running with reduced priority)
TIME	length of time the process has been running
COMMAND	command that ran the program

You can look up the **ps** command with the Librarian application to learn further details concerning this command's output.

FIGURE1. ps -aux Listing

```
localhost> ps -aux
USER        PID  %CPU %MEM VSIZE  RSIZE TT STAT   TIME COMMAND
root       1778  16.6  2.4 2.05M   800K p1 R      0:00 ps aux
simsong     153   3.6 37.7 47.0M  12.1M ?  S    651:06 - console (WindowServer)
root       1427   1.9  3.6 4.24M  1.16M ?  S      0:28 /NextApps/Terminal.app
simsong    1768   1.7 12.2 8.23M  3.90M ?  S      0:26 /LocalApps/FrameMaker.app
simsong    1428   0.6  0.9 1.53M   296K p1 S      0:01 -csh (csh)
simsong     160   0.6  5.9 6.12M  1.88M ?  S     14:21 /usr/lib/NextStep/Workspa
root          3   0.0  0.6 4.46M   184K ?  SW     0:02 /usr/etc/kern_loader -n
root         55   0.0  0.6 1.43M   192K ?  S      0:01 /usr/etc/syslogd
root         59   0.0  1.4 7.55M   456K ?  S N    0:48 /usr/etc/nmserver
root         63   0.0  0.7 1.42M   216K ?  S      0:01 (portmap)
root         66   0.0  0.7 1.45M   240K ?  S      0:00 (nibindd)
root         67   0.0  1.0 1.50M   344K ?  S      0:06 /usr/etc/netinfod local
root         71   0.0  0.9 1.52M   304K ?  S      0:08 (lookupd)
root          2   0.0  0.7 1.45M   232K co S      0:03 (mach_init)
root         -1   0.0  0.0    0K     0K ?  SW     0:00 <mach-task>
root         -1   0.0  0.0    0K     0K ?  SW<    0:00 <mach-task>
root        110   0.0  0.5 1.43M   160K ?  SW     0:00 (inetd)
root        116   0.0  0.7 1.54M   224K ?  SW     0:00 -accepting connections (s
root        121   0.0  0.6 1.98M   192K ?  S      0:00 (lpd)
root        130   0.0  0.3 1.48M    96K ?  SW     0:00 /usr/lib/lpd
root        131   0.0  0.5 1.60M   168K ?  SW     0:00 (pbs)
root         91   0.0  0.6 1.46M   208K ?  S      0:02 (autonfsmount)
root        149   0.0  0.5 1.50M   168K ?  S      0:04 (cron)
root        146   0.0  0.3 1.50M   112K ?  S      0:15 update
root        155   0.0  0.3 2.56M   112K ?  SW     0:00 (WindowServer)
root         -1   0.0  0.0    0K     0K ?  SW     0:01 <mach-task>
root         -1   0.0  0.0    8K     8K ?  S      0:09 <mach-task>
root        156   0.0  1.1 1.90M   376K ?  S      0:12 /usr/etc/pbs -a
simsong     158   0.0  0.5 1.99M   176K ?  S      0:00 (appkitServer)
root        136   0.0  1.7 4.01M   552K ?  S N    0:21 (npd)
simsong     195   0.0  2.3 4.73M   768K ?  S      1:16 /NextApps/Edit.app/Edit -
simsong     344   0.0  3.0 5.53M   976K ?  S      3:53 /NextApps/Mail.app/Mail -
simsong     448   0.0  0.8 3.89M   256K ?  SW     0:00 /NextLibrary/Services/NeX
simsong     591   0.0  2.3 4.52M   752K ?  S      0:53 /NextDeveloper/Apps/Proje
simsong    1348   0.0  2.5 5.00M   816K ?  S      0:04 /NextApps/Preferences.app
simsong    1424   0.0  2.3 8.57M   760K ?  S N    0:38 /NextApps/Librarian.app/
root          1   0.0  0.4 1.50M   144K ?  SW     0:00 /usr/etc/init -xx
root         -1   0.0  0.0    0K     0K ?  ?W<    0:00 <mach-task>
localhost>
```

Most of the processes displayed in the Figure 1 listing have an important function. Below we list what each one does.

Process	Function
ps -aux	The **ps** command that was run to display the process listing.
console (WindowServer)	The Window Server console process, which captures all output to **/dev/console**.
/LocalApps/FrameMaker.app	FrameMaker, which we used to write this book.
- (csh)	The C shell.
/usr/lib/NextStep/Work	The Workspace Manager application. It's full name is **/usr/lib/NeXT-STEP/Workspace.app/Workspace**.
/usr/etc/kern_loader -n	The Mach Kernel loader.
/usr/etc/syslogd	The system logging daemon.
/usr/etc/nmserver	The Mach name server.
(portmap)	The portmapper, for RPC (remote procedure calls).
(nibindd)	The NetInfo (network administrative information) binding daemon, responsible for finding, creating, and destroying NetInfo servers.
/usr/etc/netinfod local	The NetInfo server for the local NetInfo domain, executed by nibindd.
(lookupd)	The lookup daemon, which makes NetInfo run faster.
(mach_init)	The program that starts up Mach.
<mach-task>	An internal Mach process.
(inetd)	The inet daemon, which launches Internet servers.
-accepting connections (s	The sendmail daemon, which receives mail from the network.
/usr/lib/lpd	The line printer daemon, which handles printing.

Process	Function
(pbs)	The NeXTSTEP Pasteboard server, which coordinates sharing of data on the various pasteboards.
(autonfsmount)	The auto NFS mounter, which automatically mounts NFS filesystems when requested.
(cron)	A program that automatically runs programs listed in the file **/usr/lib/ crontab** at predetermined times.
update	A program which executes the sync(2) system call every 30 seconds to assure file system consistency.
(WindowServer)	The NeXTSTEP Window Server itself.
<mach-task>	Another internal Mach task.
/usr/etc/pbs -a	Another part of the NeXTSTEP Pasteboard server.
(appkitServer)	An internal server used by the NeXTSTEP Application Kit.
(npd)	The NeXT printer filter that handles local printing. It's full name is **/usr/lib/NextPrinter/npd**.
/NextApps/Edit.app/Edit -	The NeXTSTEP Edit program.
/NextApps/Mail.app/Mail -	The NeXTSTEP Mail program.
/NextLibrary/Services/NeX	The NeXTSTEP speller program. It's full name is **/NextLibrary/Services/ NeXTspell.service/nextspell**.
/NextDeveloper/Apps/Proje	The NeXTSTEP Project Builder application.
/NextApps/Preferences.app/	The NeXTSTEP Preferences program.
/NextApps/Librarian.app/	The NeXTSTEP Librarian program. It's full name is **/NextApps/ Librarian.app/Librarian**.
/usr/etc/init -xx	The init program.

front end

 back end

10

MathPaper and Multiple Windows

In this and the following several chapters, we are going to start over and build a new, more sophisticated calculator-like system called MathPaper. MathPaper will manage multiple windows, use fonts to convey information, and use interprocess communication to make a request to another program to do the actual calculation. In writing it we will learn a lot more about the workings of the NeXTSTEP Application Kit.

MathPaper

When we're done MathPaper will be a scratch pad mathematics application that looks like a text editor: it will display a little text window into which you can type. The neat thing about MathPaper is that when you hit the Return key, the application will automatically calculate the value of what you've typed and display the result. Figure 1 below contains an example of a main window of the running MathPaper application.

MathPaper can handle multiple windows: typing Command-n will give you another "piece" of "mathematical paper." In later chapters of this book, we'll use part of MathPaper to graph equations as well.

FIGURE 1. MathPaper Application Main Window

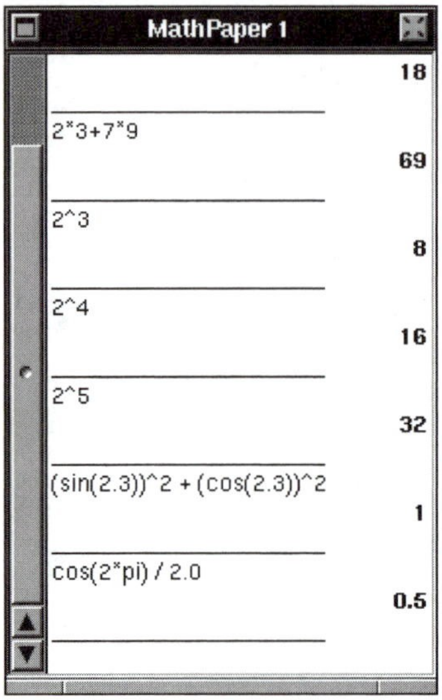

The Structure of MathPaper

MathPaper has three main parts:

- The **MathController** controlling object, which creates individual windows for solving mathematical equations.

- The **PaperControl** object, which controls one piece of math paper. There will be a separate **PaperControl** object for each piece of math paper, i.e., one for each window like the one in Figure 1.

- **Evaluator**, a separate program which can evaluate arbitrary algebraic expressions. It will communicate with a **PaperControl** object using a **Process** object.

In addition to handling multiple windows, MathPaper handles multiple processes: each piece of mathematical paper is attached to its own copy of the Evaluator program, which performs calculations solely for that window. Together **MathController** and **PaperControl** make up the application's "front end" while the Evaluator makes up the application's "back end." This technique of having separate front and back ends is similar to the way that the *Mathematica* third party application works: the advantage is that it lets you subdivide your programming efforts, concentrating on the math-solving part of the program in the back end and the user-interface part of the program in the front end. Another advantage is that the equation-solving back end can be used by more than one application program – as long as its interface is well-documented.

In the remainder of this chapter we'll build the two major modules of MathPaper: the Evaluator back end which we'll test in a UNIX shell window, and the front end which we'll test in the workspace. In the next chapter we'll hook these two modules together with an object called **Process** that manages UNIX subprocesses. In the chapter following that, Chapter 12, we'll arrange for each piece of math paper to save its data into a file and then read the data back from the file when the data file icon is double-clicked.

The "big picture" of the MathPaper application with *three* open math paper windows (all like the window in Figure 1) is shown in Figure 2 below. It indicates that the **MathController** object creates one **PaperControl** object for each window. Each **PaperControl** object will create its own **Process** object to manage a copy of the Evaluator back end.

FIGURE 2. Custom Objects and Back End in MathPaper

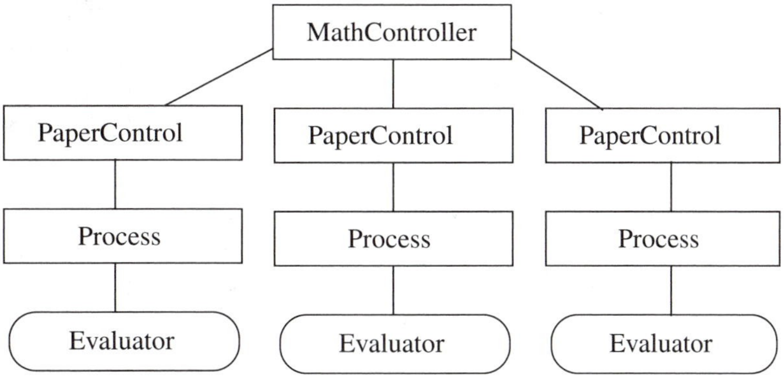

The Evaluator Back End

The MathPaper back end, which we'll call Evaluator, is a program which reads a stream of mathematical expressions and displays the result of evaluating them. That is, if you give the back end the following input:

```
1+2*3+4
2+5*sin(3)
9/4
3+
(8-76+32) / 3.2
```

It will return this output:

```
11
2.7056
2.25
Syntax Error
-11.25
```

The Evaluator writes its output directly to *standard output*, which right now displays on the screen (in a shell window). When we run the Evaluator as a subprocess from MathPaper, the Evaluator's standard output will be returned to the MathPaper application.

In the rest of this section and the next, we'll be discussing how to build the back end. These sections contain material which is not essential to understanding NeXTSTEP programming and may be skipped if you have an executable copy of the Evaluator program. If you don't have an executable copy of the Evaluator program, then you can (blindly?) follow the steps in the next section to create one without having to fully understand what's going on. All you really have to know to continue with MathPaper is that the Evaluator will perform the actual calculations for MathPaper and will run as a separate UNIX process. So, if you plan to skip this material, you should continue with the section "Building the MathPaper Front End" on page 268.

The task of the Evaluator back end breaks down into two parts: lexical analysis and parsing. *Lexical analysis* involves reading the input stream and determining which characters correspond to numbers and which correspond to operations. The character stream is then turned into a stream of *tokens*, or symbols. For example, the input to Evaluator shown above would generate the following token stream:

```
<1> <+> <2> <*> <3> <+> <4> <newline>
<2> <+> <5> <*> <sin> <(> <3> <)> <newline>
<9> </> <4> <newline>
<3> <+> <newline>
<(> <8> <-> <76> <+> <32> <)> <3.2> <newline>
```

The second part of the back end is the parser. The *parser* reads the token stream generated by the lexical analyzer, performs the requested math, and prints the correct result.

Parsers and lexical analyzers are not trivial programs to write. Fortunately UNIX comes with two programs for constructing lexical analyzers and parsers from (relatively) simple input files. These program-generating-programs are called **lex** and **yacc**. It's not important that you understand how **lex** and **yacc** work in order to understand the MathPaper program. The only thing that really matters is that, using **lex** and **yacc**, we are able to build a relatively powerful and reliable back end with a very small amount of work.

The Evaluator application is compiled from three input files:

- **Makefile** – Input for **make**; tells the computer how to compile and link the Evaluator program.
- **grammar.y** – Input to the **yacc** program.
- **rules.lex** – Input to the **lex** program.

Lex and Yacc

Lex and **yacc** are two programs that generate other programs. A full description of their use is beyond the scope of this book. For further information, use the Librarian to search the UNIX manual pages for the string "lex" and also see the book *Lex and Yacc* by Tony Mason and Doug Brown (O'Reilly and Associates, 1990).

Yacc reads an input *grammar file* (in this case, the file **grammar.y**) that describes a particular grammar and generates two C source code files: **y.tab.h** and **y.tab.c**. **Lex** reads the include file **y.tab.h** and a second file (in this case, the file **rules.lex**) that describes a set of *lexical rules* and generates a C source file called **lex.yy.c**. The source code in **y.tab.c** and **lex.yy.c** is then compiled and linked to form the Evaluator program.

We get a lot of power by using **yacc** and **lex**. Not only do we get a full-featured numerical evaluator which properly interprets parentheses and order of evaluation (for example, evaluating multiplication before addition), but we also get a system to which it is easy to add new formulas and rules. For example, adding a new function to the Evaluator simply requires adding two new lines, one to the set of rules and one to the grammar. We'll be doing much of our work from the **csh** command line, so make sure your dock contains NeXTSTEP's Terminal application.

Building the Back End

1. Create a new directory called **Evaluator** in your home directory.

2. Using an editor, create a file called **Makefile** in your **Evaluator** directory containing the following:

   ```
   CFLAGS = -O
   ```

```
Evaluator: y.tab.c lex.yy.c
           cc $(CFLAGS) -o Evaluator y.tab.c \
           lex.yy.c -ly -ll -lm

install:   Evaluator
           strip Evaluator
           cp Evaluator $(HOME)/Apps

clean:
           /bin/rm -f Evaluator lex.yy.c y.tab.?

lex.yy.c:  rules.lex y.tab.h
           lex rules.lex

y.tab.h:   grammar.y
           yacc -d grammar.y

y.tab.c:   grammar.y
           yacc grammar.y
```

This **Makefile** contains the targets **install, clean,** and so forth. **Make** *targets* were explained in Chapter 2.

3. Using an editor, create a file called **rules.lex** in your **Evaluator** directory which containing the following:

```
%{
#include "y.tab.h"
#include <stdlib.h>
%}


%%

"\n"   return('\n');

[0-9]*("."[0-9]*("e"[-+][0-9]+)?)? \
        {yylval.dval = atof(yytext); return(NUMBER);}

sin        return(SIN);
cos        return(COS);
tan        return(TAN);
asin       return(ASIN);
acos       return(ACOS);
atan       return(ATAN);
sinh       return(SINH);
cosh       return(COSH);
tanh       return(TANH);
asinh      return(ASINH);
```

```
acosh       return(ACOSH);
atanh       return(ATANH);
mod         return(MOD);
ln          return(LN);
log         return(LOG);
sqrt        return(SQRT);
pi          return(PI);

[ \t]       ;

.           {return(yytext[0]);}

%%
```

4. Using an editor, create a file called **grammar.y** in your **Evaluator**
    directory which contains the following:

```
%{
#include <libc.h>
#include <math.h>

int printingError = 0;
%}

%start list

%union
{
  int    ival;
  double dval;
}

%token <dval> NUMBER
%token <dval> SIN COS TAN ASIN ACOS ATAN
%token <dval> SINH COSH TANH ASINH ACOSH ATANH
%token <dval> SQRT MOD LN LOG PI
%type <dval> expr number

%left '+' '-'
%left '*' '/'
%left SIN COS TAN ASIN ACOS ATAN SINH COSH TANH ASINH
%left ACOSH ATANH
%left '^' SQRT MOD LN LOG
%left UMINUS /* supplies precedence for unary minus
*/

%%          /* beginning of rules section */

list : stat
```

```
      | list stat
      ;

stat : expr '\n'
{
  printf("%10g\n",$1);
  printingError = 0;
  fflush(stdout);
}
;

expr   : '(' expr ')'
{
  $$ = $2;
}
  | expr '+' expr { $$ = $1 + $3;}
  | expr '-' expr { $$ = $1 - $3;}
  | expr '*' expr { $$ = $1 * $3;}
  | expr '/' expr { $$ = $1 / $3;}
  | SIN expr    { $$ = sin($2);}
  | COS expr    { $$ = cos($2);}
  | TAN expr    { $$ = tan($2);}
  | ASIN expr   { $$ = asin($2);}
  | ACOS expr   { $$ = acos($2);}
  | ATAN expr   { $$ = atan($2);}
  | SINH expr   { $$ = sinh($2);}
  | COSH expr   { $$ = cosh($2);}
  | TANH expr   { $$ = tanh($2);}
  | ASINH expr { $$ = asinh($2);}
  | ACOSH expr { $$ = acosh($2);}
  | ATANH expr { $$ = atanh($2);}
  | expr '^' expr { $$ = pow($1,$3);}
  | expr MOD expr { $$ = fmod($1,$3);}
  | LN expr    { $$ = log($2);}
  | LOG expr   { $$ = log10($2);}
  | SQRT expr  { $$ = sqrt($2);}
  | '-' expr %prec UMINUS
  {
    $$ = -$2;
  }
  | number
  ;

number     : NUMBER   /* lex number */
  | PI       { $$ = M_PI;}
  ;

%% /* beginning of functions section */
```

```
void yyerror(char *s)
{
  if (printingError == 0) {
    printf("Syntax Error\n");
    fflush(stdout);
    printingError = 1;
  }
}

int main(int argc,char **argv)
{
  int i;
  int size = 0;

  while (!feof(stdin)) {
    yyparse();
  }
  exit(0);
}
```

Unlike most **lex** and **yacc** programs, Evaluator contains all of the auxiliary C code that it needs to run in the **grammar.y** file. **Yacc** automatically passes this code along to the C compiler with the parser that it generates.

5. Open up a UNIX shell window by double-clicking the Terminal icon.

6. Compile the Evaluator with the **make** utility by typing **make** in the Terminal shell window. What you should type is indicated in **bold**:

```
localhost> cd ~/Evaluator
localhost> make
yacc grammar.y
yacc -d grammar.y
lex rules.lex
cc -O -o Evaluator y.tab.c lex.yy.c -ly -ll -lm
localhost>
```

If you get any errors, you probably made a typo.

7. After the program is compiled, test it as follows:

```
localhost> ./Evaluator
10+20
    30
sin(2*pi)+cos(4*pi)
    1
^Clocalhost>
```

(Type Control-c to exit the program. The "**^c**", which indicates where you should type Control-c, will show up in the shell window where indicated.)

8. Install the Evaluator program in your **~/Apps** directory by typing **make install** as follows:

```
localhost> make install
strip Evaluator
cp Evaluator /simsong/Apps
localhost>
```

Stripping an executable file removes its symbol table, which has the effect of making the program dramatically smaller. In this case, the size of the Evaluator executable dropped from about 53,000 bytes to about 16,000. (Stripping the executable also makes it harder to debug the resulting executable, so be careful!)

Congratulations! You're finished with the back end! If you don't understand it all, don't worry too much. All you have to know to continue with MathPaper is that the Evaluator will perform the actual calculations for MathPaper and will run as a separate UNIX process.

Building the MathPaper Front End

The next step is to create the MathPaper front end – the user interface and the program module that starts up the Evaluator subprocesses and sends them algebraic expressions to evaluate.

The MathPaper program will consist of two nibs:

*   **MathPaper.nib** – the main nib that will control the menu, application initialization, and launching of new windows.
*   **paperwindow.nib** – the nib that will control a single MathPaper window. If we have several MathPaper windows, then one copy of **paperwindow.nib** will be loaded for each window. (Recall that we're using the convention that auxiliary nib file names are not capitalized.)

By having a separate nib for the MathPaper window, we can create new instances of the window simply by loading the nib multiple times. We'll see how this works later in this chapter.

Setting up the Main Nib

1. Launch Project Builder (PB) from your dock, choose PB's **Project→New** menu command and give your new project the name "**MathPaper**."[1]

2. Double-click the **MathPaper.nib** file name (under **Interfaces**) in PB's Files view. Interface Builder (IB) will automatically launch and display the **MathPaper.nib** interface created by PB.

3. In order to simplify the screen, hold down a Command key and double-click IB's icon. All other active applications will be hidden (in 3.0).

4. Click the menu icon button at the top of IB's Palettes window. This will cause the Palettes window to display all of the possible menus that you can drag into your application.

The Menus palette together with descriptions of its menu cells can be seen in Figure 3 below. Although you can change the name of any menu, many of the menu cells in IB's Menus palette automatically link (connect) to **Application** object instance methods. For example, if you drag the **Windows** menu cell into your application, the **Application** object will automatically update the **Windows** submenu as you create and delete main windows within your application. (Isn't object-oriented programming wonderful?!) You won't get this behavior if you simply drag out the menu item called **Submenu** and change its name to **Windows**.

In Chapter 6 we noted the difference in IB between the default **Info** menu item and the **Info** submenu in the Menus palette. Another example of how the default menu differs from a submenu on the Menus palette is the **Edit** submenu. Compare the default **Edit** submenu on the left of Figure 4 below with the extended **Edit** submenu on the right. The latter is accessible in the Menus palette.

The **Edit** submenu you prefer will depend on your application. If your users are going to be entering text, you'll probably want to delete the first **Edit** submenu and drop in the extended one, because it will give the user several useful capabilities for free. If **Cut** and **Paste** are going to be used only for graphical objects, however, the other **Edit** submenu commands probably aren't needed. For our MathPaper application, we'll keep the default **Edit** submenu.

---

1. If you're using NeXTSTEP 2.1, refer to Chapter 5 and Chapter 6 for details on how to create a project, auxiliary nib file, etc.

FIGURE 3. Menus Palette in Interface Builder

selects Menus
Palette

discussed in
Chapter 6

discussed in
this chapter

commands
automatically
affect **Text**
objects

also under
Format

Colors panel

for searching;
connections
not automatic

automatic
Services
submenu

automatic
Windows
submenu

user-defined
menus and
commands

FIGURE 4. Edit Submenus in Interface Builder

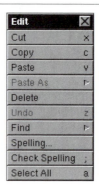

You can cut and paste menus and submenus with *Interface Builder's*
Edit→Cut and **Edit→Paste** commands. If you want a particular submenu
(like the extended **Edit** submenu) but you don't want a particular submenu
command (like **Edit→Paste As**), simply cut it out of the submenu. (You
can also delete menus by pressing the backspace key when a menu cell is
highlighted, so be careful!)

5.   In IB, select the **Info** cell in the MathPaper menu by clicking it.
MathPaper's menu should look like the one at the left of the page.

6. Type Command-x (or choose IB's **Edit→Cut**) to remove this command from the menu. (Alternatively, you can disable the button with the Menu Button Inspector. This way, you'll remember to reenable the button and write the corresponding code before you deliver your application!)

Every application should have an **Info** menu command; we'll be adding ours in Chapter 12, where we'll also create a fancy Info panel.

7. Drag **Document**, **Windows**, and **Services** submenus from the Menus palette and drop them in MathPaper's main menu so that it looks like the menu system in Figure 5 below. Make sure you follow the NeXTSTEP menu guidelines and place the cells in the main menu positions shown in Figure 5.

FIGURE 5. **MathPaper Menus in Interface Builder**

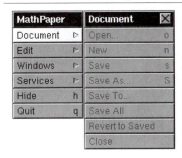
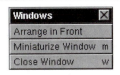

The **Document** submenu has commands for dealing with documents as a whole – creating new documents, saving them, and so on. Since the code for performing these operations will vary from application to application, and since Interface Builder doesn't know what kind of application you are writing, the **Document** submenu cells are all inactive. You should delete the ones that are not appropriate to your application program.

The **Windows** submenu has commands for dealing with windows – bringing them to the front of the window display list, miniaturizing them, and closing them. When your program is running, your **Windows** submenu will include additional menu cells for each standard window (but not panel) that your program creates: this is done automatically for you by the **Application** object which keeps a list of the application's windows. (Yes, object-oriented programming really is wonderful!) If your program can open more than one main window at a time, you should include a **Windows** submenu.

The **Services** submenu is empty: it gets filled in automatically when your program runs. NeXTSTEP applications use the **Services** submenu to send messages to other applications.

8. Change the title of the **Document** submenu to **Calculator** and set up the **Calculator** submenu so that it looks like the one in Figure 6 below.

   You *change the name* of a menu cell by double-clicking its name and typing the new name. You *enable* a menu cell using the MenuCell Attributes Inspector. You *set up a keyboard alternative* character by double-clicking in the right hand side of the menu cell and typing the character.

FIGURE 6. **MathPaper Main Menu and Calculator Submenu**

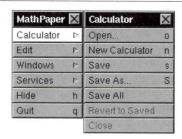

9. Select the **MyWindow** window and type Command-x to remove it.

   Deleting a window is a significant yet uncommon thing to do, so Interface Builder prompts you with the attention panel in Figure 7 below to make sure that you really want to do it. Answer **Delete.**

Don't worry that your application doesn't have any windows in it right now. We'll be adding a window in the **paperwindow.nib** file.

FIGURE 7. **Attention Panel when Deleting a Window**

10. **Subclass** the **Object** class and create a new class called **MathController** (open IB's Classes view, select **Object**, drag to the **Subclass** operation, and change the name of the new class).

11. Add an outlet called **newCalc** and two actions called **appDidInit:** and **newCalc:** to the **MathController** class (select the **MathController** class in the Classes view and then add the outlet and actions in the Class Inspector).

The **newCalc** *outlet* will be used to hold the **id** of a new piece of math paper after it's created. The **newCalc:** *action method* will create that piece of math paper. The action **appDidInit:** is the delegate initialization method which is invoked when the application starts up (we'll have to make **Math-Controller** the delegate of the **Application** object to make it work).

12. Choose the **Unparse** operation in the Classes view to create skeleton class files for the **MathController** class. Respond **Yes** to the questions in both attention panels. PB shows the new class files in its Files view.

13. Command-double-click IB's icon to activate IB and hide all other applications.

14. Create a **MathController** *instance object* by selecting **MathController** in the Classes view and dragging to the **Instantiate** operation. A new icon titled **MathController** appears in IB's File window (Objects view).

15. Connect (Control-drag from) the **File's Owner** icon (which represents the **Application** object in **MathPaper.nib**) to the **MathController** instance icon. Make **MathController** the *delegate* of the **File's Owner** by double-clicking **delegate** in the File's Owner Connections Inspector.

16. Connect the **New Calculator** menu cell to the **MathController** instance object so that it sends the **newCalc:** message. A user will be able to create new pieces (windows) of math paper by choosing this menu command.

Setting Up the paperwindow Nib

In addition to the main nib, we will use a second auxiliary nib to define the window that will be used by each piece of math paper. By putting the definition of the window in its own nib, we can load it multiple times to create multiple windows. When we're done, the method that loads the auxiliary nib (and thus creates a new math paper window) will be invoked indirectly by choosing **Calculator→New Calculator** (or by typing Command-n). We now continue with the project and set up the **paperwindow** nib.

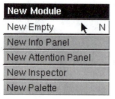

17. Choose IB's **Document→New Module→New Empty** command to create a new nib module. You'll see a new File window *without* a new menu or window, since it's a new *empty* nib.

18. Type Command-s and save this new nib in the file named **paperwindow.nib** in your **MathPaper/English.lproj** directory. Insert **paperwindow.nib** into the MathPaper project; PB will show that **paperwindow.nib** has been added to the project.

19. Command-double-click the IB icon to make IB the only visible application. Also, make sure that the **paperwindow.nib** file is active by clicking in its File window (so the remaining steps in this section affect **paperwindow.nib** and not **MathPaper.nib**).

In Chapter 6 we arranged for an auxiliary nib (**info.nib**) to "know about" a class (**Controller**) created in the main nib (**Calculator.nib**). The process took several steps. We'll do the same thing here in *one* step.

20. Add the **MathController** class to the **paperwindow.nib** class hierarchy (under **Object**) and simultaneously **Parse** the **MathController** class definition in **paperwindow.nib** by dragging the **MathController.h** icon from your File Viewer and dropping it in the **paperwindow.nib** File window.

In Chapter 6 we made the class of an auxiliary nib's File's Owner be the main nib's controller. We'll do the same thing here in the next two steps.

21. Click the Objects suitcase icon in the **paperwindow.nib** (*not* **MathPaper.nib**) File window to see the Objects view.

22. Make **paperwindow.nib**'s **File's Owner** be of the **MathController** class by clicking the **File's Owner** icon in **paperwindow.nib**'s File window and then clicking **MathController** in the File's Owner Inspector. (Note the different File's Owner icon for an auxiliary nib.)

Next we'll set up the **PaperControl** class, which will spawn a new controlling object for each new MathPaper window.

23. Subclass the **Object** class in **paperwindow.nib** and create a new class called **PaperControl**.

24. Add the following four outlets to the **PaperControl** class:

proc – to hold the **id** of the **Process** object (see the next chapter)
scroller – to hold the **id** of the **ScrollView** object (see below)
text – to hold the **id** of the **Text** object inside the **ScrollView**
window – to hold the **id** of the MathPaper window

25. **Unparse** the **PaperControl** class. Respond **Yes** to the questions in both attention panels. PB shows the new class in its Files view.

26. Back in IB, **Instantiate** a **PaperControl** object. Having this instance object in the File window causes NeXTSTEP to create a new **PaperControl** instance every time the nib is loaded.

27. Click the window icon button at the top of IB's Palettes window to view the Windows palette.

28. Drag a window icon from IB's Windows palette and drop it in the workspace; it will expand to a full window. Note the new window icon in the **paperwindow.nib** File window (Objects view).

29. Resize the new window so it's about 3 inches wide by 4 inches tall.

30. Change the title of the window to be "**MathPaper %d**" in the Window Attributes Inspector. We will use the window's title as a format string in a **sprintf** C language statement to number the MathPaper windows. NeXTSTEP itself does not directly interpret the **%d**.

31. Set the window options **Free When Closed** and **Deferred** and unset the others in the Window Attributes Inspector.

The last step above will reduce memory requirements for your application in two ways. First, when the window is closed the memory for it will be freed by the Window Server. Second, the Window Server will defer allocating memory for the window until the window is displayed on the screen.

Reducing the memory required by a NeXTSTEP program will usually make it run faster. This is because NeXTSTEP is constantly paging programs into memory from the hard disk to run them and then paging them out to make room for other programs. The less memory your program takes up, the less paging the computer has to do to run your program.

32. Click the "text" icon button at the top of IB's Palettes window to view the TextViews palette.

33. Drag a **Text ScrollView** object from IB's TextViews palette and drop it in the new window. See Figure 8 below.

We'll call this object a **Text ScrollView**, and not just a **ScrollView** (as many NeXTSTEP programmers do), because the object on the palette is really two objects – a **Text** object "inside" a **ScrollView** object. We'll describe these two objects in more detail in the next chapter.

34. Resize the **Text ScrollView** so it is the same size as the window. When you're done, it should look like the screen shot in Figure 9 below.

FIGURE 8. **TextViews Palette in Interface Builder**

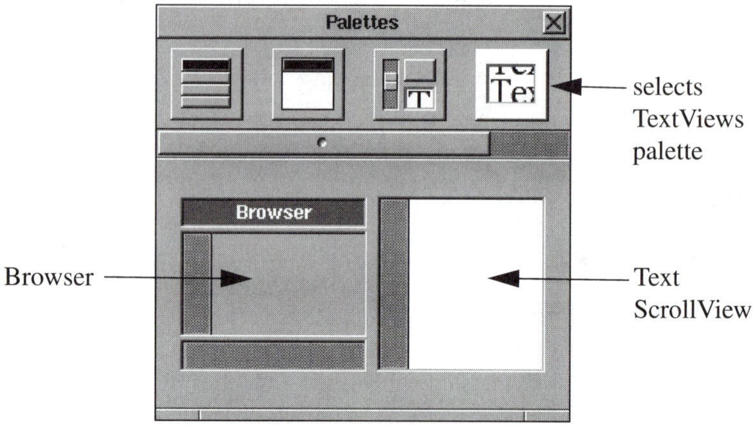

FIGURE 9. **ScrollView in a MathPaper Window**

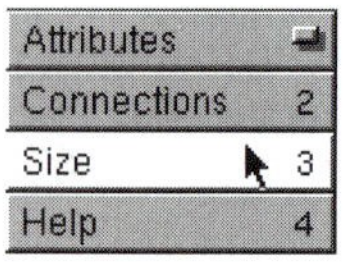

35. Select the **Text ScrollView** by clicking it. Then drag to **Size** in the ScrollView Inspector (or type Command-3) to bring up the Size Inspector as in Figure 10 below.[1]

---

1. In NeXTSTEP 2.1, it's called the **Autosizing** Inspector. Also, the Frame size is displayed in the **Miscellaneous** Inspector.

FIGURE 10. ScrollView Autosizing Inspector

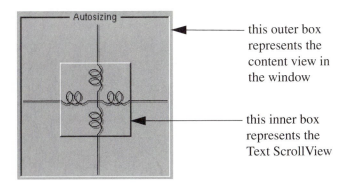

origin and size of the
Text ScrollView

straight line here
means stick to the top

spring here means
stretch when
resized vertically

straight line here means
stick to the bottom

straight line here means   spring here means stretch
stick to the left side   when resized horizontally

this outer box
represents the
content view in
the window

this inner box
represents the
Text ScrollView

The ScrollView Size Inspector lets you specify how a **View** object should change when the view's containing view, or *superview*, is resized. In this case, we are specifying the resizing characteristics of the **Text ScrollView** when the window's content **View** is resized (which occurs whenever the window is resized). In Figure 10 the small square represents the selected **View**, whereas the large square represents the superview.

36. Click the lines in the Autosizing area in the Size Inspector so it contains the "springs" as in the screen shot at the bottom of Figure 10.

This will cause the **ScrollView** to resize whenever its superview is stretched or shrunk in either the horizontal or vertical dimensions. This is precisely what we want for a **ScrollView** that covers the content area of a window.

Setting Up the paperwindow.nib Connections

We now have two nibs, **MathPaper.nib** and **paperwindow.nib**. The nib **MathPaper.nib** contains the program's main menu and the **MathController** instance object that will control the application as a whole. The nib **paperwindow.nib** will be loaded at launch time and loaded again every time the user chooses **Calculator→New Calculator**. It will instantiate another **PaperControl** instance object, together with the prototype window that will be used for every piece of math paper.

We've already made two connections in the **MathPaper.nib** file. Now let's wire up the outlets in the **paperwindow.nib** file.

37. Wire up the **newCalc**, **window**, **scroller**, and **delegate** outlets in the nib **paperwindow.nib** as specified in Figure 11 below. In this case the **File's Owner** icon represents the **MathController** instance object which loads copies of the **paperwindow** nib.

     When connecting the **scroller** outlet, release the Control-drag action in the dark gray vertical scroller area to connect the scroller outlet to the **ScrollView** and not the **Text** object within the **ScrollView**. You can see the class of the destination objects near the bottom of the Connections Inspector, as in Figure 12 below.

The connection from the **File's Owner** to the **PaperControl** instance object means that the **newCalc** outlet in **MathController** will point to the **PaperControl** instance that is created when the **paperwindow.nib** file is loaded. This lets the **MathController** send the **setUp** message (shown later) to the **PaperControl** instance to create the **Process** object which will communicate with the Evaluator.

FIGURE 11. The paperwindow.nib Connections

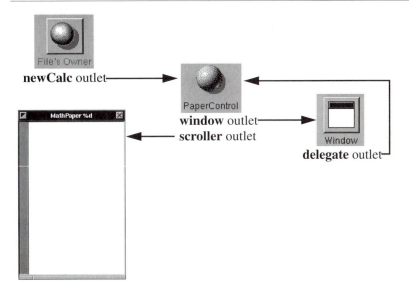

FIGURE 12. Connections Inspector for paperwindow.nib

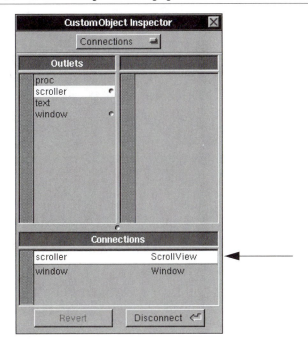

The connections involving the **window** and **scroller** outlets let the **Paper-Control** instance send messages to the MathPaper **Window** and **Scroll-View** objects, respectively. We'll discuss the connection which makes **PaperControl** instance the **Window** object's **delegate** in the next section.

Source Object	Source Outlet	Target
File's Owner	newCalc	PaperControl instance
PaperControl	window	the window
PaperControl	scroller	the scroller
Window	delegate	PaperControl instance

Window Delegates

Like the **Application** object, a NeXTSTEP **Window** object can have a delegate object that is automatically notified in response to certain conditions. You can also use a **Window** delegate to control an on-screen window's behavior. Each **Window** object has its own **delegate** outlet. All of the **Window** objects in an application can have the same delegate object, or you can specify a different delegate (possibly with a different class) for each **Window**. As with the **Application** object, you can change a **Window** object's delegate at run-time by sending it the **setDelegate:** message.

Window *Did* messages are sent to the **Window**'s delegate *after* certain changes in the window take place. They keep your application apprised of what is happening to its windows. The table below summarizes them:

Window *Did* Delegate Method	Sent When?
windowDidBecomeKey: *sender*	Sent after the window becomes a key window.
windowDidBecomeMain: *sender*	Sent after the window becomes a main window.
windowDidDeminiaturize: *sender*	Sent after the user deminiaturizes, (i.e., changes from a miniwindow to its regular size).
windowDidExpose: *sender*	Sent after the window is exposed.
windowDidMiniaturize: *sender*	Sent after the window is miniaturized.
windowDidMove: *sender*	Sent after the window moves.
windowDidResignKey: *sender*	Sent after a window relinquishes its key window status.

Window *Did* Delegate Method	Sent When?
windowDidResignMain: *sender*	Sent after a window relinquishes its main window status.
windowDidResize: *sender*	Sent after a window is resized.

Will delegate methods are sent to the delegate *before* a change in a window takes place. *Will* methods therefore let you control the behavior of the window. Here are a **Window** object's *Will* methods:

Window *Will* Delegate Method	Sent When?
windowWillClose: *sender*	Sent to the delegate when a window is about to close. If the delegate returns **nil**, then the window doesn't close.
windowWillMiniaturize: *sender* **toMiniwindow:** *miniwindow*	Sent to the delegate when a window is about to miniaturize. The delegate can then send a message to the miniwindow – for example, to change the miniwindow's title or what is drawn on it. Alternatively, the delegate can return **nil** to prevent the miniaturization from taking place.
windowWillResize: *sender* **toSize:** (NXSize *)*frameSize*	Sent to the delegate when the user tries to resize the window. By changing the value of the *frameSize* argument, the delegate can control the minimum or maximum window that the user can create, or restrict window sizes to particular values.

Did messages are sent to the delegate object *after* an action has occurred, while the *Will* messages are sent just *before* an action is about to occur. Thus *Did* messages allow the delegate to coordinate actions after certain actions occur. On the other hand, *Will* methods provide the delegate with a chance to block or modify the impending action.

For example, if a **windowWillClose:** message is sent to a delegate, then the delegate object could display an attention panel which asks "Do you want to save the contents of the window?" Depending on what the user responds, the delegate might return **self** or **nil.**

For MathPaper, we'll use the **windowWillClose:** method to do some cleanup when the user tries to close a window.

Controlling the MathPaper Application

In addition to the **newCalc** outlet, we need to add two instance variables to the **MathController** class. These variables are used to keep track of where to place new windows when they are created, as well as to keep count of the number of windows that have been created.

38. Using an editor, insert the two new instance variable declarations in **bold** below into **MathController.h**

```
#import <appkit/appkit.h>

@interface MathController:Object
{
   id newCalc;
   float offset;
   int calcNum;
}

- appDidInit:sender;
- newCalc:sender;

@end
```

The changes required in the **MathController.m** file are more substantial: we've got to implement the methods that initialize the application and manage the creation of new pieces (windows) of math paper.

39. Insert the lines in **bold** below into **MathController.m**. Also, delete the IB-generated line **return self;** in the **newCalc:** method.

```
#import "MathController.h"
#import "PaperControl.h"

@implementation MathController

- appDidInit:sender
{
   [self newCalc:self];
   return self;
}

- newCalc:sender
{
   id win;
```

```
    if ([NXApp loadNibSection: "paperwindow.nib"
            owner: self] == nil) {
      return nil;
    }

    if ([newCalc setUp]) {
      win = [newCalc window];

      if (win) {
        NXRect frame;
        char buf[256];

        [win getFrame: &frame];
        NX_X(&frame) += offset;
        NX_Y(&frame) -= offset;
        if ( (offset += 24.0) > 100.0) {
          offset = 0.0;
        }

        /* Note use of window's title as a format
         * string in the next line...
         */
        sprintf(buf, [win title], ++calcNum);
        [win setTitle: buf];
        [win placeWindowAndDisplay: &frame];
        [win makeKeyAndOrderFront: nil];
        return newCalc;
      }
    }
    return nil;
  }

@end
```

The **#import "PaperControl.h"** directive is required because messages are sent to the **PaperControl** instance (**newCalc**). The **appDidInit:** method sends the **[self newCalc:self]** message to the **MathController** (**self**) to create the initial calculator (MathPaper window and back end) at launch time.

The **newCalc:** method loads the **paperwindow** nib to create the new math paper window and **PaperControl** instance. Each time this nib is loaded, the **MathController** instance variable **newCalc** is set to be the **id** of the **PaperControl** instance that was just created. The old value of this instance variable is lost. It turns out that we really don't care about the old value because the **MathController** doesn't need to send any messages to **Paper-Control** instance after that piece of math paper is set up.

After the **paperwindow** nib is loaded, the **newCalc:** method sends the **window** message to the **PaperControl** instance that was just loaded. The **window** method (which is shown below) returns the **id** of the **paperwindow.nib** window. If the window exists, we find where its frame is and move it over a bit (by **offset**) so MathPaper's windows are not all in the same place on the screen. We then set up the window's title to distinguish it by number (**calcNum**), and finally display the window on the screen. **NX_X()** and **NX_Y()** are *macros* which return the X and Y coordinates of the **frame** rectangle in screen coordinates.

The **newCalc:** method returns the **id** of the new **PaperControl** instance if the window is successfully created; otherwise, it returns **nil**. We'll use this feature in Chapter 12 as a form of error checking.

Controlling a Piece of MathPaper

The **PaperControl** class has the task of controlling the individual pieces of math paper as we create them. We will need three new methods to complete this task. Keep in mind that a new instance of the **PaperControl** class is created each time the **paperwindow** nib section is loaded.

40. Insert the three new method declarations in `bold` below into **PaperControl.h**.

```
#import <appkit/appkit.h>

@interface PaperControl:Object
{
    id proc;
    id scroller;
    id text;
    id window;
}

- setUp;
- window;
- windowWillClose:sender;
@end
```

Below we show the implementation of the three new methods, **setUp**, **window**, and **windowWillClose:** that we made in **PaperControl.h**. The delegate notification method **windowWillClose:** will be invoked whenever the **PaperControl** window is about to close.

41. Insert the three new method implementations in **bold** below into
PaperControl.m.

```
#import "PaperControl.h"

@implementation PaperControl

- setUp
{
  return self;
}

- window
{
  return window;
}

- windowWillClose:sender
{
  [sender setDelegate: nil];
  [self free];          /* free PaperControl object */
  return self; /* Window will free itself on close */
}

@end
```

The **window** *accessor method* allows another object to get the **id** of the
window instance variable stored inside a **PaperControl** object. The **setUp**
method sets up a **PaperControl** object after the nib has been loaded. We'll
show you the code for it in the next chapter. (We can't do our initialization
in a **PaperControl init** method because it might be invoked before the rest
of **paperwindow.nib** is loaded.)

Since the **PaperControl** instance is set up as the delegate of the **Window**
object, it automatically receives the **windowWillClose:** message when the
user tries to close the window. We use this as a signal to free the memory
associated with the object. Before we do this, it is important to reset the
sender's delegate to be **nil**, so the object doesn't receive any messages after
it is freed. (If you take out the **[sender setDelegate:nil]** statement, the program will cause a bus error if you try to close the main window, because
the **Window** object will then try to send the **windowDidResignMain:**
message to the former delegate.)

42. Make an icon for the MathPaper application and put it in the file
Mathpaper.tiff. Drop the file icon in Project Builder's Attributes view
to make **Mathpaper.tiff** the MathPaper's application icon. Our attempt
at creating an icon is shown at the left.

Testing MathPaper

43. Choose **Document→Save All** from IB's menu and save all class files.

44. Compile and run your MathPaper application by clicking the **Run** button in PB. A MathPaper window will be created automatically (due to the **appDidInit:** method).

45. Press Command-n four times. Four more windows will be created, as in Figure 13 below.

46. Quit MathPaper.

FIGURE 13. Multiple MathPaper Windows

Summary

Well, that's all we've got right now – nothing else works! In the next chapter, we'll tie the front end and the back end together. To do that, we'll have to write more code for the **PaperControl** class, as well as create a new class, called **Process**, which will handle the interprocess communications.

MathPaper

11

Spawning Multiple Processes and the Text Object

In the previous chapter we built the MathPaper front and back ends; the back end was created as a separate program called Evaluator. In this chapter we'll tie the ends together, learn more about processes, and modify the **PaperControl** class to display the results of our calculations.

Spawning Processes with the Process Class

The big picture of the MathPaper application is as follows: one process is responsible for interaction with the user, and other processes are responsible for performing the actual mathematics. These processes need to be tied together. We will accomplish this with a new class called **Process**.

The **Process** class will perform the following:

- Start a subprocess (Evaluator) to perform calculations.
- Provide a means for sending data to that subprocess.
- Provide a means for specifying a function to be called when the subprocess has results ready for the controlling object.
- Provide a means for killing the subprocess when it is no longer needed.

UNIX uses the **fork()** system function to "spawn" (create) *child* subprocesses. After a subprocess is spawned, it can change what program it is running by calling the **execv()** system function. One way of communicating with subprocesses is with a *pipe,* a special kind of file object used by UNIX to transmit information between processes. The actual details of how **fork()**, **execv()** and **pipe()** work are not important for an understanding of this chapter. For further information on pipes and the **fork()** and **execv()** functions, use the Librarian to search the UNIX Manual pages for their names.

While creating and using pipes can be complicated, the **Process** class presented below does all of the hard work for you. As with any class, you need to understand the **Process** class interface in order to use it, but need not be concerned with the details of how it actually works. In order to be complete and to empower you to create similar classes, however, we'll describe this class in some detail.

1. Using an editor, create a file called **Process.h** in your **MathPaper** directory which contains the following:

```
/*
 * Process.h: spawn and control a subprocess
 */
#import <appkit/appkit.h>

@interface Process:Object
{
    int    toProcess[2];
    int    fromProcess[2];
    int    pid;
    BOOL   fdHandlerInstalled;
}

- initFromCommand:(char **)argv;
- free;
- (int)toFd;
- (int)fromFd;
- writeLine:(const char *)aLine;
- dpsWatchFD:(DPSFDProc)handler
            data:(void *)userData priority:(int)pri;
@end
```

The instance variables **toProcess** and **fromProcess** are used to hold the two pairs of file descriptors that reference the pipe. The variable **pid** is used to store the process identifier of the child (sub)process. The boolean variable **fdHandlerInstalled** works together with the **dpsWatchFD:data:priority:** method, which we'll describe a bit later.

The NeXTSTEP Display PostScript client library (DPSClient) lets you designate a function that should be automatically called whenever there is data available to read on a specified file descriptor. The file descriptor is checked for data as part of the application's event loop. This gives you a handy way for monitoring the output from a variety of processes from within your application's main event loop.

The **Process** class uses a watched file descriptor to notify the parent process whenever the child has information available for it to read. We'll now go through the implementation for the **Process** class one method at a time.

The nice thing about this class is that it works. Even if you don't understand about forks, children, and pipes, if you know how to *use* this class, you can spawn a subprocess, send the subprocess data, and set up a function to be called when that process has data to return.

2. Create a file called **Process.m** in your **MathPaper** directory which contains the following:

```
/*
 * Process.m
 */
#import "Process.h"

@implementation Process

- initFromCommand:(char **)argv
{
  [super init];

  if(argv==0 || argv[0]==0 || access(argv[0],X_OK)){
    return nil;      /* cannot execute command */
  }

  if (pipe(toProcess) == -1) {
    [self free];
    return nil;      /* could not open first pipe */
  }

  if (pipe(fromProcess) == -1) {
    close(toProcess[0]);
    close(toProcess[1]);
    [self free];
    return nil;      /* could not open second pipe */
  }

  pid = fork();
```

```
if (pid == -1){
  [self free];
  return nil;                    /* no more processes */
}

if (pid==0) {   /* executed by the child */
                /* set up and execv */
  close(0);     /* stdin  */
  close(1);     /* stdout */

  close(toProcess[1]);
  close(fromProcess[0]);

  dup2(toProcess[0], 0);     /* stdin */
  dup2(fromProcess[1], 1);   /* stdout */

  close(2);                  /* stderr */
  dup2(fromProcess[1], 2);   /* stderr */

  execv(argv[0], argv);
  perror(NXArgv[0]);
  exit(1);
}
          /* executed by the parent */
          /* close the other ends of the pipe */
close(toProcess[0]);
close(fromProcess[1]);
return self;
}
```

The **initFromCommand:** method above is by far the most complicated method in this class. It first sends a message to its superclass (**Object**) to perform its initialization. Then it creates two pipes and uses **fork()** to spawn a second process, the child. The child process file descriptors are reassigned so that its *standard input* file is connected to one of the pipes and its *standard output* is connected to the other. The child process then runs (using **execv()**) the named subprocess. The net effect of all of these manipulations is to create a child process which thinks that it is reading its data from the keyboard and sending its output to the display, when it is actually communicating with another program.

3. Insert the **free** method below at the end of your **Process.m** file.

```
- free
{
  if (fdHandlerInstalled)
                DPSRemoveFD(fromProcess[0]);
```

```
    if (toProcess[1]) close(toProcess[1]);
    if (fromProcess[0]) close(fromProcess[0]);
    if (pid>0) kill(pid, 9);
    return [super free];
}
```

The **free** method removes the function that watches the pipe for data, if the handler is installed. It then closes the pipes, if they were created, and kills the child process, if it exists. Finally it invokes the **free** method of its superclass and returns.

The next two methods, **toFd** and **fromFd,** simply make available the file descriptors that are used to communicate with the child process. We won't use them in the MathPaper application, but we will use them in an application called GraphPaper that we'll start building in Chapter 16. (When you're designing a class, it's good practice to provide functionality that you might need later on.)

4. Insert the **toFd** and **fromFd** methods below at the end of **Process.m**.

```
- (int)toFd
{
  return toProcess[1];
}

- (int)fromFd
{
  return fromProcess[0];
}
```

The **Process** class needs two more methods: one that sends data to the child process, and one that installs the function that gets called automatically when the child process has data ready to send back. The **writeLine:** method listed below performs the first of these tasks, it "writes" a line of data to the child process. If the line given by the user doesn't end with a newline character, one is added as a courtesy.

5. Insert the **writeLine:** method below at the end of **Process.m**.

```
/* send a line to the process */
- writeLine:(const char *)aLine
{
  int len = strlen(aLine);

  write(toProcess[1], aLine, len);

  if (len>0 && aLine[len-1] != '\n') {
    write(toProcess[1], "\n", 1); /* courtesy */
```

```
        }
        return self;
    }
```

To complete the **Process** class we implement the **dpsWatchFD:data:priority:** method to ask the Display PostScript system to watch the file descriptor associated with the subprocess and to call a *handler* function when data becomes available.

6. Insert the **dpsWatchFD:data:priority:** method and the **@end** directive below at the end of **Process.m**.

```
- dpsWatchFD:(DPSFDProc)handler
            data:(void *)userData priority:(int)pri
{
    DPSAddFD(fromProcess[0], handler, userData, pri);
    fdHandlerInstalled = YES;
    return self;
}

@end
```

The **Process** class uses a callback system that designates a function to be called when data is ready to be read from the child process. This is much better programming practice than executing a **read()** or **fread()** function and waiting for data to become available. The reason is that both **read()** and **fread()** are *blocking functions*: if data is not available, these functions will just wait until data is available. If something happens and the subprocess does not make data available to the controlling process, the controlling process will freeze. By using the **dpsWatchFD:data:priority:** method instead of **read()**, we prevent that from happening.

7. Launch Project Builder by double-clicking the **PB.project** file icon in the **MathPaper** project directory in the Workspace File Viewer.

8. Select the Files view in PB (if necessary) and drag the **Process.m** file icon from your File Viewer and drop it into PB's main window. PB will add *both* the **Process.m** and **Process.h** class files to the project.

The ScrollView and Text Classes

In the previous chapter we introduced the **ScrollView** and **Text** classes. We called the object on IB's TextViews Palette a "**Text ScrollView** object," since it consists of both a **ScrollView** object and a **Text** object. We'll look at these objects individually in this section.

You can think of the **ScrollView** object as a **View** that contains three other views:

- The docView, the **View** object being scrolled.
- The vertical scroller, which controls up-down scrolling and shows where you are in the document.
- The horizontal scroller, which controls left-right scrolling and shows where you are in the document.

These different **View**s are shown in Figure 1 below.

FIGURE 1. The Three Parts of a ScrollView Object

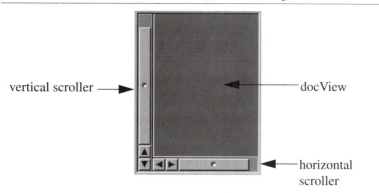

vertical scroller ⟶ | ⟵ docView

horizontal scroller

You can control whether or not each scroller is displayed by sending the **setVertScrollerRequired:** or **setHorizScrollerRequired:** messages with the arguments **YES** or **NO** to the **ScrollView**. The **Text ScrollView** that you take off IB's palette displays the vertical scroller, but not the horizontal one.

Normally **ScrollView** objects are used with **Text** objects, which is why Interface Builder gives them to us that way. We'll learn other ways to create **ScrollView**s in the GraphPaper application later in this book.

The **Text** object is NeXTSTEP's general-purpose mini-text editor. A **Text** object is used by almost every application that allows text entry. The Edit text editor uses the **Text** class as its main editing tool. It is also used by many commercial drawing programs such as *Diagram!* and *Create*.

A **Text** object can:

- Display single-font (monofont) text or multiple-font text
- Automatically word-wrap
- Work with the pasteboard
- Save its contents in a stream of either ASCII or Rich Text.

Every **Window** object has a special **Text** object called the *field editor* that can be assigned minor editing tasks for the **Window**. This **Text** object is shared among **Form**, **Matrix**, **NXBrowser**, and **TextField** objects located within the associated on-screen window. When you are working with text in one of these objects in a window, the field editor reads in the text and lets you edit it. When you're done, the field editor **Text** object spits out its contents and puts it back into the appropriate location. The shuttling about of the field editor is all fairly transparent and is handled automatically by these classes.

Text Class Basics

Like objects of the **Application** and **Window** classes, a **Text** object can have a delegate object. You can use a **Text** object's delegate to find out when the user has made changes to the text (by implementing *Did* methods in the delegate object), or prevent them from happening under certain circumstances (by implementing *Will* methods in the delegate object).

Most often, you'll use a **Text** object to display a chunk of text for the user: the contents of an article, a mail message, or some other sort of thing. Alternatively, you might use a **Text** object to let the user enter some free-form text: a mail message or other such thing. If you're writing a full-featured text editor, you probably *won't* want to use a **Text** object, because it doesn't give you enough control over the placement of characters and interpretation of keystrokes. But for most applications, a **Text** object is just fine.

When it runs, the **Text** object contains a copy of the *entire* text that you are editing. The more text that you have, the longer it will take to load the text into the **Text** object and to have it first displayed. For this reason, if you wish to display a piece of text that is longer than a few hundred kilobytes, you may wish to implement you own text object that only reads in the parts that are needed for display.

Changes to the PaperControl Class

Now that we've got the **Process** class, we'll use it to tie together the **Paper-Control** object with the Evaluator back end. In order to do this, we need to make the following changes to **PaperControl**:

- Arrange for a subprocess to be spawned whenever a new math paper window is created.

- Provide a method that waits for the user to hit Return, gets the new formula that the user has typed, and sends it to the Evaluator subprocess.

- Provide a function that watches for data from the subprocess, gets the data and displays it in the **Text** object.

Spawning the Subprocesses

Recall from the previous chapter that whenever the **MathController** object loads a copy of the **paperwindow** nib section, a **PaperControl** instance is created and its **setUp** method is invoked. At the time, we didn't have the **setUp** method do anything. Below is the complete definition for the **setUp** method; it creates a **Process** object (displaying an alert panel if the process cannot be created), and tells the **Process** object to automatically call the **printer**() function when data is available to print. We'll list and discuss the **printer**() function in the next section.

9. Insert the directive below at the *beginning* of **PaperControl.m**.

```
#define EVALUATOR_FILENAME "/Apps/Evaluator"
```

10. Insert the lines in **bold** below into the **setUp** method in **PaperControl.m**.

```
- setUp
{
  char *argv[2] = {0,0};

  argv[0] = malloc(strlen(NXHomeDirectory())+32);
  strcpy(argv[0], NXHomeDirectory());
  strcat(argv[0], EVALUATOR_FILENAME);

  proc = [ [Process alloc] initFromCommand:argv];

  if (!proc) {
   NXRunAlertPanel(0,"Cannot create calculator: %s",
                      0, 0, 0, strerror(errno));
    [window performClose: self];
    return nil;
  }
```

```
[proc dpsWatchFD:printer data:self
    priority:NX_BASETHRESHOLD];

return self;
}
```

This method uses the NeXTSTEP function **NXHomeDirectory()** to get the user's home directory. It then uses this information to construct the full path name of the Evaluator program. (Recall that we installed the Evaluator program in the **~/Apps** directory in the previous chapter.)

(Note: If you are using NeXTSTEP 3.0, you may wish to install the Evaluator program inside MathPaper's *app wrapper*. The application wrapper is the directory with the "**.app**" extension that holds the application executable and other files. Under NeXTSTEP 2.1 application wrappers were optional; Under NeXTSTEP 3.0, *all applications* are stored inside wrappers. You can use Project Builder to put the Evaluator into the wrapper. You can then use the **NXBundle** class to find its file name.)

The line with the **alloc** *class* message tries to create and initialize a **Process** object. If the **setUp** method can't create this object, then it displays an error message and sends the **performClose:** message to the **Window** object to close the on-screen MathPaper window. (Recall that we set **PaperControl**'s **window** outlet in IB in the previous chapter.) The NeXTSTEP function **NXRunAlertPanel()** displays the error message in an alert panel; the **0**'s tell the function to display the default value for the panel's title and option buttons. Use the Librarian or HeaderViewer to obtain full descriptions of the NeXTSTEP functions used here.

If the process is successfully created, the **setUp** method sends the **dps-WatchFD:data:priority:** message to the **Process** object that's been created. The first argument, **printer**, is a function that should be called automatically when data is available to display. The second argument, **self**, is a 32-bit value that is sent to the **printer()** function as an argument whenever it is called. By sending **self**, we are providing the **printer()** function with the **id** of a PaperControl instance. This is necessary if the **printer()** function wishes to send a message to the **PaperControl** instance. The last argument, **NX_BASETHRESHOLD**, specifies a priority for the part of the event loop that checks to see if data is available for the file descriptor. **NX_BASETHRESHOLD** means that the file descriptor will be checked for data during the **Application** object's main event loop, but it won't be checked when alert panels are being displayed.

Displaying Data Received From the Process

The **printer()** *function* defined below is called by the NeXTSTEP main
event loop when data is available on the watched file descriptor.

11. Insert the following lines after the **#import "PaperControl.h"**
directive but *before* the **@implementation** directive in
PaperControl.m.

```
#import "Process.h"

/* printer: This function called transparently by the
 * NXApp object when data is available to read on fd.
 * We assume that it will be a full line,
 * and less than 1024 characters
 * (both safe assumptions here).
 */

void printer(int fd, void *data)
{
  id ctl = data;
  char buf[1024];
  int size;

  size = read(fd, buf, sizeof(buf)-1);
  if (size<0) DPSRemoveFD(fd); /* error occured */
  if (size<=0) return;
  buf[size] = '\000';

  [ctl appendToText: buf fromPipe:YES];
  [ctl appendToText: "_____\n"
        fromPipe:  NO];

  /* allow new responses */

  [ [ctl text] setEditable: YES];
}
```

The arguments to the **printer()** function are the file descriptor (**fd**) which
has the data and the **void*** pointer which was originally passed to the
DPSAddFD() function. Recall that the **void*** pointer was actually the **id** of
the **PaperControl** object that controls the particular window. We need the
id if we want to send it a message.

The **printer()** function reads the data that is available on the file descriptor.
If any is present, it sends the **appendToText:fromPipe:** message to the
PaperControl object, which causes the text to be displayed. It also draws
the horizontal line that is displayed between results.

Finally the **printer** function gets the **id** of the window's **Text** object with the **text** accessor method (which we'll show later). It then sets the **Text** object to be *editable*. (In a method discussed later, we set the text to be *not editable* after the user presses return.)

Making this function work requires that we add a new method called **appendToText:fromPipe:** to the **PaperControl** class. This method will automatically add a string to the **Text** object; the **fromPipe:** flag lets us specify whether the text was returned by the Evaluator or not. Later we'll use this to indicate whether or not the text should be printed in bold.

12. Insert the **appendToText:fromPipe:** method below immediately before the **@end** directive in **PaperControl.m**.

```
- appendToText:(const char *)val fromPipe:(BOOL)flag
{
    int length = [text textLength];

    [text setSel: length : length];
    [text replaceSel: val];
    [text scrollSelToVisible];
    [text display];

    return self;
}
```

This method uses the following **Text** instance methods:

Text Method Used	Purpose
(int)**textLength**	Returns the number of characters in a **Text** object.
setSel: (int)*start* : (int)*end*	Sets the selection of text in a **Text** object. Since *start* and *end* are both equal to **length**, the selection is at the end of the text string.
replaceSel: (char *)*str*	Replaces the selection with a string, thereby appending *str* to the original string. We use this method to append text to the **Text** object.
scrollSelToVisible	Scrolls a **Text** object so that the selection is visible.
display	Forces a redisplay of a **Text** object.

In order for this method to work properly, we need the instance variable **text** to contain the **id** of the **Text** object in the MathPaper window. In

NeXTSTEP 2.1, IB does not allow an outlet to be connected to the **Text** object inside a **Text ScrollView**; fortunately this problem has been corrected in NeXTSTEP 3.0. In order to make MathPaper work in both NeXT-STEP releases and to demonstrate another NeXTSTEP technique, we'll use a *set method* to get the **id** of the **Text** object. A set method is a method that has the name **set***AnOutlet***:**, where ***anOutlet*** is the name of an outlet.

Outlet Setting Methods

NeXTSTEP normally uses the Objective-C function **object_setInstance-Variable()** to set (assign an **id** to) an outlet (search using Librarian for further details). But if a class with an outlet named ***anOutlet*** has a corresponding method called **set***AnOutlet***:** for setting it, the **Application** object will use that method for setting the outlet instead. (Note that the method name contains the outlet name with the first letter capitalized.) By using an *outlet setting* (or simply, *set*) method, we can add special initialization code to be executed when the outlet is set.

We'll use the **setScroller:** outlet-setting method to set the **scroller** outlet we defined in IB in the previous chapter. We'll also use **setScroller:** to set the **text** outlet (also defined in IB the previous chapter) to be the **id** of the **Text** object inside the **ScrollView** object.

13. Insert the **setScroller:** method below immediately before the @**end** directive in **PaperControl.m**.

```
- setScroller:aScroller
{
  scroller = aScroller;
  text = [aScroller docView];
  [text setDelegate:self];
  [text setCharFilter:NXFieldFilter];
  [text selectAll:self];
  return self;
}
```

When a **PaperControl** object is created this **setScroller:** outlet-setting method is automatically invoked. Because of the **scroller** outlet connection we made in IB in the previous chapter, the **id** of the **ScrollView** object is passed in the **aScroller** argument.

The **docView** message in **setScroller:** returns the *document view* of the associated **ScrollView** – in this case, the **Text** object. The **setScroller:** method then makes the **PaperControl** object the delegate of the **Text** object (an object can be the delegate of more than one object at the same time). Next, it sets the *character filter* of the **Text** object to be **NXFieldFil-**

ter() (more on this below). Finally, it sends the **Text** object the **selectAll:** message which, since the **Text** object starts off empty, has the same effect as clicking the mouse in the on-screen **Text** object.

Text Delegates and Field Editors

Text objects are very powerful and complicated and there are several ways to change their behavior. Two ways to do this are with text *delegates* and *field editors*.

A **Text** object delegate can receive all sorts of special messages when things happen to the **Text** object. The one that we care about here is the **textDidEnd:endChar:** message, which gets sent to the delegate when the user stops entering new text into the **Text** object. This delegate method is actually invoked when the user clicks in another **View** in the window containing the **Text** object (i.e., when the **Text** object relinquishes its first responder status) or when the user enters a *field ending character* such as the Return character.

Field ending characters are determined by the **Text** object's *character filter*. NeXT provides us with two filter functions: **NXEditorFilter()** (the default) and **NXFieldFilter()**. The **NXFieldFilter()** filter function interprets Tab and Return characters as an "end of text" command. The **NXEditorFilter()** filter function lets the user enter whatever he wishes into the text, including Tab and Return characters.

By setting our **PaperControl** object to be the delegate of the **Text** object, and by changing the **Text** object's field editor from the default **NXEditor-Filter()** to **NXFieldFilter()**, we arrange for our **PaperControl** object to be sent a message every time the user hits Return. This is how we will catch what the user typed and send it to the back end process.

14. Insert the code below for the **PaperControl(TextDelegate)** category (which includes the **textDidEnd:endChar:** delegate method) at the *end* of **PaperControl.m**, *after* the **@end** directive.

```
@implementation PaperControl(TextDelegate)

/* Invoked when the text ends.
 * Find the last line and send it down the pipe.
 */
- textDidEnd:sender endChar:(unsigned short)whyEnd
{
  NXStream *str;
  char     *lastLine;
  char     *buf;
```

```
int       len,maxlen;

str = NXOpenMemory(0, 0, NX_READWRITE);
[sender writeText:str];
NXGetMemoryBuffer(str, &buf, &len, &maxlen);
lastLine = rindex(buf, '\n');
if (lastLine) {
   lastLine++;        /* skip past '\n' */
}
else{
   lastLine = buf;    /* get first line */
}

if (strlen(lastLine) > 0){
   [proc writeLine:lastLine];
   [self appendToText:"\n" fromPipe:NO];
   [sender setEditable:NO]; /* wait for response */
}
NXCloseMemory(str, NX_FREEBUFFER);

return self;
}

@end
```

This **textDidEnd:endChar:** method uses the NeXTSTEP streams package to open a memory stream, which it then fills with the contents of the **Text** object. The programmer's interface for the streams package is very similar to the UNIX standard I/O package: you can open a stream, read or write to the stream, and then close it. The difference is that streams can be associated with memory, files, Mach ports, and any other kind of data streams. For further details on NeXTSTEP streams package, search for the function **NXOpenMemory()** using the Librarian.

Once the memory stream is filled with the contents of the **Text** object, the method gets the memory buffer associated with the stream and scans backwards to find the last complete line. If it finds a line, it sends it to the Evaluator back end and makes the **Text** object (**sender**) not editable, which prevents the user from typing anything into the **Text** object while the back end is "thinking."

The only additional method needed in **PaperControl.m** is an accessor method for returning the **id** of the **text** outlet.

15. Insert the **text** accessor method below *between the first pair of* **@implementation** *and* **@end** *statements* in **PaperControl.m**.

```
- text
{
  return text;
}
```

When a MathPaper window is closed, we should free the Evaluator process that did the calculations for that window and the associated **Process** object. We can do this easily by adding one line to **PaperControl**'s **window-WillClose:** method.

16. Insert the line in **bold** below into the **windowWillClose:** method in **PaperControl.m**:

```
- windowWillClose:sender
{
  [sender setDelegate:nil];
  [proc free]; /* free Evaluator & Process object */
  [self free]; /* free PaperControl object */
  return self; /* Window will free itself on close */
}
```

Now we'll update the **PaperControl** interface class file to reflect the newly added methods.

17. Insert the three new method declarations in **bold** below into **PaperControl.h**.

```
#import <appkit/appkit.h>

@interface PaperControl:Object
{
  id proc;
  id scroller;
  id text;
  id window;
}

- setUp;
- window;
- windowWillClose:sender;
- text;
- setScroller:aScroller;
- appendToText:(const char *)val
                      fromPipe:(BOOL)flag;
@end
```

18. Save all pertinent files (nib, class, project) and **Build** (compile) but do *not* run your MathPaper project.

19. Open up a UNIX shell window and type **ps -ux** to display all of the currently running processes that you own, as in Figure 2 below.

FIGURE 2. ps -ux Listing Before MathPaper Launched

```
localhost> ps -ux
USER        PID  %CPU %MEM VSIZE RSIZE TT STAT   TIME COMMAND
simsong     128   3.3 21.5 27.0M 5.15M ?  S     70:50 - console (WindowServer)
simsong    1435   1.3  1.5 1.53M  368K p1 S      0:00 -csh (csh)
simsong     721   2.1 10.4 5.41M 2.51M ?  S     31:41 /usr/lib/NextStep/Workspa
simsong     720   0.0  0.9 1.99M  216K ?  S      0:00 appkitServer
simsong    1391   0.0  8.1 4.44M 1.94M ?  SW     0:11 /NextApps/Edit.app/Edit
localhost>
```

The **ps** command lists processes running on the computer. The **u** option means "display a *user-oriented* listing" and the **x** option means "also display processes that are not associated with a tty." As you can see in the table below, there were five processes running on our computer when we typed the **ps** command. The number and type of processes running on your computer may differ.

PID	Process
128	The NeXTSTEP Window Server.
1435	The C-shell where the **ps -ux** command was typed.
721	The NeXTSTEP Workspace Manager. Note that this is a process that is distinct from the Window Server.
720	The Application Kit server.
1391	**/NextApps/Edit.app** is the Edit application, which we happened to be running at the time **ps -ux** was entered.

20. Now run the MathPaper application from PB or the Workspace. You'll see its application icon and its initial window appear.

21. Verify that MathPaper works by typing **2+2** and hitting Return, as in Figure 3 below.

22. Back in the shell window, type **ps -ux** again, as in Figure 4 below.

FIGURE 3. **MathPaper Main Window**

FIGURE 4. **ps -ux Listing With One MathPaper Window**

```
localhost> ps -ux
USER       PID   %CPU %MEM VSIZE RSIZE TT STAT    TIME COMMAND
simsong    128   15.0 24.0 27.0M 5.76M ?  S      71:27 - console (WindowServer)
simsong    1435   0.0  1.5 1.53M  368K p1 S       0:00 -csh (csh)
simsong    721    2.3 10.4 5.41M 2.48M ?  S      31:50 /usr/lib/NextStep/Workspa
simsong    720    0.0  0.9 1.99M  216K ?  S       0:00 appkitServer
simsong    1391   0.0  7.0 4.44M 1.69M ?  SW      0:11 /NextApps/Edit.app/Edit
simsong    205    0.0  7.3 3.80M 1.16M ?  S       0:01 /simsong/MathPaper/MathPa
simsong    206    0.0  1.4 1.37M  232K ?  S       0:00 /simsong/Apps/Evaluator
localhost>
```

Notice that there are two additional processes:

PID	Process
205	The MathPaper application.
206	A copy of the Evaluator program being used in the window titled **MathPaper 1**.

23. Click in the **MathPaper 1** window and then press Command-n three times, so that you've created four MathPaper windows in total.

24. Then try typing **ps -ux** again. Our results are shown in Figure 5 below.

FIGURE 5. ps -ux Listing With Several MathPaper Windows

```
localhost> ps -ux
USER       PID   %CPU %MEM VSIZE RSIZE TT STAT   TIME COMMAND
simsong    128   15.0 24.0 27.0M 5.76M ?  S     73:41 - console (WindowServer)
simsong    1435  0.0  1.5  1.53M  368K p1 S      0:00 -csh (csh)
simsong    721   2.3  10.4 5.41M 2.48M ?  S     32:12 /usr/lib/NextStep/Workspa
simsong    720   0.0  0.9  1.99M  216K ?  S      0:00 appkitServer
simsong    1391  0.0  7.0  4.44M 1.69M ?  SW     0:16 /NextApps/Edit.app/Edit
simsong    205   0.0  7.6  3.83M 1.22M ?  SW     0:02 /simsong/MathPaper/MathPa
simsong    206   0.0  1.4  1.37M  232K ?  SW     0:00 /simsong/Apps/Evaluator
simsong    210   0.0  1.2  1.37M  200K ?  SW     0:00 /simsong/Apps/Evaluator
simsong    211   0.0  1.2  1.37M  200K ?  SW     0:00 /simsong/Apps/Evaluator
simsong    212   0.0  1.4  1.37M  232K ?  SW     0:00 /simsong/Apps/Evaluator
localhost>
```

There are now *four* copies of Evaluator running, each one connected to its own window.

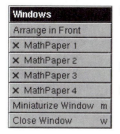

25. Choose the **Windows** menu command and notice that the four MathPaper windows are shown in separate menu cells. The **Windows** menu works without any programming effort whatsoever – fabulous!

26. Choose the **Services** menu command and note that it works too!

27. Now close one of the MathPaper windows and type **ps -ux** again in a shell window. There are now only *three* copies of Evaluator running because we properly killed one in the **windowWillClose:** method of the associated **PaperControl** object.

Getting Out of Hand

What happens if you try to create too many processes? The answer is simple: Mach won't let you. If you type Command-n too many times, you'll get the Alert panel as in Figure 6 below. (Notice that the window titled **MathPaper 88** has a dark gray title bar because it is still the main window even though it is no longer the key window. NeXTSTEP does this automatically for us.)

The text displayed in the alert panel in Figure 6 was determined by the second argument in the **NXRunAlertPanel()** function call we inserted in the **setUp** method in the **MathController** class implementation:

```
NXRunAlertPanel(0,"Cannot create calculator: %s",
                        0, 0, 0, strerror(errno));
```

The **NXRunAlertPanel()** function causes an alert panel to be displayed with a single default button that says **OK**. The panel is *modal*, which

FIGURE 6. **Too Many MathPaper Windows**

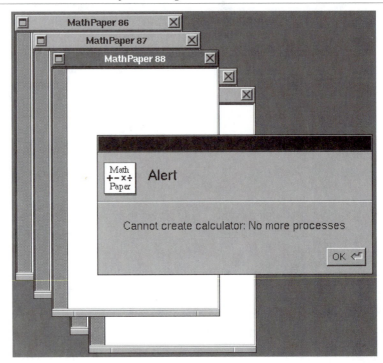

means that your application can't do anything else until the user clicks the **OK** button. The **strerror(errno)** function returns a printable string for the error number stored in the variable **errno**, which was set when the **fork()** function failed in the **initFromCommand:** method.

Summary

In this chapter we created a class which creates subprocesses and showed how to tie it together with the MathPaper application we developed in the previous chapter. In the next chapter we'll learn about Rich Text and more about the **Text** class in order to use fonts and formatting in MathPaper windows.

12

Text and Rich Text

The MathPaper window that we built in the last chapter didn't quite live up to what was promised. We promised what you see on the left of Figure 1 but gave what you see on the right.

FIGURE 1. What We Promised and What We Delivered

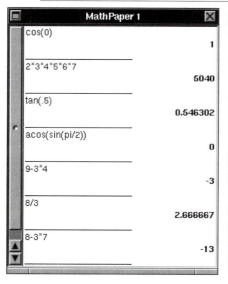
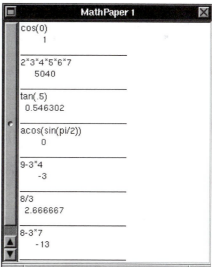

The big difference between the two windows is fonts and formatting. Although the **Text** object allows a great deal of control over fonts and formatting, when we use the **replaceSel:** method we're simply pasting plain ASCII text into the selection. That comes up as left-justified monofont text – not very interesting. In order to get the promised fonts and formatting, we need to learn about the *Rich Text Format* (*RTF*).

What Is Rich Text?

Suppose you want to amaze your friends by showing them how easy it is to create fonts with different sizes in a window. You might want the final window to look something like this:

FIGURE 2. Displaying Variable Size Fonts in a Text Object

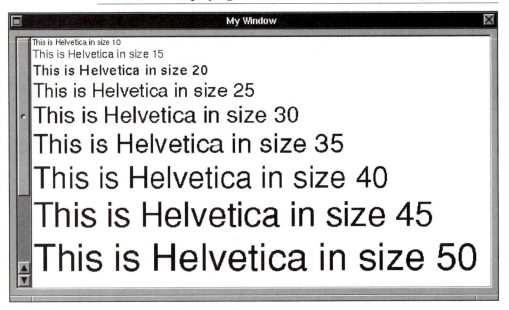

One way that you can do this is by using the **Text** class as if it were a simple text editor, sending an instance of it commands to insert text, select the text, and then change the text to the desired size. Although this is an inefficient way to manipulate the **Text** class, it is conceptually easy.

Manipulating a Text Object with Explicit Commands

A **Text** object provides lots of commands for selecting, modifying and altering the text it contains. We only need a few methods to create the text in Figure 2:

setSel:(int)*start* **:**(int)*end*   Selects the text in a **Text** object from the character at position *start* to the character at position *end*. This is the same as selecting the text by dragging the mouse across it. This method also makes the **Text** object the first responder.

replaceSel:(char *)*aString*   Replaces the selected text with *aString*, a null-terminated string.

setSelFontSize:(float)*size*   Sets the font *size* of the selected text.

Below is a method that will display the text in the **Text** object inside the **ScrollView** object (**aScroller**) in Figure 2 above:

```
- slowFontDemo:sender
{
  float s;
  id text = [aScroller docView];

  for (s=10.0 ; s<51.0 ; s += 5.0) {
    char buf[255];
    int length, newLength;

    sprintf(buf,"This is Helvetica in size %g\n",s);

    length = [text textLength];

    [text setSel: length : length];
    [text replaceSel: buf];
    newLength = [text textLength];
    [text setSel: length : newLength];
    [text setSelFontSize: s];
  }
  return self;
}
```

The method is called **slowFontDemo:** because it is very slow. Another problem that you'll see, if you actually compile and run this code, is that it *looks* like somebody is sitting down at the computer's keyboard, inserting the string "This is Helvetica in size *nnn*" into the text editor, selecting it with the mouse, and changing its size. When the method runs, it is just plain ugly.

(If you want to create an application with **slowFontDemo:**, use PB and IB to create a project with a **Text ScrollView** object in a window and a menu item called **Show RTF**. Then subclass **Object** to get the **MyObject** class and add an outlet called **aScroller** and an action called **slowFontDemo:** to it. Instantiate the subclass to get a **MyObject** instance, connect the **aScroller** outlet from the **MyObject** instance to the **ScrollView** object and make the **Show RTF** menu cell send the action message **slowFontDemo:** to the **MyObject** instance. Finally, unparse **MyObject,** type in the **slowFontDemo**: code above, make and run the application, and choose the **Show RTF** command.)

The demonstration shows some of the advantages of NeXTSTEP:

- The fonts look great, because they're automatically scaled by Display PostScript to whatever size you request.
- The text automatically wraps when you resize the window.
- The second time you run this demo it will run faster, because the Window Server will have cached bitmaps for the sizes of the fonts that you have specified.

Clearly we're on the right track. We just need a better way of writing multi-font text to the screen.

Rich Text Format (RTF)

The other way to manipulate the text is by constructing the text you want ahead of time – with all of the fonts and formatting commands already in place – and then reading it into the **Text** object in a single operation. The format for this ASCII stream is called *Rich Text*, and it was developed several years ago by the Microsoft Corporation. It looks a little like the codes used by *TeX* (pronounced "*tech*" as in the word *technique*), the document typesetting system developed by Donald Knuth.

Here's the Rich Text for the above demonstration:

```
{\rtf0\ansi{\fonttbl\f0\fswiss Helvetica;}
\paperw11440
\paperh9000
\margl120
\margr120
{\colortbl\red0\green0\blue0;}
\pard\tx520\tx1060\tx1600\tx2120\tx2660\tx3200\tx372
0\tx4260\tx4800\tx5320\f0\b0\i0\ul0\fs20\fc0 This
is Helvetica in size 10\
\fs30 This is Helvetica in size 15\
\fs40 This is Helvetica in size 20\
```

```
\fs50 This is Helvetica in size 25\
\fs60 This is Helvetica in size 30\
\fs70 This is Helvetica in size 35\
\fs80 This is Helvetica in size 40\
\fs90 This is Helvetica in size 45\
\fs100 This is Helvetica in size 50
}
```

Each Rich Text command begins with a backslash (\) and consists of a string of letters followed by an optional numeric argument. Brackets have a special meaning: they create Rich Text graphics *states*. If you change the state of a font within a graphics state, the change gets lost when the state is closed.

Don't be alarmed if Rich Text seems a little complicated! There are really only a few Rich Text commands that you need to be concerned about – and later in this chapter, we'll introduce an RTF object that handles them for you automatically.

Exploring Rich Text Commands

The bundled NeXTSTEP editor Edit is a Rich Text editor. If you create a new window with Edit, choose the **Format→Text→Make Rich Text** menu command (if necessary), and then save the empty window, you'll get a file that contains the following information:

```
{\rtf0\ansi{\fonttbl\f0\fswiss Helvetica;}
\paperw4040
\paperh9000
\margl120
\margr120
\pard\tx533\tx1067\tx1601\tx2135\tx2668\tx3202
\tx3736\tx4270\tx4803
\tx5337\f0\b0\i0\ul0\fs24
}
```

Try it and use the UNIX **cat** command to list the file's contents in a shell window. (The contents of your file may differ slightly, depending on your defaults.) If you add three lines of text, in Helvetica, you'll end up with something like this:

```
{\rtf0\ansi{\fonttbl\f0\fswiss Helvetica;}
\paperw11440
\paperh9000
\margl120
\margr120
```

```
\pard\tx533\tx1067\tx1601\tx2135\tx2668\tx3202
  \tx3736\tx4270\tx4803
\tx5337\f0\b0\i0\ul0\fs24 This is line 1\
This is line 2\
This is line 3\
}
```

When Edit reads a file, it checks the first six characters to see if they are "**{\rtf0**". If they are, Edit assumes that the file is in Rich Text Format.

Let's experiment with text *weight* and *angle* changes. The window in Figure 3 below produces the following RTF file:

```
{\rtf0\ansi{\fonttbl\f0\fswiss Helvetica;}
\paperw4720
\paperh2520
\margl120
\margr120
\pard\tx533\tx1067\tx1601\tx2135\tx2668\tx3202
  \tx3736\tx4270\tx4803
\tx5337\f0\b0\i0\ul0\fs24 This is plain\
\b This is bold\
\b0\i This is italic\
\b This is bold italic\
}
```

FIGURE 3. Weights and Angles in a Text Object

Now lets try changing the font size. The window on the left of Figure 4 below produces this RTF file:

```
{\rtf0\ansi{\fonttbl\f0\fswiss Helvetica;}
\paperw4820
\paperh2260
\margl120
\margr120
```

```
\pard\tx355\tx711\tx1067\tx1423\tx1779\tx2135\tx2490
   \tx2846
\tx3202\tx3558\f0\b0\i0\ul0\fs16 This is 8 point\
\fs20 This is 10 point\
\fs24 This is 12 point\
\fs28 This is 14 point\
\fs32 This is 16 point
}
```

FIGURE 4. **Variable Sizes and Fonts in a Text Object**

Finally, lets try changing fonts. The window on the right of Figure 4 produces this RTF file:

```
{\rtf0\ansi{\fonttbl\f0\fswiss Helvetica;
\f2\fnil Times-Roman;\f1\fmodern
Courier;\f4\fmodern Ohlfs;}
\paperw4400
\paperh2160
\margl120
\margr120
\pard\tx533\tx1067\tx1601\tx2135\tx2668\tx3202
   \tx3736\tx4270
\tx4803\tx5337\f0\b0\i0\ul0\fs24 This is Helvetica\
\f2 This is Times\
\f1 This is Courier\
\f4 This is Ohlfs\
}
```

Understanding the Rich Text Format

Microsoft Rich Text Format is a system for encoding various kinds of font information into a printable ASCII character stream. Using Rich Text, you can encode font changes, size changes, even margin changes in an application-independent fashion. There are many Rich Text commands; NeXT only implements a subset of them. This brief discussion is enough to get you going.

An RTF document begins with the character string "**{\rtf0**" and ends with a closing brace "**}**". Inside the RTF document you can have control symbols, which begin with a backslash (\), and text. Control symbols are interpreted as commands, while text is displayed or printed.

You can have additional pairs of braces within Rich Text. Any formatting commands that you issue within a pair of braces will be used but not printed when the Rich Text is printed. For example, the following sequence in an RTF file:

```
This is {\b a test} of Rich Text.
```

prints like this:

```
This is a test of Rich Text.
```

Commands can appear anywhere in the text. For example, the strings

```
This is \b a test \plain of Rich Text.
```

and

```
This is \b a test \b0 of Rich Text.
```

print like this (the same as the string with braces above):

```
This is a test of Rich Text.
```

Normally, Rich Text ignores carriage returns. If you want a carriage return, precede it with a backslash (\). If you want a backslash, type a double backslash (\\).

You can define any number of fonts within an RTF document. Fonts are given numbers; you usually define them within a set of braces at the beginning of the document. In our example above, the following string defined a single font table with font **\f0** being Helvetica:

```
{\rtf0\ansi{\fonttbl\f0\fswiss Helvetica;}
```

Here is a list of some of the more common RTF commands:

RTF Command	Meaning
\rtf	declares a file to be a Rich Text file

Font Definitions:

\fonttbl	begins definition of a font table

RTF Command	Meaning
\f0	selects font 0
\fswiss *fontname*	selects a sans serif font *fontname*
\fmodern *fontname*	same as fswiss
\froman *fontname*	selects a serif font *fontname*
\fnil *fontname*	selects another kind of font *fontname*
\fs*nn*	selects a font size – *nn* is in half points
\plain	plain
\b	bold
\b0	no bold
\i	italic
\i0	no italic
\gray*nnn*	gray; *nnn*= 0 for black, 1000 for white
\ul	underline
\ul0	no underline
\up*nn*	superscript *nn* half points
\dn*nn*	subscript *nn* half points

Formatting:

\ql	left justify text (quad left)
\qc	center justify text (quad center)
\qr	right justify text (quad right)
\tab	tabstop
\paperw*nnnn*	paper width in twips
\paperh*nnnn*	paper height in twips
\margl*nnn*	left margin
\margr*nnn*	right margin
\fi*nnnn*	first line indent in twips
\li*nnnn*	left indent in twips

There are 1440 *twips* in an inch.

The following RTF commands, while useful, aren't currently implemented by NeXT:

RTF command	Meaning
\shad	shadow
\scaps	small caps
\caps	all caps
\v	invisible text
\ulw	word underline
\uld	dotted underline
\uldb	double underline

If you specify a font which isn't available on the machine you're using, you are likely to get Courier.

A Rich Text Object

Using Rich Text can be a pain: you've got to remember far too many commands such as which characters to quote and which ones not to quote. Getting the Rich Text into a **Text** object is even more of a pain: you've got to allocate structures in memory, then create streams to get the data into the **Text** object itself, then clean up all of the memory structures. There's got to be an easier way!

Of course there is: create an Objective-C class for building and managing Rich Text segments. Below is the interface for such a class, a subclass of the **Object** class, which works with the **Text** object.

RTF.h:

```
#import <appkit/appkit.h>
#import <streams/streams.h>

@interface RTF:Object
{
   NXStream *textStream;
}
- (NXStream *)stream;
- appendRTF:(const char *)string;
- append:(const char *)string;
```

```
- bold:(BOOL)flag;
- setJustify:(int)mode;
- free;

@end
```

This time, we'll describe these methods before we show how they are coded, to demonstrate that you don't need to know how an object is implemented in order to use it. Here is a description of the instance methods declared in the **RTF** class:

RTF Method	Meaning
- (NXStream *)**stream**	Returns a stream for all of the text stored in the **RTF** object. You can pass this stream in a **Text** object's **replaceSelWithRichText:** method.
- **appendRTF:** (const char *)*string*	Appends a *Rich Text* string to the **RTF** object stream. No translation is performed on the string.
- **append:** (const char *)*string*	Appends an *ASCII* text string to the **RTF** object stream. Any "special" characters, like newline and backslash, are automatically quoted.
- **bold:** (BOOL)*flag*	If *flag* is YES, all of the following text appended is appended in bold. If *flag* is NO, all of the following text appended is not bold.
- **setJustify:** (int)*mode*	This sets the justification mode of the text that is appended to the RTF object. NeXTSTEP's justification modes are defined in the file **<appkit/Text.h>**.

Here is the implementation for the **RTF** class:

RTF.m:

```
#import "RTF.h"

const char *header =
  "{\\rtf0\\ansi{\\fonttbl\\f0\\fswiss"
  " Helvetica;}\\f0\n";

@implementation RTF
```

```
- init
{
  [super init];

  textStream = NXOpenMemory(0, 0, NX_READWRITE);
  NXWrite(textStream, header, strlen(header));
  return self;
}


- (NXStream *)stream
{
  NXSeek(textStream, 0L, NX_FROMSTART);
  return textStream;
}


/* appendRTF: appends an arbitrary RTF string
 * to the RTF object
 */
- appendRTF:(const char *)string
{
  NXSeek(textStream, 0L, NX_FROMEND);
  NXWrite(textStream, string, strlen(string));
  return self;
}


/* append: appends an ASCII text string, "escaping"
 * all of the special characters in the text.
 */
- append:(const char *)string
{
  if (string==0) return self; /* safety */

  NXSeek(textStream, 0L, NX_FROMEND);
  while (*string) {
    switch (*string) {
      /* escape special characters */
      case '\n':
      case '{':
      case '}':
      case '\\':
        NXPutc(textStream, '\\');
      break;
      default:
      break;
    }
```

```
        NXPutc(textStream, *string);
        string++;
    }
    return self;
}

- bold:(BOOL)flag
{
    [self appendRTF: flag ? "\\b " : "\\b0 "];
    return self;
}

- setJustify:(int)mode
{
    switch(mode) {
        case NX_LEFTALIGNED:
        case NX_JUSTIFIED:
            [self appendRTF: "\\ql "];
            break;
        case NX_CENTERED:
            [self appendRTF: "\\qc "];
            break;
          case NX_RIGHTALIGNED:
            [self appendRTF: "\\qr "];
            break;
    }
    return self;
}

- free
{
    NXCloseMemory(textStream, NX_FREEBUFFER);
    return [super free];
}

@end
```

The **init**, **appendRTF:**, **stream**, and **free** methods all use "**NX**" functions that are part of the NeXTSTEP *streams* package.

The **replaceSelWithRichText:** instance method in the **Text** class requires a stream as its argument; this dovetails nicely with **RTF**'s **stream** method. This **stream** method returns a pointer to a NeXTSTEP stream that contains the **RTF** object's data. The **replaceSelWithRichText:** method in the **Text** class takes a pointer to a stream that contains RTF data. No special translating or processing of the data is necessary in order to make these two methods work together.

Notice that, before the stream is returned, its pointer is set to the beginning of the stream, and before a string is appended, the pointer is reset to the end. The user of the object doesn't have any way of knowing that this is done, and indeed, as long as the stream works properly for the user, the user doesn't need to know. This is another example of why it is better to use accessor methods than using Objective-C's **@public** feature and accessing an object's instance variables directly.

Integrating the Rich Text Object with MathPaper

Now that we have defined the **RTF** class, let's integrate it into the MathPaper application to get the promised fonts and formatting.

1. Using an editor, create the **RTF.h** and **RTF.m** class files (as specified in the previous section) in your **MathPaper** directory.

2. Launch Project Builder by double-clicking the **PB.project** file icon in your **MathPaper** project directory in the Workspace File Viewer.

3. Select the Files view in Project Builder and drag the **RTF.m** file icon from your File Viewer and drop it into PB's main window. PB will add *both* the **RTF.m** and **RTF.h** class files to the project.

Now that our new **RTF** class has been added to the project, we proceed to make the necessary changes in the **PaperControl** class.

4. Insert the directive below after the other **#import** statements near the top of **PaperControl.m**.

    ```
    #import "RTF.h"
    ```

5. *Replace* the **appendtoText:fromPipe:** method implementation in **PaperControl.m** with the new implementation below.

    ```
    - appendToText:(const char *)val fromPipe:(BOOL)flag
    {
      int length = [text textLength];

      [text setSel:length :length];

      if (flag) {
        id rtf =
              [ [RTF allocFromZone:[self zone] ] init];

        [rtf bold:YES];
        [rtf setJustify:NX_RIGHTALIGNED];
        [rtf append:val];
    ```

```
                [rtf bold:NO];
                [rtf setJustify:NX_LEFTALIGNED];
                [rtf append:" "];
                [text replaceSelWithRichText:[rtf stream] ];
                [rtf free];
            }
            else {
                [text replaceSel:val];
            }

            [text scrollSelToVisible];
            [text display];

            return self;
        }
```

6. Save all pertinent files, and **make** and run your MathPaper project. The **RTF** object should behave as shown in the screen shot on the left of Figure 1, "What We Promised and What We Delivered," on page 307.

7. Quit MathPaper.

Summary

In this chapter we learned more about the **Text** class. Specifically, we learned how to exert precise control over the contents of a **Text** object by using Rich Text to encode font, size, and justification information into a stream before copying the information into the **Text** object.

In the next chapter, we'll see how to use methods built into the **Text** class to save the contents of a MathPaper window into a file. We'll also learn how to catch the message that Workspace Manager generates when a user double-clicks a file icon in the File Viewer and see how to open that file in our application program.

13

Saving, Loading, and Printing

In the previous chapter we saw how the contents of a **Text** object can be translated into a "Rich Text" stream of characters. In this chapter, we'll see how to take that stream and save it into the file; we'll also see how to load one of those files and place its contents in a new window. Finally, we will learn about printing.

Right now, our MathPaper application makes a good try at handling multiple windows, but it's missing many basic functions such as:

- Saving the contents of a window into a file.
- Loading a saved file, so that you can continue calculating where you left off.
- Marking an edited window with the "unsaved" close button (), so that you know it has been edited.
- Alerting the user when he or she tries to close an edited window without first saving it.
- Graying out menu items that are not appropriate in a given context (e.g., the **Save** menu item when there are no open documents).
- Printing the contents of a window.

We'll add all of these features as we progress through this chapter.

Saving to a File

Saving a the contents of a window means writing all of the states associated with the window into a file, so that we can reconstruct the window's current state as closely as possible when it's reloaded. In the case of a MathPaper window, not many states need to be saved. Since neither the **Process** object nor the Evaluator back end retain any states between launches, all we've got to do to reload the state of the MathPaper window is to start up a **Process** object and an Evaluator back end process and reload the former contents of the window.

We can use the **Text** class to archive the contents of the window in the form of a Rich Text stream. All we need to do is to open a stream and tell a **Text** object to send its contents into that stream. Then we copy the stream into a file. Simple! But what sort of file should contain the contents of a MathPaper window? Read on...

File Name Extensions

NeXTSTEP uses file extensions to determine what kind of information is stored in a file. A file extension is the set of letters that come after the *last* period (dot) in a file's name. This isn't the safest way to determine file type, because it lets the user accidentally change a file's type simply by changing its name, but the UNIX file system makes no other provisions for storing a file type with each file.

In the table below we list most of the commonly used extensions and their meanings. These are "standard" extensions used by NeXTSTEP.

File Extension	File Type
.a	UNIX library file
.app	Directory containing an application
.bshlf	(Digital) Librarian bookshelf file
.c	C language source file
.compressed	Compressed file in Workspace Manager
.debug	Directory containing an application with debugging information
.dsp	Binary file for the digital signal processor (DSP)
.eps	Encapsulated PostScript file
.f	FORTRAN source file

File Extension	File Type
.h	C (or Objective-C) header file
.iconheader	Header info. for __ICON segment; used by IB
.l or .lex	Lex source file
.lproj	Directory containing language-specific nibs
.lnk	File with relocatable object code for the DSP
.lod	Program that can be loaded into the DSP
.m	Objective-C language source file
.mbox	Directory containing a Mail.app Mailbox
.midi	File with binary MIDI data
.nib	NeXT Interface Builder file
.o	UNIX object code file
.project	Project file for use with Project Builder
.psw	File of wrapped PostScript commands
.pswm	File of wrapped PostScript commands for use with Objective-C
.rtf	Rich Text Format File
.rtfd	Rich Text Format Directory containing .rtf and image files such as .tiff and .eps
.s	File containing assembler source
.score	Music file in the Scorefile language
.snd	Sound file
.tar	tape archive format file (see UNIX man page for *tar*)
.tiff	File in the Tag Image File Format (TIFF)
.uu	Uuencoded file
.y	Yacc source file
.Z	File that has been compressed

The extensions in the following table have been adopted by *third party* application programs. There are many others.

File Extension	Meaning
.afm	Adobe Font Metrics
.ai	Adobe *Illustrator* file
.awk	General use (awk script)
.bepf	Adobe Bitmap font file
.book	*FrameMaker* book file
.cl	Common Lisp source code
.create	*Create* file
.diagram	*Diagram!* file
.dp	*DataPhile* file
.draw	*Draw* file (a NeXT-provided Demo)
.dvi	*TeX* (device independent format)
.el	*Emacs* Lisp source code
.elc	*Emacs* Lisp compiled format
.fdat	*StatLab* (a NeXT-provided Demo)
.frame	*FrameMaker* document file
.framemif	*FrameMaker* Maker Interchange File
.imp	Lotus *Improv* directory
.ma	*Mathematica* notebook
.mft	*TeX* (Metafont source)
.mol	*Molecule* (a NeXT-provided Demo)
.msg	Msgwrap (declaration file for msgwrap utility)
.nff	Ray, Neutral File Format (a NeXT-provided Demo)
.sty	*TeX* (style definitions)
.tex	*TeX* (TeX source file)
.tfm	TeX font
.top	*TopologyLab* (a NeXT-provided Demo)
.web	*TeX* (meta-level TeX source)
.wn	*WriteNow* file (or directory)
.wndict	*WriteNow* dictionary
.wp	*WordPerfect* file

Although NeXT is currently providing a registry of file extensions, the company will eventually have to develop a better system for designating the application program that created a particular data file.

Adding a Document File Icon and Extension to MathPaper

For our application, we'll use the extension "**mathpaper**" to specify a MathPaper document file. (Hopefully, no other programmer on the planet has decided to use that extension for something else.)

1. Create an icon for MathPaper document files and save it in your **MathPaper** directory with the name **MP_Doc_File.tiff**. We came up with the icon at the left.

PB.project

2. Launch Project Builder by double-clicking the **PB.project** file icon in your **MathPaper** project directory in the Workspace File Viewer.[1]

3. View your project's attributes by clicking the **Attributes** button at the top of PB's main window, as in Figure 1 below.

FIGURE 1. Adding a Document Icon and File Extension in PB

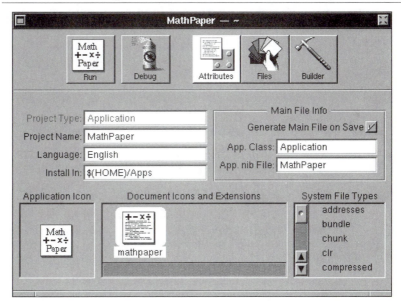

---

1. In NeXTSTEP 2.1, add the document file icon and extension in the Attributes view of IB's Project Inspector. The process is very similar to adding an application icon. Use the **Doc 1** icon well for the document icon and enter the extension name.

4. Add a document icon to the MathPaper project by dragging the **MP_Doc_File.tiff** icon from your File Viewer and dropping it in the **Document Icons and Extensions** area in PB's main window. See Figure 1. The question marks, shown at the left of this step, indicate that a document file extension must be specified.

5. Add a document file extension to be associated with the new document icon by triple-clicking the question marks (???) under the new icon in PB and entering "mathpaper" (it's not necessary to type the period). PB's main window should now look like the one in Figure 1.

Writing the Save Methods

Remember the **FirstResponder** icon we first discussed in Chapter 3? Now we're going to find out what it means.

The **FirstResponder** icon in the File window is a place holder for the application's current *first responder*, that is, the object which will be the first to try to respond to keyboard events and menu commands such as **Cut**, **Copy**, and **Paste**. You can also think of it as a pointer to a list of **Responder** objects. Any message sent to the **FirstResponder** object gets sent one-by-one to the objects listed below, until an object is found that can receive the message and respond with a value other than **nil**.

• The key window
• The key window's delegate
• The application's main window
• The application's main window's delegate
• The application's **Application** object
• The application's **Application** object's delegate

To make the **Save** and **Save As** menu commands work, we'll arrange for their menu cells to send the **save:** and **saveAs:** action messages to the **FirstResponder**; the messages will automatically be dispatched to the delegate of the currently selected (key) window. We'll then implement **save:** and **saveAs:** methods for the **PaperControl** class. Each MathPaper window has a **PaperControl** instance as its delegate, so the correct instance will get sent the **save:** (**saveAs:**) message when the user chooses the **Save** (**Save As**) menu command.

6. Double-click **MathPaper.nib** in the Files view of PB's main window to open this nib file in Interface Builder, and then Command-double-click IB's application icon to simplify the screen.

7. Select the class labeled **FirstResponder** in the **MathPaper.nib**
   Classes view, as in Figure 2 below.

Remember that the **FirstResponder** class isn't a real class; its just a holding place for messages that you might want to send to the current **FirstResponder** object.

8. If necessary, type Command-1 to see the Attributes Inspector for the
   FirstResponder class. See the Inspector in Figure 2 below.

FIGURE 2. **FirstResponder Class and Actions in IB**

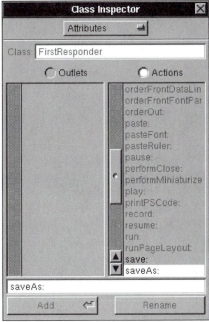

Notice that this Attributes Inspector has lots of actions. Don't worry about them – these are *all* of the actions that Interface Builder thinks you might want to send to the **FirstResponder**. If you send a message to the **FirstResponder** that is not implemented by the current first responder, or any other object in the responder chain, the message is ignored and your program continues running.

9. Add the following two new actions to the **FirstResponder** "class" (remember, *it's not really a class*), as in Figure 2:

```
save:
saveAs:
```

10. Connect the **Calculator→Save** and **Calculator→Save As** menu cells (which were previously enabled) to the **FirstResponder** icon. The **Calculator→Save** menu cell should send the **save:** action and the **Calculator→Save As** menu cell should send the **saveAs:** action.

11. Insert the four lines in **bold** below into **PaperControl.h**.

```
#import <appkit/appkit.h>

@interface PaperControl:Object
{
    id    proc;
    id    scroller;
    id    text;
    id    window;
    char *filename;
}

- setUp;
- window;
- windowWillClose:sender;
- text;
- setScroller:aScroller;
- appendToText:(const char *)val
                          fromPipe:(BOOL)flag;
- setFilename:(const char *)aFilename;
- saveAs:sender;
- save:sender;

@end
```

12. Insert the three method implementations below into **PaperControl.m**. Put them immediately before the *first* **@end** directive, *not* in the **TextDelegate** section.

```
- setFilename:(const char *)aFilename
{
```

```
      if (filename) free(filename);
      filename = malloc(strlen(aFilename)+1);
      strcpy(filename, aFilename);
      [window setTitleAsFilename:aFilename];
      return self;
  }


- saveAs:sender
{
  id panel;
  const char *dir;
  char *file;

/* prompt user for file name and save to that file */

  if (filename==0) {
    /* no filename; set up defaults */
    dir  = NXHomeDirectory();
    file = (char *)[window title];
  }
  else {
    file = rindex(filename, '/');
    if (file) {
      dir  = filename;
      *file = 0;
      file++;
    }
    else {
      dir  = filename;
      file = (char *)[window title];
    }
  }

  panel = [SavePanel new];

  [panel setRequiredFileType: "mathpaper"];
  if ([panel runModalForDirectory: dir
              file: file]) {
    [self setFilename: [panel filename] ];

    return [self save: sender];
  }
  return nil; /* didn't save */
}


- save:sender
```

```
        {
          int fd;
          NXStream *theStream;

          if (filename==0) return [self saveAs: sender];
          [window setTitle: "Saving..."];

          fd= open(filename, O_WRONLY|O_CREAT|O_TRUNC,0666);
          if (fd<0) {
            NXRunAlertPanel(0, "Cannot save file: %s",
                                 0, 0, 0, strerror(errno));
            return self;
          }

          theStream = NXOpenFile(fd, NX_WRITEONLY);
          [text writeRichText: theStream];

          NXClose(theStream);
          close(fd);

          [window setTitleAsFilename: filename];
          return self;
        }
```

We added the **filename** instance variable to the **PaperControl** class to record the file name associated with any window. The new **setFilename:** method sets **filename** to a file name that you specify, both allocating the memory necessary for the string and then setting the window's title bar to be the file name.

We also added the **saveAs:** action method that prompts the user for a file name, using a NeXTSTEP **SavePanel** object, and then saves it into the file. Lastly we added a **save:** method that first checks to see if a file name has been specified for the window. If a file name has not been specified, it invokes the **saveAs:** method, which prompts the user for a file name. Otherwise, it simply saves the file under the name that was previously specified.

Testing the Save Features

After you've made the changes, it's time to test them.

13. Save all pertinent files and **make** your application, but don't run it yet.

14. Drag the **MathPaper.app** (or **MathPaper.debug**) application icon from your File Viewer into your *dock*. Double-click the docked icon to launch MathPaper.

15. Enter some mathematical expressions into the MathPaper window.

16. Choose either the **Calculator→Save** or the **Calculator→Save As** menu command. Since you haven't given this window a file name yet, both functions do the same thing – bring up the Save panel. Note that the application icon automatically appears in the Save panel. See Figure 3 below.

FIGURE 3. Saving the Contents of a MathPaper Window

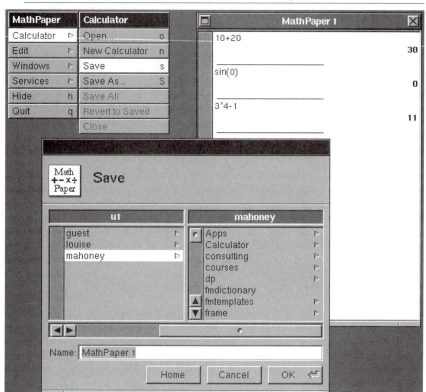

17. If necessary, click **Home** in the Save panel to open your home directory. Then type a file name and click **OK** (or hit return) to save the file in your home directory. You'll see the document icon appear above your chosen file name in your File Viewer, as in Figure 4 below.

Note also that the title bar of the MathPaper window has changed, as in the window in Figure 5 below.

18. Try **Calculator→Save As** to see that you can save the file under a different file name.

FIGURE 4. MathPaper Icons in File Viewer

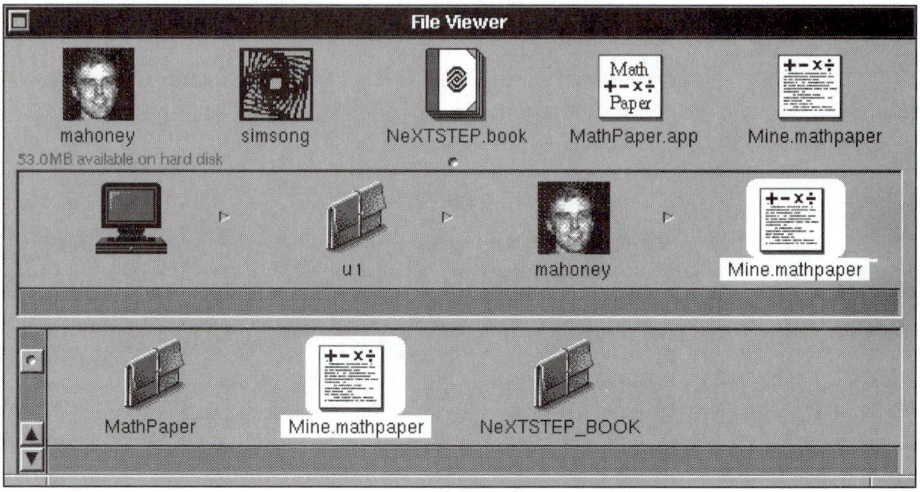

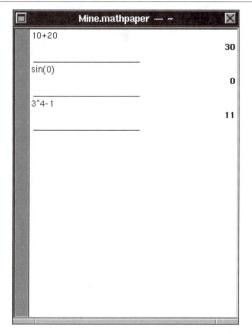

FIGURE 5. Name Change in a MathPaper Window's Title Bar

19. Quit MathPaper.

Loading From a File

Loading means that there is already a file on the computer's disk that we want to read and use in an application. Loading a file is usually considerably easier than saving it, since the hard work has (presumably) already been done.

There are two ways that the user should be able to load a file into our Math-Paper application:

- by choosing MathPaper's **Calculator→Open** menu command
- by double-clicking a MathPaper document file icon in the File Viewer.

In order to make "double-click loading" work properly, we'll need to add some code and do at least *one* of the following:

- Put the MathPaper application icon into your dock.
- Put the MathPaper application into your directory **~/Apps**, log out, and log back in.
- Put the MathPaper application into the directory **/LocalApps**, log out, and log back in. (You'll need **root** privilege to do this.)

We need to do one of these to force the Workspace Manager to read the MathPaper program's iconheader section, so that it discovers that the **mathpaper** extension is a MathPaper document file.

Now we'll add an action method that gets invoked when the user chooses MathPaper's **Calculator→Open** menu command.

1. Insert the new **loadCalc:** action method declaration below into **MathController.h**, immediately before the **@end** directive.

   ```
   - loadCalc:sender;
   ```

2. Insert the **loadCalc:** action method implementation below into **MathController.m**, immediately before the **@end** directive.

   ```
   - loadCalc:sender
   {
     char *types[2] = {"mathpaper", 0};

     if ([ [OpenPanel new] runModalForTypes:types]) {
       if ([self newCalc:self]) {
         [newCalc loadCalcFile:[ [OpenPanel new]
                                        filename] ];
       }
     }
   }
   ```

```
    return self;
}
```

This **loadCalc:** action method will be invoked in response to a user choosing the **Calculator→Open** menu command (we'll make a connection in IB later). The **[OpenPanel new]** message in **loadCalc:** returns the **id** of the MathPaper's **OpenPanel** instance object. (Each application gets precisely one **OpenPanel** object, and a pointer to it is returned by the **new** method.) We then send to the new **OpenPanel** object the **runModalForTypes:** message to display the on-screen Open panel and accept only file names with the **mathpaper** extension. The **types** argument set to the array **{"mathpaper", 0}** lets the Open panel display only files with the **mathpaper** extension and subdirectories. The array's contents determines which files will be displayed in the Open panel's browser. The zero (**0**) specifies the end of the array.

If the user clicks the **Cancel** button, the **runModalForTypes:** method returns **0**, and the rest of the **loadCalc:** method is ignored. Otherwise, a new calculator is created with the **newCalc:** method and assigned to the **newCalc** instance variable (see Chapter 10). We then send to this new calculator the **loadCalcFile:** message, which we'll discuss a bit later.

[[OpenPanel new] filename] simply returns the file name that was selected the last time that the **OpenPanel** was activated. (Remember, there is exactly one **OpenPanel** instance per application.)

Next we'll add code to **MathController** so that files with the **mathpaper** extension can be opened within MathPaper when their file icons are double-clicked in the File Viewer. The "delegate" code organized in a category below works because we made **MathController** the delegate of the **Application** object previously (in Chapter 10).

3. Insert the following code *after* the **@end** directive in **MathController.m**.

```
@implementation MathController(ApplicationDelegate)

- (BOOL)appAcceptsAnotherFile:sender
{
    return YES;
}

- (int)app:sender
    openFile:(const char *)filename
    type:(const char *)aType
{
```

```
        if ([self newCalc:self]) {
          if ([newCalc loadCalcFile:filename]) {
            return YES;
          }
        }
        return NO;
      }

      @end
```

4. For consistency, *move* **MathController**'s **appDidInit:** delegate method to the **MathController(ApplicationDelegate)** section and *delete* the **appDidInit:** declaration from **MathController.h**. (**ApplicationDelegate** methods should not be declared in the class interface file, unless they are declared in a separate **ApplicationDelegate** interface section, which is optional here.)

When you double-click a document file icon in your File Viewer, the Workspace Manager starts up the associated application (if it isn't already running). The application's **Application** delegate will then receive the **appAcceptsAnotherFile:** message to see if another file can be opened. If the application returns **YES** (1), then it can open another file. Some applications can only have a single file open at a time, and return **NO** if they already have one open.

If your **appAcceptsAnotherFile:** method returns **YES**, the **Application** object's delegate receives the **app:openFile:type:** message. The **sender** argument contains the **id** of the application, **filename** is the full path name of the file to open, and **aType** is the extension of the file name (**mathpaper** in our application). This method tries to create a new calculator, and if it is successfully created, it gets loaded. The method returns **YES** if the load was successful, and **NO** if it wasn't. If **NO** is returned, the Workspace Manager alerts the user that the application could not open the file.

Exception Handling

In **MathController**'s **loadCalc:** and **app:openFile:type:** methods above we invoked, but didn't define the **loadCalcFile:** method. We need to add this method to **PaperControl** to load a piece of math paper from a file. Before we show the method, however, we need to introduce two new concepts: *exceptions* and *exception handling*.

Exceptions are special conditions that interrupt the normal flow of a program. NeXTSTEP has a rich system for catching exceptions and handling them within the course of your program's execution. Exception handling is designed for multi-threaded applications, so that an exception generated in one thread can be handled without affecting execution in other threads.

To use the NeXTSTEP exception system, you specify a region of code that is *protected* and a second region of code that follows the protected region called the *exception handler*. If an exception is "raised" within the protected region of code – or within any function called within your protected region of code – control jumps to the exception handler. If an exception is not raised, the exception handler is skipped.

NeXTSTEP uses three macros for exception handling:

NX_DURING	Marks the beginning of the protected code
NX_HANDLER	Marks the beginning of the handler
NX_ENDHANDLER	Marks the end of the handler.

These are *macros*, not functions or compiler directives, and should *not* be followed by a semicolon. They can be found by searching in HeaderViewer or Librarian or by simply looking in the file **/NextDeveloper/Headers/ objc/error.h**. For more information about exceptions and exception handling in general, search for "exceptions" in Librarian.

The most common place to use an exception handler is when loading information from a disk file: if the file is inconsistent, an exception will be raised, and your handler will execute. We'll use this type of exception handler below to protect the **PaperControl** class while a MathPaper file is being loaded into the **Text** object.

5. Insert the new **loadCalcFile:** method declaration below into **PaperControl.h**, immediately before the **@end** directive.

```
- loadCalcFile:(const char *)aFile;
```

6. Insert the **loadCalcFile:** method implementation below into **PaperControl.m**, immediately before the *first* **@end** directive.

```
- loadCalcFile:(const char *)aFile
{
  NXStream *theStream= NXMapFile(aFile,NX_READONLY);
  if (theStream) {
    id ret = self;
    [window setTitle:"Loading..."];
```

```
        NX_DURING
        [text readRichText:theStream];
        [self setFilename:aFile];

        /* Exception handler is skipped
         * if no exception is raised.
         */
        NX_HANDLER
          switch (NXLocalHandler.code) {
          case NX_illegalWrite:
            NXRunAlertPanel(0,"Illegal write on stream",
                            0,0,0);
            ret = nil;
            break;
          case NX_illegalRead:
            NXRunAlertPanel(0,"Illegal read on stream",
                            0,0,0);
            ret = nil;
            break;
          case NX_illegalSeek:
            NXRunAlertPanel(0,"Illegal seek on stream",
                            0,0,0);
            ret = nil;
            break;
          case NX_illegalStream:
            NXRunAlertPanel(0,"invalid stream",0,0,0);
            ret = nil;
            break;
          case NX_streamVMError:
            NXRunAlertPanel(0,"VM error on stream",
                            0,0,0, aFile);
            ret = nil;
            break;
        }
        NX_ENDHANDLER   /* end of handler */


        NXCloseMemory(theStream, NX_FREEBUFFER);
        return ret;
    }
  return nil;
}
```

This **loadCalcFile:** method uses the **NXMapFile()** stream function to create an **NXStream** that contains the entire contents of the **aFile** file. This is the most efficient way to read a file into an application. If the stream is read, it is loaded into the **Text** object, the paper's file name is set (which also sets the title bar), and then the stream is closed. If the file can't be loaded, the method returns **nil**.

7. Open up **MathPaper.nib** in Interface Builder.

8. Drag the **MathController.h** file icon from your Workspace File Viewer and drop it into the **MathPaper.nib** File window in IB. IB will automatically **Parse** the outlets and actions in **MathController.h** (only **loadCalc:** is new). Make sure **MathController.h** has been saved.

9. Connect the **Calculator→Open** menu cell (which should be enabled) to the **MathController** instance so that it sends the **loadCalc:** action message.

10. Save all pertinent files, **make** and run your updated application.

11. Enter some mathematical expressions in the MathPaper window, and save the contents of a window using the **Calculator→Save** menu command.

12. Try double-clicking the file icon for the file that you saved both when MathPaper *is* and *is not* running. The Workspace Manager should automatically launch MathPaper when it isn't running and should create a window with the contents of the file that you just saved in both cases.

13. Try to open the file you saved by choosing the **Calculator→Open** command. It should work.

14. Quit MathPaper.

Marking a Document Window as Edited

An application should properly handle the closing of a document window by setting the **docEdited** flag, an instance variable declared in the **Window** class. The **docEdited** flag determines whether the on-screen window's close button contains a solid cross (, **docEdited=NO**) or a cross with a hole in it (, **docEdited=YES**). It can also be used to determine whether or not a document window can be safely closed without any loss of data. Obviously, the **docEdited** flag should be *set* when the text inside the Math-Paper page has been edited, and *unset* when it hasn't.

1. Insert the two lines in **bold** below into the **appendtoText:fromPipe:** and **save:** methods in **PaperControl.m**. They are all that's needed to properly set the **docEdited** flag:

```
-appendToText:(const char *)val fromPipe:(BOOL)flag
```

```
{
  int length = [text textLength];
  [window setDocEdited:YES];
  [text setSel:length :length];
  . . .
}

- save:sender
  . . .
  [window setTitleAsFilename:filename];
  [window setDocEdited:NO];
  return self;
}
```

We'll also modify the **windowWillClose:** delegate method so that the user will be warned before a window with edited text is closed (so he gets a chance to change his mind). We'll do this by displaying an attention (warning, alert) panel if the user attempts to close a window containing edited text.

2. Insert the lines in **bold** below into the **windowWillClose:** method in **PaperControl.m**:

```
- windowWillClose:sender
{
  if ([sender isDocEdited]) {
    const char *fname;
    int q;

    fname = filename ? filename : [sender title];
    if (rindex(fname,'/'))
                       fname = rindex(fname,'/') + 1;

    q = NXRunAlertPanel("Save",
            "Save changes to %s?",
            "Save", "Don't Save", "Cancel", fname);
    if (q==1) {        /* save */
      if (![self save:nil]) {
        return nil;   /* didn't save */
      }
    }
    if (q==-1) {       /* cancel */
      return nil;
    }
  }
                  /* tell Window we're gone */
  [sender setDelegate:nil];
  [proc free];
```

```
    [self free]; /* erase instance */
    return self; /* Window will free itself on close*/
}
```

The **NXRunAlertPanel()** function displays the panel in Figure 6 below. The function returns **1, 0,** or **-1**, depending on whether the first (**Save**), second (**Don't Save**), or third (**Cancel**) option is chosen. Recall that the **save:** method returns **nil** if the file didn't get saved. If **save:** returns **nil,** then **windowWillClose:** also returns **nil**. Recall that if the **windowWillClose:** delegate method returns **nil**, the window doesn't close. This is what prevents the window from closing if the user clicks cancel.

FIGURE 6. Attention Panel (for Saving a Window's Contents)

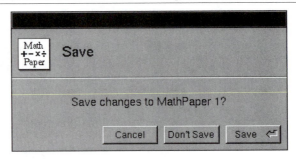

The last argument in **NXRunAlertPanel(), fname,** is the name of the file that will be displayed in the attention panel. In our case, it will be **Mathpaper 1** (or **2**, or ...) because the C string function call **rindex(fname,'/')** returns a pointer to the last occurrence of the character '/' in the full path name of the file.

Terminating an Application Properly

When the user chooses to quit an application, it is customary and appropriate for the application to scan all of its open windows and see if any of them contain edited documents which haven't been saved. If there are any, the application should give the user the opportunity to save them. This functionality is quite easy to implement with the **Application** delegate method **appWillTerminate:**.

3. Insert the two new method declarations below into **MathController.h,** immediately before the **@end** directive.

```
- (int)countEditedWindows;
- saveAll:sender;
```

4. Insert the **countEditedWindows** method implementation below into **MathController.m**, immediately before the *first* **@end** directive.

```
-  (int)countEditedWindows
{
   id  winList;
   int i;
   int count = 0;

   winList = [NXApp windowList];
   for (i=0; i<[winList count]; i++) {
      if ([ [winList objectAt: i] isDocEdited])
         count++;
   }
   return count;
}
```

The first new **MathController** method, **countEditedWindows**, counts the number of windows that have edited documents and returns the number. It gets the list of all the application's windows from the **Application** object (**NXApp**) and then uses the Window method **isDocEdited** to determine whether the contents of a window have been edited. See Chapter 7 for more on the **List** class.

The second new method, **saveAll:**, goes through the window list, looking at the delegate of each window to make sure that it's an instance of the **PaperControl** class. (We don't want to send the **save:** message to the windows that contain the application's menus or panels.) It then sends the **save:** message to each window delegate.

5. Insert the **saveAll:** method implementation below into **MathController.m**, immediately before the *first* **@end** directive.

```
-  saveAll:sender
{
   id  winList;
   int i;

   winList = [NXApp windowList];
   for (i=0; i<[winList count]; i++) {
      id win = [winList objectAt: i];
      id delegate = [win delegate];

      if ([delegate isKindOf:[PaperControl class]]) {
         [win makeKeyAndOrderFront:nil];
         [delegate save:win];
      }
   }
}
```

```
    return self;
}
```

Another new method – this time an **Application** delegate method called **appWillTerminate:** – will invoke the **countEditedWindows** method to determine if there are any edited windows. If there are, it gives the user a chance to review the unsaved documents (and possibly save them) by sending a **performClose:** message to each document window (which has the same effect as the user clicking the window's close button). Alternatively, the user can quit the application with the unsaved documents, or cancel the termination request.

6.   Insert the **appWillTerminate:** method below into **MathController.m**. For consistency, it's best to put it with the other **Application** delegate methods, in **ApplicationDelegate**.

```
- appWillTerminate:sender
{
  if ([self countEditedWindows]>0) {
    int q = NXRunAlertPanel("Quit",
            "There are edited windows.",
            "Review Unsaved",
            "Quit Anyway", "Cancel");
    if (q==1) {           /* Review */
      int i;
      id  winList;

      winList = [NXApp windowList];
      for(i=0; i<[winList count]; i++){
        id win = [winList objectAt: i];

        if([ [win delegate]
             isKindOf:[PaperControl class] ]){
          [win performClose:nil];
        }
      }
      return self;
    }
    if (q==-1) {          /* cancel */
      return nil;
    }
  }
  return self;           /* quit */
}
```

Now that we've implemented the **saveAll:** method, it's very easy to give functionality to the **Calculator→Save All** menu command.

7. Back in IB with **MathPaper.nib** active, **Parse** the **MathController** class interface. This can be done by choosing the **Parse** operation or by dragging the **MathController.h** file icon into IB's File window.

8. Connect the **Calculator→Save All** menu cell (which should be enabled) to the **MathController** instance so that it sends the **saveAll:** action message.

9. Save all the pertinent files and **make** and run MathPaper.

10. Create two new MathPaper windows, and enter some mathematical expressions in each. Note when the close buttons change.

11. Choose the **Calculator→Save All** menu command. You should be prompted to save the contents of each of the unsaved windows separately.

12. Now enter an additional mathematical expression in each of the two MathPaper windows and choose **Calculator→Save All** again.

13. Finally, enter an additional mathematical expression in each of the two MathPaper windows again and choose **Quit**. You should see the panel in Figure 7 below.

FIGURE 7. MathPaper's Quit Attention Panel

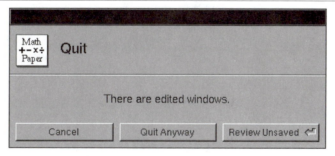

Enabling and Disabling Menu Cells

Cells (commands, items) in NeXTSTEP menus can be either *enabled* or *disabled*. When a menu cell is enabled, it's displayed in *black* type and sends a message to its target when the user clicks it with the mouse (or types its keyboard alternative). When a menu cell is disabled, it's displayed in *gray* type and it does not respond to mouse clicks or key alternatives.

NeXTSTEP provides a very sophisticated system which allows you to specify methods that get invoked automatically to determine when a menu cell should be enabled or disabled. *You should use this system rather than trying to bypass it and do something on your own.* Although NeXTSTEP's system strikes many beginning programmers as inefficient, it is actually very efficient.

Window Updates

Until now, every NeXTSTEP user interface object we've used updates itself on-screen whenever we make a change to that object's internal state. For example, when we sent the **setStringValue:** message to a **TextField** in the **displayX** method in the Calculator application, the value displayed in the on-screen text field changed immediately.

Oftentimes, objects in a window don't get notified when they need to change what they are displaying. For example, if you have an Inspector panel in a drawing program such as NeXTSTEP's IconBuilder, the Inspector doesn't get notified when the user selects a different graphic. Instead, it is the job of the Inspector (or its controller) to constantly monitor what is selected and change itself as appropriate.

NeXTSTEP uses a similar system to update the status of menu cells. For each menu cell, you define an *update action*. Whenever a menu needs to be updated, NeXTSTEP sends the update action down the responder chain for every exposed menu cell. The update action returns YES if the menu cell needs to change its state, either from enabled to disabled or vice versa. If the update action returns NO, the menu cell does not need to change its state.

But how often do menu cells need to be updated? It's impossible for NeXTSTEP to know – that depends on your application. You can force a window update by hand whenever you want by sending the **updateWindows** message to **NXApp**. Alternatively, you can send **NXApp** the message [**NXApp setAutoupdate:YES**]. Auto-updating makes NeXTSTEP update the windows after each event is processed. Although it seems that auto-updating will impose a severe performance penalty, in practice it doesn't.

Making MathPaper Update Its Menus

In this section, we'll modify the MathPaper application to automatically enable or disable the **Save** and **Save As** menu cells. The commands should be enabled whenever the main window is a piece of math paper.

An easy way to check to see if the main window is a piece of MathPaper is to look at the main window's delegate. If the window's delegate is an instance of the **PaperControl** class, then the main window is a piece of math paper.

In order to make the menu cells properly enable and disable, we also need to know the **id** of each cell and the **id** of the menu that contains them. It's easy enough to get the **id** of the **Save** and **Save As** cells: simply create outlets in the **MathController** object and connect them to the cells.

Getting the **id** of their containing menu is a little more difficult. You can't connect an outlet to the menu directly. Instead, we'll connect an outlet to the **Calculator** menu cell in the main menu. The *target* of this menu cell will be the **id** of the **Calculator** menu itself.

The first step is to create three new outlets in the **MathController** object with the **id** of the menu cells that we wish to control.

1. Insert the three new outlets and new method declaration in `bold` below into **MathController.h**.

   ```
   #import <appkit/appkit.h>

   @interface MathController:Object
   ...
      /* three outlets for updating menu cells */
      id calculatorSubmenuCell;
      id saveMenuCell;
      id saveAsMenuCell;
   }
   ...
   - saveAll:sender;
   - (BOOL)menuActive:menuCell;
   @end
   ```

2. Back in IB with **MathPaper.nib** open, **Parse** the new class definition of **MathController**.

3. Connect the **saveMenuCell** outlet in the **MathController** instance to the **Save** menu cell in the **Calculator** submenu. Note that the direction here is different from our previous connections involving menus.

4. Connect the **saveAsMenuCell** outlet in the **MathController** instance to the **Save As** menu cell in the **Calculator** submenu.

5. Connect the **calculatorSubmenuCell** outlet in the **MathController** instance to the **Calculator** menu *cell* in the *main* menu (*not* to anything in the **Calculator** submenu).

Now we need to add the code to the **MathController** class that will set the **updateAction** for these menu cells to be a new method in the class. We also need to write the **updateAction** method.

6.   Insert the **menuActive:** method implementation below into **MathController.m**, immediately before the *first* **@end** directive.

```
- (BOOL)menuActive:menuCell
{
  BOOL shouldBeEnabled;

  shouldBeEnabled = [[[NXApp mainWindow] delegate]
                        isKindOf:[PaperControl class]];

  if([menuCell isEnabled] != shouldBeEnabled) {
    /* Menu cell is either enabled and shouldn't be,
     * or it is not enabled and should be.
     * In any event, set the correct state.
     */
    [menuCell setEnabled:shouldBeEnabled];
    return YES;   /* redisplay */
  }
  return NO;      /* no change */
}
```

This method looks at the delegate of the main window to see if it is an instance of the **PaperControl** class. If it is, it sets the boolean variable **shouldBeEnabled** to be **YES**. The method then compares the menu cell's current condition with what it should be. If the cell is enabled and shouldn't be or is not enabled and should be, it sets the menu cell to the correct state and returns **YES**. Returning **YES** tells NeXTSTEP to redisplay the menu. Otherwise, the method returns **NO** and the menu cell is not redisplayed.

7.   Insert the lines in **bold** below into the **appDidInit:** delegate method in **MathController.m**.

```
- appDidInit:sender
{
  id docMenu = [calculatorSubmenuCell target];

  [self newCalc:self];

  [saveMenuCell
      setUpdateAction: @selector(menuActive:)
      forMenu: docMenu];

  [saveAsMenuCell
      setUpdateAction: @selector(menuActive:)
      forMenu: docMenu];
```

```
    [NXApp setAutoupdate: YES];
    return self;
}
```

The first new statement gets the **id** of the **Calculator** submenu. We then send a message to each menu cell telling each their update action (**menuActive:**) and the menu in which they reside. Finally, we send **NXApp** the **setAutoupdate:YES** message so that window update messages are automatically generated after every event is processed.

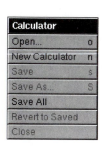

8. Save all pertinent files, **make** and run your updated MathPaper.

9. Open the **Calculator** submenu and close the (only) MathPaper main window. The **Save** and **Save As** cells will become disabled, as in the menu at the left. Note that we should also disable the **Save All** menu command; try it yourself!

10. Quit MathPaper.

Adding Printing Capability

This has been a long chapter and it's time for a quick dessert. We haven't done anything with printing so far. One of the biggest programming secrets of NeXTSTEP is that printing is extremely easy. Just as PostScript is used to display things on the screen, PostScript is used to send images to the printer. Once you set up the environment to generate PostScript and send it to the printer, it's all nearly automatic.

The NeXTSTEP **View** class provides a rich set of methods for controlling printing. The important method is **printPSCode:**, which causes the **View** to display the standard Print panel. If the user clicks the **Print** button in the Print panel, the PostScript code is turned into a bit image which is then sent to the printer. (It's a "dumb" printer – the PostScript is handled entirely in the computer – which keeps the cost of the printer down.) Thus the only thing that you need do to make a **View** object print its contents is send it the **printPSCode:** message. If you wish to capture the PostScript code that a **View** would generate if printed, you can call the method **copyPSCodeInside:to:** to send the PostScript code for a particular bounding box to a stream of your choice.

You can override methods in the **View** class to get more control over printing. For example, you can override the **beginPageSetupRect:placement:**

method to cause special PostScript code to be generated at the beginning of each page; likewise, you can override the **endPage** method to cause specific PostScript code to be generated when the page is done.

1. Back in IB, select the **FirstResponder** "class" in the **MathPaper.nib** Classes view.

2. Add the **printCalc:** action method to the **FirstResponder** class in the Class Attributes Inspector.

3. Drag an **Item** menu cell from IB's Menus palette and drop it just above the **Services** menu cell in the MathPaper main menu.

4. Change the name of the new menu cell to "**Print...**" and give it a key equivalent "**p**" as in the menu at the left of the page. (Don't forget the three dots, which indicate that the menu command brings up a panel.)

5. Connect the **Print** menu cell to the **FirstResponder** object in IB's File window (Objects view) so that it sends the **printCalc:** action method.

Recall that when a message is sent to the **FirstResponder** object, the message is sent to the following objects in the following order, until a recipient to the message is found:

- The key window
- The key window's delegate
- The application's main window
- The application's main window's delegate
- The application's **Application** object
- The application's **Application** object's delegate

We're going to modify the **PaperControl** instance, the key window's delegate, so that it responds to the **printCalc:** action method we added in IB. We'll be lazy and simply have the **printCalc:** method send the **printPSCode:** method to the window's **Text** object. The **Text** object will automatically provide for pagination if it contains more than one page of calculations.

We are being lazy because we are not going to print any nice features, such as a headline, page numbers, or vertical lines to denote the sides of the output. When we're done the output should look similar to what you see in Figure 8 below (we added the rectangular boundary).

FIGURE 8. **Printed Output from MathPaper**

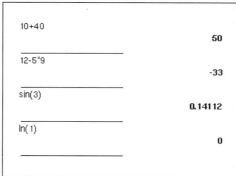

10+40

50

12-5*9

-33

sin(3)

0.14112

ln(1)

0

In order to implement the nice print features, we would have to create our own custom **View**, which we'll do in a later chapter. For now, let's just make the thing print!

6. Insert the new **printCalc:** method declaration below into **PaperControl.h**, immediately before the **@end** directive.

```
- printCalc:sender;
```

7. Insert the **printCalc:** method implementation below into **PaperControl.m**, immediately before the *first* **@end** directive.

```
- printCalc:sender
{
  [text printPSCode:nil];
  return self;
}
```

8. Save all pertinent files, **make** and run your updated application.

9. Try out the new **Print** menu command. When you type Command-p, you'll see the Print Panel appear as in Figure 9 below (note that our application icon was automatically added). Print the contents of a MathPaper window; you'll get something similar to what's in Figure 8 above.

10. Quit MathPaper and congratulate yourself on learning a heck of a lot in this chapter.

FIGURE 9. **Print Panel in MathPaper**

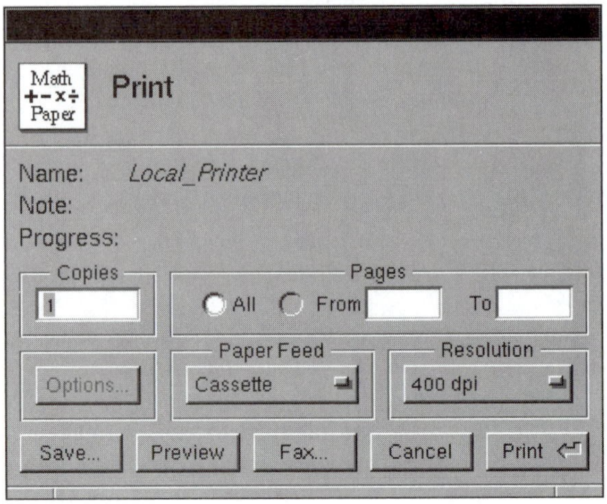

Summary

In this chapter we learned how to save and load the contents of a window using **Application** delegate, **SavePanel**, and **OpenPanel** objects and methods. We then learned how to mark a window as edited, and how to erase that mark after the window's contents are saved. We also learned how to check to see if a window is edited before closing it, how to check to see if an application has any edited windows before quitting, and how to display appropriate warning panels to ask the user what to do in these situations. Finally, as frosting on the cake, we learned a quick and dirty way to make an object print "itself."

In the next chapter, we'll have some fun with a little animation. It's the last chapter that involves MathPaper. Then in the following chapter, we'll go into more depth about custom **View**s.

DPS 14

Drawing with Display PostScript

Although we've mentioned PostScript numerous times before, we've never used it to do much in the way of actual drawing. The reason for this is largely due the power of the NeXTSTEP Application Kit: most of the objects that we've used until this point already know how to generate PostScript to display themselves on the screen. Consequentially, we haven't had to generate it ourselves.

PostScript is itself a complete programming language. It is a subject far too vast to cover in this chapter. (See Appendix B for references on PostScript.) Instead, we'll give you a sense of how PostScript drawing is done in the NeXTSTEP environment, and give you pointers on where to go from here.

Animation in an Info Panel

The goal of this chapter is to create an animated Info Panel for the MathPaper application. NeXTSTEP applications' Info Panels are often animated, even in programs that don't otherwise use animation. An impressive Info Panel shows off what a programmer can do; rightly or wrongly, the quality of the Info Panel might be taken as a representation of the overall quality of the application itself.

The MathPaper Info Panel will have two kinds of animation: *motion* and *dissolving*. Motion animation is just that – something moves on the screen. If you look at the Info Panel for the Terminal application, you'll see the string ">**MACH**" scroll up in the little terminal window. See Figure 1 below.

FIGURE 1. Animation in the Terminal Info Panel

Another kind of animation is dissolving animation, where one image literally dissolves into another. A good example of this sort of animation is the Workspace Manager Info Panel, where the NeXT icon dissolves into pictures of its four authors (Lee Boynton, Jean-Marie Hullot, Bertrand Serlet, and Keith Ohlfs) when the user clicks the NeXT icon or an author's name. Of course, it's impossible to show what these images really look like on a printed page, but Figure 2 below should give you an idea.

FIGURE 2. Dissolving in the Workspace Manager Info Panel

In our animation, we'll arrange for the *plus*, *minus*, *times*, and *divide* symbols to move from the top of MathPaper's Info Panel to the bottom. The string "MathPaper" and the MathPaper icon will then dissolve into the window, as if they were being beamed down from the *Starship PostScript*. The final panel will look like the one in Figure 3 below. Making this happen will be the subject of the rest of this chapter.

FIGURE 3. MathPaper Info Panel

pswrap: Wrapping PostScript into a C Function

One of the fundamental problems of using a PostScript-based window system is the problem of communication between a programmer's application and the Window Server. After all, most programmers write in C, not in PostScript, and their programs are designed to execute in the user's address space, rather than in the Window Server. In the Adobe Display PostScript environment, this communication is accomplished by means of a system called *PostScript wraps*.

Simply put, a *wrap* is a piece of a C-code wrapped around a cluster of Post-Script code. A program called **pswrap** in the **/usr/bin** directory processes the wrap and generates a C language function that can be called by any C program. When the generated C function is called, the PostScript is down-loaded to the Window Server and executed. NeXT provides wraps for all of the standard built-in PostScript operators, called *single-operator C functions*. You can also write your own wraps.

Let's see how **pswrap** works. Below is a simple wrap for the PostScript **show** (i.e., *show output*) operator. Suppose it is saved in the file named **PSshow.psw** (the **psw** extension means **P**ost**S**cript **w**rap).

```
defineps PSshow()
    show
endps
```

You can see that the syntax is a strange conglomeration of C and Post-Script. Procedures start with the **defineps** directive and end with the **endps** directive. The name of the function follows the keyword **defineps**; any arguments are placed within the parentheses (more on arguments later). Only valid PostScript code can be placed between the **defineps** and **endps** statements. In this case, the wrap is called **PSshow()**, and it generates a call to the PostScript **show** operator.

You can run the **pswrap** command from the command line (what you type is in **bold**):

```
localhost> pswrap PSshow.psw -h PSshow.h -o PSshow.c
localhost> ls -l PS*
total 3
-rw-r--r-- 1 simsong     627 Feb 14 14:45 PSshow.c
-rw-r--r-- 1 simsong     172 Feb 14 14:45 PSshow.h
-rw-r--r-- 1 simsong      30 Feb 14 14:45 PSshow.psw
localhost>
```

The **-h** argument tells **pswrap** the name of the **.h** file where you want the header information written, while the **-o** argument tells **pswrap** the name of the **.c** file where you want the C source code written.

Below we list the C-code generated by **pswrap** in **PSshow.c**. It's not essential that you understand what it means, so we'll spend very little time on it.

```
/* PSshow.c generated from PSshow.psw
 * by unix pswrap V1.009 Wed Apr 19 17:50:24 PDT 1989
 */
```

```
#include <dpsclient/dpsfriends.h>
#include <string.h>

#line 1 "PSshow.psw"
#line 10 "PSshow.c"
void PSshow()
{
  typedef struct {
    unsigned char tokenType;
    unsigned char topLevelCount;
    unsigned short nBytes;

    DPSBinObjGeneric obj0;
  } _dpsQ;

  static _dpsQ _dpsF = {
    DPS_DEF_TOKENTYPE, 1, 12,
    {DPS_EXEC|DPS_NAME, 0,DPSSYSNAME,160},/* show */
  }; /* _dpsQ */

  register DPSContext _dpsCurCtxt =
                        DPSPrivCurrentContext();
  DPSBinObjSeqWrite(_dpsCurCtxt,(char *) &_dpsF,12);
}
#line 3 "PSshow.psw"
```

Not very clear, is it? The two key functions used by the wrap are **DPSPrivCurrentContext()** and **DPSBinObjSeqWrite()**. The function **DPSPrivCurrentContext()** returns the current Display PostScript context. The function **DPSBinObjSeqWrite()** sends a binary-encoded sequence of objects to that context.

(Note: You should never modify or edit the contents of the **.c** file generated from a **.psw** or **.pswm** file. We have shown the contents of this file for illustrative purposes only.)

The Display PostScript system uses a mechanism called *contexts* to present each PostScript client program with its own independent copy of the Post-Script interpreter. A PostScript context can be thought of as a "virtual printer." Each has its own set of stacks, input/output facilities, dictionaries, and memory.

Sometimes a single client can have more than one context. NeXTSTEP creates a second PostScript context when you print a view. The NeXT-STEP Mail application can display EPS images in their own context for improved security.

For more information about Display PostScript contexts, see *Programming The Display PostScript System with NeXTSTEP* (the "Purple Book"), written by Adobe and published by Addison-Wesley, 1992.

Passing Arguments to pswrap Functions

The **pswrap** utility provides a simple way for passing arguments to PostScript wraps – simpler, in fact, than in standard PostScript. Below is a simple wrap for the PostScript intrinsic **rmoveto**, the *relative move to* operator:

```
defineps PSrmoveto(float x,y)
   x y rmoveto
endps
```

Wraps that Return a Value

Wraps can also return values to the calling program. This makes it considerably simpler to debug a PostScript program. For example, to see the contents of the PostScript operand stack, just write a small wrap that duplicates the value on the top of the stack and returns it.

Below is simple wrap that copies the value on the top of the PostScript stack (using the PostScript **dup** operator) and returns the value to the user. The value on the top of the stack is assumed to be a floating point number. Notice also that output arguments in a wrap are specified after the *vertical bar* (|) in the wrap definition.

```
defineps PSgettop(|float *val)
   dup
endps
```

This wrap needs to return information from the Display PostScript interpreter to your program. So, when you call this wrap, your program will wait until the Display PostScript interpreter "catches up" with all of the PostScript that you have asked the interpreter to execute. This is called "making a round-trip" and can substantially degrade the performance of your application.

Buffering

The underlying communication channel between an application and the Display PostScript interpreter is buffered and bidirectional. *Buffered* means that the PostScript commands get saved up and sent to the server in batches, to minimize the amount of communication overhead associated with any single operation. *Bidirectional* means that you can send information to the interpreter and it can send information back.

Normally, buffering is precisely what you want, because it makes your program run more efficiently. But sometimes you need to synchronize your user program with the Display PostScript interpreter. For example, if you are displaying animation on the screen, you want each PostScript draw command to be executed, one by one, rather than having them saved up and executed all in a single batch.

As we saw above, calling a wrap that returns a value is one way to force your program to synchronize with the PostScript interpreter. Another way to synchronize the two processes is to call the NeXTSTEP function **NXPing()**, which places a call to the Window Server and waits for it to return.

Occasionally, calling a function like **NXPing()** can make your program run more efficiently, because while your program is waiting for the interpreter to catch up, they are not both competing for the CPU. Usually, though, your program simply *looks* like it is running more efficiently, because its drawing is smooth rather than jerky.

A PostScript Wrap for MathPaper

For our MathPaper Info Panel, we'll create a wrap that takes four arguments and displays a given text string in a specified gray at a specific location in the panel. By combining all of these operations in a single PostScript wrap, we'll be able to cut down on the traffic between our program and the Window Server, and make the program run more efficiently.

If we were writing "raw" PostScript, we might write the operator (procedure) like this:

```
/supershow {
  setgray
  moveto
  show
} bind def
```

We could then use this **supershow** operator by first placing four PostScript arguments on the stack, like this:

```
x y graylevel string supershow
```

Below we show how the same procedure looks using **pswrap**.

1. Using an editor, type in the wrap below and save it in a file called **supershow.psw** in your **MathPaper** directory.

```
defineps supershow(float x; float y; float graylevel;
                                        char *string)
    graylevel setgray
    x y moveto
    (string) show
    flushgraphics
endps
```

One of the nice things about PostScript wrapping is that your PostScript function can use any argument at any time, without having to carry out strange gyrations with the PostScript stack.

Next, we'll arrange for Project Builder to automatically run the **pswrap** program and compile the resulting generated C code.[1]

PB.project

2. Launch Project Builder by double-clicking the **PB.project** file icon in your **MathPaper** project directory in the Workspace File Viewer.

3. View your project's "other" source files by clicking the **Files** button at the top of PB's main window and then the **Other Sources** file type in PB's browser. See Figure 4 below.

supershow.psw

4. Add the **supershow.psw** file to the project by dragging its icon from your File Viewer into PB's Files view. Figure 4 shows that **supershow.psw** has been added to your MathPaper project.

When you **make** (build) your project, the **supershow.psw** file will automatically be processed by **pswrap** to generate the files **supershow.c** and **supershow.h**. These **pswrap**-generated files will also be automatically compiled and linked.

_____

1. In NeXTSTEP 2.1, add the **pswrap** program **supershow.psw** to your project in IB's Project Inspector (Files view); **make** will call **pswrap** for you.

FIGURE 4. **Adding a pswrap File in Project Builder**

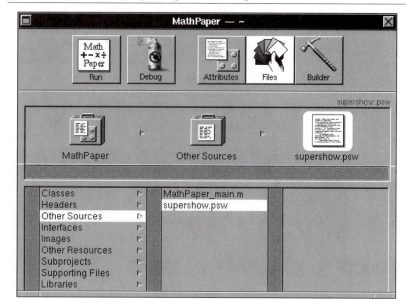

Drawing in a View with PostScript

There are two techniques we can use to draw in a **View** object:

- Place PostScript wraps calls in a **View**'s **drawSelf::** method (which is invoked whenever the **View**'s **display** method is invoked).

- Place PostScript wraps calls in *any* **View** method between **[self lockFocus]** and **[self unlockFocus]** messages. This is known as *locking the PostScript focus* on the **View**.

The first technique is used more often. When you implement code with **drawSelf::**, it gets called *automatically* when it is needed. All you need to concentrate on is *how* to draw the object; NeXTSTEP handles the *when*.

When you are learning how to draw with Display PostScript, it is often easier to draw manually by locking the focus and issuing the PostScript commands yourself. This is also the best way to create animation in your program.

Adding the Animated Info Panel to MathPaper

In this section, we'll add the animated Info Panel that we discussed earlier to the MathPaper application. First we'll add a new module for the Info Panel's nib file and arrange for the nib to be automatically loaded the first time the user chooses the **Info→Info Panel** menu command. (Recall that it's more efficient to use a separate nib module for an Info Panel, as we did in our four-function Calculator in Chapter 6. Then the nib only needs to be loaded in memory if it's used, and Info Panels aren't used very often.)

5. Double-click **MathPaper.nib** in the Files view of PB's main window to open this nib file in Interface Builder.

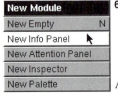

6. Choose IB's **Document→New Module→New Info Panel** command to create a new nib with an Info Panel. Save the new nib in the file **info.nib** in your **MathPaper/English.lproj** directory and insert it into the MathPaper project. PB shows the new nib has been added.[1]

As in Chapter 6, we want the main controlling object (**MathController** here) to be the **File's Owner** of the new **info.nib**, so it can easily communicate with the nib. To do this we'll need to inform **info.nib** about the **Math-Controller** class and then change the class of the **info.nib**'s **File's Owner** to be **MathController**. We'll do this the easy way this time.

7. Parse the **MathController** class definition in **info.nib** (not **MathPaper.nib**) by dragging the **MathController.h** icon from your File Viewer and dropping it in the **info.nib** File window.

8. Change the class of the **info.nib**'s **File's Owner** to **MathController** (click the **File's Owner** icon and then use the Inspector).

9. Click in the Info Panel's background, type Command-a (select all), and then Command-x to cut out every object inside the default Info Panel. We won't be needing any of them.

10. Make the empty Info Panel taller, about the same height as IB's Inspector panel.

Now that we have the Info Panel, let's create the **View** in which we'll be displaying animation.

11. **Subclass** the **View** class (under **Responder**) in the **info.nib** Classes view and rename the new class **InfoView**.

---

1. If you're using NeXTSTEP 2.1, refer to Chapter 6 for details on how to create an auxiliary nib for an Info Panel.

12. Add the **animateInfo:** action to the **InfoView** class.

13. Drag a **CustomView** icon from IB's Views palette and drop it in the Info Panel. This instantiates an instance of the **View** class.

14. Change the class of the **CustomView** to **InfoView** in the Class Inspector.

15. Resize the **InfoView** instance so that it completely covers the **Info Panel**'s content **View**. Your Info Panel should look like the panel in Figure 5 below.

FIGURE 5. **Adding an Info Panel with a Custom View**

16. **Unparse** the **InfoView** class and insert it into your MathPaper project.

Later we'll create an **Info→Info Panel** menu cell (which must be part of the main nib **MathPaper.nib**) and connect it the **MathController** instance so that it sends a message to load **info.nib**. When this nib is loaded the Info Panel and **InfoView** instance will be displayed on the screen. We'll need a way to send messages from the **MathController** instance to the **InfoView** object in order to display the animation. We'll use an outlet called **info-View** which points to the **InfoView** object to do the job.

17. Using an editor, add the **infoView** outlet below to **MathController.h** and save the file.

```
id infoView;
```

18. Back in IB, **Parse** the new definition of the **MathController** class in the **info.nib** (*not* **MathPaper.nib**) Classes view.

19. Connect the **infoView** outlet from the **info.nib**'s **File's Owner** icon (which represents the **MathController** instance) to the **InfoView** instance (the dark gray rectangle in Figure 5 above) in the Info Panel.

Adding the Info Panel Menu Cell, Method, and Connection

We still need to add the **Info Panel** menu cell to the user interface and make it send an action to the **MathController**. First we'll add the required action method, **showInfoPanel:**, which will display the Info Panel when the **Info Panel** menu command is chosen.

20. Insert the **showInfoPanel:** action method declaration below into **MathController.h**.

```
- showInfoPanel:sender;
```

21. Insert the **showInfoPanel:** action method implementation below into **MathController.m**, immediately before the *first* **@end** directive.

```
- showInfoPanel:sender
{
    if (infoView==0) {
        [NXApp loadNibSection:"info.nib" owner:self];
    }
    [ [infoView window] makeKeyAndOrderFront:self];
    [infoView animateInfo:self];
    return self;
}
```

22. Insert the **#import** directive below near the beginning of **MathController.m**.

```
#import "InfoView.h"
```

This directive is needed because messages will be sent from the **MathController** instance to the **InfoView** instance (see the **showInfoPanel:** method above). Notice that we don't need the **id** of the Info Panel itself, just the **View** to which we wish to send the **animateInfo:** message. If we needed the **id** of the window that contains the **View**, we could get it by sending the **window** message to the **View**. This is another example of the coherence that we saw in an earlier chapter.

23. **Parse** the **MathController** class in the file **MathPaper.nib** (*not* **info.nib**) Classes view to bring in the new **showInfoPanel:** action.

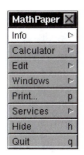

24. Add the submenu to MathPaper's main menu.

25. Enable the **Info→Info Panel** menu cell and disable the **Info→Help** menu cell.

26. Connect the **Info→Info Panel** menu cell to the **MathController** instance so that it sends the **showInfoPanel:** action message.

InfoView's Animation Code

The last thing we have to do to finish off the Info Panel is to implement the animation code in the **InfoView** class.

27. Insert the **drawSelf::** method below into **InfoView.m**.

```
- drawSelf:(const NXRect *)rects :(int)rectCount
{
    PSsetgray(NX_WHITE);
    NXRectFill(&bounds);
    return self;
}
```

A **View**'s **drawSelf::** method is invoked whenever Display PostScript wants to display the contents of a **View**. You should *not* invoke **drawSelf::** directly. Rather, you should invoke one of **View**'s **display** methods (there are several) which sets up the proper PostScript drawing context and then invokes **drawSelf::**. Our **drawSelf::** method above simply paints the background of the **InfoView** instance white.

When the **drawSelf::** method is invoked, the clipping rectangle is set to be the bounds of the **View**. Sometimes, though, you only need to redraw a part of the **View**. For these cases, your method can use the **drawSelf::** arguments **rects** and **rectCount** to tell the method which region of the **View** to redraw. We'll ignore these arguments for now and come back to them in Chapter 16.

28. Insert the **#import** statement below near the beginning of **InfoView.m**.

```
#import "supershow.h"
```

Recall that **supershow** is our PostScript wrap that displays a given string at a particular location. The **supershow.h** file contains the **supershow()** function prototype; it is important to import this prototype for two reasons:

• it avoids compiler warnings about un-prototyped functions, and

- since the function **supershow()** contains floating point arguments, calling it will not work properly unless the function is prototyped.

In addition to importing all the Application Kit class headers, the **#import <appkit/appkit.h>** statement imports the **<dpsclient/wraps.h>** file which brings in all of NeXT's standard PostScript wraps (i.e., the functions that begin with "PS").

29. Insert the **animateDrop:** method below into **InfoView.m**.

   Since it will be invoked only by another **InfoView** method (**animateInfo:**, shown below), the **animateDrop:** method declaration need not be included in **InfoView.h**. In this case, however, its implementation should be placed above the **animateInfo:** implementation.

```
- animateDrop:(float)size
{
  int i,j;
  int order[4] = {0,2,1,3};
  char *dropstrings[4] = {"+", "-", "\264", "\270"};
  float x,y;

  [self lockFocus];
  [ [Font newFont:"Symbol" size:size
          matrix:NX_IDENTITYMATRIX] set];
  for (i=0; i<4; i++) {
    float const step = 2.0;

    j = order[i];
    x = ( (size * j * 2.0)/3.0) + 10.0;

    /* Note that "frame" below is an instance
     * variable inherited from the View class.
     */
    for (y=NX_HEIGHT(&frame); y>=0; y-=step) {
      supershow(x, y+step,NX_WHITE,dropstrings[j]);
      supershow(x, y, NX_BLACK, dropstrings[j]);
      usleep(2000);   /* wait 2 ms */
      if (NXUserAborted()) {
        supershow(x, y, NX_WHITE, dropstrings[j]);
        supershow(x,0.0, NX_BLACK, dropstrings[j]);
        break;
      }
    }
  }
  [self unlockFocus];
  return self;
}
```

This **animateDrop:** method introduces the **Font** class, NeXTSTEP's class for accessing fonts stored in the Display PostScript interpreter. The **newFont:size:matrix:** *class* method returns the **id** of a **Font** instance with a specified name and size. The third argument, **matrix:**, is used to specify the scaling, rotation, and offset of the characters of the font. NeXT provides two built-in values for this parameter:

NX_IDENTITYMATRIX	Displays characters *normally* (i.e., upright) in a **View** that has a regular coordinate system (i.e., the origin is in the lower-left hand corner).
NX_FLIPPEDMATRIX	Displays the characters upside down, or right-side up in a **View** that has a flipped coordinate system.

As we said above, the **newFont:size:matrix:** method returns the **id** of the **Font** object. We then send the **Font** object the **set** message, which makes this font current font. The **set** message also alerts the **View** that you have used a particular font, so if you generate PostScript output (for printing) the fonts used by the document will be properly noted. Since fonts are managed by NeXTSTEP, you should never **free** a **Font** object.

After the **animateDrop:** method sets the current font to 72-point Symbol (the 72.0 is passed in the **size** argument), it starts two loops. The outer loop repeats for the *plus*, *subtract*, *times*, and *divide* symbols (in that order), which are stored in the **dropstrings[]** array. The inner loop does the actual animation, moving the symbols one at a time from the top of the **View** to the bottom. The inner loop calls the **NXPing()** function to synchronize the method with the Display PostScript interpreter. If you take out the call to this function, the animation will appear jerky; try it.

The inner loop also calls the **NXUserAborted()** function. This function returns **YES** if the user types "Command-." (Command-period) since the last event was read by the **Application** object's main event loop. The method uses the "Command-." user abort sequence to terminate the animation (think of the period as "the end"). Whenever you perform an animation that takes a long time and prevents the user from doing anything else while it is running, you should give the user some means for aborting the sequence.

30. Insert the two lines in **bold** below to the **animateInfo:** action method implementation in **InfoView.m**.

```
- animateInfo:sender
```

```
{
    [self display]; /* display invokes drawSelf:: */
    [self animateDrop:72.0];
    return self;
}
```

Recall that this method is invoked by the **showInfoPanel:** method in the **MathController** instance whenever the user chooses the **Info→InfoPanel** menu command.

Testing the Animation

31. Save all pertinent files, **make** and run your updated application.

    Note that **pswrap** is automatically called to generate C language code for **supershow.psw** and that this C code is automatically compiled and linked. See the compile log entries in **bold** below.

    ```
    pswrap -a -h supershow.h -o supershow.c supershow.psw
    cc -g -O -Wall   -c supershow.c -o obj/supershow.o
    cc -g -O -Wall   -ObjC   -sectcreate __ICON __header
    MathPaper.iconheader   -segprot __ICON r r -
    sectcreate __ICON app MathPaper.tiff -sectcreate
    __ICON MP_Doc_File MP_Doc_File.tiff  -o
    MathPaper.app/MathPaper  obj/InfoView.o obj/
    MathController.o obj/PaperControl.o obj/Process.o
    obj/RTF.o obj/MathPaper_main.o   obj/supershow.o
    -lMedia_s -lNeXT_s
    ```

32. Choose MathPaper's **Info→InfoPanel** menu command. The four arithmetic symbols should animate one-by-one, as advertised. Note that the "wait" cursor ( ) appears during the animation. (The animation doesn't look too good – we'll fix this later in the chapter.)

33. Choose the **Info→InfoPanel** menu command again and type "Command-." to stop the animation.

    All of the symbols should be instantly repainted along the bottom of the panel, because the function **NXUserAborted()** continues to return **YES** until the next event is received.

34. Quit MathPaper.

Displaying Pictures in a View

It's just as easy to draw pictures with NeXTSTEP as it is to draw text. In fact, in some ways, it's even easier. With NeXTSTEP version 2.0, NeXT introduced the **NXImage** class for manipulating images. You can use **NXImage** to read in the contents of a TIFF or an Encapsulated PostScript file and display it in a **View**. You can also use this class to save the image into another file – which means that you've got a simple way to convert images from TIFF to EPS representations and back. **NXImage** can also perform a variety of image manipulations.

NXImage accomplishes this magic by using objects in another class, called **NXImageRep**, to perform the actual work of storing the image. A single **NXImage** instance can have several **NXImageRep** representations of an image: it might have a bitmap representation for quick redisplay on the screen, and an EPS representation for detailed display on a printer.

Compositing

The way that the **NXImage** class transfers an image to the screen is with a process called *compositing*. Compositing is a way of combining two images, a *source image* and a *destination image* (the image already in place on the screen). The combining is done with a special function called the *compositing operator*, which combines the two images on a pixel-by-pixel basis and displays the result.

The most common compositing operators to use are **NX_COPY** and **NX_SOVER**. **NX_COPY** copies the rectangle bounded by the source image into the destination image; everything in the destination image is lost. **NX_SOVER** is similar, but the source image is placed atop the destination image. The difference is that you may be able to see parts of the destination image through any pixels in the source image that are transparent or partially transparent.

The file **/NextDeveloper/Headers/dpsclient/dpsNeXT.h** lists all 14 of the compositing operators. The most common operators are listed in the table below. As always with **NXImage**, the image stored inside the **NXImage** instance is the *source*. The *destination* can be any locked focus, including a **View**, another **NXImage** or even a PostScript graphics state.

Compositing Operation	Meaning
NX_COPY	Copies the image to the View (*destination*).
NX_CLEAR	Clears the area where the image is to be copied. This isn't used much.
NX_SOVER	"Source **OVER** destination" composites with attention to transparency in **NXImage**.
NX_XOR	Performs an exclusive-OR between the **NXImage** and the **View** destination.
NX_PLUSD	Performs mathematical addition between the source and the **View**. Whites get brighter and blacks get darker.
NX_HIGHLIGHT	Highlights the source image.

To get the image into a **View**, use the method **composite:toPoint:**, which has the form:

```
composite:(int)operator
                toPoint:(const NXPoint *)aPoint
```

The **operator** argument specifies how the image should be transferred to the **View** object. It is one of the compositing operators described above. The variable **aPoint** specifies *where* the image should be placed. Since **composite:toPoint:** is a PostScript drawing operation, it should be used only inside a **drawSelf::** method or between invocations of the **lockFocus** and **unlockFocus** methods in the **View** object in which the compositing is to occur.

The Dissolving Animation

We're going to use the **NXImage** class to perform the second half of our animation – having the application's icon and credit dissolve into the Info Panel. To accomplish this dissolving animation, we'll use another **NXImage** method called **dissolve:toPoint:**. It has the following form:

```
dissolve:(float)delta
                toPoint:(const NXPoint *)aPoint
```

This method dissolves the **NXimage** object to the location specified by
aPoint using the *dissolve* operator. The **delta** variable is a fraction between
0.0 and 1.0 that specifies how much of the resulting composite will come
from the **NXImage**.

First we'll insert the method that performs the dissolving animation.

1. Insert the **animateDissolve:** method below into **InfoView.m**. Put it
    above the **animateInfo:** method to avoid a compiler warning from
    using an undeclared method (or declare these methods in **InfoView.h**
    so the order is unimportant – we prefer the latter).

```
- animateDissolve:(float)size
{
    id        image;
    id        textFont;
    NXPoint   myPoint;
    NXSize    isize;
    float     x, y, width;
    float     gray;
    char *slgName = "Created by Simson L. Garfinkel";
    char *mkmName = " tweaking by Michael K. Mahoney";

    [self lockFocus];
    [ [Font newFont:"Times-Roman" size:size * .75
                matrix:NX_IDENTITYMATRIX ] set];

    image = [NXImage findImageNamed:"app"];
    [image getSize:&isize];

    myPoint.x = NX_X(&frame) + 10.0;
    myPoint.y = NX_Y(&frame) + size + 5.0;

    x = myPoint.x + isize.width + 10.0;
    y = myPoint.y;

    for (gray=0.0; gray<=1.0; gray+=0.005) {
      if (NXUserAborted()){
        /* User aborted. Exit loop by advancing to the
         * last value that the variable gray can take.
         */
        gray = 1.0;
      }

      [image dissolve:gray toPoint:&myPoint];
                                      /* draw image */
      PSsetgray(1.0 - (gray/2.0));   /* draw line */
```

```
        PSrectfill(NX_X(&frame), size,
                            NX_WIDTH(&frame), 2.0);
        supershow(x, y, 1.0 - gray,
                            (char *)[NXApp appName]);
    }

    textFont = [ [Font newFont:"Times-Italic"
                    size:12.0
                    matrix:NX_IDENTITYMATRIX] set];

    width  = [textFont getWidthOf:slgName];
    supershow(NX_X(&frame) +
        NX_WIDTH(&frame)-width-5.0,y-25.0,0.0,slgName);

    width  = [textFont getWidthOf:mkmName];
    supershow(NX_X(&frame) +
        NX_WIDTH(&frame)-width-5.0,y-40.0,0.0,mkmName);

    [self unlockFocus];
    return self;
}
```

The message **[NXImage findImageNamed:"app"]** gets a copy of the application's application icon.

The **animateDissolve:** method above is interesting because it uses a combination of changing gray scale and the **dissolve:toPoint:** method to make the text and the image dissolve into the **InfoView** object. We also use the **Font** instance method **getWidthOf:** to calculate the width of the string that is to be displayed. This is easier (and more accurate) than trying to parse the **afm** tables for information about the fonts that you are using and significantly faster than having Display PostScript calculate the width by using the PostScript wrap **PSstringwidth()**.

2. Insert the line in **bold** below into the **animateInfo:** method in **InfoView.m**.

```
- animateInfo:sender
{
  [self display]; /* clear the window */
  [self animateDrop:72.0];
  [self animateDissolve:72.0];
  return self;
}
```

3. Save the **InfoView.m** file, **make** and run your updated application.

4. Choose the **Info→InfoPanel** menu command. The animation and dissolving should work as advertised. See Figure 3, "MathPaper Info Panel," on page 355, for the result *after* the animation and dissolve.

5. Choose the **Info→InfoPanel** menu command again and click the panel's close button while the animation is in progress. The Info Panel won't close until the animation is complete; we'll fix this in the next section.

6. Quit MathPaper.

Display PostScript Timed Entries

The animation presented in the **animateDrop:** and **animateDissolve:** methods above can be improved. No commercial application would *ever* have the user type "Command-." to abort an animation, and no real application should ever use **sleep()** or **usleep()** to block its main event loop. That's because while the application is sleeping, it can't do anything else: it can't respond to the user, can't provide data to other applications, can't even process a **powerOffIn:andSave:** power-off message from Workspace.

Instead of doing all of this in the main command event loop, NeXTSTEP provides a system for having a small function called repeatedly at regular time intervals. The system is called *timed entries* and is managed by the NeXTSTEP functions **DPSAddTimedEntry()** and **DPSRemoveTimedEntry()**.

Adding a Timed Entry

Timed entries are based upon the notion of a *timed entry handler*, which is a short function called automatically from your application's main event loop. The timed entry handler should do its job quickly and return, so that the main event loop can quickly go on to process other events.

Here is the syntax for the **DPSAddTimedEntry()** function:

```
DPSTimedEntry DPSAddTimedEntry(
        double period,
        DPSTimedEntryProc handler,
        void *userData,
        int priority )
```

When you create a timed entry, you specify four arguments:

- The *period* of the timed entry, i.e., how often it should be called. This argument is expressed in seconds.
- A C language function, called *a handler*, that is automatically called whenever the timed entry is executed.
- Data to be provided to the handler each time it is called.
- The timed entry's priority.

For *priority*, you should usually specify NX_BASETHRESHOLD unless you want your timed entry to run when modal panels (e.g., Alert panels) are displayed or during modal loops. In these cases, you should specify a priority of NX_RUNMODALTHRESHOLD or NX_MODALRE-SPTHRESHOLD, respectively. The **DPSAddTimedEntry()** function returns the *timed entry number* of the timed entry that it creates.

The Timed Entry Handler

Your timed entry handler (named **func**() below) is a regular C language function with a predefined set of arguments. Here is its syntax:

```
void func( DPSTimedEntry teNumber,
           double now,
           char *userData )
```

The *teNumber* argument is the timed entry number that caused this function to be called. The *now* argument is a counter; it records the number of seconds from some arbitrary time in the past. The *userData* argument is the same pointer that you provided to **DPSAddTimedEntry()**. It might be a real pointer; it might also be simply a number.

Nothing is guaranteed about timed entries. If you ask that your handler be called every 5 seconds, it may actually be called every 5.3 seconds. Your handler might be called at 5 seconds, then at 10.3 second, then at 15.7 seconds, then at 20 seconds. This is one of the reasons that the argument *now* is provided.

Removing a Timed Entry

When the timed entry is no longer needed, you should remove it with the **DPSRemoveTimedEntry()** function:

```
void DPSRemoveTimedEntry(DPSTimedEntry teNumber)
```

Many timed entries remove themselves when they are no longer needed; this eliminates the need to record the timed entry number in an instance variable.

Using Timed Entries in Animation

Timed entries are ideal for animation, because they let your program animate some motion on the screen while still accepting events from the user. In many cases, this eliminates the need to call **NXUserAborted**().

Because the handler function takes a single four-byte quantity of user data, the easiest way to combine timed entries with Objective-C is to pass to the timed entry the **id** of an object cast into a **void ***. The handler function then casts its **void *** argument into an **id** and sends the object an appropriate message.

In the remainder of this chapter, we'll rewrite the **InfoView** class so that it uses timed entries instead of delayed loop.

1. *Replace* the *entire* contents of the **InfoView.h** file with the **InfoView** class interface code below.

    ```
    #import <appkit/appkit.h>

    @interface InfoView:View
    {
      DPSTimedEntry    animateTE;
      BOOL             animatingDrop;
      BOOL             animatingDissolve;
      int              animationStep;
      float            animationSize;
      float            animationFloat;
      id               symbolFont;
      id               bigTextFont;
      id               smallTextFont;
    }

    - initFrame:(const NXRect *)rect;
    - animateInfo:sender;
    - removeTE;
    - windowWillClose:sender;
    - animationClick;
    - animateDrop;
    - animateDissolve;
    - drawSelf:(const NXRect *)rects :(int)rectCount;

    @end
    ```

The **animateTE** instance variable will keep track of the timed entry number. The next five instance variables will keep track of the current stage of the animation – and what to do next. The last three instance variables will hold the **id**s of the fonts that we are using. This time we declared all of the instance methods in **InfoView.h**, which is a good way to document the methods in a class.

2. *Replace* the entire contents of **InfoView.m** with the code below.

```
#define SIZE 72.0
#import "InfoView.h"
#import "supershow.h"

@implementation InfoView

- initFrame:(const NXRect *)rect
{
  [super initFrame:rect];

  symbolFont = [Font newFont:"Symbol"
              size:SIZE
              matrix:NX_IDENTITYMATRIX];

  bigTextFont = [Font newFont:"Times-Roman"
              size:SIZE * .75
              matrix:NX_IDENTITYMATRIX];

smallTextFont = [Font newFont:"Times-Italic"
              size:12.0
              matrix:NX_IDENTITYMATRIX];

  return self;
}
```

In addition to initializing the **InfoView** instance, the **initFrame:** method creates the fonts that will be used by the animation methods. The animation will still be started by a (new) **animateInfo:** method shown below. However, instead of actually making the animation happen, this method will now just establish the timed entry and return.

3. Insert the **handler()** function below into **InfoView.m**, immediately before the **@implementation** directive.

```
void handler(DPSTimedEntry teNumber,
             double now, void *userData)
{
  id obj = (id)userData;
  [obj animationClick];
}
```

4. Insert the *updated* **animateInfo:** method below at the end of
   InfoView.m.

```
- animateInfo:sender
{
  [self display]; /* clear the window */
  [self removeTE]; /* remove timed-entry, if nec. */

  [window setDelegate:self];
  animatingDrop    = YES;      /* start with this */
  animationStep    = 0;        /* and this */
  animateTE        = DPSAddTimedEntry(.002,
                           (DPSTimedEntryProc)handler,
                           self,NX_BASETHRESHOLD);
  return self;
}
```

In addition to starting the animation, this new **animateInfo:** method sets
the animation panel's delegate to be the **InfoView** itself. This is important
so that our **View** can catch the **windowWillClose:** delegate method and
remove the timed entry if the user attempts to close the window.

5. Insert the new **removeTE** and **windowWillClose:** methods below at
   the end of **InfoView.m**.

```
- removeTE
{
  if (animateTE) {
    DPSRemoveTimedEntry(animateTE);
    animateTE = 0; /* note that it's gone */
  }
  return self;
}

- windowWillClose:sender
{
  [self removeTE]; /* make sure it is gone */
  return self;
}
```

Removing a timed entry that doesn't exist generates a PostScript error. But
since a timed entry cannot have the number 0, we can use the instance variable **animateTE** both to hold the timed entry number and to note that a
timed entry has been posted. The **removeTE** method sets the **animateTE**
instance variable to 0 after the timed entry is removed so that if the
removeTE is accidentally called a second time it won't generate an error.

6. Insert the new **animateClick** method below at the end of **InfoView.m**.

```
- animationClick
{
  if (animatingDrop)     [self animateDrop];
  if (animatingDissolve) [self animateDissolve];
  NXPing();        /* synchronize with server */
  return self;
}
```

This method is called by the timed entry. It calls the appropriate animation method depending on the values of the **animatingDrop** and **animatingDissolve** instance variables.

7. Insert the *updated* **animateDrop:** method below at the end of **InfoView.m**. Notice that this method is somewhat simpler than the *old* **animateDrop:** method that it replaces because it does not contain any loops – the looping is now performed by Display PostScript.

```
- animateDrop
{
  int    order[4] = {0,2,1,3};
  char   *dropstrings[4] = {"+","-","\264","\270"};
  float  const step=2.0;
  float  x;
  float  y = NX_HEIGHT(&frame) - animationFloat;
  int    j = order[animationStep];

  [self lockFocus];
  [symbolFont set];

  x = ((SIZE * j * 2.0) / 3.0) + 10.0;

  supershow(x, y+step, NX_WHITE, dropstrings[j]);
  supershow(x, y, NX_BLACK, dropstrings[j]);

  animationFloat += 2.0;
  if (animationFloat >= NX_HEIGHT(&frame)) {
    animationFloat = 0;      /* reset Y */
    animationStep++;          /* go to next step */
    if(animationStep==4) {   /* go to next effect */
      animationStep = 0;
      animatingDrop = NO;
      animatingDissolve = YES;
      animationFloat = 0.0;
    }
  }
  [self unlockFocus];
  return self;
}
```

8. Insert the *updated* **animateDissolve:** method below at the end of **InfoView.m**.

```
- animateDissolve
{
  id       image;
  NXPoint  myPoint;
  NXSize   isize;
  float    x, y, width;
  char   *slgName ="Created by Simson L. Garfinkel";
  char   *mkmName =" tweaking by Michael K. Mahoney";

  [self lockFocus];
  [bigTextFont set];

  image = [NXImage findImageNamed:"app"];
  [image getSize:&isize];

  myPoint.x = NX_X(&frame) + 10.0;
  myPoint.y = NX_Y(&frame) + SIZE;

  x = myPoint.x + isize.width + 10.0;
  y = myPoint.y ;

  [image dissolve:animationFloat
        toPoint:&myPoint];          /* draw image */

  PSsetgray(1.0 - (animationFloat/2.0));
  PSrectfill(NX_X(&frame),
            SIZE, NX_WIDTH(&frame), 2.0);

  supershow(x, y, 1.0 - animationFloat,
          (char *)[NXApp appName]);

  animationFloat += 0.005;
  if(animationFloat < 1.0) {
    return self;
  }

  /* finish up */
  [smallTextFont set];

  width = [smallTextFont getWidthOf:slgName];
  supershow(NX_X(&frame)
            + NX_WIDTH(&frame) - width - 5.0,
            y-20.0, 0.0, slgName);

  width = [smallTextFont getWidthOf:mkmName];
```

```
supershow(NX_X(&frame)
          + NX_WIDTH(&frame) - width - 5.0,
          y-35.0, 0.0, mkmName);

[self removeTE];
return self;
}
```

9. Insert the **drawSelf::** method (the same one as before) and the **@end** directive below at the end of **InfoView.m**.

```
- drawSelf:(const NXRect *)rects :(int)rectCount
{
  PSsetgray(NX_WHITE);
  NXRectFill(&bounds);
  return self;
}

@end
```

10. Save the new **InfoView.h** and **InfoView.m** files, **make** and run your updated application.

Your new version of MathPaper should work the same, but with one important improvement: you can now use your MathPaper windows while the animation is taking place. You can also cancel it by clicking the Info Panel's close button. The "wait" cursor ( ) does not appear during the animation.

Summary

In this chapter we learned about PostScript wraps – the way that the NeXT-STEP Application Kit communicates with the Display PostScript Window Server. We also learned a little bit about drawing directly with PostScript inside a **View** object, and then explored Display PostScript timed entries.

This chapter marks the end of our MathPaper odyssey, although we'll be using parts of it in our next major application, GraphPaper, which starts in Chapter 16. Before that in the next chapter, we'll learn much more about the **drawSelf::** method – the proper way to make your **View** show its stuff.

 # 15

Draw Yourself:
All About NeXTSTEP Views

In the previous chapter we saw how to draw in a **View** with simple Post-Script commands in two ways:

(i)   by nesting the PostScript commands between the **lockFocus** and **unlockFocus** messages to the **View** in which the drawing was to take place, and

(ii)   by placing the PostScript commands within the **drawSelf::** method of a **View**.

While it's fine to call the focus methods for simple animation as in (i), this isn't the way that most NeXTSTEP programs go about drawing in windows. Instead of explicitly invoking calls to **lockFocus** and **unlockFocus**, most NeXTSTEP programs accomplish drawing by subclassing the **View** class and then placing all of the actual PostScript drawing commands in a single method called **drawSelf::**.

The purpose of this chapter is to make you feel at home with the **drawSelf::** method and NeXTSTEP **View**s in general.

The Advantages of View's drawSelf:: Method

The advantage of the **drawSelf::** method is that it localizes all of the Post-Script code necessary to draw your **View** in a single method. This method can then be invoked under a variety of different circumstances:

- The **View** draws itself the first time that it is displayed in its window.
- If the **View**'s window is not buffered, then the **View** redraws itself every time the window is exposed.
- If the **View** is displayed in a **ScrollView**, then it redraws part of itself whenever the user makes a new part of it visible by dragging the scroll bar.
- If the user wants to print or fax the **View**, the **View** generates the appropriate PostScript code for that function.
- If the user wants to save the contents of the **View** in an Encapsulated PostScript file, the **View** can generate the PostScript for that as well.

Basically, putting the smarts of drawing a **View** in **drawSelf::** makes redisplay happen in the most efficient manner possible, and then gives you printing, faxing, and saving EPS files for free.

The **drawSelf::** method is designed to be overridden by the programmer. The **View** method **drawSelf::** does nothing; when you subclass the **View** class, you override the do-nothing **drawSelf::** method to handle the drawing for your custom **View**.

BlackView: A View That Paints Itself Black

In this chapter we'll play with a number of simple, trivial **View**s. The first is **BlackView**, a **View** whose **drawSelf::** method fills the **View** with black.

1. Launch Project Builder (PB) from your dock, choose PB's **Project→New** menu command and give your new project the name "**BlackViewDemo**."

2. Double-click the **BlackViewDemo.nib** file name (under **Interfaces**) in PB's Files view. Interface Builder (IB) will automatically launch and display the **BlackViewDemo.nib** interface created by PB.

3. **Subclass** the **View** class in IB's File window. Rename the new class **BlackView**.

4. **Unparse** the **BlackView** class and insert it into your project.

5. Using an editor, insert the **drawSelf::** in `bold` below into **BlackView.m**.

```
#import "BlackView.h"
@implementation BlackView

- drawSelf:(const NXRect *)rects :(int)rectCount
{
  [super drawSelf:rects :rectCount];
  PSsetgray(NX_BLACK);
  NXRectFill(&bounds);
  return self;
}
@end
```

The inherited **bounds** instance variable describes the frame of the **View** in its own coordinate system.

6. Back in IB, resize **MyWindow** so it's about two inches wide and one inch tall. The size you end up with isn't important.

7. Drag a **CustomView** icon from IB's Views palette and drop it in **MyWindow**.

8. Change the class of the custom **View** to **BlackView** in the CustomView Inspector.

9. Resize the **BlackView** instance so it's about the size shown in the window on the left of Figure 1 below.

FIGURE 1. BlackView in IB and in a Running Application

10. Choose IB's **Document→Test Interface** and you'll see an *empty* window. You'll also get the following messages on the system console (which can be seen by choosing **Tools→Console** from the Workspace Manager menu):

```
Jul 24 10:39:40 localhost InterfaceBuilder[168]:
objc: class 'BlackView' not linked into application
```

```
Jul 24 10:39:40 localhost InterfaceBuilder[168]:
Unknown View class BlackView in Interface Builder
file,
```

The message appears because the **BlackView** class isn't compiled into the version of Interface Builder that you're using. (You can create your own custom palettes in Interface Builder if you want; consult the Interface Builder documentation to learn how to do this.) To see **BlackView** work, you need to **make** the application.

11. Save the **BlackViewDemo.nib** and **BlackView.m** files, **make** and run your BlackViewDemo. You'll see the **BlackView** instance in all its glory, as in the window on the right of Figure 1 above.

That's all there is to it! **BlackView**'s **drawSelf::** method automatically gets invoked when the window is first drawn on the screen. There's no need to explicitly invoke **drawSelf::** method yourself. (In fact, you're not supposed to ever invoke **drawSelf::** directly. Doing so risks the wrath of NeXT's software engineering team and Steve Jobs himself!) Likewise, if we tried to print or fax this window, **BlackView**'s **drawSelf::** method would automatically be invoked again to generate the PostScript to send to the printer or fax modem.

12. To stress this point, let's modify the window by adding a few more **BlackView**s, as in the window on the left of Figure 2 below. You can do this using IB's **Edit→Copy** and **Edit→Paste** to do this.

13. When we run the program this time, we get a window that looks like the one on the right of Figure 2. NeXTSTEP automatically calls the **drawSelf::** method for each **View** when the window is displayed.

FIGURE 2. Lots of BlackViews

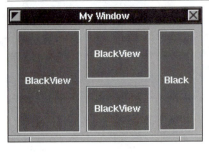 

(All **make** had to do was to copy the new **BlackViewDemo.nib** file into the **BlackViewDemo.app** (or **BlackViewDemo.debug**) directory, because we only changed the nib file and it's not bundled into the Mach-O executable.)

A Closer Look at the View Class

View is one of NeXTSTEP's most complicated classes. If you understand how it works, you can control the display of information on the computer's screen and have it updated quickly and efficiently.

View Coordinate Systems

Each NeXTSTEP **View** has its own coordinate system that can be rotated, scaled, or otherwise transformed from the coordinate system of its super-view. Each **View** also has two instance variables to describe its position in its window:

frame   Describes the **View**'s frame in the coordinate system of its *superview.*

bounds   Describe the **View**'s frame in its *own* coordinate system.

When you change a **View**'s coordinate system, its **bounds** instance variable is automatically updated to reflect the change, while its **frame** instance variable remains the same. The **View** class provides the following methods for inspecting and changing a **View**'s coordinate system:

View Method	Purpose
(float) **boundsAngle**	Returns a floating point number for the angle, in degrees, between a **View**'s coordinate system and the coordinate system of its superview.
(float) **frameAngle**	Returns the angle of the **View**'s frame relative to its superview's coordinate system. A value of 0 means that the **View** has not been rotated (but its coordinate system may have been).
(BOOL) **isRotatedFromBase**	Returns TRUE if a **View** or any of its ancestors have been rotated from the window coordinate system.
(BOOL) **isRotatedOrScaled-FromBase**	Returns TRUE if a **View** or any of its ancestors have been rotated or scaled from the window coordinate system.

View Method	Purpose
rotate: (NXCoord)*angle*	Rotates a **View**'s drawing coordinate system about the **View**'s origin (0,0). This rotates the contents of the view but not the view itself.
scale: (NXCoord)*x* :(NXCoord)*y*	Scales a **View**'s coordinate system. A value of "2" would double the size of units along the respective axis.
setDrawOrigin: (NXCoord)*x* :(NXCoord)*y*	Translates a **View**'s coordinate system so that its origin has the coordinate (x,y).
setDrawRotation :(NXCoord)*angle*	Rotates a **View**'s coordinate system so that *angle* is the angle between the **View**'s coordinate system and its frame.
setDrawSize: (NXCoord)*width* :(NXCoord)*height*	Scales a **View**'s coordinate system so that the **View**'s frame is **width** units wide and **height** units high.
translate: (NXCoord)*x* :(NXCoord)*y*	Translates the origin of the **View**'s coordinate system to (x,y).

NeXTSTEP also provides a method for disabling the coordinate transformations of a subview:

drawInSuperview	Draws the **View** in its superview's coordinate system.

You can convert a point or rectangle from a **View**'s coordinate system to or from the coordinate system of another **View** with one of these methods:

convertPoint: (NXPoint *)*aPoint* **fromView:***aView*

convertPoint: (NXPoint *)*aPoint* **toView:***aView*

convertPointFromSuperview: (NXPoint *)*aPoint*

convertPointToSuperview: (NXPoint *)*aPoint*

convertRect: (NXRect *)*aRect* **fromView:***aView*

convertRect: (NXRect *)*aRect* **toView:***aView*

convertRectFromSuperview: (NXRect *)*aRect*

convertRectToSuperview: (NXRect *)*aRect*

convertSize: (NXSize *)*aSize* **fromView:***aView*

convertSize: (NXSize *)*aSize* **toView:***aView*

If you supply **nil** as an argument to the methods that take *aView* as an argument, the methods will convert to or from window coordinates.

Moving and Resizing Views

You can move the position of a **View** relative to its superview coordinate system. This usually has the effect of changing where the **View** draws itself inside the window.

The following methods control the placement and movement of a **View**:

View Method	Purpose
moveBy: (NXCoord)*deltaX* :(NXCoord)*deltaY*	Moves the origin of the **View**'s frame by a relative amount in its superview's coordinate system.
moveTo: (NXCoord)*x* :(NXCoord)*y*	Moves the origin of the **View**'s frame to an absolute place in its superview's coordinate system.
rotateBy: (NXCoord)*deltaAngle*	Rotates a **View**'s frame by *deltaAngle*. This method and **rotateTo:** rotates the view itself in its parents coordinate system.
rotateTo: (NXCoord)*angle*	Rotates a **View**'s frame to an absolute position.
setFrame :(const NXRect *)*frameRect*	Repositions and resizes a **View** within its superview's coordinate system.
sizeBy: (NXCoord)*deltaWidth* :(NXCoord)*deltaHeight*	Resizes a **View** by a relative amount in its superview's coordinate system.
sizeTo: (NXCoord)*width* :(NXCoord)*height*	Resizes a **View** by an absolute amount in its superview's coordinate system.

Flipping

Views may be *flipped*, which means that increasing **y** coordinates move *down* the screen, instead of *up* (the way the Display PostScript coordinate system normally works). A flipped coordinate system is handy for building **View**s like the **Text** object, which naturally move down, and for which you want to be able to calculate a **y** coordinate by multiplying a line number by a constant.

The following **View** methods deal with flipped **View**s:

(BOOL)**isFlipped**	Returns whether or not the **View** is flipped.
setFlipped: (BOOL)*flag*	Flips or unflips a **View**'s coordinate system.

The View Hierarchy

All **View**s are arranged in a hierarchy. Each **View** has exactly one *superview* and can have any number of *subviews*.

View Method	Purpose
descendantFlipped: *sender*	Notifies the receiving **View** that the *sender* has flipped its coordinate system.
findAncestorSharedWith:*aView*	Searches up the hierarchy for a **View** that is in common with the receiving **View** and *aView*.
findViewWithTag: (int)*aTag*	Finds the subview or descendent **View** of the receiver that has *aTag* as its tag.
(BOOL)**isDescendantOf:** *aView*	Returns whether or not the receiver is a descendant of *aView*.
notifyAncestorWhenFrame-Changed: (BOOL)*flag*	Returns TRUE if the **View** will notify its ancestors when its frame changes. This is used with the **ScrollView** to automatically update the size of the scroll bars.
notifyWhenFlipped: (BOOL)*flag*	The **View** will notify its ancestors when it is flipped.
replaceSubview: *oldView* **with:***newView*	If *oldView* is a subview of the receiver, it is removed from the **View** hierarchy and replaced with *newView*.

View Method	Purpose
subviews	Returns the **List** object of a **View**'s subviews. Do not modify this list directly.
superview	Returns the **View**'s superview.

Opaque and Non-Rectangular Views

NeXTSTEP represents **View**s by rectangular regions on the screen. But nothing in NeXTSTEP forces the drawing that a **View** does to be rectangular. It can be an odd shape; it can even have holes, through which you can see what is behind it.

Each **View** has an instance variable called **opaque** (really a bit field) which specifies whether or not a **View** completely fills its frame when it is drawn (so that you can't see anything behind the **View**). If your **View** has holes in it, or does not completely set every pixel within its frame, **opaque** should be set to FALSE. It is important to set this variable properly to reflect what your **View** does; this minimizes the amount of redrawing that needs to be done when your **View**s are redisplayed.

These methods help you manage opaqueness:

(BOOL)**isOpaque**	Returns TRUE if a **View** is opaque.
opaqueAncestor	Returns the **View**'s nearest ancestor **View** that is opaque. If the **View** is opaque, it will return **self**.
setOpaque: (BOOL)*flag*	Indicates whether or not a **View** is opaque.

When the mouse is clicked in your **View**, the **Window** object uses the **hitTest:** method (shown below) to determine if the **View** was clicked or not. You can override this method if parts of your **View** should not be mouse sensitive – for example, if your **View** displays itself as a triangle:

hitTest: (NXPoint *)*aPoint*	Returns the lowest subview of a **View** that contains *aPoint*. The **Window** class uses this method to determine in which **View** a mouse click occurs. You can subclass this method to make some parts of your **View** "invisible" to the mouse.

Displaying Views

There are several different **display** methods, all which eventually invoke **drawSelf::**.

display	Causes the **View** to redisplay itself and its subviews.
display: (const NXRect *)*rects* :(int)*rectCount*	Redisplays the portion of the **View** and its subviews specified by the argument *rects*.
display: (const NXRect *)*rects* :(int)*rectCount* :(BOOL)*clipFlag*	Redisplays the portion of the **View** and its subviews specified by the argument *rectCount*. If *clipFlag* is FALSE, clipping is not automatically enabled, which can speed redisplay.
displayFromOpaqueAncestor :(const NXRect *)*rects* :(int)*rectCount* :(BOOL)*clipFlag*	Redisplays a **View** that is not opaque by searching up the view hierarchy for an opaque **View** that covers the region described by *rects* and redisplaying that **View**.

If your **View** will never draw beyond its boundaries, you can turn clipping off with the **setClipping:** method, which will further speed drawing:

setClipping: (BOOL)*flag*	Controls whether clipping is turned on when a **View** is drawn.

Controlling Redisplay

Most NeXTSTEP **View**s need to redisplay themselves when something about their internal state changes. For example, a **TextField** object needs to redisplay itself when the contents of the **TextField** change. If you write your own custom **View**, you may override these methods to improve drawing performance under certain circumstances.

The following methods are used for managing the redisplay of **View**s.

displayIfNeeded	Displays a **View** and any of its subviews that need to be redisplayed.
invalidate :(const NXRect *)*rects* :(int)*rectCount*	Tells a **View** that a region of itself and its subviews is no longer valid and needs to be redisplayed. This is used by the **ScrollView** class.
(BOOL)**isAutodisplay**	Returns whether or not a **View** automatically redisplays itself when it changes.
(BOOL)**needsDisplay**	Returns TRUE if the **View** needs to be redisplayed. This is used by the method **displayIfNeeded**.
setAutodisplay: (BOOL)*flag*	Enables autodisplay. Your **View** should automatically redisplay itself when its state information is changed if autodisplay is true.
setNeedsDisplay: (BOOL)*flag*	Tells the **View** that it needs to be redisplayed.

Resizing

When a window is resized, the Window class automatically sends a **resizeSubviews:** method to the Window's content view. The **resizeSubviews:** method is then passed down through the view hierarchy, resizing or not resizing the subviews as necessary.

Normally, you control resizing with Interface Builder's Autosizing inspector. But there are times that you might want to catch resize events and do something special. Here are the methods used by NeXTSTEP's resizing machinery.

resizeSubviews :(const NXSize *)*oldSize*	Informs the **View**'s subviews that the **View**'s size has been changed.
setAutoresizeSubviews :(BOOL)*flag*	Makes a **View** automatically resize its subviews when it is resized.
setAutosizing :(unsigned int)*mask*	Controls how a **View** resizes when its **View** is resized.
superviewSizeChanged :(const NXSize *)*oldSize*	Informs a **View** that its superview has changed size.

BarView: A View with a Scaled Coordinate System

In this section we'll subclass **View** to create a class called **BarView**. A **BarView** object will display a simple bar graph that draws a graph between the range 0 to 1, depending on the value of a slider. It will scale its coordinate system and control redrawing with the appropriate display methods.

1. Launch PB from your dock, choose PB's **Project→New** menu command and give your new project the name "**BarViewDemo**."

2. Double-click the **BarViewDemo.nib** file name (under **Interfaces**) in PB's Files view. IB will automatically launch and display the **BarViewDemo.nib** interface created by PB.

3. Resize **MyWindow** so it's about two inches square.

4. **Subclass** the **View** class in IB's File window. Rename the new class **BarView**.

5. Drag a **CustomView** icon from IB's Views palette and drop it in **MyWindow**.

6. Change the class of the **CustomView** to **BarView** in the Inspector.

7. Resize the **BarView** instance as in Figure 3 below.

8. Drag a horizontal slider from IB's Views palette into **MyWindow**. It has a default range from **0.0** to **1.0**.

9. Change the **Current** value of the slider to **0.0** in the Slider Attributes Inspector. Your window should look like the one in Figure 3 below.

FIGURE 3. BarView and Slider in IB

10. Add the **takePercentage:** action to the **BarView** class in the Inspector.

11. Connect the slider to the **BarView** instance so that it sends the **takePercentage:** action.

12. **Unparse** the **BarView** class and insert it into your project.

13. Insert the four lines in `bold` below into **BarView.h**.

```
#import <appkit/appkit.h>
@interface BarView:View
{
    float percentage;
}
- takePercentage:sender;
- initFrame:(NXRect *)r;
- drawSelf:(const NXRect *)rects :(int)rectCount;
- setPercentage:(float) newPercentage;
@end
```

It's not necessary to place declarations of overridden methods (e.g., **draw-Self::**) in the class interface (**.h**) file, but it's a good idea because it documents that they were overridden.

14. Insert the line in `bold` below into **BarView.m**.

```
- takePercentage:sender
{
    [self setPercentage:[sender floatValue] ];
    return self;
}
```

The **takePercentage:** method is the action that the slider takes when it's been manipulated. It gets the value of the slider using [**sender floatValue**] and then invokes the **setPercentage:** method (shown below) to set the percentage in the on-screen **BarView**.

15. Insert the three new methods implementations below into **BarView.m**. The first two override methods in the **View** class.

```
/* designated initializer */
- initFrame:(NXRect *)r
{
    [super initFrame: r];
    [self setDrawSize: 1.0 :1.0];
    [self setOpaque: YES];
    return self;
}

/* Generate PostScript to display the View */
- drawSelf:(const NXRect *)rects :(int)rectCount
{
    NXRect rect;

    rect = bounds;
```

```
        NX_HEIGHT(&rect) = percentage;
        PSsetgray(NX_WHITE);
        NXRectFill(&rect);

        NX_Y(&rect) = percentage;
        NX_HEIGHT(&rect) = 1.0 - percentage;
        PSsetgray(NX_BLACK);
        NXRectFill(&rect);
        return self;
}

/* Set the current percentage */
- setPercentage:(float)val
{
    percentage = val;
    [self setNeedsDisplay: YES];
    if ([self isAutodisplay]) [self display];
    return self;
}
```

The **initFrame:** method above invokes the inherited **setDrawSize::** method to scale **BarView**'s drawing coordinates so that width and height are both **1.0**. This makes it very easy for the **drawSelf::** method to draw the bar graph. The **drawSelf::** method draws a white rectangle from the bottom of the **View** to the line specified by the variable **percentage**, then a black box on top.

The **setPercentage:** method sets the **percentage** instance variable, tells the **View**'s superclass that redisplay is needed, and then redisplays itself if **autoDisplay** is true.

If we were not concerned about implementing autodisplay, we could have coded the **setPercentage:** method more simply as follows:

```
/* Always set the current percentage */
- setPercentage:(float)val
{
    percentage = val;
    return [self display];
}
```

The **setPercentage:** method is included in the class interface so you can set the value in the **BarView** directly from an Objective-C statement in your program, without having to use a NeXTSTEP **Control** object such as a button or a slider. When you are designing classes, you should try to include methods that will make the class useful in future application programs as well as the current program on which you are working.

16. Save all pertinent files and **make** and run BarViewDemo.

17. Drag the slider knob and the bar graph should lower and raise, as in Figure 4 below.

18. Quit BarViewDemo.

FIGURE 4. BarViewDemo Running

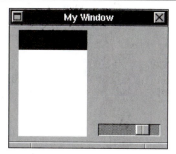

PolygonView: A Non-Opaque View

In this section we'll create a **View** called **PolygonView** that has some "holes" in it. It will draw a polygon with a specified number of sides.

1. Launch PB from your dock, choose PB's **Project→New** menu command and give your new project the name "**PolygonViewDemo**."

2. Double-click the **PolygonViewDemo.nib** file name (under **Interfaces**) in PB's Files view. IB will automatically launch and display the **PolygonViewDemo.nib** interface created by PB.

3. Resize **MyWindow** so it's about two inches square.

4. **Subclass** the **View** class in IB's File window. Rename the new class **PolygonView**.

5. Drag a **CustomView** icon from IB's Views palette and drop it in **MyWindow**.

6. Change the class of the **CustomView** to **PolygonView** in the Inspector.

7. Resize the **PolygonView** instance as in Figure 5 below.

8. Drag a vertical slider from IB's Views palette into **MyWindow** and position it as in Figure 5 below.

FIGURE 5. PolygonView and Slider in IB

9. Set the range of the slider to be from **3** to **30** and set its current value to **3** in the Slider Attributes Inspector.

10. Add the **takeNumSidesFrom:** action to the **PolygonView** class in the CustomView Inspector.

11. Connect the slider to the **PolygonView** instance so that it sends the **takeNumSidesFrom:** action message.

12. **Unparse** the **PolygonView** class and add it to your project.

13. Insert the four lines in **bold** below into **PolygonView.h**.

```
#import <appkit/appkit.h>
@interface PolygonView:View
{
   int sides;
}
- takeNumSidesFrom:sender;
- initFrame:(NXRect *)r;
- drawSelf:(const NXRect *)rects :(int)rectCount;
- setNumSides:(int)val;
@end
```

14. Insert the lines in **bold** below into **PolygonView.m**.

```
#import "PolygonView.h"

@implementation PolygonView

- takeNumSidesFrom:sender
{
   [self setNumSides:[sender intValue] ];
   return self;
```

```
}

- initFrame:(NXRect *)r
{
  [super initFrame:r];
  [self setDrawSize:2.0 :2.0];
  [self setDrawOrigin:-1.0 :-1.0];
  [self setOpaque:NO];
  sides = 3;
  return self;
}
```

The **initFrame:** method sets the coordinates for the drawing system to range from **(-1,-1)** to **(1,1)**. It then sends the **[self setOpaque:NO]** message to tell **PolygonView** that it will *not* be fully covering its frame rectangle. We'll discuss the **takeNumSidesFrom:** method after the next step.

15. Insert the two methods below into **PolygonView.m**.

```
- drawSelf:(const NXRect *)rects :(int)rectCount
{
  float theta;

  PSmoveto(sin(0.0), cos(0.0));

  /* M_PI is a predefined value of PI.
   * M_PI*2.0 is number of radians in a circle.
   * The for() statement below sweeps through each
   * pie-section of the polygon for each side.
   */
  for (theta=0.0;
        theta <= 2*M_PI;
        theta += (M_PI*2.0)/sides) {

    PSlineto(sin(theta),cos(theta));
  }
  PSsetgray(NX_BLACK);
  PSfill();
  return self;
}


- setNumSides:(int)val
{
  if (val>0 && sides!=val) {
    sides = val;

    [self setNeedsDisplay:YES];
```

```
       if ([self isAutodisplay]) {
          [self displayFromOpaqueAncestor:&bounds
                                          :0 :NO];
       }
    }
    return self;
}
```

The **drawSelf::** method above traces the outline of the polygon, sets the color that we will be drawing with, then fills it in. The **takeNumSides-From:** and **setNumSides:** methods work together to react to slider manipulations and set the number of sides of the polygon to be displayed.

Notice that instead of invoking the **display** method, **setNumSides:** invokes **displayFromOpaqueAncestor:::.** This is because the **PolygonView** is *not* opaque. It has holes around the edges of the polygon where you can see the views that are behind it. This is necessary so that the background upon which the **PolygonView** instance is drawn can be properly redrawn.

16. Save all pertinent files, **make** and run PolygonViewDemo.

17. When you drag the slider knob, the number of sides of the displayed polygon should change as in Figure 6 below.

18. Quit PolygonViewDemo.

FIGURE 6. PolygonViewDemo Running

 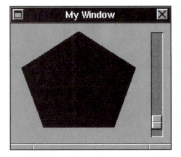

Changing the PolygonView's Size

Let's add a second control (another slider) to PolygonViewDemo which lets the user change the size of the polygon. First we'll insert the code into **PolygonView** class and then we'll work in IB.

19. Insert the two new method declarations below into **PolygonView.h**.

```
-  setSize:(float)size;
-  takeFloatSize:sender;
```

20. Insert the two new method implementations below into **PolygonView.m**.

```
-  setSize:(float)size
{
    NXRect obounds = bounds;

    [self convertRectToSuperview:&obounds];
    [self sizeTo:size :size];
    [self setDrawSize:2.0 :2.0];
    [self setDrawOrigin:-1.0 :-1.0];
    [self convertRectFromSuperview:&obounds];
    [self displayFromOpaqueAncestor:
              NXUnionRect(&obounds,&bounds) :1 :NO];
    return self;
}

-  takeFloatSize:sender
{
    [self setSize:[sender floatValue] ];
    return self;
}
```

The **setSize:** method is a little tricky, because the "size" is the coordinate system of the containing **View**, rather than the **PolygonView** itself (which is scaled from **-1** to **1** in each dimension for easy drawing).

The method first gets the "old" bounds of the **PolygonView** instance and converts it to the coordinate system of its superview (the window's content **View**). The method then resizes (**sizeTo::**), sets the scale of (**setDraw-Size::**), translates (**setDrawOrigin::**) the **PolygonView** instance (**self**) so that it ranges from **(-1,-1)** to **(1,1)**, and converts its old bounds from the superview's coordinate system back to its own coordinate system. We need to play this switching game because the coordinate system changed when we changed the size of the **PolygonView**.

The **setSize:** method then invokes **displayFromOpaqueAncestor:::** with the rectangle that is the union of the old **View** boundary and the current **View** boundary. This has the effect of redisplaying all of the region that was previously covered by the polygon and is now uncovered, which handles both the situation of the polygon getting larger and smaller.

The **takeFloatSize:** method is an action method, so it can be invoked from a slider.

21. Back in IB, **Parse** the **PolygonView** class.

22. Drag a horizontal slider from IB's Views palette and drop it in **MyWindow** as in Figure 7 below. (If necessary, resize **MyWindow** first.)

23. Using the Slider Attributes Inspector, set the slider so that it ranges from **0** to **600** and has a current value of **100**. When you're done, the window should look like the one in Figure 7 below.

FIGURE 7. PolygonViewDemo in IB with Two Sliders

24. Connect the horizontal slider to the **PolygonView** instance so that it sends the **takeFloatSize:** message.

25. Save all pertinent files and **make** and run PolygonViewDemo.

26. When you drag the horizontal slider knob to the right, you'll notice some peculiar behavior, as in window at the right of Figure 8 below.

FIGURE 8. PolygonViewDemo with Different Size Triangles

The polygon gets larger and trespasses into territory (the slider area) where it shouldn't! It looks terrible and is not the correct way to handle such a situation. We'll discuss a remedy right away.

27. Quit PolygonViewDemo.

Placing a View Inside a ScrollView

The solution that NeXTSTEP provides when you want to have a **View** that either changes size or is larger than the window is to display that **View** inside another **View** called a **ScrollView**. (Recall that we first experimented with **ScrollView**s back in Chapter 10 with MathPaper). In this section we'll learn how to put any **View** into a **ScrollView** and how to set up a window so that it can be properly resized.

28. Back in IB, select the **PolygonView** instance and make it a little smaller.

29. Choose IB's **Format→Layout→Group in ScrollView** menu command. Your **PolygonView** will be surrounded by two scroller areas as in the window on the left of Figure 9 below. (You may need to reposition the **ScrollView** so that it still fits properly in the window.)

FIGURE 9. **PolygonView Inside a ScrollView**

30. Save the updated **PolygonViewDemo.nib** file and **make** and run PolygonViewDemo.

31. Drag the knob in the horizontal scroller to the right.

This time, as you make the **PolygonView** bigger, the **ScrollView** will automatically scale the scroll knobs to accommodate the change in size, as in the window on the right of Figure 9. Notice that the scroll knobs and buttons automatically appear and disappear as needed: they are handled automatically for you by the NeXTSTEP **ScrollView** and **Scroller** objects. Furthermore, the **PolygonView** object doesn't know that it is being drawn inside a **ScrollView**: you didn't have to modify any of your code.

The **ScrollView** automatically sets the PostScript clipping rectangle so that any attempts to draw outside the **ScrollView** are not permitted. This further simplifies the task of writing our own custom **View**s.

32. Quit PolygonViewDemo.

Responding to Events in a View

In addition to drawing, the **View** class can also process events (since it's a subclass of the **Responder** abstract superclass). To receive mouse-down or mouse-up events, all your custom **View** needs to do is to override one of the event methods below that are declared in the **Responder** class:

```
- mouseDown: (NXEvent *)theEvent;
- rightMouseDown: (NXEvent *)theEvent;
- mouseUp: (NXEvent *)theEvent;
- rightMouseUp: (NXEvent *)theEvent;
```

To receive mouse-entered or mouse-exited events, your custom **View** needs to override one of the event methods below (and set up a tracking rectangle – something we will describe in Chapter 18):

```
- mouseEntered: (NXEvent *)theEvent;
- mouseExited: (NXEvent *)theEvent;
```

Additionally, if your custom **View** is made the **firstResponder** of its containing window, it will receive the following keyboard and mouse events:

```
- keyDown: (NXEvent *)theEvent;
- keyUp: (NXEvent *)theEvent;
- mouseMoved: (NXEvent *)theEvent;
- mouseDragged: (NXEvent *)theEvent;
- rightMouseDragged: (NXEvent *)theEvent;
```

In the remainder of this section, we'll show how to receive and interpret the mouse-down and mouse-up events.

Getting a Mouse-Down Event

"Overriding one of the event methods" is as simple as adding a single method to your **PolygonView** class definition. The version of a **mouse-Down:** method below tells if the user clicked inside or outside of the polygon displayed in the **PolygonView** instance.

1. Insert the **mouseDown:** method declaration below into **PolygonView.h**.

    ```
    - mouseDown:(NXEvent *)theEvent;
    ```

2. Insert the **mouseDown:** method implementation below into **PolygonView.m**.

    ```
    - mouseDown:(NXEvent *)theEvent
    {
      float theta;
      int res;
                                      /* make private copy */
      NXPoint where = theEvent->location;
                           /* get in local coordinates */
      [self convertPoint:&where fromView:nil];

      [self lockFocus]; /* now we can send PostScript */
      PSmoveto(sin(0.0), cos(0.0));
      for(theta=0.0; theta <= 2*M_PI;
                            theta += (M_PI*2.0)/sides) {
        PSlineto(sin(theta), cos(theta));
      }
      PSinfill(where.x, where.y, &res);
      [self unlockFocus];

      NXRunAlertPanel([NXApp appName],
                  "Mouse clicked %s polygon.", 0, 0, 0,
                  res ? "inside" : "outside");
      return self;
    }
    ```

This **mouseDown:** method receives the data (**theEvent**) from the mouse-down event and converts the location where the event occurred from **Window** coordinates to the **View**'s own coordinate system. It then locks the PostScript focus, redraws the path, and then uses the PostScript function **PSinfill()** to find out if the mouse click was inside or outside the filled area. The path is not redisplayed because we don't send a PostScript display operator, such as **stroke** or **fill**, to the Display PostScript interpreter.

The method then displays an Alert panel saying that the mouse was either "inside" or "outside" the polygon.

An improvement for this class would be to put the path-drawing code for both **drawSelf::** and **mouseDown:** into a module used by both – or better yet, use a PostScript *user path* to describe the path only once. For more information about user paths, see Adobe's "purple book," *Programming the Display PostScript System with NeXTSTEP.*

3. Save the **PolygonView** class files and **make** and run PolygonViewDemo.

4. Drag the vertical slider, and click the mouse outside the polygon. See Figure 10 below.

5. Click **OK** and then click the mouse inside the polygon.

6. Quit PolygonViewDemo.

FIGURE 10. Mouse Click Detection in PolygonViewDemo

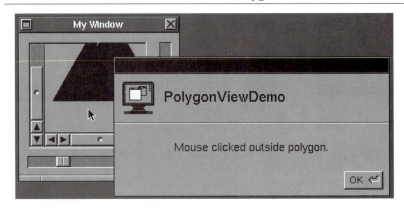

Autosizing Multiple Views in a Window

Every window that has a scroller in it should be resizable. In Chapter 10 we showed how to set up a **ScrollView** so that it would resize when its containing window was resized. This is called *Autosizing*. With the PolygonView-Demo window, however, handling window resizing requires a little more thought. Clearly, the **ScrollView** should stretch when the window is stretched. The sliders, on the other hand, should stay in place: the right-hand slider should remained anchored to the right hand side of the window, while the bottom slider should remain anchored to the bottom. Fortunately, NeXTSTEP gives us an easy way to add these features, through IB's Size Inspector.

Interface Builder's **Test Interface** mode is wonderful for experimenting around with Autosizing attributes. The diagram in Figure 11 below shows the proper settings for each object in the PolygonViewDemo window. Remember to set the Autosizing attribute for every object in the window.

The horizontal springs are for horizontal resizes; the vertical springs are for vertical ones. The inside box is for stretching, while the outside box is for anchoring. A spring in the inside box indicates that the object should stretch when it is resized. A line on the outside box indicates that the distance between the object and the side of the window should remain fixed if at all possible; a spring indicates that it should be resizable.

1. Back in IB, select the **PolygonView** instance and type Command-3 to bring up the Size Inspector. Click the lines in the inside box so four springs appear as on the left of Figure 11 below.

FIGURE 11. Autosizing PolygonView and Sliders

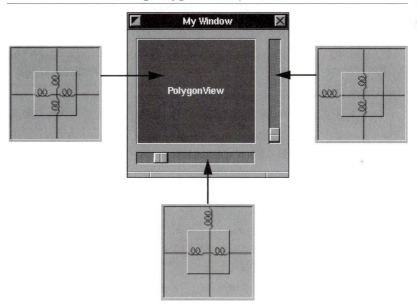

2. Select the horizontal slider and click lines in the inside and outside boxes so three springs appear as at the bottom of Figure 11.

3. Select the vertical slider and click lines in the inside and outside boxes so three springs appear as on the right of Figure 11.

4. Choose IB's **Document→Test Interface** menu command. Try stretching the PolygonViewDemo window to the right. You'll see the **ScrollView** instance and the horizontal slider resize, while the vertical slider moves. See Figure 12 below for an example. You'll get similar results for stretching the window down.

FIGURE 12. PolygonView after Resizing in IB's Test Interface Mode

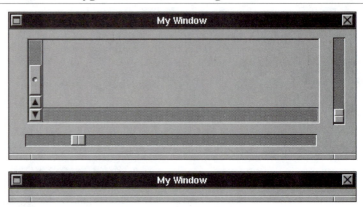

The one problem with resizing right now is not stretching, but shrinking. If you make the window too small, you'll end up with junk, as in the window at the bottom of Figure 12. In NeXTSTEP 3.0, you can use Interface Builder to set a minimum window size. We'll see how to do that in Chapter 18.

5. Quit IB's **Test Interface** mode.

6. Save the **PolygonViewDemo.nib** file and **make** and run PolygonViewDemo.

7. Drag the vertical slider knob, and then drag the different parts of the window's resize bar. It works!

8. Quit PolygonViewDemo.

Summary

In this chapter we learned a lot more about the **View** class, in particular the **drawSelf::** method, and a bit more about resizing. In the next chapter we'll start building our next major application, GraphPaper, which has a window that graphs equations.

16

GraphPaper: A Multi-Threaded Application with a Display List

In this chapter, we'll use the Evaluator back end that we built in Chapter 10 as the basis for a program that graphs single-valued functions. The program's main window will end up looking like the one in Figure 1 below.

FIGURE 1. Main Window in GraphPaper Application

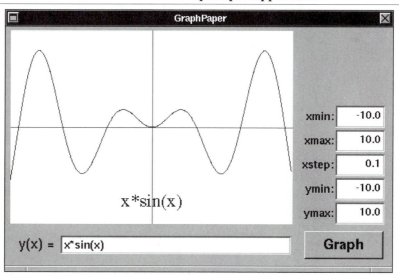

In the process of developing this program, we'll learn more about the **drawSelf::** method, see how to construct a complicated image out of many individual pieces, and learn a little bit about *threads* – Mach's system for lightweight multiprocessing.

GraphPaper's Design

Conceptually, our program to graph a function will contain four main parts:

(i) an *interface* that lets the user specify the function and the graph parameters, and start and stop the graphing process,

(ii) a *pair generator*, which takes the graph parameters and generates pairs of (**x,y**) points to be plotted,

(iii) a *graph builder*, which takes the pairs from the pair generator and builds the data structure of the graph, and

(iv) a *graph displayer*, which takes the data structure and displays it on the screen.

The Interface

We'll build GraphPaper's interface with Interface Builder (of course!). The interface will consist of a NeXTSTEP **Form** object containing several text fields (**xmin**, **ymax**, etc. in Figure 1), a button (**Graph**) to start the graphing process, and a custom **View** called the **GraphView**. The **GraphView** object will contain the brains of the GraphPaper application.

Connecting to the Back End

When GraphPaper starts up, a **GraphView** object will start up a single copy of the Evaluator program, much in the way that the MathPaper application did in Chapter 11. (In fact, GraphPaper will use the **Process** object from the MathPaper project, with no modifications. Unlike MathPaper, however, GraphPaper will use only *one* **Process** object and only *one* Evaluator.) When the user clicks the **Graph** button in GraphPaper's main window, the **GraphView** object will first check to make sure that all of the graph parameters make sense. It will then start up a second task (called a *thread*) which will send pairs of numeric algebraic expressions to the Evaluator for processing.

Each of these numeric algebraic pairs corresponds to an (**x,y**) pair. Since the Evaluator doesn't know how to process variables, **GraphView** will substitute the value of the variable **x** for the letter "x" for every point that it graphs before it sends it to the Evaluator. That's what we mean when we say "numeric" algebraic pairs. For example, suppose the user wanted the graph the equation

```
y(x) = 2*x + 1
```

over the range of **0** to **10** with a step of **1**. **GraphView**'s subsidiary thread would send the following sequence of 11 pairs to the Evaluator:

```
0, 2*0+1
1, 2*1+1
2, 2*2+1
...
10, 2*10+1
```

The Evaluator, in turn, would evaluate each of these expressions and send them back in a form that looks like this:

```
0, 1
1, 3
2, 5
...
10, 21
```

The third part of the **GraphView** object will "watch" for the results from the Evaluator and incorporate them into a data structure called a *display list*. The display list that **GraphView** will use is an Objective-C **List** object, which contains a list of other objects. Each object in this list will know how to respond to two methods: **bounds** and **drawPSInView:**. We will have to implement these methods for each class whose members we wish to put into the display list.

When an object in the display list receives the **bounds** message, the object returns a pointer to an **NXRect** structure that describes the object's size and position. When an object in the display list receives a **drawPSInView:** message, it generates the PostScript code to "draw itself."

Initially, we'll only have one kind of object that can be put into the display list. It will be called **Segment**, and it will be used to represent a line segment of the final plot, from one **(x,y)** pair to another. In addition to responding to the **bounds** and **drawPSInView:** messages, a **Segment** object will also have a special **initx1:y1:x2:y2:** method for initialization and a **free** method, which frees the memory associated with a **Segment** instance.

Why Use a Display List?

The advantage of using a display list of objects, rather than an array of **(x,y)** structures, is that we can easily add new kinds of objects to be drawn in the on-screen **GraphView** by simply creating new classes and inserting instances of those classes into the display list. For example, we might want to add a title to the graph's background. With the flexibility of the display list, all we have to do is to create a **Title** class that responds to the same **bounds** and **drawPSInView:** messages. After creating the new class, it would be easy to integrate its instances into the existing display list.

The last part of the **GraphView** object does the actual drawing of the graph. This part is taken care of by the **drawSelf::** method. The **drawSelf::** method will look at the rectangle where it has been requested to perform drawing and send a message to the objects in the display list that intersect that region. Another set of methods in the **GraphView** class will take care of scaling the **GraphView** to the size requested by the user.

Working with Multiple Threads

GraphPaper is a tricky application because it basically has to do three things at the same time:

(i)   respond to user events;

(ii) "listen" for data from the Evaluator and graph it when it arrives; and

(iii) send data to the Evaluator.

Handling (i) and (ii) at the same time is no problem: we saw how to do that with the MathPaper application in Chapter 11. The NeXTSTEP **Application** object's event loop that watches for user events will also watch for data on a file descriptor.[1] The problem is (iii) – sending data to the Evaluator process. Doing this concurrently with (i) and (ii) presents a problem with NeXTSTEP. The problem has to do with the way that UNIX handles *pipes* (interprocess communication channels).

When two programs are connected with a pipe, UNIX makes allowances for the fact that one of the programs might be able to send data before the

---

1. File descriptors are also called file handles. They are the small integers that are returned by the UNIX **open()** system call and are used by the **read()**, **write()**, and **close()** calls.

other program is ready to read it by allocating a buffer for the pipe. Instead of sending the data directly from program **A** to program **B**, UNIX sends the data from program **A** to the pipe buffer, then from the buffer to program **B**. This lets program **A** write the data and keep going.

Of course, each pipe is only so big: eventually, if program **B** doesn't read the data fast enough, the pipe gets filled. Once the pipe is filled, if program **A** tries to keep sending data down the pipe, UNIX *blocks* program **A** until the pipe has some empty space.

Since it is much faster to send data to the Evaluator than it is for the Evaluator to process the data and send it back, it's reasonable to assume that any process sending data to the Evaluator is eventually going to be blocked. Unfortunately, the Evaluator is sending data *back to the same process from which the data came*. The returned data is being sent back through another pipe. That pipe can then fill up just as easily as the pipe that sends data to the Evaluator. This could result in a *deadlock* condition, with both pipes filled and both processes blocked, each waiting for the other to empty the pipe from which it is reading. The main GraphPaper process would block because the Evaluator couldn't accept any more data, and the Evaluator would be blocked because the GraphPaper application wasn't emptying its pipe either.

The solution is to use a third process – one that only has the job of sending data to the Evaluator. In the example, we call this process the *stuffer thread*. When the Evaluator gets busy and the pipeline gets filled, the stuffer thread blocks. But since all this thread does is send data to the Evaluator, it doesn't matter if it gets blocked, because no blocked process will be waiting for the stuffer.

Although we could send the data to the Evaluator with a completely different process, a far more elegant (and efficient) way to do it is with a lightweight process, or *Mach thread*. Simply put, a thread is a second process that shares the same program and data space with the program that created it. A thread can access the same global variables as the program that creates it, but runs on its own schedule and can lock its own resources. Threads and multi-thread programming are an important part of the Mach operating system.

The Difficulty of Using Threads

The power of threads does not come without a price: it is much harder to write a multi-threaded application than to write a single-threaded one. This is because two processes executing in the same address space can cause interactions in adverse ways unless you are careful to anticipate and avoid such interactions. For example, every time you want to use a global variable, you've got to lock it, so that another thread doesn't change it out from under you.

To see how this could happen consider the following simple example. Suppose a function in a multi-threaded program wanted to increment a global variable called **count**. In a single threaded application program, you would use an expression like this:

```
extern int count;
count++;
```

This might cause problems in a multi-threaded application. Suppose the first thread of a multi-threaded application had just read the value of **count** from memory, but before it could increment the value and write it back, the thread was suspended and a second thread started up. Suppose that the second thread also read and incremented the value of **count**. It would read the old unincremented value of **count** and increment it. If the second thread wrote back the value of count before the first thread starts up again, the value of **count** would be increased by only 1 (instead of by 2) when both threads were finished.

The way around this problem is by using an exclusive lock called a *mutex*, short for *mut*ual *ex*clusion. You can create a mutex with the **mutex_alloc()** function:

```
mutex_t count_lock;
count_lock = mutex_alloc();
```

You could then write the "incrementing" code discussed above using a mutex as follows:

```
extern int count;
extern mutex_t count_lock;

mutex_lock(count_lock);
count++;
mutex_unlock(count_lock);
```

If a thread executes the **mutex_lock()** function and the mutex is already locked, that thread halts execution until the mutex is unlocked. This prevents two threads from simultaneously trying to access and modify the value of the variable **count**.

It's obviously more work to write an application that uses multiple threads. These applications are also harder to debug. For these reasons, the Application Kit isn't multi-threaded. This means that if you write a multi-threaded application, *you should send messages to App Kit objects only from your application's main thread.*

Although the Application Kit isn't multi-threaded, it doesn't mean that you shouldn't use multiple threads – just don't use them to update the screen. For example, the *Sound Kit* uses multiple threads to play music. You should generally write your application so that each thread only interacts with a single NeXTSTEP kit (such as the App Kit, DBKit, or Sound Kit).

C Threads

NeXTSTEP uses the *Mach C Threads* package to handle multiple threads. The C Threads package enables you to do the following:

- create a new thread from your main process (called *forking*),
- wait for a thread that you've created to terminate (called *joining*),
- create and lock mutexes to protect global variables from simultaneous modification, and
- synchronize execution between threads.

The **mutex_alloc()**, **mutex_lock()**, and **mutex_unlock()** functions above are all part of the C Threads package. C Threads was originally developed under Berkeley 4.2 UNIX. The difference between using C Threads under UNIX and under Mach is that Mach is a truly multi-threaded operating system. Although threads share the same address space, they are truly independent processes – each separately scheduled and separately controllable.

We'll provide only a simple introduction to multi-threaded programming here. Most of the time with NeXTSTEP, you only use threads for performing a time intensive task that you want done in the background, so that it won't interfere with your main program's handling of events.

Using C Threads

To use C Threads you must include the **cthreads.h** file (in **NextDeveloper/ Headers/mach**) in your program. Once you've done that, you can start a new thread by simply calling the **cthread_fork()** function as follows:

```
cthread_fork( (cthread_fn_t)aFunction,
                        (any_t)anArgument);
```

This function call causes a new thread to be created. The thread will start by calling the function **aFunction** with the argument **anArgument**. If you need more than one argument, you can make **anArgument** a pointer to a structure that contains more. The thread terminates either by calling the function **cthread_exit()** or by returning from the function **aFunction**.

Two other C Threads functions worth mentioning here are **cthread_detach()** and **cthread_join()**. These functions are used for synchronizing execution between multiple threads.

As mentioned previously, *joining* means waiting for a thread to finish executing. You might do this in a program if you start up a thread that accesses a database in the background, but you need the thread to finish before doing something else (like closing a data file that the thread is using). In order to rejoin the thread that you have created, you need to know the thread's identifier. This identifier is returned to your program when you execute the **cthread_fork()** call. We'll call the **cthread_join()** function in the Graph-Paper program.

If you never intend to rejoin a thread that you have created, you might want to consider detaching the thread. You can't join a thread once you detach it. The advantage is that a detached thread runs slightly more efficiently than one that isn't. (When a thread is detached, an internal variable is set which tells the C Threads package to ignore the exit value of the thread. If you don't care how your thread terminates, detach it. Otherwise, don't.) For more information about these function calls, search for "cthread" in HeaderViewer or Librarian.

Threads and Objective-C

Although you can use Objective-C from within a multi-threaded application, it's best to confine all of your Objective-C calls to your main thread. The reason is that many common Objective-C objects aren't thread safe – that is, they aren't designed for use within a multi-threaded application.[1]

---

1. In NeXTSTEP 3.0, if you *must* use Objective-C from more than one thread, you can call Objective-C function **objc_setMultithreaded()**, which will cause Objective-C to use a thread-safe version of its messaging function. Using this function results in a substantial performance penalty to the Objective-C runtime system (each message call takes three times longer than it would otherwise). Furthermore, even though the runtime system is threadsafe after calling this function, few of the Objective-C classes, such as **List** and **HashTable** – and none of the Application Kit – are threadsafe. For this reason, we do not recommend using Objective-C from any thread in your application program other than the main thread.

You can, however, access public variables in Objective-C objects from within other threads, because public variables appear to regular C functions as regular C structures. That is, the public variables are simply data stored in memory. We'll use public variables in the GraphPaper application to allow for communication between the main Objective-C function and the stuffer thread.

Building the GraphPaper Application

Now that we've thought about the program a bit, let's get on with the work of building the GraphPaper application.

Changes to the Evaluator Back End

We need to make one change to the Evaluator so that it can recognize more than a single expression on a line. One way to do this is to make the Evaluator recognize two expressions separated by a comma and terminated with a newline. Fortunately, since Evaluator is built with **lex** and **yacc**, this change is very easy to do and is confined to a single file, **grammar.y**.

1. Using an editor, insert the six lines in **bold** below into **grammar.y**.

```
stat   : expr '\n'
{
   printf("%10g\n", $1);
   printingError = 0;
   fflush(stdout);
}
| expr ',' expr '\n'
{
   printf("%g,%g\n", $1, $3);
   printingError = 0;
   fflush(stdout);
}
;
```

These changes allow us to send to the Evaluator two expressions on the same line separated by a comma. The Evaluator will evaluate each expression and print the result on a single line, each separated by a comma.

2. Open up a UNIX shell window by double-clicking the Terminal icon.

3. Compile the Evaluator with the **make** utility by typing **make** in the Terminal shell window. What you should type is indicated in **bold**:

```
localhost> cd ~/Evaluator
```

```
localhost> make
yacc grammar.y
yacc -d grammar.y
lex rules.lex
cc -O -o Evaluator y.tab.c lex.yy.c -ly -ll -lm
localhost>
```

4. Install the Evaluator program in your **~/Apps** directory by typing **make install** as follows:

```
localhost> make install
strip Evaluator
cp Evaluator /simsong/Apps
localhost>
```

5. Test the new Evaluator from the command line to be sure that it understands the new comma notation.

```
localhost> Evaluator
3,2*3+1
3,7
^Clocalhost>
```

In this example, we typed "**3,2*3+1**" and Evaluator responded with "**3,7**". We then typed Control-c to terminate the input.

Building GraphPaper's Interface

1. Launch Project Builder (PB) from your dock, choose PB's **Project→New** menu command and give your new project the name "**~/GraphPaper**."

2. Create an application icon for the GraphPaper application and save it in the file **GraphPaper.tiff** in your **~/GraphPaper** project directory. Our attempt can be seen at the left.

GraphPaper.tiff

3. Drag the **GraphPaper.tiff** icon from your File Viewer and drop it in the **Application Icon** area at the lower left of the Attributes view in PB. This will set the **GraphPaper.tiff** icon to be the application icon of your GraphPaper application.

4. Double-click the **GraphPaper.nib** file name (under **Interfaces**) in PB's Files view. Interface Builder (IB) will automatically launch and display the **GraphPaper.nib** interface created by PB.

The **GraphView** class we'll use to display function graphs will be a subclass of the **View** class. It will need outlets to point to most of the on-screen objects and actions to start and stop the graphing.

5. **Subclass** the **View** class in IB's File window. Rename the new class **GraphView**.

6. In the Class Inspector, add the following outlets and actions to **GraphView**:

```
outlets:            actions:
graphButton         graph:
xminCell            stopGraph:
xmaxCell
xstepCell
yminCell
ymaxCell
formulaField
```

7. **Unparse** the **GraphView** class and insert it into your project.

Next we'll set up the program's main window as in Figure 2 below.

FIGURE 2. **Setting up GraphPaper's Main Window in IB**

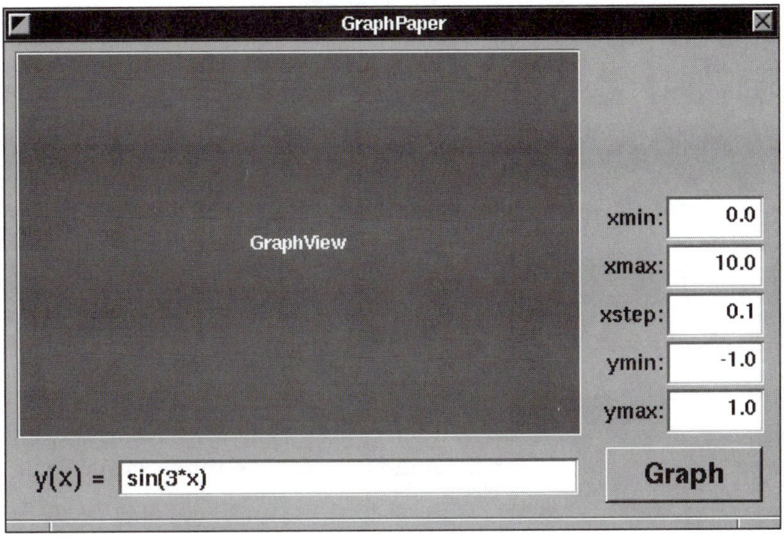

8. Using the Window Attributes Inspector, change the window's title from **MyWindow** to **GraphPaper.**

9. Make the window shorter, so that it is about four inches tall.

10. Drag a **CustomView** icon from IB's Views palette and drop it in the **GraphPaper** window. Enlarge and position it as in Figure 2.

11. Change the class of the **CustomView** to **GraphView** in the Inspector.

12. Drag a **Form** object (seen at the left) from IB's Views palette and drop it in the right side of the **GraphPaper** window.

13. Alt-drag the bottom middle handle of the **Form** object to create three more **FormCell**s, for a total of five **FormCell**s.

14. Make the **Form** labels larger by typing Command-t to bring up IB's Font panel and then selecting an appropriate font (e.g., Helvetica Bold 14 pt.).

15. Change the labels on the **FormCell**s to **xmin**, **xmax**, etc., as in Figure 2 above. (Use the tab key to move quickly from one **FormCell** to the next.)

16. Enter the numbers **0.0, 10.0, 0.1, -1.0, 1.0** in the five text areas of the **Form**, as in Figure 2 above, to set up defaults that will show the user a good looking graph at start up time.

17. Select the **Form** matrix as a whole and change the Text to be right-aligned () in the Form Attributes Inspector.

18. Drag a **TextField** icon (seen at the left) from IB's Views palette and drop it near the bottom of the **GraphPaper** window.

19. Make the text in the **TextField** larger using IB's Font panel. Make the **TextField** wider as well.

20. Enter a function which has an interesting graph in the **TextField**. We'll use **sin(3*x)**, which will lead to an interesting graph at launch time.

21. Drag a **Title** icon from IB's Views palette and drop it to the left of the **TextField** object. Change the text to "**y(x) =**" as in Figure 2 above. This **Title** icon actually represents another **TextField** object with attributes such as uneditable, gray background, etc.

22. Drag a **Button** object from IB's Views palette and drop it in the **GraphPaper** window below the **Form** as in Figure 2. Change the label on the **Button** object to "**Graph**" and make the button text larger.

23. Connect the seven **GraphView** outlets to the appropriate on-screen objects. That is, connect the **graphButton** outlet to the **Graph** button, the **xmaxCell** outlet to the **FormCell** labeled **xmax**, and so on. The **formulaField** outlet should be connected to the **TextField** object. See the Connections Inspector in Figure 3 below.

(Don't be confused that these connections are being made between two objects in the same GraphPaper window. The **GraphView** instance in the main window simply has some outlets that you are setting.)

FIGURE 3. Connections Inspector for GraphView Instance

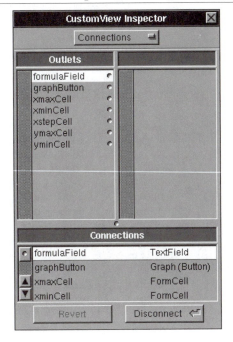

Later in this chapter we'll use the **graphButton** outlet to show how to temporarily change the title on the button from "**Graph**" to "**Stop**" while GraphPaper is drawing a graph.

24. Connect the **Graph** button to the on-screen **GraphView** instance. Make it send the **graph:** action.

We won't use the **stopGraph:** action as part of the connections we set up in IB. In fact, the only advantage of adding **stopGraph:** to the **GraphView** class in IB is that IB's **Unparse** command will save us some typing.

25. Save the **GraphPaper.nib** file.

The GraphView Class Interface File

Since **GraphView** is the most complicated class that we've built so far, we'll look at it in pieces. When learning any new class, the best place to start is with the interface file. In this case, that file is **GraphView.h**.

26. Using an editor, insert the lines in **bold** below into **GraphView.h**.

```
#import <appkit/appkit.h>
```

```
@interface GraphView:View
{
  id formulaField;
  id graphButton;
  id xmaxCell;
  id xminCell;
  id xstepCell;
  id ymaxCell;
  id yminCell;

    id         graphProc;
    id         displayList;
    BOOL       first;            /* first datapoint */
    double     lastx, lasty;  /* for drawing graph */
    char       graphBuf[17000];     /* buf to graph */
    double     ymin,ymax;
    cthread_t  stuffer_thread;

  @public            /* for use by stuffing thread */

    BOOL       graphing;
    char       *formula;
    int        toFd;
    double     xmin, xmax, xstep;
}

- graph:sender;
- stopGraph:sender;
- addBufToGraph:(const char *)buf;
- graphLine:(const char *)buf;
- addGraphSegmentx1:(float)x1 y1:(float)y1
                  x2:(float)x2 y2:(float)y2;
- drawSelf:(const NXRect *)rects :(int)rectCount;
- clear;
- awakeFromNib;

@end

#define GRAPH_TAG 0
#define LABEL_TAG 1
#define AXES_TAG 2
```

The first seven **id** statements declare the outlets we set up and connected in IB. The remaining instance variables are a little more complicated. Here is a brief description of what the first two inserted variables do:

graphProc   This variable holds the **id** of the **Process** object that connects to the Evaluator back end. It's similar to the **proc** variable that was in the MathPaper application.

displayList   This variable will hold the **id** of the display list.

The next group of variables are used for constructing the graph data structure with the **(x,y)** pairs returned by the Evaluator:

first   This boolean variable is set before the first pair is received from the Evaluator. It lets the **GraphView** object distinguish between the first pair of coordinates returned and the others.

lastx
lasty   These variables contain the **(x,y)** coordinate pair of the last point read from the Evaluator. They are only valid if **first=NO**. They are used to construct the line segment from the last point received to the current point.

graphBuf   This array is used to buffer information sent to the **GraphView** object from the Evaluator.

ymin
ymax   These two variables are used to determine the scale of the graph that is drawn.

The next group of variables (on the next page) are used by the thread process that sends data to the Evaluator. Most of them are **@public** variables that are used to provide communication between the main process and the stuffer thread. We use **@public** variables so we can access them directly from the stuffer thread, without having to message the **GraphView** instance.[1]

---

1. Don't confuse Objective-C messaging and Mach messages. Objective-C messaging and multiple threads don't mix well because much of NeXTSTEP's runtime system is not threadsafe. *Mach* messages, on the other hand, are a system for inter-process and inter-thread communication that the operating system provides. It is very threadsafe. Unfortunately, Mach messages have a significantly higher overhead than Objective-C messages.

stuffer_thread	This variable contains the thread identifier (of type **cthread_t**) of the thread that does the stuffing.
graphing	This variable is a flag, set to **YES** when graphing is taking place. If the user clicks the **Stop** button, this variable will be set to **NO**. The thread process routinely checks this variable and quits if it is set to **NO**. This is the way that the master process can halt the thread (a means for inter-thread communication).
formula	This is a copy of the string stored in the formula cell. It is important to make a copy of this variable for the stuffer thread for two reasons. First, the copy eliminates the need of having the stuffer thread message the **TextField** to find out its contents. Secondly, this copy of the **TextField**'s formula will not change, even if the user changes the contents of the **TextField** while the graph is being made.
toFd	This is the file descriptor of the pipe that sends data to the Evaluator process.
xmin **xmax** **xstep**	These variables set up the conditions for the graph; **xmin**, **xmax**, and **xstep** are used to determine the values for the variable **x** that are sent to the Evaluator.

We'll discuss the new methods as we progress through this chapter. Lastly, the **#define** statements set up the tags that we will use for various parts of the graph.

The GraphView Class Implementation File

Now let's look at the **GraphView** class implementation in **GraphView.m**. The first part of the file contains a set of **#import** directives.

27. Insert the **#import** directives below after the **#import "GraphView.h"** directive at the beginning of **GraphView.m**.

```
#import "Process.h"
#import "Segment.h"
```

We've discussed the **Process.h** include file in our description of the Math-Paper application in Chapter 11. The new **Segment** class is where a line segment element is created to draw part of the graph. We'll set up the **Segment** class later in this chapter.

The Data Stuffer Methods

The data stuffer consists of a single C function and two methods:

dataStuffer() Sends data to the Evaluator. We make this a function because it is called from a different thread.

graph: Sets up global variables and runs **dataStuffer()** with **cthread_fork()**.

stopGraph: Cleans up after a graph. Also lets a user interrupt an ongoing graph.

Although the function **dataStuffer()** appears in the source code before the two methods, we'll discuss it last for clarity. The **graph:** method starts the graphing. It's invoked when the user presses the **Graph** button.

28. Insert the lines in **bold** below into the **graph:** action method in **GraphView.m**.

```
- graph:sender
{
  /* initialize for a graph */
  [self clear];

  /* set instance variables from the form */
  xmin  = [xminCell  doubleValue];
  xmax  = [xmaxCell  doubleValue];
  xstep = [xstepCell doubleValue];
  ymin  = [yminCell  doubleValue];
  ymax  = [ymaxCell  doubleValue];
  memset(graphBuf, 0, sizeof(graphBuf));

  /* Check the parameters of the graph */
  if ( xmax-xmin<=0 || ymax-ymin<=0 ) {
    NXRunAlertPanel(0,
          "Invalid min/max combination", 0, 0, 0);
    return self;
  }

  if ( xstep<=0 ) {
    NXRunAlertPanel(0,"Need a positive step",0,0,0);
    return self;
  }

  [self setDrawSize: xmax-xmin : ymax-ymin];
  [self setDrawOrigin: xmin : ymin];
```

```
            if (formula) {
              /* Free the old formula if we have one */
              NXZoneFree([self zone], formula);
              formula = 0;
            }
            formula = NXCopyStringBufferFromZone(
                        [formulaField stringValue],
                        [self zone]);

            [ [graphButton setTitle: "Stop"]
                        setAction: @selector(stopGraph:)];

            first    = YES;   /* next pair read is the first */
            graphing = 1;     /* we are now graphing */
            stuffer_thread =
              cthread_fork((cthread_fn_t)dataStuffer, self);
            return self;
        }
```

The **graph:** action method first invokes **GraphView**'s **clear** method to clean up memory and the screen (we'll discuss the **clear** method in a later section). Then it reads the five values in the **FormCell**s and stores them in the variables **xmin**, **xmax**, **xstep**, **ymin**, and **ymax**. An Alert panel is displayed if the coordinates requested do not make any sense.

The next two lines set the scale and the origin of the graph. The inherited **View** method

- **setDrawSize:** (NXCoord) *width* : (NXCoord) *height*

sets the scale of units of the coordinate system used by **GraphView** so that it is *width* units wide and *height* units high. The inherited **View** method

- **setDrawOrigin:** (NXCoord) *x* : (NXCoord) *y*

readjusts the **GraphView**'s origin so that the point **(x,y)** is drawn in the lower-left hand corner.

The "**formula =**" line makes a copy of the contents of the formula cell. Notice that we use the NeXTSTEP function **NXCopyStringBufferFrom-Zone()** which automatically allocates a block of memory for a null-terminated string from a particular memory zone (in this case, the memory zone associated with the **GraphView** instance itself.)

The next line changes the title of the on-screen button from "**Graph**" to "**Stop**" and changes its action so that it sends the **stopGraph:** message. If the user now clicks the button, the **stopGraph:** message gets sent to the **GraphView**. This is a cute way to rewire an application while it is running.

The statement **first=YES** sets the **first** instance variable so that the method that builds the graph will know that a new graph is being created. The statement **graphing=1** sets the instance variable **graphing**, which is used to control the stuffer thread. Finally the line containing the **cthread_fork()** call causes the data stuffer thread to be created.

Stopping a Running Graph

The **stopGraph:** method below stops a running graph. It gets invoked either when the user clicks on the **stopGraph:** button or when the graph is finished.

29. Insert the lines in **bold** below into the **stopGraph:** method in **GraphView.m**.

```
- stopGraph:sender
{
    graphing = 0;
          /* wait for the stuffer thread to finish */
    cthread_join(stuffer_thread);


    [ [graphButton setTitle: "Graph"]
                   setAction: @selector(graph:)];
    return self;
}
```

This method clears the **graphing** state variable and then calls the **cthread_join()** function, which causes the main process to wait until the data stuffer thread finishes executing. The **stopGraph:** method then frees its copy of the formula. Finally, it changes the title of the **Button** object back to "**Graph**" and resets the **Button**'s action to send the **graph:** message.

The Data Stuffer Function

Finally there is the data stuffer function itself, aptly called **dataStuffer()**. The function gets started by the **cthread_fork()** function call in the **graph:** method. It has a loop which steps the variable **x** from **xmin** to **xmax**. The loop immediately stops if the **graphing** variable is set to **0** (as would happen if the user pressed the **Stop** button and the **stopGraph:** message was sent).

30. Insert the **dataStuffer()** function below into **GraphView.m**. Put it after the **#import** directives but before the **@implementation** directive.

```
/* dataStuffer: a thread fork function that
 * puts data into the pipe.
 */
int dataStuffer(GraphView *obj)
{
  double x;

  for (x=obj->xmin; obj->graphing && x<=obj->xmax;
                              x+=obj->xstep) {
    char buf[4096]; /* big enough */
    char *cc, *dd;

    /* build the expression */
    sprintf(buf, "%g,", x);
    dd = buf + strlen(buf);
    for (cc=obj->formula; *cc; cc++) {
      if (*cc=='x') {
        sprintf(dd, "%g", x);
        dd = dd + strlen(dd);
      }
      else {
        *(dd++) = *cc;
      }
    }

    *(dd++) = '\n';   /* terminate the string */
    *(dd++) = '\0';
    write(obj->toFd, buf, dd-buf);
  }
  /* Now send through terminate code */
  write(obj->toFd, "999\n", 4);
  return 0;
}
```

Recall that when the data stuffer thread was created, it was passed a single variable, namely **self**. This is the **id** of the **GraphView** object, which lets the **dataStuffer()** function access all of **GraphView**'s @**public** variables.

The body of the loop is a little complicated. It builds the expressions that are sent to the Evaluator. To do this, it must search the formula for all occurrences of the letter "x" and replace them with the current value of the variable **x**.

When the loop finishes, the function sends the number **999** to the Evaluator. This number is used as a flag to indicate that no more data is coming through the pipe. The procedure that constructs the graph looks for a **999** on a line by itself and uses that flag as its way of knowing that the graph is finished. The digits **999** really don't matter: what's important is that the Evaluator is sent a line of data with one expression and no comma. Finally the **dataStuffer()** function returns, which terminates the thread.

Constructing the Graph

Recall that the data stuffer thread sends to the Evaluator a series of expressions that looks like this:

```
0, 2*0+1
1, 2*1+1
2, 2*2+1
```

And the Evaluator sends back a series of number that look like this:

```
0, 1
1, 3
2, 5
```

The **GraphView** object needs to take those pairs of numbers and construct a graph. To do this we use a function that is called by Display PostScript when data is available, and three methods for processing the data.

gotGraphData()	Receives the data from Evaluator in blocks.
- addBufToGraph: (const char *)*buf*	Turns the blocks of data into lines of (**x,y**) pairs.
- graphLine: (const char *)*buf*	Turns (**x,y**) pairs into line segments.
- addGraphSegmentx1: y1: x2: y1:	Actually adds a line segment to the graph.

The **gotGraphData()** function gets called by Display PostScript whenever data is available on the file descriptor that connects to the Evaluator.

31. Insert the **gotGraphData()** function below to **GraphView.m**. Put it after the **#import** directives but before the **@implementation** directive.

```
/* gotGraphData: This function called by Display
 * PostScript when data is available to read on fd.
```

```
 * We assume that it will be a full line, and less
 * than 1024 characters (both good assumptions here).
 */
void gotGraphData(int fd, void *selfp)
{
  id self = selfp;
  char buf[16384];
  int len;

  if ((len = read(fd, buf, sizeof(buf))) == -1) {
    DPSRemoveFD(fd);       /* end of file */
    return;
  }
  buf[len] = '\000';
  [self addBufToGraph:buf];
}
```

This function takes the data and invokes the **addBufToGraph:** method (discussed below), which in turn adds the data to the **GraphView**'s internal buffer and then reads the data out line-by-line.

32. Insert the **addBufToGraph:** method below into **GraphView.m**.

```
- addBufToGraph:(const char *)buf
{
  char *cc;

  if (graphing==0) {
    return self;           /* not graphing */
  }

  /* The following lines take the data that we have
   * received in "buf" and concatenate it to the end
   * of our internal buffer.
   * We then extract the lines of the buffer
   * one-at-a-time and feed them to the method
   * graphLine:
   */

  strcat(graphBuf, buf);
  while (cc = index(graphBuf, '\n')) {
    *cc = '\0';              /* terminate the line */
                            /* now graph what we have */
    [self graphLine: graphBuf];
    memmove(graphBuf,
            cc+1,
            sizeof(graphBuf) - (cc-graphBuf));
  }
```

```
        return self;
    }
```

The reason for the line-by-line buffering is that the Evaluator might send more than one line of data to the **GraphView** object before it is scheduled to read the data. (This is because the data is being generated by a different execution thread.) It might also send an incomplete line, due to blocking on the pipe. The **GraphView** object therefore needs to buffer the data that it receives and then read it out a line at a time. The **addBufToGraph:** method does that buffering, and invokes the **graphLine:** method for each line.

It's important to note that the **addBufToGraph:** method ignores the data that it is sent if the **graphing** instance variable is **0**. This means that once the user clicks on the **Stop** button, all of the rest of the data in the pipeline will be ignored. This gives the application a nice snappy feeling.

The next two methods perform the actual graphing. The first is **graph-Line:**, which constructs the graph's line segments from successive **(x,y)** pairs.

33. Insert the **graphLine:** method implementation below into **GraphView.m**.

```objc
- graphLine:(const char *)buf
{
    double x, y;
    int num;

    num = sscanf(buf, "%lf , %lf", &x, &y);
    if (num!=2) {
        if (x==999.0) { /* end of graph data */
            [self stopGraph:nil];
        }
        return self; /* perhaps an invalid segment */
    }

    if (!first) {
        id seg = [self addGraphSegmentx1:lastx y1:lasty
                                    x2:x y2:y ];

        /* draw just this segment */
        [self    lockFocus];
        [seg     drawPSInView:self];
        [self    unlockFocus];
        [window flushWindow];
        NXPing();
    }
```

```
            lastx = x;
            lasty = y;
            first = NO;
            return self;
    }
```

The **graphLine:** method uses the **sscanf()** function to turn the line of text from the Evaluator back into binary numbers. If **num!=2**, then there were not two numbers separated by a comma to read; the method checks for the 999 termination code, which means that the graph is finished. If the termination code was sent, the **graphLine:** method invokes the **stopGraph:** method and the graph stops.

If this data pair is the first data pair, the execution drops down to the last four lines. These lines set the instance variables **lastx** and **lasty** to be the coordinates of the current point, then unsets the **first** variable and returns.

On all other data pairs other than the first, the middle section of this method gets executed. This conditional code first creates a **Segment** object (described below) with endpoints at **(lastx,lasty)** and **(x,y)**. The **Graph-View** then locks focus and sends the **drawPSInView:** message to the **Segment** object, which causes it to draw itself. The **NXPing()** function synchronizes the action. Finally, the segment gets added to the display list.

The last "graph-constructing" method adds the graph segment to the display list.

34. Insert the **addGraphSegmentx1:y1:x2:y2:** method below into **GraphView.m**.

```
- addGraphSegmentx1:(float)x1 y1:(float)y1
        x2:(float)x2 y2:(float)y2
{
    id seg = [ [Segment alloc]
             initx1:x1 y1:y1 x2:x2 y2:y2 ];
    [seg setTag:GRAPH_TAG];
    [displayList addObject:seg];
    return seg;
}
```

This method also sets the tag of the segment to **GRAPH_TAG**. We'll use the tags later on to distinguish between different objects stored inside the display list. Note that this method returns the **id** of the newly-created **Segment** object rather than **self**. Although the **addGraphSegmentx1:-y1:x2:y2:** method might seem a little trivial right now, this design makes it easier to change **GraphView**'s behavior by subclassing.

The drawSelf:: Method

Although the **graphLine:** method draws the graph, our **GraphView** still needs a **drawSelf::** method. The **drawSelf::** method will redraw the graph whenever the user wants to print the graph. The **drawSelf::** method also will be used to generate PostScript when we implement resizing of the graph, and when we put a scroller and a magnifying tile on the graph.

35. Insert the **drawSelf::** method below into **GraphView.m**.

```
- drawSelf:(const NXRect *)rects :(int)rectCount
{
   int i;

   for ( i=(rectCount==1 ? 0 : 1); i<rectCount; i++) {
      int j;

      /* set the background */
      PSsetgray(NX_WHITE);
      PSrectfill(NX_X(&rects[i]), NX_Y(&rects[i]),
          NX_WIDTH(&rects[i]), NX_HEIGHT(&rects[i]));

      if (displayList) {
         for (j=0; j < [displayList count]; j++) {
            id obj = [displayList objectAt: j];
            NXRect oBounds = [obj bounds];

            if (NXIntersectsRect(&rects[i],
                                 &oBounds)) {
               [obj drawPSInView:self];
            }
         }
      }
   }
   return self;
}
```

As you can see, for the first time we are using the **drawSelf::** parameters. We're finally going to find out what they mean!

The **drawSelf::** method that we constructed for the PolygonViewDemo in the previous chapter drew the entire polygon every time the method was called. This was okay because drawing the polygon involved very few PostScript operations. But when drawing complex images, it's wasteful to redraw the entire image – especially if you only need to redraw a tiny sliver of the image that's been exposed because the user has moved the slider a smidgen. That's what **drawSelf::**'s arguments are for – they tell your **drawSelf::** method which part of the screen to redraw.

The **(const NXRect *)rects** argument is an array of rectangles. In all cases, you can simply redraw the part of your image that intersects with the rectangle **rects[0]**. If the **rectCount** argument is **3**, however, you can slightly improve performance by redrawing only the parts of your image that intersect with the rectangles **rects[1]** and **rects[2]**. This is primarily an optimization for diagonal scrolling, when two rectangles get exposed that aren't adjacent. It is never necessary to redraw the parts of your image that intersect with the rectangles **rects[0]**, **rects[1]**, and **rects[2]**, since the rectangle at **rects[0]** overlaps the rectangles at **rects[1]** and **rects[2]** if they are present. To summarize:

If rectsCount is	Redraw the part of your image that intersects with
1	rects[0]
3	rects[0], or
	rects[1] and rects[2]

The NeXTSTEP function **NXIntersectsRects()** is a handy way for determining if two rectangles intersect. It's one of the many NeXTSTEP rectangle functions. Other functions will tell you if one rectangle contains another rectangle or a specified point, or if two rectangles are the same. The function **NXUnionRect()** will compute a rectangle large enough to contain two other rectangles, while **NXIntersectionRect()** will compute the region of overlap. You can find the definition for these functions as well as others using HeaderViewer or Librarian.

The **for** loop in our **drawSelf::** method above optimizes redrawing depending on whether **rectCount** is **1** or **3**. The method first sets the background of the region being redrawn to white. It then checks every element in the display list to see if that element intersects with the region that is being redrawn. If that element does, it sends the element the **drawPSInView:** message. (Now it's clear why it is also important for picture elements to respond to the **bounds** message – so **drawSelf::** can figure out the boundary of the element.)

That's it for the **drawSelf::** method. This simple method will not only handle printing and faxing, but it's optimized to redraw the absolute minimum amount of the graph that's ever required.

The clear and awakeFromNib Methods

The last two methods in our **GraphView** class definition are **clear** and **awakeFromNib**. The **clear** method gets called before the graph starts. If there was an old display list, it sends the **free** message to every element, then empties the **displayList** object itself. Otherwise, it makes a new one. It then sends the **display** method to the **GraphView** itself, which causes the **GraphView** to redraw itself empty.

36. Insert the **clear** method below into **GraphView.m**.

```
- clear
{
  /* clear the display list */
  if (displayList) {
    [ [displayList
        makeObjectsPerform:@selector(free)] empty];
  }
  else {
    displayList = [ [List alloc] init];
  }

  [self display];

  return self;
}
```

The **awakeFromNib** method starts up the Evaluator back end by creating a **Process** object. NeXTSTEP automatically sends the **awakeFromNib** message to each object loaded from a nib, after all of the objects have been created and all of the outlets have been initialized. It's not necessary to make the receiving object (e.g., **GraphView**) a delegate of any object in order for the **awakeFromNib** message to be sent.

37. Insert the **awakeFromNib** method implementation below into **GraphView.m**.

```
- awakeFromNib
{
  char *argv[2] = {0,0};
  char path[MAXPATHLEN];

  if(![[NXBundle mainBundle]
    getPath: path forResource: "Evaluator"
    ofType: ""]){
    NXRunAlertPanel(0,"Can't find Evaluator",0,0,0);
    [NXApp terminate:self];
    return nil;
  }
```

```
    argv[0] = path;

    graphProc = [ [Process alloc]
                    initFromCommand: argv];

    if (!graphProc) {
      NXRunAlertPanel(0,
                        "Cannot create calculator: %s",
                        0, 0, 0, strerror(errno));
      [NXApp terminate: self];
      return nil;
    }

    toFd = [graphProc toFd];
    [graphProc dpsWatchFD: gotGraphData
            data: self
            priority: NX_RUNMODALTHRESHOLD];

    return self;
}
```

This **awakeFromNib** method is similar to the **setUp** method in the **Paper-Control** class that we developed for the MathPaper application. The method creates a **Process** object, sets the **toFd** instance variable to be the file descriptor of the *send* pipe, installs the **gotGraphData()** function as the one to call when data is available, and returns. If the process can't be created, the method displays an Alert panel and then sends the **terminate:** message to **NXApp**, the **Application** object.[1]

One difference between this **awakeFromNib** method and the **setUp** method is that we now store the Evaluator program in the application's **.app** (or **.debug**) directory and retrieve its file name through the use of the **NXBundle** class.

38. View your project's "other" resource files by clicking the **Files** button at the top of PB's main window and then the **Other Resources** file type in PB's browser. See Figure 4 below.

---

1. Note: the **awakeFromNib** method was introduced in NeXTSTEP 3.0. If you're using NeXTSTEP 2.1, change the name of the **awakeFromNib** method to **setUp**, make **GraphView NXApp**'s delegate, and use the **appDidInit:** delegate method to invoke **setUp** when your program starts up.

FIGURE 4. Adding An "Other Resource" to GraphPaper

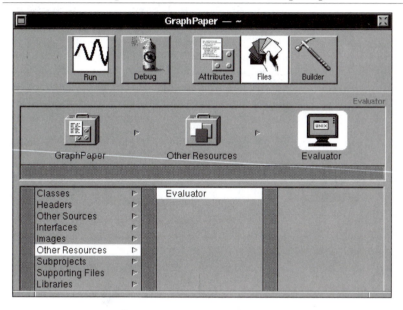

39. Add the **Evaluator** file to the project by dragging its icon from your File Viewer into PB's Files view. PB will automatically copy the file into the project directory. Figure 4 shows that **Evaluator** has been added to the MathPaper project.

When you **make** (build) your project, the **Evaluator** file will automatically be copied into the **.app** or **.debug** directory.

The Segment Class

Although a **GraphView** object constructs graphs, it relies upon a **Segment** object to actually draw the lines that make up the graph. The **GraphView** object invokes two **Segment** instance methods:

bounds Returns a rectangle bounding the **Segment**'s line.

drawPSInView: Causes the **Segment** object to draw its line.

By using a separate class which interacts with the **GraphView** class according to a well-defined protocol, we open up the possibility of adding additional objects to the graph with very little work. To make the **Segment** class even more general, it supports a **tag** internal variable, which we'll use later.

The **bounds** method returns an **NXRect** structure directly on the stack, rather than returning a pointer to the structure. We do this so that these objects will work in a multi-threaded application (although this feature is not necessary for *this* multi-threaded application, because we look at the value returned by the **bounds** message in our main thread). This method is similar to a NeXTSTEP color function returning an **NXColor** structure. Although returning large C structures on the stack can degrade performance, the penalty for small structures is relatively small, and it makes your programs easier to develop and compile.

40. Create a file called **Segment.h** containing the **Segment** class interface code below.

```
#import <appkit/appkit.h>

@interface Segment:Object
{
    NXPoint    start;
    NXPoint    end;
    float      gray;
    int        tag;
}

- initx1:(float)x1 y1:(float)y1
      x2:(float)x2 y2:(float)y2;
- setGray:(float)aGray;
- (float)x;
- (float)y;
- drawPSInView:aView;
- (NXRect)bounds;
- (int)tag;
- setTag:(int)aTag;

@end
```

41. Create a file called **Segment.m** containing the **Segment** class implementation code below.

```
#import "Segment.h"

@implementation Segment

- initx1:(float)x1 y1:(float)y1
      x2:(float)x2 y2:(float)y2
{
    [super init];    /* must init the Object class! */

    start.x = x1;
    start.y = y1;
```

```
    end.x    = x2;
    end.y    = y2;
    [self setGray: NX_BLACK];
    return self;
}


- setGray:(float)aGray
{
    gray = aGray;
    return self;
}


- (float)x
{
    return (start.x + end.x)/2.0;
}


- (float)y
{
    return (start.y + end.y)/2.0;
}


- drawPSInView:aView
{
    NXSize  sz = {1.0, 1.0}; /* a default size */

    PSsetgray(gray);
    PSmoveto(start.x, start.y);
    PSlineto(end.x, end.y);

    [aView convertSize: &sz fromView: nil];

    /* Rescale the coordinate system for stroking, so
     * that the line we draw is exactly one point wide
     * in the screen coordinate system.
     */
    PSscale(sz.width,sz.height);
    PSsetlinewidth(1.0);
    PSstroke();

    /* Restore the old scale. We could have done this
     * with a gsave/grestore, but this is much more
     * efficient.
     */
```

```
        PSscale(1/sz.width, 1/sz.height);
        return self;
}


- (NXRect)bounds
{
    NXRect bounds;

    NX_X(&bounds)       = MIN(start.x,end.x) ;
    NX_Y(&bounds)       = MIN(start.y,end.y) ;
    NX_WIDTH(&bounds)   = fabs(start.x-end.x)+MINFLOAT;
    NX_HEIGHT(&bounds)  = fabs(start.y-end.y)+MINFLOAT;

    return bounds;
}


- (int)tag
{
    return tag;
}

- setTag:(int)aTag
{
    tag = aTag;
    return self;
}

@end
```

The **Segment** class implementation is fairly straightforward. Notice that there is no **bounds** instance variable; instead, we calculate each segment's bounding box on demand from other instance variables and return what was calculated. This is known as *data hiding* – an object's internal representation of data does not have to be the same representation that is used by its accessor methods.

Notice our use of MINFLOAT in the **bounds** method. This is used so that lines that are vertical and horizontal will still have a width or height that is non-zero. MINFLOAT is the smallest floating point number that the IEEE floating point package can represent. By adding MINFLOAT to the calculated width and height, we guarantee that these values will not be zero. If they are computed to be a number that is larger than MINFLOAT – for example, the number 5 – adding MINFLOAT will have no significant effect.

The Process Class

As mentioned before, we will use the same **Process** class that we created for the MathPaper implementation to start up a copy of the Evaluator.

42. Back in PB, add the **Process** class to the GraphPaper project (otherwise the **Makefile** won't instruct **make** to compile this class). The easiest way to do this is to select the Files view in PB and drag the **Process.m** file icon from your File Viewer and drop it into PB's main window. You can also use PB's **Files→Add** menu command.

PB will add *both* the **Process.m** and **Process.h** class files to the project and copy the files into the GraphPaper project directory.

43. Add the **Segment** class to the GraphPaper project in a similar fashion.

Testing GraphPaper

Now that we've got the interface built, the connections made, and all the classes implemented, we're finally ready to **make** and test GraphPaper.

44. Save all pertinent files and then **make** (build) the GraphPaper project.

45. Drag the GraphPaper file application icon from your File Viewer into your dock and double-click it to launch GraphPaper.

46. Click the **Graph** button and you'll get a graph as in Figure 5 below.

47. Click the **Graph** button again and then quickly interrupt the graphing process by clicking the **Stop** button (the same button with a different label while the graph is being drawn). See Figure 6 below.

48. Try graphing another function such as **cos(x)/x** with a different step and ranges. See Figure 7 below.

49. Quit GraphPaper.

In Chapter 18 we'll clean up the GraphPaper application a little, make it respond to resizing properly, and then we'll make the graph report the **(x,y)** coordinates of each point as you move the mouse over the graph. We'll finish off this chapter by showing how to add different objects to GraphPaper's display list.

FIGURE 5. GraphPaper at Runtime

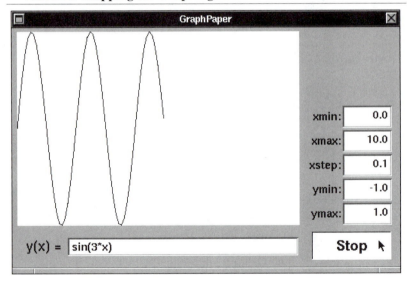

FIGURE 6. Stopping the Graphing Process

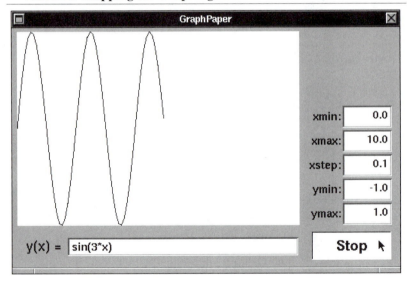

FIGURE 7. **Graphing a Different Function**

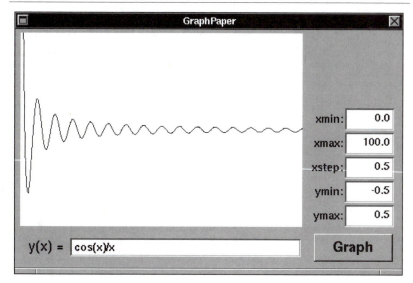

Extending the Display List

GraphView's display list and **drawSelf::** methods can be easily extended to draw other objects in the on-screen **GraphView**. In this section, we'll add axes and labels to the graph.

Adding Axes

Adding X and Y axes to **GraphView** is quite simple, since we already have the **Segment** class to draw the line. All we need to draw the axes is to create a new method that draws the axes and then arrange for it to be called by **GraphView**'s **graphLine:** method.

1. Insert the **addAxesx1:y1:x2:y2:** method declaration below into **GraphView.h**.

```
- addAxesx1:(float)x1 y1:(float)y1
    x2:(float)x2 y2:(float)y2;
```

2. Insert the **addAxesx1:y1:x2:y2:** method implementation below into **GraphView.m**.

```
- addAxesx1:(float)x1 y1:(float)y1
        x2:(float)x2 y2:(float)y2
{
    id axes = [ [Segment alloc]
```

```
                    initx1: x1    y1: y1
                        x2: x2    y2: y2 ];
    [axes setTag:AXES_TAG];
    [axes setGray:NX_DKGRAY];
    [displayList addObject:axes];
    return axes;
}
```

3. Insert the six lines in **bold** below into the **graphLine:** method into **GraphView.m**.

```
- graphLine:(const char *)buf;
...
        return self;     /* perhaps an invalid segment */
    }

    if (first) {
        /* put in graph axes */
        [self addAxesx1:xmin y1:0.0 x2:xmax y2:0.0 ];
        [self addAxesx1:0.0 y1:ymin x2:0.0 y2:ymax ];
        [self display];
    }
    if (!first) {
...
    }
```

4. Save the **GraphView** class files and then **make** and run GraphPaper.

5. To see both the axes in GraphPaper, enter the values as in Figure 8.

When the first data point comes through, the new **if** statement in the **graph-Line:** method above creates two **Segment** objects which correspond to the **X** and **Y** axes. The "color" of these segments is set to dark gray and the tags are set to 1. The axis lines are added to the display list and then the graph is displayed. The window in Figure 8 below shows what the graph looks like with axes. We set the tag to **AXES_TAG** so that we can distinguish these segments from the segments used to draw the graph itself. This distinction will be important in Chapter 18, when we want to make the graph segments sensitive to mouse clicks without making the axes sensitive.

Adding Labeling

In addition to axes, we can add a function label fairly easily by creating a **Label** class that responds to the same **bounds** and **drawPSInView:** methods as the **Segment** class. Since Objective-C uses dynamic binding – where messages are resolved when they are sent, rather than when the program is compiled – we won't need to make any changes to **GraphView**'s **drawSelf::** method. **Label** objects will be stored in the display list, along

FIGURE 8. GraphPaper Window with Axes

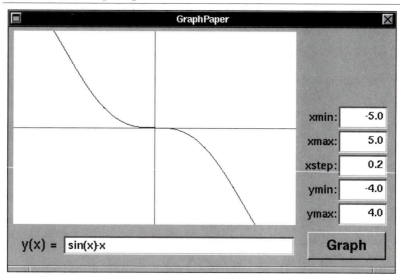

with the **Segment** objects. (The **Label** object must have its own initialization methods, however, because line segments and text labels need to be set up in different ways.)

1. Create a file called **Label.h** containing the **Label** class interface code below.

```
#import <appkit/appkit.h>

@interface Label:Object
{
    NXRect    bounds;
    char      *text;
    float     gray;
    int       tag;
    id        font;
}

- initx:(float)x y:(float)y text:(const char *)aText
                    size:(float)aSize forView:aView;
- free;
- setGray:(float)aGray;
- (NXRect)bounds;
- (int)tag;
- setTag:(int)aTag;
- drawPSInView:aView;
@end
```

Notice that this interface is remarkably similar to the interface used by **Segment**. The main difference is that the two objects use different initialization methods, which of course they must. The **Label** class implementation itself is a bit more complicated than the **Segment** class. It starts out with the **initx:y:text:size:forView:** method which we show in the next step.

2. Create a file called **Label.m** containing the (incomplete) **Label** class implementation code below.

```
#import "Label.h"

@implementation Label

- initx:(float)x y:(float)y text:(const char *)aText
                    size:(float)aSize forView:aView
{
  NXSize fontScale;
  float matrix[6];

  [super init];

  fontScale.width = 1.0;
  fontScale.height = 1.0;

  [aView convertSize:&fontScale fromView:nil];

  /* construct transform matrix */
  memset(matrix, 0, sizeof(matrix));
  matrix[0] = fontScale.width;
  matrix[3] = fontScale.height;

  font = [Font newFont:"Times-Roman"
              size:aSize matrix:matrix];

  text = NXCopyStringBufferFromZone(aText,
                            [self zone]);

  [self setGray:NX_BLACK];

  NX_WIDTH(&bounds)  = [font getWidthOf:text];
  NX_HEIGHT(&bounds) = [font pointSize];
  NX_X(&bounds)      = x - (NX_WIDTH(&bounds)/2.0);
  NX_Y(&bounds)      = y;

  return self;
}
```

This **initx:y:text:size:forView:** method is a little complicated because we are using the **View**'s scaling to scale the graph. If we just tried to draw a regular 12-point text in this **View**, it would get squashed or stretched out of shape in accordance with the **View**'s current scaling. To get around this problem, it is necessary to calculate a special transformation matrix for this font which will transform its scaling from the **View**'s coordinate system to the screen's coordinate system. This matrix is calculated by translating a 1-by-1 size with the **View**'s **convertSize:fromView:** method and then calculating a matrix with the converted size.

After the matrix is calculated, it is used to create a new font. The **Label** object then makes its own private copy of the label that it displays. We use the **NXCopyStringBufferFromZone()** method so that this string is allocated in the same memory zone as the object itself. Objects frequently run faster when all of their data is located in the same region of memory, because the computer's virtual memory system does not need to page as much in order to access the data referenced by the object.

Finally, the method calculates a bounding box for this piece of text and stores it in the **bounds** instance variable.

Since **Label** creates local storage (its private copy of the label string pointed to by **text**), this storage should be released when the object is freed. This is done by the **free** method below.

3.   Insert the **free** method below into **Label.m**.

```
- free
{
  if (text){
    NXZoneFree([self zone], text);
    text = 0;
  }
  return [super free];
}
```

The **bounds**, **setGray:**, **tag** and **setTag:** methods below simply provide access to instance variables from outside the class.

4.   Insert the four methods below into **Label.m**.

```
- setGray:(float)aGray
{
  gray = aGray;
  return self;
}
```

```
- (NXRect)bounds
{
  return bounds;
}

- (int)tag
{
  return tag;
}

- setTag:(int)aTag
{
  tag = aTag;
  return self;
}
```

Lastly, the **Label** class implements a **drawPSInView:** method to generate the PostScript necessary to display the label. Note that **Label**'s **drawPSIn-View:** method does not use the **aView** argument; this is because we have already taken care of scaling in choosing the font's matrix.

5. Insert the **drawPSInView:** method and **@end** directive below into **Label.m**.

```
/* If we are printing, we'll invoke [font set]
 * to set the font. Although we only need to do
 * this once per drawSelf::, we do it every time.
 */

- drawPSInView:aView
{
  [font set];
  PSsetgray(gray);
  PSmoveto(NX_X(&bounds), NX_Y(&bounds));
  PSshow(text);
  return self;
}
@end
```

Notice that this **drawPSInView:** method sends the **[font set]** message every time it is invoked. This is necessary to support printing. If the **GraphView** that contains this label is printed, the font used needs to be rasterized at a different resolution. A PostScript error results unless the **[font set]** message is sent before PostScript code is generated for the printer. (A more efficient approach would be to implement a protocol by which objects in the display list could be told to invoke the **set** method whenever PostScript was to be generated for a new context.)

Using the Label Class

To use this new class, we'll need to make several changes to **Graph-View.m**. First we'll add a new method to the **GraphView** class and make another modification to the **graphLine:** method.

6. Insert the **addLabel:atx:y:size:** method declaration below into **GraphView.h**.

```
- addLabel:(const char *)aTitle
          atx:(float)x y:(float)y
          size:(float)size;
```

7. Insert the **addLabel:atx:y:size:** method implementation below into **GraphView.m**.

```
- addLabel:(const char *)aTitle
          atx:(float)x y:(float)y
          size:(float)size
{
  id label = [ [Label alloc] initx:x y:y text:aTitle
                              size:size forView:self];
  [label setTag:LABEL_TAG];
  [displayList addObject:label];
  return label;
}
```

8. Insert the lines in **bold** below into the **graphLine:** method in **GraphView.m**.

```
- graphLine:(const char *)buf;
...
  if (first) {
    /* put in graph axes */
    [self addAxesx1:xmin y1:0.0 x2:xmax y2:0.0 ];
    [self addAxesx1:0.0 y1:ymin x2:0.0 y2:ymax ];
    /* add the label */
    [self addLabel:formula
        atx:(xmin+xmax)/2.0 y:(ymin*10.0+ymax)/11.0
        size:24.0];
    [self display];
  }

  if (!first) {
...
}
```

9. Insert the new **#import** directive in below into **GraphView.m**.

```
#import "Label.h"
```

10. Back in PB, add the **Label** class to the GraphPaper project.

11. Save all pertinent files and **make** and run GraphPaper.

12. Enter a function and ranges and click the **Graph** button to see the new label, as in Figure 1, "Main Window in GraphPaper Application," on page 407.

Summary

Wow, we've really done a lot in this chapter! In the first half of the chapter we got a taste of multi-threaded programming in Mach by creating an application with two execution threads – one which sends data to a back end program and another which reads the resultant values. In the second half, we learned how to draw a picture by building a display list of objects, each object knowing how to draw itself.

In the next chapter, we'll see how **GraphView**'s modular design makes it easy to add new functionality to the class. In particular, we'll see how to add color by subclassing the **GraphView** class and overriding some of its methods.

17

Color

If you are running NeXTSTEP on a color display, you may be feeling a little left out, since all of the examples so far have been in black-and-white. Fortunately, NeXTSTEP's Display PostScript makes drawing in color relatively easy.

Colors and Color Objects

NeXTSTEP colors have two components: color and alpha. *Color* is the way that the color looks when it is displayed on an empty background.[1] *Alpha* is a measure of the color's *transparency* – it tells Display PostScript

---

1. On a black-and-white system, empty windows have a white background. On a color system, they have a black background. This inconsistency was inadvertently introduced when NeXT introduced color and the alpha channel. The problem only occurs on windows that have *alpha* – that is, windows into which alpha has been painted. By default, windows do not have alpha, and they won't get alpha unless you put it there. NeXT recommends against drawing into a window with alpha. Not only does it create the white vs. black problem, but it also makes drawing and flushing such windows much slower. If you use alpha it is more efficient to do your drawing in an off-screen buffer.

how to blend a color with the colors already present in the background when the color is displayed. Alpha is measured on a scale from 0.0 to 1.0. An alpha of 0.0 is completely transparent; an alpha of 1.0 is opaque.

NeXTSTEP allows you to specify the color using several different models. Like most computer systems, you can specify values for the amount of red, green and blue (RGB) you want to mix in an *additive* color model, where the colors are added together like colored lights (mix them all and you get white). Alternatively, you can also specify a color by specifying a hue, saturation and brightness (HSB). You can also specify the amount of cyan, yellow, magenta, and black (CMYK) "inks" to mix at any point (called a *subtractive* color model since the colors are subtracted from white: mix them all and you get a muddy brown). CMYK colors are device-dependent.

NeXTSTEP 3.0 also allows the user to specify color by *PANTONE number*. PANTONE is a trademark system for specifying a color by industry-standard numbers. PANTONE colors are also device-dependent, however there are tables which specify the correct device-dependent value for different printers, allowing some degree of conversion.

On black-and-white NeXTSTEP displays, colors are automatically mapped to corresponding shades of gray by the Display PostScript system.

Colors From a Programmer's Point of View

Internally, NeXT represents color with the **NXColor**. You should *never* access the contents of the **NXColor** structure. Instead, NeXTSTEP provides a set of functions for creating **NXColor** structures and manipulating them.

The following eight functions all return an **NXColor** structure for the color specified by their arguments. Only the first four allow an alpha transparency factor.

```
NXColor NXConvertRGBAToColor(float red,
        float green, float blue, float alpha)

NXColor NXConvertCMYKAToColor(float cyan,
        float magenta, float yellow, float black,
        float alpha)

NXColor NXConvertHSBAToColor(float hue,
        float saturation, float brightness,
        float alpha)
```

NXColor **NXConvertGrayAlphaToColor**(float *gray*,
        float *alpha*)

NXColor **NXConvertRGBToColor**(float *red*, float *green*,
        float *blue*)

NXColor **NXConvertCMYKToColor**(float *cyan*,
        float *magenta*, float *yellow*, float *black*)

NXColor **NXConvertHSBToColor**(float *hue*,
        float *saturation*, float *brightness*)

NXColor **NXConvertGrayToColor**(float *gray*)

If you have a **NXColor**, you can determine its components with one these functions:

void **NXConvertColorToRGBA**(NXColor *color*,
        float **red*, float **green*, float **blue*,
        float **alpha*)

void **NXConvertColorToCMYKA**(NXColor *color*,
        float **cyan*, float **magenta*, float **yellow*,
        float **black*, float **alpha*)

void **NXConvertColorToHSBA**(NXColor *color*, float **hue*,
        float **saturation*, float **brightness*,
        float **alpha*)

void **NXConvertColorToGrayAlpha**(NXColor *color*,
        float **gray*, float **alpha*)

void **NXConvertColorToRGB**(NXColor *color*, float **red*,
        float **green*, float **blue*)

void **NXConvertColorToCMYK**(NXColor *color*,
        float **cyan*, float **magenta*, float **yellow*,
        float **black*)

void **NXConvertColorToHSB**(NXColor *color*, float **hue*,
        float **saturation*, float **brightness*)

void **NXConvertColorToGray**(NXColor *color*, float **gray*)

As a side effect, these functions give programmers an easy way to convert from one color model to another.

Colors From a User's Point of View

NeXTSTEP also gives users a variety of options for choosing colors through a standard interface called the *Colors panel*, an instance object of the **NXColorPanel** class. The Colors panel allows the user to specify a color (or gray) using any of the color models mentioned above. The panel also lets the user set the amount of alpha used by each color that he picks. Figure 1 below contains the black and white view, or *grayscale-alpha mode*, of the NeXTSTEP 3.0 Colors panel.

FIGURE 1. Colors panel in Grayscale-Alpha Mode

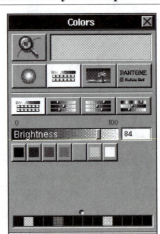

The buttons along the top of the panel change the way that the Colors panel displays colors. By selecting a color and then clicking a button at the top of the Colors panel, you can see how the color is represented in different color models. For example, in the Colors panel on the left of Figure 2 below we chose fully saturated "green" in RGB mode and then clicked a button to see the corresponding color in the CMYK mode in the Colors panel on the right of Figure 2. (Unfortunately, it's difficult to display a good "green" in a monochrome book – you'll have to play with the Colors panel on a computer which displays NeXTSTEP in color to see the real thing).

The space along the bottom of the Colors panel is a holding area for colors. You can drag a color from the color well at the panel's right into the holding area. You can also drag colors directly into application programs.

The Colors panel works closely with another NeXTSTEP class called the **NXColorWell** (the **NXColorWell** icon from Interface Builder's Views pal-

FIGURE 2. Same Color (green) in RGB and CMYK modes

ette can be seen at the left). If you press the mouse in a **NXColorWell** instance and drag it away, you'll take a little dab of color, called a *color chip*, with you (see Figure 3 below). Every **NXColorWell** has a color; you can change its color by dragging a color chip from a different **NXColor-Well** and dropping it inside. The gray rectangle at the upper right of the Colors panel is a color well whose color is linked to the current position of the Colors panel sliders.

FIGURE 3. Dragging a Color Chip From an NXColorWell

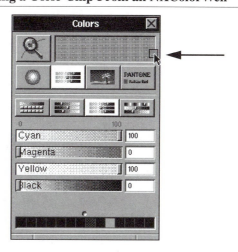

Programming with Colors

To add color to your application, you need to do two things:

- give the user a way for specifying a color; and
- modify your drawing methods so that Color PostScript code is produced.

The easiest way to let a user specify a color is by placing an **NXColorWell** object in your application. Clicking the *border* of an **NXColorWell** object brings up the Colors panel which is "linked" to the **NXColorWell**: when you change the color on the panel, the well's color gets changed automatically.

Both the **NXColorPanel** and **NXColorWell** objects support NeXTSTEP's target/action paradigm. Normally they send an action message to their target when their color is changed. But if you send the **NXColorWell** the **setContinous:TRUE** message, it will message its target each time you move a slider. This lets the user watch the drawing change color as he or she moves the Colors panel sliders. The receiver of the action message from the **NXColorWell** can find out which color was selected by sending the **NXColorWell** a **color** message, which returns the well's **NXColor** structure.

The **NXSetColor()** function is the color PostScript analog to the Display PostScript **PSsetgray()** single-operator function. To draw PostScript code in color, use the **NXSetColor()** function in your **drawSelf::** method to change the color currently being drawn in the Display PostScript context. The **NXSetColor()** function looks at its arguments and generates a PostScript **setgray** operator if the argument is a gray color.

Adding Color to GraphPaper

In the remainder of this chapter, we'll add color to the GraphPaper application. That is, we'll add a Preferences panel that will let the user choose the colors to draw the graph, the equation, and the axes.

To isolate the parts of the **GraphView** that deal solely with color, we'll create a **GraphView** subclass called **ColorGraphView**. This way, we won't need to make any changes to the **GraphView** class itself, yet we can use all its functionality. This is called *reusability* of classes. Unfortunately, we will need to make some minor changes to the **Segment** and **Label** classes so that we can change their colors and have them draw using color PostScript commands.

The user probably won't want to change the graph's colors every time the GraphPaper application is run, so we'll put the Preferences panel in its own nib file rather than in **GraphPaper.nib**. That way the Preferences panel will be loaded and take up memory only when the user chooses to see it. The **ColorGraphView** class will have three **NXColor** instance variables to keep track of the colors currently being drawn. We'll set up a new class called **PrefController** to take care of modifying these instance variables when the Preferences panel is displayed. If the Preferences panel isn't loaded, the **ColorGraphView** class will make up some reasonable defaults for the color instance variables. In Chapter 21, we'll see how to set the value for these colors from the NeXTSTEP "defaults" database the, application defaults information stored in every NeXTSTEP user's **~/.NeXT** directory.

Creating a Preferences Panel

A Preferences panel is a panel that an application provides to let users change preferences and configuration options. A Preferences panel gives the user an easy way to read the contents of the defaults database for their particular application and make modifications, without having to resort to the UNIX command line. Every configuration or installation option that your program has should be set-able through the Preferences panel.

Preference panels can be simple or complex; usually, there is little correlation between the complexity of a program's Preferences panel and the complexity of the program itself. You should endeavor to keep the options in your application's Preferences panel under control. When in doubt, let ease-of-use be your guide.

In the upcoming sections we'll make a simple Preferences panel for setting the color of a graph in GraphPaper. This panel won't be a fully-functional Preferences panel, though, because it will be missing the **OK** and **Revert** buttons for saving the Preferences information into the defaults database. We'll add those in Chapter 21.

First we'll make a **Controller** class for our application which will act as a central coordinator of the activity of the **GraphView** object and the Preferences panel.

The Controller Class

Like most NeXTSTEP applications, the purpose of GraphPaper's **Controller** class will be to load nibs and provide a central means for finding the **id**s of important objects. It won't be a very complicated class, but it will be very important.

We'll set up the **Controller** object so that it is the **NXApp** delegate. This outlet will make it possible for any object in our application to get the **id** of the **GraphView** instance by evaluating the expression:

```
[ [NXApp delegate] graphView]
```

Putting accessor methods in classes when you design them is good programming practice. It's called *planning ahead*.

In order to have the Preferences panel in its own nib, we will also need to have the **Controller** class to load the nib on demand. This is similar to code we saw in previous chapters to load the Info Panel nib on demand.

1. Open your GraphPaper project in Project Builder and the **GraphPaper.nib** file in Interface Builder.

2. **Subclass** the **Object** class. Rename the new class **Controller**.

3. Add an outlet to the **Controller** class called **graphView**.

4. Add another outlet to the **Controller** class called **prefController**.

5. Add an action to the **Controller** class called **showPrefs:**.

6. **Unparse** the **Controller** class and insert the class files to the project.

7. **Instantiate** the **Controller** class in IB's File window. A new icon labeled **Controller** will show up in the Objects view.

8. Make the **Controller** the **File's Owner**'s delegate by Control-dragging from the **File's Owner** icon to the **Controller** icon and double-clicking **delegate** in the File's Owner Inspector.

9. Connect the **Controller**'s **graphView** outlet to the on-screen **GraphView** instance in GraphPaper's main window.

10. Insert the **graphView** method declaration in `bold` below into **Controller.h**.

```
#import <appkit/appkit.h>

@interface Controller:Object
{
    id graphView;
```

```
                    id prefController;
        }

        - graphView;
        - showPrefs:sender;
        @end
```

11. Insert the lines in **bold** below into **Controller.m**.

```
#import "Controller.h"
#import "GraphView.h"

@implementation Controller

- graphView
{
    return graphView;
}

- showPrefs:sender
{
    if (!prefController) {
        [NXApp loadNibSection: "preferences.nib"
                owner: self];
    }
    [ [prefController window]
        makeKeyAndOrderFront:sender];
    return self;
}

@end
```

Controller may seem like a gratuitous class: why not just make the **GraphView** instance the delegate of the **NXApp** object? The answer will become more clear as we add more features to the GraphPaper application: having a separate **Controller** object will make it easier to add new functionality.

The **prefController** outlet will be initialized to point to a **PrefController** object (which will control the Preferences panel) that we'll create in the next section. The **showPrefs:** action will be invoked in response to a user requesting the Preferences panel and will pass the request along to the **PrefController** object through the **prefController** outlet.

The *first* time the **showPrefs:** action method is invoked it loads the preferences nib. *Every* time the **showPrefs:** action method is invoked it asks the

prefController for the **id** of its window, and then exposes the window with the **makeKeyAndOrderFront:** message.

12. Back in IB, cut (Command-x) out GraphPaper's **Info** menu cell.

13. Drag an **Info→** submenu from IB's Menus palette and drop it just below the main menu title bar, as at the left.

14. Enable the **Info→Preferences** menu cell.

15. Connect the **Info→Preferences** menu cell to GraphPaper's **Controller** instance so that it sends the **showPrefs:** action message.

16. Save **GraphPaper.nib**.

Creating the Preferences Nib, Panel, and Controller

The Preferences panel will be loaded by a **PrefController** object in response to the user choosing the **Info→Preferences** menu command. In this section we'll set up the nib and create the **PrefController** class. These steps all refer to the file **preferences.nib**, *not* **GraphPaper.nib**.

17. Choose IB's **Document→New Module→New Empty** command to create a new module for the Preferences panel.

18. Save the new nib module in the **preferences.nib** file in GraphPaper's **English.lproj** directory and insert it into the GraphPaper project.

19. Parse the **Controller** class definition in **preferences.nib** by dragging the **Controller.h** icon from your File Viewer and dropping it in the **preferences.nib** File window.

20. Change the class of the **preferences.nib**'s **File's Owner** to **Controller** in the File's Owner Inspector.

21. **Subclass** the **Object** class. Rename the new class **PrefController**.

22. Add the four outlets and two actions below to **PrefController** in IB's Inspector.

```
outlets:          actions:
graphColorWell    okay:
axesColorWell     revert:
labelColorWell
window
```

Don't be concerned with the **revert:** and **okay:** actions now; we won't be using them until Chapter 21.

23. **Unparse** the **PrefController** class and insert its class files to the GraphPaper project.

24. **Instantiate** a **PrefController** instance.

25. Connect the **prefController** outlet in the **File's Owner (Controller)** object to the **PrefController** instance in the **preferences.nib** File window.

26. Set up a panel in **preferences.nib** that looks like the one in Figure 4 below. Drag a **Panel** icon from IB's Windows palette and drop it in the workspace. Then drag three **NXColorWell**s and three **Title** icons from IB's Views palette and drop them in the new panel. Use IB's Grid feature and **Format→Layout→Alignment** menu command to align these objects and IB's **Format→Layout→Group** to get the boundary (Box) labeled **Colors** in Figure 4.

FIGURE 4. GraphPaper's Preferences Panel in IB

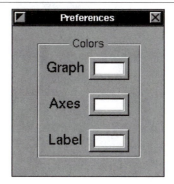

27. Connect each color well outlet in **PrefController** to the appropriate **NXColorWell** object in the Preferences panel.

28. Connect **PrefController**'s **window** outlet to the **Preferences** panel title bar.

29. Save **preferences.nib**.

PrefController Class Implementation

The **PrefController** class manages the Preferences panel. Below is the implementation of the **awakeFromNib** method and the method that it invokes (**setUpWell:defaultColor:tag:**) to set up each color well. In addition, the **window** accessor method is added so the **Controller** can get the **id** of the Preferences panel to send it the **makeKeyAndOrderFront:** message.

30. Insert the three method declarations in **bold** below into **PrefController.h**

```
#import <appkit/appkit.h>

@interface PrefController:Object
{
    id axesColorWell;
    id graphColorWell;
    id labelColorWell;
    id window;
}

- okay:sender;
- revert:sender;
- window;
- setUpWell:well defaultColor:(NXColor)aColor
            tag:(int)aTag;
- awakeFromNib;

@end
```

31. Insert the two **#imports** below into **PrefController.m**.

```
#import "Controller.h"
#import "GraphView.h"
```

32. Insert the two method implementations below into **PrefController.m**.

```
- window
{
    return window;
}

- setUpWell:well defaultColor:(NXColor)aColor
            tag:(int)aTag
{
    [well setColor:aColor];
    [well setTag:aTag];
    [well setContinuous:YES];
    [well setTarget:[ [NXApp delegate] graphView] ];
    [well setAction:@selector(setObjectColor:) ];
    return self;
}
```

The **setUpWell:defaultColor:tag:** method gives the **NXColorWell** an initial color, the appropriate tag, and sets the **continuous** flag. In the next two lines it arranges for the **NXColorWell** to send the **setObjectColor:** action message (described later) directly to the **ColorGraphView** target object. It gets the **ColorGraphView id** (**graphView**) by sending the **graphView** accessor message to the **Controller** (**NXApp**'s delegate). This is a good way to overcome NeXTSTEP's lack of flexibility for sending messages between nibs (which can only be done graphically inside Interface Builder by using the **File's Owner**).

33. Insert the method implementation below into **PrefController.m**.

```
- awakeFromNib
{
  [ [NXColorPanel sharedInstance:YES]
                 setContinuous:YES];
  [self setUpWell:axesColorWell
        defaultColor:NX_COLORDKGRAY tag:AXES_TAG];
  [self setUpWell:labelColorWell
        defaultColor:NX_COLORBLACK tag:LABEL_TAG];
  [self setUpWell:graphColorWell
        defaultColor:NX_COLORBLACK tag:GRAPH_TAG];

  return self;
}
```

The Application Kit uses a single **NXColorPanel** object for each running application. The method **[NXColorPanel sharedInstance:YES]** returns the **id** of that shared instance; if the Colors panel hasn't been created yet, it gets created. If we had specified **sharedInstance:NO**, the **id** of the panel would have been returned only if the panel had been previously created.

PrefController's **awakeFromNib** method first creates a Colors panel, then sets the **continuous** flag in the shared Colors panel. It is necessary to set the **continuous** flags in both the color well and the Colors panel if you want a color well to automatically send a message to its target as the color on the Colors panel is changed. The **awakeFromNib** method also invokes the **setUpWell:defaultColor:tag:** method for each of the three color wells.

ColorGraphView

In this section we'll create the **ColorGraphView** class which knows how to draw a graph in color and how to change the colors of the objects in the display list.

Adding Color to GraphPaper

The **ColorGraphView** class will have two jobs: managing the drawing of the graph in color and changing the color of things in the display list when requested.

34. Back in IB, select GraphPaper's main window and turn on the "**Wants to be color**" switch in the Window Attributes Inspector.

35. **Subclass** the **GraphView** class (under **View**) in the **GraphPaper.nib** Classes view. Rename the new class **ColorGraphView**.

36. Change the class of the on-screen **GraphView** instance in GraphPaper's main window to **ColorGraphView** in the Inspector.

37. If necessary, connect the **Graph** button to the on-screen **ColorGraphView** instance. Make it send the **graph:** action.

38. Add the **setObjectColor:** action to the **ColorGraphView** class in the Inspector. (Since **GraphView** is **ColorGraphView**'s superclass, its outlets and actions show up in gray, uneditable text in the Inspector.)

39. **Unparse** the **ColorGraphView** class and insert the files in the project.

40. Insert the lines in **bold** below into **ColorGraphView.h**.

```
#import <appkit/appkit.h>

#import "GraphView.h"

@interface ColorGraphView:GraphView
{
   NXColor axesColor;
   NXColor graphColor;
   NXColor labelColor;
}
- setObjectColor:sender;
- addGraphSegmentx1:(float)x1 y1:(float)y1
      x2:(float)x2 y2:(float)y2;
- addAxesx1:(float)x1 y1:(float)y1
      x2:(float)x2 y2:(float)y2;
- addLabel:(const char *)title
      atx:(float)x y:(float)y
      size:(float)size;
- setObjectColor:(NXColor)theColor forTag:(int)aTag;
- awakeFromNib;

@end
```

The **axesColor**, **graphColor**, and **labelColor** instance variables will store the color in which those objects are currently being drawn. The color wells on the Preferences panel will send the **setObjectColor:** message to tell the **ColorGraphView** when the user wants to change the color of the axes, graph, or label.

Changes to the GraphView Class

There aren't any changes we need to make to the **GraphView** class itself. However, we're going to *override* its methods for drawing the axes, graph segments, and labels in the **ColorGraphView** subclass. These override methods will invoke the methods in the **GraphView** class (by sending messages to **super**) to draw the parts of the graph and will then change their color to be the color requested by the user.

The ColorGraphView Class Implementation

The **ColorGraphView** implementation isn't very complicated because most of the work of actually drawing the class is being done in the **Graph-View** class. The only thing that the **ColorGraphView** class has to manage is the color of the newly drawn objects on the graph, as well as changing the colors of existing objects when the user changes a color in one of the color wells in the Colors panel.

41. Insert the **#imports** in `bold` below to **ColorGraphView.m**.

```
#import "Segment.h"
#import "Label.h"
```

The key definitions that we need for color are contained in the **NXColor-Well.h** and **NXColorPanel.h** files. It's a good idea to briefly look at these files, as well as **color.h**, in the **/NextDeveloper/Headers/appkit** directory, to learn the basic structures, constants, and methods provided by NeXT-STEP for handling color.

The first three methods in the class implementation below override **Graph-View**'s methods for drawing parts of the graph. Each of these methods invokes the method with the same name in the **GraphView** class (**Color-GraphView**'s superclass), and then changes the color of the newly-created object to be the color specified by the appropriate **NXColorWell**. These methods work because their corresponding methods in the **GraphView** class all return the **id** of the object that's been created, rather than **self**.

42. Insert the three method implementations below into **ColorGraphView.m**.

```
- addGraphSegmentx1:(float)x1 y1:(float)y1
     x2:(float)x2 y2:(float)y2
{
    id newSeg = [super addGraphSegmentx1:x1 y1:y1
                       x2:x2 y2:y2];
    [newSeg setColor:graphColor];
    return newSeg;
```

```
  }

- addAxesx1:(float)x1 y1:(float)y1
      x2:(float)x2 y2:(float)y2
  {
    id newAxes = [super addAxesx1:x1 y1:y1
                          x2:x2 y2:y2 ];
    [newAxes setColor:axesColor];
    return newAxes;
  }

- addLabel:(const char *)title
      atx:(float)x y:(float)y
      size:(float)size
  {
    id newLabel = [super addLabel:title
                          atx:x y:y
                          size:size];
    [newLabel setColor:labelColor];
    return newLabel;
  }
```

As this example shows, part of a good class design means being able to easily change or enhance functionality by subclassing.[1]

These three methods are all that is necessary to have newly-drawn graphs displayed in the colors wanted by the user. But if you want to let the user change the colors on an existing graph, you'll need to add a few more methods.

Setting the Colors

When the user changes a color using an **NXColorWell** object, it will send the **setObjectColor:** action to the **ColorGraphView** object (the target and action were set up in **PrefController**'s **setUpWell:defaultColor:tag:** method above). The **setObjectColor:** method in **ColorGraphView** needs to change the value of the appropriate color instance variable as well as the elements in the display list. We'll use the **NXColorWell**'s **tag** instance

---

1. An earlier version of the **GraphView** class not shown in this book didn't have these three methods, but simply drew the graph segments, axes, and labels in the **graphLine:** method. It proved to be impossible to add color to that version of **GraphView** without making changes to the **GraphView** class itself (i.e., subclassing didn't work). The new version of **GraphView**, that we showed in the previous chapter, overcame those problems through better design.

variable to figure out which **NXColorWell** sent the message. (Recall that the **setUpWell:defaultColor:tag:** method in **PrefController** set the tag of each color well to a unique value.)

43. Insert the line in `bold` below into the **setObjectColor:** method in **ColorGraphView.m**.

```
-  setObjectColor:sender
{
   [self setObjectColor:[sender color]
                         forTag:[sender tag] ];
   return self;
}
```

This method gets the **color** and the **tag** from the **NXColorWell** that sends the message and then invokes the **setObjectColor:forTag:** method shown below.

44. Insert the **setObjectColor:forTag:** method implementation below into **ColorGraphView.m**.

```
-  setObjectColor:(NXColor)theColor forTag:(int)aTag
{
   int i;

   switch(aTag) {
      case AXES_TAG:     axesColor  = theColor; break;
      case GRAPH_TAG:    graphColor = theColor; break;
      case LABEL_TAG:    labelColor = theColor; break;
   }

   if (!displayList) return nil;

   [self lockFocus];
   for (i=0; i < [displayList count]; i++) {
      id obj = [displayList objectAt:i];

      if ([obj tag]==aTag) {
         [ [obj setColor:theColor] drawPSInView:self];
      }
   }
   [self unlockFocus];
   [window flushWindow];
   return self;
}
```

This method scans the display list for objects with a given tag and changes their color to the color requested. This method relies on the fact that each kind of object in the display list has a unique tag, and that those tags are the same as the tags of the corresponding **NXColorWell**s.

Setting the Initial Color

There's a problem with the code that we've written so far: if the user tries to make a graph *without* first invoking the Preferences panel, nothing will get drawn, because all of the **NXColor** instance variables for setting the graph, axes, and label colors will be zero. The logical way to set the initial values for these instance variables is by overriding the **GraphView**'s **awakeFromNib** method; for now, we'll just "hard-code" in values. In Chapter 21, we'll see how to set these values from the defaults database system.

45. *Override* **GraphView**'s **awakeFromNib** method by adding the **awakeFromNib** method implementation below to **ColorGraphView.m**.

```
- awakeFromNib
{
  [super awakeFromNib];
  axesColor  = NX_COLORDKGRAY;
  labelColor = NX_COLORBLACK;
  graphColor = NX_COLORBLACK;
  return self;
}
```

Changes to the Segment and Label Classes

Before the color GraphPaper application will work, it is necessary to modify the **Segment** and **Label** classes so that they can respond to the **set-Color:** method and draw themselves in color. Although we could accomplish these changes with subclassing, we'll add the color attributes directly to the **Segment** and **Label** classes because color is a useful attribute for line segments and text labels to have – the ability to handle color should really have been included from the beginning.

Note that we preserve the semantics of the **setGray:** method for both these classes – the method still exists, but now it creates a gray "color." This is an example of data encapsulation. Any Objective-C code that we wrote that used the **setGray:** method will still work, even though the internal representation of colors has changed, because we have preserved a backwards-compatible interface. Below we show the changes to the **Segment.h**, **Segment.m**, **Label.h**, and **Label.m** files.

46. *Replace* the instance variable declaration

```
float gray;
```

in **Segment.h** with

```
NXColor myColor;
```

47. Insert the new **setColor:** method declaration below into **Segment.h**.

```
- setColor:(NXColor)aColor;
```

48. Insert the **setColor:** method implementation below into **Segment.m**.

```
- setColor:(NXColor)aColor
{
    myColor = aColor;
    return self;
}
```

49. *Replace* the line

```
PSsetgray(gray);
```

in the **drawPSInView:** method implementation in **Segment.m** with

```
NXSetColor(myColor);
```

50. *Replace* the line

```
gray = aGray;
```

in the **setGray:** method implementation in **Segment.m** with

```
myColor = NXConvertGrayToColor(aGray);
```

51. *Replace* the instance variable declaration

```
float gray;
```

in **Label.h** with

```
NXColor myColor;
```

52. Insert the new **setColor:** method declaration below into **Label.h**.

```
- setColor:(NXColor)aColor;
```

53. Insert the **setColor:** method implementation below into **Label.m**.

```
- setColor:(NXColor)aColor
{
    myColor = aColor;
    return self;
}
```

54. *Replace* the line

```
PSsetgray(gray);
```

in the **drawPSInView:** method implementation in **Label.m** with

```
NXSetColor(myColor);
```

55. *Replace* the line

```
gray = aGray;
```

in the **setGray:** method implementation in **Label.m** with

```
myColor = NXConvertGrayToColor(aGray);
```

By now it's becoming clear that a better initial design decision would have been to make the **Label** and **Segment** subclasses of some abstract super-class that supported the **setGray:**, **setColor:**, and **bounds** methods. Frequently these sorts of design possibilities only become obvious when you are partway into a project. With Objective-C, it would be easy to make that sort of change (which is left as an exercise for the reader).

Testing GraphPaper's Color

56. Save all pertinent files and **make** and run GraphPaper.

57. Click the **Graph** button to make a graph appear with axes and label.

58. Choose **Info→Preferences** to make the Preferences panel appear.

59. Click the border of a color well to expose the Colors panel, which will be linked to the color well.

60. Try changing the color in the Colors panel, and you'll see the color of the graph change at the same time. In Figure 5 below we have just changed the color of the label from black to gray.

61. Quit GraphPaper.

Summary

In this chapter we learned that drawing in color with Display PostScript is nearly as easy as drawing in black-and-white. Then we saw how a well-designed class makes it easy to improve its functionality through subclassing. Finally, we showed another way to use the tag facility with the display list to change the color attribute for a set of objects.

In the next chapter we'll learn more about **View**s – specifically, we'll see how to put any view in a scroller and add a pop-up magnification control, and we'll show how to subclass the **ColorGraphView** to handle mouse tracking.

FIGURE 5. **GraphPaper Running with Colors**

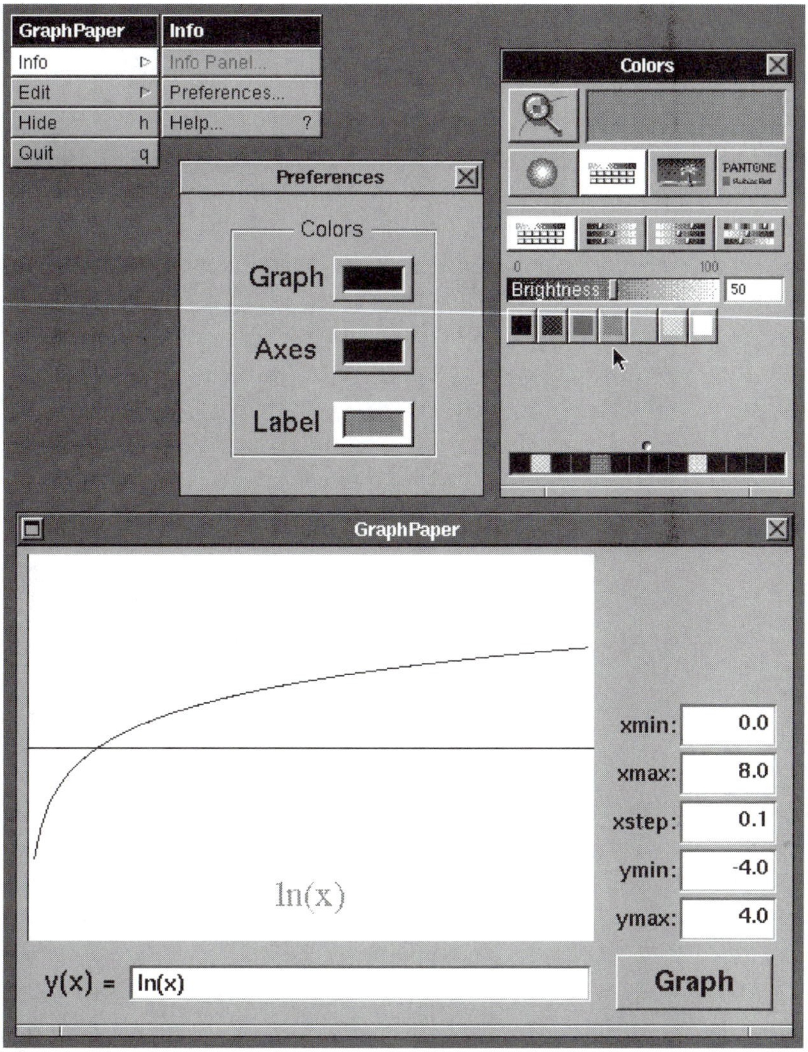

18

View Resizing and Mouse Tracking

The GraphPaper application we created in the previous chapter has two problems when its window is resized. The first problem occurs when we stretch the GraphPaper window. As seen in the window at the top of Figure 1, the white rectangular **GraphView** area doesn't resize – the margins around it just get bigger. The second problem occurs when we shrink the GraphPaper window. As seen in the window at the bottom of Figure 1, the GraphPaper window doesn't even contain the entire graph.

These two resizing problems have two different solutions which we'll show in the first part of this chapter. In the second part of this chapter we'll see how to make the **GraphView** more useful by reporting the **(x,y)** location of the cursor (mouse) as it moves over the graph and also by changing the cursor to a more appropriate image.

More About Resizing

In Chapter 15 we learned how to make a **View** object resize itself properly with Autosizing in the Size Inspector. By setting the Autosizing "springs" in the Inspector, we can make a **View** squeeze or stretch when its superview is resized. Let's try it with GraphPaper.

FIGURE 1. **Problems with Resizing the GraphPaper Window**

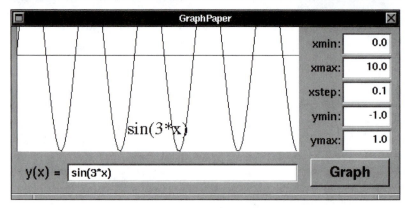

1. Open your GraphPaper project in Project Builder and the **GraphPaper.nib** file in Interface Builder.

2. Select the **ColorGraphView** instance, type Command-3 and set the Autosizing attributes as in the Inspector on the *left* of Figure 2 below.

3. Select the **Form** instance, type Command-3 and set the Autosizing attributes as in the Inspector on the *right* of Figure 2 below.

4. Save **GraphPaper.nib**, **make** and run GraphPaper.

FIGURE 2. **Autosizing "Springs" for CustomView and Form**

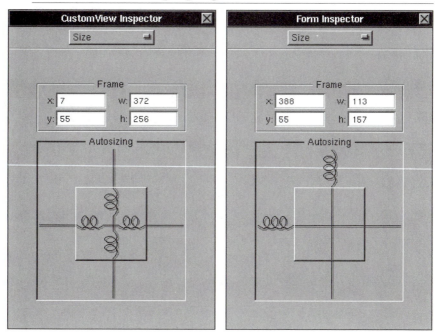

5. Click the **Graph** button and enlarge the **GraphPaper** window to get something that looks like the window in Figure 3 below.

But merely changing the size of the **GraphView** isn't enough. As you can see in Figure 3, stretching the window increases the size of the **View**, but the graph of the function is the same size. The problem is that the **Graph-View**'s coordinate system does not scale automatically when the **Graph-View** changes size. You've got to do that explicitly in your class definition.

In order to change the scale of the coordinate system, it's necessary for the **GraphView** object to be notified when its size has been changed. Fortunately, there is a **View** method that is automatically invoked to change the size of a **View**. That method is **sizeTo::**. The method's arguments are the **View**'s new width and height.

In order for the **GraphView** to change its scale automatically when it is resized, we have to override the **sizeTo::** method. Our method should first invoke the version of **sizeTo::** in the superclass, which performs the actual **View** resizing, and then scale itself. Below we present a method that does the trick.

FIGURE 3. GraphPaper with Autosizing

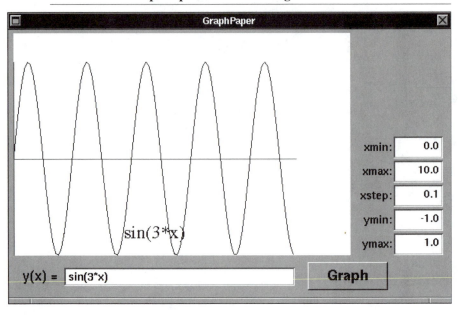

6. Insert the **sizeTo::** method declaration below into **GraphView.h**.

```
- sizeTo:(NXCoord)width :(NXCoord)height;
```

7. Insert the **sizeTo::** method implementation below into **GraphView.m**.

```
- sizeTo:(NXCoord)width :(NXCoord)height
{
    [super sizeTo:width :height];
    if (xmax!=xmin && ymax!=ymin) {
        [self setDrawSize:xmax-xmin :ymax-ymin];
        [self setDrawOrigin:xmin :ymin];
        [self display];
    }
    return self;
}
```

8. Save the **GraphView** class files, **make** and run GraphPaper.

9. Enter a function, click the **Graph** button, and drag the **GraphPaper** window's resize bar in several directions. The **View** should handle resize events properly as in Figure 4 below. (It can even handle resizing while the graph is being drawn!)

FIGURE 4. Resizing with sizeTo:: in GraphView

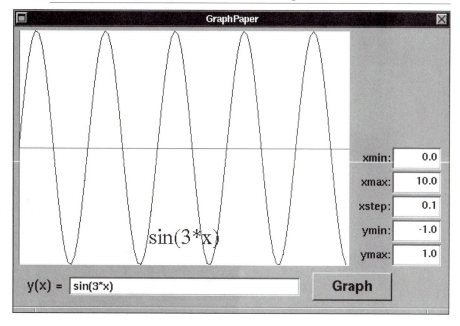

One thing that this implementation of **sizeTo::** doesn't do *properly* is resize the size text label (**sin(3*x)** in Figure 4) that is drawn inside the graph. Instead, the text simply gets scaled up with the change in resolution. This can make the text look funny. (However, the text will automatically scale itself if you click the **Graph** button after a resize because the transform matrix will be recalculated.) The problem is that we are using the **View**'s own coordinate system as the graph coordinate system – something that you probably wouldn't want to do if you were creating a commercial product.

Keeping Your Windows Big Enough

With Interface Builder 3.0, you can set the minimum size that each window may attain. The easiest way to do this is to make your window the minimum size you want in IB and then to click the **Current** button in IB's Window Inspector. (See Figure 5 below.) This will set the minimum window size to the window's current size. Go ahead and do this without our steps.

FIGURE 5. Setting a Minimum Window Size in IB

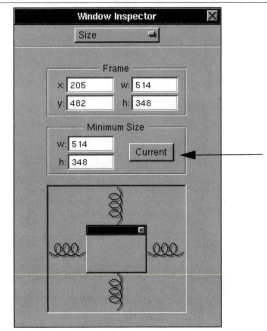

Tracking the Mouse

Some applications are downright active! Most applications just sit there and wait for you to click a mouse button or pound on a key, but some applications start doing things the moment you move the cursor over their little pieces of screen real estate.

For example, the *Adobe Illustrator* application displays a set of rulers on the side of the window and puts little gray lines in the rulers to indicate the exact **(x,y)** position of the cursor. Then there are games like Lighthouse Design's *VOID* which uses the cursor location in the window as a control stick for a starfighter. In the remainder of this chapter, we'll see how to grab the mouse location to report the **(x,y)** position of points on the Graph-Paper graph as the cursor is moved over them.

Tracking Rectangles

Until now, we've thought of NeXTSTEP events as being in two categories: mouse events and keyboard events. Another way of classifying events is according to the sort of programmatic gyrations you have to go through in order to receive them.

The simplest events to use are those that require no setup. You merely create a custom **View** and implement the event methods to receive them. Here are the *simple events*:

```
- mouseDown: (NXEvent *)theEvent
- rightMouseDown: (NXEvent *)theEvent
- mouseUp: (NXEvent *)theEvent
- rightMouseUp: (NXEvent *)theEvent
```

A second group of mouse events involve the responder chain. Usually, your **View** receives these events by making itself a First Responder. This can happen automatically if the user clicks the mouse in your **View** and your **View** responds **YES** to the message **acceptsFirstResponder:**. The responder chain events include the keyboard events as well as events that have to deal with simple mouse motion. Here are the *First Responder events*:

```
- keyDown: (NXEvent *)theEvent
- keyUp: (NXEvent *)theEvent
- flagsChanged: (NXEvent *)theEvent
- mouseMoved: (NXEvent *)theEvent
- mouseDragged: (NXEvent *)theEvent
- rightMouseDragged: (NXEvent *)theEvent
```

You might be surprised to see the **mouseMoved:** and **mouseDragged:** events in this list. They are included because it takes a fairly significant amount of time for the **Window** object to figure out which **View** should receive a mouse click and, normally, you want all of the **mouseMoved:** and **mouseDragged:** events going to the same place anyway. It's easier (and a lot more efficient) to simply tell the **Window** object where to send the events with the **makeFirstResponder:** message.

The last group of events have to do with *tracking rectangles*, rectangular regions within windows. You can arrange to have messages sent to an object whenever a tracking rectangle is *entered* or *exited* by the mouse. Here are the *tracking events*:

```
- mouseEntered: (NXEvent *)theEvent
- mouseExited: (NXEvent *)theEvent
```

You send the **setTrackingRect:inside:owner:tag:left:right:** method to a **Window**'s object to set up a tracking rectangle. Let's look at all of these arguments:

```
- setTrackingRect:(const NXRect *)aRect
          inside:(BOOL)insideFlag
          owner:anObject
```

tag:(int)*trackNum*
left:(BOOL)*leftDown*
right:(BOOL)*rightDown*

Argument	Meaning
aRect	This argument is a pointer to the tracking rectangle in the **Window**'s coordinate system. The tracking rectangle does not change if the **Window** is resized.
insideFlag	Set this flag to indicate whether you think the mouse cursor is initially inside or outside the tracking rectangle. If this flag is **NO**, then the **mouseEntered:** event will be sent the first time that the cursor moves into the tracking rectangle.
anObject	This is the object that should receive the **mouseEntered:** and **mouseExited:** messages. It's usually a **View** or an **NXCursor** object, but not always.
trackNum	You identify the tracking rectangle with this integer. You will use this integer again to destroy the tracking rectangle when you're done with it. Don't use a negative value, because NeXTSTEP uses those numbers to implement cursor rectangles.
leftDown	If this parameter is **TRUE**, the events will be sent only if the cursor crosses the tracking rectangle when the *left* mouse button is down.
rightDown	If this parameter is **TRUE**, the events will be sent only if the mouse crosses the tracking rectangle when the *right* mouse button is down.

There is no default tracking rectangle. If you don't set a tracking rectangle, you won't get **mouseEntered:** and **mouseExited:** events. Whatever you do, don't set both **leftDown** and **rightDown** to **TRUE** at the same time!

The Window Event Mask

Each window has an event mask that determines which events the Window Server will send it. The reason for this, once again, is efficiency: most applications simply don't need all of the events that are happening at any given time. For example, the Window Server is happy to send your application the **flagsChanged:** event whenever the user presses the keyboard's Shift or Control key, but most programs don't care about those keys unless the user is also pressing a letter or a number. The biggest efficiency killer is the **mouseMoved:** event, which causes the Window Server to send a message to your application every time the mouse is moved. If you set this flag, you'll get the events whether or not your application is the active application. This is the way that Lighthouse Design's *Eyecon* application works.

The *event mask* is a 32-bit number, with each bit corresponding to a different event. (This is the reason why NeXTSTEP only supports 32 different events.) A **1** in a bit position means that the event is sent to the window; a **0** in that bit position suppresses the sending of the event.

By default, there are only eight events that get sent to your application:

- **mouseDown:** (NXEvent *)*theEvent*
- **rightMouseDown:** (NXEvent *)*theEvent*
- **mouseUp:** (NXEvent *)*theEvent*
- **rightMouseUp:** (NXEvent *)*theEvent*
- **mouseEntered:** (NXEvent *)*theEvent*
- **mouseExited:** (NXEvent *)*theEvent*
- **keyDown:** (NXEvent *)*theEvent*
- **keyUp:** (NXEvent *)*theEvent*

To receive additional events, use the **Window** object's **addToEventMask:** method. For example, to get **mouseMoved:** events, you could send a **Window** the following message:

```
[aWindow addToEventMask:NX_MOUSEMOVEDMASK]
```

When you don't need these events anymore, you can send the message:

```
[aWindow removeFromEventMask:NX_MOUSEMOVEDMASK]
```

The mask also allows App Kit defined events, **Application** defined events, and system-defined events to be sent. You'll find a listing of all of the event masks in the file **/NextDeveloper/Headers/dpsclient/event.h**.

Adding Mouse Tracking to GraphPaper

With the above as an introduction, let's add mouse tracking to GraphPaper. The modifications will involve the four key parts below:

(i) Modification of the **awakeFromNib** method to set up the tracking rectangle around the on-screen **GraphView** instance.

(ii) A **mouseEntered:** method that will:

- Add the NX_MOUSEMOVEDMASK to the window's event mask, so the **Window** object starts getting **mouseMoved:** events.

- Make **GraphView** the **Window**'s First Responder, so **GraphView** will receive the **mouseMoved:** events.

(iii) A **mouseMoved:** method to process the **mouseMoved:** events.

(iv) A **mouseExited:** method that will reset the window's event mask.[1]

Rather than adding this new functionality to the **GraphView** or **ColorGraphView** classes, we'll subclass the **ColorGraphView** class to make a **TrackingGraphView**. Tracking functionality is separate from the graphing functionality and it makes sense to separate them in the code. Now let's get on with it!

Changes to the GraphPaper Interface

1. Back in IB, **Subclass** the **ColorGraphView** class. Rename the new class **TrackingGraphView**.

 2. Add outlets called **xCell** and **yCell** to the **TrackingGraphView** class.

3. Change the class of the **ColorGraphView** instance in the GraphPaper window to **TrackingGraphView** in the Class Attributes Inspector.

4. If necessary, connect the **Graph** button to the on-screen **TrackingGraphView** instance. Make it send the **graph:** action.

5. Add two **TextField** objects inside GraphPaper window and label them "**x:**" and "**y:**" as in Figure 6 below.

6. Using the Attributes Inspector, make the **TextField**s uneditable and their borders solid lines, as in Figure 6. Make the font larger as well.

7. Using the Size Inspector, set the "springs" for both **TextField**s in the same way that was done for the **Form** object (see Figure 2, "Autosizing "Springs" for CustomView and Form," on page 473).

8. Connect the **TrackingGraphView**'s **xCell** outlet to the **TextField** labeled **x:** and the **yCell** outlet to the one labeled **y:**.

9. **Unparse** the **TrackingGraphView** class and insert it into your project.

---

1. The **mouseEntered:**, **mouseMoved:** and **mouseExited:** events only pertain to mouse tracking. They do not change or effect the current first responder, although your **View** must be the first responder to get the **mouseMoved:** events.

FIGURE 6. New Text Fields and TrackingGraphView in IB

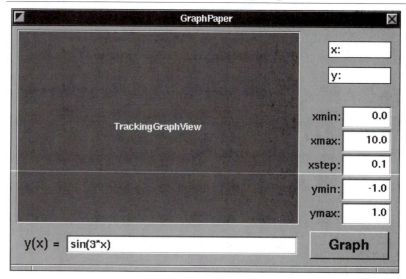

Changes to the TrackingGraphView Class Files

The **TrackingGraphView** class needs three new instance variables: **inside**, **highlightedSegment** and **trackingRect**. The **inside** variable will be used to keep track of whether the cursor is inside or outside the tracking rectangle. When processing **mouseMoved:** events, sometimes a few extra **mouseMoved:** events are sent after the mouse moves out of the tracking rectangle. (It takes a few moments before the Window Server stops sending those events.) The **inside** flag lets us ignore these events once we leave the rectangle.

The **highlightedSegment** variable will store the **id** of the highlighted **Segment** in the graph. We need to know the **id** of this segment so we can unhighlight it when the mouse moves. The **trackingRect** variable will be zero (**0**) if no tracking rectangle has been set; if a rectangle has been set, this variable will hold that tracking rectangle's number. We need to maintain this information because NeXTSTEP generates an error if you try to discard a tracking rectangle that does not exist.

10. Insert the ten lines in **bold** below into **TrackingGraphView.h**.

```
#import "ColorGraphView.h"

@interface TrackingGraphView:ColorGraphView
{
  id   xCell;
```

```
id    yCell;
BOOL  inside;
id    highlightedSegment;
int   trackingRect;
}
- setMyTrackingRect:(BOOL)flag;
- awakeFromNib;
- mouseEntered:(NXEvent *)theEvent;
- mouseExited:(NXEvent *)theEvent;
- sizeTo:(NXCoord)width :(NXCoord)height;
- unhighlightSegment;
- mouseMoved:(NXEvent *)theEvent;
@end
```

We'll set up seven methods in the **TrackingGraphView** class to make it
highlight any **Segment** of the graph over which the mouse cursor moves.
The first method, **setMyTrackingRect:**, establishes a tracking rectangle
around the **TrackingGraphView**. Although it is only meant to be used by
other methods in the class, we've included its definition in the class interface so that you can place the method anywhere in the file. (By making its
definition public, we also give other programmers a chance to build upon
the **TrackingGraphView** by subclassing the object.)

11. Insert the **#import** directive below into **TrackingGraphView.m**.

    ```
    #import "Segment.h"
    ```

12. Insert the **setMyTrackingRect:** method implementation below into
    TrackingGraphView.m.

    ```
    - setMyTrackingRect:(BOOL)flag
    {
      NXRect visible;

      /* Discard old tracking rect if present */
      if (trackingRect) {
        [window discardTrackingRect:trackingRect];
        trackingRect = 0;
      }

      if (flag){
        /* Set new tracking rect if requested
         * and if visible.
         */
        if ([self getVisibleRect:&visible]) {
          [self convertRect:&visible toView:nil];
          [window setTrackingRect:&visible
              inside:NO owner:self
              tag:1 left:NO right:NO];
    ```

```
            trackingRect = 1;
        }
    }
    return self;
}
```

The first part of the **setMyTrackingRect:** method discards any tracking rectangle, if one has been previously created, then creates a new one and assigns its number to the instance variable **trackingRect**. The second part of the method gets the visible rectangle – the portion of the **View** that is visible on the screen – and converts it to **Window** coordinates. This is necessary because the tracking rectangle is handled by the Display PostScript Window Server, which only knows about windows, not views. (The **convertRect:toView:** method with a **nil** second argument converts this rectangle's specifications to **Window** coordinates.) It then sets tracking rectangle #1 to be the visible **View**, and sets the **trackingRect** instance variable to 1 to remember the fact that the window is set.

13. Insert the **awakeFromNib** method below, which overrides the one in **ColorGraphView**, into **TrackingGraphView.m**.

```
- awakeFromNib
{
  [super awakeFromNib];
  [self setMyTrackingRect: YES];
  return self;
}
```

This method invokes the **awakeFromNib** method in the **ColorGraphView** class (the **TrackingGraphView**'s superclass) and then sets the tracking rectangle by invoking **setMyTrackingRect:**.

The next pair of methods responds to events generated by the cursor entering and exiting the tracking rectangle.

14. Insert the **mouseEntered:** and **mouseExited:** method implementations below into **TrackingGraphView.m**.

```
- mouseEntered:(NXEvent *)theEvent
{
  [window makeFirstResponder:self];
  [window addToEventMask:NX_MOUSEMOVEDMASK];
  inside = YES;
  return self;
}

- mouseExited:(NXEvent *)theEvent
{
```

```
    [self unhighlightSegment];
    [window removeFromEventMask:NX_MOUSEMOVEDMASK];
    inside = NO;
    return self;
}
```

The **mouseEntered:** method makes the **TrackingGraphView** the **Window**'s First Responder and changes the **Window**'s event mask so that it gets all mouse-moved events. The **mouseExited:** method restores the original event mask. (We'll discuss the **unhighlightSegment** method shortly.)

If the user resizes GraphPaper's main window, the tracking rectangle will no longer be correct. The **sizeTo::** method below resizes the tracking rectangle if the **TrackingGraphView** is resized.

15. Insert the **sizeTo::** method implementation below into **TrackingGraphView.m**.

```
- sizeTo:(NXCoord)width :(NXCoord)height
{
    [super sizeTo:width :height];
    return [self setMyTrackingRect: YES];
}
```

The next two methods, **unhighlightSegment** and **mouseMoved:**, are a bit more complicated. The first method unhighlights a **Segment** if one is highlighted, and erases the contents of the **xCell** and **yCell** text fields. It's invoked when the cursor (mouse) moves off the graph or, from **mouseExited:**, when the mouse moves outside of the tracking rectangle.

16. Insert the **unhighlightSegment** method below into **TrackingGraphView.m**.

```
- unhighlightSegment
{
    if (highlightedSegment) {
        [self lockFocus];
        [ [highlightedSegment setColor: graphColor]
                            drawPSInView: self];
        [self unlockFocus];
        [xCell setStringValue:"x: "];
        [yCell setStringValue:"y: "];
        highlightedSegment = nil;
    }
    return self;
}
```

17. Insert the **mouseMoved:** method below into **TrackingGraphView.m**.

```
- mouseMoved:(NXEvent *)theEvent
```

```
{
  NXPoint pt;
  char buf[256];

  pt = theEvent->location;
  [self convertPoint: &pt fromView: nil];

  if (displayList && inside) {
    int j;
    for (j=0; j<[displayList count]; j++) {
      id obj = [displayList objectAt:j];
      NXRect obounds = [obj bounds];

      if ([obj tag]==GRAPH_TAG &&
          [self mouse: &pt inRect: &obounds]) {

        if (obj != highlightedSegment) {
          [self unhighlightSegment];/* erase old */

          /* highlight new segment */
          [self lockFocus];
          [obj setGray: NX_LTGRAY];
          [obj drawPSInView: self];
          [self unlockFocus];

          /* update positions */
          sprintf(buf, "x:  %g", [obj x]);
          [xCell setStringValue: buf];
          sprintf(buf, "y:  %g", [obj y]);
          [yCell setStringValue: buf];

          highlightedSegment = obj;
        }
        return self;
      }
    }
  }
  /* no segment should be highlighted */
  [self unhighlightSegment];
  return self;
}
```

Despite the length of this **mouseMoved:** method, it isn't very complicated.
First it converts the new mouse location from **Window** to **View** coordinates. Then it iterates through the display list, searching for an object that
has the **GRAPH_TAG** tag and contains the point corresponding to the
mouse. If the **Segment** that we've found is not the point that is already

highlighted, we unhighlight the old highlighted **Segment**, draw the **Segment** that we found in light gray, and set the **x** and **y** cells to be the **Segment**'s **x** and **y** values. We then store the highlighted **Segment**'s **id** in the **highlightedSegment** variable. If the mouse doesn't correspond to any **Segment**, and a **Segment** was already highlighted, we unhighlight that **Segment** and erase the values in the **x** and **y** cells.

18. Save all pertinent files, **make** and run GraphPaper.

19. Click the **Graph** button and move the cursor over the graph.

The window in Figure 7 below shows what the **x** and **y** cells and highlighted **Segment** look like when GraphPaper runs. Note the arrow cursor.

FIGURE 7. GraphPaper Window with x and y Cells and Tracking

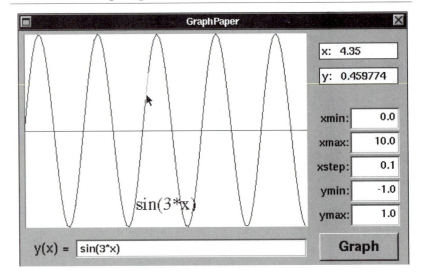

Changing the Cursor

The standard NeXTSTEP *arrow* cursor ( ) isn't the best tool for picking out points on the graph. A better one is the simple *crosshair* cursor ( ). Although you can't see it, the dots around the center of the cursor are not white, but transparent.

NeXTSTEP provides a simple way for giving **View**s or parts of **View**s their own cursors. If a **View** has its own cursor, the mouse cursor automatically changes to that **View**'s cursor when the mouse moves on top of that **View**, and automatically reverts to what it was before when the mouse cursor moves off that **View**. This section shows how to set up cursors that change automatically.

Adding a Cursor to the Nib

You can make the cursor be any TIFF or EPS image, as long as that image is 16 pixels square. If the cursor is black, it should be surrounded by a white border so that you can see it on a black background (as an example, move the arrow cursor inside a title bar). You can also use transparent pixels or semi-transparent pixels in your cursor to allow the user to see things underneath it.

To use an image as a cursor, you must make its image accessible to your program. There are three ways to do this:

- Add the cursor's image to your application's nib.
- Add the cursor's image to your project's TIFF or EPS file list.
- Place the cursor's image file in the directory in which the program resides (called a *package*).

First we'll show how to add the cursor image to your application's nib.

1. Create a cursor that you like (or use an existing one such as **cross.tiff** in **/NextDeveloper/Examples/AppKit/Draw**) and store it in a file (we'll use the name **CrossHair.tiff** here).

2. Drag the icon for the **CrossHair.tiff** file into the Project Builder's main window. The image will be added to your project (under the **Images** file type) and copied into your project directory, if necessary.

Changes to the TrackingGraphView Class

Displaying a custom cursor requires using two NeXTSTEP classes: **NXImage** and **NXCursor**. The **NXImage** class is NeXTSTEP's generic class for manipulating images. The **NXCursor** class uses an **NXImage** object that you provide and displays it as a cursor when necessary. Displaying a cursor also requires an additional method in the **View** class called **resetCursorRects**, which is invoked automatically by the **Window** object to set up the cursor rectangles when you move into the designated area on the screen.

Cursor rectangles are *only* used to change the shape of the cursor when the user moves the cursor into a particular rectangular region of the window.

Although they are implemented with mouse tracking rectangles, they have no other impact on mouse tracking.

To make all of this work, you need to add an instance variable to the **TrackingGraphView** object that will hold the **id** of the **NXCursor** object.

3. Insert the new instance variable below into **TrackingGraphView.h**.

```
id cursor;
```

4. Insert the new **resetCursorRects** method declaration below into **TrackingGraphView.h**.

```
- resetCursorRects;
```

Next, we need to modify the **awakeFromNib** method to create the **NXCursor** object and set its "hot spot" appropriately. The *hot spot* is the point in the cursor image whose location on the screen is reported as the cursor's location. The hot spot on the standard arrow cursor ( ) is the point at the tip of the arrow, whereas the hot spot on the **CrossHair.tiff** cursor ( ) is defined in the **awakeFromNib** method below to be the point at the intersection of the two lines.

5. Insert the lines in **bold** below into the **awakeFromNib** method in **TrackingGraphView.m**.

```
- awakeFromNib
{
    NXPoint hotSpot;

    [super awakeFromNib];

    cursor = [ [NXCursor alloc] initFromImage:
                [NXImage findImageNamed: "CrossHair"] ];

    hotSpot.x = 8.0;
    hotSpot.y = 8.0;

    [cursor setHotSpot: &hotSpot];

    [self  setMyTrackingRect: YES];
    return self;
}
```

The nested [**NXImage findImageNamed:**"CrossHair"] message searches the application for an image named **CrossHair**, **CrossHair.tiff** or **CrossHair.eps** and reads it into memory into an **NXImage** object. The **id** of the **NXImage** associated with the cursor image is then passed to the

NXCursor object that was previously allocated by the [**NXCursor alloc**] message.

Finally, we need to implement the **resetCursorRects** method.

6.   Insert the **resetCursorRects** method below into
     TrackingGraphView.m.

```
-  resetCursorRects
{
   NXRect visible;
   if ([self getVisibleRect:&visible]) {
      [self addCursorRect:&visible cursor:cursor];
   }
   return self;
}
```

This method sets up the cursor tracking rectangle so that the cursor automatically changes from the arrow to the crosshair when the mouse moves inside the **TrackingGraphView**. The rectangle is set to be merely the amount of the **View** that is visible; this is important if part of the **View** is hidden behind a scroller. The **resetCursorRects** message is sent to the key window by the **Application** object whenever it determines that the key window has invalid cursor rectangles (e.g., when the **View** is resized). The key window then sends the **resetCursorRects** message to each of its subviews, which includes **TrackingGraphView** in this example.

7.   Save all pertinent files, **make** and run GraphPaper.

8.   Click the **Graph** button and move the cursor over the graph. The crosshair cursor should appear, as in the middle of the GraphPaper window in Figure 8 below.

Summary

In this chapter, we continued our investigation of the NeXTSTEP **View** class by looking at the way the class handles resize events and controls cursors. In the next chapter we'll learn more about NeXTSTEP **ScrollView**s, we'll see how to put a zoom button on the GraphPaper application, and we'll make provisions for saving a graph as an EPS or TIFF file.

FIGURE 8. GraphPaper Window CrossHair Cursor

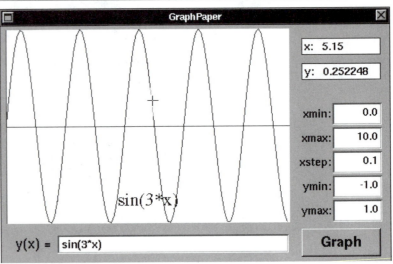

19

Zooming and Saving Graphics Files

This chapter shows you how to do a few odds and ends with **View**s. In the first part we'll show how to put a zoom pop-up list in a **ScrollView**. In the second part we'll show you how to generate encapsulated PostScript or TIFF from a **View**, how to save the graph into an EPS or TIFF file, and how to add controls to a Save panel.

Adding a Zoom Button To GraphPaper

We did things incorrectly in the previous chapter by having the **Graph-View** object rescale its coordinate system when its containing window was resized. Although it was a neat hack and a good way to show how to catch resizing events, stretching an application's window just isn't the right way for a user to get more detail about what the window contains.

The reason has to do with the NeXTSTEP user interface guidelines. The window is supposed to be just that – a window into a page of an imaginary document. The document shouldn't get bigger when you stretch its window. Stretching the window should merely let you see *more* of the document.

What NeXTSTEP applications should use to let the user see more detail is a zoom button. A zoom button is a little pop-up list button at the bottom of a **ScrollView** that allows you change the magnification of the **ScrollView**. Appsoft's word processor *WriteNow* has such a button (see Figure 1).

FIGURE 1. **Zoom Pop-Up List Button in WriteNow**

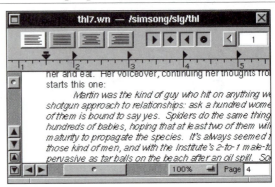

The window in Figure 1 is set to a zoom factor of 100%. Pressing the button reveals a pop-up list of different magnification settings, which in turn lets you change the size of the text that is displayed, as in Figure 2.

FIGURE 2. **Zoomed WriteNow Window**

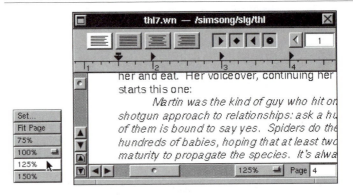

It's really quite easy to add a zoom button to any **ScrollView**. The trick requires knowing a little bit about how the **ScrollView** works.

The ScrollView Class Revisited

Recall that each **ScrollView** object has another object "inside" it called its **docView**, which is the actual **View** being displayed. In addition to the **docView**, each **ScrollView** has three other **View** objects to help it perform its scrolling tasks:

- A **Scroller** to control horizontal scrolling.
- A **Scroller** to control vertical scrolling.
- A **ClipView** that shows the part of the **docView** which is visible.

You can change the magnification of the **View** displayed in the **ScrollView** simply by sending a **scale:** message to the **ClipView**, which will cause it to scale the **View** that it contains when it is drawn. Zooming happens without the knowledge or cooperation of the **docView**.

Whenever a **ScrollView** changes size (for example, when it is resized), and whenever the **View** that it contains changes size, the **ScrollView** sends the **tile** message to itself to alert its subviews to change their sizes. By subclassing the **ScrollView** class and overriding the **tile** method, it is possible to place additional objects such as rulers and zoom buttons over or next to the scrollers that the **ScrollView** displays.

In this section, we will subclass the **ScrollView** class to make a new class called **ZoomScrollView**. This class will have outlets for its **docView** – the **TrackingGraphView** that we created in the previous chapter – as well as for the zoom pop-up list. We'll control the **ZoomScrollView** instance from the **Controller** object.

Changes to GraphPaper.nib

1. Open your GraphPaper project in Project Builder and the **GraphPaper.nib** file in Interface Builder.

2. Resize the **TrackingGraphView** in the **GraphPaper** window so that it's smaller and put it somewhere in the window that is out of the way. (Don't worry about the size or position of the **TrackingGraphView** – it will automatically be resized and placed in the proper position when GraphPaper runs.)

3. **Subclass** the **ScrollView** class and create the **ZoomScrollView** class.

4. Add the following outlets and action to the **ZoomScrollView** class in IB's Inspector.

Outlets	Action
subView, zoomButton	changeZoom:

5. Drag a **CustomView** icon from IB's Views palette and drop it in the **GraphPaper** window. Change its class to **ZoomScrollView**.

6. Resize the on-screen **ZoomScrollView** instance to be as large as the previous **TrackingGraphView**, as in Figure 3 below.

7. Choose IB's **Format→Layout→Send To Back** menu command to put the **ZoomScrollView** instance "behind" the **TrackingGraphView** instance, as in Figure 3 below. (The only reason to send the **ZoomScrollView** to the back is to see both **View**s at the same time.)

FIGURE 3. ZoomScrollView in GraphPaper Window

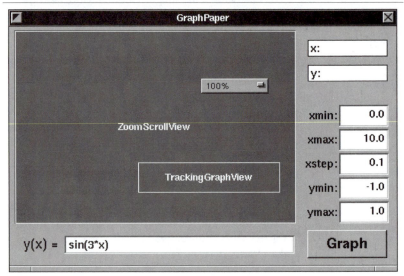

8. Type Command-3 and set the **ZoomScrollView**'s Autosizing attributes so it will stretch when the window is resized (the "springs" should be the same as for the **TrackingGraphView** instance – see page 473).

9. Drag a pop-up list button (seen at the left) from IB's Views palette and drop it on the **ZoomScrollView**.

10. Double-click the pop-up list button.

When you double-click the pop-up list button, you'll see the three menu cells that the associated pop-up list initially contains. The on-screen pop-up list is controlled by an instance of the **PopUpList** class which itself is a subclass of the **Menu** class. You can add more items to an open pop-up list in IB by dragging them from the Menus palette and dropping them in the pop-up list. (You can't add submenus to a pop-up list, however.)

The pop-up list button itself is actually an instance of the NeXTSTEP **Button** class that sends the **popUp:** message to the **PopUpList** instance. After a selection is made, the **PopUpList** automatically changes the title of the **Button** by sending it the **setTitle:** message.

11. One-by-one, drag three more menu items from the Menus palette and drop them in the pop-up list.

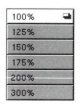

12. Name the menu cells **100%**, **125%**, **150%**, **175%**, **200%**, and **300%** and give them the tags **100**, **125**, **150**, **175**, **200**, and **300**, respectively (use the MenuCell Attributes Inspector). When you're done, the pop-up list should look like the one at the left.

13. Connect each menu cell in the pop-up list so that they all send the **changeZoom:** action message to **ZoomScrollView**. Be sure to drag the connections from each item in the menu, and not from the pop-up button, or "cover." The title in the Inspector's title bar indicates the source of the connection.

14. Click the **100%** item and close the pop-up list by clicking somewhere else in the window.

15. Connect **ZoomScrollView**'s **zoomButton** outlet to the pop-up list *button* (you'll have to temporarily move the pop-up list button outside the area covered by the **ZoomScrollView** instance).

16. Connect **ZoomScrollView**'s **subView** outlet to the **TrackingGraphView**.

17. **Unparse** the class definition for **ZoomScrollView** and insert its class files into the project.

Changes to ZoomScrollView

18. Insert the six lines in **bold** below to **ZoomScrollView.h**.

```
#import <appkit/appkit.h>

@interface ZoomScrollView:ScrollView
{
    id subView;
    id zoomButton;
    float scaleFactor;
    NXRect originalContentViewFrame;
}

- changeZoom:sender;
- initFrame:(const NXRect *)theFrame;
- awakeFromNib;
```

```
- setScaleFactor:(float)aFactor;
- tile;

@end
```

We'll use the **scaleFactor** instance variable to store the current scale factor of the **ZoomScrollView**. When the user changes the zoom factor using the pop-up list, the **PopUpList** object will send the **changeZoom:** message to the **ZoomScrollView** object, which will in turn send the **setScaleFactor:** message to itself. **ZoomScrollView**'s **setScaleFactor:** method will then compare the new zoom factor with the current one and calculate the proper arguments to the **scale:** message. If the new magnification isn't different from the old, the **ZoomScrollView** won't do anything.

19. Insert the **initFrame:** method below into **ZoomScrollView.m**.

```
- initFrame:(const NXRect *)theFrame
{
  [super initFrame: theFrame];
  [self setBackgroundGray: NX_WHITE];
  scaleFactor = 1.0;
  return self;
}
```

The **initFrame:** method is the designated initializer for the **View** class. **ZoomScrollView**'s **initFrame:** method sends the **initFrame:** message to its superview and then sets the background of the **ScrollView** to be white. Finally it sets the current scale factor to be **1.0**, which corresponds to the **100%** menu item in the pop-up list.

TrackingGraphView's **awakeFromNib** method installs the **Tracking-GraphView** instance as the **docView** inside the **ScrollView**.

20. Insert the **awakeFromNib** method below into **ZoomScrollView.m**.

```
- awakeFromNib
{
  [self setVertScrollerRequired:  YES];
  [self setHorizScrollerRequired: YES];
  [self setBorderType: NX_LINE];

  /* The next 3 lines install the subview
   * and set its size to be the same as
   * the ScrollView's contentView.
   */
  [self        setDocView: subView];
  [contentView getFrame: &originalContentViewFrame];
  [subView     setFrame: &originalContentViewFrame];
```

```
    return self;
}
```

This method also tells the **ZoomScrollView** that both scrollers are required and that its border should be of type NX_LINE (as opposed to NX_BEZEL or NX_NOBORDER). Finally it sizes the **TrackingGraphView** (**sub-View**) to be the size of the **ScrollView**'s **contentView**, which is the **Clip-View**.

The next method is the one that actually changes the magnification of the **ClipView** object. **ClipViews** are used by the **ScrollView** class to do the actual displaying of the **ScrollView**.

21. Insert the **setScaleFactor:** method below into **ZoomScrollView.m**.

```
- setScaleFactor:(float)aFactor
{
  if (scaleFactor != aFactor) {
    float delta = aFactor/scaleFactor;
    scaleFactor = aFactor;
    [contentView scale: delta : delta];
  }

  return self;
}
```

As we mentioned above, this **setScaleFactor:** method simply sends the **scale:** message to the **ClipView** (**contentView**) with the arguments being the **delta** necessary to make the **ClipView** have the magnification that the user wants. The next method is the action that is invoked when the user clicks the pop-up list button.

22. Insert the line in **bold** below into the **changeZoom:** method in **ZoomScrollView.m**.

```
- changeZoom:sender
{
  [self setScaleFactor:
              [ [sender selectedCell] tag] / 100.0];
  return self;
}
```

Lastly, there is our **tile** method, an override of **ScrollView**'s **tile** method. It is invoked automatically when the **ZoomScrollView** size changes.

23. Insert the **tile** method below into **ZoomScrollView.m**.

```
- tile
{
  NXRect scrollerRect, buttonRect;

  [super tile];

  /* The next line makes the zoomButton itself
   * one of the ZoomScrollView's subviews the
   * first time that the tile message is sent.
   */

  if ([zoomButton superview] != self) {
    [self addSubview:zoomButton];
  }

  /* make the hScroller smaller and stick the
   * pop-up list next to it.
   */
  [hScroller getFrame: &scrollerRect];
  NXDivideRect(&scrollerRect, &buttonRect, 60.0, 2);
  [hScroller setFrame: &scrollerRect];
  NXInsetRect(&buttonRect, 1.0, 1.0);
  [zoomButton setFrame: &buttonRect];

  return self;
}
```

This **tile** method gets the frame of the horizontal scroller, snips off 60 pixels, and gives that space to the zoom button. (NeXTSTEP's "Rectangle Functions" are really handy; search for "**NXDivideRect**" in HeaderViewer or Librarian to see what's available.)

Testing the Zoom Button

24. Save all pertinent files and then **make** and run GraphPaper.

25. You should get a magnification button in the lower right-hand corner of the **ZoomScrollView**, as in the window at the top of Figure 4 below. Enter a function and click the **Graph** button.

26. Press the pop-up list button and drag to **200%**. The zoom button title should change as in the window at the bottom of Figure 4.

27. Resize the GraphPaper window and drag the scroll knobs. The **ZoomScrollView** should stretch, making more of the graph visible, rather than changing its scale as it did previously.

FIGURE 4. Zoom Button in GraphPaper Window

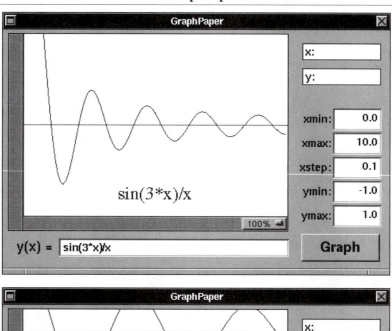

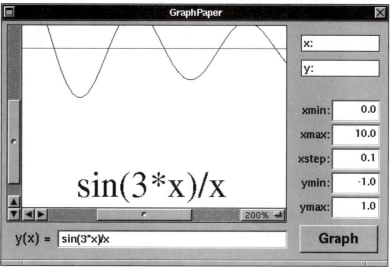

Bug Fixes

In making the **ZoomScrollView**, we've inadvertently introduced two bugs into our GraphPaper application having to do with the **TrackingGraph-View**'s tracking rectangles: when the GraphPaper window is resized, parts of the graph sometimes lose their mouse sensitivity. Another bug that we've had from the beginning is that the application continues to track the mouse even when the GraphPaper window is not key.

The problem with resizing owes itself to the fact that the **TrackingGraph-View** depends upon catching the **superviewSizeChanged:** method in order to discard its old tracking rectangle and create a new one. Unfortunately, when a **View** is placed inside a **ScrollView**, this message is not forwarded, because the **ClipView** (which is the superview of the **docView** of a **Scroll-View**) does not resize the **View** when you stretch the window. This makes sense– if you make a **ScrollView** larger, you may be able to see more of the **docView**, but the **docView** itself doesn't resize to be larger. We therefore need to pick a different strategy for noticing that the visible portion of the **TrackingGraphView** has changed, and then reset the tracking rectangle appropriately.

Because this problem arises when the window is resized, an easy way to solve it is to catch the window resize event and take the appropriate action. The way to do this is to make the **TrackingGraphView** the *delegate* of its window and to implement the **windowDidResize:** delegate method.

28. Back in IB, connect the GraphPaper window's **delegate** outlet to the **TrackingGraphView** (Control-drag from the **MyWindow** icon in the Objects view to the **TrackingGraphView** instance in the window).

29. Insert the three method declarations below into **TrackingGraphView.h** (*not* **ZoomScrollView.h**).

```
- windowDidResize:sender;
- windowDidBecomeMain:sender;
- windowDidResignMain:sender;
```

30. Insert the method below into the file **TrackingGraphView.m**.

```
- windowDidResize:sender
{
    return [self setMyTrackingRect: YES];
}
```

This will fix the resizing problem; the tracking rectangle should now automatically be resized when the window is resized.

The second bug – that the application continues to track the mouse when it is no longer the active application – is also solved through the use of window delegate methods. This time, we'll use the **windowDidBecomeMain:** and the **windowDidResignMain:** methods so that the application only tracks the mouse when it is the main window.

31. Insert the two methods below into **TrackingGraphView.m**.

```
- windowDidBecomeMain:sender
{
    return [self setMyTrackingRect: YES];
```

```
    }

    - windowDidResignMain:sender
    {
        return [self setMyTrackingRect: NO];
    }
```

32. Save all pertinent files and then **make** and run GraphPaper.

The tracking now turns off when you activate another application, and turns back on when you reactivate GraphPaper.

Saving a View as Encapsulated PostScript

Although making a graph (or any other picture) is a nice start, it's important to be able to save the graph in a format that can work with other NeXT-STEP applications. For example, you might want to put the graph in a word processor document that you are making with *WriteNow* or *WordPerfect*. One way to do this is by saving the graph into a file as an Encapsulated PostScript (EPS) image.

NeXTSTEP's **View** class makes it particularly easy to generate an EPS file: create an **NXStream** for writing and send the **copyPSCodeInside:to:** message to the **View**. The **View** object will invoke the appropriate **drawSelf::** method but instead of sending the PostScript code to the Window Server, it captures the output and sends it to the stream that you designate.

In the remainder of this section we'll add a **Save** command to GraphPaper's menu and then modify the **Controller** object to capture the EPS and write it to a file.

Changes to GraphPaper.nib

1. Back in IB, add a menu item to the GraphPaper menu. Change its title to **Save Image** and give it the "**s**" key alternative.

2. Select the **FirstResponder** class in the Classes view (under **Object**) and add an action called **save:** in the Class Attributes Inspector.

3. Connect the **Save Image** menu cell so that it sends the **save:** action message to the **FirstResponder** "object" in the Objects view.

Changes to the Controller Class

We need to add two methods to the **Controller** class to make the **Save Image** command work. The first method, **save:**, will be invoked in response to a user choosing the **Save Image** menu command. It will get the file name in which the user wishes to save the EPS file, and open an **NXStream** to receive the PostScript. The second method, **copyPSToStream:forView:**, will actually generate the PostScript. (Using a second method to generate the PostScript output will make it easier to adapt the **save:** method to save the file as either EPS or TIFF.)

4.   Insert the two method declarations below into **Controller.h**.

```
- save:sender;
- copyPSToStream:(NXStream *)aStream forView:view;
```

5.   Insert the **save:** action method below into **Controller.m**.

```
- save:sender
{
  id save;

  save = [ [SavePanel new]
           setRequiredFileType:"eps"];

  if ([save runModal]==1) {
    NXStream *aStream;

    aStream = NXOpenMemory(0, 0, NX_WRITEONLY);
    [self copyPSToStream:aStream forView:graphView];
    NXSaveToFile(aStream, [save filename]);
    NXCloseMemory(aStream, NX_FREEBUFFER);
  }
  return self;
}
```

This method displays the Save panel and asks the user for a file name with extension EPS. If the user provides a valid name, the method opens a memory-resident **NXStream**, invokes the **copyPSToStream:forView:** method to fill the stream with an EPS representation of the contents of the **Zoom-ScrollView**, and finally saves the stream to a file and frees its memory.

The following method, the one that actually generates the EPS, is even simpler.

6.   Insert the **copyPSToStream:forView:** method below into **Controller.m**.

```
- copyPSToStream:(NXStream *)aStream forView:view
```

```
{
  NXRect bounds;

  [view getBounds:&bounds];
  [view copyPSCodeInside:&bounds to:aStream];
  return self;
}
```

This **copyPSToStream:forView:** method first finds the **bounds** of the **ZoomScrollView**. Then it sends the **ZoomScrollView** the **copyPSCodeInside:to:** message, which invokes the **ZoomScrollView**'s **drawSelf::** method and redirects the output to the given stream.

Testing the Save Image Menu Command

7. Save all pertinent files and then **make** and run GraphPaper.

8. Click the **Graph** button and then choose the **Save Image** menu command. You'll see a standard NeXTSTEP Save panel as in Figure 5 below.

9. Enter a file name such **MyGraph** and click **OK**. You'll see a new icon appear in the File Viewer as in Figure 5 below.

FIGURE 5. Saving an EPS File in GraphPaper

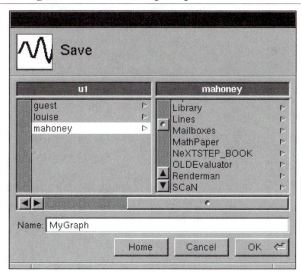

You can incorporate this EPS file directly into a word processor document. One nice thing about EPS files is that they are automatically imaged at the resolution of the PostScript device in use. For example, we can incorporate the EPS file into this book, as in Figure 6 below.

FIGURE 6. An EPS File Printed in this Book

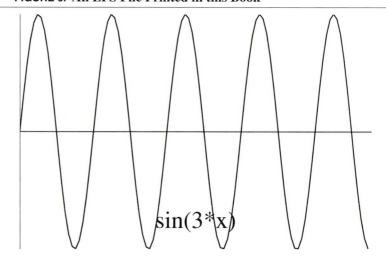

If you compare this image of the **GraphView** with the others in this book, you'll see that the letters "**sin(3*x)**" have no *jaggies* and that the line itself looks smoother. That's because the PostScript file has been imaged at the 1270 dpi (dots per inch) resolution of our phototypesetter. The other images of the **GraphView** were captured off the screen at 92 dpi and had their pixels replicated to get to the 1270 dpi of the phototypesetter.

Saving a View in Tag Image File Format

Under certain circumstances, you might want to generate a TIFF file instead of an EPS file. A TIFF (Tag Image File Format) file could be displayed on an Apple Macintosh screen (which can't handle PostScript), or could be edited pixel-by-pixel in applications such as IconBuilder.

We'll use the **NXImage** class to generate the TIFF file. First we'll capture the PostScript for the **GraphView** into a stream. Then we'll feed this stream into an instance of the **NXImage** class. Finally we'll ask the **NXImage** instance to write its image, in TIFF format, to a second stream. This second stream will then be saved to the file that the user specifies.

1. Insert the method declaration below into **Controller.h**.

```
- copyTIFFToStream:(NXStream *)aStream forView:view;
```

2. Insert the **copyTIFFToStream:forView:** method below into **Controller.m**.

```
- copyTIFFToStream:(NXStream *)aStream forView:view
{
    NXRect      bounds;
    id          image;
    NXStream    *workStream;

    /* Capture the PostScript output */
    workStream = NXOpenMemory(0,0,NX_READWRITE);
    [view getBounds: &bounds];
    [view copyPSCodeInside: &bounds to: workStream];

    /* Read the PostScript into an NXImage object */
    NXSeek(workStream,0L,NX_FROMSTART);

    image = [[NXImage alloc]
            initFromStream: workStream];

    /* The following statement forces the
     * NXImage object to set its bits-per-pixel depth
     * to be the maximum specified in the PostScript
     * stream, rather than have the depth limited by
     * the user's current display.
     */

    [image setCacheDepthBounded:NO];

    /* Have the image write its output as a TIFF
     * to requested stream
     */
    [image writeTIFF: aStream];
    [image free];

    /* Close our work output */
    NXCloseMemory(workStream,NX_FREEBUFFER);

    return self;
}
```

But how should we invoke the **copyTIFFToStream:** method? One way would be to create a second menu item – for example, **Save Image as TIFF**. But a better way would be to give the user a file format option on the **SavePanel**. The way to do this is with an *accessory View*.

Creating an Accessory View

An *accessory* **View** is a **View** that you provide to the **SavePanel** object that is automatically incorporated into the Save panel when the panel is displayed. Many applications use accessory **View**s to let the user choose options when saving.

The easiest way to put controls in an accessory **View** is to create a new window in IB and put the necessary controls in it. Then group all of the controls in a box; this will make them all subviews of the box. Finally, get the **id** of the box and pass it to the Save panel. The new window never gets displayed while the program is running.

We'll start by making the necessary changes to **Controller.h**. Then we'll create the box and make connections in IB, and finally we'll implement the necessary method in **Controller.m**.

3. Insert the two outlets **formatBox** and **formatMatrix** below into **Controller.h**.

    ```
    id formatBox;
    id formatMatrix;
    ```

4. Insert the **setFormat:** action method declaration below into **Controller.h**.

    ```
    - setFormat:sender;
    ```

5. Back in IB, **Parse** the updated **Controller** class definition in **GraphPaper.nib**.

Next we'll create a window with the accessory **View**, as at the left.

6. Drag a **Window** icon from IB's Windows palette and drop it into the workspace. The window will be added to the file **GraphPaper.nib**. Resize the window so it's about the same size as the one at the left.

7. In the Window Attributes Inspector, set the attributes of the window as **Nonretained** and *not* **Visible at Launch Time**. The window is made **Nonretained** so that it uses the least amount of computer resources. Making the window *not* **Visible at Launch Time** prevents the user from ever seeing it, since we won't be displaying it in any other way.

8. Drag a radio button matrix from IB's Views palette and drop it in the window. Give it two choices: **EPS** and **TIFF**. Make EPS the default. Change the font using the Font panel, if you like.

9. Select the radio button matrix and choose IB's **Format→Layout→Group** menu command to group it in a box.

10. Rename the box **Format**. The window should now look very similar to the one above.

11. Connect the **Controller**'s **formatBox** outlet to the box titled **Format**. Read the text near the bottom of the Inspector so you are sure which object was connected.

12. Connect the **Controller**'s **formatMatrix** outlet to the radio button matrix (a *gray*, not black rectangle should surround the button matrix).

13. Connect the radio button matrix to the **Controller** instance icon so that it sends the **setFormat:** action. You must double-click the matrix so that you select the matrix rather than its containing box.

Changes to the Controller Class Implementation

In addition to the **copyPSToStream:forView:** and **copyTIFFToStream:-forView:** methods we discussed above, we'll need to implement the **set-Format:** action method that is invoked when the user changes the file format type in the Save panel. NeXTSTEP only provides a single instance of the **SavePanel** object, and thus we can use the **[SavePanel new]** statement to get the panel's **id** inside the **setFormat:** method. The **SavePanel** object lets us change its required file types inside its modal loop, so when the user changes the format, the required file type is automatically changed.

14. Insert the **setFormat:** method below into **Controller.m**.

```
- setFormat:sender
{
    char *format;
    char *cc;

    format = NXCopyStringBuffer(
                     [ [sender selectedCell] title]);
    for (cc=format; *cc; cc++) {
      *cc = NXToLower(*cc);
    }
    [ [SavePanel new] setRequiredFileType:format];
    free(format);
    return self;
}
```

Note that this method uses the **NXCopyStringBuffer()** function to make a private copy of the contents of the matrix's selected cell's title (EPS or TIFF). This private copy is then changed to lower case and used directly as the Save panel's required file type. There's no need to mess around with tags when the title of the buttons works just fine.

Lastly we need to modify the **save:** method to rip the box (and the subviews that it contains) out of the window that we created above and put it into the Save Panel as an accessory **View**. This is done with the **SavePanel**'s **setAccessoryView:** method. The **SavePanel** object automatically resizes the on-screen Save panel to accommodate the accessory **View**.

We also need to modify the **save:** method to look at the title of the selected cell and choose the appropriate method to send output to the stream. Both of these modifications are presented below:

15. *Replace* the previous version of the **save:** method in **Controller.m** with the one below.

```
- save:sender
{
  id save = [SavePanel new];

  /* set the initial format */
  [self setFormat:formatMatrix];

  /* put format box in View */
  [save setAccessoryView:formatBox];

  if ([save runModal]==1) {
    NXStream *aStream;

    aStream = NXOpenMemory(0,0,NX_WRITEONLY);
    if (!strcmp([ [formatMatrix selectedCell]
                  title], "EPS")) {
      [self copyPSToStream: aStream
                    forView: graphView];
    }
    else {
      [self  copyTIFFToStream: aStream
             forView: graphView];
    }
    NXSaveToFile(aStream, [save filename]);
    NXCloseMemory(aStream, NX_FREEBUFFER);
  }
  return self;
}
```

Testing the "EPS or TIFF" Save Feature

16. Save all pertinent files and then **make** and run GraphPaper.

17. Click the **Graph** button and then choose the **Save Image** menu command. You should see a Save panel with the accessory **View** containing the radio button matrix, as in Figure 7 below.

18. Try saving the same graph as EPS and as TIFF. Then double-click the EPS and TIFF file icons in your File Viewer to see them in Preview. You might also try to import the files into a word processor.

FIGURE 7. Save Panel with an Accessory View

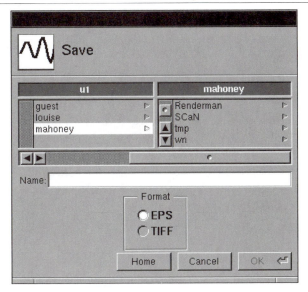

Summary

You may notice that things are starting to happen really quickly – that's because we've reached critical mass with NeXTSTEP. Everything we've learned is starting to jell and build on everything else that we've learned. The result is that with each step we now take, we can do more things with less effort.

From here on, you could probably figure out everything else yourself, since you've now mastered the basic concepts. The last two chapters of this book will walk you through the cut-and-paste system and the NeXTSTEP defaults database system.

20

The Pasteboard and Services

In the previous chapter we showed how images produced by the GraphPaper application can be incorporated into other programs by saving the images in an EPS or TIFF file. In this chapter we'll show two slicker, more direct ways that NeXTSTEP provides for making applications work together: the cut, copy, and paste system, and the **Services** menu.

Cut, Copy, and Paste with the Pasteboard

The NeXTSTEP **Pasteboard** object provides a simple and direct way for users to transfer data between applications using familiar copy, cut, and paste commands. But NeXTSTEP extends the traditional notions of cut, copy, and paste by providing multiple pasteboards, each of which can hold several different data representations simultaneously, and by providing *lazy evaluation*, a system whereby information is not put onto the pasteboard unless it is needed by a receiving application.

NeXTSTEP provides five basic pasteboards:

- the *General* pasteboard (**NXGeneralPboard**), which is used to cut, copy, and paste data between applications. This pasteboard supports ordinary **Cut**, **Copy**, and **Paste** menu commands. (This pasteboard was formerly called the **NXSelectionPboard**.)
- the *Ruler* pasteboard (**NXRulerPboard**), which holds information about margins and tab stops. This pasteboard supports **Copy Ruler** and **Paste Ruler** menu commands, such as those in *Edit* and *WriteNow*.
- the *Font* pasteboard (**NXFontPboard**), which holds information about character font size, format and style. This pasteboard supports **Copy Font** and **Paste Font** menu commands.
- the *Find* pasteboard (**NXFindPboard**), which is used to hold information about the current state of each application's Find panel. Although most applications don't use the Find pasteboard, it is designed so that you can execute a find command in one application and then execute a find-next command in another application without having to retype the search string.
- The *Drag* pasteboard (**NXDragPboard**), which is used to hold information when objects (such as color chips) are dragged from one window (or application) to another.

You can also create your own pasteboards in addition to these and use them between different applications that you write. Of course, other people's applications are not likely to know of their existence.

Pasteboards are generally transparent to the user. That is, users don't realize that there are four distinct pasteboards – they simply know that when they cut text from one application and paste it into another, it doesn't change the last ruler that they copied or pasted. Likewise, users are generally unaware that NeXTSTEP pasteboards can hold data in multiple representations at the same time. It just happens automatically, like magic!

For example, when you copy a definition from the *Webster* program to the pasteboard, *Webster* puts data on the pasteboard in both ASCII and Rich Text. If you paste the definition into a *Terminal* window, the *Terminal* application reads the ASCII definition. But if you paste the definition into a word processor document, you might get the Rich Text version (depending on which word processor).

If you copy an image with Lighthouse Design's *Diagram!* program to the pasteboard, *Diagram!* will put the image on the pasteboard in three ways: as TIFF, as Encapsulated PostScript, and in *Diagram!*'s internal format. If you paste back into *Diagram!*, it will paste objects rather than images.

Interface Builder uses the pasteboard to let you paste windows, controls, objects and practically anything else.

There's also nothing like the pasteboard for showing bugs and implementation errors with NeXTSTEP applications. For example, *FrameMaker* 3.0 has both a **Paste** and a **Paste RTF** command, even though this violates NeXT's style guidelines. *WriteNow* 2.0 won't cut or paste RTF – the program only cuts and pastes ASCII, TIFF and EPS images. Unfortunately, when you find one of these bugs, all you can do is report them to the program's author and go on: the pasteboard system doesn't give you a way for fixing the bugs in other people's programs.

Providing Data to the Pasteboard

NeXTSTEP keeps data on the pasteboard in a separate program called **pbs**, the "pasteboard server." (Enter the UNIX command "**ps aux**" in a shell window to see the running **pbs** server.) You can only communicate with the pasteboard server indirectly, by sending messages to the NeXTSTEP **Pasteboard** object.

There are six commonly used **Pasteboard** methods. The following two *class* methods return the **id** of a **Pasteboard** object:

Class Method	What it does
+ new	Returns the **id** of the *Selection* pasteboard.
+ newName: (const char *)*aName*	Returns the **id** of a pasteboard with a given name.

There are two *instance* methods for putting data onto a pasteboard. They are usually invoked by (your override of) the **cut:** or **copy:** methods that handle the **Cut** or **Copy** commands.

Instance Method	What it does
- declareTypes: num: owner:	Tells the pasteboard which types you can provide.
- writeType: data: length:	Writes the data to the pasteboard.

Two other instance methods take data from the pasteboard. These are usually called by a **paste:** method that handles the **Paste** command.

Instance Method	What it does
- types	Returns an array with the kinds of types available for pasting.
- readType: data: length:	Returns an array with the kinds of types available for pasting.

NeXTSTEP defines nine basic pasteboard data types:

Pasteboard Type	What it contains
NXAsciiPboardType	ASCII text
NXPostScriptPboardType	Encapsulated PostScript code
NXTIFFPboardType	TIFF
NXRTFPboardType	Rich Text
NXSoundPboardType	Sound object's pasteboard type
NXFilenamePboardType	Complete file names
NXTabularTextPboardType	Tabular text, for example, rows and columns in a spreadsheet
NXFontPboardType	A font, defined by Rich Text
NXRulerPboardType	A ruler, defined by Rich Text

Data on the pasteboard is stored as an array of bytes, the same way that you might store it in a file.

Programs can put data on the pasteboard in two ways:

- *Immediately.* When the user presses Command-c, the program puts all of the selected data on the pasteboard.
- *Lazily.* When the user presses Command-c, the program simply tells the pasteboard what sort of types it could provide if asked. Then, when the user does a paste in another application, the program that originally copied the data onto the pasteboard is asked to provide the requested data.

Most NeXTSTEP programs write one format onto the pasteboard when the user chooses a **cut** or **copy** operation, and lazy evaluation is used to provide the other kinds of representations that the application knows about. The representation first written should be the most "rich" representation of the data possible – a representation that can be used to reconstruct all others. If the application performing the **Paste** operation wants data in a different format, the first application reads the richest description from the pasteboard, converts the data to the requested format, and writes it back.

Using the Pasteboard in GraphPaper

To show how to use the pasteboard, we'll first modify the GraphPaper application so that a user may copy a graph to the pasteboard by choosing the **Edit→Copy** menu command.

When you choose **Document→New Application** in Interface Builder, it automatically provides an **Edit** submenu like the one at the left. Each of the four menu cells in the **Edit** submenu come pre-connected to the **FirstResponder** icon, each sending the appropriate message, **cut:**, **copy:**, **paste:** or **selectAll:**. Thus, to implement **Cut** and **Copy** commands for the graph, all we need to do is to add **cut:** and **copy:** methods to GraphPaper's **Controller** class and make **Controller** the **NXApp** delegate (we already made **Controller** the **NXApp** delegate in Chapter 17). The **cut:** and **copy:** messages will automatically be forwarded to **NXApp**'s delegate unless another responder in the responder chain intercepts them first.

GraphPaper's implementation of cut, copy, and paste will be able to provide data in two formats: EPS and TIFF. Since EPS is the richer of these two formats, it will put EPS on the pasteboard first and convert that EPS to TIFF if requested by *lazy* evaluation.

Now we're ready to discuss the implementations of **Controller**'s **copyToPasteboard:** and **copy:** methods. The supporting **copyToPasteboard:** method is the one that does most of the work.

1. Insert the four method declarations below into **Controller.h**.

    ```
    - copyToPasteboard:pboard;
    - copy:sender;
    - pasteboard:sender provideData:(NXAtom)type;
    - cut:sender;
    ```

2. Insert the **copyToPasteboard:** and **copy:** methods below into **Controller.m**.

    ```
    - copyToPasteboard:pboard
    {
        NXStream *stream;
    ```

```
        char *data;
        int length, maxlen;

        NXAtom typelist[2];

        typelist[0] = NXPostScriptPboardType;
        typelist[1] = NXTIFFPboardType;
        [pboard declareTypes: typelist num: 2 owner:self];

    /* Now put the EPS on the pasteboard */
        stream = NXOpenMemory(0, 0, NX_WRITEONLY);
        [self copyPSToStream: stream forView: graphView];
        NXGetMemoryBuffer(stream, &data, &length,&maxlen);
        [pboard writeType: NXPostScriptPboardType
                     data: data length: length];
        NXCloseMemory(stream, NX_FREEBUFFER);
        return self;
    }



    - copy:sender
    {
        [self copyToPasteboard: [Pasteboard new] ];
        return self;
    }
```

Don't be thrown by the **NXAtom** type. This is a **typedef** for **const char ***. **NXAtom**s are allocated by the function **NXUniqueString()** and reside in a special portion of the application's memory which is usually set to be read-only.

The message **[Pasteboard new]** creates a new selection pasteboard, if necessary, and returns its **id**. If a selection pasteboard has already been created, the **id** of that pasteboard is returned instead.

The **copyToPasteboard:** method begins by constructing an array of two elements, **NXPostScriptPboardType** and **NXTIFFPboardType**. The order of these two elements is important: it specifies the preferred order in which the types should be used (PostScript is better than TIFF). It then sends the **declareTypes:num:owner:** message to the pasteboard (which is passed from the **copy:** method) to do three things:

(i)   Erase any existing data on the pasteboard.

(ii) Tell the pasteboard that your object can provide data of type TIFF or EPS (see the first two arguments).

(iii) Specify an object (via the **owner:** argument) that the pasteboard can message to provide any types necessary for *lazy* evaluation. Whenever there is a request for lazy data from the Pasteboard, the pasteboard will send the **pasteboard:provideData:** message to the object specified by the **owner:** argument.

The last block of code in the **copyToPasteboard:** method creates a stream, fills it with the EPS representation for the **ZoomScrollView** object (**graph-View**), and writes the stream's buffer to the pasteboard with the **write-Type:data:length:** message. Finally, the stream is closed and its associated memory buffer freed.

Providing Data Through Lazy Evaluation

Suppose a user has copied a GraphPaper graph to the pasteboard and wants to paste it into another application such as *WriteNow* (which we'll refer to as the *receiving application*). When the user chooses the **Paste** command to paste the graph, the receiving application obtains access to the selection pasteboard with the **[Pasteboard new]** message and then sends the **types** message to find out what types are available. The **types** message will return the following array of two types that the GraphPaper put on the pasteboard with the **declareTypes:num:owner:** method:

```
{NXPostScriptPboardType, NXTIFFPboardType, 0}
```

Even if the receiving program knows what kind of data it wants, the program must first send the Pasteboard the **types** message to set it up for returning the requested data. Once the **types** message is sent, the receiving program can ask for either type and be reasonably well-assured of getting it.

If the receiving application wants the **NXPostScriptPboardType**, it will simply take the data off the pasteboard when it invokes the **readTypes:-data:length:** method. If the receiving program asks for the **NXTIFFP-boardType**, it will wait while the **Pasteboard** object sends the **pasteboard:provideData:** message to GraphPaper's **Controller** object and receives a reply. This lazy evaluation is completely transparent to the receiving program that is pasting the data.

The **pasteboard:provideData:** method that performs the conversion from EPS to TIFF is a little tricky. We can't simply use the **Controller** instance method **copyTIFFToStream:forView:** (as in the previous chapter), because it is possible that the graph that was copied to the pasteboard is no longer the one displayed in the **GraphPaper** window. Instead, this method needs to take the EPS image from the pasteboard and convert it to a TIFF image directly. It does this conversion by using an **NXImage** object.

3.   Insert the **pasteboard:provideData:** method below to **Controller.m**.

```
/* Invoked to convert EPS to TIFF.
 * Done in its own zone, which is later destroyed.
 */
- pasteboard:sender provideData:(NXAtom)type
{
  if (type==NXTIFFPboardType) {
    char *epsData;
    int epsLen;

    if ([sender readType: NXPostScriptPboardType
          data: &epsData length: &epsLen]) {
      NXZone    *zone;
      NXStream  *epsStream;
      NXStream  *tiffStream;
      char      *tiffData;
      int       tiffLen;
      id        image;
      int       maxLen;

      /* create EPS data from pasteboard */
      epsStream = NXOpenMemory(epsData, epsLen,
                      NX_READONLY);

      /* create a private zone */
      zone = NXCreateZone(vm_page_size,
                      vm_page_size, NO);
      NXNameZone(zone, "EPS Converter");

      /* create the image */
      image = [ [NXImage allocFromZone: zone]
              initFromStream: epsStream];
      [image setCacheDepthBounded: NO];

      /* write the TIFF to the new stream */
      tiffStream = NXOpenMemory(0, 0, NX_WRITEONLY);
      [image writeTIFF: tiffStream];

      /* send the TIFF back to the pasteboard */
      NXGetMemoryBuffer(tiffStream, &tiffData,
                      &tiffLen, &maxLen);
      [sender writeType: NXTIFFPboardType
              data: tiffData length: tiffLen];

      /* clean up */
```

```
        NXCloseMemory(tiffStream, NX_FREEBUFFER);
        NXDestroyZone(zone);
        vm_deallocate(task_self(),
                    (vm_address_t)epsData, epsLen);
        return self;
    }
  }
  return nil; /* failed */
}
```

This method uses *Mach memory zones*. A *zone* is a region of memory that is dedicated to a particular task. This method creates a zone with the function **NXCreateZone()** and then uses the **allocFromZone:** method to allocate an **NXImage** object from the zone that was just created. When the method is finished executing, it destroys the zone. Using zones for special purposes such as this reduces memory fragmentation and speeds application performance.

The second new thing about this method is that it reads information *off* the pasteboard in addition to putting data on the Pasteboard. The data is read off the Pasteboard with the method **readType:data:length:**. Data from the pasteboard arrives in the form of a Mach message and must be specially freed by using the **vm_deallocate()** function. Although these functions are more cumbersome than the traditional **malloc()** and **free()** C language functions, they are much faster, because the information is transferred directly from the address space of one application to another without having to be copied. This is why NeXTSTEP doesn't "choke" when you cut-and-paste hundreds or thousands of kilobytes of information at a time.

If the user quits GraphPaper after some of its data has been copied to the pasteboard, its **Application** object will automatically force the pasteboard owner to turn all of the lazy data into real data. This lets the user paste data into another application even if the source (application) of the data copied to the pasteboard is no longer running.

Implementing the Cut Command

Cutting data is similar to copying it, except the data is deleted after the copy operation is performed. For GraphPaper, it doesn't make a lot of sense to cut out a graph from the **ZoomScrollView**. But implementing it still makes sense from a user interface point of view (it's good practice to give the user the expected feedback from a well-known and widely used command). Therefore, if the user tries to cut a graph, GraphPaper copies the graph onto the pasteboard and then erases the **ZoomScrollView**.

4. Insert the **cut:** method implementation below into **Controller.m**.

```
-  cut:sender
{
  [self copy:sender];
  [graphView clear];
  return self;
}
```

Testing GraphPaper's Copy and Cut Commands

5. Save the **Controller** class files, **make** and run GraphPaper.

6. Graph an equation and move the cursor into the **ZoomScrollView** area (otherwise one of the **TextField**s might be the first responder).

7. Choose GraphPaper's **Edit→Copy** menu command to copy the graph to the pasteboard. GraphPaper's **Application** object will send the **copy:** message to its delegate **Controller** object.

8. Open a document in *WriteNow* (or your favorite word processor) and choose *WriteNow*'s **Edit→Paste** menu command. If the modifications to GraphPaper are correct and the word processor can handle the appropriate pasteboard types, you'll see the graph appear in your word processor document!

9. Now graph a different equation and move the cursor into the **ZoomScrollView** area.

10. Choose GraphPaper's **Edit→Cut** menu command this time. The graph should disappear.

11. Again choose the **Edit→Paste** menu command in the word processor and the second graph should appear.

12. Quit GraphPaper.

Services

In addition to cut, copy, and paste, NeXTSTEP provides a nearly transparent system for applications to work together called *Services*. Services work with NeXTSTEP's concept of "selection" to provide a system for automatically sending information from one application to accomplish a specific function in another. For example, if you are using the *Edit* text editor and do not have any text selected, your **Services** menu might look like the one on the left of Figure 1 below. If you select a word, say by double-clicking it, the **Services** menu will change and look like the one on the right of Figure 1. (The difference is that two services have been enabled.)

FIGURE 1. **Services Menu Before and After a Word Selection**

Edit		Services	
Info	▷	Define in Webster	=
File	▷	Grab	▷
Edit	▷	HeaderViewer	▷
Format	▷	Librarian	▷
Utilities	▷	Mail	▷
Windows	▷	NeXTtv	▷
Print...	p	Open in Workspace	
Services	▷	Project	▷
Hide	h	Terminal	▷
Quit	q		

Edit		Services	
Info	▷	Define in Webster	=
File	▷	Grab	▷
Edit	▷	HeaderViewer	▷
Format	▷	Librarian	▷
Utilities	▷	Mail	▷
Windows	▷	NeXTtv	▷
Print...	p	Open in Workspace	
Services	▷	Project	▷
Hide	h	Terminal	▷
Quit	q		

If you choose a **Services** menu command, such as **Define in Webster**, the word that you've selected, say "services," will automatically be sent to the Webster program and defined, as in Figure 2 below.

FIGURE 2. **Webster Application Defining a Selected Word**

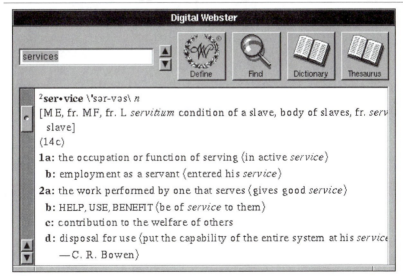

How Services Work

Unlike most menus, the **Services** menu is *not* controlled by the application in which it appears. Instead, the contents of the **Services** menu are controlled by the Workspace Manager!

When a user logs in, the Workspace Manager scans all of the applications in the standard applications paths (**/NextApps**, **/LocalApps**, **/NextDeveloper/Apps**, **/NextDeveloper/Demos**, and the user's **~/Apps** directory) looking for applications that advertise that they can handle the Services protocol.[1] This advertisement consists of a list of the messages that the program can handle, what sort of data types it can accept, and what kind it can return. For example, the *Webster* application's "advertisement" is given below:

```
Message: defineWord
Port: Webster
Send Type: NeXT plain ascii pasteboard type
Menu Item: Define in Webster
KeyEquivalent: =
```

It's also possible for an application to have a "Return Type:" field, but *Webster* doesn't. When a user runs an application, the application sends the following message to **NXApp** to register which types it can send and receive:

registerServicesMenuSendTypes : *sendTypes*
            andReturnTypes : *returnTypes*

sendTypes and *returnTypes* are both arrays of types similar to those used by **Pasteboard**'s **declareTypes:num:owner** method (except these arrays are null-terminated, instead of having their length explicitly coded). After the program starts running, the

validRequestorForSendType : (NXAtom) *typeSent*
            andReturnType : (NXAtom) *typeReturned*

method is sent down the responder chain for every combination of *send* and *return* types that the application can handle. If a responder can handle a particular combination, it should return something other than NULL. For

---

1. In NeXTSTEP 3.0, you can also control which Services appear in **Services** menus using the Preferences application.

example, the **Text** class implements this method returning **self** for the following combinations and NULL for all others:

Send Type	Return Type	Comments
NULL	NXAsciiPboardType	inserts new text
NULL	NXRTFPboardType	inserts new Rich Text
NXAsciiPboardType	NULL	send text, no return
NXRTFPboardType	NULL	send rich text, no return
NXAsciiPboardType	NXAsciiPboardType	
NXAsciiPboardType	NXRTFPboardType	
NXRTFPboardType	NXAsciiPboardType	
NXRTFPboardType	NXRTFPboardType	

The **validRequestorForSendType:andReturnType:** method is invoked often, so it should be as efficient as possible. Normally it will simply look for combinations of send and return types and return a value.

When the user selects an item from the **Services** menu, your object will be sent the message:

```
(BOOL)writeSelectionToPasteboard : pboard
                          types : (NXAtom *)types
```

This method is defined by the Application Kit as an addition (beyond the common class definition) to the **Object** class, so it can be sent to any object in your program. Normally, though, it will just be sent to objects that can handle selection. When your object gets the message, it should write whatever is selected to the paste board *pboard*. The method should return **YES** if the data can be provided and **NO** if it cannot.

If the service returns data, your object should also implement the message:

```
(BOOL)readSelectionFromPasteboard : pboard
                           types : (NXAtom *)types
```

If you are creating an object that does *not* handle selection, you do not need to implement or even worry about these methods. (The **Text** object is an example of an object that *does* handle selection.) For the remainder of this chapter, we will concentrate solely on the other half of the process – offering services to other applications.

Creating Your Own Service

Services advertisements, such as the one for the *Webster* application we
listed above, are stored in the application's __ICON section in a segment
named either __**request** or __**services**. (The **Services** menu was called
"request" under NeXTSTEP Release 1.0.) When the Workspace Manager
registers a new application, it opens up the __ICON section and looks for
the application's application icon, its document icons, and the application's
Services advertisement (if it exists). Workspace then caches this information to improve performance.

Here are all of the fields allowed in the Services advertisement:

Field	Meaning
Message:	The name of the message to be sent.
Port:	The name of the Mach port where the message should be sent.
User Data:	Additional data that should be provided to the method invoked (like a tag).
Send Type:	The pasteboard types that method can receive.
Return Type:	The pasteboard types that the method can return.
Menu Item:	The name of the menu item that should appear in the **Services** menu.
KeyEquivalent:	The key equivalent, if any, that the menu item should have.

Incoming Services messages are sent to a special delegate called the *Services delegate*. In NeXTSTEP releases 2.0 and 3.0, the Services delegate is
set by the application's **Listener** object, which is part of NeXTSTEP's
Speaker/Listener system. (In future releases of NeXTSTEP, **Speaker/Lis-
tener** will be replaced by NeXTSTEP's distributed object system.) The service methods use a private pasteboard to exchange data between the
sending and the receiving applications.

To respond to a Services message, you must implement a method in the
Services delegate object that has the form:

```
<serviceName>:pasteboard
        userData:(const char *)userData
        error:(char **)msg
```

Adding a Graph Service to GraphPaper

To show how Services work, we're going to modify the GraphPaper application so that it is accessible through the **Services** menu of other applications. The graph service will take a formula that has been selected by the user, graph it, and return the completed graph. In order to perform this operation, the method that implements the service will need to read a formula from the pasteboard, draw the graph, and then put the graph back on the pasteboard.

GraphPaper needs only a few minor modifications to work as a Service. In addition to properly advertising itself, we need to modify GraphPaper's **Controller** object so it reads the selected formula off the Services pasteboard and initiates the graph. We'll also need to modify the **GraphView** object so that it alerts the **Controller** when the graph is finished. Finally, we need to modify the **Controller** so that it sends back the completed graph when it's finished.

When GraphPaper is running as a Service, it will not use the standard NeXTSTEP event loop. Instead, it will run its own modal session.

A modal session is like the standard application event loop that we have used until now except the application object ignores events from all other windows except the window designated in the **runModalSession:** message. This is how NeXTSTEP implements Open and Save panels.

The **GraphView** object will signal that the graph is finished using the **stopModal:** method, which will return control to the **Controller** and signal for the completed graph to be sent back to the calling program.

1. Using an editor, create a file called **services.txt** in your **GraphPaper** project directory with the six lines below (it's important that there be no blank lines at the end of the advertisement, or else the Workspace Manager may not register the Service properly).

```
Message: graphEquation
Port: GraphPaper
Send Type: NXAsciiPboardType
Return Type: NXPostScriptPboardType
Return Type: NXTIFFPboardType
Menu Item: Graph/Equation
```

This advertisement tells Workspace Manager that your Service should have a single menu item called **Services→Graph→Equation** (see the last of the six lines), which responds to the message **graphEquation:userData:er-**

ror: (see the first line and the description of the **<serviceName>:userData:error:** method above).

2. Create a file called **Makefile.preamble** in your GraphPaper project directory with the following line:

```
LDFLAGS=-sectcreate __ICON __services services.txt
```

(Note that there are two underscore characters before the letters "ICON" and "services.")

This line tells the loader to create a segment called **__services** in the **__ICON** section of the executable from the **services** file.

3. Insert the instance variable below into **GraphView.h**.

```
BOOL runningAsService;
```

4. Insert the two method declarations below into **GraphView.h**.

```
- setRunningAsService:(BOOL)flag;
- formulaField;
```

We'll use the **runningAsService** instance variable to tell **GraphView** that it should stop the modal loop started in **graphEquation:userData:** method (which we'll discuss shortly).

5. Insert the three lines in **bold** below into the **stopGraph:** method in **GraphView.m**.

```
- stopGraph:sender
...
   [ [graphButton setTitle:"Graph"]
                   setAction:@selector(graph:)];

   if (runningAsService) {
      [NXApp stopModal:NX_RUNSTOPPED];
   }
   return self;
}
```

This addition causes the **stopModal:** message to be sent to GraphPaper's **Application** object when the graph is stopped or finished.

6. Insert these two accessor methods below into **GraphView.m**.

```
- setRunningAsService:(BOOL)flag
{
   runningAsService = flag;
   return self;
}
```

```
- formulaField
{
  return formulaField;
}
```

7. Insert the **graphEquation:userData:error:** and **appDidInit:** method declarations below into **Controller.h** (*not* **GraphView.m**).

```
- graphEquation:pasteboard
      userData:(const char *)userData
      error:(char **)msg;
- appDidInit:sender;
```

8. Insert the **graphEquation:userData:error:** method below into **Controller.m**.

```
- graphEquation:pasteboard
  userData:(const char *)userData error:(char **)msg
{
  id win = [graphView window];
  NXModalSession session;
  const NXAtom *types;
  char *formula;
  int formulaLen;
  char *buf;

  /* get the equation */
  for (types = [pasteboard types]; *types; types++){
    if (*types == NXAsciiPboardType) break;
  }
  if (*types == 0) {
    *msg = "Could not read equation";
    return nil;
  }

  if ([pasteboard readType: NXAsciiPboardType
        data: &formula length: &formulaLen]==nil) {
    *msg = "Could not read equation data";
    return nil;
  }

  /* create a null-terminated buffer on the stack */
  buf = alloca(formulaLen+1);
  memcpy(buf, formula, formulaLen);
  buf[formulaLen] = '\000';
  vm_deallocate(task_self(), (vm_address_t)formula,
                formulaLen);

  [ [graphView formulaField] setStringValue:buf];
```

```
   [win orderFront: nil]; /* bring window to front */
   [graphView setRunningAsService: YES];
   [graphView graph: self];

   /* run a modal session to service DPSWatchFD()
    * and get data from Evaluator
    */
   [NXApp beginModalSession: &session for: win];
   while(1) {
     if ([NXApp runModalSession:&session] !=
                                    NX_RUNCONTINUES)
       break;
   }
   [NXApp endModalSession:&session];

   [graphView setRunningAsService: NO];
   [self copyToPasteboard: pasteboard];
   [win orderBack: nil]; /* put window in back*/
   return self;
}
```

Although this **graphEquation:userData:error:** method is long, it's fairly
self-explanatory. The method first scans the pasteboard types available to
make sure that **NXAsciiPboardType** has been provided. (Note that you
must use the **types** method to find out what types are available; do not just
ask for the type that you want.) It then creates a second buffer for the formula (since the string returned by the pasteboard is not null-terminated),
and stuffs the string into the formula cell that is on the **graphView**.

Next, the method brings the GraphPaper window to the front of the display
list, sets the **runningAsService** instance variable, and starts the graph. It
then uses the application modal session commands to create a small loop
which processes events. Ideally, the lines:

```
   [NXApp beginModalSession:&session for:win];
   while(1) {
     if ([NXApp runModalSession:&session] !=
                                    NX_RUNCONTINUES)
       break;
   }
   [NXApp endModalSession:&session];
```

could be replaced with the statement:

```
   [NXApp runModalFor:win];
```

Unfortunately, this approach does not handle events properly in NeXT-STEP 3.0 due to a bug in the **Application** object.

When the modal session is finished, this method unsets the **runningAsService** flag, copies the graph to the pasteboard that was provided by the Services manager, and pushes the GraphPaper window to the back of the display list. The **copyToPasteboard:** method will put the EPS version of the graph on the pasteboard; if your application wants the TIFF version, it will be provided through lazy evaluation.

9. Insert the **appDidInit:** method below to the file **Controller.m**. (Recall that **Controller** is the delegate of the **Application** object.)

```
- appDidInit:sender
{
  [ [NXApp appListener] setServicesDelegate:self];
  return self;
}
```

This method sets the **Controller** object as the services delegate. You must do this in order to receive services messages.

Testing GraphPaper's Service

We need to install GraphPaper in one of the standard "apps" directories in order for its Service to be available to other applications. Look in Project Builder's Attributes view and you'll see **$(HOME)/Apps** in the **Install In:** text field. This refers the **Apps** directory under your home directory. If you have root access, you can install GraphPaper in other "apps" directories.

10. *Install* GraphPaper in your **~/Apps** directory by typing **install** in the **args:** field in PB's Builder view and then clicking the **Build** button. You can also install GraphPaper by typing the commands in **bold** below in a Terminal shell window.

```
localhost> cd ~/GraphPaper
localhost> make install
```

The installed version of GraphPaper is much smaller than the "regular" version because it has been "stripped."

11. Log out and log back in, so the Workspace Manager will register the GraphPaper and incorporate its Service into **Services** menus.

12. Start up a word processor (we'll use *WriteNow*) and enter an equation. Select it as in Figure 3 below.

13. Choose the **Services→Graph→Equation** menu command in the word processor. See Figure 4 below.

FIGURE 3. Selected Equation in WriteNow

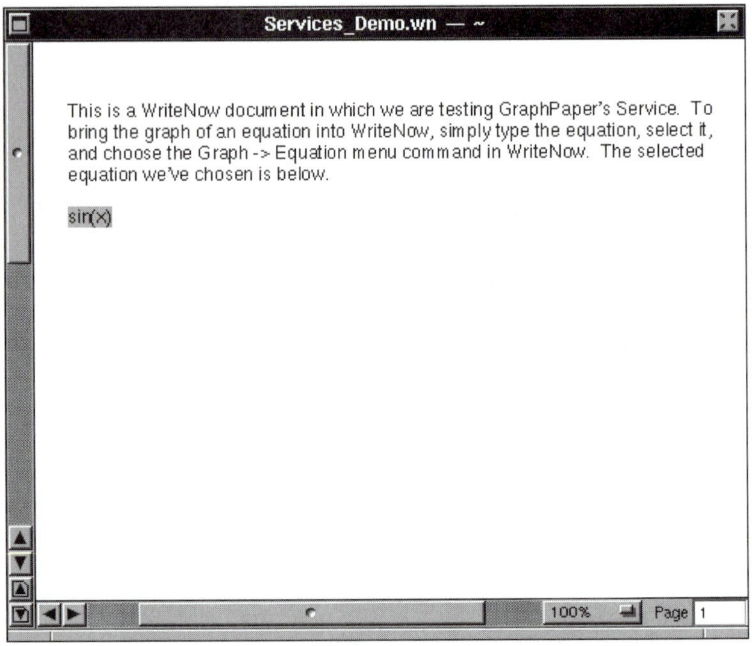

Services_Demo.wn — ~

This is a WriteNow document in which we are testing GraphPaper's Service. To bring the graph of an equation into WriteNow, simply type the equation, select it, and choose the Graph -> Equation menu command in WriteNow. The selected equation we've chosen is below.

sin(x)

100%   Page 1

FIGURE 4. The Graph Service Menu in WriteNow

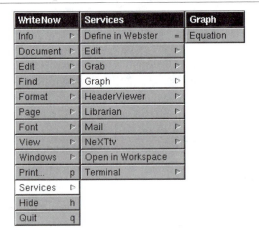

If it's not already running, the Workspace Manager will start up the Graph-Paper application. GraphPaper should then create the graph and then the graph should replace the selected formula in the word processor as in Figure 5 below.

FIGURE 5. A GraphPaper Graph in WriteNow

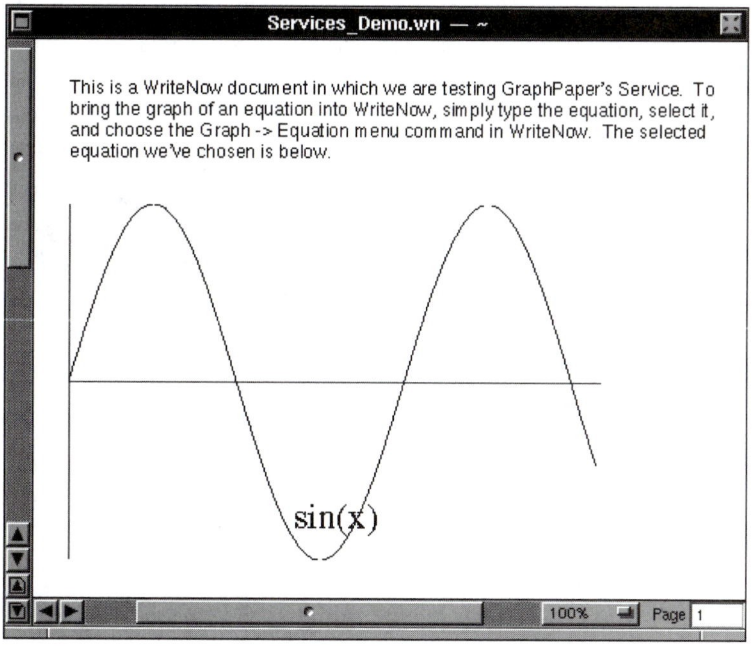

If you get an "Error providing services Equation" then you probably made a spelling error either in the **services.txt** file or the **Controller.m** file.

Unfortunately, as of this writing, few word processors are "smart" enough to realize that a service can take a text string and return an image. The GraphPaper application service does not correctly work with *Edit*, *WordPerfect*, or *FrameMaker*. Hopefully these programs will have their bugs fixed in the near future.

Summary

In this chapter we worked with two systems that NeXTSTEP uses for inter-application communication: the cut, copy, and paste system; and services. Using these features, you can greatly increase the power and usefulness of your applications by making their features available to other NeXTSTEP programs. In the next chapter, the last one in the book, we'll learn about the NeXTSTEP Preferences system.

21

Preferences and Defaults

If you've used an operating environment other than NeXTSTEP (like Microsoft Windows or X Windows), then you've probably had to worry about environment variables and configuration files. Such nuisances are pointedly missing from NeXTSTEP, which uses an object-oriented database to store all such configuration and user preference information.

The NeXTSTEP *defaults database* stores the preferences that you set in the Preferences panels of *all* applications. As a NeXTSTEP programmer, you can use the defaults system to store whatever information you want.

In this chapter, we'll modify the GraphPaper program to work with the defaults database system. We'll use the database to store the colors used to draw the graph, axes, and labels. In the second half of this chapter, we'll use the defaults system to store the initial values for the graph parameters. Then finally, we'll see how to create a multi-view inspector to switch between these two preferences options.

How Preference Defaults Work

NeXTSTEP stores your preference information in the two files, **.NeXTdefaults.D** and **.NeXTdefaults.L**, which reside in your **~/.NeXT** directory. Therefore, every user has his own defaults database. Each application can store whatever information it wishes in the database. Information in the database is stored by application name (called the *owner*) and preference name. *Global* preference values can also be stored in this database. Global preferences are used as defaults when a preference is not otherwise indicated by an application. Only printable ASCII text can be stored in the database.

Accessing the Information Stored in the Database

NeXTSTEP provides the three commands below for accessing the defaults database from the UNIX command line. For further information see the associated *man* pages.

Defaults Database Command	What It Does
dread	reads preferences from the database
dwrite	writes new preferences to the database
dremove	removes entries from the database

Let's use the "**dread -l**" command to see *all* the variables and defaults in a typical database:

```
localhost> dread -l
BackSpace priority 0
BackSpace screenSaver On
BackSpace viewType All
BackSpace windowType 0
Create ColorPickerH 200
Create ColorPickerW 318
Create ColorPickerX 61
Create ColorPickerY 446
Create NXFontPanelPreviewFrame "0 0 281 47"
Diagram ClickDragMove 1
Diagram InspectorIsOpen 0
Diagram NXFontPanelPreviewFrame "0 0 281 46"
Diagram ShowMarkers 1
Edit DeleteBackup NO
Edit "Find Panel" 53:316:391:189
Edit IndentWidth 3
Edit NXFixedPitchFontSize 14
```

```
Edit NXSwatchSize 22.000000
Edit PagesPerSheet 1
Edit Preferences 15:168:234:424
Edit Programmer YES
Edit RichText NO
FrameMaker AutoBackupOnSave On
FrameMaker AutoSave On
FrameMaker AutoSaveTime 5
FrameMaker GreekSize "7.0 pt"
FrameMaker LicenseStr <deleted>
FrameMaker NonDocWinLayer SubMenus
FrameMaker PrintPrologueCompression On
FrameMaker SerialNum 0-000
GLOBAL NXMenuX "    0"
GLOBAL NXMenuY " 833"
IconBuilder NXColorPanelMode 1
IconBuilder NXColorPickerSlidersDefaults 1
IconBuilder NXMenuLocations "4 826
IconBuilder NXSwatchSize 22.000000
IconBuilder docWidth 48
Installer ActionView "Progress View"
Installer VerboseList NO
Mail Archive YES
Mail KeyBindings YES
Mail LipService 452:538:346:103
Mail Mailboxes 864:59:191:464
Mail NXFont Helvetica
Mail NXFontPanelPreviewFrame "0 0 281 35"
Mail NXFontSize 12
Mail PollTime 1
NeXT1 AutoDimTime 40800
NeXT1 InitialKeyRepeat 15
NeXT1 KeyRepeat 2
NeXT1 MouseButtonsTied Yes
NeXT1 MouseHandedness Right
NeXT1 MouseScaling "5 2 2 3 4 4 6 5 8 6 10"
Preferences HideClockType 1
ProjectBuilder DeleteBackup Yes
ProjectBuilder Host ""
ProjectBuilder ServiceBuild Debug
SBook NXFontPanelPreviewFrame "0 0 281 47"
System Language English;French;German;Spanish
System OpenPanelFrame "328 242 463 456"
System Printer Local_Printer
System PrinterHost ""
System SavePanelFrame "411 257 418 419"
Terminal AutoFocus YES
Terminal Columns 80
```

```
Terminal Keypad NO
Terminal Meta 27
Terminal NXFixedPitchFont Ohlfs
Terminal NXFixedPitchFontSize 10
Terminal NXFontPanelFrame "178 -2 308 711"
Terminal NXFontPanelPreviewFrame "0 0 291 115"
Terminal Rows 24
Terminal Scrollback YES
Terminal Shell /bin/csh
TouchType NXFontPanelPreviewFrame "0 0 281 47"
VOID GameNumber 0
VOID Outline 0
VOID ShipType 0
VOID UserName ""
Webster DictionaryOpen YES
Webster ExactMatch YES
Webster FontSize 14
Webster Frames 115,198,515,381,2,71,303
Webster FullWordIndex NO
Webster PrintPictures YES
Webster ShowPictures YES
Webster ThesaurusOpen YES
WordPerfect NXFontPanelFrame "428 -3 298 749"
WordPerfect NXFontPanelPreviewFrame "0 0 281 133"
WriteNow InitialUntitled NO
WriteNow NXFontPanelPreviewFrame "0 0 281 40"
WriteNow NXFontSize 12.0
Yap NXFontPanelPreviewFrame "0 0 281 48"
Yap "NXWindow Frame NXFontPanel" "90 144 299 330 "
Yap "NXWindow Frame Output Window" "555 450 422 374 "
```

As you can see, practically every program used stores information in the defaults database. When storing information in the database, it is therefore important to pick a unique owner name so that the preferences from your application do not accidentally coincide with another's. NeXT recommends that commercial applications use the "full market name" of the application, which should be unique. NeXT further recommends that noncommercial applications use the name of the program and the author's name or institution name, for example, "MikeysTestProgram."

If you look through this list, you will see some common preference names stored in several applications. Two such preferences are **NXFontPanel-Frame** and **NXFontPanelPreviewFrame**, which get written into the database automatically by the NeXTSTEP **FontPanel** object. The **FontPanel** object uses the defaults database to remember its size and the size of the preview area between invocations of an application.

Adding Defaults to GraphPaper

In this section, we are going to modify the GraphPaper application to work with the defaults database. We will do this by making changes to both the **Controller** and the **ColorGraphView** classes.

NeXTSTEP provides ten functions for manipulating the preferences database from within your program. To use these functions, you need to create a *defaults registration table*, which contains a list of all of the default names that your application will use and their default values. (That is, the value that they should have for a new user running your program for the first time.)

NeXT recommends that you register your defaults in a method called **+initialize**. The **+initialize** method is a special *class* method that is invoked when your class is first used. The Objective-C runtime system assures that the **+initialize** message is sent once and only once to each class in your program. The **+initialize** message is always sent to a class's superclass before it is sent to the class itself.

1. Insert the *class* method declaration below into **Controller.h**.

```
+ initialize;
```

2. Insert the *class* method below into **Controller.m**.

```
+ initialize
{
    static NXDefaultsVector GraphPaperDefaults = {
        {"AxesColor", "0.3333333:0.3333333:0.3333333"},
        {"LabelColor", "0:0:0"},
        {"GraphColor", "0:0:0"},
        {"xstep", "0.1"},
        {"xmin", "0.0"},
        {"xmax", "10.0"},
        {"ymin", "-5.0"},
        {"ymax", "5.0"},
        {"Function", "sin(x)"},
        {NULL, NULL}
    };

    NXRegisterDefaults("GraphPaper",
                        GraphPaperDefaults);
    return self;
}
```

The **NXRegisterDefaults()** function creates the defaults registration table in memory. This table provides the default values for preference settings that have not been changed by the user.

Since the defaults system can only store printable ASCII characters, we will convert colors (e.g., *black* stored as an **NXColor**) into red, blue, and green triplets and store them in the defaults database separated by colons (e.g., "**0:0:0**"). The two functions we show below perform this conversion and its inverse.

3. Insert the two functions below into **Controller.m**. Place them *after* the **#import** directives but *before* the **@implementation** directive.

```
char *colorToASCII(NXColor color, char *buf)
{
   float   r, g, b;

   NXConvertColorToRGB(color, &r, &g, &b);
   sprintf(buf, "%f:%f:%f", r, g, b);
   return buf;
}

NXColor ASCIIToColor(const char *buf)
{
   float   r, g, b;
   sscanf(buf, "%f:%f:%f", &r, &g, &b);
   return NXConvertRGBToColor(r, g, b);
}
```

4. Insert the two function prototypes below into **Controller.h**. Place them *before* the **@interface** directive.

```
char      *colorToASCII(NXColor color, char *buf);
NXColor   ASCIIToColor(const char *buf);
```

We include these prototypes because these functions will be called from methods in the **ColorGraphView.m** file, which will import **Controller.h**.

Reading Values from the Defaults Database

When GraphPaper starts up, it will read the defaults database to discover the user's preferences for graph, axes, and label colors (we'll add the initial graph parameters to this list in a later section). To read the database we use the **NXGetDefaultValue()** function. This function has the prototype

```
const char *NXGetDefaultValue(const char *owner,
                              const char *name)
```

where *owner* is the name of your program and *name* is the name of the default that you wish to access.

The **NXGetDefaultValue()** function looks for the default value in the four locations discussed below.

(i) The function first checks the UNIX command line that was used to launch the program, if one exists. This lets you temporarily change the value of a preference for a single run of a program. The syntax on the command line is:

```
programName -name value {-name value, ...}
```

For example, suppose we had launched the GraphPaper application from the command line with

```
localhost> open GraphPaper.app -xstep 5
```

Then the function call

```
NXGetDefaultValue("GraphPaper", "xstep")
```

would return the value "5" instead of what was stored in the defaults database.[1]

(ii) If no command line value was given, the function next checks the user's defaults database for a default with the same owner/name combination.

(iii) If no owner/name combination is found in the defaults database, the function next checks for a default owned by GLOBAL with the same name.

(iv) If there is no global value for this default, the function returns the value that was specified in the registration table with the function **NXRegisterDefaults()**.

When your program starts up, it needs to read the user's default values and set the state of the associated objects in the application. **ColorGraphView**'s **setUp** method performs this function. Recall that in Chapter 17, we simply hard-coded values to use for defaults. Here's how we modify the method to work with the defaults system:

5. Insert the **#import** directive below into **ColorGraphView.m**.

```
#import "Controller.h"
```

---

1. This is the way that a program finds out if it was automatically launched by Workspace when the user logs in. If the program was auto-launched, the function call **NXGetDefaultValue(***owner***, "NXAutoLaunch")** returns the string "YES".

6. *Replace* the **awakeFromNib** method in **ColorGraphView.m** with the one below.

```
- awakeFromNib
{
  [super awakeFromNib];

  axesColor = ASCIIToColor(
    NXGetDefaultValue("GraphPaper","AxesColor") );

  labelColor = ASCIIToColor(
    NXGetDefaultValue("GraphPaper","LabelColor") );

  graphColor = ASCIIToColor(
    NXGetDefaultValue("GraphPaper","GraphColor") );

  return self;
}
```

The first time that the user runs GraphPaper, there are no values in the defaults database, and the **NXGetDefaultValue()** function calls in **awake-FromNib** return the values that were originally registered with the function **NXRegisterDefaults()** in the **+initialize** method. If the user changes his or her personal value for one of these defaults (using the Preferences panel, described below), the function **NXGetDefaultValue()** returns that new value instead.

Making the Preferences Panel Work with Defaults

Now that we've arranged for the **ColorGraphView** class to set its initial colors to those in the registration table or defaults database, we'll modify GraphPaper's Preferences panel to let the user see those values and change them. We'll use the same Preferences panel that we created back in Chapter 17, except that we'll add two new controls:

- An **OK** button, which will write the current values in the Preferences panel back into the defaults database. This button will send the **okay:** message to the Preferences panel controller object (**PrefController**).

- A **Revert** button, which will redisplay the information on the Preferences panel by reading it out of the database. This button will send the **revert:** message to **PrefController**. (Recall that we added the **okay:** and **revert:** action methods and **Unparse**(d) their skeletons in IB back in Chapter 17).

We'll modify the **PrefController** class so that it sends itself the **revert:** message the first time the panel is displayed. This will make **PrefController** read the values out of the registration table or defaults database.

Modifying the Preference Panel

7. Open GraphPaper's auxiliary nib file **preferences.nib** in Interface Builder.

8. Make the Preferences panel big enough so that you can add **Revert** and **OK** buttons as shown in Figure 1 below.

FIGURE 1. Preferences Panel with Revert and OK buttons

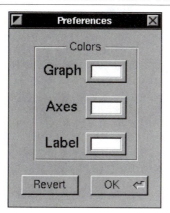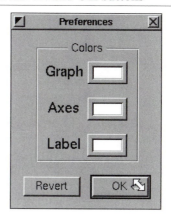

9. Add the **Revert** and **OK** buttons as in the panel on the left of Figure 1. To add the return icon (⏎) on the **OK** button, drag it from the Images view in IB's File window and drop it on the button.

    Note the link cursor (⬇) that you see when dropping the return icon on the button, as in the panel on the right of Figure 1. This link cursor means that the when the user hits the Return key while the panel is the key window, the button will act as if it was clicked. It's actually a connection involving a **performClick:** action message, which is sent to the button. It's easy!

10. Connect the **Revert** button to the **PrefController** instance icon so that it sends the **revert:** message.

11. Connect the **OK** button to the **PrefController** instance icon so that it sends the **okay:** message.

12. Save **preferences.nib**.

Changes to PrefController Class

The modifications that we need to make to the **PrefController** class are to implement the **revert:** and **okay:** methods, and to make modifications to the "set up" methods that set up the initial colors.

The **revert:** action method, which gets invoked when the user clicks the **Revert** button, simply replaces the current color of each color well on the Preferences panel with the value taken out of the defaults database.

13. Insert the lines in **bold** below into the **revert:** method in **PrefController.m** (the method stub should already be there).

```
- revert:sender
{
    [graphColorWell setColor:ASCIIToColor(
        NXGetDefaultValue("GraphPaper","GraphColor")) ];

    [labelColorWell setColor:ASCIIToColor(
        NXGetDefaultValue("GraphPaper","LabelColor")) ];

    [axesColorWell setColor:ASCIIToColor(
        NXGetDefaultValue("GraphPaper","AxesColor")) ];

    return self;
}
```

The **okay:** method is a bit more complicated.

14. Insert the lines in **bold** below into the **okay:** method in **PrefController.m** (the method stub should already be there).

```
- okay:sender
{
    char    buf[256];
    static NXDefaultsVector newDefaults = {
        {"LabelColor", ""},      /* 0 */
        {"AxesColor", ""},       /* 1 */
        {"GraphColor", ""},      /* 2 */
        {NULL, NULL}
    };

    newDefaults[0].value = alloca(256);
    strcpy(newDefaults[0].value,
            colorToASCII([labelColorWell color],buf));

    newDefaults[1].value = alloca(256);
    strcpy(newDefaults[1].value,
            colorToASCII([axesColorWell color],buf));
```

```
newDefaults[2].value = alloca(256);
strcpy(newDefaults[2].value,
       colorToASCII([graphColorWell color],buf));

NXWriteDefaults("GraphPaper", newDefaults);

[window orderOut:self];  /* dismiss panels */
[ [NXColorPanel sharedInstance:NO]
       orderOut:self];

return self;
}
```

This **okay:** method creates a new defaults vector (**newDefaults**) and fills the value for each of the properties with the ASCII representation of the appropriate color, as returned by the **NXColorWell** objects. Notice that we use the **alloca()** function to allocate memory; the memory allocated by this function is automatically freed when the method exits. This method also removes the Preferences and Colors panels from the screen after the database is updated.

Lastly, we need to modify **PrefController**'s **awakeFromNib** method so that the initial values for the **NXColorWell** objects in the Preferences panel are taken from the defaults database. The easiest way to do this is by invoking the **revert:** method we discussed above. We'll also take this opportunity to simplify the **setUpWell:tag:** method that sets up the tag and other default values of the **NXColorWell**s, so that the default color need not be specified. The simplified method has one less argument.

15. *Replace* the **awakeFromNib** method implementation in **PrefController.m** with the one below.

```
- awakeFromNib
{
  [ [NXColorPanel sharedInstance:YES]
      setContinuous:YES];
  [self setUpWell:axesColorWell tag:AXES_TAG];
  [self setUpWell:labelColorWell tag:LABEL_TAG];
  [self setUpWell:graphColorWell tag:GRAPH_TAG];
  [self revert:self];
  return self;
}
```

16. *Replace* the **setUpWell:defaultColor:tag:** method *declaration* in **PrefController.h** with the **setUpWell:tag:** declaration below.

```
- setUpWell:well tag:(int)aTag;
```

17. *Replace* the **setUpWell:defaultColor:tag:** method *implementation* in **PrefController.m** with the **setUpWell:tag:** implementation below.

```
- setUpWell:well tag:(int)aTag
{
  [well setTag:aTag];
  [well setContinuous:YES];
  [well setTarget:[ [NXApp delegate] graphView] ];
  [well setAction:@selector(setObjectColor:) ];
  return self;
}
```

Testing the Updated Preferences Panel

18. Save all pertinent files and **make** and run GraphPaper.

19. Graph a function and choose the **Info→Preferences** menu command to bring up the Preferences panel.

20. Change some colors and click the **Revert** button; notice how the old colors return to the Preferences panel.

21. Change some colors and click **OK**.

22. Quit GraphPaper.

23. Run GraphPaper again. Notice how the values that you set in the Preferences panel during the last run of the program are still in effect.

24. To see the values written into the defaults database, open up a Terminal shell window and enter the **dread** command below. Before entering the **dread** command below, we used GraphPaper's Preferences panel to change the Axes color to red, Graph color to green, and Label color to blue. The numbers are the ASCII representations of red, blue, and green values.

```
localhost> dread -o GraphPaper
GraphPaper AxesColor 1.000000:0.000000:0.000000
GraphPaper GraphColor 0.000000:1.000000:0.000000
GraphPaper LabelColor 0.000000:0.000000:1.000000
localhost>
```

There may be other GraphPaper defaults, such as

```
GraphPaper NXColorPanelMode 6
```

that will show up when you enter the **dread** command. These are automatically generated by NeXTSTEP. We'll discuss additional defaults for GraphPaper in the next section.

Setting Up a Multi-View Panel

In this section, we're going to change the Preferences panel into a multi-view panel, so that we can use it to change either the initial colors or the initial graph parameters (e.g., **xmin**, **ymax**). Figure 2 below shows the pop-up list and two **View**s which will show up in the new Preferences panel. The **View** that shows up depends on which item (**Colors** or **Initial**) in the pop-up list the user chooses. In the final section of this chapter (and the book!), we'll modify **GraphView** to read its initial graph conditions out of the defaults database.

FIGURE 2. **The Two Views of the Multi-View Preferences Panel**

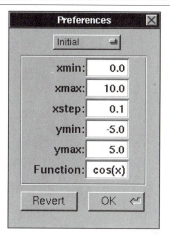

Multi-View Panels

The basic idea behind a multi-view panel is having a single panel that can be used to look at a variety of different **View**s. Usually, the **View** selection is implemented with an on-screen pop-up list.

The way we're going to implement the multi-view panel is by putting the various content **View**s for the Preferences panel on a second panel, which we'll title "Holding Place" (see Figure 3 below). The Preferences panel will contain **PopUpList** and **Box** objects, as in Figure 4 below. When a user chooses a pop-up list item in the Preferences panel, the appropriate content **View** (a **Box** with contents) will be copied from the Holding Place panel and into the **Box** in the Preferences panel. This is similar to the way that we put auxiliary **View**s in the Save panel in Chapter 19.

FIGURE 3. **The Holding Place Panel**

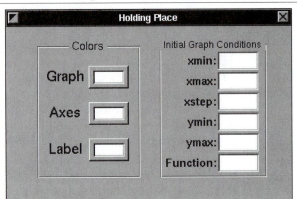

FIGURE 4. **Finished Preferences Panel in IB**

First we'll show the modifications necessary to the **PrefController** class to make all this work.

1. Insert the three instance variables and two method declarations in **bold** below into **PrefController.h**.

```
#import <appkit/appkit.h>
@interface PrefController:Object
...
    /* instance variables for multi-view inspector */
    id   colorView;
    id   initialView;
```

```
    id   multiView;
}
...
- setPref:sender;
- setPrefToView:theView;
@end
```

The **colorView** and **initialView** outlets will store the **ids** of the **View**s (**Box**es in the Holding Place panel) that we will eventually copy into our multi-view Preferences panel. The **multiView** outlet will store the **id** of the **Box** (in the Preferences panel) into which we'll copy those **View**s.

To implement the multi-view panel, we'll add two new methods to the **PrefController** class. The first, called **setPref:,** will be invoked whenever the user drags to an item in the pop-up list that changes the **View**.

2. Insert the **setPref:** method below into **PrefController.m.**

```
- setPref:sender
{
  id newView = nil;

  switch ( [ [sender selectedCell] tag]) {
    case 0:  newView = [colorView contentView];
             break;
    case 1:  newView = [initialView contentView];
             break;
  }

  [self setPrefToView:newView];
  return self;
}
```

This method determines which **View** the user chose by looking at the **tag** of the **PopUpList** cell (item) which sent the message. It then gets the content **View** of the appropriate box and invokes the **setPrefToView:** method, shown below.

3. Insert the **setPrefToView:** method below into **PrefController.m.**

```
- setPrefToView:theView
{
  NXRect boxRect, viewRect;

  [multiView getFrame:&boxRect];
  [theView getFrame:&viewRect];

  [multiView setContentView:theView];
```

```
NX_X(&viewRect) =
   (NX_WIDTH(&boxRect)-NX_WIDTH(&viewRect)) / 2.0;
NX_Y(&viewRect) =
   (NX_HEIGHT(&boxRect)-NX_HEIGHT(&viewRect))/ 2.0;

[theView setFrame:&viewRect];/* center the view */
[multiView display];
return self;
}
```

This **setPrefToView:** method is deceptively simple. First it makes **theView** the content **View** of the **Box** that is pointed to by the **multiView** outlet. The method then gets the frame of the **View** on the multi-view box, the frame of the **View** that is being dropped in, and centers the second in the first. Finally it invokes the **display** method so the appropriate **View** is displayed.

We'll also need to make a small modification to **PrefController**'s **awake-FromNib** method so that one of the **View**s is selected when the Preferences panel is initially displayed.

4.   Insert the line in **bold** below into the **awakeFromNib** method in **PrefController.m**.

```
- awakeFromNib
...
  [self revert:self];
  [self setPrefToView:[colorView contentView] ];
  return self;
}
```

Changes to the Interface

The next step is to create the **View**s for the Preferences panel and to add the appropriate connections to **preferences.nib**.

5.   Open **preferences.nib** in Interface Builder.

6.   **Parse** the **PrefController** class to bring in its new outlets and action.

7.   Drag a **Panel** icon from IB's Windows palette and drop it in the workspace. This new panel will hold the **View**s which will be displayed in the multi-view panel.

8.   Rename the panel "**Holding Place**" and set its attributes to be **Nonretained** and *not* **Visible at Launch Time**.

9. Cut the **Box** from the Preferences panel and paste it into the Holding Place panel as follows: select the "Colors" **Box** and its contents in the Preferences panel, choose IB's **Edit→Cut**, click in the **Holding Place** panel, and choose IB's **Edit→Paste**.

Note that it is critical that all of the objects you choose be grouped inside the **Box**, rather than merely be resting on top of it. In this case, the group does more than make the panel visually pleasing. It makes all of the objects subviews of the **Box** object. We can then manipulate the objects as a whole by manipulating that **Box**. You can tell if the items are in the **Box** by clicking on the **Box** to select it and then moving the **Box**. If the objects move with the **Box**, then they are grouped inside it.

10. Reconnect each "well" outlet in **PrefController** instance to the appropriate **NXColorWell** object (IB automatically breaks all connections when an object is pasted).

11. Connect the **colorView** outlet in the **PrefController** instance to the Colors **Box** in the Holding Place panel.

Now we'll set up the "Initial Graph Conditions" **Box** in the Holding Place panel as in Figure 5 below.

FIGURE 5. The Holding Place Panel

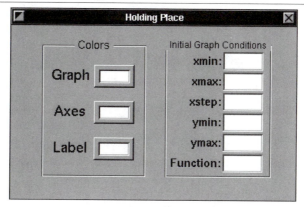

12. Drag a **Form** object from IB's Views palette and drop it in the panel.

13. Alt-drag on the bottom middle handle of the **Form** to create four more **FormCells**. Label the six **FormCells** as in Figure 5.

14. Set the text in the **Form** to be right aligned and choose a font.

15. Choose **Format→Layout→Group** to group the **FormCell**s in a **Box** and give the **Box** the title "Initial Graph Conditions."

16. Connect the **initialView** outlet in the **PrefController** instance to the Initial Graph Conditions **Box** in the Holding Place panel.

17. Connect the **Form** to the **OK** button (in the separate Preferences panel) so that it sends the **performClick:** message. This will let the user hit Return after entering initial values.

18. Drag a **Box** icon from IB's Views palette and drop it in the middle of the Preferences panel, above the **Revert** and **OK** buttons. This **Box** will hold the **View** that will change contents for the multi-view.

19. Resize the **Box** and delete its title (select **No Title** in the Box Attributes Inspector) so it looks like the one in Figure 4 above.

20. Connect the **PrefController** instance's **multiView** outlet to the **Box** in the new Preferences panel.

21. Drag a **PopUpList** from IB's Views palette and drop it above the **Box** you just added in the Preferences panel.

22. Set up two cells (items) in this **PopUpList** with the following titles and tags:

Title	Tag
Colors	0
Initial	1

23. Connect the two **PopUpList** cells to the **PrefController** instance so that they both send the **setPref:** message.

Defaults for Initial Values

Lastly, we'll modify the **GraphView** class to set up the initial parameters of the graph – **xmin**, **xmax**, and **xstep** for the **x** variable, **ymin** and **ymax** for the **y** variable, and the initial function (formula) to graph. Then we'll modify **PrefController**'s **okay:** and **revert:** methods so that they save the initial values in the database.

The changes needed in **GraphView.m** are very similar to the modifications we made to **ColorGraphView.m** to take initial values for the color wells; we simply take a default value out of the database and stuff it into a cell. We'll put those modifications in **GraphView**'s **setUp** method.

24. Insert the lines in **bold** below into the **awakeFromNib** method in **GraphView.m**.

```
- awakeFromNib
...
   [graphProc dpsWatchFD:gotGraphData data:self
     priority:NX_RUNMODALTHRESHOLD];

   [xminCell setStringValue:
       NXGetDefaultValue("GraphPaper", "xmin") ];
   [xmaxCell setStringValue:
       NXGetDefaultValue("GraphPaper", "xmax") ];
   [xstepCell setStringValue:
       NXGetDefaultValue("GraphPaper", "xstep") ];
   [yminCell setStringValue:
       NXGetDefaultValue("GraphPaper", "ymin") ];
   [ymaxCell setStringValue:
       NXGetDefaultValue("GraphPaper", "ymax") ];
   [formulaField setStringValue:
       NXGetDefaultValue("GraphPaper", "Formula")];

   return self;
}
```

We need to add six outlets to the **PrefController** so that we can read the contents of the initial values and save them in the defaults database.

25. Insert the six new outlets below into **PrefController.h**.

```
/* for initial values */
id   xminCell;
id   xmaxCell;
id   xstepCell;
id   yminCell;
id   ymaxCell;
id   formulaField;
```

26. Insert the lines in **bold** below into the **revert:** method in **PrefController.m**.

```
- revert:sender
...
   [axesColorWell setColor:ASCIIToColor(
     NXGetDefaultValue("GraphPaper", "AxesColor"))];

   [xminCell setStringValue:
       NXGetDefaultValue("GraphPaper", "xmin")];
   [xmaxCell setStringValue:
       NXGetDefaultValue("GraphPaper", "xmax")];
   [xstepCell setStringValue:
       NXGetDefaultValue("GraphPaper", "xstep")];
   [yminCell setStringValue:
```

```
            NXGetDefaultValue("GraphPaper", "ymin")];
    [ymaxCell setStringValue:
            NXGetDefaultValue("GraphPaper", "ymax")];
    [formulaField setStringValue:
            NXGetDefaultValue("GraphPaper", "Formula")];
    return self;
}
```

27. Insert the lines in **bold** below to the **okay:** method in
    PrefController.m.

```
- okay:sender
{
    static NXDefaultsVector newDefaults = {
        {"LabelColor", ""}, /* 0 */
        {"AxesColor", ""},  /* 1 */
        {"GraphColor", ""}, /* 2 */
        {"xmin", ""},       /* 3 */
        {"xmax", ""},       /* 4 */
        {"xstep", ""},      /* 5 */
        {"ymin", ""},       /* 6 */
        {"ymax", ""},       /* 7 */
        {"Formula", ""},    /* 8 */
        {NULL, NULL}
    };

    ...
    newDefaults[2].value = alloca(256);
    strcpy(newDefaults[2].value,
            colorToASCII([graphColorWell color],buf));

    newDefaults[3].value =
                (char *) [xminCell stringValue];
    newDefaults[4].value =
                (char *) [xmaxCell stringValue];
    newDefaults[5].value =
                (char *) [xstepCell stringValue];
    newDefaults[6].value =
                (char *) [yminCell stringValue];
    newDefaults[7].value =
                (char *) [ymaxCell stringValue];
    newDefaults[8].value =
                (char *) [formulaField stringValue];

    NXWriteDefaults("GraphPaper", newDefaults);

    [window orderOut:self ];  /* dismiss panels */
    [ [NXColorPanel sharedInstance:NO] orderOut:self];
```

```
    return self;
}
```

28. Back in IB, **Parse PrefController**'s updated class definition in
    preferences.nib.

29. Connect each of the six new outlets in the **PrefController** instance to
    the appropriate **FormCell** in the **Form** in the Holding Place panel.

30. Save all pertinent files and **make** and run GraphPaper.

31. Choose the **Info→Preferences** menu command to bring up the
    Preferences panel. You should see the defaults "Colors" **View**.

32. Press the pop-up list button in the Preferences panel and drag to **Initial**.

33. Enter values for all the initial parameters and click **OK** (or hit Return).
    The **OK** and **Revert** buttons work as before. See Figure 2 above.

34. Quit GraphPaper.

35. Now run GraphPaper again, and the initial values should show up in
    both the GraphPaper window and the Preferences panel.

36. Quit GraphPaper.

37. To see the values written into the defaults database, open up a Terminal
    shell window and enter the **dread** command below.

```
localhost> dread -o GraphPaper
GraphPaper AxesColor 0.333338:0.333338:0.333338
GraphPaper GraphColor 0.000000:0.000000:0.000000
GraphPaper xmax 10.0
GraphPaper xstep 0.1
GraphPaper ymax 5.0
GraphPaper ymin -5.0
GraphPaper Formula cos(x)
GraphPaper LabelColor 0.000000:0.000000:0.000000
GraphPaper NXColorPanelMode 6
GraphPaper NXSwatchSize 22.000000
GraphPaper xmin 0.0
```

38. Congratulate yourself for making it through this book! We salute you!

Summary

Well, we've finally come to the end of the book. In this chapter, you learned
the last of what you need to write a professional quality NeXTSTEP application program – how to use NeXTSTEP's defaults database.

Although there's lots more to write about NeXTSTEP, from here on you should be able to get most of what you need from the on-line documentation (or from our next book!). If you've been with us until now, you've learned the basics of NeXTSTEP's three main classes – **Application**, **View**, and **Window** – learned how they interact, and learned how to modify their functions as necessary to get done what you want.

NeXTSTEP establishes a framework into which all of the Application Kit objects neatly fit, like carved wooden pieces into a Chinese puzzle. The longer you program NeXTSTEP, the more you'll learn about using the pieces that NeXT provides, as well as adding your own.

Go out and write a killer app!

Appendix A:
Source Code Listings

The source code from the three major applications in the book, Calculator, MathPaper, and GraphPaper, is listed in this appendix. The source code consists primarily of our custom NeXTSTEP 3.0 class interface and class implementation files but also includes the **main**() function files generated by Project Builder. Within each application, the files are listed in alphabetical order.

Calculator Application

Source files included:

```
CalcWindow.h              CalcWindow.m
Calculator_main.m
Controller.h              Controller.m
```

CalcWindow.h

```
#import <appkit/appkit.h>

@interface CalcWindow:Window
{
```

```
        id keyTable;
}

- findButtons;
- checkView:aView;
- checkButton:aButton;
- checkMatrix:aMatrix;

@end
```

CalcWindow.m

```
#import "CalcWindow.h"

@implementation CalcWindow

- findButtons
{
  /* check all the views recursively */
  [keyTable empty];
  [self checkView:contentView];
  return self;
}


- checkView:aView
{
  id   subViews = [aView subviews];
  int  numSubViews = [subViews count];
  int  i;

/* Process the View if it's a Matrix or a Button. */
  if ([aView isKindOf: [Matrix class] ]) {
    return [self checkMatrix: aView];
  }

  if ([aView isKindOf: [Button class] ]) {
    return [self checkButton: aView];
  }

/* Recursively check all the subviews. */
  for (i=0; i<numSubViews; i++) {
    [self checkView:[subViews objectAt:i] ];
  }
  return self;
}
```

```
- checkButton:aButton
{
  const char *title = [aButton title];

/* Check for a cell that has a title that's exactly
 * one character long. Insert both uppercase and
 * lowercase versions for the user's convenience.
 */
  if (title && strlen(title)==1 &&
      [aButton tag] != 0x0c) { /* "c" for Clear */
    [keyTable insertKey: (void *)NXToLower(title[0])
              value: aButton];
    [keyTable insertKey: (void *)NXToUpper(title[0])
              value: aButton];
  }

  return self;
}


- checkMatrix:aMatrix
{
  id  cellList = [aMatrix cellList];
  int numCells = [cellList count];
  int i;

  for (i=0; i<numCells; i++) {
    [self checkButton: [cellList objectAt:i] ];
  }

  return self;
}


- keyDown:(NXEvent *)theEvent
{
  id button;

  button = [keyTable valueForKey:
           (void *)(int)theEvent->data.key.charCode];

  if (button) {
    return [button performClick:self];
  }

  return [super keyDown:theEvent];
}
```

```
- initContent:(const NXRect *)contentRect
    style:(int)aStyle
    backing:(int)bufferingType
    buttonMask:(int)mask
    defer:(BOOL)flag
{
  keyTable = [ [HashTable alloc] initKeyDesc:"i"];
  return [super initContent:contentRect
              style: aStyle
              backing:bufferingType
              buttonMask:mask
              defer:flag];
}

@end
```

Calculator_main.m

```
/* Generated by the NeXT Project Builder
   NOTE: Do NOT change this file --
   Project Builder maintains it.
*/

#import <appkit/Application.h>

void main(int argc, char *argv[]) {

  [Application new];
  if ([NXApp loadNibSection:"Calculator.nib"
      owner:NXApp withNames:NO])
  [NXApp run];
  [NXApp free];
  exit(0);
}
```

Controller.h

```
enum {
  PLUS     = 1001,
  SUBTRACT = 1002,
  MULTIPLY = 1003,
  DIVIDE   = 1004,
  EQUALS   = 1005
};

#import <appkit/appkit.h>
```

```
@interface Controller:Object
{
  id      readout;
  BOOL    enterFlag;
  BOOL    yFlag;
  int     operation;
  float   X;
  float   Y;
  id      infoPanel;
  int     radix;
  id      radixMatrix;
  id      keyPad;
  NXRect  originalViewSize;
}

- clear:sender;
- clearAll:sender;
- enterDigit:sender;
- enterOp:sender;
- displayX;
- doUnaryMinus:sender;
- showInfo:sender;
- setRadix:sender;
@end


@interface Controller(ApplicationDelegate)
- appDidInit:sender;
@end
```

Controller.m

```
#import "Controller.h"
#import "CalcWindow.h"

char *ltob(unsigned long val, char *buf)
{
  int i;

  for (i=0; i<32; i++) {
    buf[i] = (val & (1<<(31-i)) ? '1' : '0');
  }
  buf[32] = '\0';

  for (i=0; i<32; i++) {
    if (buf[i] != '0') return (&buf[i]);
  }
```

```
      return (&buf[31]);
}

@implementation Controller

- clear:sender
{
  X = 0.0;
  [self displayX];
  return self;
}


- clearAll:sender
{
  X = 0.0;
  Y = 0.0;
  yFlag = 0;
  enterFlag = 0;
  [self displayX];
  return self;
}


- enterDigit:sender
{
  if (enterFlag) {
    Y = X;
    X = 0.0;
    enterFlag = NO;
  }

  X = (X*radix) + [ [sender selectedCell] tag];
  [self displayX];
  return self;
}


- enterOp:sender
{
  if (yFlag) {          /* something is stored in Y */
    switch (operation) {
      case PLUS:
        X = Y + X;
        break;

      case SUBTRACT:
        X = Y - X;
```

```
              break;

          case MULTIPLY:
            X = Y * X;
            break;

          case DIVIDE:
            X = Y / X;
            break;
      }
    }

    Y = X;
    yFlag = YES;

    operation = [ [sender selectedCell] tag];
    enterFlag = 1;

    [self displayX];
    return self;
}


- displayX
{
    char buf[256];
    char bbuf[256];

    switch(radix) {
      case 10:
        sprintf( buf, "%15.10g", X );
        break;
      case 16:
        sprintf( buf, "%x", (unsigned int)X);
        break;
      case 8:
        sprintf( buf, "%o", (unsigned int)X);
        break;
      case 2:
        strcpy( buf, ltob( (int)X, bbuf ) );
        break;
    }

    [readout setStringValue:buf];
    return self;
}
```

```
- doUnaryMinus:sender
{
  X = -X;
  [self displayX];
  return self;
}


- showInfo:sender
{
  if (infoPanel == nil) {
    if ( ![NXApp
          loadNibSection: "info.nib"
          owner: self
          withNames: NO]) {
      return nil;              /* Load failed */
    }
  }
  [infoPanel makeKeyAndOrderFront: nil];
  return self;
}


- setRadix:sender
{
  int  i;
  id   cellList;
  int  oldRadix   = radix;
  id   keyWindow  = [keyPad window];

  radix = [ [sender selectedCell] tag];

  /* Disable the buttons that are
   * higher than selected radix
   */
  cellList = [keyPad cellList];
  for (i=0; i<[cellList count]; i++) {
    id cell = [cellList objectAt: i];
    [cell setEnabled: ([cell tag] < radix) ];
  }

  if (radix==16 && oldRadix != 16) {
                            /* make window bigger */
    NXRect keyFrame;
    NXRect newWindowFrame;
    [keyPad getFrame:&keyFrame];

    [keyWindow getFrame:&newWindowFrame];
```

```
        NX_WIDTH(&newWindowFrame) +=
                NX_X(&keyFrame) + NX_WIDTH(&keyFrame)
                - NX_WIDTH(&originalViewSize)
                + 4.0;
    [keyWindow
            placeWindowAndDisplay:&newWindowFrame];
  }
  /* placeWindowAndDisplay: gives a cleaner redraw
   * when making the window bigger.
   */

  if (radix != 16 && oldRadix == 16) {
                    /* make window smaller */
    [keyWindow
      sizeWindow:NX_WIDTH(&originalViewSize)
      :NX_HEIGHT(&originalViewSize)];
  }

  [self displayX];
  return self;
}

@end


@implementation Controller(ApplicationDelegate)

- appDidInit:sender
{
  id kwin = [keyPad window];

  [self setRadix:radixMatrix];
  [self clearAll:self];

  [ [kwin contentView] getFrame: &originalViewSize];
  [kwin findButtons];

  [ [ [keyPad window] contentView]
                    getFrame:&originalViewSize];
  return self;
}

@end
```

MathPaper Application

Source files included:

InfoView.h	InfoView.m
MathController.h	MathController.m
MathPaper_main.m	
PaperControl.h	PaperControl.m
Process.h	Process.m
RTF.h	RTF.m

InfoView.h

```
#import <appkit/appkit.h>

@interface InfoView:View
{
  DPSTimedEntry    animateTE;
  BOOL             animatingDrop;
  BOOL             animatingDissolve;
  int              animationStep;
  float            animationSize;
  float            animationFloat;
  id               symbolFont;
  id               bigTextFont;
  id               smallTextFont;
}

- initFrame:(const NXRect *)rect;
- animateInfo:sender;
- removeTE;
- windowWillClose:sender;
- animationClick;
- animateDrop;
- animateDissolve;
- drawSelf:(const NXRect *)rects :(int)rectCount;

@end
```

InfoView.m

```
#define SIZE 72.0
#import "InfoView.h"
#import "supershow.h"

void handler(DPSTimedEntry teNumber,
             double now, void *userData)
```

```
{
  id obj = (id)userData;
  [obj animationClick];
}

@implementation InfoView

- initFrame:(const NXRect *)rect
{
  [super initFrame:rect];

  symbolFont = [Font newFont:"Symbol"
                  size:SIZE
                  matrix:NX_IDENTITYMATRIX];

  bigTextFont = [Font newFont:"Times-Roman"
                  size:SIZE * .75
                  matrix:NX_IDENTITYMATRIX];

  smallTextFont = [Font newFont:"Times-Italic"
                  size:12.0
                  matrix:NX_IDENTITYMATRIX];

  return self;
}

- animateInfo:sender
{
  [self display]; /* clear the window */
  [self removeTE]; /* remove timed-entry, if nec.*/

  [window setDelegate:self];
  animatingDrop   = YES;     /* start with this */
  animationStep   = 0;       /* and this */
  animateTE       = DPSAddTimedEntry(.002,
                      (DPSTimedEntryProc)handler,
                      self,NX_BASETHRESHOLD);
  return self;
}

- removeTE
{
  if (animateTE) {
    DPSRemoveTimedEntry(animateTE);
    animateTE = 0; /* note that it's gone */
  }
  return self;
}
```

```
- windowWillClose:sender
{
  [self removeTE]; /* make sure it is gone */
  return self;
}


- animationClick
{
  if (animatingDrop)[self animateDrop];
  if (animatingDissolve) [self animateDissolve];
  NXPing();        /* synchronize with server */
  return self;
}


- animateDrop
{
  int    order[4] = {0,2,1,3};
  char   *dropstrings[4] = {"+","-","\264","\270"};
  float  const step = 2.0;
  float  x;
  float  y = NX_HEIGHT(&frame) - animationFloat;
  int    j = order[animationStep];

  [self lockFocus];
  [symbolFont set];

  x = ((SIZE * j * 2.0) / 3.0) + 10.0;

  supershow(x, y+step, NX_WHITE, dropstrings[j]);
  supershow(x, y, NX_BLACK, dropstrings[j]);

  animationFloat += 2.0;
  if (animationFloat >= NX_HEIGHT(&frame)) {
    animationFloat = 0;       /* reset Y */
    animationStep++;             /* go to next step */
    if(animationStep==4) {   /* go to next effect */
      animationStep = 0;
      animatingDrop = NO;
      animatingDissolve = YES;
      animationFloat = 0.0;
    }
  }
  [self unlockFocus];
  return self;
}
```

```
- animateDissolve
{
  id      image;
  NXPoint myPoint;
  NXSize  isize;
  float   x, y, width;
  char  *slgName ="Created by Simson L. Garfinkel";
  char  *mkmName =" tweaking by Michael K. Mahoney";

  [self lockFocus];
  [bigTextFont set];

  image = [NXImage findImageNamed:"app"];
  [image getSize:&isize];

  myPoint.x = NX_X(&frame) + 10.0;
  myPoint.y = NX_Y(&frame) + SIZE;

  x = myPoint.x + isize.width + 10.0;
  y = myPoint.y ;

  [image dissolve:animationFloat
          toPoint:&myPoint];        /* draw image */

  PSsetgray(1.0 - (animationFloat/2.0));
  PSrectfill(NX_X(&frame),
              SIZE, NX_WIDTH(&frame), 2.0);

  supershow(x, y, 1.0 - animationFloat,
          (char *)[NXApp appName]);

  animationFloat += 0.005;
  if(animationFloat < 1.0) {
    return self;
  }

  /* finish up */
  [smallTextFont set];

  width = [smallTextFont getWidthOf:slgName];
  supershow(NX_X(&frame)
              + NX_WIDTH(&frame) - width - 5.0,
              y-20.0, 0.0, slgName);

  width = [smallTextFont getWidthOf:mkmName];
  supershow(NX_X(&frame)
              + NX_WIDTH(&frame) - width - 5.0,
              y-35.0, 0.0, mkmName);
```

```
  [self removeTE];
  return self;
}


- drawSelf:(const NXRect *)rects :(int)rectCount
{
  PSsetgray(NX_WHITE);
  NXRectFill(&bounds);
  return self;
}

@end
```

MathController.h

```
#import <appkit/appkit.h>

@interface MathController:Object
{
  id newCalc;
  float offset;
  int calcNum;

  /* next three outlets for updating menu cells */
  id calculatorSubmenuCell;
  id saveMenuCell;
  id saveAsMenuCell;

  id infoView;
}

- newCalc:sender;
- loadCalc:sender;
- (int)countEditedWindows;
- saveAll:sender;
- (BOOL)menuActive:menuCell;
- showInfoPanel:sender;

@end
```

MathController.m

```
#import "MathController.h"
#import "PaperControl.h"
#import "InfoView.h"
```

```
@implementation MathController

- newCalc:sender
{
  id win;

  if ([NXApp loadNibSection: "paperwindow.nib"
             owner: self] == nil) {
    return nil;
  }

  if ([newCalc setUp]) {
    win = [newCalc window];

    if (win) {
      NXRect frame;
      char buf[256];

      [win getFrame: &frame];
      NX_X(&frame) += offset;
      NX_Y(&frame) -= offset;
      if ( (offset += 24.0) > 100.0) {
        offset = 0.0;
      }

      /* Note use of window's title as a format
       * string in the next line.
       */
      sprintf(buf, [win title], ++calcNum);
      [win setTitle: buf];
      [win placeWindowAndDisplay: &frame];
      [win makeKeyAndOrderFront: nil];
      return newCalc;
    }
  }
  return nil;
}


- loadCalc:sender
{
  char *types[2] = {"mathpaper", 0};

  if ([ [OpenPanel new] runModalForTypes:types]) {
    if ([self newCalc:self]) {
      [newCalc loadCalcFile:[ [OpenPanel new]
                                    filename] ];
    }
```

```
    }
    return self;
}


- (int)countEditedWindows
{
  id winList;
  int i;
  int count = 0;

  winList = [NXApp windowList];
  for (i=0; i<[winList count]; i++) {
    if ([[winList objectAt: i] isDocEdited])
      count++;
  }
  return count;
}


- saveAll:sender
{
  id winList;
  int i;

  winList = [NXApp windowList];
  for (i=0; i<[winList count]; i++) {
    id win = [winList objectAt: i];
    id delegate = [win delegate];

    if ([delegate isKindOf:[PaperControl class]]) {
      [win makeKeyAndOrderFront:nil];
      [delegate save:win];
    }
  }
  return self;
}


- (BOOL)menuActive:menuCell
{
  BOOL shouldBeEnabled;

  shouldBeEnabled = [[[NXApp mainWindow] delegate]
                      isKindOf:[PaperControl class]];

  if ([menuCell isEnabled] != shouldBeEnabled) {
    /* Menu cell is either enabled and shouldn't be,
```

```
          * or it is not enabled and should be.
          * In any event, set the correct state.
          */
        [menuCell setEnabled:shouldBeEnabled];
        return YES;   /* redisplay */
      }
      return NO;      /* no change */
    }



    - showInfoPanel:sender
    {
      if (infoView==0) {
        [NXApp loadNibSection:"info.nib"
                                          owner:self];
      }
      [ [infoView window] makeKeyAndOrderFront:self];
      [infoView animateInfo:self];
      return self;
    }

    @end



    @implementation MathController(ApplicationDelegate)

    - appDidInit:sender
    {
      id docMenu = [calculatorSubmenuCell target];

      [self newCalc:self];

      [saveMenuCell
          setUpdateAction: @selector(menuActive:)
          forMenu: docMenu];

      [saveAsMenuCell
          setUpdateAction: @selector(menuActive:)
          forMenu: docMenu];

      [NXApp setAutoupdate: YES];

       return self;
    }
```

```
- (BOOL)appAcceptsAnotherFile:sender
{
  return YES;
}


- (int)app:sender openFile:(const char *)filename
    type:(const char *)aType
{
  if ([self newCalc:self]) {
    if ([newCalc loadCalcFile:filename]) {
      return YES;
    }
  }
  return NO;
}


- appWillTerminate:sender
{
  if ([self countEditedWindows]>0) {
    int q = NXRunAlertPanel("Quit",
              "There are edited windows.",
              "Review Unsaved",
              "Quit Anyway", "Cancel");
    if (q==1) {            /* Review */
      int i;
      id winList;

      winList = [NXApp windowList];
      for(i=0; i<[winList count]; i++){
        id win = [winList objectAt: i];

        if([ [win delegate]
            isKindOf:[PaperControl class] ]){
            [win performClose:nil];
        }
      }
      return self;
    }
    if (q==-1) {          /* cancel */
      return nil;
    }
  }
  return self;            /* quit */
}

@end
```

MathPaper_main.m

```
/* Generated by the NeXT Project Builder
   NOTE: Do NOT change this file --
   Project Builder maintains it.
*/
#import <appkit/Application.h>

void main(int argc, char *argv[]) {

  [Application new];
  if ([NXApp loadNibSection:"MathPaper.nib"
       owner:NXApp withNames:NO])
  [NXApp run];
  [NXApp free];
  exit(0);
}
```

PaperControl.h

```
#import <appkit/appkit.h>

@interface PaperControl:Object
{
  id proc;
  id scroller;
  id text;
  id window;
  char *filename;
}

- setUp;
- window;
- windowWillClose:sender;
- text;
- setScroller:aScroller;
- appendToText:(const char *)val
     fromPipe:(BOOL)flag;
- setFilename:(const char *)aFilename;
- saveAs:sender;
- save:sender;
- loadCalcFile:(const char *)aFile;
- printCalc:sender;

@end
```

PaperControl.m

```
#define EVALUATOR_FILENAME "/Apps/Evaluator"

#import "PaperControl.h"
#import "Process.h"
#import "RTF.h"

/* printer: This function called transparently by the
 * NXApp object when data is available to read on fd.
 * We assume that it will be a full line,
 * and less than 1024 characters
 * (both safe assumptions here).
 */

void printer(int fd, void *data)
{
  id ctl = data;
  char buf[1024];
  int size;

  size = read(fd, buf, sizeof(buf)-1);
  if (size<0) DPSRemoveFD(fd); /* error occured */
  if (size<=0) return;
  buf[size] = '\000';

  [ctl appendToText: buf fromPipe:YES];
  [ctl appendToText: "_____\n"
          fromPipe: NO];

  /* allow new responses */

  [ [ctl text] setEditable: YES];
}


@implementation PaperControl

- setUp
{
  char *argv[2] = {0,0};

  argv[0] = malloc(strlen(NXHomeDirectory())+32);
  strcpy(argv[0], NXHomeDirectory());
  strcat(argv[0], EVALUATOR_FILENAME);

  proc = [ [Process alloc] initFromCommand:argv];
```

```
   if (!proc) {
    NXRunAlertPanel(0,"Cannot create calculator: %s",
                           0, 0, 0, strerror(errno));
      [window performClose: self];
      return nil;
   }

   [proc dpsWatchFD:printer data:self
        priority:NX_BASETHRESHOLD];
   return self;
}


- window
{
   return window;
}


- windowWillClose:sender
{
   if ([sender isDocEdited]) {
     const char *fname;
     int q;

     fname = filename ? filename : [sender title];
     if (rindex(fname,'/'))
                       fname = rindex(fname,'/') + 1;

     q = NXRunAlertPanel("Save",
             "Save changes to %s?",
             "Save", "Don't Save", "Cancel", fname);
     if (q==1) {          /* save */
       if (![self save:nil]) {
         return nil;  /* didn't save */
       }
     }
     if (q==-1) {        /* cancel */
       return nil;
     }
   }

   [sender setDelegate: nil];
   [proc free]; /* free Evaluator & Process object */
   [self free]; /* free PaperControl object */
   return self; /* Window will free itself on close */
}
```

```
- appendToText:(const char *)val fromPipe:(BOOL)flag
{
  int length = [text textLength];

  [window setDocEdited:YES];
  [text setSel:length :length];

  if (flag) {
    id rtf =
            [ [RTF allocFromZone:[self zone] ] init];

    [rtf bold:YES];
    [rtf setJustify:NX_RIGHTALIGNED];
    [rtf append:val];
    [rtf bold:NO];
    [rtf setJustify:NX_LEFTALIGNED];
    [rtf append:" "];
    [text replaceSelWithRichText:[rtf stream] ];
    [rtf free];
  }
  else {
    [text replaceSel:val];
  }

  [text scrollSelToVisible];
  [text display];

  return self;
}


- setScroller:aScroller
{
  scroller = aScroller;
  text = [aScroller docView];
  [text setDelegate:self];
  [text setCharFilter:NXFieldFilter];
  [text selectAll:self];
  return self;
}


- text
{
  return text;
}
```

```
- setFilename:(const char *)aFilename
{
  if (filename) free(filename);
  filename = malloc(strlen(aFilename)+1);
  strcpy(filename, aFilename);
  [window setTitleAsFilename:aFilename];
  return self;
}


- saveAs:sender
{
  id panel;
  const char *dir;
  char *file;

/* prompt user for file name and save to that file */

  if (filename==0) {
    /* no filename; set up defaults */
    dir = NXHomeDirectory();
    file = (char *)[window title];
  }
  else {
    file = rindex(filename, '/');
    if (file) {
      dir = filename;
      *file = 0;
      file++;
    }
    else {
      dir = filename;
      file = (char *)[window title];
    }
  }

  panel = [SavePanel new];

  [panel setRequiredFileType: "mathpaper"];
  if ([panel runModalForDirectory: dir
              file: file]) {
    [self setFilename: [panel filename] ];

    return [self save: sender];
  }
  return nil; /* didn't save */
}
```

```
- save:sender
{
  int fd;
  NXStream *theStream;

  if (filename==0) return [self saveAs: sender];
  [window setTitle: "Saving..."];

  fd= open(filename, O_WRONLY|O_CREAT|O_TRUNC,0666);
  if (fd<0) {
    NXRunAlertPanel(0, "Cannot save file: %s",
                         0, 0, 0, strerror(errno));
    return self;
  }

  theStream = NXOpenFile(fd, NX_WRITEONLY);
  [text writeRichText: theStream];

  NXClose(theStream);
  close(fd);

  [window setTitleAsFilename: filename];
  [window setDocEdited:NO];
  return self;
}


- loadCalcFile:(const char *)aFile
{
  NXStream *theStream= NXMapFile(aFile,NX_READONLY);
  if (theStream) {
    id ret = self;
    [window setTitle:"Loading..."];

    NX_DURING
    [text readRichText:theStream];
    [self setFilename:aFile];

    /* Exception handler is skipped
     * if no exception is raised.
     */
    NX_HANDLER
     switch(NXLocalHandler.code){
       case NX_illegalWrite:
         NXRunAlertPanel(0,"Illegal write on stream",
                            0,0,0);
         ret = nil;
         break;
```

```
            case NX_illegalRead:
              NXRunAlertPanel(0,"Illegal read on stream",
                                  0,0,0);
              ret = nil;
              break;

            case NX_illegalSeek:
              NXRunAlertPanel(0,"Illegal seek on stream",
                                  0,0,0);
              ret = nil;
              break;

            case NX_illegalStream:
              NXRunAlertPanel(0,"invalid stream",0,0,0);
              ret = nil;
              break;

            case NX_streamVMError:
              NXRunAlertPanel(0,"VM error on stream",
                                  0,0,0,aFile);
              ret = nil;
              break;
        }

    NX_ENDHANDLER   /* end of handler */


    NXCloseMemory(theStream, NX_FREEBUFFER);
    return ret;
  }
  return nil;
}


- printCalc:sender
{
  [text printPSCode:nil];
  return self;
}

@end


@implementation PaperControl(TextDelegate)

/* Invoked when the text ends.
 * Finds the last line and sends it down the pipe.
 */
```

```
- textDidEnd:sender endChar:(unsigned short)whyEnd
{
  NXStream *str;
  char     *lastLine;
  char     *buf;
  int      len,maxlen;

  str = NXOpenMemory(0, 0, NX_READWRITE);
  [sender writeText:str];
  NXGetMemoryBuffer(str, &buf, &len, &maxlen);
  lastLine = rindex(buf, '\n');
  if (lastLine) {
    lastLine++;        /* skip past '\n' */
  }
  else{
    lastLine = buf;    /* get first line */
  }

  if (strlen(lastLine) > 0){
    [proc writeLine:lastLine];
    [self appendToText:"\n" fromPipe:NO];
    [sender setEditable:NO]; /* wait for response */
  }
  NXCloseMemory(str, NX_FREEBUFFER);

  return self;
}

@end
```

Process.h

```
/*
 * Process.h: spawn and control a subprocess
 */
#import <appkit/appkit.h>

@interface Process:Object
{
  int toProcess[2];
  int fromProcess[2];
  int pid;
  BOOL fdHandlerInstalled;
}

- initFromCommand:(char **)argv;
- free;
```

```
- (int)toFd;
- (int)fromFd;
- writeLine:(const char *)aLine;
- dpsWatchFD:(DPSFDProc)handler
            data:(void *)userData priority:(int)pri;
@end
```

Process.m

```
#import "Process.h"

@implementation Process

- initFromCommand:(char **)argv
{
  [super init];

  if(argv==0 || argv[0]==0 || access(argv[0],X_OK)){
    return nil;      /* cannot execute command */
  }

  if (pipe(toProcess) == -1) {
    [self free];
    return nil;      /* could not open first pipe */
  }

  if (pipe(fromProcess) == -1) {
    close(toProcess[0]);
    close(toProcess[1]);
    [self free];
    return nil;      /* could not open second pipe */
  }

  pid = fork();

  if (pid == -1){
    [self free];
    return nil;                /* no more processes */
  }

  if (pid==0) {   /* executed by the child */
                  /* set up and execv */
    close(0);     /* stdin  */
    close(1);     /* stdout */

    close(toProcess[1]);
    close(fromProcess[0]);
```

```
      dup2(toProcess[0], 0);      /* stdin */
      dup2(fromProcess[1], 1);    /* stdout */

      close(2);                   /* stderr */
      dup2(fromProcess[1], 2);    /* stderr */

      execv(argv[0], argv);
      perror(NXArgv[0]);
      exit(1);
  }
                /* executed by the parent */
                /* close the other ends of the pipe */
  close(toProcess[0]);
  close(fromProcess[1]);
  return self;
}


- free
{
  if (fdHandlerInstalled)
                      DPSRemoveFD(fromProcess[0]);
  if (toProcess[1]) close(toProcess[1]);
  if (fromProcess[0]) close(fromProcess[0]);
  if (pid>0) kill(pid, 9);
  return [super free];
}


- (int)toFd
{
  return toProcess[1];
}


- (int)fromFd
{
  return fromProcess[0];
}


/* send a line to the process */
- writeLine:(const char *)aLine
{
  int len = strlen(aLine);

  write(toProcess[1], aLine, len);
```

```
    if (len>0 && aLine[len-1] != '\n') {
      write(toProcess[1], "\n", 1); /* courtesy */
    }
    return self;
}


- dpsWatchFD:(DPSFDProc)handler
              data:(void *)userData priority:(int)pri
{
  DPSAddFD(fromProcess[0], handler, userData, pri);
  fdHandlerInstalled = YES;
  return self;
}

@end
```

RTF.h

```
#import <appkit/appkit.h>
#import <streams/streams.h>

@interface RTF:Object
{
  NXStream *textStream;
}
- (NXStream *)stream;
- appendRTF:(const char *)string;
- append:(const char *)string;
- bold:(BOOL)flag;
- setJustify:(int)mode;
- free;

@end
```

RTF.m

```
#import "RTF.h"

const char *header =
  "{\\rtf0\\ansi{\\fonttbl\\f0\\fswiss"
  " Helvetica;}\\f0\n";

@implementation RTF

- init
{
```

```
  [super init];

  textStream = NXOpenMemory(0, 0, NX_READWRITE);
  NXWrite(textStream, header, strlen(header));
  return self;
}


- (NXStream *)stream
{
  NXSeek(textStream, 0L, NX_FROMSTART);
  return textStream;
}


/* appendRTF: appends an arbitrary RTF string
 * to the RTF object
 */
- appendRTF:(const char *)string
{
  NXSeek(textStream, 0L, NX_FROMEND);
  NXWrite(textStream, string, strlen(string));
  return self;
}


/* append: appends an ASCII text string, "escaping"
 * all of the special characters in the text.
 */
- append:(const char *)string
{
  if (string==0) return self; /* safety */

  NXSeek(textStream, 0L, NX_FROMEND);
  while(*string) {
    switch(*string) {
      /* escape special characters */
      case '\n':
      case '{':
      case '}':
      case '\\':
        NXPutc(textStream, '\\');
      break;
      default:
      break;
    }
    NXPutc(textStream, *string);
    string++;
```

```
  }
  return self;
}


- bold:(BOOL)flag
{
  [self appendRTF: flag ? "\\b " : "\\b0 "];
  return self;
}


- setJustify:(int)mode
{
  switch(mode) {
    case NX_LEFTALIGNED:
    case NX_JUSTIFIED:
      [self appendRTF: "\\ql "];
      break;
    case NX_CENTERED:
      [self appendRTF: "\\qc "];
      break;
     case NX_RIGHTALIGNED:
      [self appendRTF: "\\qr "];
      break;
  }
  return self;
}


- free
{
  NXCloseMemory(textStream, NX_FREEBUFFER);
  return [super free];
}

@end
```

GraphPaper Application

Source files included:

Controller.h   Controller.m
GraphPaper_main.m
GraphView.h   GraphView.m
Label.h   Label.m
PrefController.h   PrefController.m
Process.h   Process.m
Segment.h   Segment.m
TrackGraphView.h   TrackGraphView.m
ZoomScrollView.h   ZoomScrollView.m

Controller.h

```
#import <appkit/appkit.h>

   char     *colorToASCII(NXColor color, char *buf);
   NXColor  ASCIIToColor(const char *buf);


@interface Controller:Object
{
   id graphView;
   id prefController;
   id formatBox;
   id formatMatrix;
}

- graphView;
- showPrefs:sender;
- save:sender;
- copyPSToStream:(NXStream *)aStream forView:view;
- copyTIFFToStream:(NXStream *)aStream forView:view;
- setFormat:sender;
- copyToPasteboard:pboard;
- copy:sender;
- pasteboard:sender provideData:(NXAtom)type;
- cut:sender;
- graphEquation:pasteboard
       userData:(const char *)userData
       error:(char **)msg;
- appDidInit:sender;
+ initialize;

@end
```

Controller.m

```
#import "Controller.h"
#import "GraphView.h"

char *colorToASCII(NXColor color, char *buf)
{
  float   r, g, b;

  NXConvertColorToRGB(color, &r, &g, &b);
  sprintf(buf, "%f:%f:%f", r, g, b);
  return buf;
}

NXColor ASCIIToColor(const char *buf)
{
  float   r, g, b;
  sscanf(buf, "%f:%f:%f", &r, &g, &b);
  return NXConvertRGBToColor(r, g, b);
}


@implementation Controller

- graphView
{
  return graphView;
}


- showPrefs:sender
{
  if (!prefController) {
    [NXApp loadNibSection: "preferences.nib"
          owner: self];
  }
  [ [prefController window]
    makeKeyAndOrderFront:sender];
  return self;
}


- save:sender
{
  id save = [SavePanel new];

  /* set the initial format */
  [self setFormat:formatMatrix];
```

```
      /* put format box in View */
      [save setAccessoryView:formatBox];

      if ([save runModal]==1) {
        NXStream *aStream;

        aStream = NXOpenMemory(0,0,NX_WRITEONLY);
        if (!strcmp([ [formatMatrix selectedCell]
                    title], "EPS")) {
          [self copyPSToStream: aStream
                      forView: graphView];
        }
        else {
          [self  copyTIFFToStream: aStream
                  forView: graphView];
        }
        NXSaveToFile(aStream, [save filename]);
        NXCloseMemory(aStream, NX_FREEBUFFER);
      }
      return self;
}


- copyPSToStream:(NXStream *)aStream forView:view
{
  NXRect bounds;

  [view getBounds:&bounds];
  [view copyPSCodeInside:&bounds to:aStream];
  return self;
}


- copyTIFFToStream:(NXStream *)aStream forView:view
{
  NXRect     bounds;
  id         image;
  NXStream   *workStream;

  /* Capture the PostScript output */

  workStream = NXOpenMemory(0,0,NX_READWRITE);
  [view getBounds: &bounds];
  [view copyPSCodeInside: &bounds to: workStream];

  /* Read the PostScript into an NXImage object */
  NXSeek(workStream,0L,NX_FROMSTART);
```

```
    image = [[NXImage alloc]
              initFromStream: workStream];

    /* The following statement forces the
     * NXImage object to set its bits-per-pixel depth
     * to be the maximum specified in the PostScript
     * stream, rather than have the depth limited by
     * the user's current display.
     */

    [image setCacheDepthBounded:NO];

    /* Have the image write its output as a TIFF
     * to requested stream
     */
    [image writeTIFF: aStream];
    [image free];

    /* Close our work output */
    NXCloseMemory(workStream,NX_FREEBUFFER);

    return self;
}


- setFormat:sender
{
    char *format;
    char *cc;

    format = NXCopyStringBuffer(
                     [ [sender selectedCell] title]);
    for (cc=format; *cc; cc++) {
        *cc = NXToLower(*cc);
    }
    [ [SavePanel new] setRequiredFileType:format];
    free(format);
    return self;
}


- copyToPasteboard:pboard
{
    NXStream *stream;
    char *data;
    int length, maxlen;

    NXAtom typelist[2];
```

```
    typelist[0] = NXPostScriptPboardType;
    typelist[1] = NXTIFFPboardType;
    [pboard declareTypes: typelist num: 2 owner:self];

/* Now put the EPS on the pasteboard */
    stream = NXOpenMemory(0, 0, NX_WRITEONLY);
    [self copyPSToStream: stream forView: graphView];
    NXGetMemoryBuffer(stream, &data, &length,&maxlen);
    [pboard writeType: NXPostScriptPboardType
                 data: data length: length];
    NXCloseMemory(stream, NX_FREEBUFFER);
    return self;
}


- copy:sender
{
  [self copyToPasteboard: [Pasteboard new] ];
  return self;
}


/* Invoked to convert EPS to TIFF.
 * Done in its own zone, which is later destroyed.
 */
- pasteboard:sender provideData:(NXAtom)type
{
  if (type==NXTIFFPboardType) {
    char *epsData;
    int epsLen;

    if ([sender readType: NXPostScriptPboardType
          data: &epsData length: &epsLen]) {
      NXZone   *zone;
      NXStream *epsStream;
      NXStream *tiffStream;
      char     *tiffData;
      int      tiffLen;
      id       image;
      int      maxLen;

      /* create EPS data from pasteboard */
      epsStream = NXOpenMemory(epsData, epsLen,
                              NX_READONLY);

      /* create a private zone */
      zone = NXCreateZone(vm_page_size,
                        vm_page_size, NO);
```

```
        NXNameZone(zone, "EPS Converter");

        /* create the image */
        image = [ [NXImage allocFromZone: zone]
                initFromStream: epsStream];
        [image setCacheDepthBounded: NO];

        /* write the TIFF to the new stream */
        tiffStream = NXOpenMemory(0, 0, NX_WRITEONLY);
        [image writeTIFF: tiffStream];

        /* send the TIFF back to the pasteboard */
        NXGetMemoryBuffer(tiffStream, &tiffData,
                            &tiffLen, &maxLen);
        [sender writeType: NXTIFFPboardType
                data: tiffData length: tiffLen];

        /* clean up */
        NXCloseMemory(tiffStream, NX_FREEBUFFER);
        NXDestroyZone(zone);
        vm_deallocate(task_self(),
                    (vm_address_t)epsData, epsLen);
        return self;
    }
  }

  return nil; /* failed */
}


- cut:sender
{
  [self copy:sender];
  [graphView clear];
  return self;
}


- graphEquation:pasteboard
  userData:(const char *)userData error:(char **)msg
{
  id win = [graphView window];
  NXModalSession session;
  const NXAtom *types;
  char *formula;
  int formulaLen;
  char *buf;
```

```
/* get the equation */
for (types = [pasteboard types]; *types; types++){
  if (*types == NXAsciiPboardType) break;
}
if (*types == 0) {
  *msg = "Could not read equation";
  return nil;
}

if ([pasteboard readType: NXAsciiPboardType
       data: &formula length: &formulaLen]==nil) {
  *msg = "Could not read equation data";
  return nil;
}

/* create a null-terminated buffer on the stack */
buf = alloca(formulaLen+1);
memcpy(buf, formula, formulaLen);
buf[formulaLen] = '\000';
vm_deallocate(task_self(), (vm_address_t)formula,
                 formulaLen);

[ [graphView formulaField] setStringValue:buf];

[win orderFront: nil]; /* bring window to front */
[graphView setRunningAsService: YES];
[graphView graph: self];

/* run a modal session to service DPSWatchFD()
 * and get data from Evaluator
 */
[NXApp beginModalSession: &session for: win];
while(1) {
  if ([NXApp runModalSession:&session] !=
                             NX_RUNCONTINUES)
    break;
}
[NXApp endModalSession:&session];

[graphView setRunningAsService: NO];
[self copyToPasteboard: pasteboard];
[win orderBack: nil]; /* put window in back*/
return self;
}
```

```
- appDidInit:sender
{
  [ [NXApp appListener] setServicesDelegate:self];
  return self;
}


+ initialize
{
  static NXDefaultsVector GraphPaperDefaults = {
    {"LabelColor", "0:0:0"},
    {"AxesColor", "0.3333333:0.3333333:0.3333333"},
    {"GraphColor", "0:0:0"},
    {"xstep", "0.1"},
    {"xmin", "0.0"},
    {"xmax", "10.0"},
    {"ymin", "-5.0"},
    {"ymax", "5.0"},
    {"Function", "sin(x)"},
    {NULL, NULL}
  };

  NXRegisterDefaults("GraphPaper",
                        GraphPaperDefaults);
  return self;
}

@end
```

GraphPaper_main.m

```
/* Generated by the NeXT Project Builder
   NOTE: Do NOT change this file --
   Project Builder maintains it.
*/

#import <appkit/Application.h>

void main(int argc, char *argv[]) {

  [Application new];
  if ([NXApp loadNibSection:"GraphPaper.nib"
      owner:NXApp withNames:NO])
  [NXApp run];
  [NXApp free];
  exit(0);
}
```

GraphView.h

```
#import <appkit/appkit.h>

@interface GraphView:View
{
  id formulaField;
  id graphButton;
  id xmaxCell;
  id xminCell;
  id xstepCell;
  id ymaxCell;
  id yminCell;

  id          graphProc;
  id          displayList;
  BOOL        first;          /* first datapoint */
  double      lastx, lasty;   /* for drawing graph */
  char        graphBuf[17000];    /* buf to graph */
  double      ymin,ymax;
  cthread_t   stuffer_thread;
  BOOL runningAsService;

@public            /* for use by stuffing thread */

  BOOL     graphing;
  char     *formula;
  int      toFd;
  double   xmin, xmax, xstep;
}

- graph:sender;
- stopGraph:sender;
- addBufToGraph:(const char *)buf;
- graphLine:(const char *)buf;
- addGraphSegmentx1:(float)x1 y1:(float)y1
                  x2:(float)x2 y2:(float)y2;
- drawSelf:(const NXRect *)rects :(int)rectCount;
- clear;
- awakeFromNib;
- addAxesx1:(float)x1 y1:(float)y1
    x2:(float)x2 y2:(float)y2;
- addLabel:(const char *)aTitle
          atx:(float)x y:(float)y
          size:(float)size;
- sizeTo:(NXCoord)width :(NXCoord)height;
- setRunningAsService:(BOOL)flag;
- formulaField;
```

```
@end

#define GRAPH_TAG 0
#define LABEL_TAG 1
#define AXES_TAG 2
```

GraphView.m

```
#import "GraphView.h"
#import "Process.h"
#import "Segment.h"
#import "Label.h"

/* dataStuffer: a thread fork function that
* puts data into the pipe.
*/
int dataStuffer(GraphView *obj)
{
  double x;

  for (x=obj->xmin; obj->graphing && x<=obj->xmax;
                                    x+=obj->xstep) {
    char buf[4096]; /* big enough */
    char *cc, *dd;

    /* build the expression */
    sprintf(buf, "%g,", x);
    dd = buf + strlen(buf);
    for (cc=obj->formula; *cc; cc++) {
      if (*cc=='x') {
        sprintf(dd, "%g", x);
        dd = dd + strlen(dd);
      }
      else {
        *(dd++) = *cc;
      }
    }

    *(dd++) = '\n';    /* terminate the string */
    *(dd++) = '\0';
    write(obj->toFd, buf, dd-buf);
  }
  /* Now send through terminate code */
  write(obj->toFd, "999\n", 4);
  return 0;
}
```

```
/* gotGraphData: This function called by Display
 * PostScript when data is available to read on fd.
 * We assume that it will be a full line, and less
 * than 1024 characters (both good assumptions here).
 */
void gotGraphData(int fd, void *selfp)
{
  id self = selfp;
  char buf[16384];
  int len;

  if ((len = read(fd, buf, sizeof(buf))) == -1) {
    DPSRemoveFD(fd);      /* end of file */
    return;
  }
  buf[len] = '\000';
  [self addBufToGraph:buf];
}


@implementation GraphView

- graph:sender
{
  /* initialize for a graph */
  [self clear];

  /* set instance variables from the form */
  xmin = [xminCell doubleValue];
  xmax = [xmaxCell doubleValue];
  xstep = [xstepCell doubleValue];
  ymin = [yminCell doubleValue];
  ymax = [ymaxCell doubleValue];
  memset(graphBuf, 0, sizeof(graphBuf));

  /* Check the parameters of the graph */
  if ( xmax-xmin<=0 || ymax-ymin<=0 ) {
    NXRunAlertPanel(0,
          "Invalid min/max combination", 0, 0, 0);
    return self;
  }

  if ( xstep<=0 ) {
    NXRunAlertPanel(0,"Need a positive step",0,0,0);
    return self;
  }

  [self setDrawSize: xmax-xmin : ymax-ymin];
```

```
   [self setDrawOrigin: xmin : ymin];

   if (formula) {
     /* Free the old formula if we have one */
     NXZoneFree([self zone],formula);
     formula = 0;
   }
   formula = NXCopyStringBufferFromZone(
               [formulaField stringValue],
               [self zone]);

   [ [graphButton setTitle: "Stop"]
                 setAction: @selector(stopGraph:)];

   first = YES;      /* next pair read is the first */
   graphing = 1;     /* we are now graphing */
   stuffer_thread =
     cthread_fork((cthread_fn_t)dataStuffer, self);
   return self;
}


- stopGraph:sender
{
   graphing = 0;
        /* wait for the stuffer thread to finish */
   cthread_join(stuffer_thread);


   [ [graphButton setTitle: "Graph"]
                 setAction: @selector(graph:)];

   if (runningAsService) {
     [NXApp stopModal:NX_RUNSTOPPED];
   }

   return self;
}


- addBufToGraph:(const char *)buf
{
   char *cc;

   if (graphing==0) {
     return self;             /* not graphing */
   }
```

```
                    /* The following lines take the data that we have
                     * received in "buf" and concatenate it to the end
                     * of our internal buffer.
                     * We then extract the lines of the buffer
                     * one-at-a-time and feed them to the method
                     * graphLine:
                     */

                  strcat(graphBuf, buf);
                  while (cc = index(graphBuf, '\n')) {
                    *cc = '\0';                /* terminate the line */
                                            /* now graph what we have */
                    [self graphLine: graphBuf];
                    memmove(graphBuf,
                            cc+1,
                            sizeof(graphBuf) - (cc-graphBuf));
                  }
                  return self;
                }


                - graphLine:(const char *)buf
                {
                  double x, y;
                  int num;

                  num = sscanf(buf, "%lf , %lf", &x, &y);
                  if (num!=2) {
                    if (x==999.0) { /* end of graph data */
                      [self stopGraph:nil];
                    }
                    return self; /* perhaps an invalid segment */
                  }

                  if (first) {
                    /* put in graph axes */
                    [self addAxesx1:xmin y1:0.0 x2:xmax y2:0.0 ];
                    [self addAxesx1:0.0 y1:ymin x2:0.0 y2:ymax ];
                    /* add the label */
                    [self addLabel:formula
                        atx:(xmin+xmax)/2.0 y:(ymin*10.0+ymax)/11.0
                        size:24.0];
                    [self display];
                  }

                  if (!first) {
                    id seg = [self addGraphSegmentx1:lastx y1:lasty
                                        x2:x y2:y ];
```

```
        /* draw just this segment */
        [self lockFocus];
        [seg drawPSInView:self];
        [self unlockFocus];
        [window flushWindow];
        NXPing();
    }

    lastx = x;
    lasty = y;
    first = NO;
    return self;
}


- addGraphSegmentx1:(float)x1 y1:(float)y1
        x2:(float)x2 y2:(float)y2
{
    id seg = [ [Segment alloc]
                initx1:x1 y1:y1 x2:x2 y2:y2 ];
    [seg setTag:GRAPH_TAG];
    [displayList addObject:seg];
    return seg;
}


- drawSelf:(const NXRect *)rects :(int)rectCount
{
    int i;

    for ( i=(rectCount==1 ? 0 : 1); i<rectCount; i++) {
        int j;

        /* set the background */
        PSsetgray(NX_WHITE);
        PSrectfill(NX_X(&rects[i]), NX_Y(&rects[i]),
            NX_WIDTH(&rects[i]), NX_HEIGHT(&rects[i]));

        if (displayList) {
            for (j=0; j < [displayList count]; j++) {
                id obj = [displayList objectAt: j];
                NXRect oBounds = [obj bounds];

                if (NXIntersectsRect(&rects[i],
                                    &oBounds)) {
                    [obj drawPSInView:self];
                }
            }
```

```
      }
    }
    return self;
}


- clear
{
  /* clear the display list */
  if (displayList) {
    [ [displayList
        makeObjectsPerform:@selector(free)] empty];
  }
  else {
    displayList = [ [List alloc] init];
  }

  [self display];

  return self;
}


- awakeFromNib
{
  char *argv[2] = {0,0};
  char path[MAXPATHLEN];

  if(![[NXBundle mainBundle]
    getPath: path forResource: "Evaluator"
    ofType: ""]){
    NXRunAlertPanel(0,"Can't find Evaluator",0,0,0);
    [NXApp terminate:self];
    return nil;
  }
  argv[0] = path;

  graphProc = [ [Process alloc]
                initFromCommand: argv];

  if (!graphProc) {
    NXRunAlertPanel(0,
                    "Cannot create calculator: %s",
                    0, 0, 0, strerror(errno));
    [NXApp terminate: self];
    return nil;
  }
```

```
    toFd = [graphProc toFd];
    [graphProc dpsWatchFD: gotGraphData
            data: self
            priority: NX_RUNMODALTHRESHOLD];

    [xminCell setStringValue:
        NXGetDefaultValue("GraphPaper", "xmin") ];
    [xmaxCell setStringValue:
        NXGetDefaultValue("GraphPaper", "xmax") ];
    [xstepCell setStringValue:
        NXGetDefaultValue("GraphPaper", "xstep") ];
    [yminCell setStringValue:
        NXGetDefaultValue("GraphPaper", "ymin") ];
    [ymaxCell setStringValue:
        NXGetDefaultValue("GraphPaper", "ymax") ];
    [formulaField setStringValue:
        NXGetDefaultValue("GraphPaper", "Formula")];

    return self;
}


- addAxesx1:(float)x1 y1:(float)y1
        x2:(float)x2 y2:(float)y2
{
    id axes = [ [Segment alloc]
                initx1: x1 y1: y1
                    x2: x2 y2: y2 ];
    [axes setTag:AXES_TAG];
    [axes setGray:NX_DKGRAY];
    [displayList addObject:axes];
    return axes;
}


- addLabel:(const char *)aTitle
        atx:(float)x y:(float)y
        size:(float)size
{
    id label = [ [Label alloc] initx:x y:y text:aTitle
                            size:size forView:self];
    [label setTag:LABEL_TAG];
    [displayList addObject:label];

    return label;
}
```

```
- sizeTo:(NXCoord)width :(NXCoord)height
{
  [super sizeTo:width :height];
  if (xmax!=xmin && ymax!=ymin) {
    [self setDrawSize:xmax-xmin :ymax-ymin];
    [self setDrawOrigin:xmin :ymin];
    [self display];
  }
  return self;
}

- setRunningAsService:(BOOL)flag
{
  runningAsService = flag;
  return self;
}

- formulaField
{
  return formulaField;
}

@end
```

Label.h

```
#import <appkit/appkit.h>

@interface Label:Object
{
  NXRect    bounds;
  char      *text;
  NXColor myColor;
  int       tag;
  id        font;
}

- initx:(float)x y:(float)y text:(const char *)aText
                    size:(float)aSize forView:aView;
- free;
- setGray:(float)aGray;
- (NXRect)bounds;
- (int)tag;
- setTag:(int)aTag;
- drawPSInView:aView;
- setColor:(NXColor)aColor;
@end
```

Label.m

```
#import "Label.h"

@implementation Label

- initx:(float)x y:(float)y text:(const char *)aText
                    size:(float)aSize forView:aView
{
  NXSize fontScale;
  float matrix[6];

  [super init];

  fontScale.width = 1.0;
  fontScale.height = 1.0;

  [aView convertSize:&fontScale fromView:nil];

  /* construct transform matrix */
  memset(matrix, 0, sizeof(matrix));
  matrix[0] = fontScale.width;
  matrix[3] = fontScale.height;

  font = [Font newFont:"Times-Roman"
                  size:aSize matrix:matrix];

  text = NXCopyStringBufferFromZone(aText,
                                    [self zone]);
  [self setGray:NX_BLACK];

  NX_WIDTH(&bounds) = [font getWidthOf:text];
  NX_HEIGHT(&bounds)= [font pointSize];
  NX_X(&bounds)     = x - (NX_WIDTH(&bounds)/2.0);
  NX_Y(&bounds)     = y;

  return self;
}


- free
{
  if (text){
    NXZoneFree([self zone], text);
    text = 0;
  }
  return [super free];
}
```

```objc
- setGray:(float)aGray
{
  myColor = NXConvertGrayToColor(aGray);
  return self;
}


- (NXRect)bounds
{
  return bounds;
}


- (int)tag
{
  return tag;
}


- setTag:(int)aTag
{
  tag = aTag;
  return self;
}


/* If we are printing, we'll invoke [font set]
 * to set the font. Although we only need to do
 * this once per drawSelf::, we do it every time.
 */
- drawPSInView:aView
{
  [font set];
  NXSetColor(myColor);
  PSmoveto(NX_X(&bounds), NX_Y(&bounds));
  PSshow(text);
  return self;
}


- setColor:(NXColor)aColor
{
  myColor = aColor;
  return self;
}

@end
```

PrefController.h

```
#import <appkit/appkit.h>

@interface PrefController:Object
{
    id   axesColorWell;
    id   graphColorWell;
    id   labelColorWell;
    id   window;

    id   colorView;
    id   initialView;
    id   multiView;

    /* for initial values */
    id   xminCell;
    id   xmaxCell;
    id   xstepCell;
    id   yminCell;
    id   ymaxCell;
    id   formulaField;
}

- okay:sender;
- revert:sender;
- window;
- setUpWell:well tag:(int)aTag;
- awakeFromNib;
- setPref:sender;
- setPrefToView:theView;

@end
```

PrefController.m

```
#import "PrefController.h"
#import "Controller.h"
#import "GraphView.h"

@implementation PrefController

- window
{
    return window;
}
```

```objc
- setUpWell:well tag:(int)aTag
{
  [well setTag:aTag];
  [well setContinuous:YES];
  [well setTarget:[ [NXApp delegate] graphView] ];
  [well setAction:@selector(setObjectColor:) ];
  return self;
}


- awakeFromNib
{
  [ [NXColorPanel sharedInstance:YES]
      setContinuous:YES];
  [self setUpWell:axesColorWell tag:AXES_TAG];
  [self setUpWell:labelColorWell tag:LABEL_TAG];
  [self setUpWell:graphColorWell tag:GRAPH_TAG];
  [self revert:self];
  [self setPrefToView:[colorView contentView] ];
  return self;
}


- okay:sender
{
  char  buf[256];
  static NXDefaultsVector newDefaults = {
    {"LabelColor", ""},    /* 0 */
    {"AxesColor", ""},     /* 1 */
    {"GraphColor", ""},    /* 2 */
    {"xmin", ""},          /* 3 */
    {"xmax", ""},          /* 4 */
    {"xstep", ""},         /* 5 */
    {"ymin", ""},          /* 6 */
    {"ymax", ""},          /* 7 */
    {"Formula", ""},       /* 8 */
    {NULL, NULL}
  };

  newDefaults[0].value = alloca(256);
  strcpy(newDefaults[0].value,
      colorToASCII([labelColorWell color],buf));

  newDefaults[1].value = alloca(256);
  strcpy(newDefaults[1].value,
      colorToASCII([axesColorWell color],buf));

  newDefaults[2].value = alloca(256);
```

```
        strcpy(newDefaults[2].value,
               colorToASCII([graphColorWell color],buf));

        newDefaults[3].value =
                       (char *) [xminCell stringValue];
        newDefaults[4].value =
                       (char *) [xmaxCell stringValue];
        newDefaults[5].value =
                       (char *) [xstepCell stringValue];
        newDefaults[6].value =
                       (char *) [yminCell stringValue];
        newDefaults[7].value =
                       (char *) [ymaxCell stringValue];
        newDefaults[8].value =
                       (char *) [formulaField stringValue];

        NXWriteDefaults("GraphPaper", newDefaults);

        [window orderOut:self];  /* dismiss panels */
        [ [NXColorPanel sharedInstance:NO]
               orderOut:self];

        return self;
}


- revert:sender
{
  [graphColorWell setColor:ASCIIToColor(
    NXGetDefaultValue("GraphPaper","GraphColor")) ];

  [labelColorWell setColor:ASCIIToColor(
    NXGetDefaultValue("GraphPaper","LabelColor")) ];

  [axesColorWell setColor:ASCIIToColor(
    NXGetDefaultValue("GraphPaper","AxesColor")) ];

  [xminCell setStringValue:
      NXGetDefaultValue("GraphPaper", "xmin")];
  [xmaxCell setStringValue:
      NXGetDefaultValue("GraphPaper", "xmax")];
  [xstepCell setStringValue:
      NXGetDefaultValue("GraphPaper", "xstep")];
  [yminCell setStringValue:
      NXGetDefaultValue("GraphPaper", "ymin")];
  [ymaxCell setStringValue:
      NXGetDefaultValue("GraphPaper", "ymax")];
  [formulaField setStringValue:
```

```
                           NXGetDefaultValue("GraphPaper", "Formula")];

    return self;
}


- setPref:sender
{
  id newView = nil;

  switch ( [ [sender selectedCell] tag]) {
    case 0:  newView = [colorView contentView];
             break;
    case 1:  newView = [initialView contentView];
             break;
  }

  [self setPrefToView:newView];
  return self;
}


- setPrefToView:theView
{
  NXRect boxRect, viewRect;

  [multiView getFrame:&boxRect];
  [theView getFrame:&viewRect];
  [multiView setContentView:theView];

  NX_X(&viewRect)=
     (NX_WIDTH(&boxRect)-NX_WIDTH(&viewRect)) / 2.0;
  NX_Y(&viewRect) =
     (NX_HEIGHT(&boxRect)-NX_HEIGHT(&viewRect))/ 2.0;

  [theView setFrame:&viewRect];/* center the view */
  [multiView display];
  return self;
}

@end
```

Process.h

```
/*
 * Process.h: spawn and control a subprocess
 */
```

```
#import <appkit/appkit.h>

@interface Process:Object
{
   int  toProcess[2];
   int  fromProcess[2];
   int  pid;
   BOOL fdHandlerInstalled;
}

- initFromCommand:(char **)argv;
- free;
- (int)toFd;
- (int)fromFd;
- writeLine:(const char *)aLine;
- dpsWatchFD:(DPSFDProc)handler
            data:(void *)userData priority:(int)pri;
@end
```

Process.m

```
/*
 * Process.m
 */
#import "Process.h"

@implementation Process

- initFromCommand:(char **)argv
{
  [super init];

  if(argv==0 || argv[0]==0 || access(argv[0],X_OK)){
    return nil;      /* cannot execute command */
  }

  if (pipe(toProcess) == -1) {
    [self free];
    return nil;      /* could not open first pipe */
  }

  if (pipe(fromProcess) == -1) {
    close(toProcess[0]);
    close(toProcess[1]);
    [self free];
    return nil;      /* could not open second pipe */
  }
```

```
pid = fork();

if (pid == -1){
  [self free];
  return nil;                    /* no more processes */
}

if (pid==0) {   /* executed by the child */
                /* set up and execv */
  close(0);      /* stdin  */
  close(1);      /* stdout */

  close(toProcess[1]);
  close(fromProcess[0]);

  dup2(toProcess[0], 0);     /* stdin */
  dup2(fromProcess[1], 1);   /* stdout */

  close(2);                  /* stderr */
  dup2(fromProcess[1], 2);   /* stderr */

  execv(argv[0], argv);
  perror(NXArgv[0]);
  exit(1);
}
          /* executed by the parent */
          /* close the other ends of the pipe */
close(toProcess[0]);
close(fromProcess[1]);
return self;
}


- free
{
  if (fdHandlerInstalled)
                        DPSRemoveFD(fromProcess[0]);
  if (toProcess[1]) close(toProcess[1]);
  if (fromProcess[0]) close(fromProcess[0]);
  if (pid>0) kill(pid, 9);
  return [super free];
}


- (int)toFd
{
  return toProcess[1];
}
```

```
- (int)fromFd
{
    return fromProcess[0];
}


/* send a line to the process */
- writeLine:(const char *)aLine
{
    int len = strlen(aLine);

    write(toProcess[1], aLine, len);

    if (len>0 && aLine[len-1] != '\n') {
        write(toProcess[1], "\n", 1); /* courtesy */
    }
    return self;
}


- dpsWatchFD:(DPSFDProc)handler
            data:(void *)userData priority:(int)pri
{
    DPSAddFD(fromProcess[0], handler, userData, pri);
    fdHandlerInstalled = YES;
    return self;
}

@end
```

Segment.h

```
#import <appkit/appkit.h>

@interface Segment:Object
{
    NXPoint   start;
    NXPoint   end;
    NXColor myColor;
    int       tag;
}

- initx1:(float)x1 y1:(float)y1
        x2:(float)x2 y2:(float)y2;
- setGray:(float)aGray;
- (float)x;
- (float)y;
```

```
- drawPSInView:aView;
- (NXRect)bounds;
- (int)tag;
- setTag:(int)aTag;
- setColor:(NXColor)aColor;

@end
```

Segment.m

```
#import "Segment.h"

@implementation Segment

- initx1:(float)x1 y1:(float)y1
      x2:(float)x2 y2:(float)y2
{
  [super init];   /* must init the Object class! */

  start.x = x1;
  start.y = y1;
  end.x = x2;
  end.y = y2;
  [self setGray: NX_BLACK];
  return self;
}


- setGray:(float)aGray
{
  myColor = NXConvertGrayToColor(aGray);
  return self;
}


- (float)x
{
  return (start.x + end.x)/2.0;
}


- (float)y
{
  return (start.y + end.y)/2.0;
}
```

```
- drawPSInView:aView
{
  NXSize  sz = {1.0, 1.0}; /* a default size */

  NXSetColor(myColor);
  PSmoveto(start.x, start.y);
  PSlineto(end.x, end.y);

  [aView convertSize: &sz fromView: nil];

  /* Rescale the coordinate system for stroking, so
   * that the line we draw is exactly one point wide
   * in the screen coordinate system.
   */
  PSscale(sz.width,sz.height);
  PSsetlinewidth(1.0);
  PSstroke();

  /* Restore the old scale. We could have done this
   * with a gsave/grestore, but this is much more
   * efficient.
   */
  PSscale(1/sz.width, 1/sz.height);

  return self;
}


- (NXRect)bounds
{
  NXRect bounds;

  NX_X(&bounds) = MIN(start.x,end.x) ;
  NX_Y(&bounds) = MIN(start.y,end.y) ;

  NX_WIDTH(&bounds) = fabs(start.x-end.x)+MINFLOAT;
  NX_HEIGHT(&bounds) = fabs(start.y-end.y)+MINFLOAT;

  return bounds;
}


- (int)tag
{
  return tag;
}
```

```
- setTag:(int)aTag
{
  tag = aTag;
  return self;
}



- setColor:(NXColor)aColor
{
  myColor = aColor;
  return self;
}

@end
```

TrackingGraphView.h

```
#import <appkit/appkit.h>
#import "ColorGraphView.h"

@interface TrackingGraphView:ColorGraphView
{
    id      xCell;
    id      yCell;
    BOOL    inside;
    id      highlightedSegment;
    int     trackingRect;
    id      cursor;
}

- setMyTrackingRect:(BOOL)flag;
- awakeFromNib;
- mouseEntered:(NXEvent *)theEvent;
- mouseExited:(NXEvent *)theEvent;
- sizeTo:(NXCoord)width :(NXCoord)height;
- unhighlightSegment;
- mouseMoved:(NXEvent *)theEvent;
- resetCursorRects;
- windowDidResize:sender;
- windowDidBecomeMain:sender;
- windowDidResignMain:sender;

@end
```

TrackingGraphView.m

```
#import "TrackingGraphView.h"
#import "Segment.h"

@implementation TrackingGraphView
- setMyTrackingRect:(BOOL)flag
{
  NXRect visible;

  /* Discard old tracking rect if present */
  if (trackingRect) {
    [window discardTrackingRect:trackingRect];
    trackingRect = 0;
  }

  if (flag) {
    /* Set new tracking rect if requested
     * and if visible.
     */
    if ([self getVisibleRect:&visible]) {
      [self convertRect:&visible toView:nil];
      [window setTrackingRect:&visible
          inside:NO owner:self
          tag:1 left:NO right:NO];
      trackingRect = 1;
    }
  }
  return self;
}


- awakeFromNib
{
  NXPoint hotSpot;

  [super awakeFromNib];

  cursor = [ [NXCursor alloc] initFromImage:
          [NXImage findImageNamed: "CrossHair"] ];
  hotSpot.x = 8.0;
  hotSpot.y = 8.0;

  [cursor setHotSpot: &hotSpot];

  [self setMyTrackingRect: YES];
  return self;
}
```

```
- mouseEntered:(NXEvent *)theEvent
{
  [window makeFirstResponder:self];
  [window addToEventMask:NX_MOUSEMOVEDMASK];
  inside = YES;
  return self;
}



- mouseExited:(NXEvent *)theEvent
{
  [self unhighlightSegment];
  [window removeFromEventMask:NX_MOUSEMOVEDMASK];
  inside = NO;
  return self;
}



- sizeTo:(NXCoord)width :(NXCoord)height
{
  [super sizeTo:width :height];
  return [self setMyTrackingRect: YES];
}



- unhighlightSegment
{
  if (highlightedSegment) {
    [self lockFocus];
    [ [highlightedSegment setColor: graphColor]
                     drawPSInView: self];
    [self unlockFocus];
    [xCell setStringValue:"x: "];
    [yCell setStringValue:"y: "];
    highlightedSegment = nil;
  }
  return self;
}



- mouseMoved:(NXEvent *)theEvent
{
  NXPoint pt;
  char buf[256];

  pt = theEvent->location;
  [self convertPoint: &pt fromView: nil];
```

```
      if (displayList && inside) {
        int j;
        for (j=0; j<[displayList count]; j++) {
          id obj = [displayList objectAt:j];
          NXRect obounds = [obj bounds];

          if ([obj tag]==GRAPH_TAG &&
              [self mouse: &pt inRect: &obounds]) {

            if (obj != highlightedSegment) {
              [self unhighlightSegment];/* erase old */

              /* highlight new segment */
              [self lockFocus];
              [obj setGray: NX_LTGRAY];
              [obj drawPSInView: self];
              [self unlockFocus];

              /* update positions */
              sprintf(buf, "x:    %g", [obj x]);
              [xCell setStringValue: buf];
              sprintf(buf, "y:    %g", [obj y]);
              [yCell setStringValue: buf];

              highlightedSegment = obj;
            }
            return self;
          }
        }
      }

      /* no segment should be highlighted */
      [self unhighlightSegment];
      return self;
    }


- resetCursorRects
{
  NXRect visible;
  if ([self getVisibleRect:&visible]) {
    [self addCursorRect:&visible cursor:cursor];
  }

  return self;
}
```

```
- windowDidResize:sender
{
  return [self setMyTrackingRect: YES];
}


- windowDidBecomeMain:sender
{
  return [self setMyTrackingRect: YES];
}


- windowDidResignMain:sender
{
  return [self setMyTrackingRect: NO];
}

@end
```

ZoomScrollView.h

```
#import <appkit/appkit.h>

@interface ZoomScrollView:ScrollView
{
  id subView;
  id zoomButton;
  float scaleFactor;
  NXRect originalContentViewFrame;
}

- changeZoom:sender;
- initFrame:(const NXRect *)theFrame;
- awakeFromNib;
- setScaleFactor:(float)aFactor;
- tile;

@end
```

ZoomScrollView.m

```
#import "ZoomScrollView.h"

@implementation ZoomScrollView

- changeZoom:sender
{
```

```
    [self setScaleFactor:
              [ [sender selectedCell] tag] / 100.0];

    return self;
}


- initFrame:(const NXRect *)theFrame
{
    [super initFrame: theFrame];
    [self setBackgroundGray: NX_WHITE];
    scaleFactor = 1.0;

    return self;
}


- awakeFromNib
{
    [self setVertScrollerRequired: YES];
    [self setHorizScrollerRequired:YES];
    [self setBorderType:NX_LINE];

    /* The next 3 lines install the subview
     * and set its size to be the same as
     * the ScrollView's contentView.
     */
    [self setDocView: subView];
    [contentView getFrame: &originalContentViewFrame];
    [subView setFrame: &originalContentViewFrame];

    return self;
}


- setScaleFactor:(float)aFactor
{
    if (scaleFactor != aFactor) {
        float delta = aFactor/scaleFactor;
        scaleFactor = aFactor;
        [contentView scale: delta : delta];
    }

    return self;
}
```

```
- tile
{
  NXRect scrollerRect, buttonRect;

  [super tile];

  /* The next line makes the zoomButton itself
   * one of the ZoomScrollView's subviews the
   * first time that the tile message is sent.
   */
  if ([zoomButton superview] != self) {
    [self addSubview:zoomButton];
  }

  /* make the hScroller smaller and stick the
   * pop-up list next to it.
   */
  [hScroller getFrame: &scrollerRect];
  NXDivideRect(&scrollerRect, &buttonRect, 60.0, 2);
  [hScroller setFrame: &scrollerRect];
  NXInsetRect(&buttonRect, 1.0, 1.0);
  [zoomButton setFrame: &buttonRect];

  return self;
}

@end
```

Appendix B: References

It is essential that NeXTSTEP developers become familiar with NeXT's on-line documentation. It resides under the **/NextLibrary/Documentation** directory and can be easily accessed using the bundled Librarian and HeaderViewer applications. Much of this documentation has been published in hardcopy form by Addison-Wesley. We won't list these references here.

NeXT's technical summaries documentation contains an excellent list of references concerning NeXTSTEP, UNIX, Mach, and a variety of other topics. Below we have highlighted some of the most important references and include some others which we've found useful.

C, Objective-C, and Object-Oriented Programming

C by Discovery. L. Sheila Foster. Scott/Jones Publishers, 1991.

Advanced C: Tips and Techniques. Gail Anderson and Paul Anderson. Hayden Books (a division of Howard W. Sams & Company), 1988.

Object-Oriented Programming: An Evolutionary Approach, 2nd edition. Brad J. Cox and Andrew J. Novobilski. Addison-Wesley, 1991.

Objective-C: Object-Oriented Programming Techniques. Lewis J. Pinson and Richard S. Wiener. Addison-Wesley, 1991.

An Introduction to Object-Oriented Programming. Timothy Budd. Addison-Wesley, 1991.

UNIX

The Design and Implementation of the 4.3BSD UNIX Operating System. Samuel J. Leffler, Marshall Kirk McKusick, Michael J. Karels, and John S. Quarterman. Addison-Wesley Publishing Company, New York, 1988.

The Design of the UNIX Operating System. Maurice J. Bach. Prentice-Hall, 1986.

The UNIX C Shell Field Guide. Gail Anderson and Paul Anderson. Prentice-Hall, 1986.

GNU Tools

GNU Emacs Manual. Richard Stallman. Free Software Foundation, 1987. An instruction manual for GNU EMACS, one of the editors that comes with the NeXTSTEP Extended edition.

The GNU Source-Level Debugger. Richard Stallman. Free Software Foundation, February 1988. Describes how to use the debugger used in NeXTSTEP.

Although the GNU manuals are available in some bookstores, you can order them directly from the Free Software Foundation, 675 Mass Avenue, Cambridge, MA 02139.   (617) 876-3296

PostScript and Display PostScript

Programming The Display PostScript System with NeXTSTEP (the "purple book"). Adobe Systems Incorporated. Addison-Wesley, 1992.

PostScript Language Tutorial and Cookbook (the "blue book"). Adobe Systems Incorporated. Addison-Wesley, 1985.

PostScript Language Reference Manual, 2nd edition (the "red book"). Adobe Systems Incorporated. Addison-Wesley, 1991.

PostScript Language Program Design (the "green book"). Adobe Systems Incorporated. Addison-Wesley, 1988.

Display PostScript Programming. David A. Holzang. Addison-Wesley, 1990.

pswrap Reference Manual. Adobe Systems Incorporated.

Computer Security

Practical UNIX Security, Simson L. Garfinkel, and Gene Spafford. O'Reilly and Associates, Cambridge, MA, 1991. A thorough description of the UNIX operating system, from a security-minded point of view.

Computer Security Basics. Deborah Russell and G. T. Gangemi. O'Reilly and Associates, Cambridge, MA, 1991. An excellent introduction to the issues of computer security, with emphasis on the Department of Defense's so-called "Orange Book" for classifying levels of computer security.

Compositing

"Compositing Digital Images." Thomas Porter and Tom Duff. *Computer Graphics* (SIGGRAPH '84 Conference Proceedings), Vol. 18, No. 3, July 1984, pp. 253-259. The authoritative paper describing the compositing operator.

Data Formats

Rich Text Format (RTF) Specification. Microsoft Corporation.

Tag Image File Format Specification. Aldus Corporation and Microsoft Corporation. Available from Aldus Corporation; for more information, contact the Aldus Developer's Desk at (206) 628-6593.

User Interface Design

Designing the User Interface, 2nd edition. Ben Shneiderman. Addison-Wesley, 1992.

Software User Interface Design. Deborah Mayhew. Prentice-Hall, 1992.

Index